Concepts in Composition

2nd Edition

Concepts in Composition: Theory and Practice in the Teaching of Writing is designed to foster reflection on how theory impacts practice, enabling prospective teachers to develop their own comprehensive and coherent conception of what writing is or should be and to consider how people learn to write. This approach allows readers to assume the dual role of both teacher and student as they enter the conversation of the discipline and become familiar with some of the critical issues.

New to this second edition are:

- up-to-date primary source readings
- a focus on collaborative writing practices and collaborative learning
- additional assignments and classroom activities
- an emphasis on new media and information literacy and their impact on the teaching of writing.

These new directions will inform the content of this revision, reflecting significant advancements in the field. Each chapter addresses a particular theoretical concept relevant to classroom teaching and includes activities to help readers establish the connection between theoretical concepts and classroom lessons. The book's companion website provides resources for instructors, including PowerPoint presentations and lecture notes. Bringing together scholars with expertise in particular areas of composition, this text will serve as an effective primer for students and educators in the field of composition theory.

Irene L. Clark is Professor of English, Director of Composition, and Director of the Master's Option in Rhetoric and Composition at California State University, Northridge. She previously taught at the University of Southern California (USC), where she also co-directed the university's Writing Program and directed its Writing Center. She has won multiple awards from the National Writing Centers Association, and has authored several textbooks for both undergraduate and graduate students. She holds a B.A. in Music from Hunter College, an M.A. in English from Columbia University, and a Ph.D. in English Literature from USC.

Concepts in Composition

Theory and Practice in the Teaching of Writing

2nd Edition

Irene L. Clark

with Contributors

Betty Bamberg

Darsie Bowden

John R. Edlund

Lisa Gerrard

Olga Griswold

Sharon Klein

Julie Neff-Lippman

James D. Williams

Routledge
Taylor & Francis Group

NEW YORK AND LONDON

Instructors: please visit the companion website at
www.routledge.com/9780415885164

Second edition published 2012
by Routledge
711 Third Avenue, New York, NY 10017

Simultaneously published in the UK
by Routledge
2 Park Square, Milton Park, Abingdon, Oxon OX14 4RN

Routledge is an imprint of the Taylor & Francis Group, an informa business
© 2012 Taylor & Francis

First edition published 2003 by Lawrence Erlbaum Associates

Library of Congress Cataloging-in-Publication Data
Clark, Irene L.
Concepts in composition : theory and practice in the teaching of writing / Irene L. Clark ; with contributors, Betty Bamberg ... [et al.]. — 2nd ed.
p. cm.
Includes bibliographical references and indexes.
I1. English language—Rhetoric—Study and teaching. 2. English language—Composition and exercises—Study and teaching. 3. English language—Study and teaching—Foreign speakers. 4. Report writing—Study and teaching. I. Bamberg, Betty. II. Title.
PE1404.C528 2011
808'.042071—dc22
2011007099

ISBN 13: 978-0-415-88515-7 (hbk)
ISBN 13: 978-0-415-88516-4 (pbk)
ISBN 13: 978-0-203-80680-7 (ebk)

Typeset in Minion and Gill Sans
by EvS Commnication Networx, Inc.

Printed and bound in the United States of America on acid-free paper
by Edwards Brothers, Inc.

To my supportive and energetic husband, Bill,
my beautiful, growing family, and
my amazing students at California State University, Northridge,
whose insights enlighten me every day.

Brief Contents

Contents

Preface

Concepts in Composition: Theory and Practice in the Teaching of Writing focuses on scholarship in rhetoric and composition that has influenced classroom teaching. Its goal is to foster reflection on how theory impacts practice, enabling prospective teachers to become conscious of how they think about writing in the context of a first-year writing class and develop strategies that can help students improve as writers. Each chapter addresses a particular theoretical concept that impacts classroom teaching and includes suggestions for writing, discussion, and further exploration. Over the past several years, I have used this book in a number of graduate seminars, and I have found that its approach enables prospective instructors to assume the dual role of both teacher and student as they enter the conversations of the discipline and become familiar with some of its critical issues.

The initial impetus for the first edition of this book was provided by a course in composition theory and pedagogy that I had taught for prospective high school teachers and graduate teaching assistants. The course had been organized around concepts that I felt were the most important for my students to understand in terms of their influence on classroom practice and which, in many instances, had generated lively and fruitful discussion. Then, one day, when I was flying home from a conference on college composition, I thought about how useful it would be for me and perhaps for others, if I transformed my classroom notes into a book. Thus was *Concepts in Composition* conceived, and, in accordance with the organization of my course, each chapter consists of the following:

- An overview of a significant concept in composition that informs classroom teaching.
- Writing assignments and discussion prompts to foster further exploration of the concept.
- An article, sometimes two, to generate further discussion.
- Bibliographical references for further research.
- Suggestions for classroom activities to apply the concept in a pedagogical context.

High in the air, jotting down ideas, I initially thought that I would write every chapter myself. However, once on the ground, breathing fresh air, I decided that the breadth of scholarship and diversity of perspective would be significantly improved if I enlisted the aid of scholars in the field who had expertise in particular concepts in composition. The result is a more substantive book that is considerably richer, due to the contributions of my knowledgeable and gracious colleagues, who embarked on revising their chapters for this second edition with impressive expertise and remarkable good humor.

THE SECOND EDITION

Developing from the early days of the process movement in composition, the field of rhetoric and composition has emerged as a vibrant and dynamic scholarly discipline, with an impressive array of articles, books, journals, online resources, discussion groups, and conferences. Thus, although all contributors have remained committed to the "Concepts in Composition" approach that informed the first edition, the second edition reflects deepening understandings and new perspectives. Three directions, in particular, have become particularly important, both theoretically and pedagogically: the inclusion of critical reading and literacy awareness in the composition curriculum; the increased emphasis on rhetoric and genre in helping students continue to develop as writers; and the profound impact of new media and information literacy on the teaching of writing. These topics have all informed the second edition.

Some of these new emphases are manifested in altered chapter titles. For example, Chapter 1 in the first edition was titled "Process" to reflect the mantra of the process movement: "writing is a process not a product." Now, however, although it is recognized that writing is indeed a process, we understand that reading, thinking, and research are processes as well and that all of these processes interconnect when people write—hence the new title. Chapter 7 in the first edition had the title "Voice," whereas in the second edition it is called "Voice and Style," a title that reflects more complicated understandings of the term "voice," especially in the context of new media, which enables writers to assume other identities, download information from multiple sources, and write in many different "voices," even within the same text. New media has rendered every concept in composition more complicated, and its impact, both actual and potential, is discussed in every chapter. Chapter 11, in particular, titled "Writing in Multiple Media," focuses directly on this important concept, examining the many forms and genres that are emerging in an increasingly online, visual, and participatory world. How writing and the teaching of writing will or should be impacted by that world are important issues to address in our classes, as students enter the university with greater technical sophistication and different perspectives on the nature of writing and on what constitutes meaningful communication.

Nevertheless, although this second edition reflects recent scholarly insights and new possibilities for defining and teaching "writing," whatever that might mean or come to mean, the book remains committed to the idea that the teaching of writing requires willingness, enthusiasm, an interest in texts (of all kinds) as a subject of study, and a deep concern for helping students improve as writers, both within and beyond the writing class. It includes additional ideas—assignments, lessons, projects—for classroom use, but it also emphasizes the necessity of understanding the "concepts of composition" on which effective classroom pedagogy is based. Although many factors can contribute to a teacher's success in a writing class, the message in this book—that writing teachers need to be acquainted with the theories of composition and rhetoric that have influenced composition pedagogy for more than 40 years—has not changed. As our field has developed and gained prominence as a scholarly discipline, fewer academics believe that teaching writing means correcting grammatical errors and is something that anyone who reads and writes well can do. The many journals, books, conferences and organizations that are associated with this burgeoning discipline have brought the recognition that helping students improve as writers requires a thorough grounding in both theory and practice.

For all contributors to this book, the most daunting challenge has been figuring out how to address each multifaceted concept in composition within the confines of a single chapter. Composition scholarship is extensive, and the question of what to include and what to omit was the subject of many conversations among my contributors, all of whom were concerned about simplifying, but who also recognized the paradox of teaching composition: that teachers need to know a little about each concept to plan their courses effectively, but that it is only through classroom experience that they will really be able to understand the interaction of theory and practice. It is a credit to my contributors that they all managed to find a middle ground between too much and too little information, presenting a balanced perspective for beginning teachers while pointing the way to further exploration and research.

It is often the case that new teachers, worried about how to fill class time, become impatient with courses that address theory at all. "Just tell me what I need to teach," they implore. "Give me a syllabus and I'll follow it." *Concepts in Composition: Theory and Practice in the Teaching of Writing* aims to help teachers find answers for themselves by helping them understand connections between a theoretical concept and a classroom lesson. It is only when teachers understand that relationship that they will be able to teach effectively.

A companion website is available for use with this volume, with additional materials for instructors using the book in the classroom: www.routledge.com/9780415885164.

ACKNOWLEDGMENTS

I am deeply grateful to the contributors to this second edition. Their willingness to update their chapters, their breadth of scholarship, and their generosity of spirit have been crucial to the development of this second edition. I would also like to thank Linda Bathgate and the editorial staff at Taylor & Francis publishers, who provided continued support and encouragement, as did my wonderful graduate students at California State University, Northridge, whose enthusiasm for the first edition sparked my own efforts. In particular, I would like to acknowledge the contributions of Margeaux Gamboa and Michelle Mutti whose insights into new media have been so valuable. And then, finally, and always, there is my husband and family, who have always supported my publishing efforts and encouraged me in all my endeavors.

Processes

Irene L. Clark

- Why and how did writing classes become important in colleges and universities in the United States?
- What is meant by the term "process"?
- What does rhetoric have to do with the teaching of writing?
- What is the role of reading in the writing class?
- What is the role of reflection in helping students improve as writers?

In the first edition of *Concepts in Composition*, Chapter 1 was titled "Process," not "Processes," and in composition scholarship, the term "process" is still widely used. A popular statement in early journal articles and textbooks was "writing is a process, not a product," and today there is general agreement that an important goal for a writing course is to help students develop an effective writing *process*. However, it is now also recognized that there is no one writing "process" that works for everyone, that writers use various processes at different times, depending on what sort of text they wish to write, and that reading and research are also processes. So—the term "process" really refers to many *processes*, an important idea for prospective writing teachers to understand.

This chapter traces the history of the "process movement" within the emerging discipline of rhetoric and composition, discusses several competing views or theories of composing, explains connections between rhetoric and composition, and explores possibilities for integrating reading into writing courses. It will also discuss the role of reflection and the impact of new media on the idea of "process" in the teaching of writing.

THE "PROCESS" MOVEMENT

When I first began teaching writing, the hallway outside my office displayed a cartoon-like picture depicting a classroom of 100 years ago or more. In the center of the scene was a stereotypical professor, caricatured with pointed gray beard, wire spectacles, bushy gray eyebrows, and censorious expression, who was doggedly pouring knowledge through an oversized funnel into the head of a student, a sulky, somewhat plump young man. Obviously intended to be humorous, the picture ironically suggested that successful teaching involves transferring knowledge from professor to student, the professor active and determined, the student passive and submissive, perhaps uninterested, even unwilling.

I often recall that picture when I think about the term "process" in the context of composition pedagogy, because the outmoded concept of teaching it portrays constitutes the antithesis of current ideas about the teaching of writing. Over the past 40 years, the discipline of rhetoric and composition has emphasized the importance of helping students become active participants in learning to write, because, as the learning theorist Jerome Bruner (1966) has maintained:

> to instruct someone in [a] discipline is not a matter of getting him to commit results to mind. Rather, it is to teach him to participate in the process that makes possible the establishment of knowledge. … Knowledge is a process, not a product. (p. 72)

Because students do not learn to write by having knowledge poured into their heads, one of the most important goals of a writing class is to enable students to understand that writing is a "process," to develop a "process" that works well for them, and to be able to vary that process as the need arises. The term "process" is of key importance for anyone entering the field of composition, both as a teacher and as a researcher.

THE WRITING PROCESS MOVEMENT: A BRIEF HISTORY

In the long sweep of history, it is only recently that serious consideration has been given to writing in colleges and universities. The field of written rhetoric, which came to be called "composition," grew during the 19th century from an older tradition of oral rhetoric, which has been traced back to 500 B.C. However, during the 19th century, several political and technological developments had the effect of focusing academic attention on writing in English, instead of in Latin and Greek, as had previously been the case. The establishment of the land grant colleges in 1867 brought a new population of students to the university, students from less privileged backgrounds who had not studied classical languages and who, therefore, had to write in the vernacular—that is, English. Then, a number of inventions had the effect of making writing more important in a variety of settings. The invention of the mechanical pencil (1822), the fountain pen (1850), the telegram (1864), and the typewriter (1868), plus the increasing availability of cheap durable paper, paralleled and aided the increasing importance of writing at the university.

As writing became more important, the task of teaching writing was assumed by various educational institutions. The writing classes developed were viewed as "a device for preparing a trained and disciplined workforce" and for assimilating "huge numbers of immigrants into cultural norms, defined in specifically Anglo-Protestant terms" (Berlin, 1996, p. 23). In 1874, Harvard University introduced an entrance exam that featured a writing requirement; when the English faculty received the results, they were shocked by the profusion of error of all sorts—punctuation, capitalization, spelling, and syntax. In 1879, Adams Sherman Hill, who was in charge of the Harvard entrance examination for several years, complained that even the work of good scholars was flawed by spelling, punctuation, and grammar errors and urged that a required course in sophomore rhetoric that had been offered at Harvard for several years be moved to the first year. Thus was a literacy crisis born, and when Harvard instituted a first-year writing course, a number of institutions did likewise.

I am quite fond of this story and use it frequently both in lectures and in casual conversations in which someone has bemoaned the "decline" in student writing, claiming that it *used to be so much better*. The truth, though, is that each generation seems to look back on a golden age in which students were able to write "better" than they can at present, whatever "better" might mean, a time when students were more serious, more committed to learning, etc. And yet, even at Harvard, a recognized elite university, students' writing had been deemed inadequate. Even at Harvard, as Chester Noyes Greenough wrote in an early issue of the *English Journal* (February 1913), the work of undergraduate "men" was characterized by "incoherence, lack of unity in sentences and paragraphs, ignorance of certain rules of punctuation, repeated misspelling of certain words, and so on" (p. 113).

The First-Year Course and the Use of Handbooks

Greenough's article noted the writing limitations of the students at Harvard, but his primary concern was on the inadequate training provided to those assigned the task of working with these students. Although first-year writing courses abounded at a number of institutions, it was soon realized that such courses not only failed to provide an instant solution to the problem but also created a great deal of work for faculty who undertook or were assigned the task of reading and responding to student texts. However, by the turn of the century, a presumed method of addressing this situation was devised—the creation of a new sort of textbook called the "handbook," in which all of the rules and conventions of writing could be written and to which teachers could refer in the margins of student papers. The idea behind the development of the handbook was that teachers would no longer have to read and mark student papers in detail. Instead, they could skim the papers for errors, circle those errors in red, and cite rule numbers, which students could then look up in their handbooks. Handbooks became very popular, and soon every publisher had developed one, followed by a workbook of exercises that students could use to practice. Presumably, these handbooks and workbooks would lighten the teacher's load and solve the problem of teaching students to write. Yet, not surprisingly, the problems continued, and student writing did not improve.

The difficulties experienced by those attempting to teach students to write at the beginning of the 20th century were described in the lead article of the first issue of the *English Journal*, published in 1912. The title of that article was "Can Good Composition Teaching Be Done Under Present Conditions?" and the first word of the article was "No." Then, after a few sentences, the article went on as follows:

> Every year teachers resign, breakdown, perhaps become permanently invalided, having sacrificed ambition, health, and in not a few instances even life, in the struggle to do all the work expected of them. (Hopkins, p. 1)

Certainly, this was not an encouraging portrait of an emerging field!

Moreover, the composition course was often a brutal experience for students as well. Lad Tobin (1994), in his essay "How the Writing Process Was Born—and Other Conversion Narratives," recalled it like this:

> Once upon a time, in an age of disciplinary darkness and desolation ... writing students were subjected to cruel and inhuman punishments. They were assigned topics like "Compare Henry Fleming from *The Red Badge of Courage* to one of the characters in the *Iliad*; make sure to consider the definition of an anti-hero" or "Write about your most humiliating moment." They were told, with a straight face, that no decent person ever wrote without outlining first, that there is a clear distinction between description, narration, exposition, and argument;

that grammatical errors were moral and mortal sins, and that teachers' evaluations of student essays were always objective accurate and fair …

In that dark period of our disciplinary history, teachers rarely explained anything about the process of writing (unless you count "outline, write, proofread, hand in" as the student's process) … Or they would explain some of the rules governing good writing. But they would say nothing about invention, how to get started, what to do in the middle, or what to do when the middle turned back into the start, and so on. (pp. 2–3)

Of course, this picture constitutes a generalization, and it is likely that a number of teachers, intuitively understanding what was helpful to beginning writers, did not adhere to this model of "teaching" writing. Yet, that this model did indeed exist, I can attest to from my own college experience, where essay topics were assigned regardless of whether students knew or cared much about them, and where few, if any, process-oriented activities—prewriting strategies, multiple drafts, collaborative groups, student–teacher conferences—were encouraged or even mentioned. When I submitted a paper as a college student, I would wait with trepidation for the teacher to return it, which he or she would eventually do, usually without having written anything other than a grade or perhaps a brief evaluative comment on the front page.

In a recent review essay titled, "Of Pre- and Post-Process: Reviews and Ruminations," Richard Fulkerson (2001) characterized the situation of how first-year writing used to be as similar to "riding a bicycle. If you knew how to do it, then you could demonstrate your ability on demand; hence the idea of in-class and time-limited writing" (p. 96). Fulkerson (2001) described his own experience in a "pre-process program" as follows:

In the fall quarter, we had an anthology of readings, a handbook of grammar, and the 2nd edition of McCrimmon's *Writing with a Purpose*. We wrote at least five papers. One assigned topic was "My First Day at School." Another was "any philosophical issue." A third was a limited research paper about some historic person, who we were to argue was or was not "great" based on several readings in the anthology. Dr. Staton would assign *the* topic orally, and we would have about a week to write. Then he marked the paper, put a grade on it, and a brief comment. (p. 95)

Learning to write in those days meant being able to figure out what the teacher wanted in order to create an acceptable "product," and apparently, few teachers thought that helping students acquire a workable writing "process" was part of their job. Whatever process students used, they had to manage on their own.

This lack of attention to the process writers engage in when they write reflected a concept of creativity that to some extent persists in our culture—that is, that a "good" writer is someone who can produce an excellent text as quickly, independently, and effortlessly as a bird learns to fly. This idea suggests that those of us who struggle, for whom writing is a laborious, time-consuming, and often painful process (i.e., most, if not all, of us), are not, by definition, "good" writers. One could either write, or one couldn't. Such was the fantasy of that time, and even now, our culture continues to value speed and ease of production, particularly in reference to the speaking ability of our politicians, who are deemed "good speakers" if they can think on their feet.

Unlike the product orientation of pre-process days, in ancient times, classical rhetoricians were aware of how much thought and preparation went into the production of a seemingly effortless speech. In ancient Greece and Rome, rhetoricians envisioned the composing process as consisting of five stages—invention (the discovery of ideas), arrangement (putting ideas in a persuasively effective order), style (finding the right language in which to present the ideas), memory (memorizing the speech), and delivery (using voice and gesture to present the speech effectively). Apparently, no one at that time was under the impression that a "gifted" speaker did not have to engage in an elaborate process before he could deliver an effective speech.

For Writing and Discussion

Write a brief essay describing how you learned to write. To what extent was your experience similar to Fulkerson's description? Did your teachers focus on the idea of process?

The Birth of the Process "Movement"

This product-oriented view of writing continued through the 1950s and 1960s. Then, in 1963, at the Conference of College Composition and Communication, it is reported that there was a different feeling in the air, a feeling that the field had changed. That conference signaled a renewal of interest in rhetoric and composition theory, a revival that generated the "process" approach to composition and a new research area that focused on understanding how people write and learn to write. This interest in writing as a process led to the development of a number of process-oriented methods and techniques—staged writing, conferencing, strategies of invention, and revision—activities that are now considered essential components of a writing class. Suddenly, all over the country, writing teachers began to embrace a "process" approach to writing, tossing out their handbooks and grammar exercises in order to focus on process-oriented teaching. The sentence "Writing is a process, not a product" became a mantra. "Process" was in; "product" became almost a dirty word.

Can this interest in writing as a process and the emergence of composition as a research discipline be called a "movement"? Richard Fulkerson (2001) suggested that we refer to this interest in process-oriented writing as a political party, "with members frequently willing to vote together for the same candidates, and more or less united around certain slogans lacking in nuance and short enough for bumper stickers. 'Teach process not product.' 'Down with Current-Traditional Rhetoric.' 'Say no to grammar'" (pp. 98–99).

Influences on the Concept of Process Teaching

Whether one characterizes the concept of process teaching as a movement or a political party, the notion that "writing is a process" became a slogan for the enlightened. However, like all movements (or political parties), one can retrospectively note antecedent influences. One particularly important influence on the development of process teaching in the early 1960s was what has been referred to as the New Education Movement often associated with the ideas of the psychologist Jerome Bruner. Bruner viewed learning as a process that reflected "the cognitive level of the student and its relation to the structure of the academic discipline being studied" (Berlin, 1990, p. 207), and emphasized the role of student participation and individual discovery in the learning process. In the context of writing pedagogy, Bruner's ideas translated into an emphasis on students engaging in composing activities so as to discover their own composing process—rather than in analyzing someone else's text—and on teachers creating a facilitative learning environment to enable students to do so—rather than focusing on assigning grades or correcting grammar.

Another important influence on the emerging writing process movement was the Dartmouth conference of 1966, a meeting of approximately 50 English teachers from the United States and Great Britain to consider common writing problems. What emerged from the conference was the awareness that considerable differences existed between the two countries in how instruction in English was viewed. In the United States, English was conceived of as an academic discipline with specific content to be mastered, whereas the British focused on the personal and linguistic growth of the child (Appleby, 1974, p. 229). Instead of focusing on content, "process or activity ... defined the English curriculum for the British teacher" (Appleby, 1974, p. 230), its purpose being to foster the personal development of the student. As Berlin (1990) noted,

> The result of the Dartmouth Conference was to reassert for U.S. teachers the value of the expressive model of writing. Writing is to be pursued in a free and supportive environment in which the student is encouraged to engage in an act of self discovery. (p. 210)

This emphasis on the personal and private nature of composing was also manifested in the recommendations of early composition scholars such as Ken Macrorie, Donald Murray, Walker Gibson, and Peter Elbow.

What does it actually mean to view writing as a process? Broadly speaking, a process approach to writing and the teaching of writing means devoting increased attention to *writers* and the activities in which writers engage when they create and produce a text, as opposed to analyzing and attempting to reproduce "model" texts. Reacting against a pedagogy oriented toward error correction and formulaic patterns of organization, the process approach, as it evolved during the 1960s and 1970s, was concerned with discovering *how* writers produce texts, developing a model of the writing process, and helping writers find a process that would enable them to write more effectively and continue to improve as writers. Although to many writers and teachers the concept of a writing "process" was not news, the increased emphasis in the classroom on helping students acquire an effective process and on finding out what successful writers did when they wrote, constituted a new pedagogical approach and a potentially exciting research direction.

For Writing and Discussion

Reflecting on Your Own Writing Process

(Adapted from "Chronotopic Lamination: Tracing the Contours of Literate Activity." Paul Prior and Jody Shipka, *Writing Selves/Writing Societies*, Bazerman & Russell, published February 1, 2003. http://wac.colostate.edu/books/selves_societies/.)

This is an assignment that will enable you to gain conscious awareness of the process you use to write papers that are assigned in classes (and the extent to which that process might be different when you write for other purposes). It is an assignment that you can also use with your students.

Think about a paper you have written recently for a college class. Then draw two pictures:

1. The first picture should represent how you actually engaged in writing this particular piece. It might show a place or places where you did that writing.
2. The second picture should represent the whole writing process for this particular piece. The picture might show how this writing activity got started, interactions with other people and other texts, experiences that have influenced the direction or approach you used, the number and type of drafts, your evaluations of and emotions about this activity at different times.

After the two drawings are completed:

1. Describe the writing assignment and class for which it was intended. How did you feel about the assignment? Were you interested in it immediately? Did you find it difficult or confusing?
2. List as many activities associated with that writing as you possibly can recall. Some questions to consider:

- What was the first action you performed to complete the writing task? What actions followed?
- Did you think about the writing when you were involved in other activities (driving a car, for example)?
- Did you talk with anyone about the topic?
- What sort of revision did you do?
- Were these behaviors typical of what you usually do when you are given a writing assignment?
- Do you feel your writing process is effective?
- Do you use a different process when you are working on something that you, yourself, have decided to write? If so, how is it different?

THE STAGES OF WRITING

One perspective that gained prominence during the early days of the process movement was that the writing process consisted a series of sequenced, discrete stages sometimes called "planning, drafting, and revising," although today they are often referred to as "prewriting, writing, and rewriting." An article by Gordon Rohman (1965), "Prewriting: The Stage of Discovery in the Writing Process," published in *College Composition and Communication*, emphasized the importance of invention and providing students with models of how writing is actually done. Articles published during this period strongly emphasized prewriting; however, what many of them also suggested was that writing occurred in a linear sequence, each stage following neatly upon the other, the "prewriting" phase preceding the "writing" phase, which then precedes the "revising" phase. Such a model was based on the idea that writing is a reflection of what already has been formulated in the mind of the writer and, by implication, suggested that writing can occur only after the main ideas are in place. According to this model, discovery and creativity entered the process only in terms of the writer's decisions about *how* to say what has been discovered, not in discovering and selecting *what* to say. It also suggested that once a writer knew what he or she wanted to write, that part of the process was complete.

We now know that this linear model of writing as a series of discrete stages does not reflect what most writers actually do, because writers frequently discover and reconsider ideas during, as well as before, they write, moving back and forth between the prewriting, writing, and revision stages as the text emerges. For example, when I wrote this chapter, I began with a set of points I planned to discuss, but I modified them many times as I wrote, often revising sentences and generating additional material as new ideas occurred to me. In addition, with ease of access to new information, writers now can move from writing to research and back to writing without ever leaving their desks. Moreover, because every person's writing habits are different, an insistence on a lock-step sequence of stages can prove inhibiting, sometimes paralyzing, to beginning writers. Those who believe that writing cannot occur until every thought is clarified often delay actually writing until the paper is fully outlined and developed—or until time has run out and the due date forces the writer to begin. For some students, the idea that a writer must know exactly what he or she is going to say before beginning to write can create a writer's block that actually *prevents* effective writing from taking place. Although the idea that writing occurs in stages was a more helpful one than the previous emphasis on grammatical correctness, when it was interpreted rigidly, this idea did not provide sufficient insight into the composing processes of actual writers; nor was it always useful in the classroom or in other venues. As Muriel Harris (1989) argued in the article at the end of this chapter, "when students write essay exams or placement essays and when they go on to on-the-job writing where time doesn't permit multiple drafts, they need to produce first drafts which are also coherent, finished final drafts."

RENEWED INTEREST IN RHETORIC

The process movement was also characterized by a renewed interest in rhetoric and its connection to composition, a phenomenon that is often referred to as the "new rhetoric," although the term "rhetoric" was absent from early publications. However, in 1971, James Kinneavy published *A Theory of Discourse*, which established "the relation between composition and classical—specifically Aristotelian—rhetoric" (Williams, 1998, p. 30). This work helped legitimize composition as a genuine research field and suggested that anyone who is serious about teaching writing should be studying rhetoric. Providing a theoretical grounding for the new rhetoric, Kinneavy's work was also notable for its reminder that writing is an act of communication between writer and audience.

Many of the scholars who worked in composition during the early days of the process movement have "a story to tell about how and when they discovered rhetoric" (Lunsford, 2007, p. 1), and rhetoric has increasingly become an important element in many writing classes. Although the term is often associated with empty or sometimes deceptive language, such as "that's just rhetoric," the term in actuality refers to the complex interaction between the writer, the reader, and the context and is therefore neither good nor bad in itself. An ethical person will use rhetoric to explore an idea and discover truth, whereas an unethical person will use it to deceive. Plato distrusted rhetoric because of its association with the Sophists, who used it to "win" an argument, no matter where the truth might be. Aristotle, however, viewed rhetoric as the ability, in each particular case, to discover the available means of persuasion, the presumption being that persuasion should and could be used in the service of justice. Although not all writing is persuasive, awareness of how writer, audience, and situation interact in the creation of a text enables us to know the world and make informed choices in the construction of a text. John Gage in "The Reasoned Thesis" pointed out that Aristotelian rhetoric does not have to be understood strictly in terms of persuasion or coercion, but rather in terms of inquiry, of helping people discover "mutual grounds for assent" (Gage, 1996, p. 10). M. J. Killingsworth (2005) showed how rhetoric can enable writers and readers achieve mutual understanding of the values they share.

Rhetoric, Exigence, and Process

An understanding of rhetoric can help students develop an effective writing process in that the elements of rhetoric can suggest directions for exploration and revision. In particular, I have found the terms "rhetorical situation" and "exigence" to be particularly useful in writing classes at any level. Lloyd Bitzer's notion of the "rhetorical situation," which he defines as a problem, situation, or need that can be impacted or addressed in some way through writing, can enable students to find a rationale or purpose for writing. Bitzer also used the word "exigence," which he defined as a defect, an obstacle or some problem or situation that is not what it ought to be or at least needs attention. When my students are in the process of developing ideas for an essay, I will often ask them "Where's the exigence?"

The idea of "exigence" can enable students to begin the process of writing and keep them focused on a writing task as they develop ideas and formulate an approach. It can also motivate revision, as they consider the potential impact on an audience and revisit the context, occasion, and purpose for writing. Chapter 2 on "Invention" will discuss the role of rhetoric and exigence in further detail.

Rhetoric, Authority, and Values

Including rhetoric in a writing class focuses students' attention on what enables them to accept the "truth" of an idea—that is, what makes an idea convincing and what sort of evidence and authority contributes to making it so. For example, in a strongly Christian community in which the Bible is viewed as a source of values, quoting from the Bible may serve as a definitive authority and convincing evidence might be found by quoting from that source. Academic writing, however, is usually intended for a broader, more secular community, and therefore the Bible may not serve as a convincing source of authority for that audience. Moreover, as Killingsworth (2005) maintained:

> Modern rhetoric does not so much replace one authority with another; rather it attacks the very idea of absolute authority. People who use rhetoric don't have to be atheists or moral relativists, but they must realize that the constraints on how we discuss issues are different as we move from community to community, audience to audience. (p. 13)

In writing about an issue such as whether women should submit to their husband in marriage, Killingsworth pointed out, a student would have to base his or her arguments "on something more than the Bible" (p. 12). Incorporating rhetoric into a writing class will enable students to understand how the values of an intended audience impact the direction and credibility of a text.

RHETORICAL READING

The process movement focused on the idea that "writing is a process." However, it is now recognized that reading is a process as well, and that many students, while able to read or "decode" words on a page, are unable to understand the texts assigned in their college classes. The term "rhetorical reading," associated with the work of Bean, Chappell, and Gillam (2005), can be defined as "attending to an author's purposes for writing and the methods the author uses to accomplish those purposes" (p. xxiii). The concept of rhetorical reading emphasizes the importance of helping students analyze the rhetorical strategies used in academic texts and helping students understand "academic writing as a process in which writers engage with other texts" (p. xxiii). It also includes the concept of "critical" reading as a means of enabling students to recognize biased perspectives in various texts, including visual texts such as websites and advertisements.

The idea that reading is a process enables students to approach a text purposefully, not simply to begin reading passively, sentence by sentence without considering why it was written and the strategies the writer has used to accomplish a particular purpose. In working with students in a writing class, I urge them to develop a process of reading that I refer to as "the three-pass approach," which consists of the following process-oriented activities:

1. The First Pass—Reflection and Quick Overview
   During the first pass, students reflect on the subject and context that are being addressed, evaluate the qualifications and motives of the author, and examine the reading for additional clues, such as the title, publication information, and easily discernible strategies of organization.
2. The Second Pass—Reading for Meaning and Structure
   During the second pass, students read the text for meaning to determine what it is saying. To aid understanding, they are encouraged to look for structural clues within the text and summarize main points. Other activities associated with the second pass might include creating a "map" of the text or noting the "moves" the writer uses.
3. The Third Pass—Interacting with the Text
   During the third pass, students are encouraged to interact with the text, actively engaging in a critical dialogue with it, in order to understand it more deeply and determine how much of it to accept. Such interaction involves distinguishing between fact and opinion, evaluating the type of evidence cited, deciding whether the writer is aware of the complexity of the topic, and paying close attention to how language is being used to shape the reader's perspective.

(For additional information on this three-pass approach, see Clark, 2010.)

GENRE AND PROCESS

The topic of genre will be discussed in detail in a subsequent chapter. However, in the context of "process," it is important to mention that "genre knowledge" can have a significant impact on the "process" a writer will use to complete a writing task. To write a shopping list, for example, one would simply jot down items on a piece of paper, and any revision of that list would be unlikely to involve serious effort—perhaps the addition of other items, a check placed next to an item already purchased, or a line through an item that was not needed after all. More complicated genres or high-stakes genres, however, involve more serious effort, and the "process" of writing might begin with a reflection about what such a genre requires. In the reading included at the end of this chapter, Mary Jo Reiff (2006) noted that a writing assignment, particularly one that requires an unfamiliar genre, generates a number of genre-based questions. Reiff observed that when she was asked to write about the "genre of the *Pedagogical Insight* essay," she called on her "genre knowledge, her past experience with similar texts in similar situations" (p. 157) in order to orient herself to the expectations of the genre. Because she knew that she was not familiar with this genre, she asked herself several questions, such as "What are the actions that this genre performs? How will I position myself within this genre—what identity and relations will I assume?" (p. 157). These questions then prompted her to consider a potential audience and the social and cultural situation toward which her response would be directed. A consideration of genre, then, enabled Reiff to begin the process of writing her essay.

A number of scholars (in particular, see Devitt, 2004) have suggested that an important goal of a writing class is to help students become aware of the genres they are expected to produce, an approach that is particularly useful for students whose first language is not English. Such a genre-based class may focus on studying multiple examples of a genre in order to discern its features, as well as more usual process-oriented activities, such as writing multiple drafts and obtaining peer feedback.

EARLY RESEARCH ON COMPOSING

The "process" movement generated a great deal of scholarship, some based on observational studies, other focused on cognitive models of learning. In an overview of early research concerned with the writing process, Sondra Perl (1994) noted 1971 as the year when the field of composition moved from an almost exclusive focus on written products to an examination of composing processes. 1971 was the year that Janet Emig published "The Composing Processes of Twelfth Graders," which Perl describes as the first study to ask a process-oriented question, "How do 12th-graders write?" and the first to devise a method to study writing processes as they unfolded. Emig observed eight 12th-graders who spoke aloud as they composed, and from her observations, called into question the absoluteness of the stage-model theory of composing. Noting that these students did not create outlines before they composed, Emig characterized the composing process as recursive, rather than linear, noting that writers move back and forth between various phases of the process as they compose.

Although the validity of having students speak aloud as they compose can be questioned, Emig's study was important because it showed the oversimplification of the writing process inherent in the stage model, which was, and to some extent still is, reinforced in some textbooks. Moreover, it generated a number of observational studies that shed further light on the composing process, among them the work of Linda Flower and John Hayes (1980), discussed later in this chapter, that linked the development of writing ability to cognitive development and the studies by Sondra Perl (1979) and Nancy Sommers (1980) which provided valuable insight into revision.

For Further Exploration

Early Process-oriented Scholarship

Faigley, L., & Witte, S. (1980). Analyzing revision. *CCC, 32,* 400–414.

Flower, L., & Hayes, J. (1981). A cognitive process theory of writing. *CCC, 32,* 354–387.

Kroll, B., & Schafer, J. (1978). Error analysis and the teaching of composition. *CCC, 29,* 242–248.

Matsuhashi, A. (1981). Pausing and planning: The tempo of written discourse production. *Research in the Teaching of English, 15,* 113–134.

Perl, S. (1979). The composing process of unskilled college writers. *Research in the Teaching of English, 13,* 317–336.

Perl, S. (1981). Understanding composing. *CCC, 31,* 363–369.

Pianko, S. (1979). A description of the composing processes of college freshmen writers. *Research in the Teaching of English, 13,* 5–22.

Sommers, N. (1980). Revision strategies of student writers and experienced adult writers. *CCC, 31,* 378–388.

Rhetoric and the Composition Class

Gage, J. T. (1996). The reasoned thesis: The E-word and argumentative writing as a process of inquiry. In Barbara Emmel, Paula Resch, & Deborah Tenney (Eds.), *Argument revisited; Argument redefined* (pp. 3–18). Thousand Oaks, CA: Sage Publications.

Killingsworth, M. J. (2005). *Appeals in modern rhetoric: An ordinary-language approach.* Carbondale: Southern Illinois University Press.

Lunsford, A. A. (2007). *Writing matters.* Athens and London: University of Georgia Press.

Lunsford, A. A., & Glenn, C. (1990). Rhetorical theory and the teaching of writing. In Gail Hawisher, & Anne Soter (Eds.), *On literacy and its teaching* (pp. 174–189). Albany: State University of New York.

For Writing and Discussion

Compare Nancy Sommers' "The Revision Strategies of Student Writers and Experienced Adult Writers" (in Chapter 3) with Muriel Harris' essay "Composing Behaviors of One-and Multi-Draft Writers" at the end of this chapter. Note the similarities and differences between their perspectives on the writing process. What are the implications of these perspectives for working with students in a writing class?

The Role of Cognitive Psychology

Early studies of the composing process were strongly influenced by ideas associated with cognitive psychology, particularly those of Jerome Bruner, previously discussed, and those of Jean Piaget and Lev Vygotsky. The underlying idea of cognitive psychology is that to understand an observable behavior (such as writing), one must understand the mental structures that determine that behavior. Conceiving of language and thought as the primary mental structures that influence writing, cognitive psychologists maintained that to understand how students learn to write, one must understand how these structures develop as an individual matures and acquires knowledge of the world.

Cognitive psychology perceives linguistic and intellectual ability as developing in a natural sequence, and it is this concept that has had the most significant impact on the study of writing acquisition and on how a writing teacher can utilize that sequence in the classroom. Emig (1971), for example, maintained that the ability to write personal, expressive writing precedes the ability to write on literary or academic topics. She, therefore, urged teachers to use more of what she referred to as "reflexive"—that is, personal—writing in the classroom, based on students' own experiences and feelings. Beginning with personal topics before addressing more abstract topics, Emig claimed, fosters students' cognitive development. Whether or not this is absolutely true has not been established. However, in order for students to engage with a topic, it is useful for them to consider what personal involvement they might have with it. In my own writing classes, students often write about a personal experience that is related to the topic before they focus on issues or controversies that may be developed in an argument essay.

Developmental Models of the Composing Process

This notion that the development of writing ability correlates with human linguistic and intellectual development resulted in a number of publications that suggested that the English curriculum should parallel the sequence in which that development was presumed to occur. Deriving from Piaget's notion of cognitive development, James Moffett's *Teaching the Universe of Discourse* (1968) outlined a theory by which a sequential curriculum in language arts could be based. Moffett's system consisted of a progression that moved from the personal to the impersonal and from low to high levels of abstraction based on two horizontal scales. The first, the audience scale, organized discourse according to the distance between the writer and his or her audience, according to four categories (Moffett, 1968b):

Reflection (interpersonal communication within the self)

Conversation (interpersonal communication between two people within communication distance)

Correspondence (interpersonal communication between remote individuals)

Publication (impersonal communication between unconnected individuals, unknown to one another). (p. 33)

Moffett's second scale, the subject scale, categorized discourse by how far away the writer or speaker is from the subject being considered. For example, a person may be sitting at a table in a cafeteria eating lunch, noting what is happening at the given moment. Later on, he or she might report on what happened in the cafeteria during lunch, generalize about what usually happens in the cafeteria at lunch, or argue that something might or should happen in the cafeteria at lunch. These two scales, the audience scale and the subject scale, Moffett suggested, can be used to help students recreate their experience through language, enabling them to develop facility in writing. Moffett's concept of a language arts curriculum based on this sequence was explained in considerable detail in his textbook *A Student-Centered Language Arts Curriculum* (1968a).

A British study, *The Development of Writing Abilities 11–18*, published in 1975 by James Britton, Tony Burgess, Nancy Martin, Alex McLeod, and Harold Rosen, also included the notion of sequential development. Aimed at creating a model that would "characterize all mature written utterances and then go on to trace the developmental steps that led to them" (p. 6), this system of Britton and his colleagues categorized all student writing by function—the transactional, which communicates information to an unknown audience, the expressive, which communicates information to a known audience, and the poetic, which deals only tangentially with any form of audience. Britton et al. characterized most school writing as transactional, but argued that because students are most engaged in expressive writing, this is the type of writing that is most likely to foster the development of writing ability.

Both Moffett's work and the work of Britton et al., evolving from the theories of Jean Piaget, addressed the question of how children learn to move beyond their early egocentricism to reach out to an audience, a topic addressed by Linda Flower in her seminal article "Writer-Based Prose: A Cognitive Basis for Problems in Writing" (1979). According to Flower, novice writers often have difficulty transcending their own egocentric perspective to consider the needs of their intended audience. As a result, their texts are often characterized by what she refers to as "writer-based prose"—that is, texts in which information is omitted or inadequately explained, definitions unclarified—in other words, texts that reflect what might be in their writers' minds at the time of writing but that have not been sufficiently contextualized or modified for a reader. Often reflecting the order in which the writer first generated ideas, writer-based prose may be clear to the writer, but a reader may have difficulty understanding it. Awareness of writer-based prose in the writing class can be used to help novice writers transform "writer-based" to "reader-based" prose, enabling them to develop a better understanding of the concept of audience.

Pursuing a similar direction, Andrea Lunsford, in an article titled "Cognitive Development and the Basic Writer" (1979), claimed that the difficulties novice or "basic" writers have with writing are because of their not having reached a level of cognitive development that would enable them to form abstractions. To remedy this problem, Lunsford suggested a variety of workshop activities focusing on analysis and active thinking. During that same year (1979), Sharon Pianko published "A Description of the Composing Processes of College Freshman Writers," in which she claimed that the composing process of basic writers is less developed than that of more skillful writers.

The Work of Flower and Hayes

Several articles by Flower and Hayes continued to explore the writing process based on theories of cognitive psychology. Concerned with avoiding models that suggest that the writing process is linear, Flower and Hayes (1981) set up a cognitive theory based on four points:

1. The process of writing is best understood as a set of distinctive think processes that writers orchestrate or organize during the act of composing.
2. These processes have a hierarchical, highly embedded organization in which any process can be embedded within any other.
3. The act of composing itself is a goal-directed thinking process, guided by the writer's own growing network of goals.
4. Writers create their own goals in two key ways: by generating both high-level goals and supporting subgoals that embody the writer's developing sense of purpose, and then, at times, by changing major goals or even establishing new ones based on what has been learned in the act of writing. (p. 366)

Flower and Hayes also focused on the role of problem definition in the writing process, noting in their article "The Cognition of Discovery: Defining a Rhetorical Problem" (1980) that although a teacher may give "20 students the same assignment, the writers themselves create the problem they solve" (p. 23). Using the technique of "protocols" (having students speak aloud as they compose), Flower and Hayes constructed a model of the rhetorical problem itself, which consisted of two major units: the rhetorical situation, which consists of the "writer's given," including the audience and the assignment, and the set of goals that the writer creates for himself. The four goals they noted involved the reader, creating a persona or voice, building a meaning, and producing a formal text, which, as they point out, "closely parallel the four terms of the communication triangle: reader, writer, world, word" (p. 25).

EXPRESSIVISM AND THE CONCEPT OF PERSONAL VOICE

The initial phase of the process movement has often been associated with an emphasis on the importance of students being able to "express" their thoughts and feelings through writing, a perspective that is often referred to as "expressivism." Teachers adhering to an expressivist philosophy tended to assign essays concerned with personal experience and self-reflection, the goal being to enable students to discover their own personal "voice" that would result in "authentic" writing and self-empowerment. Ken Macrorie, in his 1970 textbook *Telling Writing*, insisted on the importance of truth telling by avoiding what he refers to as "Engfish," which he defines as institutional language, or language that conceals rather than reveals a personal self. In the preface to that work, Macrorie (1970) defined composition teaching in the following terms:

> Enabling students to use their own powers, to make discoveries, to take alternative paths. It does not suggest that the world can best be examined by a set of rules ... The program gives the student first, freedom to find his voice and let his subjects find him ... for both teacher and student, a constant reading for truth, in writing and commenting on that writing. This is a hard requirement, for no one speaks truth consistently. (pp. vii–viii)

For Macrorie, good writers speak in honest voices and tell some kind of truth, a perspective similar to that of Donald Stewart (1972), for whom the most important goal of a writing course was for students to engage in a process of self-discovery, manifested in the student's text by the appearance in the text of an authentic voice; Donald Graves (1983) also referred to voice as infusing a text with the writer's presence. Perhaps the best-known proponent of the concept of voice, Peter Elbow (1986), although acknowledging the difficulty of defining voice, nevertheless viewed the discovery of voice as a necessary prerequisite of growth. "I can grow or change," Elbow maintained, but "not unless I start out inhabiting my own voice or style. ... In short, I need to accept myself as I am before I can tap my power or start to grow" (p. 204). Voice, for Elbow, constitutes both a motivating force and a source of power. In its emphasis on empowering the inner self, the expressivist approach to writing is sometimes referred to as the "romantic" school of writing, in contrast to the "classical" or "cognitive" school, which view writing in terms of intellectual development as manifested in problem solving.

Of course, there is no reason that the "process" approach should be so closely connected to expressivist writing. As Ladd Tobin (1994) points out, "a teacher could assign a personal essay but ignore the writing process or assign a critical analysis yet nurture the process" (p. 6). Nevertheless, process and personal or expressivist writing were often associated with one another in the early days of the process movement, and today the expressionists remain "a force in rhetoric and composition studies. Such figures as Peter Elbow, Donald Murray, Ken Macrorie … continue to explore writing as a private and personal act. It is this group that continues to insist on the importance of the individual against the demands of institutional conformity, holding out for the personal as the source of all value" (Berlin, 1990, pp. 218–219).

SOCIAL CONSTRUCTIONISM

Although cognitive and expressivist approaches to composition dominated scholarship during the 1970s and 1980s, during the mid-1980s, publications began to appear that questioned both the validity and the utility of focusing on the individual. Patricia Bizzell's "Cognition, Convention, and Certainty: What We Need to Know About Writing" (1983) argued that writers are not autonomous individuals, distinct and removed from culture, but, rather, that individual consciousness is shaped by culture through language. This perspective implied that all writers, even when they are presumably composing only for themselves or writing notes for a subsequent piece of writing, are mentally influenced by the "inner speech," as Vygotsky (1978) referred to it, that develops in response to a particular culture's concept of language and thought. From this perspective, then, writing is *socially constructed* because it both reflects and shapes thinking, a position that in composition studies is known as *social constructionism*. Social constructionist approaches to composition emphasize the role of community in shaping discourse and the importance of understanding community expectations when working with students. Bizzell's article (1983), for example, pointed out that although Flower and Hayes' cognitive-based model described how writing occurs, it focused too strongly on the individual writer and did not help composition teachers "advise students on difficult questions of practice" (p. 222).

Social constructionist approaches to composition derive from perspectives in philosophy, as well as other fields, that emphasize the importance of community consensus in determining knowledge. This view is based on the idea that individuals perceive the world according to the shared beliefs and perceptions of the community or communities to which they belong; it is one that writers in fields such as history or ethnography have supported for some time. The philosopher, Richard Rorty, for example, in *Philosophy and the Mirror of Nature* (1979), maintained that knowledge is a "socially constructed belief," a viewpoint that straddles a middle position between absolute relativism, in which an individual may choose to believe anything, and the positivist notion of objective truth derived from an absolute reality. The anthropologist, Clifford Geertz (1983), similarly argued that modern consciousness is an "enormous multiplicity" of cultural values, and Charles Bazerman (1981) has emphasized the role of the scientific community in shaping the writing of scientists.

In composition, social constructionist approaches have been associated with the work of David Bartholomae, Kenneth Bruffee, Patricia Bizzell, and James Berlin, who all focused on the social context of writing and the role of community in determining the appropriateness and effectiveness of a text. Kenneth Bruffee's "Collaborative Learning and the 'Conversation of Mankind'" (1984) maintained that every person is born into the "conversation of mankind" and that it is this conversation that gives meaning and value to what we do, influencing both thinking and writing. "We can think because we can talk, and we think in ways we have learned to talk" (p. 87), Bruffee explained. For writing teachers, it is important to realize (Bruffee, 1984):

> that our task must involve engaging students in conversation among themselves at as many points in both the writing and the reading process as possible and that we should contrive to ensure that students' conversation about what they read and write is similar in as many ways as possible to the way we would like them eventually to read and write. The way they talk with each other determines the way they will think and the way they will write. (p. 89)

Collaborative Learning

Social constructionism has often associated with collaborative learning, although this pedagogical approach has been around for some time. Bruffee's work acknowledged the use of collaborative learning in teaching medical students through group diagnosis, and Albert DeCiccio (1988) has noted its association with progressive education and the educational approach of John Dewey. Moreover, as Bruffee (1984) has noted, the uses of collaborative learning in the composition class in the 1970s derived more from practical need than from a particular philosophical or theoretical perspective on learning. Because open admission policies brought a large number of students to the university who were educationally disadvantaged, collaborative learning developed as a means of enabling students to assist one another. As Bruffee (1984) pointed out, "For American college teachers, the roots of collaborative learning lie neither in radical politics nor in research." Rather it was based primarily on "a pressing educational need" (p. 637).

Whatever its roots, the concept of collaborative learning has significant implications for what occurs in the writing class. Most important, it implies a decentering of the writing class, a balancing of authority between students and teacher, so that students can participate in their own learning through peer editing and writing groups. This idea, as Bruffee pointed out, is actually quite similar to the work of the early process theorists such as Peter Elbow, who has long advocated the effectiveness of the "teacherless" classroom and the necessity of delegating authority to writing groups. According to this perspective, students learn only when they have assumed responsibility for their own learning. They do not develop writing skills by listening to a teacher lecture about the writing process. Rather they must engage fully in that process themselves, working together with peers.

Collaborative Learning in the Classroom

Although the concept of collaborative learning is easy to endorse in the abstract, successful implementation in the classroom requires the teacher to plan carefully all activities involving group work, whether they be peer editing sessions, group discussions, or team research projects. All of us who have blithely assumed that simply telling students to work together or putting them into pairs or groups without providing specific instructions can attest to the problems that often occur. Unless collaborative activities are carefully orchestrated by the teacher, students may not take group work seriously, socializing instead of working, allocating most of the work to one member, completing the activity superficially, and generally not engaging fully in the process. Sometimes they will offer innocuous compliments to one another such as "I liked your paper. I could relate to it." Or "It flowed." Or else they will complete the group activity quickly so that they can leave the class early.

Wendy Bishop (1997), in "Helping Peer Writing Groups Succeed," emphasized the importance of carefully scripting and modeling what is expected from peer writing groups. Below are some additional suggestions for maximizing the value of collaborative activities in the writing class:

- Model the activity by first engaging in it yourself in front of the class. Before putting students into groups for peer editing, ask students to volunteer a paper to be edited, or use one from another class. Make copies for the class and demonstrate how you expect students to proceed.
- Determine the procedures for group work, such as whether students should read papers silently or aloud, how many copies of the paper students should bring in, how much time should be allotted for each paper, and the sort of comments that should be encouraged.
- Assign the groups yourself through random selection. If students choose their own groups, they may spend the time socializing instead of working. To enable the groups to develop a productive working relationship, keep the groups constant throughout the semester, unless there is a good reason for changing them.
- For peer editing, develop assignment-specific questions (see the following "For Writing and Discussion" for an example).
- When possible, require students to report their discussion results to the class. This works well when students engage in group research because it requires them to take responsibility for their work. They should be aware that they will be standing in front of the class and that inadequate preparation will be apparent to everyone!

For Writing and Discussion

The following assignment is provided as an example of how peer questions should be oriented toward a specific assignment. Work through this process by writing a response to the assignment, bringing your response to class, and working in groups to respond to the questions. By completing the process yourself, you will gain insight into how to use it in your writing class.

Writing Assignment

One important insight arising from research into the composing process is that no approach or strategy is appropriate for all writers and that, as Muriel Harris points out, "there is a very real danger in imposing a single 'ideal' composing style on students." In fact, the more we engage in research about the composing process, the more we realize how much more we need to learn.

As a writer and a student of writing, you have learned a great deal about the writing process from your own experiences, some of them useful, some less so, and it is your writing background that will serve as the primary resource for this assignment. Think about your own history as a writer—your classroom successes and failures, teachers and writers who have influenced you, assignments you have completed, and strategies you have developed as you grappled with various types of writing assignments throughout your academic career. Then in an essay of **three to five pages**, respond to the following question:

Based on your experience as a writer and a student, what insights into the composing process do you consider to be the most important?

In discussing insights you have gained, please enliven your prose with specific examples and anecdotes.

First draft: 3 copies due in class on __. First drafts must be typed.

Final draft due on __.

Peer Editing Question Sheet

Name of Writer _____ Feedback Provided by _____

1. Does the essay respond to the prompt—that is, what insights into the composing process does the writer consider most important?
2. Examine the introduction. What function does it serve? To attract attention? To indicate a direction for the essay? How does the introduction prepare the reader for other sections in the essay?
3. Examine the essay for support. What are the main ideas or themes? What specific examples, anecdotes, or explanations are used to support these ideas or themes?
4. Examine the essay for coherence. What strategies are used to connect each paragraph with the next?
5. Examine the essay for style and sentence structure. What specific words does the writer use to illustrate main points? What kind of person do you sense behind the prose? How does the writer make this person seem real? How does the writer use sentence structure to develop the essay? Is the essay's style sufficiently varied? Are the sentences choppy?
6. What has the writer done to make the essay interesting? What did you learn from this essay? What did the writer do to enhance the audience appeal of this essay?

Collaborating Online

Recently, increased access to new media has enabled students to collaborate virtually—sharing ideas and drafts online, working in groups on various projects without meeting face to face. Beach, Anson, Breuch, and Swiss (2009) discuss a number of options for using "digital discussion environments to enhance writing instruction and student engagement" (p. 48). Defining "digital discussion environments" as those that promote conversation and collaboration, these authors provide an overview of both *synchronous* (real-time) discussions, used when students are on the computer at the same time, and *asynchronous discussions*, when students write separate messages at different times. Synchronous discussions tend to be more conversational and are sometimes used even when all students are in a classroom; asynchronous discussions occur when students are not in the same location and can serve as a written transcript of an ongoing discussion. Both can be useful in enabling students to learn from one another and build upon one another's ideas.

Online writing and collaboration can take many forms: having students respond to a reading, discovering a purpose for writing, finding additional research, responding to drafts, discussing ideas for a project, or enabling students to become aware of audience. Whatever purpose it might serve, however, planning is crucial, just as it is in a face-to-face classroom. When they engage in a digital collaboration, students should have a clear idea of what they are expected to do or learn in the context of a particular assignment or task.

For Further Exploration

Social Constructionism

Bartholomae, D., & Petrosky, A. (1986). *Facts, artifacts, and counterfacts.* Portsmouth, NH: Heinemann.

Bazerman, C. (1981). What written knowledge does: Three examples of academic discourse. *Philosophy of the Social Sciences, 11,* 361–387.

Bruffee, K. Social construction, language and the authority of knowledge. *College English, 48,* 773–790.

Geertz, C. (1983). *Local knowledge.* New York: Basic Books.

Harris, J. (1989). The idea of community in the study of writing. *CCC, 40,* 11–22.

Rorty, R. (1979). *Philosophy and the mirror of nature.* Princeton, NJ: Princeton University Press.

Vygotsky, L. (1978). *Mind in society* (M. Cole, V. John Steiner, S. Scribner, & E. Souberman Eds.). Cambridge, MA: Harvard University Press.

Collaborative Learning

Bizzell, P. (1983). Cognition, convention, and certainty: What we need to know about writing. *PRETEXT, 3,* 213–243.

Brooke, R. (1991). *Writing and sense of self: Identity negotiation in writing workshops.* Urbana, IL: NCTE.

Brooke, R., Mirtz, R., & Evans, R. (1994). *Small groups in writing workshops.* Urbana, IL: NCTE.

Bruffee, K. A. (1984, November). Collaborative learning and the "conversation of mankind." *College English, 46,* 635–652.

Elbow, P. (1973). *Writing without teachers.* New York: Oxford University Press.

Forman, J. (Ed.). (1992). *New visions of collaborative writing.* Portsmouth, NH: Boynton/ Cook.

George, D. (1984) Working with peer groups in the composition classroom. *CCC, 35,* 320–326.

Gere, A. R. (1987). *Writing groups: History, theory, and implications.* Carbondale, IL: Southern Illinois University Press.

Lunsford, A., & Ede, L. (1990). *Singular texts/plural authors: Perspectives on collaborative writing.* Carbondale, IL: Southern Illinois University Press.

Mason, E. (1970). *Collaborative learning.* London: Ward Lock.

Smith, D. (1989). Some difficulties with collaborative learning. *Journal of Advanced Composition, 9,* 45–57.

Spellmeyer, K. (1994). On conventions and collaboration: The open road and the iron cage. In J. Clifford, & J. Schilb (Eds.), *Writing theory and critical theory.* New York: MLA.

Trimbur, J. (1989, October). Consensus and difference in collaborative learning. *College English, 51,* 602–616.

Collaborating Online

Beach, R., Anson, C. Breuch L. B., & Swiss, T. (2009). *Teaching writing using blogs, wikis, and other digital tools.* Norwood, MA: Christopher-Gordon.

Gane, N., & Beer, D. (2008). *New media.* Oxford: Berg.

Wysocki, A. F., Johnson-Eilola, J., & Selfe, C. L. (2004). *Writing new media: Theory and applications for expanding the teaching of composition.* Logan, UT: Utah State University Press.

CRITICISM OF THE PROCESS MOVEMENT

The process movement resulted in important developments in the teaching of writing, notably a flowering of interest in composition pedagogy, the creation of an established research discipline concerned with writing and the teaching of writing, the realization that people learn to write by actually writing and revising, rather than by completing decontextualized exercises, and a renewed attention to individualized instruction. However, although recognizing its pedagogical importance, some critics maintain that because "the process model focuses on writers and their psychological states ... it offers little insight into the relationship between writers and audience" (Williams, 1998, p. 45). Other critics have pointed out that the process model does not address the issue of how gender, race, class, and culture influence writers' goals, standards, and methods, or even the concept of literacy itself. Scholars such as Catherine Dorsey-Gaines and Denny Taylor (1988) examined how the concept of "process" is influenced by race, and Nancie Atwell (1988) and Julie Neff (1994) wrote about how a process approach must be specially tailored to the needs of the learning disabled. Mike Rose, in *Lives on the Boundary: The Struggle and Achievements of America's Underprepared* (1989), and Shirley Brice Heath, in *Ways with Words: Language, Life, and Work Communities and Classrooms* (1983), discussed the impact of social class on the acquisition of literacy.

Another critical perspective questioned the extent to which the process model was successful in addressing the literacy crisis. Some scholars noted that it neither provided a magic solution to student writing problems, nor influenced the writing class as drastically as has sometimes been claimed. Lad Tobin (1994) characterized the movement as a type of "fairy tale," not because "it is false or childish or naïve," but, rather, because its "disciples" tended to oversimplify the problems inherent in composing and in the teaching of writing. Tobin argued that although we can appreciate the usefulness of the process model, we also "need to acknowledge and confront the extent of the difficulties we face ... to stop pretending that we have everything under control, that everything is proceeding according to plan" (pp. 144–145).

In a similar vein, Joseph Harris noted that "while it seems clear to me that the process movement helped establish composition as a research field, I am not nearly so sure it ever transformed the actual teaching of writing as dramatically as its advocates have claimed" (1997, p. 55). Harris also pointed out that although "the older current-traditional approach to teaching writing focused relentlessly on surface correctness, the advocates of process focused just as relentlessly on "algorithms, heuristics, and guidelines for composing" (p. 56). No system, Harris argued, should be adopted without qualification.

Post-Process Theory

Concern about the effectiveness and validity of the process movement has been manifested in literature concerned with "post-process theory," a term that refers to the idea that the process movement is no longer pertinent, either theoretically or pedagogically. In *Post-Process Theory: Beyond the Writing-Process Paradigm* (1999), Thomas Kent asserted that because every communication act requires the writer to "guess" how a text will affect a reader, it is impossible to model communication, and, therefore, there is no writing process that can be presented in the classroom. "No single course can teach a student how to produce or analyze discourse," Kent maintains, "for the hermeneutic guessing required in all discourse production and analysis can be only refined; it cannot be codified and then taught" (p. 39). In his essay in that collection, Gary Olson (1999) took this position further, asserting not only that writing cannot be taught but also that it cannot even be adequately described. To construct a model of the writing process, Olson states, is to be in conflict with the postmodern rejection of certainty and the corresponding emphasis on assertion as a valued academic skill. For Olson, "the vocabulary of process is no longer useful" (p. 9), and, therefore, compositionists must move away from "a discourse of mastery and asser-tion toward a more dialogic, dynamic, open-ended, receptive, nonassertive stance" (p. 14). Olson, however, did not suggest how this perspective can benefit students or be applied in a pedagogical context.

Another criticism of the process movement focused on the emphasis on formula with which the writing process has been presented in the classroom. Joseph Petraglia and David Russell both rejected the rigidity of a "prewrite, write, revise, edit" model, Petraglia noting in "Is There Life after Process?" (1999) that composition scholarship seems to be increas-ingly irrelevant to working effectively with students. Russell, embracing an activity theory orientation, emphasized that there are many writing processes. Instead of teaching one pro-cess, Russell (1999) maintains, compositionists study those various processes to "(re)classify them, commodify them, and involve students with (teach) them in a curriculum" (p. 88) that acknowledges that some writing activities can be performed mechanistically, whereas others cannot. As yet, post-process theory has not been applied to effective classroom teach-ing. However, for an excellent and enjoyable review of post-process scholarship, read Rich-ard Fulkerson's "Of Pre-and Post-Process: Reviews and Ruminations" (2001).

Genre Theory and the Concept of Process

Although the original goals of the process "movement" focused on promoting student lit-eracy, a number of scholars associated with recent notions of genre theory have maintained that process pedagogy in its most rigid manifestations has resulted in only limited success for the groups that it was originally intended to help. This perspective emphasizes that the progressive classroom, with its focus on individual expression and personal voice, has not resulted in writing improvement in those groups who were most in need of improvement. In fact, according to several critics associated with the genre-based curriculum in Sydney, Australia, the process-oriented classroom, despite its original goal of validating culturally marginalized groups, has actually served "to sustain the powerlessness of children and pre-serve the class divisions in western culture" (Richardson, 1994, p. 55). According to Cope and Kalantzis, 1993, those involved in implementing the Australian curriculum argue that:

> Many working-class, migrant and Aboriginal children have been systematically barred from competence with those texts, knowledges, and 'genres' that enable access to social and mate-rial resources. The culprits, they argue, are not limited to traditional pedagogies that disregard children's cultural and linguistic resources and set out to assimilate them into the fictions of mainstream culture. But the problem is also located in progressive 'process' and 'child-centered' approaches that appear to 'value differences but in so doing leave social relations of inequity fundamentally unquestioned. (p. vii)

Contributors to Cope and Kalantzis' book *The Powers of Literacy: A Genre Approach to Teaching Writing* (1993), which is intended to explain the Australian genre approach to non-Australians, have maintained that the emphasis on personal voice and the corresponding reluctance of teachers to intervene directly in changing students' texts has, ironically, promoted a situation in which only the brightest middle-class children, those whose voices are already in tune with those in power and whose backgrounds include acquaintanceship with the genres of privilege, will be able to learn what is needed for social, and, ultimately, economic success. Noting that "by the 1980s it was clear that the new progressivist curriculum was not producing any noticeable improvement in patterns of educational attainment" (Cope & Kalantzis, 1993, p. 1), Cope and Kalantzis also pointed out that such a curriculum "encourages students to produce texts in a limited range of written genres, mostly personalised recounts" (p. 6).

It is clear that the process movement has not solved every problem associated with helping students to learn to write. Nevertheless, it was characterized by an intellectual and moral energy that generated an exciting new discipline and an important ideological focus that continues to influence composition pedagogy at various levels. Although in many institutions the concepts of expressive writing and personal voice have been superseded by other academic emphases, the idea that writing is a recursive process and that teaching writing means helping students develop a process that works effectively for them now constitutes a basis for writing curricula across the country.

For Further Exploration

Process

Bartholomae, D. (1980). The study of error. *College Composition and Communication, 31,* 253–269.

Daniell, B. (1994). Theory, theory talk, and composition. In J. Clifford, & J. Schilb (Eds.), *Writing theory and critical theory* (pp. 127–140). New York: MLA.

Dyer, P. M. (1990). What composition theory offers the writing teacher. In L. A. Arena (Ed.), *Language proficiency: Defining, teaching, and testing* (pp. 99–106). New York: Plenum.

Elbow, P. (1973). *Writing without teachers.* New York: Oxford University Press.

Elbow, P. (1981). *Writing with power: Techniques for mastering the writing process.* New York: Oxford UP.

Elbow, P. (1981). *Embracing contraries: Explorations in learning and teaching.* New York: Oxford University Press.

Elbow, P. (1991). Reflections on academic discourse. *College English, 53,* 135–155.

Faigley, L. (1986). Competing theories of process: A critique and a proposal. *College English, 48,* 527–542.

Hairston, M. (1982). The winds of change: Thomas Kuhn and the revolution in the teaching of writing. *College Composition and Communication, 33,* 76–86.

Knoblauch, C. H., & Brannon, L. (1984). *Rhetorical traditions and the teaching of writing.* Upper Montclair, NJ: Boynton Cook.

Scardamalia, M., Bereiter, C., & Goelman, H. The role of production factors in writing ability. In M. Nystrand (Ed.), *What writers know: The language, process, and structures of academic discourse* (pp. 173–210). New York: Academic.

Selzer, J. (1984). Exploring options in composing. *College Composition and Communication, 35,* 276–284.

Writing Assignment

Understanding Yourself as a Writer[1]

Although all writers engage in planning, drafting, and revising, they do so in a variety of ways and no writer approaches every writing task the same way. One way to move away from writing habits that have not worked well for you in the past is to understand what type of writer you are. Think about the models of writers described here. In the space provided, indicate the extent to which this description pertains to your own writing habits.

Writers Who Plan in Advance. These people tend to think about their ideas and plan their writing in their minds or on paper before they begin to write. As a result, their first drafts are usually better than most first drafts often are, even though these drafts will probably still need additional revision before they can be submitted. People who plan in advance use spare moments of their time to think—while they eat lunch, drive, and wait in line. When they start to write, they usually have at least some idea about what they want to say.

Writers Who Discover Ideas Through Writing. Although every writer discovers ideas through writing, at least sometimes, these writers use writing to find out what they want to say, planning and revising while they write. They begin by writing whatever comes into their minds and then reconsider and rewrite again and again. Writers who discover ideas through writing may even throw out a whole first draft and begin again.

Writers Who Spend Equal Time on Planning, Writing, and Revising. Some writers divide the writing task into stages, a method that is probably the most effective in writing a college essay as long as adequate time is allowed for each stage of the process. However, it is important to keep in mind that an effective plan involves more than a few notes scratched on a sheet of paper, that sufficient time must be allowed for drafting, and that a revision means a great deal more than correcting a few sentences.

Writers Who Delay. This is a familiar type of writer—those who delay writing until right before the paper is due. These writers sometimes stay up all night, trying to write a complete draft of a paper, and, thus, when they submit their work, they are really submitting a first draft, not usually their best work. Of course, for various reasons, all writers probably procrastinate sometimes. But those who always write first drafts under conditions of pressure or panic are unlikely to do as well as they could.

Writing Assignment

Assessing Your Own Writing Process

This self-assessment will enable you to look at your own writing process, to evaluate the strategies you use when you write. Try to answer each question as fully as possible.

1. Mark the scale below to indicate how easy or difficult you find the process of writing.
   Easy _____ Difficult
   Please explain your selection, indicating the reasons for your response.
2. Describe how you usually write your papers.
3. What practices or "rules of writing" do you find to be useful? Which do you find to be phony or not useful?
4. Which of the following problems have you experienced?
   - Beginning the paper
   - Knowing what you want to say
   - Writing an introduction
   - Getting a first sentence
   - Finding a thesis
   - Organizing the paper
   - Deciding how to structure your ideas
   - Writing an outline
   - Addressing the needs of your audience
   - Knowing what your reader wants
   - Deciding what information to include
   - Working on coherence and style
   - Connecting each paragraph to your overall point
   - Writing sentences that connect with one another
   - Making your writing lively and interesting to read
   - Finding the right words.
5. Based on your responses to the previous questions, what changes would you like to make in your writing behavior?

Writing Assignment

Writing Class Observation

If you currently attend a college or university where writing classes are taught, arrange to observe at least three classes over a two-week period. Then, based on your observations, write a two-part report of five to seven pages that addresses the following:

Part I. Describe the writing class you observed, including many specific details such as the name of the teacher, the level of the class, how often the class meets, the number of students, the textbook used, the assignment the students are working on, the handouts that were used, the seating arrangement—any details that will enable a reader to understand what the teacher and students were doing during various segments of the class.

Part II. Discuss how observing these classes has provided you with information that you will use to plan your own writing class. Specific points to address in this section include the teacher, students, classroom dynamics, methodology, and materials. What did you learn in this class from both the teacher and the students that will be helpful to you?

Note that your purpose is NOT to evaluate the teacher or the methods in any way, but rather to reflect on what you have learned and can apply to your own teaching.

Classroom Observation Guidelines

1. Select the "teacher volunteer" whose class you plan to observe.
2. Plan to observe at least three successive class meetings, or a total of four class meetings over a three-week period.
3. Contact the teacher (via telephone, e-mail, or mail) and make certain that you will be the only observer in class on the days of your visits. Request that he or she provides you with a copy of the course syllabus and any other important handouts when you observe your first class.
4. Find out if the teacher has any preference regarding your "role" as observer in his/her class. For example, should you get up and walk around if group work is in progress or remain in your seat and listen in on the closest group?
5. During your first observation, take as many notes as you feel are necessary to provide you with a full record of your experience.
6. During your second and subsequent observations, focus on what you consider to be the most informative and important insights you have gained.
7. If possible, have a short "debriefing" session with the instructor when you have finished the sequence of observations.
8. Be sure to arrive on time for the class. Do not leave until the class has ended.

Points to Note When Observing Composition Classes

Physical Arrangement of Class. How seats are arranged and placement of teacher.

Atmosphere in Classroom/Classroom Dynamics. Formal? Informal? Friendly?

The Lesson. The day's agenda, the day's topic, specific skills to be taught, activities planned (group work, writing/thinking activities, revision, invention, and exercises), sequencing of activities, materials used, quality of discussion, and applicability of lesson to student writing/language skills.

Student Behaviors

- What kind of writing are the students doing?
- How many students are participating?
- What are students doing who are not participating?
- Are students reading their work aloud?
- Are students speaking to one another?
- Are students working in groups?
- How are students reacting to the day's agenda and topic?

Teacher Behaviors

- What sort of voice does the teacher use?
- Has the teacher engaged the students?
- What kind of working relationship does the teacher have with the students?

- What is the evidence that suggests that kind of working relationship?
- What does the teacher do when students participate or ask questions? Characterize the teacher's strategies for listening and promoting dialogue.

Teacher Activities

- Presenting the assignment/lesson.
- Modeling a particular writing strategy.
- Teacher addressing class as a whole.
- Teacher addressing a small group.
- Teacher speaking with an individual student.
- Teacher presenting the lesson.

Overall, you should be aware of how writing and reading are addressed in the class, how students are engaged, with the instructor and with each other, how the lesson has been planned, and how much student participation drives and supports the action of the class.

THE IMPORTANCE OF REFLECTION

Readers of this book are likely to be teaching a one- or perhaps two-semester writing class, but the ideas associated with "process" should, of course, enable students to continue to improve as writers, beyond the expectations of a first-year writing course. To help students to develop a writing process that works well in various contexts and to continue to develop as writers, it is important for them to "reflect" on what they have learned—to develop a metacognitive awareness of what it means to write at various stages and in various contexts. The following assignments focus on fostering student reflection.

Writing Assignment

Keeping a Reflective Writing Journal

A useful strategy for gaining insight into your own writing process is to keep a reflective writing journal. A reflective writing journal will enable you to recall writing experiences in your past, from which you can develop your own "theory" of writing. Insights fostered by this means will be useful for helping your students to develop an effective writing process. The following are some suggestions for entries into your reflective writing journal:

1. Discuss your history as a writer, focusing on particular highlights.
2. Describe your own writing process.
3. Write about one of your best teachers.
4. Find some examples of what you feel is "good writing." What makes this writing good?
5. Why have you chosen to study rhetoric and composition?

Writing a Reflective Memo *(to be used to help students reflect on a draft)*

REFLECTIVE MEMO[1]

To accompany a draft

1. My thesis is _____

2. This thesis needs to be argued because _____

3. My thesis needs to be read because _____

4. If I had two more days to work on this, I would _____

5. My favorite section is _____

6. My favorite sentence is _____

7. What could we spend more time on in class that would enable me to do this assignment more competently?

    _____

NOTE

1   This form is based on a discussion of various types of writers in Lisa Ede. (1995). *Work in Progress* (3rd ed.). Boston/New York: St. Martin's Press.

REFERENCES

Appleby, A. N. (1974). *Tradition and reform in the teaching of English: A history*. Urbana IL: NCTE.

Atwell, N. (1988). A special writer at work. In T. Newkirk and N. Atwell (Eds.), *Understanding writing: Ways of learning, observing, and teaching K–8* (2nd ed.). Portsmouth, NH: Heinemann.

Bazerman, C. (1981). What written knowledge does. Three examples of academic discourse. *Philosophy of the Social Sciences, 11*, 361–388.

Beach, R. Anson, C. Breuch L. B., & Swiss, T. (2009). *Teaching writing using blogs, wikis, and other digital tools*. Norwood, MA: Christopher-Gordon.

Bean, J. C., Chappell, V. A., & Gillam, Alice (2005). *Reading rhetorically: A reader for writers*. New York: Pearson Longman.

Berlin, J. (1990). Writing instruction in school and college English. In J. Murphy (Ed.), *A short history of writing instruction*. Davis, CA: Hermagoras Press.

Berlin, J. (1996). *Rhetorics, poetics, and cultures: Refiguring English studies*. Urbana, IL: NCTE.

Bishop, W. (1997). Helping peer writing groups succeed. In *Teaching lives: Essays and stories* (pp. 14–24). Logan, UT: Utah State University Press.

Bizzell, P. (1983). Cognition, convention, and certainty: What we need to know about writing. *PRETEXT, 3*, 213–243.

Britton, J., Burgess, T., Martin, N., McLeod, A., & Rosen, H. (1975). *The development of writing abilities 11–18*. London: Macmillan Education Ltd.

Bruffee, K. A. (1984, November). Collaborative learning and the "conversation of mankind." *College English, 46*, 635–652.

Bruner, J. (1966). *Toward a theory of instruction*. Cambridge, MA: The Belknap Press of Harvard University Press.

Clark, I. L. (2010). *College argument: Understanding the genre*. Dubuque, IA: Kendall Hunt.

Cope, B., & Kalantzis, M. (Eds.). (1993). *The powers of literacy: A genre approach to teaching writing*. Pittsburgh, PA: University of Pittsburgh Press.

De Ciccio, A. (1988). *Social constructionism and collaborative learning: Recommendations for teaching writing*. CCCC paper: ERIC ED 282212.

Devitt, A. J. (2004). *Writing genres*. Carbondale, IL: Southern Illinois Press.

Dorsey-Gaines, C., & Taylor, D. (1988). *Growing up literate: Learning from inner-city families*. Portsmouth, NH: Heinemann.

Elbow, P. (1986). *Embracing contraries: Explorations in learning and teaching*. New York: Oxford University Press.

Emig, J. (1971). The composing process of twelfth graders. *Research report No. 13*. Urbana: NCTE.

Flower, L. (1979, September). Writer-based prose: A cognitive basis for problems in writing. *College English, 41*, 19–38.

Flower, L., & Hayes, J. (1981). A cognitive process theory of writing. *College Composition and Communication, 32*, 365–388.

Flower, L. S., & Hayes, J. (1980, February). The cognition of discovery: Defining a rhetorical problem. *CCC, 31*, 21–32.

Fulkerson, R. (2001). Of pre- and post-process: Reviews and ruminations. *Composition Studies, 29* (2), 93–119.

Gage, J. T. (1996). The reasoned thesis: The E-word and argumentative writing as a process of inquiry. In Barbara Emmel, Paula Resch, & Deborah Tenney (Eds.), *Argument revisited: Argument redefined* (pp. 3–18). Thousand Oaks, CA: Sage Publications.

Geertz, C. (1983). *Local knowledge*. New York: Basic Books.

Graves, D. (1983). *Writing, teachers and children at work*. Portsmouth: Heinemann.

Greenough, C. N. (1913, February). An experiment in the training of teachers of composition for work with college freshmen. *The English Journal, 2* (2), 109–121.

Harris, J. (1997). *A teaching subject: Composition since 1966*. New Jersey: Prentice Hall.

Harris, M. (1989, February). Composing behavior, of one- and multi-draft writers. *College English, 51* (2), 174–190.

Heath, S. B. (1983). *Ways with words: Language, life, and work communities and classrooms*. Cambridge: Cambridge University Press.

Hopkins, L. T. (1912, January). Can good composition teaching be done under present conditions? *English Journal, 1*, 1–12.

Kent, T. (1999). *Post-process theory: Beyond the writing-process paradigm*. Carbondale: Southern Illinois University Press.

Killingsworth, M. J. (2005). *Appeals in modern rhetoric: An ordinary-language approach*. Carbondale: Southern Illinois University Press.

Kinneavy, J. (1971). A theory of discourse. Englewood Cliffs, NJ: Prentice Hall. (Reprinted 1980. New York: Norton.)

Lunsford, A. (1979). Cognitive development and the basic writer. *College English, 41*, 38–46.

Lunsford, A. A. (2007). *Writing matters*. Athens and London: University of Georgia Press.

Lunsford, A. A., & Glenn, C. (1990). Rhetorical theory and the teaching of writing. In Gail Hawisher, & Anne Soter (Eds.), *On literacy and its teaching* (pp. 174–189). Albany: State University of New York.

Macrorie, K. (1970). *Telling writing*. Rochelle Park, NJ: Hayden.

Moffett, J. (1968a). *Student-centered language arts curriculum, grades K-13*. Boston: Houghton-Mifflin.

Moffett, J. (1968b). *Teaching the universe of discourse*. Portsmouth, NH: Boynton/Cook.

Neff, J. (1994). Learning disabilities and the writing center. In J. A. Mullin, & R. Wallace (Eds.), *Intersections: Theory-practice in the writing center* (pp. 81–95). Urbana, IL: NCTE.

Olson, G. (1999). Toward a post-process composition: Abandoning the rhetoric of assertion. In T. Kent (Ed.), *Post-process theory: Beyond the writing-process paradigm* (pp. 7–15). Carbondale: Southern Illinois University Press.

Perl, S. (1979). The composing process of unskilled college writers. *Research in the Teaching of English, 13*, 317–336.

Perl, S. (1994). Writing process: A shining moment. In S. Perl (Ed.), *Landmark essays on writing process* (pp. xi–xx). Davis, CA: Hermagoras Press.

Petraglia. J. (1999). Is there life after process? The role of social scientism in a changing discipline. In T. Kent (Ed.), *Post-process theory: Beyond the writing-process paradigm* (pp. 49–64). Carbondale: Southern Illinois University Press.

Pianko, S. (1979). A description of the composing processes of college freshman writers. *Research in the Teaching of English, 13*, 5–22.

Richardson, P. W. (1994). Language as personal resource and as social construct: Competing views of literacy pedagogy in Australia. In A. Freedman, & P. Medway (Eds.), *Learning and teaching genre* (pp. 117–142). Portsmouth, NH: Boynton/Cook.

Rohman, D. G. (1965). Pre-writing: The stage of discovery in the writing process. *College Composition and Communication, 16*, 106–112.

Rorty, R. (1979). *Philosophy and the mirror of nature*. New Jersey: Princeton University Press.

Rose, M. (1989). *Lives on the boundary: The struggles and achievements of America's underprepared*. New York: Free Press.

Russell, D. (1999). Activity theory and process approaches: Writing (power) in school and society. In T. Kent (Ed.), *Post-process theory: Beyond the writing-process paradigm* (pp. 80–95). Carbondale: Southern Illinois University Press.

Sommers, N. (1980). Revision strategies of student writers and experienced adult writers. *College Composition and Communication, 31* (4), 378–388.

Stewart, D. C. (1972). *The authentic voice: A prewriting approach to student writing*. Dubuque, IA: William C. Brown.

Tobin, L. (1994). How the writing process was born—and other conversion narratives. In T. Newkirk, & L. Tobin (Eds.), *Taking stock: The writing process movement in the '90s*. Portsmouth, NH: Boynton/Cook.

Vygotsky, L. (1978). *Mind in society* (M. Cole, V. John-Steiner, S. Scrivner, & E. Souberman, Eds). Cambridge, MA. Harvard University Press.

Williams, J. D. (1998). *Preparing to teach writing: Research, theory, and practice* (2nd ed.). Mahwah, NJ: Lawrence Erlbaum Associates.

Readings

COMPOSING BEHAVIORS OF ONE-
AND MULTI-DRAFT WRITERS

Muriel Harris

A belief shared by teachers of writing, one that we fervently try to inculcate in our students, is that revision can improve writing. This notion, that revision generally results in better text, often pairs up with another assumption, that revision occurs as we work through separate drafts. Thus, "hand in your working drafts tomorrow and the final ones next Friday" is a common assignment, as is the following bit of textbook advice: "When the draft is completed, a good critical reading should help the writer re-envision the essay and could very well lead to substantial rewriting" (Axelrod and Cooper 10). This textbook advice, hardly atypical, is based on the rationale that gaining distance from a piece of discourse helps the writer to judge it more critically. As evidence for this assumption. Richard Beach's 1976 study of the self-evaluation strategies of revisers and non-revisers demonstrated that extensive revisers were more capable of detaching themselves and gaining aesthetic distance from their writing than were non-revisers. Nancy Sommers' later theoretical work on revision also sensitized us to students' need to re-see their texts rather than to view revision as an editing process at the limited level of word changes.

A logical conclusion, then, is to train student writers to re-see and then re-draft a piece of discourse. There are other compelling reasons for helping students view first or working drafts as fluid and not yet molded into final form. The opportunities for outside intervention, through teacher critiques and suggestions or peer evaluation sessions, can be valuable. And it is equally important to help students move beyond their limited approaches and limiting tendency to settle for whatever rolls out on paper the first time around. The novice view of a first draft as written-in-stone (or fast-drying cement) can preclude engaging more fully with the ideas being expressed. On the other hand, we have to acknowledge that there are advantages in being able, where it is appropriate, to master the art of one-draft writing. When students write essay exams or placement essays and when they go on to on-the-job writing where time doesn't permit multiple drafts, they need to produce first drafts which are also coherent, finished final drafts. Yet, even acknowledging that need, we still seem justified in advocating that our students master the art of redrafting to shape a text into a more effective form.

The notion that reworking a text through multiple drafts and/or visible changes is generally a beneficial process is also an underlying assumption in some lines of research. This had been particularly evident in studies of computer-aided revision, where counts were taken of changes in macrostructure and microstructure with and without word processing. If more changes were made on a word processor than were written by hand, the conclusion was that word processors are an aid to revision. Such research is based on the premise that revision equals visible changes in a text and that these changes will improve the text.

Given this widely entrenched notion of redrafting as being advantageous, it would be comforting to turn to research results for clearcut evidence that reworking of text produces better writing. But studies of revision do not provide the conclusive picture that we need in order to assert that we should continue coaxing our students into writing multiple drafts. Lillian Bridwell's 1980 survey of revision studies led her to conclude that "questions about the relationship between revision and qualitative improvement remain largely unanswered" (199), and her own study demonstrated that the most extensively revised papers "received a range of quality ratings from the top to the bottom of the scale" (216). In another review of research on revision, Stephen Witte cities studies which similarly suggest that the amount of re-drafting (which Witte calls "retranscription") often bears little relation to the overall quality of completed texts ("Revising" 256). Similarly, Linda Flower and John Hayes, et al., citing studies which also dispute the notion that more re-drafting should mean better papers, conclude that the amount of change is not a key variable in revision and that revision as an obligatory stage required by teachers doesn't necessarily produce better writing. (For a teacher's affirmation of the same phenomenon, see Henley.)

Constricting revision to retranscription (i.e., to altering what has been written) also denies the reality of pre-text, a composing phenomenon studied by Stephen Witte in "Pre-Text and Composing." Witte defines a writer's pre-text as "the mental construction of 'text' prior to transcription" (397). Pre-text thus "refers to a writer's linguistic representation of intended meaning, a 'trial locution' that is produced in the mind, stored in the writer's memory, and sometimes manipulated mentally prior to being transcribed as written text" (397). Pre-texts are distinguished from abstract plans in that pre-texts approximate written prose. As the outcome of planning, pre-text can also be the basis for further planning. In his study Witte found great diversity in how writers construct and use pre-text. Some writers construct little or no pre-text; others rely heavily on extensive pre-texts; others create short pre-texts; and still others move back and forth between extensive and short pre-texts. The point here is that Witte has shown us that revision can and does occur in pre-texts, before visible marks are made on paper. In an earlier paper, "Revising, Composing Theory, and Research Design," Witte suggests that the pre-text writers construct before making marks on paper is probably a function of the quality, kind, and extent of planning that occurs before transcribing on paper. The danger here is that we might conclude that the development from novice to expert writer entails learning to make greater use of pre-text prior to transcribing. After all, in Linda Flower's memorable phrase, pre-text is "the last cheap gas before transcribing text" (see Witte, "Pre-Text" 422). But Witte notes that his data do not support a "vote for pre-text" ("Pre-Text" 401). For the students in Witte's study, more extensive use of pre-text doesn't automatically lead to better written text. Thus it appears so far that the quality of revision can neither be measured by the pound nor tracked through discreet stages.

But a discussion of whether more or fewer drafts is an indication of more mature writing is itself not adequate. As Maxine Hairston reminds us in "Different Products, Different Processes," we must also consider the writing task that is involved in any particular case of generating discourse. In her taxonomy of writing categories, categories that depict a variety of revision behaviors that are true to the experience of many of us, Hairston divides writing into three classes; first, routine maintenance writing which is simple communication about uncomplicated matters; second, extended, relatively complex writing that requires the writer's attention but is self-limiting in that the writer already knows most of what she is going to write and may be writing under time constraints; and third, extended reflective writing in which the form and content emerge as the writing proceeds. Even with this oversimplified, brief summary of Hairston's classes of writing, we recognize that the matter of when and if re-drafting takes place can differ according to the demands of different tasks and situations as well as the different skills levels of writers.

Many—or perhaps even most—of us may nod in agreement as we recognize in Hairston's classes of writing a description of the different types of writing we do. But given the range of individual differences that exist among writers, we still cannot conclude that the nature of effective revision is always tied to the writing task, because such a conclusion would not account for what we know also exists—some expert writers who, despite the writing task, work at either end of the spectrum as confirmed, consistent one-drafters or as perpetual multi-drafters. That writers exhibit a diversity of revising habits has been noted by Lester Faigley and Stephen Witte in "Analyzing Revision." When testing the taxonomy of revision changes they had created, Faigley and Witte found that expert writers exhibited "extreme diversity" in the ways they revised:

> One expert writer in the present study made almost no revisions; another started with an almost stream-of-consciousness text that she then converted to an organized essay in the

second draft; another limited his major revisions to a single long insert; and another revised mostly by pruning. (410)

Similarly, when summarizing interviews with well-known authors such as those in the *Writers at Work: The Paris Review Interviews* series, Lillian Bridwell notes that these discussions reveal a wide range of revision strategies among these writers, from rapid producers of text who do little revising as they proceed to writers who move along by revising every sentence (198).

More extensive insights into a variety of composing styles are offered in Tom Waldrep's collection of essays by successful scholars working in composition, *Writers on Writing*. Here too as writers describe their composing processes, we see a variety of approaches, including some writers who plan extensively before their pens hit paper (or before the cursor blips on their screens). Their planning is so complete that their texts generally emerge in a single draft with minor, if any, editing as they write. Self-descriptions of some experienced writers in the field of composition give us vivid accounts of how these one-drafters work. For example, Patricia Y. Murray notes that prior to typing, she sees words, phrases, sentences, and paragraphs taking shape in her head. Her composing, she concludes, has been done before her fingers touch the typewriter, though as she also notes, she revises and edits as she types (234). William Lutz offers a similar account:

> Before I write, I write in my mind. The more difficult and complex the writing, the more time I need to think before I write. Ideas incubate in my mind. While I talk, drive, swim, and exercise I am thinking, planning, writing. I think about the introduction, what examples to use, how to develop the main idea, what kind of conclusion to use. I write, revise, rewrite, agonize, despair, give up, only to start all over again, and all of this before I ever begin to put words on paper. ... Writing is not a process of discovery for me. ... The writing process takes place in my mind. Once that process is complete the product emerges. Often I can write pages without pause and with very little, if any, revision or even minor changes. (186–87)

Even with such descriptions from experienced writers, we are hesitant either to discard the notion that writing *is* a process of discovery for many of us or to typecast writers who make many visible changes on the page and/or work through multiple drafts as inadequate writers. After all, many of us, probably the majority, fall somewhere along the continuum from one- to multi-drafters. We may find ourselves as both one- and multi-drafters with the classes of writing that Hairston describes, or we may generally identify ourselves as doing both but also functioning more often as a one- or multi-drafter. Just as we have seen that at one end of the spectrum there are some confirmed one-drafters, so too must we recognize that at the other end of that spectrum there are some confirmed multi-drafters, expert writers for whom extensive revising occurs when writing (so that a piece of discourse may go through several or more drafts or be reworked heavily as the original draft evolves.) David Bartholomae, a self-described multi-drafter, states that he never outlines but works instead with two pads of paper, one to write on and one for making plans, storing sentences, and taking notes. He views his first drafts as disorganized and has to revise extensively, with the result that the revisions bear little resemblance to the first drafts (22–26). Similarly, Lynn Z. Bloom notes that she cannot predict at the outset a great deal of what she is going to say. Only by writing does she learn how her content will develop or how she will handle the structure, organization, and style of her paragraphs, sentences, and whole essay (33).

Thus, if we wish to draw a more inclusive picture of composing behaviors for revision, we have to put together a description that accounts for differences in levels of ability and experience (from novice to expert), for differences in writing tasks, and also for differences in the as yet largely unexplored area of composing process differences among writers. My interest here is in the composing processes of different writers, more particularly, the reality of those writers at either end of that long spectrum, the one-drafters at one end and the multi-drafters at the other. By one-draft writers I mean those writers who construct their plans and the pre-texts that carry out those plans as well as do all or most of the revising of those plans and pre-texts mentally, before transcribing. They do little or no retranscribing. True one-drafters have not arrived at this developmentally or as a result of training in writing, and they should not be confused with other writers who—driven by deadlines, lack of motivation, insufficient experience with writing, or anxieties about "getting it right the first time"—do little or no scratching out of what they have written. Multi-drafters, on the other hand, need to interact with their transcriptions in order to revise. Independent of how much planning they do or pre-text they compose, they continue to revise after they have transcribed words onto paper. Again, true multi-drafters have not reached this stage developmentally or as a result of any intervention by teachers. This is not to say that we can classify writers into two categories, one- and multi-drafters, because all the evidence we have and, more importantly, our own experience tells us that most writers are not one or the other but exist somewhere between these two ends of the continuum.

However, one- and multi-drafters do exist, and we do need to learn more about them to gain a clearer picture not only of what is involved in different revising processes but also to provide a basis for considering the pedagogical implications of dealing with individual differences. There is a strong argument for looking instead at the middle range of writers who do some writing in single drafts and others in multiple drafts or with a lot of retranscribing as they proceed, for it is very probable that the largest number of writers cluster there. But those of us who teach in the individualized setting of conferences or writing lab tutorials know that we can never overlook or put aside the concerns of every unique individual with whom we work. Perhaps we are overly intrigued with individual differences, partly because we see that some students can be ill-served in the group setting of the classrooms and partly because looking at individual differences gives us such enlightening glimpses into the complex reality of composing processes. Clinicians in other fields would argue that looking at the extremes offers a clearer view of what may be involved in the behaviors of the majority. But those who do research in writing also acknowledge that we need to understand dimensions of variation among writers, particularly those patterned differences or "alternate paths to expert performance" that have clear implications for instruction (Freedman et al. 19). In this case, whatever we learn about patterns of behavior among one- and multi-drafters has direct implications for instruction as we need to know the various trade-offs involved in any classroom instruction which would encourage more single or multiple drafting. And, as we will see when looking at what is involved in being able to revise before drafting or in being able to return and re-draft what has been transcribed, there are trade-offs indeed. Whatever arguments are offered, we must also acknowledge that no picture of revision is complete until it includes all that is known and observed about a variety of revision behaviors among writers.

But what do we know about one- and multi-drafters other than anecdotal accounts that confirm their existence? Much evidence is waiting to be gathered from the storehouse of various published interviews in which well-known writers have been asked to describe their writing. And Ann Ruggles Gere's study of the revising behaviors of a blind student gives us a description of a student writer who does not redraft but writes "first draft/final draft" papers, finished products produced in one sitting for her courses as a master's degree candidate. The student describes periods of thinking about a topic before writing. While she doesn't know exactly what she will say until actually writing it, she typically knows what will be contained in the first paragraph as she types the title. Her attention is not focused on words as she concentrates instead on images and larger contexts. A similar description of a one-drafter is found in Joy Reid's "The Radical Outliner and the Radical Brainstormer." Comparing her husband and herself, both composition teachers, Reid notes the differences between herself, an outliner (and a one-drafter), and her husband, a brainstormer (and a multi-drafter), differences which parallel those of the writers in *Writers on Writing* that I have described.

The descriptions of all of the one- and multi-draft writers mentioned so far offer a fairly consistent picture, but these descriptions do little more than reaffirm their existence. In an effort to learn more, I sought out some one- and multi-drafters in order to observe them composing and to explore what might be involved. Since my intent was not to determine the percentage of one- and multi-drafters among any population of writers (though that would be an interesting topic indeed, as I suspect there are more than we may initially guess—or at least more who hover close to either end of the continuum). I sought out experienced writers who identify themselves as very definitely one- or multi-drafters. The subjects I selected for observation were graduate students who teach composition or communications courses, my rationale being that these people can more easily categorize and articulate their own writing habits. From among the group of subjects who described themselves as very definitely either one- or multi-drafters, I selected those who showed evidence of being experienced, competent writers. Of the eight selected subjects (four one-drafters and four multi-drafters), all were at least several years into their graduate studies in English or communications and were either near completion or had recently completed advanced degrees. All had received high scores in standardized tests for verbal skills such as the SAT or GRE exams; all had grade point averages ranging from B+ to A in their graduate courses; and all wrote frequently in a variety of tasks, including academic papers for courses and journal publications, conference papers, the usual business writing of practicing academics (e.g., letters of recommendation for students, memos, instructional materials for classes, etc.), and personal writing such as letters to family and friends. They clearly earned their description as experienced writers. Experienced writers were used because I also wished to exclude those novices who may, through development of their writing skills, change their composing behaviors, and also those novices whose composing habits are the result of other factors such as disinterest (e.g., the one-drafter who habitually begins the paper at 3 a.m. the night before it's due) or anxiety (e.g., the multi-drafter who fears she is never "right" and keeps working and re-working her text).

The experienced writers whom I observed all confirmed that their composing behaviors have not changed over time. That is, they all stated that their writing habits have not altered as they became experienced writers and/or as they moved through writing courses. However, their descriptions of themselves as one- or multi-drafters were not as completely accurate as might be expected. Self-reporting, even among teachers of writing, is not a totally reliable measure. As I observed and talked with the eight writers, I found three very definite one-drafters, Ted, Nina, and Amy; one writer, Jackie, who tends to be a one-drafter but does some revising after writing; two very definite multi-drafters, Bill and Pam; and two writers, Karen and Cindy, who described themselves as multi-drafters and who tend to revise extensively but who can also produce first draft/final draft writing under some conditions. To gather data on their composing behaviors, I interviewed each person for an hour, asking questions about the types of writing they do, the activities they engage in before writing, the details of what happens as they write, their revision behaviors, the manner in which sentences are composed, and their attitudes and past history of writing. Each person was also asked to spend an hour writing in response to an assignment. The specific assignment was a request from an academic advisor asking for the writers' descriptions of the skills needed to succeed in their field of study. As they wrote, all eight writers were asked to give thinking-aloud protocols and were videotaped for future study. Brief interviews after writing focused on eliciting information about how accurately the writing session reflected their general writing habits and behaviors. Each type of information collected is, at best, incomplete because accounts of one's own composing processes may not be entirely accurate, because thinking-aloud protocols while writing are only partial accounts of what is being thought about, and because one-hour writing tasks preclude observing some of the kinds of activities that writers report. But even with these limitations I observed patterns of composing behaviors that should differentiate one-draft writers from multi-draft writers.

Preference for Beginning with a Developed Focus vs. Preference for Beginning at an Exploratory Stage

Among the consistent behaviors that one-drafters report is the point at which they can and will start writing. All of the four one-drafters expressed a strong need to clarify their thinking prior to beginning to transcribe. They are either not ready to write or cannot write until they have a focus and organization in mind. They may, as I observed Jacky and Ted doing, make some brief planning notes on paper or, as Amy and Nina did, sit for awhile and mentally plan, but all expressed a clearly articulated need to know beforehand the direction the piece of writing would take. For Nina's longer papers, she described a planning schedule in which the focus comes first, even before collecting notes. Ted too described the first stage of a piece of writing as being a time of mentally narrowing a topic. During incubation times before writing, two of these writers described some global recasting of a paper in their minds while the other two expressed a need to talk it out, either to themselves or friends. There is little resorting of written notes and little use of written outlines, except for some short lists, described by Ted as "memory jogs" to use while he writes. Amy explained that she sometimes felt that in high school or as an undergraduate she should have written outlines to please her teachers, but she never did get around to it because outlines served no useful purpose for her. Consistent throughout these accounts and in my observation of their writing was these writers' need to know where they are headed beforehand and a feeling that they are not ready to write—or cannot write—until they are at that stage. When asked if they ever engaged in freewriting, two one-drafters said they could not, unless forced to, plunge in and write without a focus and a mental plan. Ted, in particular, noted that the notion of exploration during writing would make him so uncomfortable that he would probably block and be unable to write.

In contrast to the one-drafters' preference for knowing their direction before writing, the two consistent multi-drafters, Pam and Bill, explained that they resist knowing, resist any attempt at clarification prior to writing. Their preference is for open-ended exploration as they write. They may have been reading and thinking extensively beforehand, but the topic has not taken shape when they decide that it is time to begin writing. Bill reported that he purposely starts with a broad topic while Pam said that she looks for something "broad or ambiguous" or "something small that can grow and grow." As Bill explained, he doesn't like writing about what he already knows as that would be boring. Pam too expressed her resistance to knowing her topic and direction beforehand in terms of how boring it would be. Generally, Bill will do about four or five drafts as he works through the early parts of a paper, perhaps two to four pages, before he knows what he will write about. He and Pam allow for—and indeed expect—that their topic will change as they write. Pam explained: "I work by allowing the direction of the work to change if it needs to. ... I have to allow things to go where they need to go." When I observed them writing, Pam spent considerable time planning and creating pre-texts before short bursts of transcribing while Bill wrote several different versions of an introduction and, with some cutting and pasting, was about ready to define his focus at the end of the hour. He reported that he depends heavily on seeing what he has written in order to find his focus, choose his content, and organize. Pam also noted that she needs to see chunks of what she has transcribed to see where the piece of discourse is taking her.

The other two writers who characterized themselves as multi-drafters, Karen and Cindy, both described a general tendency to plunge in before the topic is clear. Karen said that she can't visualize her arguments until she writes them out and generally writes and rewrites as she proceeds, but for writing tasks that she described as "formulaic" in that they are familiar because she has written similar pieces of discourse, she can write quickly and finish quickly—as she did with the writing task for this study. Since she had previously written the same kind of letter assigned in this study, she did not engage in the multi-drafting that would be more characteristic, she says, of her general composing behaviors. Cindy, the other self-described multi-drafter, almost completed the task in a single draft, though as she explained with short pieces, she can revert to her "journalistic mode" of writing, having been a working journalist for a number of years. For longer papers, such as those required in graduate courses, her descriptions sound much like those of Bill, Pam, and Karen. All of these writers, though, share the unifying characteristic of beginning to write before the task is well defined in their minds, unlike the one-drafters who do not write at that stage.

Preference for Limiting Options vs. Preference for Open-ended Exploring

Another consistent and clearly related difference between one-and multi-drafters is the difference in the quantity of options they will generate, from words and sentences to whole sections of a paper, and the way in which they will evaluate those options. As they wrote, all four of the one-drafters limited their options by generating several choices and then making a decision fairly quickly. There were numerous occasions in the think-aloud protocols of three of the four one-drafters in which they would stop, try another word, question a phrase, raise the possibility of another idea to include, and then make a quick decision. When Ted re-read one of his paragraphs, he saw a different direction that he might have taken that would perhaps be better, but he accepted what he had. ("That'll do here, OK … OK" he said to himself and moved on.) Nina, another one-drafter, generated no alternate options aloud as she wrote.

As is evident in this description of one-drafters, they exhibited none of the agonizing over possibilities that other writers experience, and they appear to be able to accept their choices quickly and move on. While observers may question whether limiting options in this manner cuts off further discovery and possibly better solutions or whether the internal debate goes on prior to transcribing, one-drafters are obviously efficient writers. They generate fewer choices, reach decisions more quickly, and do most or all of the decision-making before transcribing on paper. Thus, three of the four one-drafters finished the paper in the time allotted, and the fourth writer was almost finished. They can pace themselves fairly accurately too, giving me their estimates of how long it takes them to write papers of particular lengths. All four one-drafters describe themselves as incurable procrastinators who begin even long papers the night before they are due, allowing themselves about the right number of hours in which to transcribe their mental constructs onto paper. Nina explained that she makes choices quickly because she is always writing at the last minute under pressure and doesn't have time to consider more options. Another one-drafter offered a vivid description of the tension and stress that can be involved in these last minute, all-night sessions.

While they worry about whether they will finish on time, these one-drafters generally do. Contributing to their efficiency are two time-saving procedures involved as they get words on paper. Because most decisions are made before they commit words to paper, they do little or no scratching out and re-writing; and they do a minimum of re-reading both as they proceed and also when they are finished. The few changes I observed being made were either single words or a few short phrases, unlike the multi-drafters who rejected or scratched out whole sentences and paragraphs. As Nina wrote, she never re-read her developing text, though she reported that she does a little re-reading when she is finished with longer papers. The tinkering with words that she might do then, she says, is counterproductive because she rarely feels that she is improving the text with these changes. (Nina and the other one-drafters would probably be quite successful at the kind of "invisible writing" that has been investigated, that is, writing done under conditions in which writers cannot see what they are writing or scan as they progress. See Blau.)

In contrast to the one-drafters' limited options, quick decisions, few changes on paper and little or no re-reading, the multi-drafters were frequently observed generating and exploring many options, spending a long time in making their choices, and making frequent and large-scale changes on paper. Bill said that he produces large quantities of text because he needs to see it in order to see if he wants to retain it, unlike the one-drafters who exhibit little or no need to examine their developing text. Moreover, as Bill noted, the text he generates is also on occasion a heuristic for more text. As he writes, Bill engages in numerous revising tactics. He writes a sentence, stops to examine it by switching it around, going back to add clauses, or combining it with other text on the same page or a different sheet of paper. For the assigned writing task, he began with one sheet of paper, moved to another, tore off some of it and discarded it, and added part back to a previous sheet. At home when writing a longer paper, he will similarly engage in extensive cutting and pasting. In a somewhat different manner. Pam did not generate as many options on paper for this study. Instead, her protocol recorded various alternative plans and pre-texts that she would stop to explore verbally for five or ten minutes before transcribing anything. What she did write, though, was often heavily edited so that at the end of the hour, she, like Bill, had only progressed somewhat through an introductory paragraph of several sentences. Thus, while Bill had produced large amounts of text on paper that were later rejected after having been written, Pam spent more of her time generating and rejecting plans and pre-texts than crossing out transcriptions.

Writing is a more time-consuming task for these multi-drafters because they expect to produce many options and a large amount of text that will be discarded. Both Bill and Pam described general writing procedures in which they begin by freewriting, and, as they proceed, distilling from earlier drafts what will be used in later drafts. Both proceed incrementally, that is, by starting in and then starting again before finishing a whole draft. Both writers are used to re-reading frequently, partly to locate what Pam called "key elements" that will be retained for later drafts and partly, as Bill explained, because the act of generating more options and exploring them causes him to lose track of where he is.

Because both Bill and Pam seem to be comfortable when working within an as-yet only partially focused text, it would be interesting to explore what has been termed their "tolerance for ambiguity," a trait defined as a person's ability to function calmly in a situation in which interpretation of all stimuli is not completely clear. (See Budner, and Frenkel-Brunswick.) People who have little or no tolerance for ambiguity perceive ambiguous situations as sources of psychological discomfort, and they may try to reach conclusions quickly rather than to take the time to consider all of the essential elements of an unclear situation. People with more tolerance for ambiguity enjoy being in ambiguous situations and tend to seek them out. The relevance here, of course, is the question of whether one-drafters will not begin until they have structured the task and will also move quickly to conclusions in part, at least, because of having some degree of intolerance for ambiguity. This might be a fruitful area for further research.

For those interested in the mental processes which accompany behaviors, another dimension to explore is the Myers-Briggs Type Indicator (MBTI), a measure of expressed preferences (i.e., not performance tasks) in four bi-polar dimensions of personality. The work of Geroge H. Jensen and John K. DiTiberio has indicated some relationships between the personality types identified by the MBTI and writing processes. Of particular interest here is that Bill, who had independently taken the MBTI for other reasons, reported that he scored highly in the dimensions of "extraversion" and "perceiving." Extraverts, say Jensen and DiTiberio, "often leap into tasks with little planning, then rely on trial and error to complete the task" (288), and they "often find freewriting a good method for developing ideas, for they think better when writing quickly, impulsively, and uncritically" (289). Perceivers, another type described by Jensen and DiTiberio, appear to share tendencies similar to those with a tolerance for ambiguity, for perceivers "are willing to leave the outer world unstructured. ... Quickly made decisions narrow their field of vision" (295). Perceiving types tend to select broad topics for writing, like a wide range of alternatives, and always want to read one more book on the subject. Their revisions thus often need to be refocused (296). The similarities here to Bill's writing behaviors show us that while the MBTI is somewhat circular in that the scoring is a reflection of people's self-description, it can confirm (and perhaps clarify) the relationship of writing behaviors to more general human behaviors.

The Preference for Closure vs. Resistance to Closure

From these descriptions of one- and multi-drafters it is readily apparent that they differ in their need for closure. The one-drafters move quickly to decisions while composing, and they report that once they are done with a paper, they prefer not to look back at it, either immediately to re-read it or at some future time, to think about revising it. Ted explained that he generally is willing to do one re-reading at the time of completing a paper and sometimes to make a few wording changes, but that is all. He shrugged off the possibility of doing even a second re-reading of any of his writing once it is done because he says he can't stand to look at it again. All of the one-drafters reported that they hardly, if ever, rewrite a paper. This distaste for returning to a completed text can be the source of problems for these one-drafters. Forced by a teacher in a graduate course who wanted first drafts one week and revisions the next week, Nina explained that she deliberately resorted to "writing a bad paper" for the first submission in order to submit her "real" draft as the "revised" paper. Writing a series of drafts is clearly harder for one-drafters such as Nina than we have yet acknowledged.

These one-drafters are as reluctant to start as they are impatient to finish. Although they tend to delay the drafting process, this does not apply to their preparation which often starts well in advance and is the "interesting" or "enjoyable" part for them. With writing that produces few surprises or discoveries for any of them because the generative process precedes transcription, drafting on paper is more "tedious" (a word they frequently used during their interviews) than for other writers. Said Ted, "Writing is something I have to do, not something I want to do." Even Jackie, who allows for some revising while drafting in order to develop the details of her plan, reported that she has a hard time going back to revise a paper once it is completed. She, like the others, reported a sense of feeling the paper is over and done with. "Done, dead and done, done, finished, done," concluded another of these one-drafters.

On the other hand, the multi-drafters observed in this study explained that they are never done with a paper. They can easily and willingly go back to it or to keep writing indefinitely. Asked when they know they are finished, Bill and Pam explained that they never feel they are "done" with a piece of discourse, merely that they have to stop in order to meet a deadline. As Pam said, she never gets to a last draft and doesn't care about producing "neat packages." Understandably, she has trouble with conclusions and with "wrapping up" at the end of a piece of discourse. Asked how pervasive her redrafting is for all of her writing, Pam commented that she writes informal letters to parents and friends every day and is getting to the point that she doesn't rewrite these letters as much. Bill too noted that he fights against products and hates to finish. As a result, both Bill and Pam often fail to meet their deadlines. Cindy, bored by her "journalistic one-draft writing," expressed a strong desire to return to some of her previously completed papers in order to rewrite them.

Writer-Based vs. Reader-Based Early Drafts

One way of distinguishing the early drafts produced by the multi-drafters for this study from the drafts produced by the one-drafters is to draw upon Linda Flower's distinction between Writer-Based and Reader-Based prose. Writer-Based prose, explains Flower, is "verbal expression written by a writer to himself and for himself. It is the working of his own verbal thought. In its *structure*, Writer-Based prose reflects the associative, narrative path of the writer's own confrontation with her subject" (19–20). Reader-Based prose, on the other hand, is "a deliberate attempt to communicate something to a reader. To do that it creates a shared language and shared context between writer and reader. It also offers the reader an issue-oriented rhetorical structure rather than a replay of the writer's discovery process" (20). Although Flower acknowledges that Writer-Based prose is a "problem" that composition courses are designed to correct, she also affirms its usefulness as a search tool, a strategy for handling the difficulty of attending to multiple complex tasks simultaneously. Writer-Based prose needs to be revised into Reader-Based prose, but it can be effective as a "medium for thinking." And for the multi-drafters observed in this study, characterizing the initial drafts of two of the multi-drafters as Writer-Based helps to see how their early drafts differ from those of the one-drafters.

One feature of Writer-Based prose, as offered by Flower, is that it reflects the writer's method of searching by means of surveying what she knows, often in a narrative manner. Information tends to be structured as a narrative of the discovery process or as a survey of the data in the writer's mind. Reader-Based prose, on the other hand, restructures the information so that it is accessible to the reader. Both the protocols and the written drafts produced by the two confirmed multi-drafters, Bill and Pam, reveal this Writer-Based orientation as their initial way into writing. Bill very clearly began with a memory search through his own experience, made some brief notes, and then wrote a narrative as his first sentence in response to the request that he describe to an academic counselor the skills needed for his field: "I went through what must have been a million different majors before I wound up in English and it was actually my first choice." Pam spent the hour exploring the appropriateness of the term "skills."

In distinct contrast, all four of the one-drafters began by constructing a conceptual framework for the response they would write, most typically by defining a few categories or headings which would be the focus or main point of the paper. With a few words in mind that indicated his major points, Ted then moved on to ask himself who would be reading his response, what the context would be, and what format the writing would use. He moved quickly from a search for a point to considerations of how his audience would use his information. Similarly, Amy rather promptly chose a few terms, decided to herself that "that'll be the focus," and then said, "OK, I'm trying to get into a role here. I'm responding to someone who … This is not something they are going to give out to people. But they're going to read it and compile responses, put something together for themselves." She then began writing her draft and completed it within the hour. Asked what constraints and concerns she is most aware of when actually writing, Amy said that she is generally concerned with clarity for the reader. The point of contrast here is that the search process was both different in kind and longer for the multi-drafters. Initially, their time was spent discovering what they think about the subject, whereas the one-drafters chose a framework within a few minutes and moved on to orient their writing to their readers. Because the transformation or reworking of text comes later for the multi-drafters, rewriting is a necessary component of their writing. The standard bit of advice, about writing the introductory paragraph later, would be a necessary step for them but would not be a productive or appropriate strategy for one-drafters to try. For the one-drafters, the introductory paragraph is the appropriate starting point. In fact, given what they said about the necessity of knowing their focus beforehand, the introductory paragraph is not merely appropriate but necessary.

Because the early stages of a piece of writing are, for multi-drafters, so intricately bound up with mental searching, surveying, and discovering, the writing that is produced is not oriented to the reader. For their early drafts, Bill and Pam both acknowledged that their writing is not yet understandable to others. When Pam commented that in her early drafts, "the reader can't yet see where I'm going," she sighed over the difficulties this had caused in trying to work with her Master's thesis committee. If some writers' early drafts are so personal and so unlikely to be accessible to readers, it is worth speculating about how effective peer editing sessions could be for such multi-drafters who appear in classrooms with "rough drafts" as instructed.

Conclusions

One way to summarize the characteristics of one- and multi-drafters is to consider what they gain by being one-drafters and at what cost they gain these advantages. Clearly, one-drafters are efficient writers. This efficiency is achieved by mentally revising beforehand, by generating options verbally rather than on paper, by generating only a limited number of options before settling on one and getting on with the task, and by doing little or no re-reading. They are able to pace themselves and can probably perform comfortably in situations such as the workplace or in in-class writing where it is advantageous to produce first-draft, final-draft pieces of discourse. Their drafts are readily accessible to readers, and they can expend effort early on in polishing the text for greater clarity. But at what cost? One-drafters are obviously in danger of cutting themselves off from further exploration, from a richer field of discovery than is possible during the time in which they generate options. When they exhibit a willingness to settle on one of their options, they may thereby have eliminated the possibility of searching for a better one. In their impatience to move on, they may even settle on options they know could be improved on. Their impulse to write dwindles as these writers experience little or none of the excitement of discovery or exploration during writing. The interesting portion of a writing task, the struggle with text and sense of exploration, is largely completed when they begin to commit themselves to paper (or computer screen). Because they are less likely to enjoy writing, the task of starting is more likely to be put off to the last minute and to become a stressful situation, thus reinforcing their inclination not to re-read and their desire to be done and to put the paper behind them forever once they have finished. And it appears that it is as hard for true one-drafters to suspend the need for closure as it is for multi-drafters to reach quick decisions and push themselves rapidly toward closure.

Multi-drafters appear to be the flip side of the same coin. Their relative inefficiency causes them to miss deadlines, to create Writer-Based first drafts, to produce large quantities of text that is discarded, and to get lost in their own writing. They need to re-read and re-draft, and they probably appear at first glance to be poorer writers than one-drafters. But they are more likely to be writers who will plunge in eagerly, will write and re-write, and will use writing to explore widely and richly. They also are more likely to affirm the value of writing as a heuristic, the merits of freewriting, and the need for cutting and pasting of text. They may, if statistics are gathered, be the writers who benefit most from collaborative discussions such as those in writing labs with tutors. Their drafts are truly amenable to change and available for re-working.

Implications

Acknowledging the reality of one- and multi-drafting involves enlarging both our perspectives on revision and our instructional practices with students. In terms of what the reality of one-drafting and multi-drafting tells us about revision, it is apparent that we need to account for this diversity of revision behaviors as we construct a more detailed picture of revision. As Stephen Witte notes, "revising research that limits itself to examining changes in written text or drafts espouses a reductionist view of revising as a stage in a linear sequence of stages" ("Revising" 266). Revision can and does occur when writers set goals, create plans, and compose pre-text, as well as when they transcribe and re-draft after transcription. Revision can be triggered by cognitive activity alone and/or by interaction with text; and attitudes, preferences, and cognitive make-up play a role in when and how much a writer revises—or is willing to revise—a text.

Yet, while recognizing the many dimensions to be explored in understanding revision, we can also use this diversity as a source for helping students with different types of problems and concerns. For students who are one-drafters or have tendencies toward single drafting, we need to provide help in several areas. They'll have to learn to do more reviewing of written text both as they write and afterwards, in order to evaluate and revise. They will also need to be aware that they should have strategies that provide for more exploration and invention than they may presently allow themselves. While acknowledging their distaste for returning to a draft to open it up again, we also need to help them see how and when this can be productive. Moreover, we can provide assistance in helping one-drafters and other writers who cluster near that end of the spectrum recognize that sometimes they have a preference for choosing an option even after they recognize that it may not be the best one. When Tim, one of the one-drafters I observed, noted at one point in his protocol that he should take a different direction for one of his paragraphs but won't, he shows similarities to another writer, David, observed by Witte ("Pre-Text and Composing" 406), who is reluctant to spend more than fifteen seconds reworking a sentence in pre-text, even though he demonstrates the ability to evoke criteria that could lead to better formulations if he chose to stop and revise mentally (David typically does little revision of written text). This impatience, this need to keep moving along, that does not always allow for the production of good text, can obviously work against producing good text, and it is unlikely that such writers will either recognize or conquer the problem on their own. They may have snared themselves in their own vicious circles if their tendency to procrastinate puts them in a deadline crunch, which, in turn, does not afford them the luxury of time to consider new options. Such behaviors can become a composing habit so entrenched that it is no longer noticed.

As we work with one-drafters, we will also have to learn ourselves how to distinguish them from writers who see themselves as one-drafters because they are not inclined, for one reason or another, to expend more energy on drafting. Inertia, lack of motivation, lack of information about what multiple drafts can do, higher priorities for other tasks, and so on are not characteristic of true one-drafters, and we must be able to identify the writer who might take refuge behind a label of "one-drafter" from the writer who exhibits some or many of the characteristics of one-draft composing and who wants to become a better writer. For example, in our writing lab I have worked with students who think they are one-drafters because of assorted fears, anxieties, and misinformation. "But I have to get it right the first time." "My teachers never liked to see scratching out on the paper, even when we wrote in class," or "I hate making choices, so I go with what I have" are not the comments of true one-drafters.

With multiple-drafters we have other work to do. To become more efficient writers, they will need to become more proficient planners and creaters of pre-text, though given their heavy dependence on seeing what they have written, they will probably still rely a great deal on reading and working with their transcribed text. They will also need to become more proficient at times at focusing on a topic quickly, recognizing the difficulties involved in agonizing endlessly over possibilities. In the words of a reviewer of this paper, they will have to learn when and how "to get on with it."

Besides assisting with these strategies, we can help students become more aware of their composing behaviors. We can assist multi-drafters in recognizing that they are not slow or inept writers but writers who may linger too long over making choices. For writers who have difficulty returning to a completed text in order to revise, we can relate the problem to the larger picture, an impatience with returning to any completed task. Granted, this is not a giant leap forward, but too many students are willing to throw in the towel with writing skills in particular without recognizing the link to their more general orientations to life. Similarly, the impatient writer who, like Ted, proclaims to have a virulent case of the "I-hate-to-write" syndrome may be a competent one-drafter (or have a preference for fewer drafts) who needs to see that it is the transcribing stage of writing that is the source of the impatience, procrastination, and irritation. On the other hand, writers more inclined to be multi-drafters need to recognize that their frustration, self-criticism, and/or low grades may be due to having readers intervene at too early a stage in the drafting. What I am suggesting here is that some writers unknowingly get themselves caught in linguistic traps. They think they are making generalizations about the whole act of "writing," that blanket term for all the processes involved, when they may well be voicing problems or attitudes about one or another of the processes. What is needed here is some assistance in helping students define their problems more precisely. To do this, classroom teachers can open conferences like a writing lab tutorial, by asking questions about the student's writing processes and difficulties.

In addition to individualizing our work with students, we can also look at our own teaching practices. When we offer classroom strategies and heuristics, we need to remind our students that it is likely that some will be very inappropriate for different students. Being unable to freewrite is not necessarily a sign of an inept writer. One writer's written text may be just as effective a heuristic for that writer as the planning sheets are for another writer. Beyond these strategies and acknowledgments, we have to examine how we talk about or teach composing processes. There is a very real danger in imposing a single, "ideal" composing style on students, as Jack Selzer found teachers attempting to do in his survey of the literature. Similarly, as Susan McLeod notes, teachers tend to teach their own composing behaviors in the classroom and are thus in danger either of imposing their redrafting approaches on students whose preference for revising prior to transcribing serves them well or of touting their one- or few-draft strategies to students who fare better when interacting with their transcribed text. Imposing personal preferences, observes McLeod, would put us in the peculiar position of trying to fix something that isn't broken. And there's enough of that going around as is.

Works Cited

Axelrod, Rise B., and Charles R. Cooper. *The St. Martin's Guide to Writing.* New York: St. Martin's, 1985.

Bartholomae, David. "Against the Grain." Waldrep 1:19–29.

Beach, Richard. "Self-Evaluation Strategies of Extensive Revisers and Non-revisers." *College Composition and Communication* 27 (1976): 160–64.

Blau, Sheridan. "Invisible Writing: Investigating Cognitive Processes in Composition." *College Composition and Communication* 34 (1983): 297–312.

Bloom, Lynn Z. "How I Write." Waldrep 1:31–37.

Bridwell, Lillian S. "Revising Strategies in Twelfth Grade Students' Transactional Writing." *Research in the Teaching of English* 14 (1980): 197–222.

Budner, S. "Intolerance of Ambiguity as a Personality Variable." *Journal of Personality* 30 (1962): 29–50.

Faigley, Lester, and Stephen Witte. "Analyzing Revision." *College Composition and Communication* 32 (1981): 400–14.

Flower, Linda. "Writer-Based Prose: A Cognitive Basis for Problems in Writing." *College English* 41 (1979): 19–37.

Flower, Linda, John R. Hayes, Linda Carey, Karen Shriver, and James Stratman. "Detection, Diagnosis, and the Strategies of Revision." *College Composition and Communication* 37 (1986): 16–55.

Freedman, Sarah Warshauer, Anne Haas Dyson, Linda Flower, and Wallace Chafe. *Research in Writing: Past, Present, and Future.* Technical Report No. 1. Center for the Study of Writing. Berkeley: University of California, 1987.

Frenkel-Brunswick, Else. "Intolerance of Ambiguity as an Emotional and Perceptual Personality Variable." *Journal of Personality* 18 (1949): 108–43.

Gere, Ann Ruggles. "Insights from the Blind: Composing Without Revising." *Revising: New Essays for Teachers of Writing.* Ed. Ronald Sudol. Urbana, IL: ERIC/NCTE, 1982, 52–70.

Hairston, Maxine. "Different Products, Different Processes: A Theory about Writing." *College Composition and Communication* 37 (1986): 442–52.

Henley, Joan. "A Revisionist View of Revision." *Washington English Journal* 8.2 (1986): 5–7.

Jensen, George, and John DiTiberio."Personality and Individual Writing Processes." *College Composition and Communication* 35 (1984): 285–300.

Lutz, William. "How I Write." Waldrep 1:183–88.

McLeod, Susan. "The New Orthodoxy: Rethinking the Process Approach." *Freshman English News* 14.3 (1986): 16–21.

Murray, Patricia Y. "Doing Writing." Waldrep 1:225–39.

Reid, Joy. "The Radical Outliner and the Radical Brainstormer: A Perspective on Composing Processes." *TESOL Quarterly* 18 (1985): 529–34.

Selzer, Jack. "Exploring Options in Composing." *College Composition and Communication* 35 (1984): 276–84.

Sommers, Nancy. "Revision Strategies of Student Writers and Experienced Adult Writers." *College Composition and Communication* 31 (1980): 378–88.

Waldrep, Tom, ed. *Writers on Writing.* Vol. 1, New York: Random House, 1985. 2 vols.

Witte, Stephen P. "Pre-Text and Composing." *College Composition and Communication* 38 (1987): 397–425.

—— "Revising, Composing Theory, and Research Design." *The Acquisition of Written Language: Response and Revision.* Ed. Sarah Warshauer Freedman. Norwood, NJ: Ablex, 1985, 250–84.

MOVING WRITERS, SHAPING MOTIVES, MOTIVATING CRITIQUE AND CHANGE: A GENRE APPROACH TO TEACHING WRITING

Mary Jo Reiff
University of Tennessee

What prompted me to write this essay for this anthology? My "assignment" was to write about the genre of the *Pedagogical Insight* essay. I immediately called on my genre knowledge—my past experience with reading and writing similar texts in similar situations—to orient me to the expectations of this genre. While I am familiar with the genre of "the essay"—and my awareness alerted me to the fact that my piece could be less formal than an article, a piece based more in experience than in research—I was not as familiar with the expectations of this particular genre, a Pedagogical Insight essay. I began, then, with these questions: What are the actions that this genre performs? How will I position myself within this genre—what identity and relations will I assume? In what ways will the genre define and sustain the field's discussions of pedagogy or pedagogical approaches? What are the potential sites of resistance and transformation?

I looked for clues about how the assignment located me within a situation and provided me with the rhetorical means for acting within that situation. From the authors' invitation, I constructed the rhetorical situation that helped motivate and shape my response. The audience was described as "new teachers," and the purpose was "to ground abstract composition theory, as presented by the anthologized articles, in the immediacy of a real classroom context and a real teacher's lived experience." There was a specified length (1,500 words), but within the constraints of audience, purpose, and format, there was also a great deal of choice within this genre, with the authors noting that they "hope for a great diversity in tone, stance, and focus." A sample Pedagogical Insight essay was included in the materials sent—an example of one writer's "appropriate" response.

Writing an effective response would mean conceiving of my role as a writer not only in relation to readers and other writers and their purposes, but also in relation to the social and cultural formations in which they interact. As a result, the larger cultural context beyond the immediate situation of this Pedagogical Insight essay also helped to generate and organize my response. In the materials passed along to help contextualize my response, I was given the proposal (shaped in response to the editors at the National Council of Teachers of English as well as to a secondary audience of contributors and reviewers) that positioned the imagined readers of this anthology, positioned the book intertextually (among "competing texts"), and provided an overview of how the book responds to material conditions and functions epistemologically. My response, then, is situated very purposefully and mediated by various contextual factors, not the least of which is a response to the multiple and related voices included in this section on relations.

Genre in the Classroom (or "How Our Students Can Relate")

Our students are similarly positioned within and by genres. When confronted with a writing assignment, students are suspended within a complex web of relations—from the institutional, disciplinary, and/or course objectives that frame the assignment to the defined roles for writers, their purposes, their subjects, and their conventions for writing. More important, a genre approach allows students to see a writing assignment itself as a social action—a response to the whole disciplinary and institutional context for the assignment, not just a response to the teacher. Students can access and participate effectively in academic situations by identifying the assumptions and expectations regarding subject, their roles as writers (as critics, knowledgeable professionals in the field), the roles of readers (teacher-readers, specialist audiences, implied audiences), and purposes for writing (to describe, analyze, argue, evaluate, etc.) that are embedded in the assignment.

Approaching writing through a contextual genre theory consists of using genre as a lens for accessing, understanding, and writing in various situations and contexts. A genre approach to teaching writing is careful not to treat genres as static forms or systems of classification. Rather, students learn how to recognize genres as rhetorical responses to and reflections of the situations in which they are used; furthermore, students learn how to use genres to intervene in situations. Students begin by (1) collecting samples of a wide range of responses within a particular genre; (2) identifying and describing the larger cultural scene and rhetorical situation from which genre emerges (setting, subject, participants, purposes); (3) identifying and describing the patterns of the genre, including content, structure, format, sentences, and diction; and (4) analyzing genres for what they tell us about situation and making an argumentative or critical claim about what these patterns reveal about the attitudes, values, and actions embedded in the genre.

For example, a prelaw student in my advanced composition class explored the genre activities of the law community by first examining the genre system—the textualized sites such as opinions, wills, deeds, contracts, and briefs—that defines and sustains the legal community. After choosing to focus her study on the genre of case briefs, the student began by collecting samples of constitutional law briefs, discovering that the shared purposes and functions "illustrated the legal community's shared value of commitment to tradition, as well as the need for a standard and convenient form of communicating important and complex legal concepts." Through her study of the repeated rhetorical patterns and social actions of legal briefs, the student gained access to the habits, beliefs, and values of the law community. She not only learned about the genre features of case briefs—such as the technical terminology, rigid format, and formal style—but she also become more aware of how these formal patternings reflected and reinforced the goals of the community. Recognizing that all the briefs follow the same organizational strategy of presenting sections labeled "case information," "facts of the case," "procedural history," "issue," "holding," and "court reasoning," she surmised that "Even the rigid structure of the format [suggests] the community's emphasis on logic and order, which are two esteemed values of the profession." The genre not only reflects the legal community's valuing of logic and order but, as the student discovered, also reinscribes these values by "maintaining a system of communication that relates the scientific and the complex world of law," establishing a relationship, in effect, between scientific, technical precision and the less precise interpretation of law and, as a result, reinforcing the belief that legal cases are unambiguous and clearcut. Furthermore, reflecting on the legal jargon, such as *writ of mandamus*, or the formal language of verbs like *sayeth* and *witnesseth* or words like *hereunder* and *wherewith*, the student makes the following connections among text, contexts, and the ideological effects of genres:

> Legal language is part of a lawyer's professional training, so the habit of "talking like a lawyer" is deeply rooted in the practices of the community. This tells us that lawyers feel compelled to use established jargon to maintain a legitimate status in the eyes of other community members. In addition, formal language is needed to surround legal proceedings with an air of solemnity, and to send the message that any legal proceeding is a significant matter with important consequences.

The writer also notes how this use of legal language reinscribes a power relationship of sorts, separating "insiders" (members of the profession) from "outsiders" (the public) by cultivating a language "that reads like a foreign language to those outside the profession." For students like this one, using genre as a lens for inquiry cultivates a consciousness of the rhetorical strategies used to carry out the social actions of a group or disciplinary community, thus making the complex, multitextured relations of the legal community more tangible and accessible.

Relating and Resisting

Students' critical awareness of how genres work—their understanding of how rhetorical features are connected to social actions—enables them to more effectively critique and resist genres by creating alternatives. For example, a student's critique of the wedding invitation as a genre allowed the discovery of a particular cultural view of women or gender bias in its rhetorical patterns and language (particularly in the references to the bride's parents who "request the honor of your presence"). Embedded in the invitation are cultural assumptions of women as objects or property to be "handed over" from parents to spouse. The textual patternings of the genre, such as references to the parents and the bride as "their daughter" and the omission of the bride's name (while naming the bride's parents and the groom), reinforce what the student describes as a cultural attitude toward marriage that involves a loss of identity for women. Wedding invitations, then, in the student's final analysis, are cultural artifacts that through their repeated use in similar situations—the repeated cultural event of formally announcing marriages—not only reflect but reinscribe gender inequality and unequal distributions of power in relationships (Devitt, Reiff, and Bawarshi).

Classroom genres, too, reflect and enact the social relations of classrooms, and because of the recurring forms of language use of genres, the institutionally sanctioned academic genres might be more easily perpetuated, thus excluding students for whom these genres are less accessible. Brad Peters, in "Genre, Antigenre, and Reinventing the Forms of Conceptualization," describes a college composition course in which students read about the United States invasion of Panama in a book that takes a Panamanian perspective. The students were then told to write an essay exam that followed a particular format moving from a summary of the argument, to the three most compelling points for a Latin American reader, to the three most fallacious points for a Latin American reader, and finally to the student's reaction compared to that of the Latin American reader. One student, Rita, wrote the essay exam from the fictional perspective of her close friend Maria, a native Latin American, and after completing the rhetorical analysis part of the exam, dropped the persona and took up her own in the form of a letter to Maria. Peters identifies this as an "antigenre" but points out that Rita's response satisfies the social purpose of the genre while reconstituting voice and varying the format of the genre. This demonstrates that even when the writing assignment is fairly prescriptive and students are asked to write a fairly traditional genre, there is room for them to maneuver within (and because of) the constraints of the genre.

Toward Changing Relations and Developing New Textual Relations

One criticism leveled against a genre approach to literacy teaching is that it focuses on analysis and critique of genres, stopping short of having writers use genres to enact change. Genres—as they function to define, critique, and bring about change—can provide rich pedagogical sites, sites for intervention. Bruce McComiskey, for example, pairs academic and public genres—having students write a critical analysis of education followed by a brochure for high school students, or following an analysis of the cultural values of advertisements with letters to advertisers arguing the negative effect on consumers. Genre analysis encourages students to critique sites of intervention, analyzing how such genres enable participation in the process while also limiting intervention. Students identify linguistic and rhetorical patterns and analyze their significance, while simultaneously critiquing the cultural and social values encoded in the genre (what the genre allows users to do and what it does not allow them to do, whose needs are most/least served, how it enables or limits the way its users do their work).

But the final step would be to ask students to produce new genres or genres that encode alternative values for the purpose of intervening. Students could create their own genres that respond to those they analyzed. Or, after interrogating the sites at which change happens, students can more directly intervene in these sites by writing their own alternative genres or "antigenres" in response. I often have my students follow their analysis of genres by inventing and formulating their own generic response or by writing a manual for others on how to write that genre. The idea is that as students critique genres as sites of rhetorical action and cultural production and reproduction, they also see how genres function as motivated social actions, enabling them to enter into the production of alternatives.

Teaching Alternatives (or Coming Full Circle)

As is typical in the genre of the essay, I am going to conclude by returning to my introduction, where I invoked the genre of the Pedagogical Insight essay. This genre seeks to intervene in the theoretical readings in this section on *Relations* by reflecting, according to the authors' goals, "some concrete, practical instantiations of theoretical positions." Ideally this genre will function for new teachers as a "conversation starter" about how teaching writing means teaching relations, and how genre analysis can move teachers beyond teaching academic forms to teaching purposeful rhetorical instruments for social action. By teaching students to interrogate how social groups organize and define kinds of texts and how these genres, in turn, organize and define social relations and practices, teachers can construct assignments that enable students to engage more critically in situated action and to produce alternative ways of interacting.

More important, perhaps, is an understanding of how our own work as teachers is also situated institutionally and organized and generated by genres ranging from textbooks to syllabi to assignments to the end comments we write on papers (see, for instance, Summer Smith's "The Genre of the End Comment" and her research on how our comments on papers both enable and restrict writing choices). From the conversations we have with other teachers about our classroom practices to the syllabi that we write that position us as teachers, define our roles in the classroom, establish relationships between us and our students, and reflect and reinforce the goals of our writing courses, the genres we use are sites of action—sites in which we, as teachers, communicate, enact, and carry out our teaching lives. Just as genres may provide a framework for facilitating both inquiry and intervention for our students, as teachers we can use our understanding of the institutional genres that situate us and our teaching—our understanding of our "teaching assignment"—to prompt us to explore ways we might enter into the production of alternative approaches.

Works Cited

Devitt, Amy, Mary Jo Reiff, and Anis Bawarshi. *Scenes of Writing: Strategies for Composing with Genres*. New York: Longman, 2004.

McComiskey, Bruce. *Teaching Composition as a Social Process*. Logan, UT: Utah State UP, 2000.

Peters, Brad. "Genre, Antigenre, and Reinventing the Forms of Conceptualization." *Genre and Writing: Issues, Arguments, Alternatives*. Portsmouth: Boynton/Cook, 1997.

Smith, Summer. "The Genre of the End Comment: Conventions in Teacher Responses to Student Writing." *College Composition and Communication* 48.2 (1997): 249–68.

2

Invention

Irene L. Clark

- Where do ideas come from?
- How does invention reflect its heritage in classical rhetoric?
- What controversies are associated with the concept of invention?
- Why do people experience writer's block?
- What approaches to invention are most useful for students?

This chapter presents an overview of invention, tracing its origins in classical rhetoric, and discusses approaches and classroom strategies that prospective teachers can experiment with in their own writing and then adapt for their students.

My experience in teaching writing at various levels suggests that there are two main reasons that students have difficulty "inventing," "generating," or "discovering" material for the essays they are assigned in their college classes. The first is that they don't understand the assignment and therefore don't know how to proceed. The second is that they wait until the last minute to begin. And, of course, both of these reasons are interconnected. When students are confused about an assignment, they may wait until the last minute to begin working on it. And when they haven't spent enough time thinking about it, they may be unable to figure out what to do. Whichever comes first, the process causes considerable anxiety.

We are all familiar with the scene: students up all night, staring at a blank screen, tossing unsatisfactory drafts into an already overflowing waste basket, and still unable to write anything they are proud to submit. Or they manage to write a draft or part of a draft but then discover that it doesn't fulfill the requirements of the assignment because they didn't engage with it seriously. Because students so frequently experience problems with generating or locating ideas, helping them develop effective invention strategies is an important part of the writing class and should be addressed many times over the semester.

As a concept in composition, "invention" refers to the process writers use to search for, discover, create, or "invent" material for a piece of writing, and at one time, people thought that invention was a first step that must be completed before beginning to write. Now we understand that invention occurs throughout the writing process and can be both a conscious and an unconscious process. For a few writers, it seems to happen effortlessly, involving little more than thinking about the topic and jotting down a few ideas. But for most writers, generating ideas, particularly for an unfamiliar topic, involves considerable effort, often accompanied by stress. Even people who write frequently in their professional lives say that they have at least some difficulty with invention, and for students, who have had little experience with the composing process and who often don't allow sufficient time for ideas to percolate, a writing assignment can be formidable.

THE HERITAGE OF INVENTION

In considering the role of invention in the writing process, both as a writer and as a prospective teacher, it is important to understand the following concepts:

1. Current approaches to and debates about invention have their roots in the past, particularly in classical rhetoric.
2. What is deemed an "appropriate" subject is strongly influenced by societal values.
3. The process of invention is strongly influenced by the subject and rhetorical situation being addressed.

For invention to occur, a writer must have the capacity to invent, that is, he or she must have a store of experience and/or knowledge that is sufficient enough to generate ideas, either through the imagination or a quest for information. This statement seems self-evident, but it raises the question of how writers develop this capacity and what should be done in the writing class to aid the process. Does any person, simply on the basis of being human, have the ability to invent material for a piece of writing? Or is invention the province of only highly educated, intelligent, or imaginative people? Debate on this issue has occurred for a long time and has implications for how writers should be educated and for how writing should be approached in the classroom.

Robert Connors (1987), in his article "Personal Writing Assignments," noted that throughout the history of rhetoric, a true "rhetor" (anyone who composes discourse that is intended to affect community thinking or events) was supposed to know everything, so as to be able to write on any possible subject. Cicero (106–43 B.C.) in *De Oratore* (1942) asserted that "no one can be an absolutely perfect orator unless he has acquired a knowledge of all important subjects and arts" (I, 4, 20), and Quintilian (35–95 A.D.), although not stating this idea so forcefully, nevertheless, in *Institutio Oratorio* (1920), recommended a complete literary and philosophical education as preparatory to the learning of rhetoric, "for there is nothing which may not crop up in a cause or appear as a question for discussion" (II, 21, 22). Thus, one position in the debate about invention maintains that, to have anything worthwhile to say, speakers or writers must be highly educated and possess such a wealth of knowledge that ideas will flow from them as easily and effortlessly as water in a stream.

On the other hand, more practical or realistic rhetoricians recognized that although it might be desirable for writers and speakers to be so broadly educated, in actuality, this level of knowledge is impossible for most people to acquire. Epitomized in the works of Aristotle, this more realistic and practical approach acknowledges that many writers and speakers need approaches and invention strategies to investigate a subject and generate ideas. According to Aristotle's perspective, potential writers and orators can prepare by familiarizing themselves with argumentative approaches and text structures that will enable them to respond to any rhetorical situation.

Another debatable issue addressed during classical times concerned the question of where ideas come from, a question that is of interest today as well. Are ideas "created" through the active mind, and generated, fresh and new from within? Or are ideas "out there," waiting to be discovered? In the ancient world, the term "invent" was almost synonymous with "discover," and the focus was on where ideas could be discovered. Tracing the origins of this issue, W. Ross Winterowd pointed out that the concept of invention took two directions, one associated with Plato, the other with Aristotle, and he referred to this split as "the idealist-empiricist dialectic" (Winterowd & Blum, 1994, p. 2). For Plato (428–348 B.C.), ideas existed independently and were available through the mind, the goal of invention being the discovery of truth obtained through an inner-directed search. But for Aristotle, ideas were "out there," waiting to be discovered, their purpose being to convince an audience of the persuasiveness of a concept or belief. Winterowd maintained that Plato's conception of ideas as being "inner directed" was the source of the "transcendental tradition," which provided the basis for the romantic view of composing associated with Peter Elbow and Donald Murray, whereas Aristotle was the founder of the "empirical tradition."

For Writing and Discussion

Briefly describe the invention strategies you use to generate ideas for assigned essays, indicating the extent to which you are satisfied with the process you use. How do you feel about teaching students particular invention strategies? Share your response in small groups.

Invention in Classical Rhetoric

Historians usually locate the classical period in rhetoric from the 5th century B.C. to around the 5th century A.D., the period that saw the flowering of rhetorical scholarship in Athens and Rome. As was discussed in Chapter 1, the word "rhetoric" does not refer to empty or deceptive words, as a modern reader might think; rather, it refers to the art that helps people compose effective discourse. For ancient rhetoricians, rhetoric was an important means of helping "people to choose the best course of action when they disagreed about political, religious, or social issues" (Crowley, 1994, p. 1), and "invention" (*heuresis* in Greek, *inventio* in Latin) was a significant division of rhetoric. It referred to the means of discovering possible arguments, providing "speakers and writers with sets of instructions to help them find and compose proofs appropriate for any rhetorical situation" (Crowley, 1990, p. 30). The word "invenire" meant "to find" or "to come upon" in Latin, and the Greek equivalent, "heuriskein," also meant "to find out" or "discover," a word that has given us "heuristic," which means "an aid to discovery." To Plato and Aristotle, "rhetoric" was oriented toward the construction of "proofs"—that is, any statement or statements that could be used to persuade an audience to think or act in a certain way, because ancient rhetoricians were concerned primarily with persuasion. Those studying rhetoric at that time became familiar with many invention strategies, which they could then apply to any rhetorical situation that arose. Usually those situations occurred in a public context, growing out of the life of the community.

The idea of community was inextricably linked to invention in the ancient world because knowledge was located in communal learning. In fact, according to rhetorical theorist Sharon Crowley, the idea that knowledge exists outside of people and has to be taken in or absorbed and then transferred to others by speaking and writing is a modern one. Ancient rhetoricians defined knowledge as the collected wisdom of those who are knowledgeable. Thus, they would have had difficulty understanding the problem students have with finding something to write about, because they assumed that anyone who wanted to compose would have had a clear reason for doing so. They would not be grappling with a topic such as "The Problem With My Roommate" or "Describe a Moment When You Learned Something About Yourself." Rather, they would be addressing issues of public interest that had generated some disagreement or dispute. This perspective has relevance for many writing classes today as well.

In ancient Greece, the need to train orators gave rise to two traditions: the techne, which prescribed how to structure an oration, and the sophistic, which "offered set speeches that students of oratory could memorize, analyze, and imitate" (Covino & Jolliffe, 1995, p. 39). Plato questioned both of these traditions as being too mechanistic and not sufficiently concerned with the discovery of truth, which he saw as absolute. Plato had this same criticism of a group known as the "sophists," who conceived of "rhetoric as epistemic, that is, as an art that creates rather than reflects knowledge" (p. 84). Plato distrusted the sophists for believing in the relativity of truth and for being manipulators of language; he was concerned that the linguistic facility obtained through the teaching of the sophists was a trick that could be used for ignoble purposes, such as influencing young people to believe what is false. He would, no doubt, have had great difficulty with the language of advertising.

It must be noted here, however, that although the term "sophist" today suggests a person who uses language to deceive, sophists in 5th century B.C. Athens were initially professors who "lectured on the 'new learning' in literature, science, philosophy, and especially oratory. The Sophists set up small private schools and charged their pupils a fee for what amounted in many cases to tutoring" (Corbett & Connors, 1999, p. 491). In 392 B.C., Isocrates set up a school of oratory, which was apparently quite lucrative, enabling him to amass "a considerable fortune from his teaching" (Corbett & Connors, 1999, p. 491). Plato, however, held the sophists in low esteem, arguing in the *Gorgias* and the *Phaedrus,* that:

> Rhetoric could not be considered a true art because it did not rest on universal principles. Moreover, rhetoricians, like poets, were more interested in opinions, in appearances, even in lies, than in the transcendental truth that the philosopher sought. They made the "worse appear the better reason." They were mere enchanters of the soul, more interested in dazzling their audiences than in instructing. (Quoted in Covino and Joliffe [1995] p. 492)

These objections to those who use language to manipulate still pertain today; often we disdain the "sophistry" of politicians or advertisers.

For Writing and Discussion

Plato's criticism of the sophists was based on their ability to manipulate language to suit particular audiences and situations as well as on their belief in the relativity and contingency of truth. To what extent do you agree with Plato's criticism? Consider the following questions:

1. Is it ethical to teach persuasive strategies if they can be used to manipulate?

2. Are the means of persuasion simply a *knack*, a trick of language that anyone can learn?
3. When students write an essay in which they are asked to express and support an "opinion," must they really believe what they write?
4. Is it ethical to write an essay that expresses an opinion that the author does not really hold?

Aristotle

Aristotle's *The Art of Rhetoric*, composed between 360 and 334 B.C., is an important source of information about how invention was conceived of in the ancient world. Born in 384 B.C., Aristotle went to Athens to study with Plato in 367 B.C. and then, at Plato's death in 347 B.C., stayed on as a teacher, where he eventually taught rhetoric, dividing it into five parts: invention, arrangement, style, memory, and delivery, although only the first three are considered important in the context of writing. Aristotle is associated with two important overall claims that pertain to invention: that rhetoric is an art that can be taught (thus, students can be "taught" to invent), and that subject matter can be discovered in the world. Seeking to rescue rhetoric from Plato's low opinion of it, Aristotle asserted that although individual rhetors might use rhetoric for unscrupulous ends, it is a skill, like a number of others, such as physical strength or the ability to decipher codes, that can be used for either noble or ignoble purposes. In fact, he argued, the study of rhetoric would enable people to understand and evaluate the quality of ideas, thereby helping them to assess their own beliefs and recognize poor or fallacious arguments. This is a belief that many of us share today.

For Aristotle, rhetoric was a system that enabled a rhetor to perceive the available means of persuasion or "proofs" (*pisteis*), which he classified as either "artistic" or "non-artistic." As Corbett and Connors (1999) explained:

> Non-artistic proofs are unimportant to the concept of invention because they consisted of appeals to physical evidence, such as contracts or testimony. These are not invented by the speaker because they involve the interpretation of already existing material such as laws, witnesses, contracts, tortures, oaths. Apparently, the lawyer pleading a case in court made most use of this kind of proof, but the politician or the panegyrist could use them too. (p. 18)

However, "artistic" proofs (called "artistic" because they are part of the "art" of rhetoric) could be discovered, and these constituted the subject matter of *The Art of Rhetoric*, which focused on three types of artistic proofs or appeals which still have validity today. The first was *ethos*, usually translated as the character of the speaker as it comes across in a speech. According to Covino and Jolliffe (1995),

> theorists in ancient Greece and Rome did not agree among themselves whether ethos exists solely in the text a *rhetor* creates, or whether the *rhetor* must evince *ethos* in his or her life as well as in his or her texts. (p. 15)

But Aristotle believed that "a rhetor could not depend … on the audience's knowing more about the rhetor's ethos than the text itself established" (Covino & Joliffe, 1995, p. 15). In other words, the text must speak for itself—that is, it must demonstrate that the rhetor is a person of good sense, virtue, and will. In the context of the composition class, *ethos* refers to a writer rather than a speaker, but the principle is the same, because a writer who has established trustworthiness and good will in a text will be more convincing than one who has not. All of us are more likely to accept another person's ideas if we think of that person as knowledgeable, trustworthy, logical, and fair, as opposed to ignorant, untrustworthy, illogical, and biased.

Aristotle's idea of the credible rhetor has been affirmed in a recent study of academic writing in multiple disciplines by Chris Thaiss and Terri Zawacki, which they reported on in *Engaged Writers, Dynamic Disciplines* (2006). The primary characteristics they discovered as relevant across the disciplines were "clear evidence that the writer(s) have been persistent, open-minded, and disciplined in study" (p. 5). Apparently, these characteristics are as important today as they were in ancient Greece.

The second type of proof Aristotle discussed was *pathos,* which is sometimes called the emotional or pathetic appeal. The main idea behind *pathos* was that an effective discourse will appeal to or move an audience, and Aristotle's (333 B.C.) *Rhetoric* contains a list of emotions that could be used for this purpose, such as pity, fear, indignation, or anger. Aristotle also categorized potential audiences into character types such as the young, the old, aristocrats, and the wealthy, assigning various emotions to each character type. This type of appeal also has relevance to the composition class, in that an effective text will take into consideration what is likely to move an intended audience. Moreover, a consideration of audience can serve as an effective invention strategy that can aid in discovery.

Aristotle's third and most important proof was *logos,* the appeal to reason, which in ancient Greece did not refer simply to logic, but rather to "thought plus action." As Covino and Jolliffe (1995) explained,

> just as *ethos* moves an audience by activating their faith in the credibility of the rhetor and *pathos* stimulates their feelings and seeks a change in their attitudes and actions, so *logos,* accompanied by the other two appeals, mobilizes the powers of reasoning. (p. 17)

The Topoi

In addition to discussing the types of proofs that can be used to develop a more persuasive text, Aristotle also referred to places in the memory, or topoi, where ideas can be stored and retrieved. These topoi can be considered types of argumentative strategies and reasons that can be useful in various rhetorical situations, and his idea was for orators to ask themselves questions that the topoi generated, thereby developing content. The most frequently used and most usable topics deriving from Aristotle's system are definition, comparison, cause-and-effect, and authority. Aristotle was the first rhetorician to introduce the topics, but others such as Cicero and Quintilian developed them further, often describing "the places as though they were hidden away." Quintilian (1994), for example, defined the topoi as "the secret places where arguments reside and from which they must be drawn forth." (p. 50)

It must be clarified here, however, that the word "topic" as it was conceived of in ancient times, is not synonymous with the way in which the term is used today. When a teacher asks a class to list "topics" they would like to write about, he or she means a subject, drawn either from books, general knowledge, or personal experience. Ancient rhetoricians, however, thought of topics as existing in "the structures of language or in the issues that concerned the community. That is why they were called common places—they were available to anyone who spoke or wrote the language in which they were couched and who was reasonably familiar with the ethical and political discussions taking place in the community" (Crowley, 1994, p. 50).

Emphasis on Community in Classical Rhetoric

Classical invention was directed outward, based almost entirely on logos, rather than on ethos, concerned with the community, and focused on questions that were of concern to all members of society. As Connors (1987) phrased it:

> Rhetorical exercises mirrored the classical belief that the world—the brute facts of it, the doings of the persons in it, the nature of their feelings, judgments, beliefs—was the grist for the mill of rhetoric. From the earliest age, students were to be trained to see the world, to know what has been thought and said about it, and to hammer that knowledge into discourse that could change it. (p. 16).

THE HERITAGE OF PERSONAL WRITING

Given the public orientation of classical rhetoric, argument that was based on personal opinion or that used personal experience as its main subject was considered self-centered and unconvincing. Yet many composition classrooms today focus on, or at least include, assignments concerned with personal writing, invention being directed toward individual recollection, feeling, and opinion. Given the emphasis on argumentation and corresponding de-emphasis on personal opinion in classical and neo-classical rhetoric, how did personal writing gain such a position of importance in the writing class today?

Connors (1987) traced the beginnings of this trend to the 17th century, in which the individual—personal tastes, feelings, experiences—began to be considered important to public life, epitomized in the "rise of novels, books of personal essays, travel books, realistic narrative and overly personal poems" (p. 169). This emphasis on the individual gained importance in the latter part of the 18th and early 19th centuries, with the shift from a classical outlook to a romantic one, with the individual writer beginning to occupy a position of greater prominence in education. The focus of George Campbell's *The Philosophy of Rhetoric* (1776) was on the thoughts and perceptions of the individual, and, according to Winterowd and Blum (1994), "moved invention to the ivory tower of the individual mind" (p. 20), placing a new emphasis on creativity (genius, imagination, fancy). Invention in this context did not mean "discovering" content; it meant "creating" something completely new. Sharon Crowley (1990, p. 32) noted that with the publication of Campbell's *The Philosophy of Rhetoric* (1776), "for the first time in the history of rhetoric, the inventional process was focused solely on the individual creative mind of a rhetor working in relative isolation." This tendency was further emphasized in the writing of Hugh Blair, whose influential *Lectures on Rhetorical and Belles Lettres* (1783) focused attention on individual understanding as the goal of knowledge, culminating in the development of creativity and taste. The dissemination of what Winterowd referred to as "romantic rhetoric" thus resulted in the exaltation of self-expression, and the privileging of imagination and inspiration over invention.

Personal Writing in the Early Phase of the Process Movement

Emphasis on the personal also characterized the initial phase of the process movement of the 1960s and 1970s, when the need to provide "at-risk" student populations with successful writing experiences led to an emphasis on simple writing assignments concerned with topics with which students were presumably familiar—that is, assignments concerned with their own lives. An important goal at this time was to enable students to develop self-confidence by accessing their own personal voice and to validate their experiences. As expressed by Ken Macrorie (1970) in *Telling Writing*:

> The New English Movement has begun. ... The program gives the student first, freedom, to find his voice and let his subjects find him; and second, discipline, to learn more professional craft to supplement his already considerable language skills. (Preface, pp. vii–viii)

In this context, personal topics were considered more relevant than academic ones, enabling students to write about what they know so that they could focus on the "craft" of writing.

THE POSSIBILITY OF TEACHING INVENTION

Whether the emphasis on personal writing during the early phases of the process movement was really helpful to at-risk students can be debated, but, certainly, scholars of that time devoted significant attention to invention, considerably more than they do today. Ken Macrorie and Peter Elbow emphasized the importance of freewriting as a means of helping students find a voice in writing. Janice Lauer (1970) in "Heuristics and Composition" set up criteria for judging the effectiveness of heuristic procedures, which, she maintains, have both generative and evaluative powers. Such procedures, she emphasizes, must be distinguished both from trial and error methods, which are nonsystematic and, hence, inefficient, and from rule-governed procedures, which are overly rigorous. Lauer's article also establishes the criteria of transcendency, flexibility, and generative capacity for judging the effectiveness of a heuristic procedure. Translated into questions, these characteristics may be perceived as follows:

1. Transcendency
   How can writers transfer this model's questions or operations from one subject to another?
2. Flexible Order
   Is the model flexible so that a thinker can return to a previous step or skip to an inviting one as the evolving idea suggests?
3. Generative Capacity
   Is the model generative so that it involves the writer in various operations—such as visualizing, classifying, defining, rearranging, and dividing?

Lauer's attempt to develop useful strategies for composition students, however, was criticized by Ann Berthoff (1971) who condemned heuristics as being overly mechanical in an article titled "The Problem of Problem Solving." Berthoff's criticism was then countered by Lauer (1972) who argued that heuristics were, by definition, open ended, not rigid, flexible, and not oriented toward finding a "right" answer.

The Lauer–Berthoff debate over heuristics was indicative of the interest in invention that characterized the process movement in the 1960s and 1970s. In "Pre-Writing: The Stage of Discovery in the Writing Process," D. Gordon Rohman (1965) claimed that engaging in pre-writing enabled students to produce writing that "showed a statistically significant superiority to essays produced in control sections" (p. 112). Young, Becker, and Pike in their book, *Rhetoric: Discovery and Change* (1970), devised an elaborate invention scheme derived from tagmemic linguistics, which approached composing in terms of a complex invention strategy that requires a writer to examine a subject from nine different perspectives. The tagmemicists maintained that because people conceive of the world in terms of repeatable units that are part of a larger system, understanding those units can enable writers to investigate and, thus, generate material for a wider range of subjects. The tagmemic system is quite complicated, and only a few writers use it on a regular basis, but it became the subject of significant scholarship during the 1970s. Those who are interested in this approach to invention can find additional information in the following publications.

For Further Exploration

Kenupper, C. W. (1980). Revising the tagmemics heuristic: Theoretical and pedagogical consideration. *CCC, 3,* 161–167.

Odell, L. (1978). Another look at tagmemic theory: A response to James Kinney. *CCC, 29,* 146–152.

Young, R. E., & Becker, A. L. (1965). Toward a modern theory of rhetoric: A tagmemic contribution. *Harvard Education Review, 35,* 450–468.

WRITER'S BLOCK[1]

Writer's block or writer's anxiety are experienced by most, if not all, writers from time to time, not only by student writers but also by professional and acclaimed writers. In fact, Mike Rose (1984) began his ground-breaking *Writer's Block: The Cognitive Dimension* with a quotation from Flaubert that describes the agony of staying "a whole day with your head in your hands, trying to squeeze your unfortunate brain so as to find a word." Rose's study suggested that at least "10% of college students block frequently, and the boom of 'writer's block' workshops stands as a reminder that writer's block is a problem outside of the classroom as well" (p. 1). Rose (1984) cited the following factors as contributing to writer's block:

1. The rules by which students guide their composing processes are rigid, inappropriately invoked, or incorrect.
2. Their assumptions about composing are misleading.
3. They edit too early in the composing process.
4. They lack appropriate planning and discourse strategies or rely on inflexible or inappropriate strategies.
5. They invoke conflicting rules, assumptions, plans, and strategies.
6. They evaluate their writing with inappropriate criteria or criteria that are inadequately understood.

Rose maintained that students who block seem to be depending on rules and plans that impede rather than aid the composing process. He cited the example of "Ruth," who believed that every sentence she wrote had to come out grammatically correct the first time around. This belief led Ruth to edit each sentence before she proceeded to the next, thus closing off the flow of ideas. Another example was "Martha," who spent days developing a complex plan for her paper, leaving her little time to actually write.

In terms of invention, Rose asserted that people who suffer from writer's block are more likely to generate material if the strategies they use are well-structured. Nonstructured techniques, such as freewriting and brainstorming, can be useful, Rose (1984) maintained; however, the resulting morass of ideas "can sometimes lead to more disorder than order, more confusing divergence than clarifying focus" (p. 91).

Another work concerned with writer's block that was prominent during the early days of the process movement was James Adams' *Conceptual Blockbusting* (1974), which suggested that most of us, but particularly anxiety-ridden students, are prevented from exploring ideas freely because of emotional blocks that inhibit us from doing so. A few of these blocks contribute to the problem students have in generating ideas for papers, in particular:

1. *The fear of taking a risk.* Adams pointed out that because most of us have grown up rewarded when we produced the "right answer" and punished when we made a mistake, we tend to avoid risk whenever possible. Yet exploring ideas for papers means taking risks, to some extent. To come up with anything new means considering, at least for a short time, a notion that has not been mentioned before, a notion that one may later reject as inappropriate in some way. Because students fear the rejection associated with risk taking, they are often unable to entertain new ideas and will reject even a glimmer of creative thought, which may prove to be unsuitable and subject them to ridicule.

2. *No appetite for chaos.* Because the fear of making a mistake is rooted in insecurity, most of us tend to avoid ambiguity whenever possible, opting for safety over uncertainty, a condition Adams (1974) referred to as "having no appetite for chaos." Thus, because they are uncomfortable with the "chaos" that characterizes the stage in the writing process that exists before one generates an idea or focuses a topic, many students reach for order before they have given the topic sufficient exploration. Thus, they find themselves "stuck" with dead-end or uninteresting topics.

3. *Preference for judging, rather than generating ideas.* This emotional block, according to Adams, also has its root in our preference for safety, rather than for risk, producing in students a tendency to judge an idea too early or indiscriminately. Adams (1974) stated, "If you are a compulsive idea-judger, you should realize that this is a habit that may exclude ideas from your own mind before they have had time to bear fruit" (p. 47).

4. *Inability to incubate.* There is a general agreement that the unconscious plays an important role in problem solving, and it is, therefore, important for students to give their ideas an opportunity to incubate, to wrestle with a problem over several days. Yet students often procrastinate, putting off work on their papers until the day before they are due. They often find themselves blocked before they can even get started.

5. *Lack of motivation.* Students are often asked to write about topics in which they have little interest; their motivation lies only in the grade they hope to receive. Yet, as Adams pointed out, it is unlikely that students can come up with an interesting idea for a paper if they aren't motivated, at least somewhat, by the topic.

Writer's block and writing anxiety continue to be addressed in writing scholarship, recent approaches addressing psychological or emotional factors. Cynthia A. Arem in *Conquering Writing Anxiety* (2011) distinguished between writer's anxiety and writer's block. In her view, writer's *anxiety* is "characterized by dread, nervousness, worry, or hatred of writing. Some face anguish and panic" (p. 1) and is a condition that is deep seated. In contrast, Arem defined writer's *block* as "a condition producing a transitory inability to express one's thoughts on paper. It is characterized by feelings of frustration, rather than dread, hatred or panic" (p. 1). Arem's book contains self-assessment charts and strategies to break cycles of both writer's anxiety and writer's block and considers the influence of individual learning styles. Among the ways suggested include creating a positive writing mindset, calming techniques, visualization strategies, and the therapeutic use of writing journals.

For Writing and Discussion

Write a short paper discussing rules of composing that you find most useful when you write. Include in your paper responses to the following questions:

1. What rules of writing do you think about when you compose?
2. Do any of these rules make writing more difficult for you?
3. Have you ever experienced writer's block?
4. Share your responses in small groups.

INVENTION AND THE COMPOSITION CLASSROOM

In the conclusion to his study on writer's block, Rose (1984) emphasized the importance of selecting an *invention strategy that is suited to the writing task*, and it is important to remember this idea when teaching invention in the classroom. Students should understand that the kind of essay being written (e.g., a personal essay or an academic argument) and the subject being addressed strongly determine the type of invention strategy that is most appropriate for generating material. Heuristics direct writers' attention in particular directions, encouraging them to approach a topic from one direction or perspective as opposed to another. Thus, instructors should consider the effects of using one strategy instead of another, helping students understand their differences.

Helping Students Understand the Assignment

Ancient rhetoricians recognized that to "invent" material for a discourse, a rhetor had to be familiar with the subject under consideration, an idea that seems obvious. Yet in presenting assignments to students, some teachers do not seem to recognize the importance of this basic concept. Scribbling a writing assignment on the board or handing it out hastily in class, they send students home to write an essay, or, even more unrealistically, to generate an essay right on the spot. A fundamental invention concept derived from ancient rhetoricians, then (and in accord with common sense), is that it is important to familiarize students with the topic they are going to be writing about, to help them feel comfortable with the subject, and to make sure that they understand what is expected of them. This is true whether the essay is concerned with a public controversy or with students' own personal experiences. When the assignment is first distributed, the teacher should read it aloud to the class and then students should reread it on their own. They can also use worksheets to be completed either at home, online, or in class, to help them understand what is required.

Most importantly, all assignments should be scaffolded—that is, segmented—not only as a way to familiarize students with the topic, but also to prevent students from postponing work until the night before the essay is due. Assign due dates for each component of the process, encourage students to present their ideas in class, perhaps using PowerPoint, have students write annotated bibliographies as a preparatory activity, and incorporate group and online work into each segment of the process.

Creating an Invention-Oriented Classroom Atmosphere

In introducing a writing topic in the classroom, it is important to foster a classroom atmosphere that invites experimentation and exploration so that students will be able to entertain possibilities without fear of ridicule or negative evaluation. To create a classroom atmosphere that is "invention oriented," you can share your own invention process with students and encourage students to try out new ideas. Assure them that everyone finds invention difficult, and help them understand that discovery of a main topic or subtopic can occur at any stage of the writing process, not only at the beginning. An important goal of the writing class is to enable students to explore new ideas—even in a half-written draft—and to investigate directions not previously considered.

An invention-oriented writing class also means stressing the importance of developing ideas *actively*. Although for some writers "invention" means sitting at a desk and waiting for an idea to strike like a bolt of lightning, most people find it useful to explore a subject by engaging in preliminary exploratory writing activities. Such activities enable writers to assess what they already know about the subject, although there is no guarantee that something wonderful will be discovered immediately; in fact, writers often reject a significant portion of what they have written at this stage. But even if this is the case, it is likely that the process will stimulate the discovery of something that is useful or, at least, bring the realization that additional information is needed.

INVENTION STRATEGIES

Class and Group Discussion

The most useful method of helping students generate ideas for a writing assignment is to have them discuss the topic in pairs, small groups, with the whole class, or online, using programs such as WebCT, Blackboard, or Moodle. Sharing ideas will enable students of all levels to engage with a topic, fostering insight that will stimulate the imagination. This is a principle that seems self-evident; yet it is often overlooked and little research exists that demonstrates its effectiveness. An early study, published in 1969, was conducted by Robert Zoellner, who published the results in an article entitled "Talk-Write: A Behavioral Pedagogy for Composition." In that article Zoellner asserted that students will be able to write more clearly and expansively if they approach writing through another behavior (speaking) that has already proven at least reasonably successful. Zoellner's article focused on the importance of actual talk, but today's students are also quite familiar with online chats, so it makes sense to incorporate electronic discussions as well.

Although Zoellner's ideas have not been tested rigorously, a number of years ago, George Kennedy (1983) conducted some research that suggested the validity of Zoellner's work. Kennedy divided a group of basic writers into two groups: the experimental "Speakwrites" and the control "Writeonlys," and both groups watched a film, which was used as the stimulus for a writing assignment. The Speakwrites were interviewed individually on the subject of the film and were then asked to write a 30-minute essay on a general topic generated by the film. The Writeonlys had no opportunity to discuss the film and were asked only to write the 30-minute essay. When the essays were graded by independent evaluators, the Speakwrites' essays received significantly higher scores than did the Writeonly's. Kennedy's research, therefore, highlighted the importance of "talking" to the invention process and the necessity of preparing students before they begin to write. Online discussions are likely to have a similar benefit.

Journals

Journals are another source of ideas for an essay, and students often enjoy writing them. For journals to be useful to the invention process, though, it is important to explain that a journal in a composition class is not a diary of daily events, but, rather, a place for grappling with ideas or responding to readings. Students will be able to distinguish between journals and diaries if you prompt journal entries with specific questions, at least in the beginning of the class, and to ask those whose entries are particularly well developed if you might share them with other students.

Freewriting and Brainstorming

Many students find that writing freely about a topic, either by hand or on a computer, enables them to generate preliminary ideas about it, particularly if the topic has affected them personally. Jotting down ideas or brainstorming about a topic can thus be extremely helpful both as a classroom exercise and as a homework assignment. Images that come to mind can suggest other images, and frequently students find that they can then generate ideas that they didn't even know they had.

Clustering

Clustering is similar to freewriting and brainstorming in that its aim is to elicit as many ideas as possible. Clustering, however, enables students to group ideas visually and to see possible connections between ideas. To use clustering, the writer places the central idea or topic in the center of the paper and circles it. Around this circled word, he or she writes other words that are associated with this central idea and puts circles around them as well. Then they write other words that are associated with these other ideas and use lines to connect them either to each other or to other words on the page. Clustering helps writers develop details and find connections that might not have been discovered otherwise.

THINKING ABOUT YOUR ASSIGNMENT: A WORKSHEET

This worksheet will enable you to learn as much as possible about your assignment, so that you will be able to write your essay with greater insight. Follow each of the steps below, writing your response in the space provided.

1. Read the assignment aloud to yourself, paying particular attention to the place where the *writing task* is discussed.
2. List the *key terms* in the assignment that give directions.

   List any terms that need to be defined.

3. Summarize in your own words the type of writing task that the assignment requires. Remember that most college writing assignments require a thesis or main point and that although you may not know yet what that thesis will be, eventually you will have to formulate one.

4. What type of information does this paper require? Will the information be based primarily on personal experience or opinion? Will you need to find information from the library or the Internet?
5. Locate any requirements of the assignment that may not be directly stated, but which are necessary in order for the assignment to be completed satisfactorily.
   - Does this assignment require you to define terms? If so, which ones?
   - Does this assignment require you to develop a relationship between ideas? If so, which ideas must be connected?
   - Does this assignment require you to take a position on a controversial subject? If so, list two opposing views. Does this assignment require you to consider questions of degree or make a judgment (does it say "to what extent" for example)?
6. Who is the audience for this paper, aside from your teacher? What sort of knowledge about the topic do you assume your audience has?
   Respond to the following questions about audience:
   - *Before* the people in my audience have read this paper, they are likely to have the following beliefs about this topic:

   - *After* the people in my audience have read this paper, I would like them to have the following beliefs about this topic:

7. Why does this topic matter? Why would anyone care about it? Why is it important to think about? Are there implications or consequences that should be addressed?
8. A possible thesis or main point for this paper might be _____

FIG. 2.1 A Worksheet for Thinking About an Assignment.

The Points to Make List

Brainstorming is usually just the first step in generating an interesting and well-thought-out essay, with ideas that go beyond the superficial. A useful invention strategy that follows brainstorming and precedes the drafting of an essay is the *Points to Make List,* which enables a writer to sort and narrow ideas. Although different writers do this in individual ways, most good writers will take time to write down, examine, and revise their ideas in an informal list that is not as rigid as an outline. It is also an important tool to help develop an effective rough plan and thesis statement. See Fig. 2.3.

Exploring a Topic Through Questioning

Learning to ask oneself questions about a topic is a useful invention strategy, loosely derived from Aristotelian rhetoric. Responding to questions enables writers to reflect on experiences, facts, opinions, and values they already have about the topic, determine what they *don't* know about the topic, decide what they need to find out, and then evaluate the material they find. Several of the following strategies are based on the use of questions.

Exploration Questions

Exploration questions are useful for exploring a topic that is concerned with a controversy, one that requires the writer to develop a thesis or position (a characteristic of most college writing assignments). Responding in writing to these questions enables the writer to understand a controversy in terms of background and issue, an insight that helps writers construct a point of view. A sheet that can be used for this purpose appears in Fig. 2.3.

Topical Questions

Another questioning strategy, loosely based on Artistotle's *On Rhetoric* (1991), uses the idea of "topics" as a means of discovering material for an argument, a strategy that was developed by Edward Corbett (1981) in *The Little Rhetoric and Handbook*. Corbett's questions are listed below.

Questions about concepts:

1. How has the term been defined by others?
2. How do you define the term?
3. What other concepts have been associated with the term?
4. In what ways has this concept affected the lives of people?
5. How might this concept be changed?

Questions about a statement or proposition:

1. What must be established before a reader will believe the proposition?
2. What are the meanings of key words in the proposition?
3. By what evidence or argument can the proposition be proved or disproved?
4. What counterarguments must be confronted and refuted?
5. What are the practical consequences of the proposition?

THE POINTS TO MAKE LIST[2]

Procedure:

1. *Create a preliminary list*:
   Review your brainstorming notes and readings. It might be useful to do this with a high-lighter or different-colored pen so that you can clearly mark the ideas that you think might be effective in your essay. At this stage, don't worry if you're interested in a number of different (and possibly unrelated) ideas. In fact, be as inclusive as you can. Just develop a primary list of points (ideas and/or opinions you have about this topic) and evidence (facts, examples, and quotes) that you like for your essay. Then in the space provided below, list those points.

   _____   _____
   _____   _____
   _____   _____

Reminder:

The above list will probably include many different kinds of ideas, some broad, some nar-row, some opinions, some explanations. Don't be concerned about this variety of ideas, and don't try to jump to a thesis statement too soon. Sometimes you need to work with ideas for a while before you finally arrive at what you "really want to say." Especially be aware of the trap that many students fall into—A MERE LIST OF POINTS IS *NOT* A THESIS STATEMENT.

2. *Re-read the writing task for this assignment, comparing your list to the actual question you are supposed to address.* In any writing situation, you need to compare your brainstorming with the assigned task, because it is very easy to move in other directions.

3. *Examine, narrow and reorder your list.* Decide which points you like best, listing them below.

   _____   _____
   _____   _____
   _____   _____
   _____   _____

4. *Look over your list and see if you can find a preliminary thesis statement or argument that responds to the assignment prompt. List that preliminary thesis below.*

Possible Thesis: _____

_____

FIG. 2.2 The Points to Make List.

EXPLORATION QUESTIONS

(Useful for developing ideas for an essay concerned with a controversy)

1. Is there a controversy associated with this topic? If so, briefly outline the nature of the controversy.

2. What was your opinion on this controversy when you were growing up? What opinion did your family and community have on this topic?

3. How did your school experiences influence your conception of the topic? Did your teachers and classmates feel the same way about it as did your family? Were there any points of disagreement?

4. Can you think of at least two people who hold differing views about this topic? If so, describe these people and summarize what you believe were their points of view.

5. Has your opinion changed about this topic in any way? Why or why not?

6. Do you think that this topic is important for people to think about? Why or why not?

FIG. 2.3 Exploration Questions.

Journalistic Questions

The five questions journalists frequently ask to generate information about a topic can be used effectively as an invention strategy. They are particularly useful in writing about a problem, a focus that characterizes a number of writing assignments, but they can also be adapted to other situations or experiences. The following are the five questions, phrased in the context of a problem.

What is the problem?
Who finds this a problem?
When is this a problem?
Where is this a problem?
How can this problem be solved?

The Pentad

The author/scholar/rhetorician Kenneth Burke contributed many ideas to the field of rhetoric, but in terms of invention, he is best known for the strategy known as the "pentad." The pentad is a scheme for investigating pretty much anything, and, indeed, Burke regarded the field of rhetoric as inclusive of almost all human actions, defining it as "the use of language in such a way as to produce a desired impression on the reader or hearer" (1953, p. 165). Thus, Burke, like Aristotle, conceived of rhetoric in terms of audience, claiming in *The Rhetoric of Motives* (1950) that meaning always involves an element of persuasion. The pentad was first introduced in *A Grammar of Motives* (1952) as a device for analyzing literature, and, indeed, it is well suited for this purpose. However, it can also be used to investigate other subjects.

The pentad consists of five terms that can be used to "invent" material. These are as follows:

- Act (What does it say? What happened? What sort of action is it?)
- Agent (Who wrote it? Who did it? What kind of agent is it?)
- Agency (How was it done? What were the methods of accomplishing it?)
- Scene (Where did it happen? What background is necessary to understand? When did it happen?)
- Purpose (Why did it happen? What is its purpose?)

Whatever questioning strategy you recommend to your students, it is important to demonstrate it by working with it in class on the board. Only when students have observed how an invention strategy functions—to see it in action—will they be ready to work with it on their own.

DISCOVERING IDEAS BY ENGAGING WITH A TEXT

A number of invention strategies, particularly those associated with the early days of the process movement, focus students' attention inwardly; the student uses the strategy to elicit ideas from their own backgrounds and experiences and they then expand those ideas outwardly to discover new ideas. This is a useful approach if the student has had relevant experiences that can be elicited and the assignment calls for such experiences. Sharon Crowley (1994), however, defined invention as "the practice of looking for the arguments that are available in a given situation" (p. 231), situating it within a rhetorical situation, and in this context, it can be helpful for students to begin with an argument-based reading and engage with the ideas in it as a way to discover ideas.

A useful approach that utilizes this perspective on invention may be found in Joseph Harris's book, *Rewriting: How to Do Things With Texts* (2006), which discussed several "moves" that writers use to write in response to the work of others. Harris conceived of all writing as "rewriting," and since invention can occur throughout the writing process, his approach can help students discover new directions and perspectives. Below is a summary of these moves, which can be applied to an article that is distributed in class.

1. *Coming to Terms.* The concept of "coming to terms" involves "translating" a text written by another writer into one's own words. The focus is on trying to understand the writer's "project"—the ideas the writer wants to argue and the methods and strategies he uses to do so. To "translate" a text, students find keywords, passages, or "flashpoints" they find most important, examine how the writer connects examples to ideas, and the type of experience and evidence used.
2. *Forwarding.* The idea of forwarding involves "taking words, images, or ideas from a text and putting them to use in new contexts" (p. 37). The analogy Harris uses is that of e-mail, in which a writer will "forward" a post that they think will interest particular friends and make some comment about it, sometimes in the form of text-message symbols. Forwarding a text can involve using a text as an illustration, citing a text to support one's own argument, drawing on ideas from a text in discussing a topic, and extending a concept or definition from a text in one's own writing.
3. *Countering.* The idea of "countering," as Harris defines it, involves looking at other texts in order to suggest a different way of thinking. It can mean arguing the other side of an

issue, redefining or reexamining "a term that a text has left undefined or unexamined" (p. 57), or showing the limits of an idea.

All of these activities or "moves" can help students generate ideas for an essay, ultimately enabling them to construct their own approach or position. What is particularly valuable about this approach is that it involves students with other texts as a means of discovering ideas and requires students to participate actively in the invention process, rather than wait for an idea to strike. It also focuses students' attention on the intertextuality that characterizes academic writing.

They Say/I Say

Related to the concept of "moves" in using readings to generate ideas is a very useful book entitled *They Say/I Say: The Moves That Matter in Academic Writing*, by Gerald Graff and Cathy Birkenstein (2006). Graff and Birkenstein maintained that that statement, "they say/I say," helps students understand that academic writing involves entering a conversation and that this move constitutes a

> template that represents the deep, underlying structure, the internal DNA as it were, of all effective argument. Effective persuasive writers do more than make well-supported claims ("I say"); they also map those claims relative to the claims of others ("they say"). (p. xii)

An example provided in the book is the following:

> Some say that *The Sopranos* presents caricatures of Italian Americans. In fact, …

However, the characters in the series are very complex!

Graff and Birkenstein maintained that the "they say/I say" model can help students with invention, enabling them to find something to say. They argue that students are

> more likely to discover what they want to say not by thinking about a subject in an isolation booth, but by reading texts, listening closely to what other writers say, and looking for an opening in which they can enter the conversation. In other words, listening closely to others and summarizing what they have to say can help writers generate their own ideas. (p. xiii)

I have found the "they say/I say" approach very useful for students who are unclear about how to develop a thesis—not only first-year writing students, but upper division and graduate students as well. However, some composition scholars are uncomfortable with the word "template" and with some of the other templates that are illustrated in *They Say/I Say*, fearing that this approach will result in mechanical, formulaic writing. Anticipating this concern, Graff and Birkenstein emphasized that their approach can help students "enter" the academic conversation by demystifying what academic writing is, and that their templates "have a generative quality, prompting students to make moves in their writing that they might not otherwise make or even know they should make" (p. xiii). They pointed out that these "moves" are the same as those that seasoned writers have picked up unconsciously and that templates have a long and rich history that "reflect the classical rhetorical tradition of imitating established models" (p. xv).

For Writing and Discussion

1. How do you feel about the use of templates or consciously chosen "moves" as a means of helping students discover ideas?
2. Do you use templates or moves in your own writing?
3. Assign a short text on a problematic or controversial issue. Have students read the article and practice the invention moves discussed above.

INVENTION AND IMITATION

Although in the past, imitation was considered an important invention strategy, concern with plagiarism, particularly now that information online is so easily available, has caused many teachers and scholars to avoid using it in the invention process. Another factor is based on the value placed on "originality" and the importance of helping students find their own "voice." However, I have always maintained that inexperienced writers can gain a great deal from imitation, particularly when they are unfamiliar with the writing genre they are expected to produce, and that imitation can enable students to expand their repertoire of possibilities. Anis Bawarshi (2003) similarly argued that imitation has an inventive power and explored the concept of invention in terms of genre in *Genre and the Invention of the Writer: Reconsidering the Place of Invention in Composition*. For ideas about how to use imitation as an invention strategy, I suggest Corbett and Connors' *Classical Rhetoric for the Modern Student* (1994), which includes several imitation-based exercises. Imitating a particular style or form, Corbett and Connor maintained, can help students generate new ideas and develop their own style.

For Further Exploration

Invention and New Media

Bacci, Tina. (2008, Nov.–Dec.). Invention and drafting in the digital age: New approaches to thinking about writing. *Clearing House: A Journal of Educational Strategies, Issues and Ideas, 82,* 75–81.

Jenkins, H. (2009). *Confronting the challenges of participatory culture: Media education for the 21st century.* Cambridge: MIT Press.

Lessner, S., & Collin, C. (2010). Finding your way in: Invention as inquiry based learning in first year writing. In C. Lowe, & P. Zemliansky (Eds). *Writing spaces: Readings on writing* Vol. 1. West Lafayette: Parlor Press.

Nicotra, J. (2009, Sept.). "Folksonomy" and the restructuring of writing space. *CCC, 61,* 259–276.

Trim, M. D., & Isaac. M. L. (2010). Reinventing invention: Discovery and investment in writing. In C. Lowe, & P. Zemliansky (Eds.). *Writing spaces: Readings on writing* Vol. 1. West Lafayette: Parlor Press.http://www.parlorpress.com/pdf/writing-" http://www.parlorpress.com/pdf/writing-spaces-v1.pdf.

For Writing and Discussion

Read Mike Rose's article at the end of this chapter, "Rigid Rules, Inflexible Plans, and the Stifling of Language: A Cognitivist Analysis of Writer's Block." This article was written in 1980, over 30 years ago, before many of the seminal ideas and approaches explored through the writing process movement had been incorporated into composition pedagogy. We are now in a new century, and it is worth examining whether Rose's article is relevant to the writing scene today.

In this context, consider whether Rose's ideas pertain to experiences with writing that you personally have encountered, either in school or elsewhere. Discuss these ideas in small groups. Then write an essay that addresses the following question:

To what extent is Rose's position on writer's block still relevant?

In developing ideas for this assignment, work with at least one invention strategy previously described.

For Further Exploration

Bawarshi, A. (2003). *Genre and the invention of the writer: Reconsidering the place of invention in composition.* Logan: Utah State University Press.

Brady, L. L. (2002). To whom it might actually concern: Letter writing as invention in first-year composition. In Duane Roen, Veronica Pantoja, Lauren Yena, Susan K. Miller, & Eric Waggoner (Eds.), *Strategies for teaching first year composition* (pp. 249–251). Urbana, IL: NCTE.

Coe, R. M. (1981, October). If not to narrow, then how to focus: Two techniques for focusing. *CCC, 32,* 272–277.

Connors, R., & Glenn, C. (1999). *The new St. Martin's guide to teaching writing.* Boston: Bedford/St/Martin's.

Emig, J. (1977, May). Writing as a mode of learning. *CCC, 28,* 122–128.

Howard, R. (2009). *Invention: A bibliography for composition and rhetoric.* http://wrt-howard.syr.edu/Bibs/Invention.htm

LeFevre, K. B. (1987). *Invention as a social act.* Carbondale: Southern Illinois University Press.

Rickert, T. (2007). Invention in the wild: On locating kairos in space-time. In Keller, C. J., & Weisser, C. R. (Eds.). *The locations of composition.* Albany, NY: New York State University Press.

Roen, D., Pantoja, V., Yena, L., Miller, S. K., & Waggoner, E. (Eds). (2002). *Strategies for teaching first year Composition.* Urbana, IL: NCTE.

Witte, S. (1987). Pre-text and composing. *CCC, 38,* 397–425.

NOTES

1 Some of the material on writer's block is also discussed in Irene L. Clark. *Writing in the Center,* 3rd Ed. Dubuque, IA: Kendall Hunt, 2008.
2 The Points to Make List was developed by Jack Blum at the University of Southern California.

REFERENCES

Adams, J. L. (1974). *Conceptual blockbusting: A pleasurable guide to better problem solving.* San Francisco, CA: W. H. Freeman.

Arem, C. A. (2011). *Conquering writing anxiety.* Engleword, CO: Morton Publishing.

Aristotle. (1991). *Aristotle on rhetoric: A theory of civic discourse.* Ed. & trans. George A. Kennedy, New York: Oxford University Press.

Bawarshi, A. (2003). *Genre and the invention of the writer: Reconsidering the place of invention in composition.* Logan: Utah State University Press.

Berthoff, A. (1971). The problem of problem solving. *College Composition and Communication, 22,* 237–242.

Blair, H. (1966/1783). *Lectures on Rhetoric & Belles Lettres.* Ed. H. Harding. Carbondale: Southern Illinois University Press.

Burke, K. (1950). *A rhetoric of motives.* Englewood Cliffs, NJ: Prentice Hall.

Burke, K. (1952). *A grammar of motives.* Englewood Cliffs, NJ: Prentice Hall.

Burke, K. (1953). *Counterstatement.* Los Altos, CA: Hermes.

Campbell, G. (1963/1776). *The philosophy of rhetoric.* Ed. Lloyd Bitzer. Carbondale, Southern Illinois University Press.

Cicero. (1942). *De Oratore.* Trans. E. W. Sutton, & H. Rackham. Cambridge, MA: Harvard University Press.

Connors, R. (1987, May). Personal writing assignments. *College Composition and Communication, 38,* 166–183.

Corbett, E. P. (1981). *The little rhetoric and handbook.* New York: John Wiley.

Corbett, E. P., & Connors, R. J. (1999). *Classical rhetoric for the modern student* (4th ed.). New York: Oxford University Press.

Covino, W. A., & Jolliffe, D. A. (1995). *Rhetoric: Concepts, definitions, boundaries.* Boston: Allyn and Bacon.

Crowley, S. (1990). *The methodical memory: Invention in current-traditional rhetoric.* Carbondale IL: Southern Illinois University Press.

Crowley, S. (1994). *Ancient rhetorics for contemporary students.* New York: Macmillan.

Graff, G., & Birkenstein, C. (2006). *They say/I say: The moves that matter in academic writing.* New York: W.W. Norton.

Harris, J. (2006). *Rewriting: How to do things with texts.* Logan, Utah: Utah State University Press.

Kennedy, G. E. (1983). The nature and quality of compensatory oral expression and its effects on writing in students of college composition. *Report to the National Institute of Education.* Washington State University.

Lauer, J. (1970). Heuristics and composition. *College Composition and Communication, 21,* 396–404.

Lauer, J. (1972). Response to Anne E. Berthoff, "The problem of problem solving." *College Composition and Communication, 23,* 208–210.

Macrorie, K. (1970). *Telling writing* (4th ed.). Upper Montclair, NJ: Boynton/Cook.

Quintilian. (1920). *Institutio oratoria.* Trans. H. E. Butler. Cambridge: Harvard University Press.

Quintilian. (1994). Ancient rhetorics. In S. Crowley (Ed.), *Ancient rhetorics for contemporary students.* New York: Macmillan.

Rohman, D. G. (1965). Pre-writing: The stage of discovery in the writing process. *College Composition and Communication, 16,* 106–112.

Rose, M. (1980). Rigid rules, inflexible plans, and the stifling of language: A cognitivist analysis of writer's block. *College Composition and Communication, 31,* 389–401.

Rose, M. (1984). *Writer's block: The cognitive dimension.* Carbondale, IL: Southern Illinois University Press.

Thaiss, C., & Zawacki, M. T. (2006). *Engaged writers, dynamic disciplines.* Portsmouth, NH: Boynton/Cook Heinemann.

Winterowd, W. R., & Blum, J. (1994). *Composition in the rhetorical tradition.* Urbana, IL: NCTE.

Young, R. E., Becker, A. L., & Pike, K. L. (1970). *Rhetoric: Discovery and change.* New York: Harcourt.

Zoellner, R. (1969). Talk-write: A behavioral approach to writing. *College English, 30,* 267–320.

Reading

RIGID RULES, INFLEXIBLE PLANS, AND THE STIFLING OF LANGUAGE: A COGNITIVIST ANALYSIS OF WRITER'S BLOCK

Mike Rose

Ruth will labor over the first paragraph of an essay for hours. She'll write a sentence, then erase it. Try another, then scratch part of it out. Finally, as the evening winds on toward ten o'clock and Ruth, anxious about tomorrow's deadline, begins to wind into herself, she'll compose that first paragraph only to sit back and level her favorite exasperated interdiction at herself and her page: "No. You can't say that. You'll bore them to death."

Ruth is one of ten UCLA undergraduates with whom I discussed writer's block, that frustrating, self-defeating inability to generate the next line, the right phrase, the sentence that will release the flow of words once again. These ten people represented a fair cross-section of the UCLA student community: lower-middle-class to upper-middle-class backgrounds and high schools, third-world and Caucasian origins, biology to fine arts majors, C+ to A- grade point averages, enthusiastic to blasé attitudes toward school. They were set off from the community by the twin facts that all ten could write competently, and all were currently enrolled in at least one course that required a significant amount of writing. They were set off among themselves by the fact that five of them wrote with relative to enviable ease while the other five experienced moderate to nearly immobilizing writer's block. This blocking usually resulted in rushed, often late papers and resultant grades that did not truly reflect these students' writing ability. And then, of course, there were other less measurable but probably more serious results: a growing distrust of their abilities and an aversion toward the composing process itself.

What separated the five students who blocked from those who didn't? It wasn't skill; that was held fairly constant. The answer could have rested in the emotional realm—anxiety, fear of evaluation, insecurity, etc. Or perhaps blocking in some way resulted from variation in cognitive style. Perhaps, too, blocking originated in and typified a melding of emotion and cognition not unlike the relationship posited by Shapiro between neurotic feeling and neurotic thinking.[1] Each of these was possible. Extended clinical interviews and testing could have teased out the answer. But there was one answer that surfaced readily in brief explorations of these students' writing processes. It was not profoundly emotional, nor was it embedded in that still unclear construct of cognitive style. It was constant, surprising, almost amusing if its results weren't so troublesome, and, in the final analysis, obvious: the five students who experienced blocking were all operating either with writing rules or with planning strategies that impeded rather than enhanced the composing process. The five students who were not hampered by writer's block also utilized rules, but they were less rigid ones, and thus more appropriate to a complex process like writing. Also, the plans these non-blockers brought to the writing process were more functional, more flexible, more open to information from the outside.

These observations are the result of one to three interviews with each student. I used recent notes, drafts, and finished compositions to direct and hone my questions. This procedure is admittedly non-experimental, certainly more clinical than scientific; still, it did lead to several inferences that lay the foundation for future, more rigorous investigation: (a) composing is a highly complex problem-solving process[2] and (b) certain disruptions of that process can be explained with cognitive psychology's problem-solving framework. Such investigation might include a study using "stimulated recall" techniques to validate or disconfirm these hunches. In such a study, blockers and non-blockers would write essays. Their activity would be videotaped and, immediately after writing, they would be shown their respective tapes and questioned about the rules, plans, and beliefs operating in their writing behavior. This procedure would bring us close to the composing process (the writers' recall is stimulated by their viewing the tape), yet would not interfere with actual composing.

In the next section I will introduce several key concepts in the problem-solving literature. In section three I will let the students speak for themselves. Fourth, I will offer a cognitivist analysis of blockers' and non-blockers' grace or torpor. I will close with a brief note on treatment.

Selected Concepts in Problem Solving: Rules and Plans

As diverse as theories of problem solving are, they share certain basic assumptions and characteristics. Each posits an *introductory period* during which a problem is presented, and all theorists, from Behaviorist to Gestalt to Information Processing, admit that certain aspects, stimuli, or "functions" of the problem must become or be made salient and attended to in certain ways if successful problem-solving processes are to be engaged. Theorists also believe that some conflict, some stress, some gap in information in these perceived "aspects" seems to trigger problem-solving behavior. Next comes a *processing period,* and for all the variance of opinion about this critical stage, theorists recognize the necessity of its existence—recognize that man, at the least, somehow "weighs" possible solutions as they are stumbled upon and, at the most, goes through an elaborate and sophisticated information-processing routine to achieve problem solution. Furthermore, theorists believe—to varying degrees—that past learning and the particular "set," direction, or orientation that the problem solver takes in dealing with past experience and present stimuli have critical bearing on the efficacy of solution. Finally, all theorists admit to a *solution period,* an end-state of the process where "stress" and "search" terminate, an answer is attained, and a sense of completion or "closure" is experienced.

These are the gross similarities, and the framework they offer will be useful in understanding the problem-solving behavior of the students discussed in this paper. But since this paper is primarily concerned with the second stage of problem-solving operations, it would be most useful to focus this introduction on two critical constructs in the processing period: rules and plans.

Rules

Robert M. Gagné defines "rule" as "an inferred capability that enables the individual to respond to a class of stimulus situations with a class of performances."[3] Rules can be learned directly[4] or by inference through experience.[5] But, in either case, most problem-solving theorists would affirm Gagné's dictum that "rules are probably the major organizing factor, and quite possibly the primary one, in intellectual functioning."[6] As Gagné implies, we wouldn't be able to function without rules; they guide response to the myriad stimuli that confront us daily, and might even be the central element in complex problem-solving behavior.

Dunker, Polya, and Miller, Galanter, and Pribram offer a very useful distinction between two general kinds of rules: algorithms and heuristics.[7] Algorithms are precise rules that will always result in a specific answer if applied to an appropriate problem. Most mathematical rules, for example, are algorithms. Functions are constant (e.g., pi), procedures are routine (squaring the radius), and outcomes are completely predictable. However, few day-to-day situations are mathematically circumscribed enough to warrant the application of algorithms. Most often we function with the aid of fairly general heuristics or "rules of thumb," guidelines that allow varying degrees of flexibility when approaching problems. Rather than operating with algorithmic precision and certainty, we search, critically, through alternatives, using our heuristic as a divining rod—"if a math problem stumps you, try working backwards to solution"; "if the car won't start, check x, y, or z," and so forth. Heuristics won't allow the precision or the certitude afforded by algorithmic operations;

heuristics can even be so "loose" as to be vague. But in a world where tasks and problems are rarely mathematically precise, heuristic rules become the most appropriate, the most functional rules available to us: "a heuristic does not guarantee the optimal solution or, indeed, any solution at all; rather, heuristics offer solutions that are good enough most of the time."[8]

Plans

People don't proceed through problem situations, in or out of a laboratory, without some set of internalized instructions to the self, some program, some course of action that, even roughly, takes goals and possible paths to that goal into consideration. Miller, Galanter, and Pribram have referred to this course of action as a plan: "A plan is any hierarchical process in the organism that can control the order in which a sequence of operations is to be performed" (p. 16). They name the fundamental plan in human problem-solving behavior the TOTE, with the initial T representing a *test* that matches a possible solution against the perceived end-goal of problem completion. O represents the clearance to *operate* if the comparison between solution and goal indicates that the solution is a sensible one. The second T represents a further, post-operation, *test* or comparison of solution with goal, and if the two mesh and problem solution is at hand the person *exits* (E) from problem-solving behavior. If the second test presents further discordance between solution and goal, a further solution is attempted in TOTE-fashion. Such plans can be both long-term and global and, as problem solving is underway, short-term and immediate.[9] Though the mechanicality of this information-processing model renders it simplistic and, possibly, unreal, the central notion of a plan and an operating procedure is an important one in problem-solving theory; it at least attempts to metaphorically explain what earlier cognitive psychologists could not—the mental procedures (see pp. 390–391) underlying problem-solving behavior.

Before concluding this section, a distinction between heuristic rules and plans should be attempted; it is a distinction often blurred in the literature, blurred because, after all, we are very much in the area of gestating theory and preliminary models. Heuristic rules seem to function with the flexibility of plans. Is, for example, "If the car won't start, try x, y, or z" a heuristic or a plan? It could be either, though two qualifications will mark it as heuristic rather than plan. (A) Plans subsume and sequence heuristic and algorithmic rules. Rules are usually "smaller," more discrete cognitive capabilities; plans can become quite large and complex, composed of a series of ordered algorithms, heuristics, and further planning "sub-routines." (B) Plans, as was mentioned earlier, include criteria to determine successful goal-attainment and, as well, include "feedback" processes—ways to incorporate and use information gained from "tests" of potential solutions against desired goals.

One other distinction should be made: that is, between "set" and plan. Set, also called "determining tendency" or "readiness,"[10] refers to the fact that people often approach problems with habitual ways of reacting, a prepriate to a specific problem,[11] but much of the literature on set has shown its rigidifying, dysfunctional effects.[12] Set differs from plan in that set represents a limiting and narrowing of response alternatives with no inherent process to shift alternatives. It is a kind of cognitive habit that can limit perception, not a course of action with multiple paths that directs and sequences response possibilities.

The constructs of rules and plans advance the understanding of problem solving beyond that possible with earlier, less developed formulations. Still, critical problems remain. Though mathematical and computer models move one toward more complex (and thus more real) problems than the earlier research, they are still too neat, too rigidly sequenced to approximate the stunning complexity of day-to-day (not to mention highly creative) problem-solving behavior. Also, information-processing models of problem-solving are built on logic theorems, chess strategies, and simple planning tasks. Even Gagné seems to feel more comfortable with illustrations from mathematics and science rather than with social science and humanities problems. So although these complex models and constructs tell us a good deal about problem-solving behavior, they are still laboratory simulations, still invoked from the outside rather than self-generated, and still founded on the mathematico-logical.

Two Carnegie-Mellon researchers, however, have recently extended the above into a truly real, amorphous, unmathematical problem-solving process—writing. Relying on protocol analysis (thinking aloud while solving problems), Linda Flower and John Hayes have attempted to tease out the role of heuristic rules and plans in writing behavior.[13] Their research pushes problem-solving investigations to the real and complex and pushes, from the other end, the often mysterious process of writing toward the explainable. The latter is important, for at least since Plotinus many have viewed the composing process as unexplainable, inspired, infused with the transcendent. But Flower and Hayes are beginning, anyway, to show how writing generates from a problem-solving process with rich heuristic rules and plans of its own. They show, as well, how many writing problems arise from a paucity of heuristics and suggest an intervention that provides such rules.

This paper, too, treats writing as a problem-solving process, focusing, however, on what happens when the process dead-ends in writer's block. It will further suggest that, as opposed to Flower and Hayes' students who need more rules and plans, blockers may well be stymied by possessing rigid or inappropriate rules, or inflexible or confused plans. Ironically enough, these are occasionally instilled by the composition teacher or gleaned from the writing textbook.

"Always Grab Your Audience"—The Blockers

In high school, *Ruth* was told and told again that a good essay always grabs a reader's attention immediately. Until you can make your essay do that, her teachers and textbooks putatively declaimed, there is no need to go on. For Ruth, this means that beginning bland and seeing what emerges as one generates prose is unacceptable. The beginning is everything. And what exactly is the audience seeking that reads this beginning? The rule, or Ruth's use of it, doesn't provide for such investigation. She has an edict with no determiners. Ruth operates with another rule that restricts her productions as well: if sentences aren't grammatically "correct," they aren't useful. This keeps Ruth from toying with ideas on paper, from the kind of linguistic play that often frees up the flow of prose. These two rules converge in a way that pretty effectively restricts Ruth's composing process.

The first two papers I received from *Laurel* were weeks overdue. Sections of them were well written; there were even moments of stylistic flair. But the papers were late and, overall, the prose seemed rushed. Furthermore, one paper included a paragraph on an issue that was never mentioned in the topic paragraph. This was the kind of mistake that someone with Laurel's apparent ability doesn't make. I asked her about this irrelevant passage. She knew very well that it didn't fit, but believed she had to include it to round out the paper. "You must always make three or more points in an essay. If the essay has less, then it's not strong." Laurel had been taught this rule both in high school and in her first college English class; no wonder, then, that she accepted its validity.

As opposed to Laurel, *Martha* possesses a whole arsenal of plans and rules with which to approach a humanities writing assignment, and, considering her background in biology, I wonder how many of them were formed out of the assumptions and procedures endemic to the physical sciences.[14] Martha will not put pen to first draft until she has spent up to two days generating an outline of remarkable complexity. I saw one of these outlines and it looked more like a diagram of protein synthesis or DNA structure than the time-worn pattern offered in composition textbooks. I must admit I was intrigued by the aura of process (vs. the static appearance of essay outlines) such diagrams offer, but for Martha these "outlines" only led to self-defeat: the outline would become so complex that all of its elements could never be included in a short essay. In other words, her plan locked her into the first stage of the composing process. Martha would struggle with the conversion of her outline into prose only to scrap the whole venture when deadlines passed and a paper had to be rushed together.

Martha's "rage for order" extends beyond the outlining process. She also believes that elements of a story or poem must evince a fairly linear structure and thematic clarity, or—perhaps bringing us closer to the issue—that analysis of a story or poem must provide the linearity or clarity that seems to be absent in the text. Martha, therefore, will bend the logic of her analysis to reason ambiguity out of existence. When I asked her about a strained paragraph in her paper on Camus' "The Guest," she said, "I didn't want to admit that it [the story's conclusion] was just hanging. I tried to force it into meaning."

Martha uses another rule, one that is not only problematical in itself, but one that often clashes directly with the elaborate plan and obsessive rule above. She believes that humanities papers must scintillate with insight, must present an array of images, ideas, ironies gleaned from the literature under examination. A problem arises, of course, when Martha tries to incorporate her myriad "neat little things," often inherently unrelated, into a tightly structured, carefully sequenced essay. Plans and rules that govern the construction of impressionistic, associational prose would be appropriate to Martha's desire, but her composing process is heavily constrained by the non-impressionistic and non-associational. Put another way, the plans and rules that govern her exploration of text are not at all synchronous with the plans and rules she uses to discuss her exploration. It is interesting to note here, however, that as recently as three years ago Martha was absorbed in creative writing and was publishing poetry in high school magazines. Given what we know about the complex associational, often non-neatly-sequential nature of the poet's creative process, we can infer that Martha was either free of the plans and rules discussed earlier or they were not as intense. One wonders, as well, if the exposure to three years of university physical science either established or intensified Martha's concern with structure. Whatever the case, she now is hamstrung by conflicting rules when composing papers for the humanities.

Mike's difficulties, too, are rooted in a distortion of the problem-solving process. When the time of the week for the assignment of writing topics draws near, Mike begins to prepare material, strategies, and plans that he believes will be appropriate. If the assignment matches his expectations, he has done a good job of analyzing the professor's intentions. If the assignment *doesn't* match his expectations, however, he cannot easily shift approaches. He feels trapped inside his original plans, cannot generate alternatives, and blocks. As the deadline draws near, he will write something, forcing the assignment to fit his conceptual procrustian bed. Since Mike is a smart man, he will offer a good deal of information, but only some of it ends up being appropriate to the assignment. This entire situation is made all the worse when the time between assignment of topic and generation of product is attenuated further, as in an essay examination. Mike believes (correctly) that one must have a plan, a strategy of some sort in order to solve a problem. He further believes, however, that such a plan, once formulated, becomes an exact structural and substantive blueprint that cannot be violated. The plan offers no alternatives, no "sub-routines." So, whereas Ruth's, Laurel's, and some of Martha's difficulties seem to be rule-specific ("always catch your audience," "write grammatically"), Mike's troubles are more global. He may have strategies that are appropriate for various writing situations (e.g., "for this kind of political science assignment write a compare/contrast essay"), but his entire approach to formulating plans and carrying them through to problem solution is too mechanical. It is probable that Mike's behavior is governed by an explicitly learned or inferred rule: "Always try to 'psych out' a professor." But in this case this rule initiates a problem-solving procedure that is clearly dysfunctional.

While Ruth and Laurel use rules that impede their writing process and Mike utilizes a problem-solving procedure that hamstrings him, *Sylvia* has trouble deciding which of the many rules she possesses to use. Her problem can be characterized as cognitive perplexity: some of her rules are inappropriate, others are functional; some mesh nicely with her own definitions of good writing, others don't. She has multiple rules to invoke, multiple paths to follow, and that very complexity of choice virtually paralyzes her. More so than with the previous four students, there is probably a strong emotional dimension to Sylvia's blocking, but the cognitive difficulties are clear and perhaps modifiable.

Sylvia, somewhat like Ruth and Laurel, puts tremendous weight on the crafting of her first paragraph. If it is good, she believes the rest of the essay will be good. Therefore, she will spend up to five hours on the initial paragraph: "I won't go on until I get that first paragraph down." Clearly, this rule—or the strength of it—blocks Sylvia's production. This is one problem. Another is that Sylvia has other equally potent rules that she sees as separate, uncomplementary injunctions: one achieves "flow" in one's writing through the use of adquate transitions; one achieves substance to one's writing through the use of evidence. Sylvia perceives both rules to be "true," but several times followed one to the exclusion of the other. Furthermore, as I talked to Sylvia, many other rules, guidelines, definitions were offered, but none with conviction. While she *is* committed to one rule about initial paragraphs, and that rule is dysfunctional, she seems very uncertain about the weight and hierarchy of the remaining rules in her cognitive repertoire.

"If It Won't Fit My Work, I'll Change It"—The Non-blockers

Dale, Ellen, Debbie, Susan, and Miles all write with the aid of rules. But their rules differ from blockers' rules in significant ways. If similar in content, they are expressed less absolutely—e.g., *Try to* keep audience in mind." If dissimilar, they are still expressed less absolutely, more heuristically—e.g., "I can use as many ideas in my thesis paragraph as I need and then develop paragraphs for each idea." Our non-blockers do express some rules with firm assurance, but these tend to be simple injunctions that free up rather than restrict the composing process, e.g., "When stuck, write!" or "I'll write what I can." And finally, at least three of the students openly shun the very textbook rules that some blockers adhere to: e.g., "Rules like 'write only what you know about' just aren't true. I ignore those." These three, in effect, have formulated a further rule that expresses something like: "If a rule conflicts with what is sensible or with experience, reject it."

On the broader level of plans and strategies, these five students also differ from at least three of the five blockers in that they all possess problem-solving plans that are quite functional. Interestingly, on first exploration these plans seem to be too broad or fluid to be useful and, in some cases, can barely be expressed with any precision. Ellen, for example, admits that she has a general "outline in [her] head about how a topic paragraph should look" but could not describe much about its structure. Susan also has a general plan to follow, but, if stymied, will quickly attempt to conceptualize the assignment in different ways: "If my original idea won't work, then I need to proceed differently." Whether or not these plans operate in TOTE-fashion, I can't say. But they do operate with the operate-test fluidity of TOTEs.

True, our non-blockers have their religiously adhered-to rules: e.g., "When stuck, write," and plans, "I couldn't imagine writing without this pattern," but as noted above, these are few and functional. Otherwise, these non-blockers operate with fluid, easily modified, even easily discarded rules and plans (Ellen: "I can throw things out") that are sometimes expressed with a vagueness that could almost be interpreted as ignorance. There lies the irony. Students that offer the least precise rules and plans have the least trouble composing. Perhaps this very lack of precision characterizes the functional composing plan. But perhaps this lack of precision simply masks habitually enacted alternatives and sub-routines. This is clearly an area that needs the illumination of further research.

And then there is feedback. At least three of the five non-blockers are an Information-Processor's dream. They get to know their audience, ask professors and T.A.s specific questions about assignments, bring half-finished products in for evaluation, etc. Like Ruth, they realize the importance of audience, but unlike her, they have specific strategies for obtaining and utilizing feedback. And this penchant for testing writing plans against the needs of the audience can lead to modification of rules and plans. Listen to Debbie:

In high school I was given a formula that stated that you must write a thesis paragraph with *only* three points in it, and then develop each of those points. When I hit college I was given longer assignments. That stuck me for a bit, but then I realized that I could use as many ideas in my thesis paragraph as I needed and then develop paragraphs for each one. I asked someone about this and then tried it. I didn't get any negative feedback, so I figured it was o.k.

Debbie's statement brings one last difference between our blockers and non-blockers into focus; it has been implied above, but needs specific formulation: the goals these people have, and the plans they generate to attain these goals, are quite mutable. Part of the mutability comes from the fluid way the goals and plans are conceived, and part of it arises from the effective impact of feedback on these goals and plans.

Analyzing Writer's Block

Algorithms Rather Than Heuristics

In most cases, the rules our blockers use are not "wrong" or "incorrect"—it is good practice, for example, to "grab your audience with a catchy opening" or "craft a solid first paragraph before going on." The problem is that these rules seem to be followed as though they were algorithms, absolute dicta, rather than the loose heuristics that they were intended to be. Either through instruction, or the power of the textbook, or the predilections of some of our blockers for absolutes, or all three, these useful rules of thumb have been transformed into near-algorithmic urgencies. The result, to paraphrase Karl Dunker, is that these rules do not allow a flexible penetration into the nature of the problem. It is this transformation of heuristic into algorithm that contributes to the writer's block of Ruth and Laurel.

Questionable Heuristics Made Algorithmic

Whereas "grab your audience" could be a useful heuristic, "always make three or more points in an essay" is a pretty questionable one. Any such rule, though probably taught to aid the writer who needs structure, ultimately transforms a highly fluid process like writing into a mechanical lockstep. As heuristics, such rules can be troublesome. As algorithms, they are simply incorrect.

Set

As with any problem-solving task, students approach writing assignments with a variety of orientations or sets. Some are functional, others are not. Martha and Jane (see footnote 14), coming out of the life sciences and social sciences respectively, bring certain methodological orientations with them—certain sets or "directions" that make composing for the humanities a difficult, sometimes confusing, task. In fact, this orientation may cause them to misperceive the task. Martha has formulated a planning strategy from her predisposition to see processes in terms of linear, interrelated steps in a system. Jane doesn't realize that she can revise the statement that "committed" her to the direction her essay has taken. Both of these students are stymied because of formative experiences associated with their majors—experiences, perhaps, that nicely reinforce our very strong tendency to organize experiences temporally.

The Plan that Is Not a Plan

If fluidity and multi-directionality are central to the nature of plans, then the plans that Mike formulates are not true plans at all but, rather, inflexible and static cognitive blueprints.[15] Put another way,

Mike's "plans" represent a restricted "closed system" (vs. "open system") kind of thinking, where closed system thinking is defined as focusing on "a limited number of units or items, or members, and those properties of the members which are to be used are known to begin with and do not change as the thinking proceeds," and open system thinking is characterized by an "adventurous exploration of multiple alternatives with strategies that allow redirection once 'dead ends' are encountered."[16] Composing calls for open, even adventurous thinking, not for constrained, no-exit cognition.

Feedback

The above difficulties are made all the more problematic by the fact that they seem resistant to or isolated from corrective feedback. One of the most striking things about Dale, Debbie, and Miles is the ease with which they seek out, interpret, and apply feedback on their rules, plans, and productions. They "operate" and then they "test," and the testing is not only against some internalized goal, but against the requirements of external audience as well.

Too Many Rules—"Conceptual Conflict"

According to D. E. Berlyne, one of the primary forces that motivate problem-solving behavior is a curiosity that arises from conceptual conflict—the convergence of incompatible beliefs or ideas. In *Structure and Direction in Thinking*,[17] Berlyne presents six major types of conceptual conflict, the second of which he terms "perplexity":

> This kind of conflict occurs when there are factors inclining the subject toward each of a set of mutually exclusive beliefs. (p. 257)

If one substitutes "rules" for "beliefs" in the above definition, perplexity becomes a useful notion here. Because perplexity is unpleasant, people are motivated to reduce it by problem-solving behavior that can result in "disequalization":

> Degree of conflict will be reduced if either the number of competing ... [rules] or their nearness to equality of strength is reduced. (p. 259)

But "disequalization" is not automatic. As I have suggested, Martha and Sylvia hold to rules that conflict, but their perplexity does *not* lead to curiosity and resultant problem-solving behavior. Their perplexity, contra Berlyne, leads to immobilization. Thus "disequalization" will have to be effected from without. The importance of each of, particularly, Sylvia's rules needs an evaluation that will aid her in rejecting some rules and balancing and sequencing others.

A Note on Treatment

Rather than get embroiled in a blocker's misery, the teacher or tutor might interview the student in order to build a writing history and profile: How much and what kind of writing was done in high school? What is the student's major? What kind of writing does it require? How does the student compose? Are there rough drafts or outlines available? By what rules does the student operate? How would he or she define "good" writing? etc. This sort of interview reveals an incredible amount of information about individual composing processes. Furthermore, it ofen reveals the rigid rule or the inflexible plan that may lie at the base of the student's writing problem. That was precisely what happened with the five blockers. And with Ruth, Laurel, and Martha (and Jane) what was revealed made virtually immediate remedy possible. Dysfunctional rules are easily replaced with or counter-balanced by functional ones if there is no emotional reason to hold onto that which simply doesn't work. Furthermore, students can be trained to select, to "know which rules are appropriate for which problems."[18] Mike's difficulties, perhaps because plans are more complex and pervasive than rules, took longer to correct. But inflexible plans, too, can be remedied by pointing out their dysfunctional qualities and by assisting the student in developing appropriate and flexible alternatives. Operating this way, I was successful with Mike. Sylvia's story, however, did not end as smoothly. Though I had three forty-five minute contacts with her, I was not able to appreciably alter her behavior. Berlyne's theory bore results with Martha but not with Sylvia. Her rules were in conflict, and perhaps that conflict was not exclusively cognitive. Her case keeps analyses like these honest; it reminds us that the cognitive often melds with, and can be overpowered by, the affective. So while Ruth, Laurel, Martha, and Mike could profit from tutorials that explore the rules and plans in their writing behavior, students like Sylvia may need more extended, more affectively oriented counseling sessions that blend the instructional with the psychodynamic.

Notes

1   David Shapiro, *Neurotic Styles* (New York: Basic Books, 1965).

2   Barbara Hayes-Ruth, a Rand cognitive psychologist, and I are currently developing an information-processing model of the composing process. A good deal of work has already been done by Linda Flower and John Hayes (see p. 393 of this article). I have just received—and recommend—their "Writing as Problem Solving" (paper presented at American Educational Research Association, April, 1979).

3   *The Conditions of Learning* (New York: Holt, Rinehart and Winston, 1970), p. 193.

4   E. James Archer, "The Psychological Nature of Concepts," in H. J. Klausmeier and C. W. Harris, eds., *Analysis of Concept Learning* (New York: Academic Press, 1966), pp. 37–44; David P. Ausubel, *The Psychology of Meaningful Verbal Behavior* (New York: Grune and Stratton, 1963); Robert M. Gagné, "Problem Solving," in Arthur W. Melton, ed., *Categories of Human Learning* (New York: Academic Press, 1964), pp. 293–317; George A. Miller, *Language and Communication* (New York: McGraw-Hill, 1951).

5   George Katona, *Organizing and Memorizing* (New York: Columbia Univ. Press, 1940); Roger N. Shepard, Carl I. Hovland, and Herbert M. Jenkins, "Learning and Memorization of Classifications," *Psychological Monographs,* 75, No. 13 (1961) (entire No. 517); Robert S. Wood-worth, *Dynamics of Behavior* (New York: Henry Holt, 1958), chs. 10–12.

6   *The Conditions of Learning,* pp. 190–91.

7   Karl Dunker, "On Problem Solving," *Psychological Monographs,* 58, No. 5 (1945) (entire No. 270); George A. Polya, *How to Solve It* (Princeton: Princeton University Press, 1945); George A. Miller, Eugene Galanter, and Karl H. Pribram, *Plans and the Structure of Behavior* (New York: Henry Holt, 1960).

8   Lyle E. Bourne, Jr., Bruce R. Ekstrand, and Roger L. Dominowski, *The Psychology of Thinking* (Englewood Cliffs, N.J.: Prentice-Hall, 1971).

9   John R. Hayes, "Problem Topology and the Solution Process," in Carl P. Duncan, ed., *Thinking: Current Experimental Studies* (Philadelphia: Lippincott, 1967), pp. 167–81.

10 Hulda J. Rees and Harold E. Israel, "An Investigation of the Establishment and Operation of Mental Sets." *Psychological Monographs,* 46 (1925) (entire No. 210).

11 Ibid.; Melvin H. Marx, Wilton W. Murphy, and Aaron J. Brownstein, "Recognition of Complex Visual Stimuli as a Function of Training with Abstracted Patterns," *Journal of Experimental Psychology,* 62 (1961), 456–60.

12 James L. Adams, *Conceptual Blockbusting* (San Francisco: W. H. Freeman, 1974); Edward DeBono, *New Think* (New York: Basic Books, 1958); Ronald H. Forgus, *Perception* (New York: McGraw-Hill, 1966), ch. 13; Abraham Luchins and Edith Hirsch Luchins, *Rigidity of Behavior* (Eugene: Univ. of Oregon Books, 1959); N. R. F. Maier, "Reasoning in Humans. I. On Direction," *Journal of Comparative Psychology,* 10 (1920), 115–43.

13 "Plans and the Cognitive Process of Writing," paper presented at the National Institute of Education Writing Conference, June 1977; "Problem Solving Strategies and the Writing Process," *College English,* 39 (1977), 449–61. See also footnote 2.

14 Jane, a student not discussed in this paper, was surprised to find out that a topic paragraph can be rewritten after a paper's conclusion to make that paragraph reflect what the essay truly contains. She had gotten so indoctrinated with Psychology's (her major) insistence that a hypothesis be formulated and then left untouched before an experiment begins that she thought revision of one's "major premise" was somehow illegal. She had formed a rule out of her exposure to social science methodology, and the rule was totally inappropriate for most writing situations.

15 Cf. "A plan is flexible if the order of execution of its parts can be easily interchanged without affecting the feasibility of the plan ... the flexible planner might tend to think of lists of things he had to do; the inflexible planner would have his time planned like a sequence of cause-effect relations. The former could rearrange his lists to suit his opportunities, but the latter would be unable to strike while the iron was hot and would generally require considerable 'lead-time' before he could incorporate any alternative sub-plans" (Miller, Galanter, and Pribram, p. 120).

16 Frederic Bartlett, *Thinking* (New York: Basic Books, 1958), pp. 74–76.

17 *Structure and Direction in Thinking* (New York: John Wiley, 1965), p. 255.

18 Flower and Hayes, "Plans and the Cognitive Process of Writing," p. 26.

3

Revision

Betty Bamberg

- How can I change the introduction to make it more interesting to my readers?
- How can I construct a more valid and convincing argument?
- What example could I add to make this point clearer?
- What is the most logical way to organize my argument?
- How can I reword this sentence so it will read more smoothly?
- How can I make this sentence less wordy?
- What might be a better word to use here?

This chapter traces varying perspectives on what is involved in revision and discusses what research and theory have revealed about the ways that writers, especially student writers, revise. It suggests ways for teachers to encourage students to revise in ways that develop and shape the meaning of their texts and result in more effective pieces of writing.

The questions beginning this chapter are just a few of those that writers might ask themselves when they are composing or that readers might ask writers after reading drafts of their writing. Such questions help writers rethink and reconsider their initial rhetorical choices about content, development, organization, sentence structure, and word choice so they can revise their work and improve it. Some writers, however, especially student writers, typically ask different questions: Is my grammar correct? Is this word spelled correctly? Do I need a comma here? This second set of questions reflects an older view of revision, which considered it to be a mechanical process involving little more than correcting errors or making minor changes in sentence structure or word choice to improve style. The first set of questions, on the other hand, illustrates a perspective on revision that has emerged from composing process research and theory over the last 30 years. This perspective, which is concerned primarily with issues of audience, purpose, content, organization, and style, reconceptualizes revision as a primary means of developing, elaborating, and shaping the intended meaning of a text.

This chapter discusses "revision" as an important theoretical and pedagogical concept in composition, focusing on the following aspects of the topic:

1. Why "revision" was initially seen as a process of correcting errors.
2. How research and theory in cognitive development and the composing process have led to a new concept of revision.

3. What research tells us about the ways that writers, especially student writers, revise.

4. What factors tend to inhibit or encourage meaningful revision.

5. What teachers can do to encourage students to revise in ways that develop and shape the meaning of their texts.

OLDER CONCEPTS OF REVISION

Unlike invention, which was a key concept in classical rhetoric, commentary that could be construed as revision was rare in classical rhetorical theory. For Aristotle, composing involved finding and structuring content, then polishing the sentences, and he "relegates [alterations] to the sentence level, to the editing of forms and their arrangement" (Hodges, 1982, p. 26). Although Quintilian (1921) also commented on the importance of sentence-level corrections, he recognized the possibility that new ideas could suddenly arise while delivering a speech or reviewing a written composition and advocated integrating these new insights into the discourse rather than rejecting them. However, the narrow definition of the revision process as surface editing and correction continued to prevail. Throughout the Middle Ages, imitation rather than invention was emphasized, and style was further separated from content. During the Renaissance, the idea that revision primarily involved changes at the sentence-level was further strengthened when Ramus reorganized Aristotle's rhetoric, moving invention, arrangement, and logic to philosophy. Although both Francis Bacon and Ben Jonson spoke out against the preoccupation with style and proposed a more holistic view that would allow for revisioning of content and arrangement, their ideas failed to gain acceptance (Hodges, 1982). As a result, rhetoric was limited to considering how language might be used to "dress thought," and rhetoricians became concerned with finding the most effective tropes—"figures of thought"—which included metaphor, personification, and synecdoche (the substitution of the part for the whole), or "schemes," which included structures such as parallelism, ellipsis, and anaphora (repeating the same words at the beginning of successive phrases or clauses to create emphasis) to express ideas (Covino & Jolliffe, 1995, p. 23). Although the 18th-century rhetoricians Hugh Blair and George Campbell explicitly rejected the narrow emphasis on style that characterized Renaissance rhetoric and, instead, revived a concern for ideas and persuasion in rhetoric, nevertheless their treatises focused on correctness and sentence-level changes insofar as they considered revision (Hodges, 1982).

In the United States, error correction as a major emphasis in writing instruction initially arose more from social conditions in late 19th-century America than from the rhetorical tradition (Berlin, 1987; Connors, 1997). Robert Connors argues that the emphasis on error correction in composition instruction arose from a linguistic insecurity that resulted from changes in American society in the second half of the 19th century. As universities moved away from studying classical languages and moved toward educating the new professional classes, the place of rhetoric in the university curriculum changed dramatically from the advanced study of effective persuasion to a concern with the ability to write acceptable compositions in English. In 1874, Harvard established an entrance examination, soon copied by other universities, that required students "to write a short English composition, correct in spelling, punctuation, grammar, and expression" (Bizzell, Herzberg, & Reynolds, 2000, p. 4). When more than half of Harvard's prospective students failed the exam, the university and the press condemned students' prior preparation and called for reform of

[handwritten margin note: New age thinking]

the secondary curriculum to improve their writing ability. However, Adams Sherman Hill, who oversaw the Harvard entrance exam, thought that results from improved secondary instruction would not be rapid enough and proposed that, Harvard require "a temporary course in remedial writing instruction ... of all incoming freshmen" (Connors, 1997, p. 11). In the instructional model instituted at Harvard, subsequently copied by many other universities, students wrote frequent short compositions, which their instructors then read and marked to indicate grammatical errors. After these essays were returned, students were often expected to rewrite them to correct the errors. This approach to revision became an integral part of the "current-traditional" approach to rhetoric that dominated both university and high school composition instruction until the 1960s, and it firmly established a concept of revision as rewriting to correct grammatical errors.

CONTEMPORARY CONCEPTS OF REVISION
IN THE COMPOSING PROCESS

Revival of classical rhetoric in the 1960s led to a renewed interest in Aristotle's rhetorical principles, particularly his concern for audience and purpose, adapted for written rather than oral discourse. Rhetorical theorists reclaimed invention as an essential component of composing and drew on research in cognitive and developmental psychology to argue that language created meaning. In this context, knowledge and meaning were, thus, viewed as "constructed," rather than observed and reported. In addition, scholarly and pedagogical interest in how writers compose focused attention on revision as an important stage in the composing process. Initially, composing was viewed as linear, with writers moving through discrete steps: first, prewriting or invention, then drafting, revision, and finally editing. Murray (1978), for example, divided the process into three stages: first, prevision, which includes everything that precedes the first draft; second, vision, the completion of a first or discovery draft in which the writer "stakes out a territory to explore" (p. 87); and third, revision, which consists of everything a writer does to the draft to develop a meaning that can be communicated to a reader. However, later theorists and researchers rejected the linear model in favor of a recursive one in which writers moved back and forth among the activities of invention, drafting, and revision throughout the composing process (Flower & Hayes, 1981; Perl, 1979). During this ongoing process, writers could revise at any point during composing and at any level—from the major units of discourse such as the thesis or the main arguments to individual words and sentences. However, their primary concern was always developing meaning in terms of purpose and audience. _still true_

Donald Murray (1978) characterized the new approach to revision as "everything writers do to discover and develop what they have to say, beginning with the reading of a completed first draft" (p. 87), as "internal revision." He identified four aspects of discovery in the process of internal revision. First, writers discover content and information, which leads them to the second aspect—the discovery of form and structure. Third, writers discover meaning through language itself. Fourth, writers find a voice or point of view pertaining to their subject. Murray labeled the old approach to revision—proofreading that focused on conventions of form, style, language, and mechanics—as "external revision." Because the process paradigm made discovering and developing meaning central to the composing process, composition teachers became concerned with encouraging what Murray called "internal revision." Questions of correctness—once the primary focus of revision—were to be addressed at the end, only after questions regarding content, organization, and audience had been resolved. To clearly distinguish the older concept of revision from the newer one, all changes involving correctness were increasingly referred to as editing rather than as revision.

Murray's expressivist approach to revision focused on self-expression and developing a personal voice. However, when later theorists and researchers looked at revision in academic and professional writing, they found that writers needed to draw on their knowledge of discipline-specific forms or genres and discourse conventions when revising. Alice Horning (2002), who studied the revision processes of academic and workplace professional writers, discovered that they draw on three different kinds of awareness as they revise: awareness of themselves as writers, awareness of strategies that reflect their personality preferences, and awareness of language as language. These writers also rely on skills such as collaboration with colleagues, familiarity with relevant genres, and focusing successfully on text and context to revise effectively.

For Writing and Discussion

What kinds of questions do you ask yourself when you reread your writing to revise it? How well do they help you revise your writing? Are you aware of genre conventions that you need to follow? Has past instruction or experience in composition influenced the questions you ask yourself or the strategies you use to revise?

REVISION STRATEGIES OF STUDENT WRITERS

Although this new concept of revision emphasized its role in discovering and shaping meaning, early composing process research showed that student writers typically viewed revision as error correction and made only superficial changes in their texts. In Janet Emig's (1971) groundbreaking study of the composing processes of 12th graders, Lynn, the student writer she described most extensively, recalled that her teacher made her revise by recopying essays to correct errors and described the process as "punishment work" (p. 68).

Charles Stallard (1974) analyzed the writing behaviors of 12th-grade writers and observed a number of aspects of composing, including revision. He found that the kind and amount of revision characteristic of good writers differed from that of a group of randomly selected student writers. Even though both groups were concerned about spelling and mechanics in general, good writers made almost three times more revisions than writers in the random group. Their major emphasis involved word choice, but they were more likely to make multiple word, syntactic, and paragraph revisions. Even for the good writers, however, the number of syntactic and paragraph changes was small.

In an exploratory study of upper-division college students, Beach (1976) found that some students followed the approach to revision used by students in Stallard's study. Identifying these students as nonrevisers, he found they relied on textbook formulas, expressed less interest in the writing tasks, and limited the time and effort they spend on writing. However, other students revised extensively and saw revision as an opportunity to discover and shape their meaning. These extensive revisers conceived of their papers in holistic terms and used subsequent drafts to work out their arguments and to make any necessary changes.

Beach attributed these differences to the students' ability to evaluate their writing critically, an ability present in the extensive revisers but lacking in the nonrevisers.

Bridwell's (1980) research, which focused exclusively on revision strategies, compared more and less successful 12th-grade writers. To analyze her data, she developed a comprehensive classification system to describe the types of revisions that students made. Each revision was categorized according to one of six levels, beginning with surface-level changes in mechanics and moving up to progressively more complex changes—individual words, then phrases, clauses, sentences, multiple sentences, and finally the whole text. She also counted the number of revisions made at three points during composing: in-process first-drafts, between drafts, and in-process second drafts. Bridwell found that both groups of students revised substantially more during the two in-process stages and made the greatest number of changes at all levels while writing the second draft. However, the more successful writers made more changes between drafts. Despite these differences, she found that surface- and word-level revision accounted for over half of all revisions made by *both* the more and the less successful writers. None of the students made revisions that involved the whole-text level, and very few revisions were made at the sentence or multiple-sentence level.

Research on basic or developmental writers shows that they focus almost exclusively on editing individual words and sentences for correctness rather than making meaning-based changes. In Perl's case study of "unskilled college writers" (1979), the students continuously proofread and edited their writing during composing. She concluded that they focused on correct form to a degree that interfered with generating ideas and drafting. Despite these students' emphasis on proofreading and editing, many errors remained in their work.

A key research study on revision, conducted by Nancy Sommers (1980), compared revisions made by college freshmen with those of experienced writers, including journalists, editors, and academics, and found striking differences between their approaches to revision. Because of its important insights, this essay is included as the reading at the end of this chapter.

For Reading and Discussion

Read "Revision Strategies of Student Writers and Experienced Adult Writers," pp. 100–107. Be prepared to discuss the following questions in small groups:

1. What kind of revisions do experienced writers make? How are these different from the revisions of student writers?
2. What is the attitude of student writers toward revising? What are their main concerns? How do these differ from the attitudes and concerns of experienced writers?
3. How do the revising strategies of student and adult writers in Sommers' study relate to Donald Murray's conception of internal and external revision?

For Writing and Discussion

How would you describe your revision process? Do you engage primarily in external revision, focusing on words and sentences, or do you also use revision as a way of discovering, shaping, and developing your meaning (internal revision)? How has past writing instruction influenced your approach to revision?

OBSTACLES TO REVISION

afraid of change

Why do students tend to regard revision as rewording and error correction rather than as an activity for discovering meaning and shaping their ideas for readers? One explanation blames the nature of school-sponsored writing and classroom instructional approaches for creating obstacles to revision: school writing assignments often don't give students an opportunity to write for real audiences or purposes, while teachers may reinforce a view of revision as error hunting. Monahan (1984), for example, found that seven of the nine teachers in his study taught revision by having students write second drafts using a grammar-based checklist. Moreover, an emphasis on editing and sentence-level revision can occur even in a class in which a teacher employs a process approach and strategies such as peer revision and multiple drafts to emphasize revision. Yagelski (1995) studied such a class and found that students still focused their revision on surface and stylistic concerns. Despite the writing workshop structure of the class, students revised in response to the teacher's conception of "good" writing, which emphasized grammatical correctness, tight organization, and a straightforward prose style. Most of the teacher's comments on drafts focused on lower-level concerns with virtually no attention given to ideas, and peer responses to drafts reflected similar concerns. As a result, students revised primarily to improve their grades and considered the teacher to be the primary audience.

In addition, when revision involves larger textual elements and focuses on meaning, it becomes a complex cognitive process. Flower, Hayes, Carey, Schriver, and Stratman (1986) studied this complexity by comparing the cognitive processes used by experts and novice student writers while revising. Basing their study on the Flower–Hayes cognitive model of composing, they attempted to model the basic thinking process underlying revision and looked for places where experts and novices made different decisions or handled the process itself differently. They identified three major obstacles for beginning writers: detecting problems in the text, diagnosing the problems, and choosing a strategy to remedy the problems. In their model, revision begins as writers review their text and evaluate it. To detect problems, writers must evaluate the draft in terms of their goals or intentions and criteria for effective writing. Detection, therefore, involves two complex constructive processes: first, representing the text through the act of reading and then representing one's intentions. Expert writers are able to represent both their text and their intentions clearly and also have extensive knowledge of criteria for effective writing. As a result, they are able to read their drafts for rhetorical problems related to content, organization, genre, and audience as well as for sentence-level problems of style and correct form. Novice writers, on the other hand, typically work with a vague representation of their texts. They may read meanings in their head into the text and fail to realize these meanings are not actually present for a reader. In addition, they have difficulty representing the overall structure of a draft and so have trouble reading a draft for rhetorical problems. Finally, because they are likely to have a very limited set of criteria for evaluating writing, they are able to detect only a few problems.

Once writers sense that something is wrong in their texts, they must be able to turn that detection into a diagnosis that suggests what needs to be done to correct the problem. However, diagnosis requires writers to recognize and categorize problems, an ability that novices don't have. Experts are able to see the problems they identify as fitting within meaningful, familiar categories and are then able to use their past experience and knowledge to select strategies for revision. Novices, however, are able to categorize only a small number of problems—usually at the word or sentence level—and possess a limited repertoire of revision strategies. Therefore, the complex cognitive processes involved in revising, particularly at the rhetorical level, explain why novice student writers consistently revise in more narrow and limited ways than experienced writers.

For Writing and Discussion

What kinds of difficulties do you experience when you revise your drafts? Are you able to identify problems in content, development, or organization as well as those involving sentences and correct form? What techniques or strategies do you use when you revise?

HELPING STUDENTS REVISE EFFECTIVELY: INTERVENING IN THE COMPOSING PROCESS

Given the importance of revision in composing, students' consistent tendency to view revision as correcting errors or making small changes in wording or sentence structure has led rhetoricians and composition specialists to search for strategies that would encourage more meaning-based revision. Beach (1976), who concluded that his nonrevisers' concept of revision reflected the attitudes of teachers and textbooks, recommended that we "provide alternative, helpful models of the revision process" (p. 164). Sommers (1980) also concluded that students had been taught to revise in a "narrow and predictable way." She observed that students "have strategies for handling words and phrases, but don't know what to do when they sense something larger is wrong" (p. 383). Composition instruction, therefore, has focused on expanding students' understanding of revision to include developing and shaping meaning, finding ways to intervene during the composing process that encourages meaning-based revision, and teaching students strategies for revising at the rhetorical level.

Using Whole-Class Workshops and One-to-One Conferences to Encourage Revision

Ken Macrorie and Donald Murray, early proponents of the process approach, were among the first to develop intervention strategies to help students revise drafts. Adapting a structure used in creative writing classes, Macrorie created an in-class workshop that engaged the whole class, guided by the teacher, in reading and responding to work in progress. Murray also focused on students' in-progress drafts, but he relied primarily on one-to-one conferences. Both strategies continue to be used today, either in their original form or modified for different settings and types of students.

In *Writing to Be Read,* Macrorie (1968) provided the rationale for his approach by explaining that beginning writers need to gain experience "through engaging in critical sessions with peers" (p. 85) if their writing is to improve. He later (1985) described the peer response group as a "helping circle," where students and the teacher give truthful responses to drafts that students read aloud to the group. Because writers are anxious about receiving criticism, Macrorie prohibited negative criticism at the beginning and allowed students to comment only about those parts of the drafts that they liked. Once students experienced success by hearing positive comments, then other students, assisted by the teacher, could begin to criticize the drafts. Although teachers led the writing workshop, they gave up some of their authority in what Macrorie (1970) called his "Third Way" of teaching. Rather than controlling all aspects of the class, teachers must allow "students [to] operate with freedom and discipline," by giving them "real choices" and by encouraging them "to learn the way of experts" (p. 27). Although he acknowledged that students cannot criticize writing unless they have developed evaluation standards, Macrorie argued that students learn such standards primarily from the responses of other students, rather than by having them imposed by the teacher, and that a teacher "needs to encourage the writers to criticize upon their own two feet, and to evolve their own standards" (1968, p. 85). Teachers assisted in this process by stating their opinions and pointing out examples of what they consider to be good and bad writing by both student and professional writers.

Like Macrorie, Donald Murray also endorsed supportive criticism of in-progress drafts and diminished the authority of the teacher in order to increase students' responsibility for their writing. However, he relied primarily on teacher–student conferences, rather than on class workshops to encourage revision. Murray (1985) structured conferences with students according to a basic pattern: first, students commented on their drafts; next the teacher read or reviewed the drafts and responded to the students' comments. Finally, the students responded to the teacher's responses. Murray (1985) explained that the purpose of this structure is "to help students learn to read their own drafts with increasing effectiveness" (p. 148). He described the conference as a "co-reading" of students' texts, which helps them read their writing more intensively and see its features more clearly. The teacher focused on "what is working and what needs work," made comments that were designed to stimulate and encourage students to revise their drafts, and avoided offering evaluative generalizations. Over the course of several conferences, students began to develop criteria for evaluating their own work. After students had a grasp of evaluative criteria, Murray added in-class workshops in which student writers read their work either to a small group or the whole class. However, unlike Macrorie's students, who offered first-draft freewriting for peer response, Murray's students revised their initial drafts before presenting them to a group.

Using Peer Response Groups to Encourage Revision

Peter Elbow's work popularized peer response groups as a strategy for encouraging revision. As the title of his book *Writing without Teachers* (1973) indicates, Elbow's approach further de-emphasized the role of the teacher by placing full responsibility for responding to drafts on writers themselves. Elbow's initial guidelines for listeners outlined a descriptive approach to giving feedback: pointing to words and phrases they find particularly striking and effective or weak and empty; summarizing what they consider to be the main point, feelings, or center of gravity; telling the writer what they experienced as they tried to read the writer's words carefully; and describing their perceptions through metaphors or analogies (e.g., talking about the writing by comparing it to voices, the weather, motion, clothing, terrain, color, shape, etc.). However, Elbow's later books and articles provided more structured guidelines for peer response groups and placed a greater emphasis on helping students learn criteria for good writing. In *Sharing and Responding*, Elbow and Belanoff (1989) expanded Elbow's earlier descriptive approach to responding and also added sections on analytic responding, reader-based responding, and criterion-based or judgment-based responding. For example, readers may ask for responses to specific features or dimensions of writing such as structure, point of view, attitude toward the reader, diction, or syntax. In analytic responding, readers ask for "skeleton feedback" about three main dimensions of a paper—reasons and support, assumptions, and audience. They may also play the "doubting and believing game," in which the reader is first asked to "believe (or pretend to believe) everything I have written" and give more facts to build the writer's case. Next, the reader is asked to "doubt everything" and give arguments against the writer's case (p. 66). In criterion-based or judgment-based responding, which Elbow identified as useful when writers want to know how their writing measures up to specific criteria, response groups respond in terms of traditional criteria for different types of writing. For example, criteria for expository or essay writing include such dimensions as focus on the task, content, clarity, organization, and mechanics. With these additions, Elbow not only provided more direction for peer response groups but also encouraged writers to respond to writing in terms of traditional evaluative criteria.

Using Computers to Encourage Revision

With the advent of computers and word-processing programs, theorists and researchers anticipated that the new technology, which eliminated the need to retype or recopy entire texts when revising, would encourage students to revise more extensively. They also hoped that the greater ease of manipulating text (i.e., adding, deleting, or moving) would encourage more meaning-based revisions. However, research results regarding the effect of computers and word-processing programs on revision has been mixed. An early study by Hawisher (1987) compared the amount of revision and quality of writing when advanced college freshmen used computers and when they used pen and paper. In addition to receiving specific instruction on revising their writing, students also received specific instruction on the mechanics of using a word processor to revise, completed self-assessment forms designed to prompt revision, and wrote out plans for revising their final drafts. Hawisher found that students not only revised more when using paper and pen than when using the computer but also that there seemed to be no relationship between frequency of revision and quality ratings received by the essays. In addition, there were no significant differences in quality rating between paper and pen essays and those done on the computer. A later study involving average and above average 8th graders also found that papers produced using word processors were not higher in quality than those written with pen and paper (Joram, Woodruff, Bryson, & Lindsay, 1992).

On the other hand, some research has shown word processing to have a positive effect on revision and writing quality. For example, Owston, Murphy, and Wideman (1992) compared revision strategies and writing quality when 8th-grade students, all experienced computer users, composed on a computer or by hand. They found that papers written on computer received significantly higher quality ratings than those written by hand. However, computer revisions were likely to be microstructural rather than macrostructural changes, and most revision took place at the initial drafting stage. In a study of basic college writers, McAllister and Louth (1988) found that those students who used computers produced higher quality revisions of assigned paragraphs than basic writers who did not use computers. Reynolds and Bonk (1996) investigated the use of computer prompts to encourage revision. In their study, half of the students in an intermediate college composition class had access to 24 generative and evaluative prompts that supported previous ideas and instruction in the course about revision. The prompts could be self-initiated by writers, but were also available through a keyboard template. Results showed that students using the prompting system made more meaning-related changes in their texts and produced higher-quality texts. Walker (1997), who compared the on-screen and off-screen revision processes of developmental writers, found that results varied depending on students' attitudes toward revision. Those who were open to revision made more meaning changes when revising on-screen, but others had difficulty revising both on- and off-screen. Pennington (2003) reviewed a number of studies on the effects of computer use on the writing of ESL students. Although results were mixed, later studies were more likely to have positive results and showed that students revised more when using computers.

Despite some positive results, the effects of computers and word processing on composing remain problematic. Crafton (1996), who surveyed studies conducted after computer use had become more common and students were routinely using word-processing programs to write their papers, concluded that the computer introduces new problems and complexities into the writing process and may, in some cases, emphasize the written product rather than support the composing process. Eklund (1994) found that computers encouraged localized revision because the size of the screen limits the amount of text that can be reread and reviewed, whereas Sharples (1994) suggested that the ease of making low-level revisions might actually disrupt the composing process by encouraging students to engage in continuous editing throughout the composing process. Moreover, text-editing tools such as grammar and spelling checkers seem to reinforce a concept of revision as error correction and surface-level changes. Heilker (1992) observed that students often respond to suggestions from text-analysis programs as if they were directives from a person rather than a machine. As a result, he concluded that "the writer–computer relationship is displacing and replacing the writer–audience relationship in the rhetorical situation" (p. 65).

Recent research on the effect of computers on revision has shifted from the effect of word processing on revision to the use of computers to facilitate peer revision, often in composition classes taught in a computer lab. Brown (1997) discusses the benefits of "serial collaboration," in which students have an opportunity to have their work reviewed by five or more peers. After training students to respond effectively to their peers, she advocates using the computer for serial collaboration because it greatly simplifies the logistics of the process. Honeycutt (2001), who compared e-mail and synchronous conferencing, found that students rated email as more serious and helpful than chats even though they made greater reference to writing and response tasks using chats. Tuzi (2001), who looked at the impact of e-feedback on the revisions of ESL writers, found that although students could see benefits to e-feedback, they generally preferred oral feedback. Liu and Sadler (2003) also found that face-to-face communication between L2 peers was more effective even though students using computers made more comments.

Today, many high school and most college students use word processing when writing essays, and computer use has been integrated into all aspects of composing and composition instruction. (See Lisa Gerard's Chapter 11 in this volume for a comprehensive discussion.) Given the widespread use of computers and word processing, teachers need to be aware of their limitations as well as their potential. As the research makes clear, computers and word processing do not automatically lead students to make substantive revisions. Instead, the kinds of revision that students make reflect their conception of revision and their goals in revising. In some cases, therefore, computers may reinforce a focus on editing and sentence-level revision. Computers and word processing will facilitate meaning-based revision only if students view revision as a process of shaping the text in terms of purpose and audience. Students must also be able to identify the types of larger changes that are needed and have a repertoire of rhetorical strategies at their command to make the needed changes. As a result, teachers need to provide classroom instruction and responses to drafts that will prepare students to take advantage of the computer's potential for facilitating substantive revision.

For Writing and Discussion

Do you use a computer when writing essays? If so, do you compose your first draft on the computer or by hand? How does the computer affect the way you revise? Do most of your computer revisions involve sentence-level changes in words and incorrect forms rather than changes in content, development, or organization? How frequently do you revise when composing on a computer? Do you print out a draft and revise on paper at any point in the process? Share your response in small groups.

Using Direct Instruction to Encourage Revision

Growing awareness of the importance of genre in shaping texts and the complexity of revision has led teachers to provide direct instruction that helps students understand criteria for evaluating different genres and develop a repertoire of revision strategies. For example, writers of narrative texts are often admonished to "show, don't tell," while writers of analytic arguments are expected to provide well-supported claims. The type of instruction, therefore, needs to be tailored to the kind of writing students are being asked to do. Calkins and Bleichman (2003), who teach revision to elementary children and focus on narratives, offer mini-lessons on topics such adding dialogue and showing rather than telling as well as suggestions for adding and deleting text. Gilmore (2007), whose book *"Is It Done Yet? Teaching Adolescents the Art of Revision"* targets adolescents and the formal analytic essay, provides instruction on revising each section of an essay's content—introductions, organization, incorporating evidence, conclusions, and interpreting texts and passages.

Instruction designed to help students compose texts in specific genres may also assist them in revising their texts. For example, Felton and Herko (2004) use in-class dialogue to conduct an argumentative writing workshop that helps students develop a complex two-sided argument that acknowledges an opposing-side claim and offers a counterargument to that claim. To help students move from oral to written argument, they give them a graphic organizer (PREP—position, reason, explanation, and proof) that asks them to state their position on the issue, their reason for the position, an explanation for the reason, and proof or evidence for the explanation. After students have written their arguments, they use a revision worksheet based on the PREP organizer to evaluate their work and make needed revisions. Hillocks (1979, 1983) developed an instructional program in which high school students observed and recorded sensory perceptions to help them write descriptive essays with more specific details and another program in which students engaged in inquiry to help them write more effective definitions. Research studies confirmed that students receiving instruction wrote papers superior to those who received only an assignment. Because both instructional programs used a process approach that emphasized invention and revision, students undoubtedly made use of their genre knowledge when revising their texts as well as when initially drafting them.

Instruction can also help more advanced students learn rhetorical strategies that could be used for both drafting and revising essays. Harris (2006) in *Rewriting: How to Do Things with Texts* presents sophisticated strategies for developing and revising critical academic essays that analyze one or more complex texts. In *They Say/I Say: The Moves that Matter in Academic Writing,* Graff and Birkenstein (2006) give students "templates" that help them move between the ideas in texts and their own response to those ideas. They argue that these templates help students focus not only on "what is being said, but on the *forms* that structure what is being said" (p. xi). For example, to show agreement with another writer's position, students might write "She argues _____, and I agree because _____" (p. 8), while writers can express disagreement using a template such as "I think X is mistaken because she overlooks _____" (p. 55).

Although most instruction in revision has focused on global revision, students can also benefit from sentence-level revision that moves beyond correcting errors and helps them write more stylistically effective sentences. In *Writing to be Read* (1970), Macrorie gives guidelines for improving style through techniques such as eliminating forms of "to be" (e.g., is, was, etc.), "tightening" by eliminating unnecessary words, and using active rather than passive voice. Gilmore (2007) includes a chapter on revising style that shows students how to revise sentences to improve syntax and clarity by using precise word choice, concise language, and grammatically correct syntax. Williams' (2003) *Style: The Basics of Clarity and Grace* presents ten sentence-level revision lessons, each of which addresses a different aspect of style and includes advanced topics such as sentence emphasis, shape, and elegance.

RESEARCH ON THE EFFECTIVENESS OF INTERVENTION STRATEGIES

What evidence do we have that intervening during the composing process prompts more extensive and meaningful revision? Because peer group and teacher responses to drafts are usually part of a general instructional approach, it is difficult to isolate the effect of these strategies on revision. In addition, researchers have been more interested in whether instructional strategies improve students' writing rather than in the effect on students' revision practices. For example, Clifford (1981) studied the effect of composing in stages where writing was taught as a process, and students wrote multiple drafts of their essays. In the experimental classes, students engaged in brainstorming, freewriting, and peer response groups that used feedback sheets to guide group discussion about sentence structure and syntax, paragraph patterns and structure, and support for generalizations. Students also evaluated their peers' papers, using an evaluation sheet, based on criteria developed collaboratively by the class, that indicated the strongest and weakest parts of the paper, and made specific suggestions for revisions. At the end of the term, the writing of these students was compared to that of students who were taught by a traditional "product" approach, in which the teacher read and evaluated only finished essays. In these classes, revision was optional and occurred only after students had received comments and a grade from their teacher. Clifford found that students in the process writing classes wrote essays that were significantly better than those written by students in the traditional classes. Although he attributed much of the improvement in writing ability to the peer workshops that focused on revision, undoubtedly other aspects of the class also had an effect, so the total approach, rather than peer response alone, was responsible for students' improved writing.

Although peer response groups have been a popular and highly recommended instructional strategy for encouraging students to revise, a number of studies have discovered difficulties that may arise when they are used. For example, Kraemer (1993) found that some students were uncomfortable being critical and, therefore, chose to be nice rather than helpful. When Styslinger (1998) investigated students' views on peer revision, students reported that they generally focused on sentence-level problems and discussed ways to edit papers. Many of her students also expressed frustration with the peer revision process. They complained about the comments made by peers, describing them as too limiting, general, or nice and not always based on a careful reading of the paper. Students also judged the value of peer comments in relation to their perceptions of a peer's ability and course grade. In general, they wanted teachers to play a larger role during the peer revision process. Styslinger concluded that teachers could improve peer groups by teaching students how to comment, reinforcing careful readings and responses, and allowing enough time for the process.

Further insights into the difficulties of using peer response groups effectively can be found in studies that focus on the interaction and dynamics within these groups. Carol Berkenkotter (1984) studied the comments made by three students participating in a peer response group in her freshman composition class. After discovering that students responded to peer readers in "significantly different ways depending on the writer's personality, level of maturity, and ability to handle writing problems" (p. 313), she concluded that these differences made it difficult to make generalizations about the effect of peer response groups on revision and that using peer response groups effectively was neither simple nor straightforward. In another study, Thomas Newkirk (1984) investigated the differences between instructor and peer evaluation by comparing the responses that freshman English students and instructors gave to four papers, in which students were asked to use personal experience to support generalizations. Before the papers were evaluated, mechanical errors in spelling and punctuation were corrected so that these factors would not enter into the evaluations. When Newkirk compared students' and teachers' evaluations, he found that they often used different criteria in judging student work. For example, students consistently responded to papers in terms of whether they could "relate to" the topic, whereas teachers rarely expressed a concern for such personal identification. Given their use of different criteria, Newkirk concluded that peer groups might be limited in their ability to provide an adequate response to student papers without careful preparation and training.

In a study specifically designed to investigate the effect of teacher comment and self-evaluation on revision, Beach (1979) compared students who used a self-evaluation guide to revise drafts, received teacher responses to drafts, or were told to revise on their own. After analyzing the amount and kind of revision that resulted with each of these instructional strategies, he found that students who received teacher evaluation showed a greater degree of change, higher fluency, and more support in their final drafts than students who received no evaluation or who used the self-evaluation forms. Moreover, students who used the self-evaluation guides engaged in no more revising than those who were asked to revise on their own without any assistance. Beach concluded the self-evaluation forms were ineffective because students had received little instruction in self-assessment and were not used to detaching themselves critically from their writing. As a result, he recommended that teachers "provide evaluation during the writing of drafts" (p. 119).

Audience and purpose are central concerns of experienced writers when they revise, and several research studies examined the effect of directing students' attention to these aspects of composing. Roen and Wylie (1988) conducted a study that asked students to focus on audience before revising an essay by asking them to list things their readers (specified as their teacher and peers) would know about their topic and those things they would not know. Students who considered their audience during revision received higher holistic scores than those who did not. Studies by Wallace and Hayes (1991) and Wallace, Hatch, Hayes, Miller, Moser, and Silk (1996) focused on changing students' task definition when revising by illustrating strategies for making global revisions. In both studies, students received eight minutes of instruction that used overhead transparencies to contrast the difference between local and global revisions of a text. Instruction also contrasted an expert revision procedure—first reading through the entire text to identify major problems—with a novice approach—correcting local errors line-by-line. Results found a significant increase in global revision and essay quality for students enrolled in regular first-year composition sections, but not for basic writers. Therefore, the authors concluded that the regular composition students probably possessed fundamental revision skills, and the instruction prompted or reminded them to use these skills.

Although peer response groups and teacher feedback during the composing process can promote revision, the kinds of revision and their effectiveness will depend upon the type of comments students receive. Teacher comments that focus on sentence-level correctness will reinforce students' tendency to see revision as editing rather than an opportunity to re-envision their content and organization. Peer comments may be ineffective or misleading if students are unable to identify weaknesses in a text and to suggest alternatives. In the cognitive model of revision proposed by Flower, Hayes, Carey, Schriver, and Stratman (1986), writers must first be able to detect a problem, then diagnose the problem, and finally draw on a knowledge of rhetorical strategies and use them to modify the text to remedy the problem. Direct instruction in the characteristics of specific genres and learning to evaluate these genres is therefore critical to the success not only of peer response groups but also to writers' ability to revise independently.

Adapting Intervention Strategies for a Wide Range of Contemporary Students

Because of the difficulties encountered in intervening effectively during the composing process, the individual conferences, writing workshops, and peer response groups popularized by Macrorie, Murray, and Elbow, along with the classroom structures for implementing them, have been adapted by later rhetoricians and composition specialists to make them more workable and effective. Because these strategies were initially designed for students in regular first-year or advanced composition classes, they often did not work for younger or less able students. In addition, they initially relied primarily on an inductive approach to developing criteria for effective writing. Most adaptations are more structured and directive than the strategies originally proposed and, thus, are appropriate for a wider range of students and classroom settings.

Adapting the Whole-Class Workshop

The whole-class workshop is now often used as an instructional strategy to teach students criteria for evaluating writing and to model the peer review process. Most students, especially younger and less able writers, need direct instruction in evaluating writing and guidance in responding to the writing of peers. Connors and Glenn (1995) offer the following guidelines for conducting successful whole-class workshops: "(1) Use examples of strong writing so students can easily recognize a paper's strengths. (2) Hand out copies of a student's paper in advance and ask other students to read and write comments before the class workshop begins. (3) Have the writer read his/her paper aloud and then ask for guidance on specific concerns" (p. 45). Axelrod, Cooper, and Warriner (1994) suggest an alternative approach that uses an anonymous draft on the same or a similar assignment written by a student in another class. During the whole-class workshop, teachers explain the evaluative criteria to be used and consciously model the kinds of question and response that students should use in responding to each other's drafts.

Adapting Individual Conferences
Nancie Atwell (1987) has adapted Murray's conference approach for the secondary school curricula by conducting all conferences within the classroom. These conferences are at the center of an overall approach to writing instruction in which all class activities center on writing and responding. To increase student involvement, Atwell refers to students as "authors," and students write primarily for themselves and their peers. In the first edition of *In the Middle,* Atwell (1987) recommends scheduling large blocks of class time for writing, ideally every day, but at least three consecutive days a week. In her classroom, students choose the topics and forms for their writing projects, and also move through the writing process at their own pace. They revise their drafts in response to feedback received during short conferences with the teacher, with each conference focusing on only one aspect of writing at a time (i.e., content, organization, development, etc.). In addition, students may confer with a peer or use a list of questions that help them confer with themselves about possible revisions. They develop criteria for evaluating and revising their writing through various activities: participating in brief mini-lessons where the teacher presents writing strategies, by seeing what works in the writing of other students and professional writers, and participating in "share" sessions, where they read their own work and respond to the writing of other students. Finally, students learn grammar and mechanics in context, primarily through editing conferences with the teacher.

Adapting Peer Response Groups
Elbow's "teacherless" peer response groups have been widely adopted as a strategy for encouraging revision. However, these groups have often worked better in theory than in practice (typical problems were discussed earlier in the section that examined research on intervention strategies), and Elbow himself adapted peer response groups by providing the more structured and directive approaches found in *Sharing and Responding* (1989). When peer response groups work, however, they have many benefits. Anne Gere (1987) pointed out that they are particularly effective in addressing the problem of audience awareness and provide an opportunity for collaborative learning in which students come to understand how knowledge is socially constructed. Lindemann (1995) believes that the peer workshop is "one of the best ways to teach students to become independent critics" (p. 202).

Given their potential value in developing students' writing skills, many teachers and researchers have looked for ways to overcome the difficulties that can arise when using peer response groups. For example, Hacker (1996) focused on systematically training students in peer response techniques. For each of the first three writing assignments, he modeled examples of successful peer response episodes. In addition, some students had two individual conferences with him where they reviewed two drafts that they had read prior to the conference. In the conferences, he and the student discussed issues to be addressed in an upcoming peer evaluation workshop. Hacker found that those students who had conferences with him asked more questions of their peers when they were in the role of writer and made more responses when in the role of responder. He concluded that students generally don't know how to respond to drafts in "consistent, systematic ways" and "[t]he time and care taken by writers before peer response determines in large part the types and amount of commentary" that students give (p. 125). Although conferring with students before they participate in peer response groups is time-consuming and too labor-intensive to be practical in most settings, Hacker's success with his approach illustrates the importance of carefully preparing and guiding students before they respond to papers written by their peers.

Lindemann (1995) outlines procedures for improving the effectiveness of peer response workshops that can be used in many classroom settings. She observes that writing workshops need careful planning because "students aren't accustomed to working in groups" and "need explicit instructions for using their time in groups constructively" (p. 199). Teachers must also give students a language for discussing their work and assign concrete, manageable tasks. She recommends dividing the class into heterogeneous groups of five to seven students that remain together for the entire term and suggests beginning with brief tasks. At the beginning of a term, workshop groups might, for example, examine only the first paragraph of an essay or a single paragraph in detail for 10 or 15 minutes. As they become more experienced, they would gradually address larger and more difficult tasks that would require more time to complete. She also recommends that students, guided by the teacher, generate their own list of evaluative criteria stated in language they understand. Although teachers monitor the groups to ensure that they stay on task or to help them refocus the discussion, it is important for them to stay in the background if students are to become independent critics.

Virtually all adaptations recommend that students write as well as talk during the peer response workshops so that writers have a written record of critical comments that they can refer to when they revise. Sometimes students are asked to write comments on a peer's draft or on a blank piece of paper that is stapled or clipped to the draft. However, structured peer response forms are a popular method for guiding students' responses and providing specific feedback. For these forms to work successfully, they must be carefully designed and linked to prior classroom instruction. According to the model developed by Flower and her colleagues (1986), the first steps in the revision process are detecting and diagnosing problems. Because novice student writers have difficulty with these steps, particularly in identifying rhetorical problems, a well-designed peer response form will help students focus on the relevant rhetorical issues.

The following is an example of a peer response form that could be used in conjunction with the draft essay on pages 95–96. It focuses the reader's attention on argument strategies, audience, and development. If students were evaluating a different type of essay, a personal narrative for example, the form would need to be modified to focus students' attention on different aspects of writing (i.e., those that make for an effective narrative). The form assumes that students have had previous instruction regarding the rhetorical principles that it asks them to analyze. In addition, students need instruction on strategies that can be used to eliminate the problems that have been identified if they are to revise successfully.

__English 1__   Title of Essay: _____

__Peer Suggestion Sheet__

__Your Name:__ _____   __Writer:__ _____

1. Is there a clear thesis in the essay? If so, locate and write down the thesis statement. If not, what do you think that the thesis statement seems to be? What do you think about the writer's thesis?
2. What are two reasons that the writer gives to support his/her thesis? Are these effective? Why or why not?
3. Has the writer considered any objection(s) that a reader might make to the position he/she takes? If so, how does the writer deal with the objection(s)? If not, what objections can you think of that the writer should consider?
4. Where would you like to see more development, specifics, or details? In other words, where do you want to know more?
5. How well could you follow the general flow or arrangement of the essay? Were there places that confused you? If so, explain what they were and why they were confusing? Is the essay written in a five-paragraph form? If so, what suggestions can you make to the writer to change that structure?
6. Are the transitions between sentences and paragraphs easy to follow? Point to places where the transitions are unclear.

FIG. 3.1 Peer Response Form.

For Writing and Discussion

The essay below is a draft written in response to an assignment that asked the writer to take and support a position on an issue. If this writer were a student in your class, what would be the main rhetorical problems—audience, content, development, and organization—that you would point out as needing revision? Select two or three rhetorical problems and write comments that you might put on a paper to guide this writer's revision.

PC is Ridiculous!

A debate has scourged the United States for several decades regarding the issue of "PC." The abbreviation is often confused with several different means, such as Personal Computer, President's Choice, but instead I am addressing the coined term "Political Correctness." Everyday the debate about PC becomes a more prominent topic in the classroom, the newspapers, and casual conversation and people are getting sick of it.

The truth of the matter is actually simple. No matter what Stanley Fish might claim, political correctness stifles free speech and will ultimately lead to a completely repressive society. At this point, students are afraid to open their mouths and say what they really think because they are afraid of being labeled "racist" or "sexist." Is this what education is about? Is this what our society has come to? Isn't it time we stopped being afraid of telling the truth?

Our country was founded on the Bill of Rights and the first amendment to that document guarantees freedom of speech. If the PC people continue to make policy in our colleges and universities, free speech will no longer be a guaranteed right for students. Are students supposed to be considered second citizens? Isn't the university a place where people can speak freely? The PC movement has gotten completely out of hand and all policies concerned with it on campus ought to be eliminated.

Helping Students Become Independent Revisers

If students are to write effectively for different audiences and purposes throughout their academic and professional lives, they must become confident writers who can move through the composing process independently. Classroom instruction, along with feedback from teachers and peers, all contribute to helping students become independent revisers. However, most students will benefit from developing procedures and strategies for revising without the support of teachers and peers.

In her text *Work in Progress,* Lisa Ede (1989) asks students to identify their preferred composing style and to analyze and monitor their writing process. Drawing on these insights, students then develop personal guidelines for revision that include reminders about typical problems, strategies successfully used in the past to address these problems, and productive work habits that will lead to successful revision. Ede provides students with a practical, three-stage process for revising that begins with asking the "BIG" questions about focus, content, and organization, next considers coherence, and finally examines stylistic options.

The St. Martin's Guide to Writing by Axelrod and Cooper (1997) offers a comprehensive approach to revision that is linked to instruction on critical features of different genres of writing and fits within the overall writing process. The authors advise students to begin their revisions by getting a critical reading from a classmate, friend, or family member. Then, they outline a detailed procedure for students to follow when revising. First, students reread their draft straight through to get an objective overview and identify possible problems. Next, they make a scratch outline of the essay's development and a two-column chart of a revision plan. In the left column, the student lists the basic features of the writing task assigned. For example, if the purpose of the assignment was to explain a concept, the list would include such features as concept focus, a logical plan, clear definitions, and careful use of sources. However, if students were writing about a remembered event, they would need to consider different features: a well-told story, vivid presentation of significant scenes and people, and an indication of the event's significance. Students then analyze their drafts in terms of the basic features, identifying problems to be solved by referring to questions provided in a critical reading guide. Finally, using detailed suggestions from the book, students consider ways to solve the problems identified. The revision process created by Axelrod and Cooper models the strategies characteristic of expert, experienced writers. If students repeat these procedures as they revise each assignment, they are likely to learn strategies and internalize an approach that will enable them to revise independently whenever they have a writing project.

For Writing and Discussion

Do you usually find that teachers' oral or written comments on your writing, either drafts or final copies, are helpful? How do you make use of their comments? What has been your experience with peer response groups? Have you found them helpful? If so, in

what ways? If not, why weren't they helpful? Has class instruction given you strategies
for revising content? Style? Do you have a specific plan or strategy for revising independently? If so, what is it? Share your answers in small groups.

CONCLUSION

Revision is now seen as crucial to shaping and discovering meaning during composing.
However, helping students learn to make meaning-based revisions is a challenging task.
To begin, students must develop a different concept of revision. Instead of viewing it as
changing sentences and words or hunting for errors, they need to see it as a process of making changes in content and organization and of shaping the text in terms of their purpose
and audience. Next, students must learn criteria for evaluating writing. Most students need
direct instruction not only in gaining an understanding of these criteria but also in applying
them. Teachers play a crucial role in providing this instruction, but providing such instruction can be challenging. Not only is the writing process itself complex, but school-sponsored
writing also often lacks real purposes and audiences. Moreover, classroom structures usually constrain and limit the composing process. Despite these difficulties, knowledgeable
teachers can create classroom environments that encourage and support substantive revision. If students learn criteria for evaluating their own writing and that of their peers and
are able to draw on a repertoire of rhetorical strategies for revision, they will be able to use
revision as a means of discovering meaning and shaping their texts for specific audiences
and purposes.

For Writing and Discussion

Look at a composition textbook designed for high school students and a rhetoric used by
first-year composition classes. Compare the concept of revision that each presents. What
strategies does each book recommend to help students revise effectively? How would
you evaluate these concepts and strategies based on what you have read in this chapter?

For Further Exploration

Calkins, L., & Bleichman, P. (2003). *The craft of revision*. Portsmouth, NH: Firsthand.
    Although designed for elementary students, the revision strategies illustrated could be
adapted for use with older writers who are writing narrative/descriptive essays.

Felton, M. K., & Herko, S. (2004). From dialogue to two-sided argument: Scaffolding ado-
    lescents' persuasive writing. *Journal of Adolescent & Adult Literacy, 47*, 672–683.
Describes classroom activities that enable students to draft and then revise persuasive
essays to create effective arguments.

Gilmore, B. (2007). *"Is it done yet?" Teaching adolescents the art of revision*. Portsmouth,
    NH: Heinemann.
    An excellent resource that gives specific classroom activities for revising both content
and style.

Graff, G., & Birkenstein, C. (2006). *They say/I say: The moves that matter in academic writing*. New York and London: W. W. Norton & Company.

Focuses on strategies for responding to texts and incorporating them in researched academic essays. Designed for college freshmen or advanced high school students.

Horning, A, & Becker, A. (Eds.) (2006). *Revision history, theory, and practice*. West Lafayette, IN: Parlor Press.

Comprehensive overview of current views on revision. Includes chapters on revision strategies of basic, ESL, and professional writers, best classroom practices, and guidelines for teachers and writers.

REFERENCES

Atwell, N. (1987). *In the middle: Writing, reading, and learning with adolescents*. Portsmouth, NH: Boynton/Cook Publishers.

Axelrod, R. B., & Cooper, C. R. (1997). *The St. Martin's guide to writing* (5th ed.) New York: St. Martin's Press.

Axelrod, R. B., Cooper, C. R., & Warriner, A. M. (1994). *Instructor's resource manual: The St. Martin's guide to writing*. New York: St. Martin's Press.

Beach, R. (1976). Self-evaluation strategies of extensive revisers and nonrevisers. *College Composition and Communication, 27* (2), 160–163.

Beach, R. (1979). The effects of between-draft teacher evaluation versus student self-evaluation on high school students' revising of rough drafts. *Research in the Teaching of English, 13* (2), 111–120.

Berkenkotter, C. (1984). Student writers and their authority over texts. *College Composition and Communication, 36* (3), 312–319.

Berlin, J. A. (1987). *Rhetoric and reality: Writing instruction in American colleges, 1900–1985*. Carbondale and Edwardsville, IL: Southern Illinois University Press.

Bizzell, P., Herzberg, B., & Reynolds, N. (2000). *Bedford bibliography of writing* (5th ed.) Boston and New York: Bedford/St. Martin's.

Bridwell, L. S. (1980). Revising strategies in twelfth grade students' transactional writing. *Research in the Teaching of English, 14* (3), 197–222.

Brown, J. L. (1997). Emphasizing the "what if?" of revision: Serial collaboration and quasi-hypertext. *Teaching English in the Two-Year College, 24* (1), 34–41.

Calkins, L., & Bleichman, P. (2003). *The craft of revision*. Portsmouth, NH: Firsthand.

Clifford, J. (1981). Composing in stages: The effects of a collaborative pedagogy. *Research in the Teaching of English, 15* (1), 37–53.

Connors, R. J. (1997). *Composition-rhetoric: Backgrounds, theory, and pedagogy*. Pittsburgh: University of Pittsburgh Press.

Connors, R. J., & Glenn, C. (1995). *The St. Martin's guide to teaching writing* (3rd ed.). New York: St. Martin's Press.

Covino, W. A., & Jolliffe, D. A. (1995). *Rhetoric: Concepts, definitions, boundaries*. Boston: Allyn & Bacon.

Crafton, R. E. (1996). Promises, promises: Computer-assisted revision and basic writers. *Computers and Composition, 13*, 317–326.

Ede, L. (1989). *Work in progress: A guide to writing and revising*. New York: St. Martin's Press.

Eklund, K. S. (1994). Linear and nonlinear strategies in computer-based writing. *Computers and Composition, II*, 227–235.

Elbow, P. (1973). *Writing without teachers*. New York: Oxford University Press.

Elbow, P., & Belanoff, P. (1989). *Sharing and responding*. New York: Random House.

Emig, J. (1971). *The composing process of twelfth graders*. Urbana, IL: NCTE.

Felton, M. K., & Herko, S. (2004). From dialogue to two-sided argument: Scaffolding adolescents' persuasive writing. *Journal of Adolescent & Adult Literacy, 42* (8), 672–683.

Flower, L., & Hayes, J. R. (1981). A cognitive process theory of writing. *College Composition and Communication, 32* (4), 365–387.

Flower, L., Hayes, J. R., Carey, L., Schriver, K., & Stratman, J. (1986). Detection, diagnosis, and the strategies of revision. *College Composition and Communication, 37* (1), 16–55.

Gere, A. R. (1987). *Writing groups: History, theory, and implications*. Carbondale & Edwardsville, IL: Southern Illinois University Press.

Gilmore, B. (2007). *"Is it done yet?" Teaching adolescents the art of revision*. Portsmouth, NH: Heinemann.

Graff, G., & Birkenstein, C. (2006). *They say/I say: The moves that matter in academic writing*. New York and London: W. W. Norton & Company.

Hacker, P. (1996). The effect of teacher conferences on peer response discourse. *Teaching English in the Two-Year College, 23* (2), 112–126.

Harris, Joseph. (2006). *Rewriting: How to do things with texts*. Logan, UT: Utah State University Press.

Hawisher, G. (1987). The effects of word processing on the revision strategies of college freshmen. *Research in the Teaching of English, 21* (2), 145–159.

Heilker, P. (1992). Revision worship and the computer as audience. *Computers and Composition, 9* (3), 59–69.

Hillocks, G. Jr. (1979). The effects of observational activities on student writing. *Research in the Teaching of English, 13* (1), 23–35.

Hillocks, G. Jr. (1983). Teaching defining strategies as a mode of inquiry: Some effects on student writing. *Research in the Teaching of English, 17* (3), 275–284.

Hodges, K. (1982). A history of revision: Theory versus practice. In R. A. Sudol (Ed.), *Revising: New essays for teachers of writing* (pp. 24–42). Urbana, IL: NCTE.

Honeycutt, L. (2001). Comparing e-mail and synchronous conferencing in online peer response. *Written Communication, 18* (1), 26–60.

Horning, A. (2002). *Revision revisited*. Cresskill, NJ: Hampton Press, Inc.

Joram, E., Woodruff, E., Bryson, M., & Lindsay, P. H. (1992). The effects of revising with a word processor on written composition. *Research in the Teaching of English, 26* (2), 167–193.

Kraemer, K. (1993). Revising responding. In K. Spear (Ed.), *Peer response groups in action* (pp. 133–150). Portsmouth, NH: Heinemann.

Lindemann, E. (1995). *A rhetoric for writing teachers* (3rd ed.). New York & Oxford: Oxford University Press.

Liu, J., & Sadler, R. W. (2003). The effect and affect of peer review in electronic versus traditional modes on L2 writing. *Journal of English for Academic Purposes, 2* (3), 193–227.

Macrorie, K. (1968). *Writing to be read*. New York: Hayden Book Company.

Macrorie, K. (1970). *Uptaught*. New York: Hayden Book Company.

Macrorie, K. (1985). *Telling writing* (4th ed.). Upper Montclair, NJ: Boynton/Cook.

McAllister, C., & Louth, R. (1988). The effect of word processing on the quality of basic writers' revisions. *Research in the Teaching of English, 22* (4), 417–427.

Monahan, B. D. (1984). Revision strategies of basic and competent writers as they write for different audiences. *Research in the Teaching of English, 18* (3), 288–304.

Murray, D. M. (1978). Internal revision: A process of discovery. In C. R. Cooper & L. Odell (Eds.), *Research on composing: Points of departure* (pp. 85–104). Urbana, IL: NCTE.

Murray, D. M. (1985). *A writer teaches writing* (2nd ed.). Boston: Houghton Mifflin Company.

Newkirk, T. (1984). Direction and misdirection in peer response. *College Composition and Communication, 35* (3), 300–311.

Owston, R. D., Murphy, S., & Wideman, H. H. (1992). The effects of word processing on students' writing quality and revision strategies. *Research in the Teaching of English, 26* (3), 249–276.

Pennington, M. C. (2003). The impact of the computer in second language writing. In B. Kroll (Ed.), *Exploring the dynamics of second language writing* (pp. 287–310). Cambridge: Cambridge University Press.

Perl, S. (1979). The composing processes of unskilled college writers. *Research in the Teaching of English, 13*, 317–336.

Quintilian (1921). The institutio oratoria. Trans. H. E. Butler. Cambridge: Harvard University Press.

Reynolds, T. H., & Bonk, C. J. (1996). Facilitating college writers' revisions within a generative evaluative computerized prompting framework. *Computers and Composition, 13* (1), 93–108.

Roen, D. H., & Wylie, R. J. (1988). The effects of audience awareness on drafting and revising. *Research in the Teaching of English, 22* (1), 75–88.

Sharples, M. (1994). Computer support for the rhythms of writing. *Computers and Composition, II*, 237–250.

Sommers, N. (1980). Revision strategies of student writers and experienced adult writers. *College Composition and Communication, 31* (4), 378–388.

Stallard, C. (1974). An analysis of the writing behavior of good student writers. *Research in the Teaching of English, 8* (2), 206–218.

Styslinger, M. (1998). Some milk, a song, and a set of keys: Students respond to peer revision. *Teaching and Change, 5* (2), 116–138.

Tuzi, F. (2001). E-feedback's impact on ESL writers' revisions. ED 46365. 15 pp.

Walker, C. L. (1997). Computers, revision, and the developmental writer: A case study of on-screen versus off-screen revision processes. *Research and Teaching in Developmental Education, 14* (1), 23–34.

Wallace, D. L., & Hayes, J. R. (1991). Redefining revision for freshmen. *Research in the Teaching of English, 25* (1), 54–66.

Wallace, D. L., Hatch, J. A., Hayes, J, R., Miller, W., Moser, G., & Silk, C. M. (1996). Better revision in eight minutes? Prompting first-year college writers to revise globally. *Journal of Educational Psychology, 88* (4), 682–688.

Williams, J. M. (2003). *Style: The basics of clarity and grace*. New York: Longman.

Yagelski, R. P. (1995). The role of classroom context in the revision strategies of student writers. *Research in the Teaching of English, 29* (2), 216–238.

Reading

REVISION STRATEGIES OF STUDENT WRITERS AND EXPERIENCED ADULT WRITERS

Nancy Sommers

Although various aspects of the writing process have been studied extensively of late, research on revision has been notably absent. The reason for this, I suspect, is that current models of the writing process have directed attention away from revision. With few exceptions, these models are linear; they separate the writing process into discrete stages. Two representative models are Gordon Rohman's suggestion that the composing process moves from prewriting to writing to rewriting and James Britton's model of the writing process as a series of stages described in metaphors of linear growth, conception—incubation—production.[1] What is striking about these theories of writing is that they model themselves on speech: Rohman defines the writer in a way that cannot distinguish him from a speaker ("A writer is a man who ... puts [his] experience into words in his own mind"—p. 15); and Britton bases his theory of writing on what he calls (following Jakobson) the "expressiveness" of speech.[2] Moreover, Britton's study itself follows the "linear model" of the relation of thought and language in speech proposed by Vygotsky, a relationship embodied in the linear movement "from the motive which engenders a thought to the shaping of the thought, *first* in inner speech, *then* in meanings of words, and *finally* in words" (quoted in Britton, p. 40). What this movement fails to take into account in its linear structure—"first ... then ... finally"—is the recursive shaping of thought by language; what it fails to take into account is *revision*. In these linear conceptions of the writing process revision is understood as a separate stage at the end of the process—a stage that comes after the completion of a first or second draft and one that is temporally distinct from the prewriting and writing stages of the process.[3]

The linear model bases itself on speech in two specific ways. First of all, it is based on traditional rhetorical models, models that were created to serve the spoken art of oratory. In whatever ways the parts of classical rhetoric are described, they offer "stages" of composition that are repeated in contemporary models of the writing process. Edward Corbett, for instance, describes the "five parts of a discourse"—*inventio, dispositio, elocutio, memoria, pronuntiatio*—and, disregarding the last two parts since "after rhetoric came to be concerned mainly with written discourse, there was no further need to deal with them,"[4] he produces a model very close to Britton's conception [*inventio*], incubation [*dispositio*], production [*elocutio*]. Other rhetorics also follow this procedure, and they do so not simply because of historical accident. Rather, the process represented in the linear model is based on the irreversibility of speech. Speech, Roland Barthes says, "is irreversible":

> A word cannot be retracted, except precisely by saying that one retracts it. To cross out here is to add: if I want to erase what I have just said, I cannot do it without showing the eraser itself (I must say: "*or rather ...*" "*I expressed myself badly ...*"); paradoxically, it is ephemeral speech which is indelible, not monumental writing. All that one can do in the case of a spoken utterance is to tack on another utterance.[5]

What is impossible in speech is *revision:* like the example Barthes gives, revision in speech is an afterthought. In the same way, each stage of the linear model must be exclusive (distinct from the other stages) or else it becomes trivial and counterproductive to refer to these junctures as "stages."

By staging revision after enunciation, the linear models reduce revision in writing, as in speech, to no more than an afterthought. In this way such models make the study of revision impossible. Revision, in Rohman's model, is simply the repetition of writing; or to pursue Britton's organic metaphor, revision is simply the further growth of what is already there, the "pre-conceived" product. The absence of research on revision, then, is a function of a theory of writing which makes revision both superfluous and redundant, a theory which does not distinguish between writing and speech.

What the linear models do produce is a parody of writing. Isolating revision and then disregarding it plays havoc with the experiences composition teachers have of the actual writing and rewriting of experienced writers. Why should the linear model be preferred? Why should revision be forgotten, superfluous? Why do teachers offer the linear model and students accept it? One reason, Barthes suggests, is that "there is a fundamental tie between teaching and speech," while "writing begins at the point where speech becomes *impossible*."[6] The spoken word cannot be revised. The possibility of revision distinguishes the written text from speech. In fact, according to Barthes, this is the essential difference between writing and speaking. When we must revise, when the very idea is subject to recursive shaping by language, then speech becomes inadequate. This is a matter to which I will return, but first we should examine, theoretically, a detailed exploration of what student writers as distinguished from experienced adult writers *do* when they write and rewrite their work. Dissatisfied with both the linear model of writing and the lack of attention to the process of revision, I conducted a series of studies over the past three years which examined the revision processes of student writers and experienced writers to see what role revision played in their writing processes. In the course of my work the revision process was redefined as *a sequence of changes in a composition—changes which are initiated by cues and occur continually throughout the writing of a work.*

Methodology

I used a case study approach. The student writers were twenty freshmen at Boston University and the University of Oklahoma with SAT verbal scores ranging from 450–600 in their first semester of composition. The twenty experienced adult writers from Boston and Oklahoma City included journalists, editors, and academics. To refer to the two groups, I use the terms *student writers* and *experienced writers* because the principal difference between these two groups is the amount of experience they have had in writing.

Each writer wrote three essays, expressive, explanatory, and persuasive, and rewrote each essay twice, producing nine written products in draft and final form. Each writer was interviewed three times after the final revision of each essay. And each writer suggested revisions for a composition written by an anonymous author. Thus extensive written and spoken documents were obtained from each writer.

The essays were analyzed by counting and categorizing the changes made. Four revision operations were identified: deletion, substitution, addition, and reordering. And four levels of changes were identified: word, phrase, sentence, theme (the extended statement of one idea). A coding system was developed for identifying the frequency of revision by level and operation. In addition, transcripts of the interviews in which the writers interpreted their revisions were used to develop what was called a *scale of concerns* for each writer. This scale enabled me to codify what were the writer's primary concerns, secondary concerns, tertiary concerns, and whether the writers used the same scale of concerns when revising the second or third drafts as they used in revising the first draft.

Revision Strategies of Student Writers

Most of the students I studied did not use the terms *revision* or *rewriting*. In fact, they did not seem comfortable using the word *revision* and explained that revision was not a word they used, but the word their teachers used. Instead, most of the students had developed various functional terms to describe the type of changes they made. The following are samples of these definitions:

Scratch Out and Do Over Again: "I say scratch out and do over, and that means what it says. Scratching out and cutting out. I read what I have written and I cross out a word and put another word in; a more decent word or a better word. Then if there is somewhere to use a sentence that I have crossed out, I will put it there."

Reviewing: "Reviewing means just using better words and eliminating words that are not needed. I go over and change words around."

Reviewing: "I just review every word and make sure that everything is worded right. I see if I am rambling; I see if I can put a better word in or leave one out. Usually when I read what I have written, I say to myself, 'that word is so bland or so trite,' and then I go and get my thesaurus."

Redoing: "Redoing means cleaning up the paper and crossing out. It is looking at something and saying, no that has to go, or no, that is not right."

Marking Out: "I don't use the word rewriting because I only write one draft and the changes that I make are made on top of the draft. The changes that I make are usually just marking out words and putting different ones in."

Slashing and Throwing Out: "I throw things out and say they are not good. I like to write like Fitzgerald did by inspiration, and if I feel inspired then I don't need to slash and throw much out."

The predominant concern in these definitions is vocabulary. The students understand the revision process as a rewording activity. They do so because they perceive words as the unit of written discourse. That is, they concentrate on particular words apart from their role in the text. Thus one student quoted above thinks in terms of dictionaries, and, following the eighteenth century theory of words parodied in *Gulliver's Travels,* he imagines a load of things carried about to be exchanged. Lexical changes are the major revision activities of the students because economy is their goal. They are governed, like the linear model itself, by the Law of Occam's razor that prohibits logically needless repetition: redundancy and superfluity. Nothing governs speech more than such superfluities; speech constantly repeats itself precisely because spoken words, as Barthes writes, are expendable in the cause of communication. The aim of revision according to the students' own description is therefore to clean up speech; the redundancy of speech is unnecessary in writing, their logic suggests, because writing, unlike speech, can be reread. Thus one student said, "Redoing means cleaning up the paper and crossing out." The remarkable contradiction of cleaning by marking might, indeed, stand for student revision as I have encountered it.

The students place a symbolic importance on their selection and rejection of words as the determiners of success or failure for their compositions. When revising, they primarily ask themselves: can I find a better word or phrase? A more impressive, not so cliched, or less hum-drum word? Am I repeating the same word or phrase too often? They approach the revision process with what could be labeled as a "thesaurus philosophy of writing"; the students consider the thesaurus a harvest of lexical substitutions and believe that most problems in their essays can be solved by rewording. What is revealed in the students' use of the thesaurus is a governing attitude toward their writing: that the meaning to be communicated is already there, already finished, already produced, ready to be communicated, and all that is necessary is a better word "rightly worded." One student defined revision as "redoing"; "redoing" meant "just using better words and eliminating words that are not needed." For the students, writing is translating: the thought to the page, the language of speech to the more formal language of prose, the word to its synonym. Whatever is translated, an original text already exists for students, one which need not be discovered or acted upon, but simply communicated.[7]

The students list repetition as one of the elements they most worry about. This cue signals to them that they need to eliminate the repetition either by substituting or deleting words or phrases. Repetition occurs, in large part, because student writing imitates—transcribes—speech: attention to repetitious words is a manner of cleaning speech. Without a sense of the developmental possibilities of revision (and writing in general) students seek, on the authority of many textbooks, simply to clean up their language and prepare to type. What is curious, however, is that students are aware of lexical repetition, but not conceptual repetition. They only notice the repetition if they can "hear" it: they do not diagnose lexical repetition as symptomatic of problems on a deeper level. By rewording their sentences to avoid the lexical repetition, the students solve the immediate problem, but blind themselves to problems on a textual level; although they are using different words, they are sometimes merely restating the same idea with different words. Such blindness, as I discovered with student writers, is the inability to "see" revision as a process: the inability to "re-view" their work again, as it were, with different eyes, and to start over.

The revision strategies described above are consistent with the students' understanding of the revision process as requiring lexical changes but not semantic changes. For the students, the extent to which they revise is a function of their level of inspiration. In fact, they use the word *inspiration* to describe the ease or difficulty with which their essay is written, and the extent to which the essay needs to be revised. If students feel inspired, if the writing comes easily, and if they don't get stuck on individual words or phrases, then they say that they cannot see any reason to revise. Because students do not see revision as an activity in which they modify and develop perspectives and ideas, they feel that if they know what they want to say, then there is little reason for making revisions.

The only modification of ideas in the students' essays occurred when they tried out two or three introductory paragraphs. This results, in part, because the students have been taught in another version of the linear model of composing to use a thesis statement as a controlling device in their introductory paragraphs. Since they write their introductions and their thesis statements even before they have really discovered what they want to say, their early close attention to the thesis statement, and more generally the linear model, function to restrict and circumscribe not only the development of their ideas, but also their ability to change the direction of these ideas.

Too often as composition teachers we conclude that students do not willingly revise. The evidence from my research suggests that it is not that students are unwilling to revise, but rather that they do what they have been taught to do in a consistently narrow and predictable way. On every occasion when I asked students why they hadn't made any more changes, they essentially replied, "I knew something larger was wrong, but I didn't think it would help to move words around." The students have strategies for handling words and phrases and their strategies helped them on a word or sentence level. What they lack, however, is a set of strategies to help them identify the "something larger" that they sensed was wrong and work from there. The students do not have strategies for handling the whole essay. They lack procedures or heuristics to help them reorder lines of reasoning or ask questions about their purposes and readers. The students view their compositions in a linear way as a series of parts. Even such potentially useful concepts as "unity" or "form" are reduced to the rule that a composition, if it is to have form, must have an introduction, a body, and a conclusion, or the sum total of the necessary parts.

The students decide to stop revising when they decide that they have not violated any of the rules for revising. These rules, such as "Never begin a sentence with a conjunction" or "Never end a sentence with a preposition," are lexically cued and rigidly applied. In general, students will subordinate the demands of the specific problems of their text to the demands of the rules. Changes are made in compliance with abstract rules about the product, rules that quite often do not apply to the specific problems in the text. These revision strategies are teacher-based, directed towards a teacher-reader who expects compliance with rules—with pre-existing "conceptions"—and who will only examine parts of the composition (writing comments about those parts in the margins of their essays) and will cite any violations of rules in those parts. At best the students see their writing altogether passively through the eyes of former teachers or their surrogates, the textbooks, and are bound to the rules which they have been taught.

Revision Strategies of Experienced Writers

One aim of my research has been to contrast how student writers define revision with how a group of experienced writers define their revision processes. Here is a sampling of the definitions from the experienced writers:

Rewriting: "It is a matter of looking at the kernel of what I have written, the content, and the thinking about it, responding to it, making decisions, and actually restructuring it."

Rewriting: "I rewrite as I write. It is hard to tell what is a first draft because it is not determined by time. In one draft, I might cross out three pages, write two, cross out a fourth, rewrite it, and call it a draft. I am constantly writing and rewriting. I can only conceptualize so much in my first draft—only so much information can be held in my head at one time; my rewriting efforts are a reflection of how much information I can encompass at one time. There are levels and agenda which I have to attend to in each draft."

Rewriting: "Rewriting means on one level, finding the argument, and on another level, language changes to make the argument more effective. Most of the time I feel as if I can go on rewriting forever. There is always one part of a piece that I could keep working on. It is always difficult to know at what point to abandon a piece of writing. I like this idea that a piece of writing is never finished, just abandoned."

Rewriting: "My first draft is usually very scattered. In rewriting, I find the line of argument. After the argument is resolved, I am much more interested in word choice and phrasing."

Revising: "My cardinal rule in revising is never to fall in love with what I have written in a first or second draft. An idea, sentence, or even a phrase that looks catchy, I don't trust. Part of this idea is to wait a while. I am much more in love with something after I have written it than I am a day or two later. It is much easier to change anything with time."

Revising: "It means taking apart what I have written and putting it back together again. I ask major theoretical questions of my ideas, respond to those questions, and think of proportion and structure, and try to find a controlling metaphor. I find out which ideas can be developed and which should be dropped. I am constantly chiseling and changing as I revise."

The experienced writers describe their primary objective when revising as finding the form or shape of their argument. Although the metaphors vary, the experienced writers often use structural expressions such as "finding a frame-work," "a pattern," or "a design" for their argument. When questioned about this emphasis, the experienced writers responded that since their first drafts are usually scattered attempts to define their territory, their objective in the second draft is to begin observing general patterns of development and deciding what should be included and what excluded. One writer explained, "I have learned from experience that I need to keep writing a first draft until I figure out what I want to say. Then in a second draft, I begin to see the structure of an argument and how all the various sub-arguments which are buried beneath the surface of all those sentences are related." What is described here is a process in which the writer is both agent and vehicle. "Writing," says Barthes, unlike speech, "develops like a seed, not a line,"[8] and like a seed it confuses beginning and end, conception and production. Thus, the experienced writers say their drafts are "not determined by time," that rewriting is a "constant process," that they feel as if (they) "can go on forever." Revising confuses the beginning and end, the agent and vehicle; it confuses, *in order to find,* the line of argument.

After a concern for form, the experienced writers have a second objective: a concern for their readership. In this way, "production" precedes "conception." The experienced writers imagine a reader (reading their product) whose existence and whose expectations influence their revision process. They have abstracted the standards of a reader and this reader seems to be partially a reflection of themselves and functions as a critical and productive collaborator—a collaborator who has yet to love their work. The anticipation of a reader's judgment causes a feeling of dissonance when the writer recognizes incongruities between intention and execution, and requires these writers to make revisions on all levels. Such a reader gives them just what the students lacked: new eyes to "re-view" their work. The experienced writers believe that they have learned the causes and conditions, the product, which will influence their reader, and their revision strategies are geared towards creating these causes and conditions. They demonstrate a complex understanding of which examples, sentences, or phrases should be included or excluded. For example, one experienced writer decided to delete public examples and add private examples when writing about the energy crisis because "private examples would be less controversial and thus more persuasive." Another writer revised his transitional sentences because "some kinds of transitions are more easily recognized as transitions than others." These examples represent the type of strategic attempts these experienced writers use to manipulate the conventions of discourse in order to communicate to their reader.

But these revision strategies are a process of more than communication; they are part of the process of *discovering meaning* altogether. Here we can see the importance of dissonance; at the heart of revision is the process by which writers recognize and resolve the dissonance they sense in their writing. Ferdinand de Saussure has argued that meaning is differential or "diacritical," based on differences between terms rather than "essential" or inherent qualities of terms. "Phonemes," he said, "are characterized not, as one might think, by their own positive quality but simply by the fact that they are distinct."[9] In fact, Saussure bases his entire *Course in General Linguistics* on these differences, and such differences are dissonant; like musical dissonances which gain their significance from their relationship to the "key" of the composition which itself is determined by the whole language, specific language (parole) gains its meaning from the system of language (langue) of which it is a manifestation and part. The musical composition—a "composition" of parts—creates its "key" as in an over-all structure which determines the value (meaning) of its parts. The analogy with music is readily seen in the compositions of experienced writers: both sorts of composition are based precisely on those structures experienced writers seek in their writing. It is this complicated relationship between the parts and the whole in the work of experienced writers which destroys the linear model; writing cannot develop "like a line" because each addition or deletion is a reordering of the whole. Explicating Saussure, Jonathan Culler asserts that "meaning depends on difference of meaning."[10] But student writers constantly struggle to bring their essays into congruence with a predefined meaning. The experienced writers do the opposite: they seek to discover (to create) meaning in the engagement with their writing, in revision. They seek to emphasize and exploit the lack of clarity, the differences of meaning, the dissonance, that writing as opposed to speech allows in the possibility of revision. Writing has spatial and temporal features not apparent in speech—words are recorded in space and fixed in time—which is why writing is susceptible to reordering and later addition. Such features make possible the dissonance that both provokes revision and promises, from itself, new meaning.

For the experienced writers the heaviest concentration of changes is on the sentence level, and the changes are predominantly by addition and deletion. But, unlike the students, experienced writers make changes on all levels and use all revision operations. Moreover, the operations the students fail to use—reordering and addition—seem to require a theory of the revision process as a totality—a theory which, in fact, encompasses the *whole* of the composition. Unlike the students, the experienced writers possess a non-linear theory in which a sense of the whole writing both precedes and grows out of an examination of the parts. As we saw, one writer said he needed "a first draft to figure out what to say," and "a second draft to see the structure of an argument buried beneath the surface." Such a "theory" is both theoretical and strategical; once again, strategy and theory are conflated in ways that are literally impossible for the linear model. Writing appears to be more like a seed than a line.

Two elements of the experienced writers' theory of the revision process are the adoption of a holistic perspective and the perception that revision is a recursive process. The writers ask: what does my essay as a *whole* need for form, balance, rhythm, or communication. Details are added, dropped, substituted, or reordered according to their sense of what the essay needs for emphasis and proportion. This sense, however, is constantly in flux as ideas are developed and modified; it is constantly "re-viewed" in relation to the parts. As their ideas change, revision becomes an attempt to make their writing consonant with that changing vision.

The experienced writers see their revision process as a recursive process—a process with significant recurring activities—with different levels of attention and different agenda for each cycle. During the first revision cycle their attention is primarily directed towards narrowing the topic and delimiting their ideas. At this point, they are not as concerned as they are later about vocabulary and style. The experienced writers explained that they get closer to their meaning by not limiting themselves too early to lexical concerns. As one writer commented to explain her revision process, a comment inspired by the summer 1977 New York power failure: "I feel like Con Edison cutting off certain states to keep the generators going. In first and second drafts, I try to cut off as much as I can of my editing generator, and in a third draft, I try to cut off some of my idea generators, so I can make sure that I will actually finish the essay." Although the experienced writers describe their revision process as a series of different levels or cycles, it is inaccurate to assume that they have only one objective for each cycle and that each cycle can be defined by a different objective. The same objectives and sub-processes are present in each cycle, but in different proportions. Even though these experienced writers place the predominant weight upon finding the form of their argument during the first cycle, other concerns exist as well. Conversely, during the later cycles, when the experienced writers' primary attention is focused upon stylistic concerns, they are still attuned, although in a reduced way, to the form of the argument. Since writers are limited in what they can attend to during each cycle (understandings are temporal), revision strategies help balance competing demands on attention. Thus, writers can concentrate on more than one objective at a time by developing strategies to sort out and organize their different concerns in successive cycles of revision.

It is a sense of writing as discovery—a repeated process of beginning over again, starting out new—that the students failed to have. I have used the notion of dissonance because such dissonance, the incongruities between intention and execution, governs both writing and meaning. Students do not see the incongruities. They need to rely on their own internalized sense of good writing and to see their writing with their "own" eyes. Seeing in revision—seeing beyond hearing—is at the root of the word *revision* and the process itself; current dicta on revising blind our students to what is actually involved in revision. In fact, they blind them to what constitutes good writing altogether. Good writing disturbs: it creates dissonance. Students need to seek the dissonance of discovery, utilizing in their writing, as the experienced writers do, the very difference between writing and speech—the possibility of revision.

Notes

1 D. Gordon Rohman and Albert O. Wlecke, "Pre-writing: The Construction and Application of Models for Concept Formation in Writing," Cooperative Research Project No. 2174, U.S. Office of Education, Department of Health, Education, and Welfare; James Britton, Anthony Burgess, Nancy Martin, Alex McLeod, Harold Rosen, *The Development of Writing Abilities (11–18)* (London: Macmillan Education, 1975).

2 Britton is following Roman Jakobson, "Linguistics and Poetics," in T. A. Sebeok, *Style in Language* (Cambridge, Mass: MIT Press, 1960).

3 For an extended discussion of this issue see Nancy Sommers, "The Need for Theory in Composition Research," *College Composition and Communication.* 30 (February, 1979), 46–69.

4 *Classical Rhetoric for the Modern Student* (New York: Oxford University Press, 1965), p. 27.

5 Roland Barthes, "Writers, Intellectuals, Teachers," in *Image-Music-Text.* trans. Stephen Heath (New York: Hill and Wang, 1977), pp. 190–191.

6 "Writers, Intellectuals, Teachers," p. 190.

7 Nancy Sommers and Ronald Schleifer, "Means and Ends: Some Assumptions of Student Writers," *Composition and Teaching,* II (in press).

8 *Writing Degree Zero* in *Writing Degree Zero and Elements of Semiology,* trans. Annette Lavers and Colin Smith (New York: Hill and Wang, 1968), p. 20.

9 *Course in General Linguistics,* trans. Wade Baskin (New York, 1966), p. 119.

10 Jonathan Culler, *Saussure* (Penguin Modern Masters Series; London: Penguin Books, 1976), p. 70.

Acknowledgment

The author wishes to express her gratitude to Professor William Smith, University of Pittsburgh, for his vital assistance with the research reported in this article and to Patrick Hays, her husband, for extensive discussions and critical editorial help.

4

Audience

Irene L. Clark

- Who is your audience?
- How does the concept of audience influence other elements in the text?
- Why should your audience care about what you have to say?
- Where is the audience located? In the room? In your head? In Cyberspace?

These are a few of the questions that college students need to consider about audience, a concept in composition that has always been "slippery" (to use James Porter's term) and has become more so with the insights brought about through studies in new media. As Knobel and Lankshear have noted in *A New Literacies Sampler* (2007), new literacies are "more 'participatory,' 'collaborative,' and 'distributed' in nature," characteristics that have a significant impact on the meaning of audience. Recent scholarship in new media has called attention to the blurring of boundaries between audience and creators, the difficulty of knowing who one's audience actually is, and issues involving intellectual property and shared knowledge, among others. How, then, should teachers address the concept of audience in an undergraduate writing class? This chapter discusses varying perspectives and controversies associated with audience, examines how the concept of audience has been complicated by new media, and suggests possibilities for addressing audience in the writing class.

THE COMPLICATED ISSUE OF AUDIENCE

Even before new media broadened and complicated the meaning of "audience," the term generated considerable scholarly discussion. Once equated simply with the reader or readers of a text, "audience" in composition scholarship was referred to as "audiences" and accompanied by a set of complex terms such as "invoked," "evoked," "fictionalized," "intended," or "general." More recently, in recognition of those who have been excluded from traditional academic discourse, additional terms have been added, such as "ignored, rejected, excluded or denied" (Lunsford & Ede, 2009, p. 174).

Nevertheless, despite the flurry of attention given to audience as a theoretical issue, the concept has had less of an impact in the writing class. Students think of "audience" only in terms of the teacher who will grade their work and lack awareness of how audience affects other aspects of a text, such as purpose, form, style, and genre. Teachers may tell students to "consider your audience," which is good advice, but difficult for students to follow, unless the teacher helps them understand the complexity of the concept and demonstrates how audience awareness is manifested within a text, in whatever medium that text has been produced.

PERSPECTIVES ON AUDIENCE

Audience has been a significant component of rhetoric since classical times. Plato, in the *Phaedrus* (370 B.C.), asserted that the rhetorician should adapt a speech to the characteristics of an audience, classifying "the type of speech appropriate to each type of soul" (1952, p. 147). Aristotle also conceived of audience in terms of actual "hearers" of persuasive discourse. In Book II of the *Rhetoric* (1991), Aristotle discussed the ways a speaker might adapt his discourse to various audiences, categorizing audiences according to their time in life (youth, age, the prime of life, etc.) and discussing various appeals by means of which a rhetor could be persuasive. This rhetorical model, as Kirsch and Roen (1990) have pointed out, rests on several assumptions: that the audience is known, the values and needs of the audience can be identified, and the audience is separate from the discourse and its social context. Although somewhat applicable to oral communication, the notion that an audience is completely knowable does not transfer easily to written discourse, in which an audience is often completely removed in both time and space from the writer, and this is particularly the case with the use of new media. From the perspective of the composition class, this model characterizes a rhetorical interaction as moving in only one direction, from the rhetor (the speaker or writer) to the audience or reader. The writer, according to this model, is conceived of as a sender and the audience as merely a receiver.

Nevertheless, insights into audience from classical rhetoric remain relevant, in particular, Aristotle's discussion of three persuasive appeals: *pathos*, the appeal to the emotions of the audience, *ethos*, appeal to the credibility of the speaker, and *logos*, the appeal to logic and reason. Familiarizing students with these appeals can help students consider what is likely to have an impact on an audience. But in presenting these appeals in the classroom, it is important that students not only know the definitions, but also understand how they work so that they can use them in their own writing. In order for an appeal to work, "it must focus the audience's attention, push the counterarguments into the background, and encourage the audience members to play along for a while" (Killingsworth, 2005, p. 36). Killingsworth maintained that the word "attention" here is key, pertinent to whatever medium is being used because "the root of the word attention—'to attend'—literally means to listen" (p. 36). "Listening" for Aristotle's audience meant an audience who was physically present and could actually hear what was being said. For 21st-century audiences "listening" or "attending" can occur in Cyberspace.

Rediscovering Audience

Mary Jo Reiff, in an overview of perspectives on audience that are relevant for the teaching of writing, noted that after Aristotle, attention to audience diminished, although it was revived in the 18th century in its association with psychology. However, 19th-century rhetoric did not emphasize audience, focusing instead on formal features of language such as style and correctness. The 20th century, then, "rediscovered" rhetoric, and with the rediscovery came renewed recognition of the writer–audience relationship in constructing an effective text. Redefining rhetoric more broadly as "the use of language as a symbolic means of inducing cooperation in beings that by nature respond to symbols," Kenneth Burke, in *The Philosophy of Literary Form* (1973, p. 43), revived the importance of audience in communication, as did Chaim Perelman and Lucie Olbrechts-Tyteca in *The New Rhetoric: A Treatise on Argument* (1958). These texts affirmed the classical view of audience as existing outside the discourse, and the composition textbooks of the 1970s and 1980s, reflecting this view, emphasized the importance of knowing the characteristics of particular audiences in terms of their "educational and social backgrounds, how old they are, what kind of work they do, and whether they are, on the whole, liberal or conservative about religion, sex and politics" (Hairston, 1978, pp. 107–108, qtd in Reiff, 2004, p. 17). This approach to audience was essentially demographic, the assumption being that if a writer understood the external characteristics of an audience, such as education, occupation, or religious belief, he or she would be able to persuade that audience more effectively. Similar to Aristotle's perspective, this concept of audience presumes that the audience consists of real people whose ideas and values can be known and understood by a writer.

Cognitive Perspectives

The cognitive perspective on audience, building on the work of cognitive theorists such as Jean Piaget (*The Language and Thought of the Child*, 1926/1959) and Lev Vygotsky (*Thought and Language*, 1934/1962), viewed the ability to understand audience as a mark of cognitive maturity. They maintained that a writer's ability to consider the ideas and views of others—that is, to move beyond the egocentricity of early childhood—reflected a more developed form of thinking. Piaget's work discussed various stages in cognitive development, showing that younger children are less able to consider a listener's point of view than older ones, and in a related approach, Vygotsky used the term "inner speech" to refer to the uncontextualized transformation of thought into language. Vygotsky contrasted the difference between an audience for speech with the audience for writing, noting that the task of writing for an unknown abstract audience is a more complex task than that of a speaker addressing listeners who are physically present. Vygotsky's concept of "inner speech" influenced the work of Linda Flower, whose cognitive perspective on writing was very important in the late 1970s and 1980s. In "Writer-Based Prose: A Cognitive Basis for Problems in Writing" (1979), Flower used the term "egocentric or writer-based prose" to characterize writing that does not consider audience, and "reader-based" prose to characterize writing that does. Writer-based prose often omits contextual information or elaboration that an audience would need or includes information that an audience would not be able to understand without further explanation.

The idea of writer- versus reader-based prose is a useful one to address in the writing class because it helps students understand that the first drafts of all writers, even experienced and accomplished writers, may be characterized by writer-based prose. First drafts often contain initial thoughts about a topic, and it is only when the draft has been written that a writer may be able to consider the needs of an audience and add necessary explanation, elaboration, or examples. In fact, Peter Elbow (1987), in "Closing My Eyes as I Speak: An Argument for Ignoring Audience," maintained that first drafts *should ignore* audience altogether. This "weak writing," Elbow argued, "can help us in the end to better writing than we would have written if we'd kept readers in mind from the start" (p. 50). Some audiences may be inviting or enabling; others may be inhibiting. If writers are too aware of such an audience, they may experience writer's block. Therefore, it can be liberating for writers to forget about audience altogether during the writing of a first draft.

For Writing and Discussion

1. How do you consider audience in your own writing?
2. Classical rhetoricians conceived of audience in terms of oral discourse, a model that has only limited applicability to the concept of audience in the composition class. List as many differences as you can think of between an audience that "hears" a speech and an audience that "reads" an essay.
3. How can the concept of audience help a writer explore a topic?
4. How does your concept of audience change when you post on a blog or contribute to an online discussion?

THE FICTIONALIZED AUDIENCE

An important perspective on audience that is sometimes more difficult for students to understand is that although an audience may exist outside of a text in the form of actual readers or listeners, an author also *creates* an audience and provides cues within a text about who that audience might be. This idea is the basis of a widely anthologized essay, "The Writer's Audience is Always a Fiction" (1975), in which Walter Ong maintained that "the historian, the scholar or scientist, and the simple letter writer all fictionalize their audiences, casting them in a made-up role and calling on them to play the role assigned" (p. 17). Claiming that all writers, even student writers, must fictionalize their audience, Ong illustrated his point by citing the following passage from *A Farewell to Arms*:

> In the late summer of that year we lived in a house in a village that looked across the river and the plain to the mountains. (p. 15)

This passage, Ong pointed out, fictionalizes a reader who is close to the writer, close enough to know which year is meant by "that" year, which river, which plain, and which mountains, thereby fostering a "you and me" relationship between writer and reader that the writer develops and the reader reacts to when he or she "reads" the text. All authors, Ong claimed, fictionalize their audience, even Homer, who constructed his audience through a "once upon a time" framework. Ong's main position is that student writers will be more successful if they, too, can learn to fictionalize their audiences.

How can a student envision an audience when he or she is assigned to write an essay for a class? Ong suggested that to develop awareness of audience for a particular writing task, student writers should not begin with the traditional question "Who *is* my audience?" but, rather, with the question "Who do I *choose* as my audience?" This question, of course, becomes more complicated when students are posting texts over the Internet.

Ong's view of audience as being created by the writer has been supported by a number of scholars, among them, Douglas Park (1982), who noted in his essay "The Meanings of

Audience" that even when an audience really exists outside of the text, the argumentative context or situation requires the writer to "invent" an audience that goes beyond a specific individual to encompass a set of attitudes toward or acquaintance with the subject. Park cited the example of an article concerned with how to plant asparagus root, which postulates an audience as an enthusiastic "home gardener, eager for hard work and fresh vegetables" (p. 249). Park also noted that even when the audience seems to be a particular person who really exists, the President of the United States, for example, the audience is not only the president as an individual that the text addresses but also the president in his presidential position, someone who represents a set of attitudes toward the subject. Writing a request to the President, thus, involves an act of imagination beyond that of simply knowing that particular president's attitudes and political position. The writer must also use the text to "create" a president that under the right circumstances will be receptive to the request, a president who is concerned about the subject, and a president who is open to new suggestions. Were the president not perceived as receptive, concerned, and open, there would be no rhetorical aim in writing to him. But once the writer conceives of these qualities, he or she must then address that conception of the president by indicating through cues in the text that the audience is perceived in this way. Thus, regardless of whether a real reader exists, most writing tasks, and particularly argumentative or persuasive writing, require the writer to create a fictionalized audience that embodies "a complex set of conventions, estimations, implied responses, and attitudes" (Park, 1982, p. 251).

Audience Addressed/Audience Invoked: Fictionalized and Real Audiences

The idea that audience can be both real and imagined was clarified and elaborated on in an award-winning article published in 1984 titled "Audience Addressed/Audience Invoked: The Role of Audience in Composition Theory and Pedagogy," by Lisa Ede and Andrea Lunsford. Distinguishing between what they term the "audience addressed" and the "audience invoked," Ede and Lunsford maintained that writers must both analyze a possible real audience and invent a chosen one, that the two are not incompatible, and that the concept of audience encompasses a synthesis of both:

> The addressed audience, the actual or intended readers of a discourse, exists outside of the text. Writers may analyze these readers' needs, anticipate their biases, even defer to their wishes. But it is only through the text, through language, that writers embody or give life to their conception of the reader. In so doing, they do not so much create a role for the reader—a phrase which implies that the writer somehow creates a mold to which the reader adjusts—as invoke it. (p. 169)

Citing the example of a student who wishes to persuade her neighbors that a proposed home for mentally retarded adults would not be a disaster for the neighborhood, Ede and Lunsford pointed out that the student must not only analyze the real audience—that is, not only know demographic factors such as age, race, and class—but also assess how much the real audience actually knows about mental retardation, in particular, what fears the subject might raise and what values might be used in making an appeal to change the audience's beliefs or attitudes. But beyond learning as much as possible about the real audience and tailoring the text to suit the needs of that real audience, the student might also invite that audience to see itself in an especially admirable light, that is, to *create* a role for that audience as enlightened and humanitarian; an audience who would be inclined to behave charitably once it was properly informed. Ede and Lunsford also pointed out that writers play the additionally creative roles as the readers of their own writing, testing the effectiveness of the cues within the text during rereading. They maintained that "it is the writer who, as writer and reader of his or her own text, one guided by a sense of purpose and by the particularities of a specific rhetorical situation, establishes the range of potential roles an audience may play" (Ede & Lunsford, 1984, p. 166).

This dual concept of real and created audience was further problematized by Barbara Tomlinson (1990), in "Ong May Be Wrong: Negotiating with Non-fictional Readers." Tomlinson agreed that writers must both address actual readers as well as invoke fuller representations of audiences, but she emphasized that writers must first consider real readers on whom we depend for esteem and approval. "It is only because we have those idiosyncratic, individual readers that we can ever learn to generalize about readers, to fictionalize our audiences effectively," Tomlinson observed. "These are the readers we learn to generalize from" (p. 88). This idea that the fictionalized audience derives from one that a writer has had acquaintance with was supported by Jack Selzer (2000), who noted that "like the intended reader ... and like other fictional characters, narratees and implied readers can be based on real people, can be idealizations of real people, or can be pure creations" (p. 78). More concrete is the term "informed reader," suggested by Stanley Fish (1980), denoting "neither an abstraction nor an actual living reader but a hybrid—a real reader (me) who does everything within his power to make himself informed" (p. 49). The informed reader is both the communal reader of the discourse community and an individual real reader who is actively engaged in understanding the text.

Recent Articles by Ede and Lunsford on the Topic of Audience

Ede and Lunsford followed up their seminal article "Audience Addressed, Audience Invoked: The Role of Audience in Composition Theory and Pedagogy" (1984) with two additional articles published in 1996 and 2009. The 1996 article, "Representing Audience: 'Successful' Discourse and Disciplinary Critique," reflected on the original article, reaffirming the importance of considering audience in the context of the rhetorical situation. However, it also noted that the original article privileged the tradition of individualism inherent in classical rhetoric and ignored potential tensions between the audience addressed and the audience invoked when a power imbalance exists between the two, which is certainly the case when a student writes to a teacher. Classrooms are permeated with ideologies that construct both writers and readers, Lunsford and Ede argued, inhibiting the range of possibilities for assuming a writer identity and invoking potential readers. "Teachers and students are ... not free individual agents writing their own destinies but rather constructed subjects embedded in multiple discourses, and the classroom is not a magic circle free of ideological and institutional influence" (Lunsford & Ede, 1996, p. 172).

In their 2009 article, "Among the Audience: On Audience in an Age of New Literacies," Lunsford and Ede questioned what relevance the term "audience" might have in "a world of participatory media" (p. 43) and the extent to which the invoked and addressed audiences discussed in the "1984 essay need to be revised and expanded" (p. 44). The article reaffirmed the importance of the term "audience," but acknowledged the need for a more flexible and complex perspective. "In a digital world … speakers and audiences communicate in multiple ways and across multiple channels, often reciprocally" (p. 48). Anyone and everyone can be both an author and an audience, and the concepts of audience and collaboration will merge, particularly in blogs and interactive sites such as Wikipedia. The most significant changes, the article suggested, will be reflected in new approaches to intellectual property and common knowledge:

> If you go to the Web with a question and get thousands of "hits" in answer to it … shouldn't that answer be considered as common knowledge that doesn't need to be cited? And even if we answer "no" to that question, which one of the thousands of sources should be the one to be cited? (p. 62)

STUDENT PERSPECTIVES ON AUDIENCE

Writing teachers frequently encourage students to consider their intended audience and sometimes they specify a particular audience such as a congressperson, a principal, or the director of a particular organization. Students, however, understand the concept quite simply: the audience is the teacher who will evaluate their work and assign a grade. Indeed, teachers do read their students' essays, acting as a type of audience that exists in no other rhetorical context. School-based writing constructs a reader–writer relationship that is unlike any communication in the real world because as Reid and Kroll (1995) have noted, its purpose "is not to inform, persuade, or entertain the teacher—it is to demonstrate understanding of the assignment in ways that the teacher-reader already anticipates" (p. 18). The type of relationship that exists in a school setting, is thus unlike any other:

> Instead of an expert-to-expert relationship or a colleague-to-colleague relationship between the writer and the reader (as in "real" writing–reading events), the relationship is skewed: novice-to-expert (teacher-reader) assessing the novice (student-writer) in ways that have consequences for the writer's life. (p. 18)

Academic writing tasks are tests and students understand this. They ask themselves, "what does the teacher want?" and they view their audience as the person who wields the corrective pen and assigns the grade.

College writing assignments, however, are not intended to teach students to write directly to their teacher. Rather, their goal is to enable students to construct discourse for a wider academic audience and to master the text genres that such audiences expect. Therefore, although the teacher is a significant actual reader, he or she serves as a *representative* of the audience toward which the writing is oriented. Before the Internet enabled students to write for a wider audience, college writing assignments required students to "pretend" that they were writing for a more encompassing, general audience and to address their discourse toward that audience even though the only "reader" of the discourse was usually the teacher.

Actually, as Paretti (2009) pointed out, "the teacher is always the wrong audience with the wrong needs and the wrong goals:

> For example, a letter to the editor submitted only to a composition instructor for a grade would be "inauthentic" because the stated purpose (to express one's views to a newspaper audience) and the actual purpose (to have one's writing ability evaluated) do not match. (p. 173)

Moreover, no matter what audience they are supposed to be writing for, students know "that they are always writing for the teacher, and that the teacher who is grading them has expectations, standards, and preferences that may or may not overlap with those they will find elsewhere" (p. 176).

If students think of audience solely in terms of their teacher, the nature of the discourse instantly changes. Sometimes, students may omit necessary explanations, definitions, or support, because they assume, quite reasonably, that the teacher is already familiar with the topic and, therefore, does not need such information. In fact, in some instances, students may actually address the teacher directly, almost as if they were writing personal letters instead of formal essays. One of my students, for example, began his paper as follows:

> My paper is about how the traditional family will not be a workable social entity in the twenty-first century. When we discussed Stephanie Coontz's book in class, it showed that the idea of the ideal traditional family is only a myth.

Other problems associated with students' obliviousness to audience are the assumption of an inappropriate tone or, when students write about controversial topics, the presentation of only one side of an issue. Seemingly insensible to the rhetorical goals of college writing, students may write blatantly opinionated, aggressive, or poorly reasoned diatribes on the topic, rather than an appropriately thoughtful, reasoned response. They don't seem to realize that an outrageous or insulting statement such as "Anyone who believes this is just a racist," or "Women are naturally inferior to men," might have a negative, rather than a persuasive, effect on a reader. Of course, if a student wrote a blatantly offensive statement on a blog, the outraged responses of the wider audience would immediately indicate its effect.

Actually, as Joseph Harris has observed in *Rewriting: How to Do Things With Texts* (2006), although writing is often depicted as a conversation, "academic writing is almost always intended to persuade a third reader" (p. 36):

> One scholar will criticize the work of another less in the hope of having her rival recant than in persuading other readers to see the good sense of her (rather than his) views. Even an indignant author writing to protest a wrong-headed review of his latest book addresses his letter "To the Editor." (p. 36)

Understanding the role of audience in the production of discourse, then, means that students need to choose a discoursal role that is appropriate for the intended audience and to anticipate as much as possible who might be interested in that discourse. A posting on a classroom blog will be read by students in that class; but it is also possible that others beyond the class will read it as well. The potential of new media to expand the audience has the advantage of involving students in a wider community, but it also makes it impossible for them to envision an audience with the same precision one might have had in the past. Nevertheless, in the context of academic writing, one can imagine a *range* of possible readers and construct a text with that range in mind.

CONNECTIONS BETWEEN THE WRITER AND THE AUDIENCE

The 2009 article by Lunsford and Ede emphasized the increased interactivity and collaborative interaction between writer and audience with the use of new media. However, although we may not have been as aware of it, such interactivity and involvement have always charac-terized the writer–audience relationship. Writers and audiences have always been dynami-cally linked, working cooperatively to make meaning; the writer creates an audience within the text during composing and readers recreate that text when they read it. Peter Elbow, in *Writing with Power* (1981), suggested that we picture readers and writers as two riders on the same bicycle. As writers, we can steer, but the readers have to pedal. If we don't explain where we are going and why, and convince our readers that they should keep pedaling, the bicycle will stop and both will tumble off. This is still the case, whether we are reading online or perusing a dusty tome in a library.

This interactive relationship between writers and readers was described by George Dillon (1981) through a metaphor of musical notation. He noted that:

> The written marks on the page more resemble a musical score than a computer program: they are marks cueing or prompting an enactment or realization by the reader, rather than a code requiring deciphering. (p. xi)

Other models of composing depicting this interactivity included one that was developed by James Kinneavy (1971), who, in *A Theory of Discourse*, constructed a dynamic model of communication between the writer, topic, and audience interacting dynamically with one another and Wayne Booth's concept of the rhetorical triangle. Booth (1963) maintained that audience exerts a formative influence on the text, because whether one emphasizes the writer, subject, or audience determines one's "rhetorical stance," which Booth defined as follows:

> What makes the differences between effective communication and mere wasted effort … is something I shall call the rhetorical stance, a stance which depends on discovering and main-taining in any writing situation a proper balance among the three elements that are at work in any communicative effort, the available arguments about the subject itself, the interests and peculiarities of the audience, and the voice, the implied character, of the speaker. (pp. 139–145)

For Writing and Discussion

Which metaphor depicting the relationship between writer and audience do you feel is most useful? Write a paragraph indicating which one you prefer, considering how this model can be helpful to novice writers. Are these metaphors pertinent to writing with new media?

The Work of James Moffett

James Moffett's *Teaching the Universe of Discourse* (1968) presented a view of audience based on an interrelationship between the writer, subject, and reader. According to Moffett, com-munication involves two relationships: how the writer views the subject, which he calls the "I–it" relation, and how the writer views the reader, which he calls the "I–you" relation. Moffett characterizes the "I–it" relationship as a continuum between reporting an event at the time it occurs and generalizing about that event at a more distant time. This continuum between the concrete and the abstract "indicate when events occurred in relation to when the speaker is speaking about them" (p. 244) and the main points along this continuum are conceived of in terms of four levels of increasing abstraction:

What is happening?
What happened?
What happens?
What may happen?

To give an example, suppose you were standing in the post office with a friend, commenting on how long the lines were. As you observed the lines, you would not be very distant from your subject matter—that is, the experience of standing in the line. Later on, you might recall those lines in narrative form to another friend, a process that would require you to select and incorporate details of the experience from memory. Still later, recalling those lines, you might write a report in expository form about the line at the post office, a process that would involve further generalization and abstraction, and then, months or years later, you might use that experience of waiting in line and other experiences occurring since then to argue a position about those long lines, a process that would involve still greater abstraction and generalization.

In terms of the "I-you" relation, Moffett defines degrees of distance not between the writer and the subject, but, rather, between the writer and the audience. Students might begin by writing for themselves and then move beyond to write for increasingly abstract audiences, from the known to the unknown. Moffett maintains that an effective writing curriculum would enable students to write about "what is happening" for a variety of audiences, from recreating an experience for oneself, to narrating the experience to a close friend, to writing formally about the experience for a public audience whom the writer does not know. Moffett's curriculum, then, is based on a "universe of discourse," which moves the student from concrete experience to abstract idea, and from the self to the world. The teacher's role within this universe is to construct writing assignments that enable students to move in this progression and to gain consciousness of how different audiences require different conceptual and textual strategies.

For Writing and Discussion

Moffett's *Teaching the Universe of Discourse* was published in 1968. To what extent is his concept of the I–you and I–it relationships relevant to working in new media?

USING FICTIONAL CHARACTERS AND DIALOGUE TO FOCUS STUDENT ATTENTION ON THE CONCEPT OF AUDIENCE

A classroom strategy that is useful in helping students gain awareness of audience involves having students create a fictional character who is likely to have a strong position on the topic they are writing about. Students try to understand that character's opinion on the topic, and they then write a hypothetical dialogue between this character and themselves in which they discuss the issue for the paper. Having students create a fictional audience and engage in a dialogue with that audience not only makes the class interesting and lively as students share their creations but it also fosters several important insights associated with audience, in particular:

1. It helps students understand that the teacher is not the only audience for an assigned essay.
2. It serves as a heuristic to generate ideas.
3. Because it fosters respect for an audience's humanity and opinions, it helps students understand that an essay is not simply a vehicle for the writer to express his or her own ideas, but, rather, that its goal is for the writer to engage in a cooperative activity with the reader. In this context, rhetoric is conceived of as inherently social.
4. It enables students to distinguish when it is appropriate to confront an opponent directly and when it is appropriate to strive for change through mutual acceptance and understanding by each party of the other's views.
5. It helps students determine which cues in their own text are likely to be effective in addressing their created audience.

When students create their characters and attempt to imitate these characters' voices in writing, they gain a more immediate sense of their potential audience and a greater insight into the audience's beliefs, attitudes, and values. Such understanding enables students to become sensitive to when such an audience would experience a sense of threat and anticipate potential areas of conflict. It also helps students understand the complexity of the issues involved. Working with dialogue also has the advantage of tapping into students' skills at speaking and listening, which are often better developed than their writing skills. Students can, thus, use their knowledge of what is appropriate in oral discourse to detect what may be inappropriate in their writing. The inappropriateness of statements such as "this idea is just ridiculous" or "that idea is just crazy" or "anyone who believes that is just a racist" is more easily discerned if students imagine themselves actually saying them to real people; they are better able to gauge the effect of extreme statements on the persuasiveness of their papers. The term "audience," then, becomes something real for them, not just an abstract concept.

The following section includes an exercise based on the idea of fictionalizing an audience. I suggest that you work through this exercise yourself and also adapt it for your students.

Creating Characters

Although new media greatly expands and complicates the concept of audience, the creation of specific, potentially recognizable characters can help students gain an understanding of how audience shapes discourse. To use this strategy, imagine that you are at a gathering (e.g., a party, dinner, or meeting) where the subject of your assignment is being discussed. You listen to the conversation for a while and then notice someone who has a particularly strong opinion about it. Study this character and pay close attention to what he or she is saying. Try to gain insight into his or her values and ideas and to understand the feelings behind the words. Then answer the following questions:

1. What is this person's name, age, and profession? Describe this person's physical appearance.

2. What is this person's current attitude toward this topic?
3. How much does this person know about the topic?
4. Describe this person's value system.
5. How does this person's value system influence his or her attitude toward the topic?
6. What aspect of the topic does this character find most important?
7. What aspect of the topic does this character find most disturbing?

Writing a Dialogue

To utilize dialogue in the exploration of a topic, recall the character you created through the above "character prompts." Then, assume that after listening to the character you have imagined, you decide to enter the discussion and engage in a dialogue with him or her. Script this exchange in a dialogue of one to two pages, remembering that both participants should be presented as polite and intelligent people. In this interchange, no one should make outrageous or insulting statements and no one should win. The aim is to generate an exchange of ideas, not to score points over an adversary.

For Writing and Discussion

The following assignment will enable you to practice creating characters and writing dialogues as a means of focusing attention on audience.

The Controversy Over School Uniforms

At Madison High School, located in a large American city, Principal Martin Blair has drafted a memo to the Board of Education arguing in favor of requiring all students to wear school uniforms beginning next year. Principal Blair is concerned primarily with the issue of safety, and he feels that the uniform requirement will protect children from attacks by gang members. He also believes that requiring all students to dress alike will focus their attention on their studies, rather than on their clothes. The President of the Parent–Teachers Association, Beverly Woodson, however, opposes the uniform requirement and thinks that whether a child wears a uniform to a public school should be the parents' and even the children's choice. President Woodson feels that schools should not be allowed to dictate personal decisions regarding clothing and that the imposition of such a requirement would stifle children's creativity.

How do you (or your students) feel about the issue of school uniforms? Were you (or your students) required to wear a uniform in school? If so, how did you (or they) feel about it? Do you perhaps have children of your own who are required to wear a uniform to school? If so, are you in favor of such a policy? If not, do you wish they had such a requirement?

Choose a position in this controversy and write a dialogue between yourself and either Principal Blair or President Woodson discussing this issue.

Other possibilities: start a blog on the topic of school uniforms or locate one on the Internet and summarize the discussion.

MULTIPLE CONCEPTS OF AUDIENCE IN THE CONTEXT OF NEW MEDIA

Recent scholarship concerned with audience, such as the 2009 article by Lunsford and Ede, recognizes that the concept has become more complex in the context of new media. But even before the widespread use of technology, the concept was considered more complicated than students realize. Peter Elbow (1987) observed that "there are many different entities called audience" (p. 50), among them actual readers of the text, the writer's conception of those readers (which may or may not be accurate), and the audience that the genre of the text implies, to name a few. Barry Kroll (1984), in "Writing for Readers: Three Perspectives on Audience," examined three types of audience: the rhetorical, the informational, and the social. The rhetorical, which Kroll maintained is the traditional view of many composition textbooks, is addressed to a speaker whom one wants to persuade, a process that means finding out as much as possible about this particular audience. Kroll noted a number of problems with this approach to audience: that students will then see all discourse as antagonistic, encouraging them to become overly strident and ultimately unpersuasive, that the belief in a completely knowable audience is simplistic, and that this model encompasses only a limited account of the relationship between writer and reader.

Kroll's second perspective conceived of audience "as a process of conveying information, a process in which the writer's goal is to transmit, as effectively as possible, a message to the reader" (p. 176). However, this perspective is also limited in that it doesn't acknowledge the role of the reader in constructing the text. As Kroll phrases it, "filling a reader's head with information is not nearly as simple as filling a glass of water" (p. 176). Writing is not simply encoding, nor is reading simply decoding.

Kroll's third perspective conceived of writing as social interaction, a view that emphasizes the importance of peer response and cooperative learning. The social perspective suggests that:

> novice writers need to experience the satisfactions and conflicts of reader response—both the satisfaction that comes from having successfully shaped the reader's understanding and experience, and the conflict that arises when a concept that seemed clear to the writer baffles the reader, when a phrase which held special meaning for the writer evokes no response, or when an omitted detail—clear enough in the writer's mind—causes the reader to stumble. (p. 181)

This emphasis on writing as social interaction is made apparent when students write for one another in a classroom chat room such as Moodle and is greatly expanded when students post ideas on a blog.

In terms of classroom pedagogy, a particularly useful means of categorizing different types of writer–audience relationship was presented by Ryder, Vander Lei, and Roen (1999), who based their distinction on whether a writer is writing solely for oneself, for an actual person or persons, or for a third party. These distinctions were explained as follows:

> The student who writes to express herself might imagine that she is in a monadic writing situation. She is both the writer and the audience; no one else need be involved. A second writing/speaking situation is dyadic. Such cases, where the writer/speaker is addressing a particular person, are often seen as the most important kinds of persuasion because of the relationship between the author/speaker and reader/listener. ... A third option is a triadic situation. Here, the author/speaker is one of two opponents before an audience. We see this happen during

public debates, when two candidates spar before a crowd. The two are not trying to persuade each other; rather, each is trying to persuade the audience, the third party. (p. 55)

Ryder, Vander Lei, and Roen claimed that the triadic situation is the one that is most suited to college writing assignments, and that it is, therefore, important for teachers to articulate their expectations in their assignments, because students will otherwise assume a dyadic relationship between student and teacher. Persuasive topics, they suggest, forefront the importance of audience and lend themselves to audience analysis more effectively than other types of writing assignments.

AUDIENCE AND THE EXPANDED DISCOURSE COMMUNITY

Another perspective on how writers and audience interact with one another can be obtained through the concept of discourse community. Discourse communities consist of members who share language, values, generic conventions, and a set of expectations of the requirements for an effective text. Lawyers, English teachers, and doctors all belong to different discourse communities and each adheres to different ideas about how a text should be written. Thus, if a student wishes to become an attorney, he or she will have to learn how to write and "sound" like an attorney. Otherwise, that person will always be perceived as an outsider, and his or her opinion will not be considered credible. Bennet Rafoth (1988) suggested that the term "discourse community" may be more helpful for students because it is more encompassing than the term "audience." Rafoth noted that "discourse community" more effectively captures:

> the language phenomena that relate writers, readers, and texts. Whereas the audience metaphor tends naturally to represent readers or listeners as primary, and to admit writers and texts only as derivatives, discourse community admits writers, readers and texts all together. Instead of forcing the question "Who is the audience for this writer or this text" … discourse community directs attention to the contexts that give rise to a text, including the range of conventions that govern different kinds of writing. (p. 132)

For Writing and Discussion

Do you prefer the term "discourse community" to "audience"? Why or why not? Which term do you think would be most helpful for students?

DISTINGUISHING BETWEEN NEW AND COMMON KNOWLEDGE: COMPLICATIONS

The term "discourse community" can provide insight into purpose, genre, language, and convention, and this remains true, even if the text appears online. However, when students write essays for college classes, especially when they are in their first year, they are unlikely to be actual members of the discourse communities for which they are writing, and, in fact, must try or even *pretend* to be so, doing the best they can to imagine a discourse community and fictionalizing their own insider status within it. This problem becomes particularly apparent when students must decide what information they should include in a text as "new" knowledge, as opposed to what can be omitted because it is assumed to be "common knowledge." This distinction is confusing not only because students are not true members of the academic discourse communities for which they are writing, and are therefore unfamiliar with what members of that community are likely to know or need to know, but also because they are frequently given ambiguous advice. They are told to omit what might be considered "shared" or "common" knowledge, yet the knowledge that students "share" is changing on a daily basis. Two weeks ago, for example, students may not have heard of the term "discourse community," but now they are supposed to write as if the term is quite familiar to them and does not need explanation. Moreover, in terms of shared knowledge, students are often told "not to assume that the reader knows what the writer is talking about," but also "not to tell the reader what he or she already knows." Of course, this confusion becomes compounded when students utilize new media.

Students' inability to distinguish between shared and new knowledge within a discourse community may be manifested in an opening line such as "Shakespeare was a well-known English playwright" or "Abraham Lincoln was the President of the United States during the Civil War"—information that members of an English-speaking academic discourse community would be expected to know. But this issue is difficult to address in terms of a fail-safe classroom strategy or maxim, because we learn to interact in any community only by observing the conventions of discourse within that group over a long period of time.

FOSTERING AUDIENCE AWARENESS IN THE WRITING CLASS

To help students develop greater audience awareness, composition instructors have used a variety of consciousness-raising approaches for the classroom. One approach involves focusing student attention on the audience in assigned readings, the assumption being that when students examine how experienced writers consider their audience, they will then be able to apply their insights to their own writing. Usually, though, this hoped-for carryover rarely happens when students write their own essays. A slightly more successful approach has been to provide students with broad demographic characteristics of a specified audience, a strategy that has been criticized, not only because it encourages stereotypes but also because it is questionable whether students gain sufficient insight into a potential audience when information is simply fed to them in the form of lists or facts. Finally, some instructors require students to write to "real" audiences, people who actually exist—such as the school principal or the president of the United States, for example. This approach will sometimes result in writing that is, indeed, directed to a specific audience. Its limitation is that it does not foster student awareness of audience as a generic construct—that is, it does not enable students to understand that the projection of an audience pertains to all writing tasks, regardless of whether the writer can define a so-called "real" one. The other limit of this approach is that it gives students the impression that the "audience" always exists independently of the text, the "sender-to-recipient model." Students, therefore, gain little insight into the role that envisioned audiences play in generating text and in determining the role of the writer within that text.

My recommendation is that whatever strategies a teacher may try, a focus on audience is most useful during revision (and before students send their texts out into Cyberspace). A study by Roen and Willey conducted in 1988 indicated that it is during revision that attention to audience can most contribute to the quality of a text. In that study, 60 students were randomly assigned to one of three treatment conditions: no attention to audience, attention to audience before and during drafting, and attention to audience before and during revision. The treatment consisted of four questions:

1. Make a list of things your readers most likely already know.
2. List what they don't know and most likely need to know.
3. Explain how you decided what the audience's prior knowledge or lack of prior knowledge was about the topic.
4. Consider responses to 1, 2, and 3. How will you adapt your essay to accommodate readers?

The results of this study indicated that the essays for which students addressed audience before and during revision were rated the highest, suggesting that an audience analysis guide sheet can be an effective intervention tool for student writers. The worksheet that follows can be used for this purpose, even when students are using new media.

Audience Analysis Sheet

1. Who is my audience? Who do I want my audience to be? What knowledge about the subject does my audience already have?
2. What does my audience think, believe, or understand about this topic before he or she reads my essay?
3. What do I want my audience to think, believe, or understand about this topic after he or she reads my essay?
4. How do I want my audience to think of me? What role do I want to play in addressing my audience?

Invoking Audience Cues in a Text

In the composition class, examining texts for audience-based cues can help students understand the concept more fully, whether the text is in print or electronic. Obviously, in a text written only for oneself, as in a diary or list, no audience cues need be provided. If the writer is writing for a specific person or organization, such as NOW or the Audubon Society, he or she can signal those readers directly about which position they are expected to take. Ryder, Vander Lei, and Roen (1999) refer to these cues as "naming moves," which "involve particular pronouns, such as you/your or we/our" (p. 57). They also name those groups their readers belong to, using phrases such as "those of us at MADD," or refer to positions that their readers are likely to hold, such as "those of us who care about preserving wildlife." "Naming moves" specify an intended audience, enabling other audiences to realize that the text was not intended for them and to situate themselves in relation to the writer and the intended audience.

Another cueing device concerns how much background information or context to include or exclude. This is an aspect of writing with which students often have considerable difficulty if they are under the impression that they are writing solely for their teacher, causing them to omit necessary information or explanation. How much background information should be included in a college essay? When students ask me whether they should include contextual information in their essays, I tell them that if it is a print essay, they should pretend that they have left their essay on a table in the college library where it can be read by any student who happens to find it. If they have explained and supported their ideas adequately and have included sufficient background and context for the topic, an intelligent student who comes upon the essay would be able to understand its central point, even if he or she were not thoroughly familiar with the topic or the assignment. If the student is posting online, similar contextual information would have to be included, depending on the genre. A blog, for example, would contain necessary introductory material, and the thread of the blog would provide additional cues for a reader.

Peer Feedback

Peer feedback is one of the most useful strategies I know of for helping students gain awareness of audience, one that lends itself easily to online exchange of papers through class discussion lists or Moodle. Even if a classroom has no access to computers, students can bring in several copies of their *first* (not rough!) draft and devote class time for peer review. Wherever the peer review workshop takes place, however, it is crucial to distribute a list of specific questions; otherwise, students are likely either to focus on stylistic or grammatical concerns or simply to offer praise (It flows. I can relate to it. It speaks to me). The questions you hand out or post can be tailored to the particular assignment or can be sufficiently general to apply to many different assignments. Ryder, Vander Lei, and Roen (1999) offer the following set of questions to structure a peer response session:

1. I identify with _____ in your writing.
    This is a way for peer readers to tell the writer that they have had a common experience. It is a way of beginning the conversation.
2. I like _____ about your writing.
    A little praise is always reassuring.
3. I have these questions about what you have written.
    This enables the writer to understand what readers need to know that might not be included in the text. Additional information might include additional detail, definition of terms, narration of background, or establishing a context for a controversy.
4. I have these suggestions.
    Suggestions are likely to develop from the questions.

Audience and the Potential of New Media

In an online article dated July 9, 2010 titled "Can the Internet Save the Book?" Andrew Keen discusses the value of using the Internet to help students improve as writers, helping them understand that writing is, in essence, a communicative act:

I'll tell you two things I've done here at NYU with the writing my students do for me. One, I assign them to write for each other. So they think, "My peers are going to read this and also my professor is going to read this." You'd think they'd be more concerned about me reading it, but the quality goes up when they know their friends are going to read it.

The other thing I do, with some of their stuff, is publish it online. I took a whole bunch of papers by my students from a class we did on the effect of the Internet on the 2008 Presidential election, and I just put them in a big folder and put them online. People's reaction to this was: "Oh, I may actually be communicating something; I'd better get it together here." (Keen, 2010)

Audience awareness is a crucial component of learning to write. Helping students understand multiple notions of audience, incorporating the concept of audience into writing assignments, and spending time in class examining audience cues in texts will enable students to write for a broad range of readers in both their educational and professional lives. New media offers wonderful possibilities for enhancing students' understanding of this important concept in composition.

For Writing and Discussion

Read the student essay "PC is Ridiculous!" in Chapter 3. How would attention to audience have improved this essay? Construct a peer review sheet that would generate revision of this essay.

For Writing and Discussion

Respond to Peter Elbow's (1987) essay "Closing My Eyes As I Speak: An Argument for Ignoring Audience." To what extent do you agree with Elbow's position on the role of audience during early stages in the composing process?

For Further Exploration

Harris, J. (2006). *Rewriting: How to do things with words.* Logan, UT: Utah State UP.

    Although not concerned specifically with audience, it examines various "moves" one can make with texts and the functions each aspect of a text fulfills. The writer–audience relationship provides a basis for these various moves.

Kirsch, G., & Roen, D. H. (1990). *A sense of audience in written communication.* Newbury Park, CA: Sage Publications.

    This collection consists of 16 essays on the subject of audience, ten concerned with the history and theory of audience as a rhetorical concern and six discussing empirical studies.

Kroll, B. M. (1984, May). Writing for readers: Three perspectives on audience. *College Composition and Communication, 35,* 172–185.

Kroll presents three conceptions of audience that have influenced composition teaching: the rhetorical, the informational, and the social. The article also raises issues about whether the effectiveness of a text is more fully connected to genre and convention than to social knowledge.

Long, R. C. (1980, May). Writer–audience relationships. *College Composition and Communication, 31,* 221–226.

Long distinguishes readers from audience, noting that audience exists within the text as well as external to it.

Park, D. B. (1982). The meanings of audience. *College English, 44,* 246–257.

Park advocates the importance of the created rather than real audience. The question to ask is not "Who is my audience?" but, rather, "Who do I want my audience to be?"

Porter, J. E. (1992). *Audience and rhetoric: An archeological composition of the discourse community.* Englewood Cliffs, NJ: Prentice Hall.

Porter surveys conceptions of audience from Aristotle through the new rhetoric, discussing a number of theoretical positions that impact audience, such as reader-response criticism and social constructionism. His focus tends to be on social constructionist perspectives in which the audience collaborates with the writer in composing a text.

Reiff, M. J. (2004). *Approaches to audience: An overview of the major perspectives.* Superior, Wisconsin: Parlay Press.

As its title indicates, this book provides an overview of major perspectives on audience: rhetorical, cognitive, textual, contextual, and social constructionist. The book concludes with a chapter that advocates the value of acknowledging multiple audiences.

Shilb, J. (2007). *Rhetorical refusals: Defying audiences' expectations.* Carbondate, IL: Southern Illinois University Press.

This book defines "rhetorical refusal" as an act of speaking or writing in which the rhetor refuses to do what the audience considers rhetorically normal. Analysis of how such refusals function is applied to several case studies.

Weiser, M. E., Fehler, B. M., & Gonzales, A. M. (Eds.). (2009). *Engaging audience: Writing in an age of new literacies.* Urbana, IL: NCTE.

This excellent collection of essays brings together theorists and practitioners to examine the concept of audience from multiple perspectives. It begins with Lisa Ede and Andrea Lunsford's seminal essay, "Audience Addressed, Audience Invoked: The Role of Audience in Composition Theory and Pedagogy," followed by two additional articles by these authors. Subsequent articles draw from a variety of fields: communication, history, professional writing and new media studies, all building on and engaging with the work of Lunsford and Ede.

Wilson, W. D. (1981). Readers in texts. *PMLA, 96,* 848–863.

Wilson isolates three distinct kinds of reading presences: the real reader, the implied reader, and the characterized reader.

REFERENCES

Aristotle. (1991). *Aristotle on rhetoric: A theory of civic discourse.* Ed. & trans. George A. Kennedy. New York: Oxford University Press.

Booth, W. (1963). The rhetorical stance. *College Composition and Communication, 14,* 139–145.

Burke, K. (1973). *The philosophy of literary form* (3rd ed.). Berkeley: University of California Press.

Dillon, G. (1981). *Constructing texts: Elements of a theory of composition and style.* Bloomington, IN: Indiana University Press.

Ede, L., & Lunsford, A. (1984, May). Audience addressed/audience invoked: The role of audience in composition theory and pedagogy. *College Composition and Communication, 35*, 155–171.

Elbow, P. (1981). *Writing with power.* New York: Oxford University Press.

Elbow, P. (1987). Closing my eyes as I speak: An argument for ignoring audience. *College English, 49*, 50–69.

Fish, S. (1980). *Is there a text in this class?* Cambridge, MA: Harvard University Press.

Flower, L. (1979, September). Writer-based prose: A cognitive basis for problems in writing. *College English, 41*, 19–38.

Hairston, M. (1978). *A contemporary rhetoric, 2nd ed.* Boston: Houghton Mifflin.

Harris, J. (2006). *Rewriting: How to do things with texts.* Logan, UT: Utah State University Press.

Keen, A. (2010). Can the Internet save the book? Barnes and Noble Review. www.salon.com/books/feature/2010/07/09/clay_shirky/index.html.

Killingsworth, M. J. (2005). *Appeals in modern rhetoric: An ordinary-language approach.* Carbondale: Southern Illinois University Press.

Kinneavy. J. (1971). *A theory of discourse.* New York: Norton.

Kirsch, G., & Roen, D. H. (1990). *A sense of audience in written communication.* Newbury Park, CA: Sage Publications.

Knobel, M., & Lankshear, C. (Eds.). (2007). *A new literacies sampler.* New York: Peter Lang.

Kroll, B. M. (1984, May). Writing for readers: Three perspectives on audience. *College Composition and Communication, 35*, 172–185.

Lunsford, A., & Ede, L. (1996, May). Representing audience: "Successful" discourse and disciplinary critique. *College Composition and Communication, 47*, 167–179.

Lunsford, A., & Ede, L. (2009). Among the audience: On audience in an age of new literacies. In Weiser, M. E., Fehler, B. M., & Gonzales, A. M. (Eds.), *Engaging audience: Writing in an age of new literacies* (pp. 42–69). Urbana, IL: NCTE.

Moffett, J. (1968). *Teaching the universe of discourse.* New York: Boynton Cook.

Ong, W. (1975). The writer's audience is always a fiction. *PMLA, 90*, 9–21.

Paretti, M. C. (2009). When the teacher is the audience. In Weiser, M. E., Fehler, B. M., & Gonzales, A. M. (Eds.), *Engaging audience: Writing in an age of new literacies* (pp. 165–185). Urbana, IL: NCTE.

Park, D. (1982). The meanings of audience. *College English, 44*, 247–257.

Perelman, C., & Olbrechts-Tyteca, L. (1958/1969). *The new rhetoric: A treatise on argumentation.* Trans. John Wilkinson and Purcell Weaver. Rpt. Notre Dame, IN: University of Notre Dame Press.

Plato. (1952). *Phaedrus.* Trans. A. Hackforth. Indianapolis, IN: Bobs Merrill.

Rafoth, B. (1988). Discourse community: Where writers, readers, and texts come together. In B. Rafoth, & D. Ruden (Eds.), *The social construction of written communication.* Norwood, NJ: Ablex.

Reid, J., & Kroll, B. (1995). Designing and assessing effective classroom writing assignments for NES and ESL students. *Journal of Second Language Writing, 4*, 17–41.

Reiff, M. J. (2004). *Approaches to audience: An overview of the major perspectives.* Superior, Wisconsin: Parlay Press.

Roen, D. H., & Willey, R. J. (1988). The effects of audience awareness on drafting and revising. *Research in the Teaching of English, 22*, 75–88.

Ryder, P. M., Vander Lei, E., & Roen, D. H. (1999). Audience considerations for evaluating writing. In C. R. Cooper & L. Odell (Eds.), *Evaluating writing* (pp. 53–71). Urbana, IL: NCTE.

Selzer, J. (2000). More meanings of audience. In J. C. McDonald (Ed.), *The Allyn and Bacon sourcebook for college writing teachers.* Needham, MA: Pearson.

Tomlinson, B. (1990). Ong may be wrong: Negotiating with non-fictional readers. In G. Kirsch, & D. H. Roen (Eds.), *A sense of audience in written communication* (pp. 85–93). Newbury Park, CA: Sage.

Reading

CLOSING MY EYES AS I SPEAK: AN ARGUMENT FOR IGNORING AUDIENCE

Peter Elbow

> Very often people don't listen to you when you speak to them. It's only when you talk to yourself that they prick up their ears.
>
> John Ashberry

When I am talking to a person or a group and struggling to find words or thoughts, I often find myself involuntarily closing my eyes as I speak. I realize now that this behavior is an instinctive attempt to blot out awareness of audience when I need all my concentration for just trying to figure out or express what I want to say. Because the audience is so imperiously *present* in a speaking situation, my instinct reacts with this active attempt to avoid audience awareness. This behavior—in a sense impolite or anti-social—is not so uncommon. Even when we write, alone in a room to an absent audience, there are occasions when we are struggling to figure something out and need to push aside awareness of those absent readers. As Donald Murray puts it, "My sense of audience is so strong that I have to suppress my conscious awareness of audience to hear what the text demands" (Berkenkotter and Murray 171). In recognition of how pervasive the role of audience is in writing, I write to celebrate the benefits of ignoring audience.[1]

It will be clear that my argument for writing without audience awareness is not meant to undermine the many good reasons for writing *with* audience awareness some of the time. (For example, that we are liable to neglect audience because we write in solitude; that young people often need more practice in taking into account points of view different from their own; and that students often have an impoverished sense of writing as communication because they have only written in a school setting to teachers.) Indeed I would claim some part in these arguments for audience awareness—which now seem to be getting out of hand.

I start with a limited claim: even though ignoring audience will usually lead to weak writing at first—to what Linda Flower calls "writer-based prose," this weak writing can help us in the end to better writing than we would have written if we'd kept readers in mind from the start. Then I will make a more ambitious claim: writer-based prose is sometimes better than reader-based prose. Finally I will explore some of the theory underlying these issues of audience.

A Limited Claim

It's not that writers should never think about their audience. It's a question of when. An audience is a field of force. The closer we come—the more we think about these readers—the stronger the pull they exert on the contents of our minds. The practical question, then, is always whether a particular audience functions as a helpful field of force or one that confuses or inhibits us.

Some audiences, for example, are *inviting* or *enabling*. When we think about them as we write, we think of more and better things to say—and what we think somehow arrives more coherently structured than usual. It's like talking to the perfect listener; we feel smart and come up with ideas we didn't know we had. Such audiences are helpful to keep in mind right from the start.

Other audiences, however, are powerfully *inhibiting*—so much so, in certain cases, that awareness of them as we write blocks writing altogether. There are certain people who always make us feel dumb when we try to speak to them: we can't find words or thoughts. As soon as we get out of their presence, all the things we wanted to say pop back into our minds. Here is a student telling what happens when she tries to follow the traditional advice about audience:

> You know _____ [author of a text] tells us to pay attention to the audience that will be reading our papers, and I gave that a try. I ended up without putting a word on paper until I decided the hell with _____; I'm going to write to who I damn well want to; otherwise I can hardly write at all.

Admittedly, there are some occasions when we benefit from keeping a threatening audience in mind from the start. We've been putting off writing that letter to that person who intimidates us. When we finally sit down and write *to* them—walk right up to them, as it were, and look them in the eye—we may manage to stand up to the threat and grasp the nettle and thereby find just what we need to write.

Most commonly, however, the effect of audience awareness is somewhere between the two extremes: the awareness disturbs or disrupts our writing and thinking without completely blocking it. For example, when we have to write to someone we find intimidating (and of course students often perceive teachers as intimidating), we often start thinking wholly defensively. As we write down each thought or sentence, our mind fills with thoughts of how the intended reader will criticize or object to it. So we try to qualify or soften what we've just written—or write out some answer to a possible objection. Our writing becomes tangled. Sometimes we get so tied in knots that we cannot even figure out what we *think*. We may not realize how often audience awareness has this effect on our students when we don't see the writing processes behind their papers: we just see texts that are either tangled or empty.

Another example. When we have to write to readers with whom we have an awkward relationship, we often start beating around the bush and feeling shy or scared, or start to write in a stilted, overly careful style or voice. (Think about the cute, too-clever style of many memos we get in our departmental mailboxes—the awkward self-consciousness academics experience when writing to other academics.) When students are asked to write to readers they have not met or cannot imagine, such as "the general reader" or "the educated public," they often find nothing to say except cliches they know *they* don't even quite believe.

When we realize that an audience is somehow confusing or inhibiting us, the solution is fairly obvious. We can ignore that audience altogether during the *early* stages of writing and direct our words only to ourselves or to no one in particular—or even to the "wrong" audience, that is, to an *inviting* audience of trusted friends or allies. This strategy often dissipates the confusion; the clenched, defensive discourse starts to run clear. Putting audience out of mind is of course a traditional practice; serious writers have long used private journals for early explorations of feeling, thinking, or language. But many writing teachers seem to think that students can get along without the private writing serious writers find so crucial—or even that students will *benefit* from keeping their audience in mind for the whole time. Things often don't work out that way.

After we have figured out our thinking in copious exploratory or draft writing—perhaps finding the right voice or stance as well—*then* we can follow the traditional rhetorical advice: think about readers and revise carefully to adjust our words and thoughts to our intended audience. For a particular audience it may even turn out that we need to *disguise* our point of view. But it's hard to disguise something while engaged in trying to figure it out. As writers, then, we need to learn when to think about audience and when to put readers out of mind.

Many people are too quick to see Flower's "writer-based prose" as an analysis of what's wrong with this type of writing and miss the substantial degree to which she was celebrating a natural, and indeed developmentally enabling, response to cognitive overload. What she doesn't say, however, despite her emphasis on planning and conscious control in the writing process, is that we can *teach* students to notice when audience awareness is getting in their way—and when this happens, consciously to put aside the needs of readers for a while. She seems to assume that when an overload occurs, the writer-based gear will, as it were, automatically kick into action to relieve it. In truth, of course, writers often persist in using a malfunctioning *reader*-based gear despite the overload thereby mangling their language or thinking. Though Flower likes to rap the knuckles of people who suggest a "correct" or "natural" order for steps in the writing process, she implies such an order here: when attention to audience causes an overload, start out by ignoring them while you attend to your thinking; after you work out your thinking, turn your attention to audience.

Thus if we ignore audience while writing on a topic about which we are not expert or about which our thinking is still evolving, we are likely to produce exploratory writing that is unclear to anyone else—perhaps even inconsistent or a complete mess. Yet by doing this exploratory "swamp work" in conditions of safety, we can often coax our thinking through a process of new discovery and development. In this way we can end up with something better than we could have produced if we'd tried to write to our audience all along. In short, ignoring audience can lead to worse drafts but better revisions. (Because we are professionals and adults, we often write in the role of expert: we may know what we think without new exploratory writing; we may even be able to speak confidently to critical readers. But students seldom experience this confident professional stance in their writing. And think how much richer *our* writing would be if we defined ourselves as *in*expert and allowed ourselves private writing for new explorations of those views we are allegedly sure of.)

Notice then that two pieties of composition theory are often in conflict:

1. Think about audience as you write (this stemming from the classical rhetorical tradition).
2. Use writing for *making new meaning*, not just transmitting old meanings already worked out (this stemming from the newer epistemic traditon I associate with Ann Berthoff's classic explorations).

It's often difficult to work out new meaning while thinking about readers.

A More Ambitious Claim

I go further now and argue that ignoring audience can lead to better writing—immediately. In effect, writer-based prose can be *better* than reader-based prose. This might seem a more controversial claim, but is there a teacher who has not had the experience of struggling and struggling to no avail to help a student untangle his writing, only to discover that the student's casual journal writing or freewriting is untangled and strong? Sometimes freewriting is stronger than the essays we get only because it is expressive, narrative, or descriptive writing and the student was not constrained by a topic. But teachers who collect drafts with completed assignments often see passages of freewriting that are strikingly stronger *even* when they are expository and constrained by the assigned topic. In some of these passages we can sense that the strength derives from the student's unawareness of readers.

It's not just unskilled, tangled writers, though, who sometimes write better by forgetting about readers. Many competent and even professional writers produce mediocre pieces *because* they are thinking too much about how their readers will receive their words. They are acting too much like a salesman trained to look the customer in the eye and to think at all times about the characteristics of the "target audience." There is something too staged or planned or self-aware about such writing. We see this quality in much second-rate newspaper or magazine or business writing: "good-student writing" in the awful sense of the term. Writing produced this way reminds us of the ineffective actor whose consciousness of self distracts us: he makes us too aware of his own awareness of us. When we read such prose, we wish the writer would stop thinking about us—would stop trying to "adjust" or "fit" what he is saying to our frame of reference. "Damn it, put all your attention on what you are saying," we want to say, "and forget about us and how we are reacting."

When we examine really good student or professional writing, we can often see that its goodness comes from the writer's having gotten sufficiently wrapped up in her meaning and her language as to forget all about audience needs: the writer manages to "break through." The Earl of Shaftesbury talked about writers needing to escape their audience in order to find their own ideas (Cooper 1:109; see also Griffin). It is characteristic of much truly good writing to be, as it were, on fire with its meaning. Consciousness of readers is burned away; involvement in subject determines all. Such writing is analogous to the performance of the actor who has managed to stop attracting attention to her awareness of the audience watching her.

The arresting power in some writing by small children comes from their obliviousness to audience. As readers, we are somehow sucked into a more-than-usual connection with the meaning itself because of the child's gift for more-than-usual concentration on what she is saying. In short, we can feel some pieces of children's writing as being very writer-based. Yet it's precisely that quality which makes it powerful for us as readers. After all, why should we settle for a writer's entering our point of view, if we can have the more powerful experience of being sucked out of our point of view and into her world? This is just the experience that children are peculiarly capable of giving because they are so expert at total absorption in their world as they are writing. It's not just a matter of whether the writer "decenters," but of whether the writer has a sufficiently strong focus of attention to make the *reader* decenter. This quality of concentration is what D. H. Lawrence so admires in Melville:

> [Melville] was a real American in that he always felt his audience in front of him. But when he ceases to be American, when he forgets all audience, and gives us his sheer apprehension of the world, then he is wonderful, his book *[Moby Dick]* commands a stillness in the soul, an awe. (158)

What most readers value in really excellent writing is not prose that is right for readers but prose that is right for thinking, right for language, or right for the subject being written about. If, in addition, it is clear and well suited to readers, we appreciate that. Indeed we feel insulted if the writer did not somehow try to make the writing *available* to us before delivering it. But if it succeeds at being really true to language and thinking and "things," we are willing to put up with much difficulty as readers:

> [G]ood writing is not always or necessarily an adaptation to communal norms (in the Fish/Bruffee sense) but may be an attempt to construct (and instruct) a reader capable of reading the text in question. The literary history of the "difficult" work—from Mallarme to Pound, Zukofsky, Olson, etc.—seems to say that much of what we value in writing we've had to learn to value by learning how to read it. (Trimbur)

The effect of audience awareness on *voice* is particularly striking—if paradoxical. Even though we often develop our voice by finally "speaking up" to an audience or "speaking out" to others, and even though much dead student writing comes from students' not really treating their writing as a communication with real readers, nevertheless, the opposite effect is also common: we often do not really develop a strong, authentic voice in our writing till we find important occasions for *ignoring* audience—saying, in effect, "To hell with whether they like it or not. I've got to say this the way *I* want to say it." Admittedly, the voice that emerges when we ignore audience is sometimes odd or idiosyncratic in some way, but usually it is stronger. Indeed, teachers sometimes complain that student writing is "writer-based" when the problem is simply the idiosyncrasy—and sometimes in fact the *power*—of the voice. They would value this odd but resonant voice if they found it in a published writer (see "Real Voice," Elbow, *Writing with Power*). Usually we cannot *trust* a voice unless it is unaware of us and our needs and speaks out in its own terms (see the Ashberry epigraph). To celebrate writer-based prose is to risk the charge of *romanticism*: just warbling one's woodnotes wild. But my position also contains the austere *classic* view that we must nevertheless *revise* with conscious awareness of audience in order to figure out which pieces of writer-based prose are good as they are—and how to discard or revise the rest.

To point out that writer-based prose can be *better* for readers than reader-based prose is to reveal problems in these two terms. Does *writer-based* mean:

1. That the text doesn't work for readers because it is too much oriented to the writer's point of view?
2. Or that the writer was not thinking about readers as she wrote, although the text *may* work for readers?

Does *reader-based* mean:

3. That the text works for readers—meets their needs?
4. Or that the writer was attending to readers as she wrote although her text may *not* work for readers?

In order to do justice to the reality and complexity of what actually happens in both writers and readers, I was going to suggest four terms for the four conditions listed above, but I gradually realized that things are even too complex for that. We really need to ask about what's going on in three dimensions—in the *writer,* in the *reader,* and in the *text*—and realize that the answers can occur in virtually any combination:

— Was the *writer* thinking about readers or oblivious to them?
— Is the *text* oriented toward the writer's frame of reference or point of view, or oriented toward that of readers? (A writer may be thinking about readers and still write a text that is largely oriented towards her own frame of reference.)
— Are the readers' needs being met? (The text may meet the needs of readers whether the writer was thinking about them or not, and whether the text is oriented toward them or not.)

Two Models of Cognitive Development

Some of the current emphasis on audience awareness probably derives from a model of cognitive development that needs to be questioned. According to this model, if you keep your readers in mind as you write, you are operating at a higher level of psychological development than if you ignore readers. Directing words to readers is "more mature" than directing them to no one in particular or to yourself. Flower relates writer-based prose to the inability to "decenter" which is characteristic of Piaget's early stages of development, and she relates reader-based prose to later more mature stages of development.

On the one hand, of course this view must be right. Children do decenter as they develop. As they mature they get better at suiting their discourse to the needs of listeners, particularly to listeners very different from themselves. Especially, they get better at doing so *consciously*—thinking *awarely*—about how things appear to people with different viewpoints. Thus much unskilled writing is unclear or awkward *because* the writer was doing what it is so easy to do—unthinkingly taking her own frame of reference for granted and not attending to the needs of readers who might have a different frame of reference. And of course this failure is more common in younger, immature, "egocentric" students (and also more common in writing than in speaking since we have no audience present when we write).

But on the other hand, we need the contrary model that affirms what is also obvious once we reflect on it, namely that the ability to *turn off* audience awareness—especially when it confuses thinking or blocks discourse—is also a "higher" skill. I am talking about an ability to use language in "the desert island mode," an ability that tends to require learning, growth, and psychological development. Children, and even adults who have not learned the art of quiet, thoughtful, inner reflection, are often unable to get much cognitive action going in their heads unless there are other people present to have action *with*. They are dependent on live audience and the social dimension to get their discourse rolling or to get their thinking off the ground.

For in contrast to a roughly Piagetian model of cognitive development that says we start out as private, egocentric little monads and grow up to be public and social, it is important to invoke the opposite model that derives variously from Vygotsky, Bakhtin, and Meade. According to this model, we *start out* social and plugged into others and only gradually, through learning and development, come to "unplug" to any significant degree so as to function in a more private, individual and differentiated fashion: "Development in thinking is not from the individual to the socialized, but from the social to the individual" (Vygotsky 20). The important general principle in this model is that we tend to *develop* our important cognitive capacities by means of social interaction with others, and having done so we gradually learn to perform them alone. We fold the "simple" back-and-forth of dialogue into the "complexity" (literally, "foldedness") of individual, private reflection.

Where the Piagetian (individual psychology) model calls our attention to the obvious need to learn to enter into viewpoints other than our own, the Vygotskian (social psychology) model calls our attention to the equally important need to learn to produce good thinking and discourse *while alone*. A rich and enfolded mental life is something that people achieve only gradually through growth, learning, and practice. We tend to associate this achievement with the fruits of higher education.

Thus we see plenty of students who lack this skill, who have nothing to say when asked to free-write or to write in a journal. They can dutifully "reply" to a question or a topic, but they cannot seem to *initiate* or *sustain* a train of thought on their own. Because so many adolescent students have this difficulty, many teachers chime in: "Adolescents have nothing to write about. They are too young. They haven't had significant experience." In truth, adolescents don't lack experience or material, no matter how "sheltered" their lives. What they lack is practice and help. Desert island discourse is a learned cognitive process. It's a mistake to think of private writing (journal writing and freewriting) as merely "easy"—merely a relief from trying to write right. It's also hard. Some exercises and strategies that help are Ira Progoff's "Intensive Journal" process, Sondra Perl's "Composing Guidelines," or Elbow's "Loop Writing" and "Open Ended Writing" processes (*Writing with Power* 50–77).

The Piagetian and Vygotskian developmental models (language-begins-as-private vs. language-begins-as-social) give us two different lenses through which to look at a common weakness in student writing, a certain kind of "thin" writing where the thought is insufficiently developed or where the language doesn't really explain what the writing implies or gestures toward. Using the Piagetian model, as Flower does, one can specify the problem as a weakness in audience orientation. Perhaps the writer has immaturely taken too much for granted and unthinkingly assumed that her limited explanations carry as much meaning for readers as they do for herself. The cure or treatment is for the writer to think more about readers.

Through the Vygotskian lens, however, the problem and the "immaturity" look altogether different. Yes, the writing isn't particularly clear or satisfying for readers, but this alternative diagnosis suggests a failure of the private desert island dimension: the writer's explanation is too thin because she didn't work out her train of thought fully enough *for herself*. The suggested cure or treatment is *not* to think more about readers but to think more for herself, to practice exploratory writing in order to learn to engage in that reflective discourse so central to mastery of the writing process. How can she engage readers more till she has engaged herself more?

The current emphasis on audience awareness may be particularly strong now for being fueled by *both* psychological models. From one side, the Piagetians say, in effect, "The egocentric little critters, we've got to *socialize* 'em! Ergo, make them think about audience when they write!" From the other side, the Vygotskians say, in effect, "No wonder they're having trouble writing. They've been bamboozled by the Piagetian heresy. They think they're solitary individuals with private selves when really they're just congeries of voices that derive from their discourse community. Ergo, let's intensify the social context—use peer groups and publication: make them think about audience when they write! (And while we're at it, let's hook them up with a better class of discourse community.)" To advocate ignoring audience is to risk getting caught in the crossfire from two opposed camps.

Two Models of Discourse: Discourse as Communication and Discourse as Poesis or Play

We cannot talk about writing without at least implying a psychological or developmental model. But we'd better make sure it's a complex, paradoxical, or spiral model. Better yet, we should be deft enough to use two contrary models or lenses. (Bruner pictures the developmental process as a complex movement in an upward reiterative spiral—not a simple movement in one direction.)

According to one model, it is characteristic of the youngest children to direct their discourse to an audience. They learn discourse *because* they have an audience; without an audience they remain mute, like "the wild child." Language is social from the start. But we need the other model to show us what is also true, namely that it is characteristic of the youngest children to use language in a *non-social* way. They use language not only because people talk to them but also because they have such a strong propensity to play and to build—often in a *non*-social or non-audience-oriented fashion. Thus although one paradigm for discourse is social communication, another is private exploration or solitary play. Babies and toddlers tend to babble in an exploratory and reflective way—to themselves and not to an audience—often even with no one else near. This archetypally private use of discourse is strikingly illustrated when we see a pair of toddlers in "parallel play" alongside each other—each busily talking but not at all trying to communicate with the other.

Therefore, when we choose paradigms for discourse, we should think not only about children using language to communicate, but also about children building sandcastles or drawing pictures. Though children characteristically show their castles or pictures to others, they just as characteristically trample or crumple them before anyone else can see them. Of course sculptures and pictures are different from words. Yet discourse implies more media than words; and even if you restrict discourse to words, one of our most mature uses of language is for building verbal pictures and structures for their own sake—not just for communicating with others.

Consider this same kind of behavior at the other end of the life cycle: Brahms staggering from his deathbed to his study to rip up a dozen or more completed but unpublished and unheard string quartets that dissatisfied him. How was he relating to audience here—worrying too much about audience or not giving a damn? It's not easy to say. Consider Glenn Gould deciding to renounce performances before an audience. He used his private studio to produce recorded performances for an audience, but to produce ones that satisfied *himself* he clearly needed to suppress audience awareness. Consider the more extreme example of Kerouac typing page after page—burning each as soon as he completed it. The language behavior of humans is slippery. Surely we are well advised to avoid positions that say it is "always X" or "essentially Y."

James Britton makes a powerful argument that the "making" or poesis function of language grows out of the expressive function. Expressive language is often for the sake of communication with an audience, but just as often it is only for the sake of the speaker—working something out for herself (66–67, 74ff). Note also that "writing to learn," which writing-across-the-curriculum programs are discovering to be so important, tends to be writing for the self or even for no one at all rather than for an outside reader. You throw away the writing, often unread, and keep the mental changes it has engendered.

I hope this emphasis on the complexity of the developmental process—the limits of our models and of our understanding of it—will serve as a rebuke to the tendency to label students as being at a lower stage of cognitive development just because they don't yet write well. (Occasionally they *do* write well—in a way—but not in the way that the labeler finds appropriate.) Obviously the psychologistic labeling impulse started out charitably. Shaughnessy was fighting those who called basic writers *stupid* by saying they weren't dumb, just at an earlier developmental stage. Flower was arguing that writer-based prose is a natural response to a cognitive overload and indeed developmentally enabling. But this kind of talk can be dangerous since it labels students as literally "retarded" and makes teachers and administrators start to think of them as such. Instead of calling poor writers *either* dumb or slow (two forms of blaming the victim), why not simply call them poor writers? If years of schooling haven't yet made them good writers, perhaps they haven't gotten the kind of teaching and support they need. Poor students are often deprived of the very thing they need most to write well (which is given to good students): lots of extended and adventuresome writing for self and for audience. Poor students are often asked to write *only* answers to fill-in exercises.

As children get older, the developmental story remains complex or spiral. Though the first model makes us notice that babies start out with a natural gift for using language in a social and communicative fashion, the second model makes us notice that children and adolescents must continually learn to relate their discourse better to an audience—must struggle to decenter better. And though the second model makes us notice that babies also start out with a natural gift for using language in a *private,* exploratory and playful way, the first model makes us notice that children and adolescents must continually learn to master this solitary, desert island, poesis mode better. Thus we mustn't think of language only as communication—nor allow communication to claim dominance either as the earliest or as the most "mature" form of discourse. It's true that language is inherently communicative (and without communication we don't develop language), yet language is just as inherently the stringing together of exploratory discourse for the self—or for the creation of objects (play, poesis, making) for their own sake.

In considering this important poesis function of language, we need not discount (as Berkenkotter does) the striking testimony of so many witnesses who think and care most about language: professional poets, writers, and philosophers. Many of them maintain that their most serious work is *making,* not *communicating,* and that their commitment is to language, reality, logic, experience, not to readers. Only in their willingness to cut loose from the demands or needs of readers, they insist, can they do their best work. Here is William Stafford on this matter:

> I don't want to overstate this … but … my impulse is to say I don't think of an audience at all. When I'm writing, the satisfactions in the process of writing are my satisfactions in dealing with the language, in being surprised by phrasings that occur to me, in finding that this miraculous kind of convergent focus begins to happen. That's my satisfaction, and to think about an audience would be a distraction. I try to keep from thinking about an audience. (Cicotello 176)

And Chomsky:

> I can be using language in the strictest sense with no intention of communicating. … As a graduate student, I spent two years writing a lengthy manuscript, assuming throughout that it would never be published or read by anyone. I meant everything I wrote, intending nothing as to what anyone would [understand], in fact taking it for granted that there would be no audience. … [C]ommunication is only one function of language, and by no means an essential one. (Qtd. in Feldman 5–6.)

It's interesting to see how poets come together with philosophers on this point—and even with mathematicians. All are emphasizing the "poetic" function of language in its literal sense—"poesis" as "making." They describe their writing process as more like "getting something right" or even "solving a problem" for its own sake than as communicating with readers or addressing an audience. The task is not to satisfy readers but to satisfy the rules of the system: "[T]he writer is not thinking of a reader at all; he makes it 'clear' as a contract with *language*" (Goodman 164).

Shall we conclude, then, that solving an equation or working out a piece of symbolic logic is at the opposite end of the spectrum from communicating with readers or addressing an audience? No. To draw that conclusion would be to fall again into a one-sided position. Sometimes people write mathematics *for* an audience, sometimes not. The central point in this essay is that we cannot answer audience questions in an *a priori* fashion based on the "nature" of discourse or of language or of cognition—only in terms of the different *uses* or *purposes* to which humans put discourse, language, or cognition on different occasions. If most people have a restricted repertoire of uses for writing—if most people use writing only to send messages to readers, that's no argument for constricting the *definition* of writing. It's an argument for helping people expand their repertoire of uses.

The value of learning to ignore audience while writing, then, is the value of learning to cultivate the private dimension: the value of writing in order to make meaning to oneself, not just to others. This involves learning to free oneself (to some extent, anyway) from the enormous power exerted by society and others, to unhook oneself from external prompts and social stimuli. We've grown accustomed to theorists and writing teachers puritanically stressing the *problem* of writing: the tendency to neglect the needs of readers because we usually write in solitude. But let's also celebrate this same feature of writing as one of its glories: writing *invites* disengagement too, the inward turn of mind, and the dialogue with self. Though writing is deeply social and though we usually help things by enhancing its social dimension, writing is also the mode of discourse best suited to helping us develop the reflective and private dimension of our mental lives.

"But Wait a Minute, ALL Discourse Is Social"

Some readers who see *all* discourse as social will object to my opposition between public and private writing (the "trap of oppositional thinking") and insist that *there is no such thing as private discourse*. What looks like private, solitary mental work, they would say, is really social. Even on the desert island I am in a crowd.

> [B]y ignoring audience in the conventional sense, we return to it in another sense. What I get from Vygotsky and Bakhtin is the notion that audience is not really out there at all but is in fact "always already" (to use that poststructuralist mannerism ...) inside, interiorized in the conflicting languages of others—parents, former teachers, peers, prospective readers, whomever—that writers have to negotiate to write, and that we do negotiate when we write whether we're aware of it or not. The audience we've got to satisfy in order to feel good about our writing is as much in the past as in the present or future. But we experience it (it's so internalized) as *ourselves*. (Trimbur)

(Ken Bruffee likes to quote from Frost: "'Men work together, ... /Whether they work together or apart'" ["The Tuft of Flowers"]). Or—putting it slightly differently—when I engage in what seems like private non-audience-directed writing, I am really engaged in communication with the "audience of self." For the self is multiple, not single, and discourse to self is communication from one entity to another. As Feldman argues, "The self functions as audience in much the same way that others do" (290).

Suppose I accept this theory that all discourse is really social—including what I've been calling "private writing" or writing I don't intend to show to any reader. Suppose I agree that all language is essentially communication directed toward an audience—whether some past internalized voice or (what may be the same thing) some aspect of the self. What would this theory say to my interest in "private writing"?

The theory would seem to destroy my main argument. It would tell me that there's no such thing as "private writing"; it's impossible *not* to address audience; there are no vacations from audience. But the theory might try to console me by saying not to worry, because we don't *need* vacations from audience. Addressing audience is as easy, natural, and unaware as breathing—and we've been at it since the cradle. Even young, unskilled writers are already expert at addressing audiences.

But if we look closely we can see that in fact this theory doesn't touch my central practical argument. For even if all discourse is naturally addressed to *some* audience, it's not naturally addressed to the *right* audience—the living readers we are actually trying to reach. Indeed the pervasiveness of past audiences in our heads is one more reason for the difficulty of reaching present audiences with our texts. Thus even if I concede the theoretical point, there still remains an enormous practical and phenomenological difference between writing "public" words for others to read and writing "private" words for no one to read.

Even if "private writing" is "deep down" social, the fact remains that, as we engage in it, we don't have to worry about whether it works on readers or even makes sense. We can refrain from doing all the things that audience-awareness advocates advise us to do ("keeping our audience in mind as we write" and trying to "decenter"). Therefore this social-discourse theory doesn't undermine the benefits of "private writing" and thus provides no support at all for the traditional rhetorical advice that we should "always try to think about (intended) audience as we write."

In fact this social-discourse theory reinforces two subsidiary arguments I have been making. First, even if there is no getting away from *some* audience, we can get relief from an inhibiting audience by writing to a more inviting one. Second, audience problems don't come only from *actual* audiences but also from phantom "audiences in the head" (Elbow, *Writing with Power* 186ff). Once we learn how to be more aware of the effects of both external and internal readers and how to direct our words elsewhere, we can get out of the shadow even of a troublesome phantom reader.

And even if all our discourse is *directed to* or *shaped by* past audiences or voices, it doesn't follow that our discourse is *well directed to* or *successfully shaped for* those audiences or voices. Small children *direct* much talk to others, but that doesn't mean they always *suit* their talk to others. They often fail. When adults discover that a piece of their writing has been "heavily shaped" by some audience, this is bad news as much as good: often the writing is crippled by defensive moves that try to fend off criticism from this reader.

As teachers, particularly, we need to distinguish and emphasize "private writing" in order to teach it, to teach that crucial cognitive capacity to engage in extended and productive thinking that doesn't depend on audience prompts or social stimuli. It's sad to see so many students who can reply to live voices but cannot engage in productive dialogue with voices in their heads. Such students often lose interest in an issue that had intrigued them—just because they don't find other people who are interested in talking about it and haven't learned to talk reflectively to *themselves* about it.

For these reasons, then, I believe my main argument holds force even if I accept the theory that all discourse is social. But, perhaps more tentatively, I resist this theory. I don't know all the data from developmental linguistics, but I cannot help suspecting that babies engage in *some* private poesis—or "play-language"—some private babbling in addition to social babbling. Of course Vygotsky must be right when he points to so much social language in children, but can we really trust him when he denies *all* private or nonsocial language (which Piaget and Chomsky see)? I am always suspicious when someone argues for the total nonexistence of a certain kind of behavior or event. Such an argument is almost invariably an act of definitional aggrandizement, not empirical searching. To say that *all* language is social is to flop over into the opposite one-sidedness that we need Vygotsky's model to save us from.

And even if all language is *originally* social, Vygotsky himself emphasizes how "inner speech" becomes more individuated and private as the child matures. "[E]gocentric speech is relatively accessible in three-year-olds but quite inscrutable in seven-year-olds: the older the child, the more thoroughly has his thought become inner speech" (Emerson 254; see also Vygotsky 134). "The inner speech of the adult represents his 'thinking for himself' rather than social adaptation. ... Out of context, it would be incomprehensible to others because it omits to mention what is obvious to the 'speaker'" (Vygotsky 18).

I also resist the theory that all private writing is really communication with the "*audience of self.*" ("When we represent the objects of our thought in language, we intend to make use of these representations at a later time. ... [T]he speaker-self must have audience directed intentions toward a listener-self" [Feldman 289].) Of course private language often *is* a communication with the audience of self:

- When we make a shopping list. (It's obvious when we can't decipher that third item that we're confronting *failed* communication with the self.)
- When we make a rough draft for ourselves but not for others' eyes. Here we are seeking to clarify our thinking with the leverage that comes from standing outside and reading our own utterance as audience—experiencing our discourse as receiver instead of as sender.
- When we experience ourselves as slightly split. Sometimes we experience ourselves as witness to ourselves and hear our own words from the outside—sometimes with great detachment, as on some occasions of pressure or stress.

But there are other times when private language is *not* communication with audience of self:

- Freewriting to no one: for the *sake* of self but not *to* the self. The goal is not to communicate but to follow a train of thinking or feeling to see where it leads. In doing this kind of freewriting (and many people have not learned it), you don't particularly plan to come back and read what you've written. You just write along and the written product falls away to be ignored, while only the "real product"—any new perceptions, thoughts, or feelings produced in the mind by the freewriting—is saved and looked at again. (It's not that you don't experience your words *at all* but you experience them only as speaker, sender, or emitter—not as receiver or audience. To say that's the same as being audience is denying the very distinction between 'speaker' and 'audience.')

  As this kind of freewriting actually works, it often *leads* to writing we look at. That is, we freewrite along to no one, following discourse in hopes of getting somewhere, and then at a certain point we often sense that we have *gotten* somewhere: we can tell (but not because we stop and read) that what we are now writing seems new or intriguing or important. At this point we may stop writing; or we may keep on writing, but in a new audience-relationship, realizing that we *will* come back to this passage and read it as audience. Or we may take a new sheet (symbolizing the new audience-relationship) and try to write out for ourselves what's interesting.
- Writing as exorcism is a more extreme example of private writing *not* for the audience of self. Some people have learned to write in order to get rid of thoughts or feelings. By freewriting what's obsessively going round and round in our head we can finally let it go and move on.

I am suggesting that some people (and especially poets and freewriters) engage in a kind of discourse that Feldman, defending what she calls a "communication-intention" view, has never learned and thus has a hard time imagining and understanding. Instead of always using language in an audience-directed fashion for the sake of communication, these writers unleash language for its own sake and let *it* function a bit on its own, without much *intention* and without much need for *communication,* to see where it leads—and thereby end up with some intentions and potential communications they didn't have before.

It's hard to turn off the audience-of-self in writing—and thus hard to imagine writing to no one (just as it's hard to turn off the audience of *outside* readers when writing an audience-directed piece). Consider "invisible writing" as an intriguing technique that helps you become less of an audience-of-self for your writing. Invisible writing prevents you from seeing what you have written: you write on a computer with the screen turned down, or you write with a spent ball-point pen on paper with carbon paper and another sheet underneath. Invisible writing tends to get people not only to write faster than they normally do, but often better (see Blau). I mean to be tentative about this slippery issue of whether we can really stop being audience to our own discourse, but I cannot help drawing the following conclusion: just as in freewriting, suppressing the *other* as audience tends to enhance quantity and sometimes even quality of writing; so in invisible writing, suppressing the *self* as audience tends to enhance quantity and sometimes even quality.

Contraries in Teaching

So what does all this mean for teaching? It means that we are stuck with two contrary tasks. On the one hand, we need to help our students enhance the social dimension of writing: to learn to be *more* aware of audience, to decenter better and learn to fit their discourse better to the needs of readers. Yet it is every bit as important to help them learn the private dimension of writing: to learn to be *less* aware of audience, to put audience needs aside, to use discourse in the desert island mode. And if we are trying to advance contraries, we must be prepared for paradoxes.

For instance if we emphasize the social dimension in our teaching (for example, by getting students to write to each other, to read and comment on each others' writing in pairs and groups, and by staging public discussions and even debates on the topics they are to write about), we will obviously help the social, public, communicative dimension of writing—help students experience writing not just as jumping through hoops for a grade but rather as taking part in the life of a community of discourse. But "social discourse" can also help private writing by getting students sufficiently involved or invested in an issue so that they finally want to carry on producing discourse alone and in private—and for themselves.

Correlatively, if we emphasize the private dimension in our teaching (for example, by using lots of private exploratory writing, freewriting, and journal writing and by helping students realize that of course they may need practice with this "easy" mode of discourse before they can use it fruitfully), we will obviously help students learn to write better reflectively for themselves without the need for others to interact with. Yet this private discourse can also help public, social writing—help students finally feel full enough of their *own* thoughts to have some genuine desire to *tell* them to others. Students often feel they "don't have anything to say" until they finally succeed in engaging themselves in private desert island writing for themselves alone.

Another paradox: whether we want to teach greater audience awareness or the ability to ignore audience, we must help students learn not only to "try harder" but also to "just relax." That is, sometimes students fail to produce reader-based prose because they don't *try* hard enough to think about audience needs. But sometimes the problem is cured if they just relax and write *to* people—as though in a letter or in talking to a trusted adult. By unclenching, they effortlessly call on social discourse skills of immense sophistication. Sometimes, indeed, the problem is cured if the student simply writes in a more social *setting*—in a classroom where it is habitual to share lots of writing. Similarly, sometimes students can't produce sustained private discourse because they don't try hard enough to keep the pen moving and forget about readers. They must persist and doggedly push aside those feelings of, "My head is empty, I have run out of anything to say." But sometimes what they need to learn through all that persistence is how to relax and let go—to unclench.

As teachers, we need to think about what it means to *be an audience* rather than just be a teacher, critic, assessor, or editor. If our only response is to tell students what's strong, what's weak, and how to improve it (diagnosis, assessment, and advice), we actually *undermine* their sense of writing as a social act. We reinforce their sense that writing means doing school exercises, producing for authorities what they already know—*not* actually trying to say things to readers. To help students experience us as *audience* rather than as assessment machines, it helps to respond by "replying" (as in a letter) rather than always "giving feedback."

Paradoxically enough, one of the best ways teachers can help students learn to turn off audience awareness and write in the desert island mode—to turn off the babble of outside voices in the head and listen better to quiet inner voices—is to be a special kind of private audience to them, to be a reader who nurtures by trusting and believing in the writer. Britton has drawn attention to the importance of teacher as "trusted adult" for school children (67–68). No one can be good at private, reflective writing without some *confidence and trust in self.* A nurturing reader can give a writer a kind of permission to forget about other readers or to be one's own reader. I have benefitted from this special kind of audience and have seen it prove useful to others. When I had a teacher who believed in me, who was interested in me and interested in what I had to say, I wrote well. When I had a teacher who thought I was naive, dumb, silly, and in need of being "straightened out," I wrote badly and sometimes couldn't write at all. Here is an interestingly paradoxical instance of the social-to-private principle from Vygotsky and Meade: we learn to listen better and more trustingly to *ourselves* through interaction with trusting *others.*

Look for a moment at lyric poets as paradigm writers (instead of seing them as aberrant), and see how they heighten *both* the public and private dimensions of writing. Bakhtin says that lyric poetry implies "the absolute certainty of the listener's sympathy" (113). I think it's more helpful to say that lyric poets learn to create more than usual privacy in which to write *for themselves*—and then they turn around and let *others overhear.* Notice how poets tend to argue for the importance of no-audience writing, yet they are especially gifted at being public about what they produce in private. Poets are revealers—sometimes even grandstanders or showoffs. Poets illustrate the need for opposite or paradoxical or double audience skills: on the one hand, the ability to be private and solitary and tune out others—to write only for oneself and not give a damn about readers, yet on the other hand, the ability to be more than usually interested in audience and even to be a ham.

If writers really need these two audience skills, notice how bad most conventional schooling is on both counts. Schools offer virtually no privacy for writing: everything students write is collected and read by a teacher, a situation so ingrained students will tend to complain if you don't collect and read every word they write. Yet on the other hand, schools characteristically offer little or no social dimension for writing. It is *only* the teacher who reads, and students seldom feel that in giving their writing to a teacher they are actually communicating something they really want to say to a real person. Notice how often they are happy to turn in to teachers something perfunctory and fake that they would be embarrassed to show to classmates. Often they feel shocked and insulted if we want to distribute to classmates the assigned writing they hand in to us. (I think of Richard Wright's realization that the naked white prostitutes didn't bother to cover themselves when he brought them coffee as a black bellboy because they didn't really think of him as a man or even a person.) Thus the conventional school setting for writing tends to be the least private and the least public—when what students need, like all of us, is practice in writing that is the most private and also the most public.

Practical Guidelines about Audience

The theoretical relationships between discourse and audience are complex and paradoxical, but the practical morals are simple:

1. Seek ways to heighten both the *public* and *private* dimensions of writing. (For activities, see the previous section.)
2. When working on important audience-directed writing, we must try to emphasize audience awareness *sometimes*. A useful rule of thumb is to start by putting the readers in mind and carry on as long as things go well. If difficulties arise, try putting readers out of mind and write either to no audience, to self, or to an inviting audience. Finally, always *revise* with readers in mind. (Here's another occasion when orthodox advice about writing is wrong—but turns out right if applied to revising.)
3. Seek ways to heighten awareness of one's writing process (through process writing and discussion) to get better at taking control and deciding when to keep readers in mind and when to ignore them. Learn to discriminate factors like these:
   (a) The writing task. Is this piece of writing *really* for an audience? More often than we realize, it is not. It is a draft that only we will see, though the final version will be for an audience; or exploratory writing for figuring something out; or some kind of personal private writing meant only for ourselves.
   (b) Actual readers. When we put them in mind, are we helped or hindered?
   (c) One's own temperament. Am I the sort of person who tends to think of what to say and how to say it when I keep readers in mind? Or someone (as I am) who needs long stretches of forgetting all about readers?
   (d) Has some powerful "audience-in-the-head" tricked me into talking to it when I'm really trying to talk to someone else—distorting new business into old business? (I may be an inviting teacher-audience to my students, but they may not be able to pick up a pen without falling under the spell of a former, intimidating teacher.)
   (e) Is *double audience* getting in my way? When I write a memo or report, I probably have to suit it not only to my "target audience" but also to some colleagues or supervisor. When I write something for publication, it must be right for readers, but it won't be published unless it is also right for the editors—and if it's a book it won't be much read unless it's right for reviewers. Children's stories won't be bought unless they are right for editors and reviewers *and* parents. We often tell students to write to a particular "real-life" audience—or to peers in the class—but of course they are also writing for us as graders. (This problem is more common as more teachers get interested in audience and suggest "second" audiences.)
   (f) Is *teacher-audience* getting in the way of my students' writing? As teachers we must often read in an odd fashion: in stacks of 25 or 50 pieces all on the same topic; on topics we know better than the writer; not for pleasure or learning but to grade or find problems (see Elbow, *Writing with Power* 216–36).

To list all these audience pitfalls is to show again the need for thinking about audience needs—yet also the need for vacations from readers to think in peace.

Note

1   There are many different entities called audience: (a) The actual readers to whom the text will be given; (b) the writer's conception of those readers—which may be mistaken (see Ong; Park; Ede and Lunsford); (c) the audience that the text implies—which may be different still (see Booth); (d) the discourse community or even genre addressed or implied by the text (see Walzer); (e) ghost or phantom "readers

in the head" that the writer may unconsciously address or try to please (see Elbow, *Writing with Power* 186ff. Classically, this is a powerful former teacher. Often such an audience is so ghostly as not to show up as actually "implied" by the text). For the essay I am writing here, these differences don't much matter: I'm celebrating the ability to put aside the needs or demands of *any* or all of these audiences. I recognize, however, that we sometimes cannot fight our way free of unconscious or tacit audiences (as in b or e above) unless we bring them to greater conscious awareness.

Works Cited

Bakhtin, Mikhail. "Discourse in Life and Discourse in Poetry." Appendix. *Freudianism: A Marxist Critique*. By V. N. Volosinov. Trans. I. R. Titunik. Ed. Neal H. Bruss. New York: Academic, 1976. (Holquist's attribution of this work to Bakhtin is generally accepted.)

Berkenkotter, Carol, and Donald Murray. "Decisions and Revisions: The Planning Strategies of a Publishing Writer and the Response of Being a Rat—or Being Protocoled." *College Composition and Communication* 34 (1983): 156–72.

Blau, Sheridan. "Invisible Writing." *College Composition and Communication* 34 (1983): 297–312.

Booth, Wayne. *The Rhetoric of Fiction*. Chicago: U of Chicago P, 1961.

Britton, James. *The Development of Writing Abilities, 11–18*. Urbana: NCTE, 1977.

Bruffee, Kenneth A. "Liberal Education and the Social Justification of Belief." *Liberal Education* 68 (1982): 95–114.

Bruner, Jerome. *Beyond the Information Given: Studies in the Psychology of Knowing*. Ed. Jeremy Anglin. New York: Norton, 1973.

——. *On Knowing: Essays for the Left Hand*. Expanded ed. Cambridge: Harvard UP, 1979.

Chomsky, Noam. *Reflections on Language*. New York: Random, 1975.

Cicotello, David M. "The Art of Writing: An Interview with William Stafford." *College Composition and Communication* 34 (1983): 173–77.

Clarke, Jennifer, and Peter Elbow. "Desert Island Discourse: On the Benefits of Ignoring Audience." *The Journal Book*. Ed. Toby Fulwiler. Montclair, NJ: Boynton, 1987.

Cooper, Anthony Ashley, 3rd Earl of Shaftesbury. *Characteristics of Men, Manners, Opinions, Times, Etc.* Ed. John M. Robertson. 2 vols. Gloucester, MA: Smith, 1963.

Ede, Lisa, and Andrea Lunsford. "Audience Addressed/Audience Invoked: The Role of Audience in Composition Theory and Pedagogy." *College Composition and Communication* 35 (1984): 140–54.

Elbow, Peter. *Writing with Power*. New York: Oxford UP, 1981.

——. *Writing Without Teachers*. New York: Oxford UP, 1973.

Emerson, Caryl. "The Outer Word and Inner Speech: Bakhtin, Vygotsky, and the Internalization of Language." *Critical Inquiry* 10 (1983): 245–64.

Feldman, Carol Fleisher. "Two Functions of Language." *Harvard Education Review* 47 (1977): 282–93.

Flower, Linda. "Writer-Based Prose: A Cognitive Basis for Problems in Writing," *College English* 41 (1979): 19–37.

Goodman, Paul. *Speaking and Language: Defense of Poetry*. New York: Random, 1972.

Griffin, Susan. "The Internal Voices of Invention: Shaftesbury's Soliloquy." Unpublished. 1986.

Lawrence, D. H. *Studies in Classic American Literature*. Garden City: Doubleday, 1951.

Ong, Walter. "The Writer's Audience Is Always a Fiction." *PMLA* 90 (1975): 9–21.

Park, Douglas B. "The Meanings of 'Audience' ." *College English* 44 (1982): 247–57.

Perl, Sondra. "Guidelines for Composing." Appendix A. *Through Teachers' Eyes: Portraits of Writing Teachers at Work*. By Sondra Perl and Nancy Wilson. Portsmouth, NH: Heinemann, 1986.

Progoff, Ira. *At A Journal Workshop*. New York: Dialogue, 1975.

Shaughnessy, Mina. *Errors and Expectations: A Guide for the Teacher of Basic Writing*. New York: Oxford UP, 1977.

Trimbur, John. Letter to the author. September 1985.

——. "Beyond Cognition: Voices in Inner Speech." Forthcoming in *Rhetoric Review*.

Vygotsky, L. S. *Thought and Language*. Trans. and ed. E. Hanfmann and G. Vakar. 1934. Cambridge: MIT P, 1962.

Walzer, Arthur E. "Articles from the 'California Divorce Project': A Case Study of the Concept of Audience." *College Composition and Communication* 36 (1985): 150–59.

Wright, Richard. *Black Boy.* New York: Harper, 1945.

I benefited from much help from audiences in writing various drafts of this piece. I am grateful to Jennifer Clarke, with whom I wrote a collaborative piece containing a case study on this subject. I am also grateful for extensive feedback from Pat Belanoff, Paul Connolly, Sheryl Fontaine, John Trimbur, and members of the Martha's Vineyard Summer Writing Seminar.

5

Assessing Writing

Julie Neff-Lippman

- Why do we assess writing?
- What is the difference between "direct" and "indirect" assessment?
- What is the difference between formative assessment and summative assessment and how should we use each?
- How can we provide classroom assessment that fosters student learning and engagement?

Looking forward to reading his students' first essays, the new teacher of writing pours a cup of coffee and sits down at his desk to assess the papers. The first essay, printed on good quality paper, has only one punctuation error, but little specific content. While the second paper has many punctuation and usage errors, it has passages that seem to be insightful and poignant. The third has no point. After two hours, the instructor has rewritten whole sentences and marked numerous errors in grammar and punctuation, but he has not written a comment or put a grade on a single essay. He wonders how he will respond to these papers and what he could have done to guide students to a more acceptable product.

Many teachers of writing have experienced this same frustration with assessing and responding to student writing. Whether assessment is occurring in the classroom or on a programmatic scale, whether it involves the work of an individual or the entire campus, evaluation of student writing continues to present teachers and administrators with a plethora of challenges. Assessment is a complex (Sommers, 2006) and often political topic that has been debated at every level from the individual classroom to state legislatures. This chapter will discuss these challenges, putting them in historical and programmatic contexts, and will provide strategies for helping teachers design assignments, shape the writing process, and assess and respond to student writing.

WRITING ASSESSMENT: AN OVERVIEW

Indirect Assessment: Objective Tests

As early as the late 19th century, Harvard University and other highly selective colleges instituted writing assessment as a way to place students in appropriate classes. Growing out of the notion that the current students were ill-prepared for college-level work, these early assessments, which attempted to ferret out deficits in student preparation, continue to influence assessment in the 21st century (Huot, 2002).

In the l950s, writing assessment focused on objective testing and was used to determine who would take the pre-college writing courses and who would be excused from required composition courses. During the 1950s and 1960s, this *indirect* assessment of writing reflected ideas about composition that were current at the time—that is, that writing ability could be measured by having students answer questions about grammar, usage, and punctuation in a multiple choice test. The objective tests were popular with teachers and administrators because they were easy and inexpensive to administer and score. Perhaps most importantly, they were *reliable*; in other words, test administrators could easily control the test (answers were either right or wrong) and testing situation. However, the problem became obvious: the objective tests were not *valid* in that they did not measure what they purported to measure—the student's ability to write (Yancey, 1999, pp. 484–485). A student's score on a grammar test could not predict whether the student could actually write an essay any more than the written drivers' test can predict whether a person can drive a car.

Because the tests decontextualize knowledge and meaning making, indirect assessment has been widely criticized by groups such as the National Council of Teachers of English (NCTE) and the International Reading Association (IRA). The tests also pay too much attention to lower-order skills and usurp classroom time (teaching to the test) that could be used for more relevant instruction. However, these tests have continued to be used because they are easy and inexpensive to administer, and they provide results that can be charted across schools and across districts (Wolcott, 1998).

Direct Assessment: Essay Tests

Since then, writing assessment has changed dramatically, in many ways reflecting the changes in the field of composition. From about 1970 to the mid-1980s, assessment relied primarily on essay tests that students wrote in a single session (Yancey, 1999, p. 484). Most compositionists considered these tests, called *direct* assessment, to be an improvement over the objective tests because the writing tests were *valid*; they measured what they were intended to measure—writing. By writing essay tests for assessment purposes, students demonstrate writing competence rather than recognizing the correct answer; teachers exercise their judgment, which replaces the scoring by a scantron (Wolcott, 1998, p. 5).

While most compositionists consider direct assessment to be superior to indirect assessment, they questioned the efficacy of timed essay tests written in a single setting. Direct assessment does not reflect recent thinking about process (Flower & Hayes, 1981) or social constructivist theory (Bruffee, 1986). Were students who had been trained in invention and revision put at a disadvantage by a timed test that did not allow for process or take the rhetorical situation into account? The advantage to writing tests was that they measured "writing" proficiency rather than grammar proficiency, but they defined writing in a narrow, reductive way. Lee Odell (1981) has argued that direct writing assessment defines competence too narrowly. Students should be able to demonstrate "the ability to discover what one wishes to say and to convey one's message through language, syntax and content that are appropriate for one's audience and purpose" (p. 103). Direct assessment does not give writers the opportunity to demonstrate these rhetorical abilities or to revise over time nor does it take into account the rhetorical situation and classroom context.

Although there are numerous problems with direct assessment, many schools employ it to determine who takes certain courses, who may pass over a requirement, and who may receive a diploma. Because direct assessment is still widely used, it may be useful to take a few moments to reflect on the qualities of the most successful direct assessment. Students do their best writing when they care about their topics (Atwell, 1987; Graves, 1983; Sommers, 2006) and when they have a clearly defined audience and purpose. Therefore, topics for direct assessment should be:

- accessible
- stated clearly
- broad based
- engaging, but not so emotional that students lose control of their writing
- encouraging of the type of writing sought by the curriculum (Wolcott, 1998, pp. 24–25).

The audience and purpose of the writing should also be clearly stated. While these are admirable goals for essay prompts, they are not easily attained if we consider the many kinds of difference that students bring to any testing prompt—ethnicity, gender, religion, culture, disability, and economic disparity.

Portfolios

In the late 1980s, in answer to the problems with direct assessment and to reflect changing theory and research in the field of composition, portfolios became an increasingly common assessment tool (Yancey, 1999, p. 485) and have continued to be important into the 21st century. A collection of papers chosen by the student at the end of a course, portfolios are used for both large-scale and classroom assessment. Many instructors regularly use portfolios to build assessment into their classroom practices. Portfolio assessment takes into account the need for the generation of ideas and thoughtful revision over time and allows the student to choose what goes into the portfolio. In addition to choice about content, the student has the opportunity to write a reflective piece, making the portfolio even more effective because it involves the student in his or her own learning (Yancey, 1992). Ed White (2005) argued that we regard the reflective piece as a central piece of portfolio scoring, asking students to use their reflective essay to make an argument for why their selections for the portfolio meet the goals for the course. A portfolio can play an important role in helping students take responsibility for their own writing and learning, something that is important to student growth (Huot, 2002).

Many instructors find the portfolio the ideal assessment tool because it allows instructors to act as "coaches" providing feedback that the students can use to revise the papers for the portfolio. Still some critics question the reliability of portfolios. Pointing to the number of times a paper can be revised before it goes into the portfolio, they claim it is often impossible to determine how competent the student writer is or how much help a student has received during the revision process (Wolcott, 1998, p. 52).

Despite the criticisms, most compositionists believe the benefits of portfolios far outweigh the problems: portfolios are valid because they measure students' ability to write and revise in a rhetorical setting, they involve student choice and reflection, and they are *authentic*—that is, the assessment, as much as possible, occurs in a meaningful, real-life context. Portfolios are consistent with the values expressed by the CCCC Executive Committee on Writing Assessment: A Position Statement (CCCC Committee on Assessment, 2009).

Electronic Portfolios (e-portfolios)

Electronic portfolios, like paper portfolios, contain a sample of the student's work chosen by the student along with the student's reflection about the work and why it was chosen. Electronic portfolios have all of the pedagogical advantages of paper portfolios along with the advantages of portability and the possibility for nonprint artifacts. Some universities, such as Virginia Tech, have put resources into the development of e-portfiolios across the curriculum, encouraging the use of e-portfolios within departments or schools (Zaldivar, 2010). Other schools (University of Georgia and Portland State University) use e-portfolios to provide assessment data that are deep and complex and can be useful for multiple constituencies (Yancey, Cambridge, & Cambridge, 2009). Because they may include a range of products including performances, artistic compositions, and evidence of proficiency in foreign languages, electronic portfolios go far beyond tests in demonstrating a student's learning or programmatic accomplishments. In addition, the portfolios involve students in significant self-reflection that can be carried across the entire curriculum and extended throughout the student's college career (Yancey, Cambridge, & Cambridge, 2009). While electronic portfolios are unlikely to replace testing completely, they solve many of the problems related to paper portfolios and are likely to become increasingly popular as a tool for promoting student learning (Yancey, Cambridge, & Cambridge, 2009).

Some critics of using portfolios for large-scale assessment have claimed there are too many variables with portfolio assessment and that portfolios do not hold up well enough to statistical measures for them to be considered a reliable assessment instrument (Wolcott, 1998, p. 1). Within individual classrooms, critics noted that some students do not take early assignments seriously because they know they will have opportunities for revision later in the course.

Still supporters of portfolios believe that the validity of portfolio assessment and the student involvement in it outweigh the reliability problems associated with it and that portfolio assessment is the kind of evaluation most consistent with the values of compositionists (CCCC, 2009). With appropriate safeguards, the advantages of portfolios for students and stakeholders seem to far outweigh the risks and provide a balance between process and product.

Scoring

Whether the assessment is being done through evaluating timed writing or portfolios, the scoring of the texts to be assessed is extremely important. One of the first decisions organizers of scoring must make is the kind of scoring they will use: primary trait scoring that focuses on certain traits in the writing (thesis, appropriate transitions, etc.); analytical scoring that focuses on traits that tend to be universal (word choice, punctuation, etc.); discourse scoring that uses counts of T-units and other discourse units; or holistic scoring that looks at the writing sample as a whole piece of discourse. Increasingly, holistic scoring is seen as the scoring method of choice, perhaps because it sees that the whole is greater than the sum of its parts (Myers, 1980, p. 1). John Mellon in *The National Assessment and the Teaching of English* (1975) and Charles Cooper (1977, p. 19) in *Evaluating Writing: Describing, Measuring, Judging* have found holistic scoring to be a reliable way to measure writing samples when well-trained readers from similar backgrounds use it to evaluate student writing. Others have found that holistic scoring using well-trained readers is the best method for scoring because it is valid and reliable and requires each scorer to look at the essay or portfolio as a whole (White, 1994, 2000; Wolcott, 1998). When they are used as part of a writing program, the scoring of the portfolios ideally involves the instructors who teach within the program (Yancey, 1992).

The design of a scoring rubric is important to the success of holistic scoring. Many (White, 1994, Wolcott, 1998) believe that the scorers must develop their own rubric in order for the assessment to be successful. Others have argued that as long as the group agrees to the rubric, the scoring can proceed with equal success (Cooper, 1977). Whether the rubric is developed by the group or not, all of the scorers must agree to the rubric they will use to score the papers. Before beginning the scoring, scorers are carefully trained in a norming session in which they agree to the criteria that characterize papers at each level—for instance, exceptional, good, fair, poor, or unacceptable work. Norming sessions are often difficult and intense, but if the norming has been successful, the scorers will be able to rate the students' work reliably (White, 2002). The reliability of raters' scores can be checked through a process called *inter-rater reliability*.

Internal and External Assessment

We can also divide assessment into *internal* and *external* assessment. Internal assessment, whether papers, tests, or portfolios, focus on the individual's learning and will be tied to the curriculum for the class. Internal assessment has two main advantages. First, if an essay test is being given, the teacher will be able to give extra help to students who do not understand the test directions, and she can extend the time if students have not finished. Second, when the student has finished a paper or test, the evaluation is usually given to the student or in K-12, to the parents. With internal assessment, teachers have a great deal of control over the evaluation process; they can even throw out a whole set of results if they see a problem with the test or the testing situation (Wolcott, 1998).

External assessment, considered top down because it is initiated by those outside the classroom, is not tied to a particular class and instructors are not involved in the writing assessment. Collegiate Learning Assessment (CLA) and the Collegiate Assessment of Academic Proficiency (CAAP) are examples of external learning assessments. The tests are used to prove an institution's success with student outcomes rather than to measure the learning of individual students (Adler-Kassner & Harrington, 2010). Proponents of external assessment claim that the test's directions and the prompts have usually been created with great care to improve the validity of the sample. In addition, external assessment gives administrators a chance to compare student achievement among campuses and across districts or states. The reporting of the results is much more public, as they are sent to state legislatures and occasionally to newspapers. Students and parents may not even see the results of the tests (Wolcott, 1998, p. 3).

Programmatic Assessment

Over the last 50 years in many universities, the focus of large-scale assessment has shifted from the individual learner to the program (Yancey, 1999). Measuring how well the program as a whole is working, *programmatic assessment* focuses on the *outcomes* that the program can demonstrate rather than on the accomplishments of the individual student. For example, over the past 14 years, the University of Puget Sound has been using "folders" and random sampling to gather a body of student work for programmatic assessment. Faculty, who are paid stipends for their effort, score the folders holistically to measure the success of the writing program, rather than the writing development of individual students. While this type of assessment has passed the tests for validity and reliability, it does not involve students in choosing or revising papers for their folders. Thus the assessment—done after the students graduate—provides data about the writing program, but not about individual learners. Kathleen Yancey (1999) has challenged us to think about how programmatic assessment can be used to help the individual as well as the institution.

Outcomes Assessment

Outcomes assessment, an increasingly popular term in political and educational circles, has also influenced how writing teachers think about assessment. William Spady (1994) defined outcomes assessment in the following way: "Outcomes are high-quality, culminating demonstrations of significant learning in context" (p. 18). Outcomes, based on clearly defined goals at the beginning of a course or an educational experience, measure students' achievement of the goals.

Summative and Formative Assessment

When and why assessment is conducted and what is done with the results will help determine whether it will be summative or formative. *Summative assessment* aims to measure the success of a particular endeavor after it is completed and there is no opportunity for revision. SATs, GREs, and end of the term grades provide summative assessment because they measure ability at a certain point. External assessment is always summative as are programmatic or outcomes assessment. The goal of summative writing assessment is not to shape students' thinking or learning, but rather to judge how well students have accomplished the writing task. All instructors who are obligated to give grades engage in summative assessment. In contrast, *formative assessment*, which is generally internal, puts emphasis on shaping students' writing while they are still in the process of writing. The goal of most formative assessment is to help students improve their writing and writing ability (Huot, 2002).

Assessment is often political and contentious because the *stakeholders*, those who have an interest in assessment, have agendas that are sometimes at odds. Many administrators want summative assessment that is inexpensive and easy to control with outcomes that can be reduced to tables and graphs. Teachers generally favor formative assessment that grows out of the curriculum and resides in the classroom where they can shape the progress of individual students. Parents want assessment that holds schools accountable but emphasizes the growth of the individual child—especially their child. School boards and legislators want to see that their investment in schools is paying off in terms of improved test scores. With so many people having competing agendas, the real challenge with any kind of assessment is bringing together all of the stakeholders to develop a plan that parents, teachers, school boards, community groups, and state legislators all can agree on (Banta, 2002; Wolcott, 1998).

Although writing assessment has changed over the years, it has also stayed the same depending on the geography and institution. Some universities continue to administer an objective grammar test as part of an institutional exit exam, whereas others use the holistically-scored essay exam, portfolio assessment, programmatic assessment, or some combination of assessment techniques.

Looking Forward

Assessment seems to come in waves that are sometimes overlapping (Yancey, 1999). Currents, some strong, some weak, also influence writing assessment. One of these stronger currents is the call for accountability through timed-essay tests such as the Collegiate Learning Assessment or CLA, a test that measures students' ability to "write persuasively" and "think analytically." Tests such as the CLA are designed to allow colleges to demonstrate positive gains as a result of their curriculum. Used at 400 colleges across the country, the results of this nationally normed test will be made public in 2012 (Glenn, 2010). The criticisms of all timed standardized writing tests hold true for these: they disregard process and decontextualize knowledge. Yet as the results are made public more colleges are likely to institute such tests.

The other current is e-portfolios, which bring the advantages of portfolio assessment as explained above along with the advantages of portability and student initiative and creativity. The CCCC position statement on assessment (2009) and before it Haswell and Wyche-Smith (1994), have encouraged compositionists to become advocates for the kinds of assessment that are true to their values. In the years to come, the tension between those who advocate a timed test and those who advocate portfolios, electronic or not, may give compositionists an even greater reason to become advocates for ethical, responsible assessment. Adler-Kassner and Harrington (2010) called for a new era of responsibility that includes three components: "Identifying and working from principle and best practice, building alliances with others, and engaging in (and assessing) shared actions based on common interest" (p. 86).

ASSESSMENT IN THE CLASSROOM

Let's go back to our composition teacher, who, for now, doesn't care about university-wide writing assessment but, rather, about assessing his set of compositions before dawn. Unhappy with the papers, he wonders what he could have done differently before the papers were turned in. "How do I write assignments that help my students understand what I want from their papers? How can I shape the writing process in a way that will help engage the students in their writing? How much should I correct? Should I read drafts? How can I write comments that will help students grow as writers and learners?" Because the ultimate goal of assessment is to improve student learning, at the heart of our inquiry lies this key question: How do we use assignments and assessment of them to help students become better writers?

Designing Assignments

The students who have been given the following topics for an essay are certain to have difficulty writing the paper with only this information:

- Define "educational progress"
- Write an assessment plan

- Describe your classroom
- Comment on the new salary scale for adjunct instructors.

Many of the problems with these prompts grow out of the missing rhetorical context—the purpose of the paper, the audience for it, the genre the audience expects, and the context within which it would be produced. Because all writing has a rhetorical context, it is important to give students information about the rhetorical situation. Furthermore, Charles Cooper (1999) in "What We Know about Genres" encourages teachers to give students explicit information about the genre the teacher is expecting the students to write in. Broadening the concept beyond literary categories (novel, romance, epic), Cooper defined genre as "types of writing produced every day in our culture, types of writing that make possible certain kinds of learning and social interaction" (p. 25).

Similarly, because each assignment offers students an "invitation" to write, the inadequate "invitation" may lead students astray. Weak papers may be the fault of the assignment or "invitation" rather than the fault of the student (Lindemann, 1995, p. 207). Although there will always be variables in the directions for an assignment, the writer must have explicit information about some of them: (a) the purpose of the writing, (b) the audience, (c) the role the writer is to take in relation to the subject and the audience, (d) the form the writing should take, and (e) criteria for success (Lindemann, 1995, p. 212). In each of these previous examples, the prompt does not provide enough rhetorical context for the writer. The appendix at the end of this book further addresses the importance of crafting well-thought-out writing prompts.

Ryder, Vander Lei, and Roen (1999) have pointed out that it is especially important that students know from the beginning who they are writing for: "Because writing is an interactive process, an audience has an impact on all parts of a text—the way a topic is developed, the organization, the diction, the tone, and so on. Clearly then, questions of audience cannot be left to the end of the writing process" (p. 59). Teachers might also consider taking the different kinds of relationships with audience into account when they design and sequence assignments: monadic relationship occurs when the writer writes for herself (personal journals or exploratory writing), dyadic relationship occurs when the writer writes with one other person in mind (an essay for a teacher or a letter to a friend), and triadic relationship occurs when the writer takes a side against an opponent before an audience (Ryder, Vander Lei, & Roen, 1999, p. 212).

In *Teaching and Assessing Writing*, Edward White has provided a list of questions that guide teachers as they make assignments. The following list is adapted from White's book (1994, pp. 22–23).

1. What do I want the writer to do? Is it worth doing? Why? Is it interesting and appropriate? What will it teach—specifically? What will the assignment tell me?
2. How do I want the writer to do the assignment? Will the writers collaborate or work alone?
3. Does the assignment give enough information about required length and the use of sources?
4. For whom are the writers writing? Who is the audience? What do they know about the topic? What are their predispositions toward it? Is the teacher the only audience or part of the audience?

5. How much time do the writers need for the assignment? How much class time is needed for the process? How much time outside of class is necessary?

For Writing and Discussion

1. Supplying the necessary information, rewrite the prompts at the beginning of this section so that you or someone else could actually carry out the writing. Indicate what kind of relationship the writer should have with the audience. When you've finished, share your writing prompts with others in the class and use Ed White's list to evaluate and revise the prompts.
2. Evaluate a prompt that you have received for a writing assignment in one of your classes. What additional information would have been useful? What tacit understanding, if any, did you bring to the assignment? Discuss the prompts with others in a small group.
3. Exchange a writing prompt that you have created for your students with another member of the class. As you evaluate your colleague's prompt, take on the role of a first-year student. What questions do you have? What rhetorical or cultural assumptions might you, the student, bring to the assignment? Share your response with your partner. Revise your prompt based on your partner's response.

Some teachers object to specificity in assignments, claiming that the students should have the freedom to approach the assignment as they see fit. But a rhetorical situation is inherent in most of the writing we do. For instance, when I agreed to write this chapter, I knew the approximate length, the audience, the purpose of the book, and the purpose of my chapter. I also had an outline of the book so I could see how my chapter would complement the others. And I had a sample chapter that gave me ideas about voice, tone, stance, format, and level of detail. Shouldn't students have the benefit of similar details about audience, purpose, and reader expectations?

The writing teacher need not, however, spell out every variable of an assignment. In fact, doing so would take away the students' agency and make writing a rote activity rather than a rhetorical one, which allows the students to solve problems as they produce a text. On the other hand, vague assignments with mixed messages almost guarantee that only a few papers will actually meet the readers' or the teachers' expectations.

Shaping the Process

Our new instructor of writing realizes that the writing prompt he gave his students lacked a rhetorical context and other information that the students would have found useful. But he also realizes that had he intervened in the writing process, he might have helped his students explore the subject matter and their attitudes toward it. Having students engage in activities between the time the assignment is made and the time it is due will allow the students to work with the materials in a variety of ways that will deepen their understanding of their writing project.

Below are a few ways that teachers might engage students in the writing process between the time the paper is assigned and the time it is ready for an early response. These activities will be most effective if the instructor explains the value of engaging in them and makes them part of the requirements for the course.

1. Ask students to spend 5–10 minutes writing down everything they know about the assigned topic. Ask students to share their lists in small groups or on an electronic discussion board. The respondent should respond with questions or ideas for extending the ideas.
2. Review the student's topics early in the writing process in class or electronically.
3. Show students a sample of the genre you expect them to produce and explain the features of it to them. Also explain the successes and problems with the example. First-time teachers might write the sample essay and share it with their students.
4. Ask students to write summaries of related readings, share their summaries in groups or on an electronic discussion board.
5. Ask students to write an impromptu introduction. They may not choose to use this introduction, but writing it will give students another way to see their beginning paragraph. The instructor or other students should comment without correcting or grading the introductions.
6. To help students develop the counterargument, ask students to write a few paragraphs from the point of view of someone who disagrees with their thesis. Students should seek responses from others in the class.

Sometimes instructors skip pre-writing activities because they fear the amount of grading that such activities will produce. However, pre-writing activities do not need to be graded: some instructors give a "check" for completing the task; others spot check the work; still others use electronic discussion boards where students engage with each other, and the instructor looks to see if the students are on task. While pre-writing might seem as if it would take too much class time, Richard Haswell (2006) pointed out that "shrewd preparation of students for a writing assignment saves the teacher time in responding to it" (p. 12).

For Writing and Discussion

1. Examine the previous list of pre-writing activities and decide what you might add. Jot down other ideas and share them with the class or in a small group. Try out a couple of the activities on one of your own writing projects. Which activities did you find useful? Why?
2. Discuss the advantages and disadvantages of the ideas presented here and the ones you added. Which promote creative and critical thinking? Which might save the instructor time?

Providing Formative Assessment

Once students have a draft of a paper, instructors provide formative assessment through comments on the draft. However, we need to be careful that the comments are balanced, clear, and encouraging. Researchers have found many of these teacherly comments are ineffective because they are harsh, mean spirited, and vague (Connors & Lunsford, 1988, 1993; Straub, 1997). In addition, the comments often put too much attention on surface errors and stress fixing the paper to satisfy the teacher, seldom giving the student a reason to engage in deep revision (Sommers, 1982). When instructors focus on the local features of the text (grammar, spelling, usage), they communicate that commas or other surface errors are more important than the students' ideas. I had a similar experience several years ago. A senior colleague and I had struggled mightily with the tone and content of an all-faculty e-mail about our WAC program. Once I was confident I had the tone and content just right, I rushed to meet my colleague. He looked at it and responded, "There's a spelling error in the first sentence." I was furious that he had focused on a typo rather than on the tone and content of my revision. Once he had corrected the typo with his pencil, he agreed the message was perfect. When I pick up a student paper, I try to remember how I felt when my colleague focused on an easily corrected flaw rather than on the global aspects of the text.

To give students a reason to revise, instructors should first focus on global issues —thesis or argument, appropriate development and analysis of the evidence, organization, appropriateness of tone, and attention to audience and purpose. Once students figure out what they have to say and how they are going to organize their thoughts, many of their sentence-level problems will disappear. They may also find that whole sentences or paragraphs will disappear as they develop some ideas and trim others. If we encourage students to focus on sentence-level errors early in the process, they will be less likely to give up those sentences if even the sentences no longer serve their purpose.

To focus on the global first means that sentence-level issues such as grammar and word choice will receive attention only after the more global issues have been dealt with. Focusing on the "big issues" helps ensure that students' ideas are being taken seriously. The instructor's attention to the author's ideas and the communication of those ideas is more likely to motivate student writers (Sommers, 2006). Furthermore, focusing on surface errors during the process suggests that the paper can be made acceptable by merely correcting errors and puts the instructor in the position of copyeditor rather than coach or mentor. To put inordinate emphasis on correctness takes the focus off the students' thinking and analysis.

Sometimes problems with local issues indicate a larger problem with the text. For instance, a transitional problem might indicate a problem with the structure of the essay rather than the need for a connecting a transitional phrase. Similarly, a sentence that lacks clarity because of syntactical problems may indicate problems with content or the student's understanding of it. Although we know that words and ideas are inextricably linked, giving attention to the global issues first lets students know that the instructor values their thinking and ideas over their ability to use "spell check." And in the end, the instructor will help students become better writers if they pay attention to the students' ideas first. If we think about the compelling, insightful writing that we read, we are likely to overlook a small error, but if the writing is dull, unfocused, or pointless, we are likely to dismiss it entirely.

For Writing and Discussion

1. In a small group, share a paper that has received feedback from an instructor. Look at the comments. Count how many dealt with global issues. Count how many dealt with local issues. Which were most helpful? Which were unclear or vague?
2. What kinds of comments do not inspire a writer to revise? Share these in small groups and collectively make a list of those you believe would inspire a student to revise the paper.

Providing formative assessment that provides specific ideas for improving the text will help students revise their essays in substantial ways. Instructors might explain to students that they are getting their feedback early while they can still make changes. To provide formative assessment, instructors might use peer response groups. Chris Anson (1999) stated, "Hearing other people's response to their work helps writers to develop a kind of internal monitor, a 'reading self,' which informs their decisions as they enter new and more sophisticated worlds of writing" (p. 302). Faculty might also have students do self-evaluation or visit the writing center. Still many instructors want to make comments themselves, either through the effective though labor-intensive one-on-one conferences or with notes on the text. Some have found technology to be helpful. As technological possibilities grow, we can expect to find it playing an even greater role in classroom assessment. Below are a few of the technologies that faculty have found useful.

1. Voice-activated software such as JING, which is free and downloadable. JING allows the instructor to speak to the student while highlighting particular places in the text.
2. A recorded response to the paper that the student can play on a computer or iPod.
3. Word-processing programs that allow instructors to cut and paste advice and then customize it for the individual student.
4. Text expansion software that eliminates the need to write out phrases and whole sentences that the writer often uses (Cordell, 2010; Williams, 2010).

Some instructors wonder about using machine scoring of essays. Because of the complexity of responding to students and their writing (Sommers, 2006), it is unlikely that we will be able to rely on machine-generated responses to papers. As Richard Haswell (2006) and others (Brent & Townsend, 2006) have speculated, if we thought machines could do the job effectively, we might think about turning our assessing of writing over to them. But even if they could handle the complexities of reading the papers, it is unlikely they would be able to take into account the complexities of the individual writer and the classroom context.

Summative Responses

Although formative assessment will help students and instructors, whether through portfolios or individual assignments, eventually instructors will need to engage in summative assessment. While Sommers (1982) examined the responses of instructors to first and second drafts, Donald Daiker (1989) looked at the proportion of negative to positive comments on student papers that are turned in for a final grade. "Learning to Praise," which can be found at the end of this chapter, addresses this issue in more detail.

For Writing and Discussion

1. Summarize "Learning to Praise." Share your one- to two-page summary with others in your small group and make changes in your summary as needed before you turn it in.
2. Read "An Initiation" along with the prompt and classroom context provided below.
3. Make a list of the positive and negative comments you might make in response to the essay.
4. In small groups, share and evaluate your comments. Have you included enough praise? Are the positive comments clear and specific? Do they engage the student?

Writing Prompt for "An Initiation"

For the first assignment in the course, I'd like you to write a personal narrative that tells us something about who you are or what your interests are. The audience for this paper is the instructor and the class and the purpose is to introduce yourself to us in a way that will help all of us get to know each other. Be sure to include specific details that show rather than tell. Consult your class notes about writing successful narratives. Your narrative should be two to four pages long.

An Initiation

I walked into Michael's and started to drop my clothes leaving nothing on my cold scared body but a hot pink two-piece bikini. This is it. I want to leave my goody two shoes straight A image behind and jump into the wild party at Michael's. My best friend Jenn was already there, but she was wearing sweats. I looked around and saw many people I knew and many people I didn't know.

Most were drinking Heineken and listening to music. The lights were on in the back-yard many students sat around the pool. Michael himself pushed me towards the sliding glass doors and onto the pool deck. It was cold. I jump into the freezing pool as Michael had told me to do, I thrashed through the pool loaded with ice cubes, and at least it felt like icecubes. Minute after minute went by as I tried to move my arms through the frigid water. I thought of the Titanic, and Leonardo Di Caprio. And all I could think of was drowning. Like the poor lost souls on the Titanic. But I couldn't cry, I was too cold. My life passed before my eyes. People were laughing and cheering. Was it for me?

I finally dragged myself into the hottub that was tingling hot on my freezing cold body. I had made it. Kim handed me a beer. "Well that's it," Michael said as I gasped for air. "You've passed the initiation, now you're one of us." Ryan put his hand on my leg. I smiled, but moved away. I looked around and wondered if I could ever be goody two shoes again. I wished I were home eating popcorn with my sister and watching TV. But I had to stay for awhile. What would they think of me if I left now? The party began to move inside. As soon as I was out, I put my clothes on over my wet swimsuit, and went to the kitchen to look for a coke. I found one and quickly poured it into a shiny red beer cup. I found Jenn, who had also put coke in the beer cup. Would I ever be the same again? No, I wouldn't, but that was okay. Maybe my straight A/goody two shoes image is who I truly am. I had taken the road less traveled.

Providing a Note to the Instructor

Sometimes instructors fail to engage their students because they don't have the students' perspective on the paper. One way to engage students in a conversation about their writing is to ask them to write a note to their instructor about the essay. Below is an example of a prompt that the instructor might provide when the paper is ready for a first reading, followed by a sample note from the author of "An Initiation." Students can provide such a note either for their drafts or for the final submission of the essay. Either way, the note helps the instructor respond to the student. Below is a prompt the instructor might give to the student.

Prompt for the Note

Write a note to me explaining what you would like me to pay special attention to as I read your essay. What did you work hard on? What did you struggle with? What are you most proud of? Were there issues that you were not able to resolve to your satisfaction? What changes would you make if you had another week to work on the paper? What questions do you have about the work you've done so far?

Student Note for "An Initiation"

Dear Professor,

This story is really, really important to me. In my high school and in my first semester here, I studied a lot and didn't have many friends. Going to Michael's party over Christmas break was a turning point for me. I'm hoping I conveyed this. I tried to have an eye-catching beginning. Please comment on this. I worked hard to include specific description, but as always, I struggled with a narrative essay. Is there too much? I struggled with conveying my anxiety about the party and how to write the conclusion. I guess I wanted to say that I'm still the same person, but I discovered a side to myself that I had covered up. I hope you enjoy my narrative and I hope I have explained a part of myself to the class.

Thank you,

Alli

Students should turn in the note with their papers. Having the student's thoughts next to the paper allows the instructor to engage in a conversation with the student about her work whether the comments are formative or summative. When we can envision our student audience for our comments, we are more likely to write comments that engage the student in positive and productive ways. The note also helps us focus on issues that are important to the student even as we add our own readerly comments.

For Writing and Discussion

1. Consider the comments you wrote taking into account the note from the student. Would your comments change based on the note from the student? If so, in what ways?
2. Rewrite your comments and share them with your small group.

Grading Scales

Before the paper is due, the students should be aware of the criteria that will guide the evaluations of their work. Below is a sample of a grading scale.

A Paper
- Answers a question at issue and provides a thesis that helps organize the paper.
- Has a strong sense of the audience and purpose.
- Has an introduction that provides adequate context and identifies a problem.
- Makes excellent use of sources for analysis, discussion, and development.
- Has a title that anticipates the essay.
- Has paragraphs that have a central idea and purpose related to the thesis.
- Has smooth transitions between paragraphs, which clarify reasoning.
- Is untroubled by numerous spelling, punctuation, and syntax errors.
- Correctly uses the MLA format for citation of sources.

B Paper
- Has a thesis, which helps organize the paper.
- Makes use of sources for analysis, discussion, and clarity.
- Has an imprecise sense of audience and/or appropriate tone.
- Has a title that relates to the content of the paper.
- Has paragraphs that have a central idea and purpose.
- Has some sense of transition or development from paragraph to paragraph.
- Is untroubled by numerous spelling, punctuation, and syntax errors.
- Correctly uses the MLA format for citation of sources.

C Paper
- Has a purpose but is not organized around a thesis or a question at issue.
- Has not provided adequate context or identified a problem in the introduction.
- Provides some evidence and analysis, but it is not always tied to the thesis.
- Has no title or uses the paper assignment as the title.
- Has paragraphs that have a discernible purpose.
- Has spelling, punctuation, and syntax errors.
- Provides some consistent form of documentation of sources.

D Paper
- Purpose is not clear and does not have an adequate thesis or question.
- Evidence and analysis are weak or nonexistent.
- Has a significant number of paragraphs that are confused by lack of purpose, contradictory ideas.
- Has no title.
- Has a significant number of spelling, punctuation, and syntax errors.
- Has little or no documentation.

F Paper (Fail)
- Has no discernible purpose, question, or thesis.
- Discussion rambles from topic to topic and paragraphs are without purpose.

- Has little relevant evidence and is not tied to the thesis.
- Has no title.
- Is plagued with spelling, punctuation, and syntax errors.
- Has little or no documentation.

Grading Rubrics

Many faculty would not consider grading a paper without including an *analytic scale* or *grading rubric*. Similar to the grading scale, an analytic scale sets out the criteria by

TABLE 5.1
Language for Feedback: Grading Rubric

Grading Rubric	Poor	Fair	Good	Excellent
Answers a question posed by the assignment or created by the writer				
Has a strong sense of audience and purpose				
Thesis, evidence, and their connections bring a fresh analysis or insight				
Makes use of sources, details, or other evidence				
Has paragraphs that have a central idea and purpose related to the thesis				
Has smooth, logical transitions between paragraphs, which reinforce the main point				
Is untroubled by numerous spelling, punctuation, and syntax errors				
Correctly uses a documentation format for citation of sources				
Has a title that creates expectations				
Has a title appropriate to the rhetorical situation				

which the paper will be judged, making the teacher's expectations for the paper explicit. Some instructors believe the rubric saves them time when they are grading and helps their students understand the expectations; some add a point value to each item on the scale. However, specific point values ignore the fact that the whole may be greater than the sum of the parts (White, 1994). Furthermore, the rubric may not be sensitive to purpose, speaker role, and audience that occur within the same kind of paper (Cooper, 1977, p. 14).

Whether or not instructors decide to use a rubric, they should be aware of how one might be constructed and the reasons for using one or not. The following analytic scale was designed for an argumentative paper. Of course, the assessment criteria will change, depending on the kind of writing the students are producing and the assignment's place in the term.

Marking Grammar and Other Sentence-level Errors

Those who believe that student writing becomes worse every year (something I hear regularly on my campus) have something in common with Harvard professors of the 19th century (Huot, 2002). These same colleagues mark every error, re-write whole sentences throughout the paper, and cite pages in the handbook, expecting these marks will make students eager to revise. Generally, none of these happen to be true. Here are a few principles that grow out of the research and have been borne out in practice by legions of us who teach writing. Of course, all of these need to be offered in the context of the classroom (Mathison Fife & O'Neill, 2001; Sommers, 1982).

1. Less is more (Haswell, 1983). Pick out two or three of the sentence-level problems that are most likely to obscure clear communication. Mark them in a few places throughout the text or mark them in a single paragraph and give the student a brief specific explanation. For the next paper, pick another two or three errors.
2. Do not re-write the paper sentence by sentence. See above.
3. Do not use lines, circles, or other marks that students will see as vague (Sommers, 1982).
4. If a concept has been presented in class, comment specifically when you see it used correctly or incorrectly referring the student to the handbook or to the classnotes. Put the comments in the context of the class (Sommers, 2010).
5. Use specific positive comments to reinforce things the writer has done well (Daiker, 1989).
6. Insist that students use a spell check and/or grammar check on their computers. (Surprisingly, some students just don't bother unless it is a requirement.)

For Writing and Discussion

1. Keeping in mind the narrative assignment ("An Initiation"), consider the Grading Rubric on p. 160. What changes does the rubric need in order to suit the assignment? Make these changes and share them with others in the class. Then use the rubric to evaluate "An Initiation" and share your scores and the reasons for them. Compare your written comments to your marking of the rubric. Which better communicates with students? Could you use both?

2. Consider an assignment that you intend to give your students. Change the grading rubric to fit the assignment or create a new one. Share these with others in a small group. What ideas do others have for improving your rubric?

3. If you are teaching a class, ask your students to help you create a grading rubric.

For Writing and Discussion

In "Across the Drafts," Nancy Sommers brought additional research and fresh insights to the work on responding to student writing that she has done over the last two decades. Read "Across the Drafts" at the end of this chapter. Then read the following student essays that represent two different responses to an assignment given in a first-year writing class.

First-year Seminar: The Poetry of William Blake

Assignment

In this first section of the course, we have read several poems from William Blake's "Songs of Innocence" and "Songs of Experience." Please choose one of the poems that we have not discussed in class and write an analysis of it. Your goal in this assignment is to help others in the class understand the poem in more depth. You can anticipate that your readers have read the poem but have not explored it in depth.

1. Experiencing Life

Blake's time was one of great change. People had many challenges as they went about their lives. Blake wants to write about people and their challenges in his poems. He writes many many poems and most of them moved people. One poem that I thought was interesting and enjoyable was "The Clod and the Pebble."

In his poem, Black has many thoughts about love. I don't think he was talking about romantic love though. The clod is ugly but he is still happy. But the clod can not protect itself from the cattle who tromp along, sometimes tromping on the clod. Even so he has a bright out look on life and a warm heart. He is also innocent.

The pebble is the opposite of the clod. It is beautiful. It sits in the water, and sings. But the song doesn't sound like much it doesn't sound like the beautiful song of the clod because the pebble has a hard heart. The pebble has had experience and that makes him unhappy.

This demonstrates that the clod is full of love and the pebble is not. The love idea relates to the Bible where it says that: "Love does not delight in evil but rejoices in the truth." The clod represents truth because it is happy. The pebble represents "sin" because it is unhappy.

William Blake does an excellent job of bring together the ideas of innocence and experience especially in this poem.

2. The Clod and the Pebble: The Marriage of Innocence and Experience

All throughout his Songs of innocence and of Experience, William Blake makes comparisons between the naivete and goodness of youth and the cynicism and pain of age. Many of his innocence poems have parallel lyrics of experience, showing the two sides of the same social or political coin. It is through these comparisons that Blake seeks to compare the harsh realities that come with age and with the clear, unsullied ideals of youth. Yet a few of his poems attempt to contain both aspects of life, exposing innocence and experience within the same context and effectively linking the two. In "The Clod & the Pebble," Blake discusses the Christian virtue love, first ideally and then pessimistically.

The Clod of Clay represents all that is rough on the edges, still moldable, and unaffected by life and time. Not only does the Clod express its joy and love, it does so in song, with the happiness and melody of an unharmed innocence. At the same time, the Clod is not impressive to look at; one must truly look deep to find any beauty in a piece of clay. But appearance is not the goal of the Clod. Instead, its focus is upon pleasing those around it, making any attempt possible to create a "Heaven in Hell's despair" (ln 4). Although recognizing the sadness, pain, and death of hell, The Clod does not give up hope that, with enough love, the despair of hell can be changed into the hope of heaven. The Clod is idealistic, optimistic, and most of all selfless. It seeks to exemplify the principles of 1 Corinthians 13, specifically the phrases "It is not self-seeking" (vs 5). The Clod has not been hardened by sin, by pain, by experience of any kind. Yet the Clod is also easily moved— quickly "trodden with the cattle's feet" (ln 6). It has not yet built any sort of protective shell and is, therefore, quite susceptible to any outside force. The cattle of the world have every power to move the Clod because it does not suspect any interference and cannot protect itself.

The Pebble of the brook is clearly the opposite of the Clod. The Pebble, hard, smooth, and immutable, warbles out its tuneless words of woe. As the Clod looked rugged and ugly on the outside so the Pebble, refined by the constant stream of water, shines and glistens. It looks beautiful on the outside, but has nothing of softness or warmth on the inside. As the Clod sought to make a heaven out of hell, so the Pebble manages to create a hell despite the power and existence of heaven. Hurt and used by the experiences of coming of age, the Pebble is selfish and egocentric. It directly opposes 1 Corinthians 13, not just in seeking its own delight but also in taking joy in the pain of another (1 Cor. 13:6 says that "Love does not delight in evil but rejoices with the truth." The Pebble has become hard and cold by sin, pain, and experience, but it has also somewhat established itself. Constantly opposing the water of the brook the Pebble has learned to rely upon itself. It remains where it is, despite the continual pressure to submit to the power of the water. As time has pressed forward, the Pebble has learned to stand on its own, to be only mildly affected by the things of life, to look at life through tainted eyes.

Most of Blakes' poetry only focuses upon one aspect of existence—either the ideal or the reality. In "The Clod & the Pebble," Blake effectively sets the two extremes against each other to truly bring out their opposites. By doing so, he has in many ways summed up the who effect of the rest of his work on innocence and experience and, consequently, the futility of either perspective. To look at life as the Clod would, without defense or protection is just as meaningless as taking the Pebble's hardened and unloving perspective. It must be, then, that reality is a focus of the two extremes.

For Writing and Discussion

1. After reading "Across the Drafts," summarize it. What is Sommers' argument?
2. Break into small groups and discuss the ways in which "Across the Drafts" extends the notions of how we respond to student writers as expressed in "Learning to Praise"?
3. Do your own experiences with teacherly comments mirror what Sommers has found? Explain in a few paragraphs. Be sure to be specific.
4. Sommers' research was conducted at Harvard. How might Harvard's student population have influenced the study? Do you believe a similar study conducted at another institution would come to the same conclusions? Answer these questions in a two- to three-page paper. Be specific and draw from your own experiences.
5. Using "Learning to Praise" and "Across the Drafts," write responses to "The Clod and the Pebble: The Marriage of Innocence and Experience" and to "Experiencing Life." Before you turn them in, share them with others in a small group. Revise as necessary keeping in mind that you are responding to a student rather than to a paper. Would a note from the students have helped you with your responses?

CONCLUSION

Assessing student writing is a complicated task that has become increasingly complex as we learn more about the teaching of writing and the assessment of it. You may have found these assessment exercises both enlightening and frustrating. No one wants to do assessment (Yancey & Huot, 1997); however, if we can tie assessment more closely to our pedagogical goals, we are likely to find it more rewarding and productive (Huot, 2002). When instructors develop a clear approach tied to the goals of the course, good assessment can improve student writing and learning. If we hope to help students become better writers, we need to engage them in their text, not only to offer praise or criticism of the text but also to become engaged, to take seriously the individual student and his or her ideas (Sommers, 2006).

Whether assessment is summative assessment conducted system-wide or formative assessment conducted in the classroom, assessment should be an integral part of teaching writing. Because assessing writing is complex, contextual, and integrally tied to good teaching and learning, it is essential that we do it thoughtfully and well.

For Writing and Discussion

The writing instructor we met at the beginning of the chapter now realizes what he could have done differently during the process to make his job of assessing the essays easier and more productive. But he still has 25 papers on his desk, and he will have 25 writers in his class tomorrow. At this point, what should he do with the essays?

1. Using the ideas presented in this chapter as basis, write a three- to five-page letter of advice to the instructor outlining his options for dealing with or responding to

the papers. Recommend a course of action to achieve the best pedagogical outcome and convince him of it.

2. Using the syllabus for a class you will be teaching, build both formative and summative assessment into the syllabus. Share your syllabi in small groups and make changes based on the responses of your colleagues.

Teachers' Checklist for In-class Writing Assessment

* Is my assessment of writing tied to my goals for the course?
* Have I made the goals and the criteria for the course and for assessment clear to students?
* Have I focused on global issues?
* Have I made specific, positive comments?
* Have I limited the number of sentence-level comments or corrections?
* Have I engaged the students in the assessment process?
* Have I provided formative assessment during the writing process?
* Have I used students' errors to correct problems with my teaching or assignments?
* Are my comments specific, useful, balanced, and encouraging?
* Have I provided enough context for the writing assignments?
* Will the assignments and the evaluation of them be important to the students' learning?
* Have I written comments that take the writer and her learning seriously?
* Have my comments been addressed to a living, breathing human being?

For Further Exploration

Cambridge, D., Cambridge, B., & Yancey, K. (Eds.). (2009). *Electronic portfolio 2.0: Emergent research on implementation and impact.* Stirling, VA: Stylus Publishers.

This collection brings together articles from researchers on two continents regarding e-portfolios. In the conclusion, the editors see electronic portfolios as part of the future of higher education.

CCCC Committee on Assessment (2009, March). *Writing assessment: A position statement.* Retrieved from www.ncte.org/cccc/resources/positions/writing assessment.

This document sets out the principles and guidelines for ethical, responsible assessment. Guiding large-scale and classroom assessment, it was developed in 2006 and updated in 2009 by the CCCC Committee on Assessment and approved by the CCCC Executive Committee.

Huot, B. (2002). (Re) *Articulating writing assessment for teaching and learning.* Logan, UT: Utah State University.

Huot looks at ways writing assessment can be tied to teaching and learning, emphasizing the role of self-evaluation and the local control of assessment.

Meyers, M. (1994). *A procedure for writing assessment and holistic scoring.* Urbana, IL: NCTE.

Meyers provides a nuts and bolts guide for those who want to conduct large-scale holistic scoring.

White, E. (1994). *Teaching and assessing writing.* New York: Jossey-Bass.

This book, arguably one of the most important books in the field, explores all aspects of assessment but focuses on portfolio assessment.

White, E. (2005, June). The scoring of writing portfolios: Phase II. *College Composition and Communication, 56*, 4.

This article updates White's earlier work calling for portfolio assessment to be tied to the goals through the reflective letter.

Wolcott, W., & Legg, S. (1998). *An overview of writing assessment: Theory, research, and practice*. Urbana, IL: NCTE.

Willa Wolcott with Sue Legg provide a description of the controversies and theories that have shaped current assessment practices.

REFERENCES

Adler-Kassner, L., & Harrington, S. (2010, Sept.). Responsibility and composition's future in the twenty-first century: Reframing "accountability." *College Composition and Communication, 62*, 73–99.

Anson, C. (1999). Reflective reading: Developing thoughtful ways to respond to students' writing. In C. R. Cooper, & S. L. Odell (Eds.), *Evaluating writing: The role of teachers' knowledge about text, learning and culture* (pp. 302–324). Urbana, IL: NCTE.

Atwell, N. (1987). *In the middle: Writing, reading and learning with adolescents*. Portsmouth, NH: Boynton/Cook, Heinemann.

Banta, T. W. (2002). *Building a scholarship of assessment*. San Francisco: Jossey-Boss.

Brent, E., & Townsend, M. (2006). Automated essay-grading in the sociology classroom: Finding common ground. In P. S. Ericsson, & R. Haswell (Eds.), *Machine scoring of student essays: Truth and consequences* (pp. 117–198). Logan, UT: Utah State University.

Bruffee, K. A. (1986). Social construction, language and authority of knowledge: A bibliographic essay. *College English, 48*, 773–790.

CCCC Committee on Assessment (2009, March). *Writing assessment: A position statement*. Retrieved from www.ncte. org/cccc/resources/positions/writing assessment.

Connors, R. J., & Lunsford, A. A. (1988). Frequency of formal errors in current college writing, or Ma and Pa Kettle do research. *College English and Communication, 39*, 395–409.

Connors, R. J., & Lunsford, A. A. (1993). Teachers' rhetorical comments on student papers. *College English and Communication, 44*, 200–223.

Cooper, C. R. (1977). Holistic evaluation of writing. In C. R. Cooper & S. L. Odell (Eds.), *Evaluating writing: Describing, measuring, judging* (p. 10). Urbana, IL: NCTE.

Cooper, C. R. (1999). What we know about genres and how it can help us assign and evaluate writing. In C. R. Cooper & S. L. Odell (Eds.), *Evaluating writing: The role of teachers' knowledge about text, learning, and culture*. Urbana: National Council of Teachers of English.

Cordell, R. (2010). Smarter typing through text expansion. Retrieved from http://chronicle.com/blogPost/ Smarter-Typing-Through-Text/23725/.

Daiker, D. (1989). Learning to praise. In C. Anson (Ed.), *Writing and response: Theory, practice, and research* (pp. 103–113).Urbana, IL: NCTE.

Flower, L., & Hayes, J. (1981). A cognitive process and theory of writing. *College Composition and Communication, 32*, 365–387.

Glenn, D. (2010). A measure of education is put to the test. *Chronicle of Higher Education*. Retrieved from http:// chronicle-com/article/A-Measure-of-Learning-Is-Put/12459/.

Graves, D. H. (1983). *Writing: Teachers and children at work*. Exeter, NH: Heinemann Educational Books.

Haswell, R. (1983, Oct.). Minimal marking. *College English, 45*, 600–604.

Haswell, R. (2006). The complexity of teacher response to student writing; or, Looking for shortcuts via the road of excess. Across the disciplines. Retrieved October 5, 2010 from http://wac.colostate.edu/atd/articles/haswell.

Haswell, R., & Wyche-Smith, S. (1994, May). Adventuring into writing assessment. *College Composition and Communication, 45*, 220–236.

Huot, B. (2002). *(Re) Articulating writing assessment for teaching and learning*. Logan, UT: University of Utah.

Lindemann, E. (1995). *A rhetoric for writing teachers*. New York: Oxford University Press.

Mathison Fife, J., & O'Neill, P. (2001, Dec.). Moving beyond the written comment: Narrowing the gap between response practice and research. *College Composition and Communication, 53*, 300–321.

Mellon, J. (1975). *National assessment and the teaching of English*. Urbana, IL: NCTE.

Myers, M. (1980). *A procedure for writing assessment and holistic scoring*. Urbana, IL: NCTE.

Odell, L. (1981). Defining and assessing competence in writing. In C. Cooper (Ed.), *The nature and measurement of competency in English* (pp. 95–138). Urbana, IL: National Council of Teachers of English.

Ryder, P. M., Vander Lei, E., & Roen, D. H. (1999). Audience considerations for evaluating writing. In C. R. Cooper, & S. L. Odell (Eds.), *Evaluating writing: The role of teachers' knowledge about text, learning and culture* (pp. 55–60). Urbana, IL: NCTE.

Sommers, N. (1982, May). Responding to student writing. *College Composition and Communication, 33,* 148–156.

Sommers, N. (2006, Dec.). Across the drafts. *College Composition and Communication, 58,* 248–257.

Sommers, N. (2010, Oct. 6). *Responding to student writers.* Talk to the University of Puget Sound faculty.

Spady, W. G. (1994). Choosing outcomes of significance. *Educational Leadership, 51,* 18–22.

Straub, R. (1997). Students' reactions to teacher comments: An exploratory study. *Research in the Teaching of English, 31,* 91–119.

White, E. (1994). *Teaching and assessing writing.* New York: Jossey-Bass.

White, E. (2000, Nov.). Bursting the bubble sheet: How to improve evaluations of teaching. *Chronicle of Higher Education,* B11.

White, E. (2005, June). The scoring of writing portfolios: Phase II. *College Composition and Communication, 56,* 4.

Williams, G. (2010, Sept.). Using text-expansion software to respond to student writing. *Chronicle of Higher Education.* Retrieved from http://chronicle.com/blogs/profhacker/using-text-expansion-software-to-respond-to-student-writing/27119.

Wolcott, W. (1998). *An overview of writing assessment theory, research, and practice.* Urbana, IL: NCTE.

Yancey, K. (1992). *Portfolios in the writing classroom: An introduction.* Urbana, IL: NCTE.

Yancey, K. (1999, Feb.). Looking back as we look forward: Historicizing writing assessment. *College Composition and Communication, 50,* 483–503.

Yancey, K., & Huot, B. (1997). *Assessing writing across the curriculum.* Greenwich, CT: Ablex.

Yancey, K., Cambridge, B., & Cambridge, D. (2009, Jan.). Making common cause: Electronic portfolios, learning, and the power of community. Retrieved from www.academiccommons.org/commons/essay/making-common-cause-electronic-portfolios.

Zaldivar, M. (2010, Aug. 16). *E-portfolios.* Talk to the University of Puget Sound faculty.

Readings

LEARNING TO PRAISE

Donald A. Daiker
Miami University

In A *Moveable Feast*, Ernest Hemingway recounts his first meeting with F. Scott Fitzgerald. One night while Hemingway is sitting with friends at the Dingo Bar in Paris, Fitzgerald unexpectedly walks in, introduces himself, and proceeds to talk nonstop about Hemingway's writing, especially "how great it was." Hemingway reports that he was embarrassed by Fitzgerald's lavish compliments—not because he felt flattered by them, but because he and his fellow expatriates "still went under the system, then, that praise to the face was open disgrace" (Hemingway 1964, 150).

The distrust of praise among American writers abroad seems to have rubbed off on composition teachers at home. In a 1985 study at Texas A&M University, Sam Dragga analyzed forty freshman essays that had been graded and marked by four randomly chosen and traditionally trained teaching assistants. They wrote a total of 864 comments on the essays, but only 51 of them were comments of praise. This means that 94% of the comments focused on what students had done poorly or incorrectly, only 6% on what had been done well (Dragga 1986). The same pattern apparently prevails in high school as well. A study of responses by thirty-six secondary English teachers revealed that although 40% of their end-of-paper comments were positive, the percentage of positive marginal comments was a meager .007% (Harris 1977).

The conclusion that college composition teachers find error more attractive than excellence is consistent with a pilot study of my own conducted in 1982 at Miami University (Daiker 1983). I asked twenty-four colleagues to grade and comment on "Easy Street," a student essay chosen because it combines strength with weakness in both content and style (see pp. 108). I asked my colleagues to mark the essay as if it had been submitted in their freshman composition course. They made a total of 378 separate markings or comments on the student essay: 338, or 89.4%, of them cited error or found fault; only 40, or 10.6%, of them were comments of praise. What may make the predominance of correction over commendation even more significant is that during the previous month, a departmental memorandum reported scholarly consensus on two matters of grading: (1) an instructor should not mark every writing error, because students cannot psychologically cope with a deluge of deficiencies; and (2) an instructor should use praise and positive reinforcement as a major teaching strategy.

Scholarship notwithstanding, composition teachers have traditionally withheld praise from papers they have considered less than perfect. A case in point is the well-known "Evaluating a Theme," published in the *Newsletter of the Michigan Council of Teachers of English* (Stevens 1958). The issue consists of twenty-five responses—twenty-one by college teachers, four by secondary teachers—to a single composition, and the issue's popularity carried it through sixteen printings. According to my figures, the proportion of criticism to praise is roughly the same as in the Texas A&M and Miami studies; the Michigan teachers identified nine errors or problems for every instance of praiseworthy writing. Just as important, fifteen of the twenty-five teachers found nothing in the paper deserving of praise. In three of those instances, college professors sufficiently skilled to ferret out thirty flaws apiece in a brief essay could not—or would not—identify a single source of strength. Their wholly negative comments reminded me of a grade-appeal procedure in which I was asked to evaluate eight compositions written for a colleague's freshman English class. I read the compositions in order, paper one through paper eight, and I read them with increasing despair—not because of what the student had written, but because in responding to a semester's worth of writing, my colleague had offered not a single word of praise. Not an idea, not an example, not a sentence or clause or phrase or punctuation mark—nothing, apparently, merited a compliment. I began to wonder why the student was appealing only a grade, and I had visions of Bartleby the scrivener at work in a dead-letter office.

Francis Christensen observed a quarter century ago that there are two sharply contrasting points of view toward the teaching of English (Christensen 1962). The first he calls the "school" tradition, the second the "scholarly" tradition. The school tradition, nourished by a view of language that regards all change as decay and degeneration, encourages instructors to respond to student writing primarily by identifying and penalizing error. Because of the school tradition, it has long been common to speak of "correcting" themes. There is no clearer embodiment of the negative and narrowly conformist values of the school tradition than the popular correction chart. The 1985 "Harbrace College Handbook Correction Chart," to take a recent example of the species, provides seventy-one correction symbols for instructors to use and students to interpret. Why are correction symbols needed? Why write "d" rather than "diction," or "frag" rather than "This is not a complete sentence because it lacks a verb"? Presumably because instructors find so many errors to mark that not enough time remains for them to use whole words or complete sentences themselves. Significantly, what the correction charts never include is a symbol for approval or praise.

To become teachers of English in a "positive, joyous, creative, and responsible sense," Christensen urges us to replace the inert, rule-encumbered school tradition with more enlightened scholarly views. For several decades now, composition scholars have reported the value of praise in improving student writing. Paul B. Diederich (1963, 1974), senior research associate for the Educational Testing Service, concluded from his research in evaluation that "noticing and praising whatever a student does well improves writing more than any kind or amount of correction of what he does badly, and that it is especially important for the less able writers who need all the encouragement they can get" (1974, 20).

Since writing is an act of confidence, as Mina Shaughnessy reminds us (1977, 85), it is not surprising that the scholarly tradition emphasizes responding with encouragement. Ken Macrorie (1968) recommends that we "encourage and encourage, but never falsely" (688). E. D. Hirsch (1977), who believes that written comments may turn out to be "the most effective teaching device of all" (159), agrees that "the best results are likely to be produced by encouragement" (161). For William F. Irmscher, "the psychology of positive ... should be the major resource for every writing teacher" (1979, 150). All of these individuals would support Diederich's statement that "The art of the teacher—at its best—is the reinforcement of good things" (1963, 58).

Praise may be especially important for students who have known little encouragement and, in part for that reason, suffer from writing apprehension. Writing apprehension is a measure of anxiety established through the research of John Daly and Michael Miller (1975b). According to these researchers, the highly apprehensive writer is one for whom anxiety about writing outweighs the projection of gain from writing. Because they fear writing and its consequences, "high apprehensives" seek to avoid writing situations: they are reluctant to take courses in writing, and they choose academic majors and occupations with minimal writing requirements. When they do write, they use language that is significantly less intense than people with low writing apprehension; that is, they are more reluctant to take a stand or to commit themselves to a position. They try to play it safe not only by embracing neutrality, but by saying less: in response to the same assignment, high apprehensives write fewer words and make fewer statements than low apprehensives (Daly 1977; Daly and Miller 1975a; Daly and Shamo 1978; Holland 1980). The problem for highly apprehensive writers is circular. Because they anticipate negative consequences, they avoid writing. Yet the avoidance of writing—the lack of practice—leads to further negative consequences: writing of poor quality that receives low grades and unfavorable comments.

One's attitude toward the act of writing, Daly concludes, clearly affects not only how one writes and how often one writes, but even how others evaluate that writing (Daly 1977). What may be equally important—since writing is a powerful and perhaps even unique mode of learning (Emig 1977)—is that by systematically avoiding writing situations, high apprehensives close off opportunities for learning and discovery.

But the cause of writing apprehension may suggest its cure—or at least its treatment. A major cause of writing apprehension is past failure or a perception of past failure; high apprehensives perceive their writing experiences as significantly less successful than low apprehensives. Daly says that the "highly apprehensive writer expects, due to a history of aversive responses, negative evaluations for writing attempts. This expectation likely becomes self-fulfilling" (1977, 571). These "aversive responses" include negative comments on assignments and low grades on papers and in writing courses. The connection between writing apprehension and teacher response is supported by the research of Thomas C. Gee (1972). Working with 139 eleventh graders, Gee found that students whose compositions received either criticism alone or no commentary at all developed significantly more negative attitudes toward writing than students whose compositions received only praise. Moreover, after just four weeks, students who received only negative comments or none at all were writing papers significantly shorter than those of students who were praised.

Since positive reinforcement, or its lack, is so crucial to a student's level of writing apprehension (Daly and Miller 1975c), one way of reducing apprehension is by allowing students to experience success with writing. They will experience success, of course, whenever their writing is praised. For students who do not share their writing with others—and high apprehensives fear negative responses from their peers as well as their instructors—the writing teacher is likely their only potential source of praise.

But praise, however beneficial as a remedy for apprehension and as a motivator of student writing, is more easily enjoined than put into practice. Dragga notes in his study, for instance, that the four teaching assistants trained in praiseworthy grading all experienced "difficulty in labeling and explaining the desirable characteristics of their students' writing." He concludes that teacher training must emphasize explicit criteria for praiseworthy grading. The title of this article implies that praise does not flow readily from the marking pens of writing teachers; it must be learned.

Still, an instructor's conscious decision to praise the work of students is a promising starting point. Sometimes all that's needed is a gimmick. My own method is to allow myself nothing but positive comments during an initial reading of a student paper; I lift my pen to write words of praise only. Another practice is to ask, just before moving to another essay, "Have I told Melissa two or three things about her paper that I like?" R. W. Reising's technique is even more effective: he has developed a grading form that requires him to write one to three positive comments before he even considers noting a weakness (1973, 43).

But sometimes what we need is not a gimmick but understanding. We need to understand that what deserves praise is, for a teacher of writing, a relative and not an absolute question. As Ben Jonson says, "I will like and praise some things in a young writer which yet, if he continue in, I cannot but justly hate him for the same" (1947, 617). Following relative standards, we are in no sense dishonest or condescending in praising one writer for what we might ignore or criticize in another—even within the same class. Diederich urges us to praise everything a student has done that is "even a little bit above his usual standard" (1974, 20).

After all, we follow relative standards in most of the teaching we do outside the classroom. In helping children learn how to talk or how to color or how to swim, we don't hold them up to the absolute standards of Demosthenes, van Gogh, or Mark Spitz; we don't even expect them to match their older friends or siblings. In fact, we praise them for the most modest achievements. I still remember trying to help my six-year-old daughter Pam learn how to hit a softball in our backyard on Withrow Avenue. Although I pitched the ball as gently as I knew how, trying to make it eminently hittable, Pam just could not get her bat on the ball. We tried all sorts of minor adjustments in her batting stance—hands held closer together, feet placed further apart, head turned at a more acute angle—but Pam kept missing. Despite my encouragement, she was losing heart in the enterprise. Finally, on perhaps the thirtieth pitch, Pam did hit the ball—nothing like solid contact, but still a distinctly audible foul tip. Of course, I jumped up and down; of course, I shouted, "Way to go, Pammy!"; and of course, she smiled. I praised her lots more when she managed first a foul pop, then a dribbler to the mound, and then a genuine ground ball. As a high school student, Pam started at first base for the varsity softball team.

Even with relative standards, a commitment to positive reinforcement, and perhaps a gimmick or two, most of us could benefit from some practice in praise. For that purpose, let's work with an essay written several years ago by a Miami University freshman in response to an open assignment.

Easy Street

The crowd screams and chants, as a bewildered contestant nervously jumps up and down in search of help. Excitedly, Monty Hall comments on the washer and dryer behind box number two in trade for the big curtain where Carol Marroll is standing. The contestant, with glamour and greed in her eyes; wildly picks the curtain. But when raised there stands a 300 pound cow munching on a bail of hay. Embarrassed and sad, the woman slowly sits down.

The old American ideal of hard work and get ahead had traditionally been one followed by many men. But with the arrival of the twentieth century, there seems to be a new way to get ahead. The new American ideal of something for nothing. It seems to have taken the place of honest work. In our popular television game shows, the idea of being able to win prizes and cash by just answering a few simple questions seems to thrill the average American. It is so popular and fascinating that the morning hours are consumed with five to six hours of the programs. The viewer is thrown into a wonderland where everything is free for the taking. The reason for such interest in these programs is that they show life as most of us really wish it be to be—soft, easy, free. Our society now enjoys the simplicities of life, and our television game shows exemplify that.

One of the newest of all American dreams is to win a state lottery. What easier way is there to become a millionaire with such a small investment? The state makes it as easy as just reading a couple of numbers off a card, or scratching away a secret spot. Who hasn't at least once in their life, dreamed of hitting the big one, and living off the fat the rest of their life; without ever having to work again? Our country clubs, local junior football teams, even our churches have lotteries now thriving on that dream.

In our whole vocabulary there is no word that can command as much attention as the word "free." It sums up our modern culture and feelings. Advertisers use the word as frequently as possible knowing its strong effect on the public. The idea of giving something away without the consumer having to pay for it has made many a company successful.

The old American ideal seems to have moved over for the new. No longer does a man have to work late or get up early. By just guessing the right tune in five notes; he could be ordering caviar in the morning rather than toast.

When "Easy Street" was evaluated by college instructors, grades ranged from *B* to *F*, with *C* and *C-* by far the most common. But my colleagues found much to praise even in an essay they rated average or slightly below average in quality. Their comments of praise are categorized below, according to the four levels Nina Ziv (1984) used in her study of teacher response: conceptual, structural, sentential, and lexical.

A. Conceptual level.

1. "Your thesis—that the new American ideal is 'something for nothing'—is strong and clear."
2. "Your thesis is interesting and clear, and your use of particular, graphic details to support the thesis greatly aids your reader's understanding. The conversational tone of your paper also helps the reader understand you."
3. "The content of this paper is interesting & to the point, the essay is fairly well unified, and you show the ability to use effective details."
4. "There is much that is strong here; your sense of detail is good and your ideas are insightful."
5. "You have provided some excellent examples which capture the essence of the 'new' American ideal."
6. "Your ideas are brilliant and the way you have argued your point is convincing. Keep up with original and thought-provoking ways of looking at life around you."
7. "I like the scope of your commentary, which moves from the initial, interest-provoking example, to the statement of American ideals in paragraph #2, to the further example—of the state lottery—in paragraph #3."
8. "You come across as being perceptive and as concerned about an important trend in our culture."
9. "Your ideas here are strong and clear" (refers to second paragraph).
10. "Your paper has fine unity and some precise illustrations."

B. Structural level.

1. "The paper is well-organized and well-focused, with some nice paragraph transitions."
2. "Good details" (refers to next-to-last sentence of first paragraph and to middle sentence of third paragraph).
3 "An effective opening paragraph—good detail!"
4. "Well put, effective use of specific detail" (refers to last sentence of third paragraph).
5. "A superb choice of topic—and a good natural organization from specific to general—from private to public—and from analysis to significance."
6. "Effective introduction—your detailed description gets the reader interested and draws him into your analysis."
7. "Good strategy for your opening; you caught my attention."
8. "Good details here" (refers to opening sentences of third paragraph).
9. "I like this" (refers to the whole of first paragraph).
10. "I got a good first impression of this paper. You've started off well with an anecdote that gives the reader a good visual picture and gets her into your thesis."

C. Sentential level.

1. "Good sentences" (refers to middle sentences of second paragraph).
2. "Good parallelism" (refers to third sentence of third paragraph and to first two sentences of last paragraph).
3. "Very nice pair of sentences—clear and concise" (refers to first two sentences of fourth paragraph).
4. "Effective closing image. Good!"
5. "Nice structure" (refers to last sentence of fourth paragraph).

D. Lexical level.

  1. "Good—effective word choice here" (refers to "chants, as a bewildered, contestant").
  2. "You have a vigorous and full vocabulary."
  3. "Nice title."
  4. "Nice series—good climax" (refers to "soft, easy, free" of second paragraph).
  5. "Nice phrase" (refers to "with glamour and greed in her eyes").

Although these positive comments show that "Easy Street" has much to praise, instructors marking the paper more readily recognized error than they identified strengths, especially on the sentential and lexical levels. For example, many instructors pointed out the dangling modifier in the next-to-last sentence of the first paragraph ("But when raised"), but no one applauded the effective use of appositive adjectives ("Embarrassed and sad") as modifiers in the following sentence. It seems clear that we have been better trained to spot comma splices and fragments and other syntactic slips than to notice when students take risks: Only one of two dozen evaluators commended the student for "soft, easy, free," a notable instance of series variation with the coordinating conjunction eliminated. Instructors routinely called attention to the misused semicolon in "By just guessing the right tune in five notes; he could be ordering caviar in the morning rather than toast." Far fewer heard the interesting sentence rhythms created by the sophisticated use of repetition.

So perhaps we need to go back to school ourselves to learn how to recognize what merits praise in student writing. A good starting point for syntax are the chapters on free modifiers in *Notes toward a New Rhetoric* (Christensen and Christensen 1978) and in *The Writer's Options* (Daiker, Kerek, and Morenberg 1986), and the articles on coordination by Winston Weathers (1966) and Robert L. Walker (1970). But probably even more useful are sessions at conferences, at department meetings, and at workshops for teaching assistants in which we help each other learn what to praise and how to praise. But, if we listen to students, the "how" may not be all that important. At the same time that students tell us that criticism must be specific to work—a comment like "diction" or "logic" or "awkward" is almost always misunderstood unless explained in detail—they receive even vague compliments like "nice" and "good" and "well written" with gratitude and thanksgiving (Hayes and Daiker 1984). Don Murray once casually remarked at a Wyoming Conference on Freshman and Sophomore English that one of his favorite responses to student writing begins with the five words "I like the way you." He told us we could complete the sentence in any way we chose: "I like the way you use dialogue here" or "I like the way you started your paper with a story" or "I like the way you repeated the key word *animal* in this paragraph."

In his preface to John Gardner's *On Becoming a Novelist*, Raymond Carver (1983) recalls his experience as a college freshman in Gardner's creative writing class at Chico State College. Carver remembers, above all, that Gardner lavished more attention and care on his work than any student had a right to expect. Although Gardner would cross out what he found unacceptable in Carver's stories and add words and even sentences of his own,

> he was always looking to find something to praise. When there was a sentence, a line of dialogue, or a narrative passage that he liked, something that he thought "worked" and moved the story along in some pleasant or unexpected way, he'd write "Nice" in the margin or else "Good!" And seeing these comments, my heart would lift. (xvi–xvii)

It's a good bet that genuine praise can lift the hearts, as well as the pens, of the writers who sit in our own classrooms, too.

References

Carver, R. 1983. Preface to *On Becoming a Novelist*, by J. Gardner, xvi–xvii. New York: Harper.

Christensen, F. 1962. Between Two Worlds. Paper delivered to the California Association of Teachers of English, February, San Diego. Reprinted in *Notes toward a New Rhetoric*, edited by F. Christensen, and B. Christensen, [1967] 1978.

Christensen, F., and B. Christensen, editors. [1967] 1978. *Notes toward a New Rhetoric: Nine Essays for Teachers*. 2d ed. New York: Harper.

Daiker, D. A. 1983. The Teacher's Options in Responding to Student Writing. Paper presented at the annual Conference on College Composition and Communication, March, Washington, D.C.

Daiker, D. A., A. Kerek, and M. Morenberg. 1986. *The Writer's Options: Combining to Composing*. 3d ed. New York: Harper.

Daly, J. A. 1977. The Effects of Writing Apprehension on Message Encoding *Journalism Quarterly* 54:566–72.

Daly, J. A, and M. D. Miller. 1975a. Apprehension of Writing as a Predictor of Message Intensity. *The Journal of Psychology* 89:175–77.

Daly, J. A, and M. D. Miller. 1975b. The Empirical Development of an Instrument to Measure Writing Apprehension. *Research in the Teaching of English* 9:242–49.

Daly, J. A., and M. D. Miller. 1975c. Further Studies on Writing Apprehension: SAT Scores, Success Expectations, Willingness to Take Advanced Courses and Sex Differences. *Research in the Teaching of English* 9:250–56.

Daly, J. A., and W. Shamo. 1978. Academic Decisions as a Function of Writing Apprehension. *Research in the Teaching of English* 12:119–26.

Diederich, P. B. 1963. In Praise of Praise. *NEA Journal* 52:58–59.

Diederich, P. B.1974. *Measuring Growth in English*. Urbana, Ill.: National Council of Teachers of English.

Dragga, S. 1986. Praiseworthy Grading: A Teacher's Alternative to Editing Error. Paper presented at the Conference on College Composition and Communication, March, New Orleans, La.

Emig, J. 1977, Writing as a Mode of Learning. *College Composition and Communication* 28:122–28.

Gee, T. C. 1972. Students' Responses to Teacher Comments, *Research in the Teaching of English* 6:212–21.

Harris, W. H. 1977. Teacher Response to Student Writing: A Study of the Response Pattern of High School Teachers to Determine the Basis for Teacher Judgment of Student Writing, *Research in the Teaching of English* 11:175–85.

Hayes, M. F., and D. A. Darker. 1984. Using Protocol Analysis in Evaluating Responses to Student Writing. *Freshman English News* 13:1–4, 10.

Hemingway, E. 1964. *A Moveable Feast* New York: Scribners.

Hirsch, E. D., Jr. 1977. *The Philosophy of Composition*. Chicago: University of Chicago Press.

Holland, M. 1980. The State of the Art: The Psychology of Writing. Paper presented at the Inland Area Writing Project's Summer Writing Conference, July, University of California at Riverside.

Irmscher, W. F. 1979. *Teaching Expository Writing*. New York: Holt, Rinehart, and Winston.

Jonson, B. 1947. Timber, or Discoveries. In *Ben Jonson*, vol. 8, edited by C. H. Herford Percy and E. Simpson. Oxford, England: Clarendon.

Macrorie, K. 1968. To Be Read. *English Journal* 57:688–92.

Reising, R. W. 1973. Controlling the Bleeding. *College Composition and Communication* 24:43–44.

Shaughnessy, M. 1977. *Errors and Expectations: A Guide for the Teacher of Basic Writing*. New York: Oxford University Press.

Stevens, A. K., editor. 1958. Evaluating a Theme. *Newsletter of the Michigan Council of Teachers of English* 5 (6). Ann Arbor: Michigan Council of Teachers of English.

Walker, R. L. 1970. The Common Writer: A Case for Parallel Structure. *College Composition and Communication* 21:373–79.

Weathers, W. 1966. The Rhetoric of the Series. *College Composition and Communication* 17:217–22.

Ziv, N. D. 1984. The Effect of Teacher Comments on the Writing of Four College Freshmen. In *New Directions in Composition Research*, edited by R. Beach and L. S. Bridwell, 362–80. New York: Guilford.

ACROSS THE DRAFTS

Nancy Sommers
Harvard University

For the past thirty years, I have been a teacher of writing—work that I love, especially teaching first-year students. I have always been curious about the ways in which students read and interpret my comments—why they find some responses useful, others distracting, and how these comments work together with the lessons of the classroom. In 1982, I published an article in *CCC* on this very topic, but rereading this essay twenty-four years later, I feel the absence of any "real" students who, through voice, expertise, and years of being responded to, could offer their teachers valuable lessons. In returning to a topic that has captured my imagination for over a quarter of a century, I'm also returning to a topic that is part of our collective imagination, with so much scholarly attention paid to it that if you search "responding to student writing" on Google, you arrive in 2.7 seconds at the first of about 230,000 entries (Harvey 44).[1] Our collective interest in responding, I suspect, is deeply professional and *personal*. We feel a weighty responsibility when we respond to our students' words, knowing that we, too, have received comments that have given us hope—and sometimes made us despair—in our abilities as writers. The words teachers scribbled on our papers, inscribed in memory, are often the same words we scribble in the margins or at the bottom of our own students' pages—well-intended, most often written with great care, though sometimes carelessly, often caffeine-induced, usually late at night. These words, we hope, our students will take with them as they move from our class to the next, from one paper assignment to another, across the drafts. We don't take this responsibility lightly. The work of entering into our students' minds and composing humane, thoughtful, even inspiring responses is serious business. Given the enormous amount of time it takes to comment fairly upon a single paper, let alone twenty or thirty, we often wonder whether our students actually read our comments and what, if anything, they take from them.

As I look back across a quarter of a century of my own drafts, I remember that my first impulse when researching the topic of response was to imagine a hierarchy of effective and ineffective comments that could be isolated, identified, even memorized by new writing teachers. I quickly learned the limits of such research when I tried to separate comments from the context in which they were written—that is, the language established in the classroom. There is a story behind each effective comment that animates it for a student, making it more than mere marks on a page. But in our professional literature about responding, we too often neglect the role of the student in this transaction, and the vital partnership between teacher and student, by focusing, almost exclusively, on the role of the teacher. We offer prescriptions to new teachers that imply a hierarchy of comments: offering praise, for instance, is more constructive than criticism; posing questions is better than issuing commands; and using green or blue ink is always preferable to red.

The new perspective I bring to this topic today comes from the Harvard Study of Undergraduate Writing, which followed four hundred students for four years to see college writing through their eyes. With the leisurely perspective of time, and with the collection of over six hundred pounds of student writing, five hundred hours of taped interviews, and countless megabytes of survey data, my fellow researchers and I have witnessed the wide range of comments that students receive, not just in one course or from one teacher, but over four years and across the disciplines.[2] To see these comments through the eyes of college students is a kaleidoscopic experience: papers never returned; papers returned with bewildering hieroglyphics—dots, check marks, squiggly or straight lines; papers with responses that treat students like apprentice scholars, engaging with their ideas, seriously and thoughtfully. That students might benefit from a decoding ring to determine whether the check marks and squiggles are a good or bad thing will not surprise us. That students might find comments useful throughout the process—before and between drafts, not just at the end—will also not surprise us. What did surprise us, though, is the role feedback plays in the complex story of why some students prosper as college writers while others lag.[3]

It would be comforting to think that those fortunate students who receive the most useful comments make the greatest leaps in writing development. And it would be equally comforting to think we could link the lack of writing development to a student's scorecard of useful and useless comments. But in the matter of writing development, nothing is straightforward. The movement from first-year writing to senior, from novice to expert, if it happens at all, looks more like one step forward, two steps back, isolated progress within paragraphs, one compositional element mastered while other elements fall away. For some students, progress is uneven but continuous. Other students stall and become stuck writing the same kind of formulaic paper, again and again, no matter what assignment they receive. We wondered—would more or better comments have made a difference to these stalled writers? And what relationship could we perceive between those who progressed as writers and the comments they received?

A quarter of a century ago, I wouldn't have known how to ask such questions, let alone answer them. At that point, I focused entirely upon comments written in first-year composition courses to prompt revisions. And I concluded, "We do not know in any definitive way what constitutes thoughtful commentary or what effect, if any, our comments have on helping our students become more effective writers" (148). In the Harvard Study, though, we looked at all comments students received over four years. Outside the first-year or upper-division writing courses, we learned, students rarely receive writing instruction and are rarely required to revise. Consequently, instructors' comments on final drafts take on an even greater role; they often become the only place for writing instruction. After following four hundred students for four years, I now challenge my earlier conclusion by arguing that feedback plays a leading role in undergraduate writing development when, but only when, students and teachers create a partnership through feedback—a transaction in which teachers engage with their students by treating them as apprentice scholars, offering honest critique paired with instruction. The role of the student in this exchange is to be open to an instructor's comments, reading and hearing their responses not as personal attacks or as isolated moments in a college writing career but, rather, as instructive and portable words to take with them to the next assignment, across the drafts.

Colleges have great expectations for their students. But if we understand how slow writing development is—that is, how long it takes to learn *how* to write a college paper, to have something to say to a reader who wants to hear it—we become rather humble about the enterprise of commenting. If our comments move students forward as writers, they do so because such comments resonate with some aspect of their writing that our students are already thinking about. As we learned from the students we followed, most comments, unfortunately, do not move students forward as writers because they underwhelm or overwhelm them, going unread and unused. As one student suggested, "Too often comments are written to the paper, not to the student." The underwhelming comments look a lot like check marks and squiggles, or papers returned with the most cryptic of comments like "B+; your style needs improvement; otherwise, a good treatment of the topic." The overwhelming comments assume too much on the part of a student, as if instructors imagine their job is to comment on every compositional element all at once, and as if they believe that pointing out such errors will prevent students from ever making them again.

What emerged in every conversation we had with students about their college writing is the power of feedback, its absence or presence, to shape their writing experiences. As one student told me, "Without a reader, the whole process is diminished." That students care deeply about the comments they receive was revealed in our survey of four hundred students, who were asked as juniors to offer one piece of advice to improve writing instruction at Harvard. Overwhelmingly—almost 90 percent—they responded: urge faculty to give more specific comments. And when we asked students each year to describe their best writing experiences, two overriding characteristics emerged: the opportunity to write about something that matters to the student, and the opportunity to engage with an instructor through feedback. What became clear from students' testimonials is that feedback plays a much larger role than we might expect from mere words scribbled in the margins or at the end of a paper; feedback plays an important social role, especially in large lecture classes, to help students feel less anonymous and to give them a sense of academic belonging. As we learned from the students we followed, it isn't just that without a reader "the whole process is diminished"; rather, it is *with* a thoughtful reader that the whole process is enriched, deepened, and inscribed in memory.

One might easily imagine that this partnership around feedback is so valuable to students because it affirms them as writers. And, yes, affirmation is often the end result, but a key finding is that constructive criticism, more than encouraging praise, often pushes students forward with their writing; constructive criticism more than praise reveals instructors' investments in their students' untapped potential. In the case of praise, the messages it contains—*you* belong at this college; you are *not* the admissions committee's one mistake—are vitally important to propel first-year students forward with their writing and to inspire them to work harder. But over a college career, when such praise is not paired with constructive criticism, when it doesn't involve a back-and-forth exchange between student and teacher, writer and reader, it has the opposite effect. Instead, undeserved praise neglects to offer students an incentive to improve, nor does it provide any alternative approaches for future papers. Students who repeatedly receive comments from their instructors such as "I have nothing to say about this well-written paper," often stall as writers because they are never asked to do anything differently, never shown what skills they need to develop, nor are they engaged in a dialogue that challenges their own thinking.

The surprise was watching so many students make great leaps in their writing development after receiving what they identified as tough and honest assessment of their work. For one student, Ellery, the harsh critique he received as a junior was the only thing that could shake him from his glibness. His political science instructor wrote: "Ellery, this is supposed to be an essay, not a rush-hour radio talk show. What you write is a good piece of entertainment, but it is not the kind of writing that goes under the label of academic." Though blunt, this response was written not as a pronouncement, but in the context of a lengthy comment in which the instructor engaged with Ellery and his ideas. She goes on to model the kind of questions he might have asked and to model the way in which skeptical readers might look at the same evidence. Although tough in her assessment, Ellery's instructor treated him as a colleague, someone capable of great things, even if not yet achieved. This kind of intellectual partnership created through feedback showed Ellery that he was part of an academic community, made up of thinkers sorting out ideas, arguing with each other, and questioning each other's thinking. Criticism is not enough; like praise, it has to be paired with instruction. But in the call and response of feedback, when instructors model for their students a live, listening person, they offer students an image of a reader at the other end of the writing process, someone willing to listen and comment, critically yet constructively.

The success of this partnership has as much to do with students' willingness to hear and accept honest assessment of their work as it does with instructors' willingness to offer such responses. Ellery, for instance, received honest assessments of his writing his first and second years, but these assessments didn't help him become a stronger writer because he dismissed these responses as his instructors' idiosyncrasies. Or, in the case of Jackson, another student in our study, who, when asked as a junior how he might use his instructors' comments in future assignments, responded: "I don't think I can use these comments since each paper is a different assignment and a different kind of paper to work through." Jackson intuited the great challenge of undergraduate writing: to move from discipline to discipline, writing about Confucius in a philosophy course one semester, a Haydn piano sonata in a music course the next. But on another level, Jackson's observation makes clear that it will be difficult for him to apply even the best comments to future writing assignments since he believes that each essay assignment is defined by its topic, a discrete unit. In Jackson's view of writing, comments are tailored to each essay but also isolated from all other essays, and their purpose is, simply, to show students what they did wrong on a particular assignment.

We learn from Jackson's undergraduate writing career that part of becoming a good writer involves learning to receive criticism, both in understanding what an instructor intends and in the practical sense of knowing how to put that advice into effect in other courses and contexts. Jackson is correct that his essay on Confucius is a text onto itself, but part of Jackson's stasis as a writer stems from his belief that there is no continuity from one assignment to another. Because he sees no way to transport lessons from one paper to the next, he reads his instructors' comments as isolated moments in his college writing career, not as bridges between assignments. Even the best, most thoughtful comments will not move students like Jackson forward as writers.

But for any writer learning *how* to receive and accept critique, how to read comments not as judgment about one's limitations as a human being, or about one's failings as a writer, is not simple, especially for beginners who are quick to dismiss or deflect feedback. For first-year students, feedback is *monumental*, their most personal, most intimate and direct interaction with their college writing culture. And feedback comes, implicitly or explicitly, with messages of hope or despair about who they are and who they might become as students. While one student will respond, "My greatest reaction to all that red ink is gratitude," another first-year will shrug and say, "I guess all these comments mean he didn't really like my paper." Or, if a first-year student believes, as one told me, that the purpose of her composition course was to teach her how to "write quickly, adequately, and painlessly," we understand why such an attitude might prevent her from being open to comments that ask her to slow down, read texts closely and carefully, and, in a word, change. The differences among first-year students, we found, are less about ability and more about an openness and receptivity to comments, a way of seeing their writing experiences as something under their control, not random and outside of themselves. We found that one of the important predictors of undergraduate writing development is a first-year student's willingness to accept and benefit from feedback, to see it as instruction, not merely as judgment.

At its best, feedback comes out of an exchange in which instructors explain to their students what is expected of them as college writers, and students are open to learning about these expectations. By giving students a generalized sense of the expectations of academic writing, teaching *one* lesson at a time, and not overwhelming them by asking them to improve all aspects of their writing at once, instructors show their students how to do something differently the next time. The comments that students identify as the most helpful are responses that straddle the present world of the paper at hand with a glance to the next paper, articulating one lesson for the future. Consider, for instance, the feedback Louisa, another student in our study, received in response to her weak thesis and introduction. Here is her instructor's comment: "Louisa, a technique that can work well for opening a paper is to begin with an intriguing detail, especially one you find difficult to account for. Beginning in this manner not only draws in your reader, but also forces you as a writer to grapple with a troubling aspect of the text, which can often be a key aspect that you had previously set aside. This, in turn, can focus your thesis and argument."

As a sophomore, Louisa had complained in an interview: "It's tough getting better as a writer when nobody is showing you how." But as a junior, she was fortunate to work with an instructor who didn't assume that she arrived in his class as a fully formed writer. Instead, the instructor treated Louisa as an apprentice, an evolving writer. The tone of his comment is phrased, respectfully, as a writing lesson on how to arrive at a thesis, and how to engage a reader with an arguable claim. By giving Louisa a generalized sense of what academic writing calls for—write about what you don't understand; those things you have dismissed might be more important than you first imagined; start with details because they engage readers—Louisa's instructor composes his comment to offer a bridge for her to cross to future writing assignments. We concluded that when students have been taken seriously as apprentice writers, when instructors model the role of an attentive reader, such comments function to anchor students in their academic lives and, ultimately, make a vast difference in their college writing.

Writing development is painstakingly slow because academic writing is not a mother tongue; its conventions require instruction and practice, years of imitation and experimentation in rehearsing other people's arguments before being able to articulate one's own. The conclusion from the Harvard Study is that feedback shapes the way students learn to write, but feedback alone, even the best feedback, doesn't move students forward as writers if they are not open to its instruction and critique, or if they don't understand how to use their instructors' comments as bridges to future writing assignments. For students to improve as writers, a number of factors are necessary: in addition to honest comments, they need plenty of opportunities to practice writing throughout their college careers, not merely in one course or in one year, and plenty of opportunities to receive writing instruction in and beyond the first year, especially instruction in one discipline's method.

Feedback is rooted in the partnership between student and teacher, and as in any relationship, it develops its own language and meaning. That this relationship provides students their most direct contact with their college writing culture seems simple enough. But what isn't simple is the profound influence the relationship created through feedback has, not only upon students' writing development, but also upon students' sense of themselves as thinkers. When students receive feedback telling them they have "great insights" that their instructors have "never seen the topic discussed this way before," or that there might be "a whole level of other questions" for them to imagine, students understand that their teachers view them as people "with things to say," thinkers capable of insight and asking other levels of questions. Or, when a student tells us that he will always hear his instructor's voice telling him to change his ideas, revise his thinking, it is not just the instructor's words the student hears and carries with him across the drafts; it is also the instructor's belief in the student as a thinker, someone capable of doing good work, even if as a first-year student he is not yet accomplishing it. When students respond to feedback as an invitation to contribute something of their own to an academic conversation, they do so because students imagine their instructors as readers waiting to learn from their contributions, not readers waiting to report what they've done wrong on a given paper.

I once read a definition of a "true gift" not just as a possession passed from giver to receiver but, rather, something that is kept in motion, moving back and forth between giver and receiver, and outward into the world. One college senior, reflecting on the role of feedback in his undergraduate writing career, told me about such a gift: "If I bumped into one of my professors twenty years from now, I would know what this professor thought of my work; our minds connected at this juncture of my paper, and I will always be indebted." The word *indebted* caught me off guard. Indebtedness, after all, carries with it a connotation of obligation, of being beholden. But indebtedness also carries with it a feeling of appreciation and gratitude, a legacy of connectedness. And indebtedness goes two ways, like any bridge. As teachers, we respond to our students' great insights because we are grateful for the insights they have given us. And in encouraging our students to imagine other levels of questions, we, too, are inspired to think more widely and deeply. Feedback doesn't need to be monumental, but its influence often is.

As our students teach us, their papers don't end when they turn them in for a grade, nor do our comments end when we write them. The partnership between writer and reader, between student and teacher, creates something new—a collection of ideas that are larger than the paper itself, ideas milling around, moving forth into the world, across the drafts.

Acknowledgments

As I worked through the various drafts of this essay, I have been fortunate to receive comments from wise colleagues and friends. I would like to acknowledge the enormous contributions of the following colleagues to my own thinking about this topic: Joshua Alper, David Bartholomae, Patricia

Bellanca, Faye Halpern, Gordon Harvey, Karen Heath, Jim Herron, Tom Jehn, Suzanne Lane, Soo La Kim, Emily O'Brien, Stuart Pizer, Maxine Rodburg, Jane Rosenzweig, Susanna Ryan, Laura Saltz, Mimi Schwartz, Dawn Skorczewski, Stephen Sutherland, Kerry Walk, and Suzanne Young.

Notes

1   A rich and abundant literature exists on the topic of responding to student writing. In particular, I would mention the important work of Chris Anson, Lil Brannon and Cy Knoblauch, Summer Smith, Richard Straub and Ronald Lunsford, and Kathleen Blake Yancey.

2   To learn more about the Harvard Study of Undergraduate Writing, see   http://www.fas.harvard.edu/~expos. To date, scholars in our field—Marilyn Sternglass, Anne Herrington, Marcia Curtis, Lee Ann Carroll, and Jenn Fishman, Andrea Lunsford and colleagues have demonstrated the value of longitudinal studies to provide a wider perspective than research focused upon one college course or one undergraduate year.

3   To bring the voices of undergraduates into a larger pedagogical discussion about responding, my colleague, Jane Rosenzweig, and I created a film, *Across the Drafts: Students and Teachers Talk about Feedback.* In this film, we follow one student, Jon Stona, and his writing teacher, Tom Jehn, as they move through the process of composing the last assignment in Jon's first-year writing course. The film also features a wide range of students, first-years through seniors, as well as their professors, speaking about the challenges and rewards of receiving and giving feedback. The film can be viewed on the Harvard Study Web site, http://www.fas.harvard.edu/~expos; copies of the film can be obtained by writing to wrstudy@fas.harvard.edu.

Works Cited

Anson, Chris M. "Response Styles and Ways of Knowing." *Writing and Response: Theory, Practice, and Research.* Ed. Chris M. Anson. Urbana: NCTE, 1989. 332–66.

Brannon, Lil, and C. H. Knoblauch. "On Students' Rights to Their Own Texts: A Model of Teacher Response." *College Composition and Communication* 33.2 (1982): 157–66.

Carroll, Lee Ann. *Rehearsing New Roles: How College Students Develop as Writers.* Carbondale: Southern Illinois University Press, 2002.

Fishman, Jenn, et al. "Performing Writing, Performing Literacy." *College Composition and Communication* 57.2 (2005): 224–52.

Harvey, Gordon. "Repetitive Strain: The Injuries of Responding to Student Writing." *ADE Bulletin* 134–135 (Spring-Fall 2003): 43–48.

Herrington, Anne J., and Marcia Curtis. *Persons in Process: Four Stories of Writing and Personal Development in College.* Urbana: NCTE, 2000.

Smith, Summer. "The Genre of the End Comment: Conventions in Teacher Response to Student Writing." *College Composition and Communication* 48.2 (1997): 249–68.

Sommers, Nancy. "Responding to Student Writing." *College Composition and Communication* 33.2 (1982): 148–56.

Sternglass, Marilyn S. *Time to Know Them: A Longitudinal Study of Writing and Learning at the College Level.* Mahwah, NJ: Erlbaum, 1997.

Straub, Richard, and Ronald F. Lunsford. *Twelve Readers Reading: Responding to College Student Writing.* Cresskill, NJ: Hampton, 1995.

Yancey, Kathleen Blake. "Looking Back as We Look Forward: Historicizing Writing Assessment." *College Composition and Communication* 50.3 (1999): 483–503.

Reprinted from Nancy Sommers. "Across the Drafts." *College Composition and Communication*, Vol. 58, No. 2, December 2006, 248–257. Copyright 2006 by the National Council of Teachers of English. Reprinted with permission.

6

Genre

Irene L. Clark

- How has the concept of genre been reconceptualized?
- How can this concept of genre be helpful for teaching composition?
- What is genre awareness?
- Which text genres should be emphasized in a college writing class?

During the early days of the process movement, articles in composition journals rarely addressed the concept of "genre." Because the movement focused on self-expression and the discovery of personal voice as a means of empowering marginalized populations, "genre" was viewed as an old-fashioned, traditional, and outmoded concept, associated with an emphasis on literary texts, rigidity, and formalist conventions. Over the past 30 years, however, the word "genre" has been used outside of literary study, and it now pertains to more encompassing elements of a text. Reconceptualized as a rhetorical construct, genre is now defined not simply in terms of formal textual or structural characteristics, but rather in terms of *function*. Moreover, this new conception incorporates the idea that genre is associated with particular discourse communities and disciplines, that familiarity with particular genres constitutes a mark of membership or "belonging," and that privileged genres are correlated with educational and professional accomplishment. Understanding genre, then, can help students achieve success, academically, socially, and economically, and this chapter will provide an overview of theoretical issues and pedagogical applications that are relevant to teaching writing.

TRADITIONAL NOTIONS OF GENRE

Genre has been a subject of scholarly interest at least since Aristotle, who defined literary genres in *The Poetics* and characterized various types of oratory in the *Rhetoric*. For Aristotle, genre was simply a way of classifying text types, and it is this concept of genre that has persisted until only fairly recently. As Freedman and Medway (1994) noted in their introduction to *Learning and Teaching Genre*, the traditional view was that genres were (a) primarily literary, (b) entirely defined by textual regularities in form and content, (c) fixed and immutable, and (d) classifiable into neat and mutually exclusive categories and subcategories (p. 1). Defined in this way, the concept of genre was perceived as unrelated to, and even incompatible with, the new ideology of composition and the pedagogy that evolved from it. As represented in the work of Elbow, Emig, and Murray, process and expressivist pedagogy defined effective learning in terms of its relevance to the individual, rather than through the imposition of institutional goals, certainly not through learning particular genres (see Chapter 1).

RECONCEIVING GENRE IN TERMS OF FUNCTION[1]

Over the past 30 years, the concept of genre has been broadened and redefined as *typified social action* that responds to a recurring situation, that is, "that people use genres to do things in the world (social action and purpose) and that these ways of acting become typified through occurring under what is perceived as recurring circumstances" (Devitt, 2000, p. 698). Carolyn Miller's important article titled "Genre as Social Action" (1984) redefined genre by building on earlier work in 20th-century rhetorical theory, first drawing on Kenneth Burke's (1969) discussion of rhetorical acts in terms of responding to particular situations and then referring to Lloyd Bitzer's definition of the rhetorical situation as a "complex of persons, events, objects, and relations" presenting an "exigence" or necessity (Miller, 1984, p. 152) that the rhetorical act addresses. Miller's article thus extended notions of genres beyond their association with a relatively stable set of discourse conventions, defining them in terms of purpose and action.

How can the concept of genre be viewed in terms of function? Consider a genre that many of us receive frequently in the mail—a fundraising letter for a charity. In analyzing this genre, one could note a number of relatively stable and easily identifiable textual features: the heart-rending sketch of the situation or cause in need of additional funds (often presented in terms of an individual case selected for its potential in eliciting an emotional response), praise of the recipient's presumed charitable impulses and humanitarian concerns, a reference to other citizens who have contributed to this worthy cause, and a concluding section in which the request for a donation is made. From a traditional point of view, one might examine this genre in terms of its formal features—structure, tone, and style—whereas current conceptions of genre would view the letter as a typical rhetorical action (the request for money) in response to a recurring situation (the need of charitable organizations for contributions), in which the structure, tone, and style contribute to the genre's effectiveness and thereby become typical.

This new way of understanding a genre in terms of its social context provides a perspective that has potential for examining many different genres, real-world genres such as business letters or greeting cards as well as academic genres such as lab reports or school essays. This perspective views a text as a typical rhetorical interaction that is situated within a social context. Because genres develop through writers' effective responses to those situations, the new concept of genre views generic conventions as arising from suitability and appropriateness, rather than from arbitrary formal conventions. As Devitt (1993) explained the current view of genre:

> Genres develop ... because they respond appropriately to situations that writers encounter repeatedly. In principle, that is, writers first respond in fitting ways and hence similarly to recurring situations; then the similarities among those appropriate responses become established as generic conventions. (p. 576)

common problems / pattern [handwritten]

Devitt cited lab reports or letters to a friend as examples of genres that developed in response to recurring situations. However, the recent reconceptualization of genre goes beyond the development of appropriate text forms. As Anis Bawarshi (2000) pointed out in a thoughtful article titled "The Genre Function," genres also help shape and maintain the ways we act within particular situations—helping us as both readers and writers to function within those situations while also shaping the ways we come to know them. As an example, Bawarshi used the first State of the Union Address given by George Washington, who was confronted with a situation that had never been encountered before (an American president addressing Congress). Never having given a State of the Union Address, Washington based his speech on those given by British kings to parliament, even though Washington and Congress were both opposed to the very notion of kings and the concept of inequality from which the notion derived. (In fact, Washington had led a successful rebellion against the British monarchy.) As a result, Washington's speech, reminiscent of the king's authority, elicited in Congress a response characterized by homage and subservience, an example that illustrates the powerful role that genre plays in influencing not only the text itself but also the roles played by both writers and readers as they are constructed by that text within a social context. *genre = influential   assigns a role* [handwritten]

For another example of how genres are not only constructed by a rhetorical situation but also play a role in constructing it, consider the example of a syllabus in a college course. When I hand out a course syllabus, I am, in essence, assigning those receiving it to the role of "student," a role that generates perspectives and behaviors that are associated with that identity. Of course, everyone plays multiple roles in their lives, and some of my students are also parents, managers of businesses, health professionals, etc. However, when they receive my syllabus, they are thrust into the role of "student" and may begin feeling and acting like students: feeling anxious about fulfilling teacher expectations, asking about page-lengths and deadlines, looking around the room to see how other students are reacting, worrying about their rank in the class. The syllabus, then, although created for use in a particular scene, also plays a role in creating that scene.

As Bazerman notes in his introduction to Bawarshi and Reiff's important book *Genre: An Introduction to History, Theory, Research, and Pedagogy* (2010),

> The longer you work with genre, the more it reveals and the more it connects with—perhaps because genre is at a central nexus of human sense-making, where typification meets utterance in pursuit of human action. To communicate effectively we need to know what kind of situation we are in, what kinds of things are being said, and what kinds of things we want to accomplish. ... Many aspects of communication, social arrangements, and human meaning-making are packaged in genre recognition. (p. xi)

For Writing and Discussion

1. In the context of recent genre theory, text genres are viewed as typified responses to recurring rhetorical situations, both reflecting and creating the social contexts in which they occur. Lab reports or letters to a friend are examples of genres that developed in response to recurring situations. Moreover, the concept of genre goes

beyond the development of appropriate text forms, revealing how we think about and react to particular situations, as well as telling us a great deal about a community's or culture's attitudes and beliefs.

Select a genre (or two, if you wish to compare one with the other) and analyze it for what it tells us about the people and/or culture or community who use it and the situation to which it responds. *Your thesis for this assignment, then, will be a claim about what a particular genre tells us about how people respond to and experience a particular situation.*

You may select any written genre that interests you, although you should not choose a broad topic about which many books have been written (such as novels or plays). Some examples might be greeting cards, letters of recommendation, personal letters, postcards, billboards, and the like. Whichever genre you use, you should make sure that you describe what the genre is, paying special attention to its features (physical and textual), who uses it, and when and why it is used. Here are some questions to consider:

- What is the history of this genre?
- What do the genre conventions reveal about the culture, community, and people?
- What is its primary function?
- What textual and formal features are associated with it?
- What style is associated with it?

2. Find a genre that utilizes new media. What is its primary function? To what extent do new media enable that genre to fulfill its function?

For examples of how other students have addressed this assignment, please see the essay by Clifton Justice at the end of this chapter.

GENRE THEORY AND OTHER RHETORICAL PERSPECTIVES

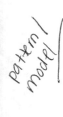

Although the rhetorical view of genre has become important only recently, it has significant roots in previous concepts of how texts interact with experience. In *Counterstatement,* philosopher Kenneth Burke (1968) observed that texts can be viewed as symbolic actions that have meaning only in terms of situation and motive. Burke noted that although there are "stock patterns of experience which seem to arise out of any system of living" (p. 171), such as the return of youth as in Faust, or betrayal, as in Brutus conspiring against Caesar, the effect of these patterns as manifested in literature are strongly influenced by formal elements of the particular time and scene. "Elizabethan audiences, through expecting the bluster of the proscenium speech, found it readily acceptable—but a modern audience not schooled in this expectation will object to it as 'unreal,'" Burke stated, arguing that what is perceived as effective or eloquent is strongly influenced by audience expectation:

> The distinction between style and manner is also fluctuant, as a change in conventional form can make one aspect of a style very noticeable and thus give it the effect of manner. (p. 173)

Burke's perspective emphasized connections between genre expectations and situation—that is, as writing has been increasingly perceived as a way of responding to readers within a given context, the resulting texts have correspondingly been viewed as incorporating particular strategies and approaches that have proven effective under similar circumstances.

Genre theory, then, views texts in a social context, a perspective that parallels other socially oriented theories that emphasize the rhetorical goal of text. Because genre theory conceives of writing as a way of responding to a specific reader or readers within a specific context on a specific occasion (Freedman & Medway, 1994, p. 5), it is consistent with the social constructionist privileging of context, audience, and occasion as well as with speech act theory, which emphasizes the function of language as a way of acting in the world and the importance of context in creating meaning.

CONTROVERSIES ASSOCIATED WITH GENRE IN THE WRITING CLASS

In my work with students at various levels, both undergraduate and graduate, in the United States as well as in England, Holland, and New Zealand, and in the classroom as well as in the writing center, I have found the concept of genre to be extremely helpful in enabling students to understand and produce both academic and "real-world" writing genres. Nevertheless, the idea of applying the concept of genre to work in the classroom has generated considerable scholarly debate. Two of the most important areas of controversy concern the extent to which an unfamiliar genre can be taught explicitly and whether an understanding of genre can enable students to learn new genres—that is, to *transfer* genre knowledge from one genre to another. Other controversies are concerned with the ethics of privileging particular genres at the university, and the extent to which genre knowledge enables or inhibits creativity.

THE DEBATE ABOUT EXPLICIT TEACHING

Significant genre scholarship has focused on whether the direct teaching of genre is useful in helping students acquire and apply genre knowledge. Aviva Freedman (1995) maintained that the explicit teaching of genre is not even possible because genre knowledge requires immersion into a discourse community, which will enable students to "ventriloquate the social language, to respond dialogically to the appropriate cues from this context" (p. 134). Freedman argued that:

> The accomplishment of school genres is achieved without either the writers or those eliciting the writing being able to articulate the sophisticated rules that underlie them. These rules are complex, nuanced, variable, context-specific, and as yet unamenable to complete reconstruction even by skilled researchers. (pp. 130–131)

Only in the disciplinary classroom, an environment that provides a rich context of reading, lecture, and discussion, does Freedman perceive that students can acquire the necessary "felt sense" of the genre that will yield successful writing.

Freedman maintained that people acquire genres below the conscious level, and her body of work does not include the teaching of explicit features of the genre, modeling, or a focus on particular strategies for learning to write in that genre. In "Learning to Write Again," she advocated an "implicit pedagogical model" that involves the following:

1. The learners approach the task with a "dimly felt sense of the new genre they are attempting."
2. They begin composing by focusing on the specific content to be embodied in this genre.
3. In the course of the composing, this "dimly felt sense" of the genre is both formulated and modified by the act of composing.
4. On the basis of external feedback (the grade assigned), the learner's either confirm or modify their map of the genre. (1987, p. 102)

The idea that explicit teaching is both desirable and possible, however, also has its advocates. Responding to Freedman, Williams, and Colomb (1993) supported the explicit teaching of genre because "what you don't know won't help you," and John Swales (1990), one of the most widely known of the genre theorists, applied genre theory to what he referred to as the characteristic "moves" within a scientific article. Working in the area of ESP (English for Special Purposes), Swales defined genre primarily by its common communicative purposes, arguing that a genre-centered approach to teaching would enable students to understand why a particular genre had acquired its characteristic features and ultimately help them to create that genre more successfully.

THE SYDNEY SCHOOL GENRE-BASED CURRICULUM

An early pedagogical approach that advocated the explicit teaching of genre, particularly in primary and secondary schools and adult education, was developed in Sydney, Australia, and is referred to as the Sydney School. This approach, while acknowledging the value of the process movement, questioned whether process pedagogy has been helpful for all students. Sydney School advocates maintained that despite its original goal of validating culturally marginalized groups, the process approach has done nothing to empower those groups or break entrenched class divisions in Western culture. Outlining what they refer to as an education experiment that has international significance, Cope and Kalantzis (1993) argued that:

> Many working-class, migrant and Aboriginal children have been systematically barred from competence with those texts, knowledges, and "genres" that enable access to social and material resources. The culprits, they argue, are not limited to traditional pedagogies that disregard children's cultural and linguistic resources and set out to assimilate them into the fictions of mainstream culture. But the problem is also located in progressive "process" and "child-centered" approaches that appear to "value differences" but in so doing leave social relations of inequity fundamentally unquestioned. (p. vii)

Contributors to Cope and Kalantzis' book *The Powers of Literacy: A Genre Approach to Teaching Writing,* which was intended to explain the Australian genre approach to non-Australians, maintained that the "progressivist" stress on text ownership and personal voice and the corresponding reluctance of teachers to intervene directly in changing students' texts has, ironically, promoted a situation in which only the brightest middle-class children, who are already familiar with the genres of privilege, will be able to learn what is needed for social, and, ultimately, economic success. Noting that "by the 1980's it was clear that ... the new progressivist curriculum was not producing any noticeable improvement in patterns of educational attainment" (Cope & Kalantzis, 1993, p. 1), these critics also point out that such a curriculum "encourages students to produce texts in a limited range of written genres, mostly personalised recounts" (p. 6).

A key point in the Australian perspective on genre is that school genres should be taught more explicitly, and that a more directive approach is not incompatible with helping students acquire a workable writing process. In fact, it may yield more fruitful results in terms of helping students master unfamiliar genres. The rationale was explained as follows:

> For those outside the discourses and cultures of certain realms of power and access, acquiring these discourses requires explicit explanation: the ways in which the "hows" of text structure produce the "whys" of social effect. If you live with the "hows"—if you have a seventh sense of how the "hows" do their social job by virtue of having been brought up with those discourses— then they will come to you more or less "naturally." Students from historically marginalised groups, however, need explicit teaching more than students who seem destined for a comfortable ride into the genres and cultures of power. (Cope & Kalantzis, 1993, p. 8)

To help these marginalized groups, the Australian School of genre, explored in *The Powers of Literacy,* edited by Bill Cope and Mary Kalantzis, advocates the following principles:

- Genres of writing are identifiable and fixed and boundaries can be drawn around them.
- Genres ought to be consciously chosen by writers and their writing should conform to the particular genre's structure.
- Structures of genres ought to be taught to pupils so that they will model their writing on the genre structure.
- There is too much emphasis on narrative forms in primary school and this is poor preparation for working in expository modes in secondary school, especially because such modes are characterized by an impersonal, neutral tone not provided for in most primary school narrative.

Two recent publications that also advocate the explicit teaching of genre are J. R. Martin and David Rose's book *Genre Relations: Mapping Culture* (2008) and Mary Macken-Horarik's "Something to Shoot For: A Systemic Functional Approach to teaching Genre in Secondary School Science" (2002). Martin and Rose presented an overview of a scaffolded curriculum and staged genre-based pedagogy; Macken-Horarik presented what she referred to as the "teaching-learning cycle," which consists of three stages: modeling, joint negotiation of text in which teachers and learners work together, and an independent construction of text, in which learners work independently (p. 26).

GENRE AWARENESS AND TRANSFERABILITY

Whether or not genres can be taught explicitly, a number of scholars have maintained the value of helping students acquire "genre awareness"—that is—understanding texts in terms of genre, viewing a text in terms of its rhetorical and social purpose, and recognizing how various elements of a text derive from its rhetorical function. Presumably, this insight will enable students to abstract principles from one rhetorical situation and apply them to other situations—that is, to *transfer* knowledge from one genre to another. Genre awareness is quite different from *explicit teaching* of a particular genre, which involves teaching students to write in a particular genre, a sort of "do it like this" approach that is often formulaic and omits analysis of its underlying rhetorical and ideological elements. In contrast, when students acquire genre *awareness*, they are learning not only how to write in a particular genre, but also gaining insight into how a given genre fulfills a rhetorical purpose and how the various components of a text, the writer, the intended reader, and the text itself, are informed by that purpose. Through explicit teaching of a particular genre, students may be able to create a text that imitates its form and style—sometimes quite successfully. But without genre awareness, they will not understand how the text "works" to fulfill its purpose, and when they encounter a new genre in another course, they may lack the tools to engage with it effectively.

Devitt's perspective was supported by Ann Beaufort, who maintained that students need to acquire a metacognitive understanding of how the elements of a familiar writing context can transfer to another less familiar one. In her longitudinal study of one writer's transfer of skills, Beaufort advocated the importance of "genre knowledge as one of the domains or mental schema that writers invoke as they analyze new writing tasks in new contexts—a domain that can bridge rhetorical and social knowledge" (2007, p. 188). Beaufort argued that "talking about genres can facilitate students' meta-cognitive reflection" (p. 188).

The issue of whether genre *awareness* can facilitate genre *transfer* has generated considerable debate and ongoing research (see Clark, 2010; Hernandez, 2010), and other scholars question the extent to which transfer is possible. David Russell, in "Activity Theory and Its Implications for Writing Instruction" (1995), claimed that although genre awareness is a desirable goal for a writing class, the goal of facilitating transfer is "over ambitious." Activity theory is concerned with various systems that involve "goal-directed, historically situated, cooperative human interactions" (p. 52), and an activity "system" is characterized by particular goals and ideologies. In the context of activity theory, Russell maintained that any attempt to teach students to improve their writing by taking a General Writing Skills Improvement (GWSI) course, "is something like trying to teach people to improve their ping-pong, jacks, volleyball, basketball, field hockey, and so on by attending a course in general ball using" (p. 58). According to Russell, the only way a novice writer will learn a new genre is to participate in the activity systems in which that genre functions. In other words, unless students are immersed in a particular discipline, they cannot learn how to write in the genres of that discipline. All they will be doing is mimicking a form, not really engaging with the genre.

need 1st hand experience

Russell's perspective was echoed in Douglas Downs and Elizabeth's Wardle's article "Teaching about Writing, Righting Misconceptions: (Re)Envisioning 'First Year Composition' as 'Introduction to Writing Studies'" (2007). Although Downs and Wardle acknowledge that transfer of writing knowledge can happen, they maintain that it is difficult to achieve. More recently, Wardle in "'Mutt Genres' and the Goal of FYC: Can We Help Students Write the Genres of the University?" affirmed the difficulty of using the first-year writing class to prepare "students to write at the university and beyond" (2009, p. 765). Referencing a number of composition scholars, Wardle argued that genres are context-specific and "cannot be easily or meaningfully mimicked outside their naturally occurring rhetorical situations and exigencies" (p. 767).

hard to fabricate

The Cognitive Perspective

A perspective worth considering in the debate about genre awareness and transfer was that of Foertsch who cites research in cognitive psychology. Foertsch (1995) argued that

> A teaching approach that uses higher-level abstractions and specific examples *in combination* will be more effective in promoting transfer-of-learning than will either method alone. Most cognitive psychologists now agree that generalized, decontextualized knowledge and

specialized, context-dependent knowledge are intertwined, differing not so much in character as in degree. According to the latest evidence, general knowledge and specialized knowledge arise from the same pool of memories, the same set of learning experiences. (p. 364, emphasis in original)

Foertsch maintained that it is valuable to "teach developing writers generic principles as well as strategies for transferring and generalizing their knowledge when faced with new tasks (p. 370), allowing students to apply "high road" or abstract principles to new problems (see Perkins & Salomon, 1988, p. 6).

In fact, the Wardle study, although arguing against the possibility of transfer, cited several pedagogical methods that can be useful for generating awareness: These include:

- Explicitly abstracting principles from a situation (Gick and Holyoak, 1983, cited in Wardle, 2009, p. 771).
- Self-reflection—asking subjects not simply to apply a strategy but to monitor their own thinking processes (Belmont, Butterfield, & Ferretti, 1982, cited in Wardle, 2009, p. 771).
- Mindfulness—defined as "a generalized state of alertness to the activities one is engaged in and to one's surroundings, in contrast with a passive reactive mode in which cognitions, behaviors and other responses unfold automatically" (Perkins & Salomon, 1988, par 19, cited in Wardle, 2009, p. 771).

The idea that "abstracting explicit principles" can be used to teach genre presumes that genres are stable, at least at a given time, that teachers have an understanding of what these principles are, and that genre insight can lead to genre performance. And of course, not everyone agrees with this view. An early work associated with the process movement, *The Development of Writing Abilities* (Britton, Burgess, Martin, McLead, & Rosen, 1975), maintained that genre boundaries are fluid, not identifiable and fixed, and others have argued against the explicit teaching of genre because of its association with authoritarian "top-down" pedagogy and an emphasis on form. Critics such as Sawyer and Watson (1987) were suspicious of the use of modeling, arguing that there is little evidence to indicate that modeling is effective and questioning whether conscious knowledge of structure makes for more effective performance in writing. Their position was that although students may be unfamiliar with a genre, it does not necessarily have to be explicated directly to become known (p. 48).

For Writing and Discussion

1. Think about the writing classes you have had. To what extent did they enable you to acquire genre awareness and/or understanding of how rhetorical elements impact a text?
2. Locate a text from the discipline with which you are most familiar. How might you use the concept of genre awareness to help a student learn to write in that discipline?
3. What is your position on the explicit teaching of genre? Where do you situate yourself in the explicit/impicit debate?

THE ETHICS OF PRIVILEGING ACADEMIC WRITING

Many college and university writing courses focus on academic writing, which is sometimes referred to as academic "argument," and even at universities where separate writing courses do not exist, academic writing, in some form, seems to pertain across disciplines. Although not everyone agrees on how to define "academic" writing, Thaiss and Zawacki, in their book *Engaged Writers, Dynamic Disciplines* (2006), present three criteria derived from a study they conducted from faculty in various disciplines. These are:

1. Clear evidence that the writer(s) have been persistent, open-minded, and disciplined in study.
2. Dominance of reason over emotion or sensual perception.
3. An imagined reader who is coolly rational, reading for information, and intending to formulate a reasoned response.

These criteria construct the image of a particular type of discourse, and it is the perspective of this book that this type of discourse is a useful genre for students to understand and be able to produce. Nevertheless, it is important to consider the viewpoints of those who consider academic writing as inherently elitist because it endorses a particular set of values that may be alien to those who come from a working-class background or another culture.

Shirley Brice Heath (1993), in particular, not only has questioned the relevance of the argument essay to other academic and professional writing tasks but also has castigated it for what she perceives as its exclusion of "many of our current students from the educational process" (p. 106). In her discussion of the origins of the "school essay," Heath pointed out that originally:

> English Composition emerged as a gatekeeping mechanism for immigrants and the increasing portion of working-class students attempting to make their way into secondary and higher education at the end of the 19th century ... The school essay stood as the external evidence of one's capacity to organize thought, to be logical, and to think in an orderly and predicable fashion. (p. 116)

Heath maintained that this genre of writing excludes a significant portion of the school population:

> Collaborative voices at leisure in the freedom to think and explore ideas; it excludes those whose habits of argument and uses of ideas as prompts to action depend on explorations of alternatives ... It excludes narratives, quick asides of witty observation, brief question-answer dyads that challenge but do not drive to a single truth. (p. 122)

Heath thus criticized the school essay as an example of what happens "when belief systems are taken up as institutional rules and practices." She maintained that we should "look at texts, not as autonomous artifacts but as open interwoven forms backed by belief systems and highly interdependent with both oral and written channels" (p. 124).

More recently, Donna LeCourt discussed the "classed nature of academic genres" (2006, p. 30) and presented what she has characterized as the "alienation narrative" (p. 33). According to this narrative,

> Working-class and academic discourses exist in dichotomous relationship where one discourse
> is depicted as in almost complete opposition to the other. Following this logic, working-class
> students succeed only if their class identity is stripped away in favor of a middle-class habitus,
> generating the feelings of loss and alienation depicted so vividly in the narratives of working-
> class academics. (pp. 30–31)

This perspective views the teaching of academic writing as a means of colonizing marginalized groups, and the writing class thus becomes a scene in which students are required
to change their identity. "You must think and write like us," is the approach that is used,
according to this narrative, "Otherwise you cannot succeed."

Certainly, this is an argument worth considering. Given what is now understood about
genre, we acknowledge that academic writing is not simply a particular form. It is based on
a way of thinking, incorporates particular ideologies and values and influences not only
people's actions but also people's identities. As Bazerman (2002) points out,

> The places you habituate will develop those parts of you that are most related to and oriented
> toward the activities of that space. As our grandmothers warned, if you hang around the race
> track long enough, you become one of those race track characters. (p. 14)   *experience*

Can people become proficient academic writers without accepting the values of a particular scene and perhaps the social inequities embodied in that scene? Is it ethical to privilege
academic argument in a writing class if it involves a transformation that can wipe out class
or cultural identity?

Autobiographical versus Discoursal Identity

LeCourt (2006) presents a response to these questions in the context of her own background, arguing that people can adopt a discoursal self without rejecting the self that is
associated with autobiographical experiences. LeCourt pointed out that her father, a high
school dropout, held a subscription to two academic political science journals and that for
most of his life derived

> his argumentative performance from such academic sources. To actually acknowledge cita-
> tions from them, however, would be anathema. He understands how such citations would
> "mark him in the context of a working-class bar." (p. 42)

LeCourt's position, then, was that although all learning is likely to have an impact on a
learner's identity, the idea that a person's "authentic identity" is in danger of being obliter-
ated by an emphasis on a particular academic genre underestimates the strength of that
identity. As Roz Ivanic (1998) pointed out, all writers bring an "autobiographical self" to
any act of writing, which continues to influence whatever "discoursal" selves a writer may
choose to project. A discoursal self, according to Ivanic, is created through the "discourse
characteristics of a text, which relate to values, beliefs, and power relations in the social
context in which they were written" (p. 25). Moreover, neither the autobiographical nor the
discoursal self is fixed and static. Both are subject to change over time and circumstance,
and if writers have self-awareness and insight into the concept of genre, they will be able to
choose which self they project in a text.

For Writing and Discussion

1. What is your position on the ethics of privileging academic writing?
2. In your own writing, can you discern differences between your autobiographical and discoursal identities? To what extent do you have control over these identities?

WRITING GENRES IN THE COMPOSITION CLASS

Personal Narrative

The controversies discussed above continue to be addressed in genre scholarship and generate questions about which writing genres should be privileged in a stand-alone writing class. One idea that informed the Australian genre-based curriculum was that the early days of the process movement placed too much emphasis on narrative forms in primary school and that narrative writing does not prepare students for working in expository modes. Victor Villanueva (1997), however, viewed personal writing as a means of generating student self-awareness, a perspective that is associated with the work of Paulo Freire, who constructed the idea of "critical consciousness" as a means of bridging the gap between the private and the public. Freire (1968) stressed the importance of having students look at their individual histories and cultures, to compare them with what they have been led to believe are their social places in the world—that is, to distinguish myth from reality. For Freire, the more students are aware of how their personal environment has been affected by social, political, and economic factors, the more they will be able to institute necessary change, both in themselves and in their environment. From Freire's political perspective, the self-awareness generated through writing personal narratives becomes an important source of political empowerment.

The use of personal narrative has also been justified in terms of helping novice writers find their "voice," a position that is often associated with the work of Peter Elbow. In his article "Being a Writer vs. Being an Academic: A Conflict in Goals," Elbow (1995) maintained that the goals of the "writer" conflict with the goals of the "academic," because academics "carry on an unending conversation, not just with colleagues, but with the dead and unborn—the Burkean Parlor metaphor." Elbow acknowledged that students, eventually, will need to enter that conversation as academics; however, in the composition class, students must first be *writers*. Toward this end, Elbow argued the value of having his students write from a personal perspective, pretending that no one has written about their subject before:

> I invite them to write as though they are a central speaker at the center of the universe—rather than feeling, as they often do, that they must summarize what others have said and only make modest rejoinders from the edge of the conversation. (p. 80)

Elbow maintained that for students to be writers (rather than academics), they must write about something that they know better than the teacher, and that "something" is usually their own experience. Otherwise, they are writing as test-takers, not as writers. For Elbow, the writing of first-person narrative is empowering, celebrating a world approached from a private perspective.

Others, of course, have disagreed. In a published interchange with Peter Elbow, David Bartholomae (1995) argued that academic writing, not narrative, is the real work of the university; if an important goal in the university is to help students understand how power, tradition, and authority are transmitted, then we must ask students to do what academics do—work with the past; work with key texts; work with others' terms; and struggle with the problems of quotation, citation, and paraphrase. Bartholomae maintained that although many students will not feel the pleasure of power of authorship unless we provide them with opportunities to write in the first person, they will ultimately need to engage in "critical writing," which, he maintained, is "at the heart of academic writing."

Robert Connors and Mike Rose assumed a middle position between those of Elbow and Bartholomae. Connors (1987) traced the question of what students are supposed to know and write about from classical times until the present, showing that there have always been two positions on the subject. In the ancient world, lines of argument were all impersonal, "the idea being that until a speaker had established his own ethos, usually through community service or previous rhetorical success, his own experiences were not important to the discourse" (p. 167). "Ancient rhetoric was a public discipline," Connors (1987) pointed out, "devoted to examining and arguing questions that could be shared by all members of the polity" (p. 167). He noted that proofs of argument were impersonal and that "to argue from personal opinion was both hubristic and stupid" (p. 167). This was a perspective on rhetoric that persisted up until the middle of the 19th century—when interest in impersonal abstract topics was replaced by a strong emphasis on personal experience, novelty, and the use of the senses. Connors noted that recent history of rhetoric has been characterized by a revival of the "romantic" notion of authorship, exemplified in the work of Peter Elbow, Ken Macrorie, and James Britton, and that the controversy over what sort of writing should be taught in school, "honest personal writing" or "writing that gets the world's work done," has yet to be resolved.

Addressing this question, Mike Rose, whose internationally known books, *Lives on the Boundary* and *Possible Lives,* discussed the needs of at-risk students in the context of the writing genres privileged in college writing classes. In "Remedial Writing Courses: A Critique and a Proposal," Rose argued personal topics are not necessarily more relevant than academic ones and that some students, particularly those from minority cultures, "might not feel comfortable revealing highly personal experiences" (1983, p. 113). Rose also problematized the notion of "authenticity" that is often associated with expressivist writing, questioning whether personal genres are any more "authentic" than nonpersonal ones. Moreover, in the context of remedial writing courses—which frequently assign fairly simple topics to put students at ease and help them avoid error—Rose observed that such assignments do not prepare students for their "university lives" (p. 110). He advocated a remedial curriculum that "slowly but steadily and systematically introduce[s] remedial writers to transactional/expositional academic discourse" (p. 112), the genre that students will need to be familiar with as they proceed in their academic and professional careers.

Academic Argument

On the other side of the controversy, others maintain that several modes of thought and conventions associated with academic argument pertain in other academic and professional contexts, and, therefore, that students need to be familiar with it. Gerald Graff (2003), in

Clueless in Academe, maintained that "one of the most closely guarded secrets that academia unwittingly keeps from students and everybody else is that all academics, despite their many differences, play a version of the same game of persuasive argument" (p. 22), which he referred to as "arguespeak." In earlier work, Susan Peck MacDonald (1987) argued for the pervasiveness of "problem definition" in multiple academic venues, noting that "the subject of academic writing either already is or is soon turned into a problem before the writer proceeds. No matter how tentative the solutions are, it is problem-solving that generates all academic writing" (p. 316). Similarly, in a comparative study of two hundred essays, Ellen Barton (1993) discussed the importance of "evidentials" as a distinguishing mark between arguments written by experienced academic writers and those written by students. Barton maintains that "argument is more unified than is commonly understood and far more unified than the fragmentation of academic fields might imply. Every scientist or scholar, regardless of field, relies on common devices of rhetoric, on metaphors, invocations of authority, and appeals to audiences" (p. 4).

Even Peter Elbow, whose work is most often associated with voice and personal writing, has acknowledged the existence of "academic writing in general," which he characterized as the:

> Giving of reasons and evidence rather than just opinions, feelings, experiences: being clear about claims and assertions rather than just employing or insinuating; getting thinking to stand on its own two feet rather than leaning on the authority of who advances it or the fit with who hears it. In describing academic discourse in this general way, surely I am describing a major goal of literacy, broadly defined. Are we not engaged in schools and colleges in trying to teach students to produce reasons and evidence which hold up on their own rather than just in terms of the tastes or prejudices of readers or how attractively they are packaged? (1991, p. 140)

Elbow's definition implied that students are more likely to acquire academic literacy through exposure to argumentation.

For Writing and Discussion

Consider the perspectives of McDonald, Bartholomae, and Heath on the importance of the argument essay in the writing class. Write an essay in which you explore the reasons for focusing or not focusing on this genre in college writing courses.

For Writing and Discussion

Read the following essays:
Rose, M. (1983). Remedial writing courses: A critique and a proposal. *College English, 45* (2), 109–122.
Elbow, P. (1995). Being a writer vs. being an academic: A conflict in goals. *College Composition and Communication, 46* (1), 72–83.
Bartholomae, D. (1995). Writing with teachers: A conversation with Peter Elbow. *College Composition and Communication, 46* (1), 62–71.

Compare the perspectives in each essay. Then write an essay that addresses the following question:

To what extent should the personal essay be included in the freshman writing class?

GENRE AND CREATIVITY

An issue that frequently arises in a discussion of genre is that of creativity and the extent to which attention to genre could produce formulaic, mechanical texts, all of them alike. This potential problem is exemplified in the importance given to the five-paragraph essay that many students have been taught in high school and continue to write, whatever the assignment happens to be. However, there is no evidence to suggest that helping students understand the purpose and conventions of academic discourse will necessarily result in dull, formulaic writing or preclude creative exploration of a topic.

In fact, a number of scholars have recently begun to acknowledge that genre awareness may actually contribute to creativity, fostering, rather than inhibiting, creative variation. Christie (1987) argued that genre enables choice and that "choice is enhanced by constraint, made possible by constraint" (p. 53). Devitt (1997) similarly maintained that "meaning is enhanced by both choice and constraint … in genre no less than in words" (p. 53) and that "within any genre there is a great deal of free variation" (p. 52). In fact, one might make the case that creativity can exist *only* within the context of genre, that genre awareness is actually a prerequisite for creativity, and that students will be unable to engage in creative adaptation of a genre if they are unaware of what the genre is.

This association between genre and creativity suggests that for any text to be considered "creative," it must push across the boundaries that define it, but that at least some of those boundaries must be present for creativity to occur. A work is designated "creative" when it incorporates both constraint and choice. Thus, Mozart's achievement in the sonata form had to occur within the context of that form, as did Picasso's visual juxtapositions within an established tradition of form and color. Because creativity rattles established certitudes, it cannot occur without some element of certitude. This association suggests that in order for any piece of writing to be considered "creative," it must be recognizable for what it is—a school essay, poem, short story, and the like—as opposed to some other genre.

If one assumes a connection between creativity and genre, then it is likely that the explicit teaching of genre will enable, rather than stifle, opportunities for creative variation. As Bakhtin (1986) pointed out:

> Where there is style, there is genre. The transfer of style from one genre to another not only alters the way a style sounds under conditions of a genre unnatural to it but also violates or renews the given genre. (p. 66)

This idea that genre awareness facilitates rather than constrains creativity was implicit in Wendy Bishop's criticism of how academic writing is presented in the writing classroom. Bishop (1997) noted that writing teachers tend to accept only one rigidly defined genre of writing from their students, even though their own scholarship utilizes "alternative styles, mixed genres, co-authored texts" (p. 5). Referring to teachers who do not encourage experimentation with genre as "discourse autocrats" (p. 5), Bishop argued that excellence in writing occurs when resources from one genre are superimposed on another and pointed out that scholars in composition have recently learned to broaden their writing and thinking so that "thesis and data driven work now thrives side by side with narrative and metaphor-rich investigations" (p. 4). Good writing is characterized by both "control and carnival," Bishop maintained; moreover, it is important for composition teachers to rethink "the ways we teach convention making and convention breaking in first-year writing classrooms" (p. 4). And such a rethinking, Bishop argued, requires understanding of genre.

In fact, recent work in creativity by Clark, Hale, and Neff-Lippmann (2010) has indicated that the definition of creativity varies a great deal according to the depth of understanding one has with a genre. On the basis of questionnaires that were administered to lower division students, upper division students and faculty, Clark, Hale, and Lippman found that notions of creativity changed as students gained expertise within a field, becoming more similar to perspectives expressed by faculty. Lower division students tended to view creativity as tied to external stylistic features of a text; moreover they did not see creativity as a way of making "new" meaning within a disciplinary community. These students had only vague notions of "genre awareness" but because they wanted to be creative, they tended to add creativity in the only way they knew how: as an add-on. In contrast, juniors and seniors, more deeply involved in their majors, had a different understanding of the relationship between creativity and genre, understanding it not as a stylistic add-on, but as growing out of connections among ideas—framing an interesting research question, presenting a good argument, or thinking "outside the box." Their perspectives were close to those expressed by faculty, who viewed creativity as closely linked to immersion in a field and aligned with genre expectations.

The conclusions of the Clark, Hale, and Neff-Lippman study were as follows:

- that creativity and genre are compatible
- that creativity requires understanding of and familiarity with genre
- that insight into the interconnections between genre and creativity increases with genre knowledge
- that novice students define creativity differently from more advanced students and faculty.

For Writing and Discussion

How do you define creativity? What do you think is the relationship between genre awareness and creativity?

Write an essay that explores the extent to which creativity should be considered important in the writing class. If you are teaching a class yourself, discuss the extent to which you reward creative papers with higher grades.

For Writing and Discussion

Gunter Kress, in *Learning to Write* (1982), argued that "there is a small and fixed number of genres in any written tradition" and that "the individual can no more create a new genre type than he or she can create a new sentence type" (pp. 98–99). Kress went on to say that "the creativity which is permitted to the individual exists in deciding in which type or sentence or genre to encode the idea" (p. 99), thereby limiting the possibilities of creativity to those of form and the choice of form.

Discuss this perspective among fellow students. Then write an essay in which you respond to Kress's perspective.

GENRE AND NEW MEDIA

There is no question that technology has become an increasingly important component of many writing classes, raising the issue of how new media are likely to impact academic writing genres. Will academic writing genres change significantly under the influence of new media? Or will new media become just another tool? Outlining two major perspectives on this issue, Knobel and Lankshear (2007) have argued that new technologies can be used simply to "replicate longstanding literacy practices" (p. 7), but, on the other hand, new literacies may "mobilize very different kinds of values and priorities and sensibilities than the literacies we are familiar with, changing the nature of the academic genres we want our students to acquire" (p. 7). At the point of this writing, new media are already playing an increasingly important role in the writing class. Many instructors allow or require their students to submit their writing on blogs, create websites, and incorporate visual and interactive elements into their work, and it is certainly possible that the expectations of academic writing genres will change as these media-oriented genres become commonplace.

A potentially new genre that has emerged as a product of new media is the "weblog," which has drawn considerable scholarly attention. Carolyn Miller and Dawn Shepherd have studied this potential new genre in terms of substance, form, and rhetorical action, examining a large corpus of blogs. In the English department at California State University, Northridge, for example, the blog has become a genre that is used for a culminating assignment at the end of a semester. Although a blog is often associated with the voicing of opinions, as in restaurant or movie blogs, blogs in the department are being used more like websites. Students use the blog as a repository for research materials and eventually post their final essays on the blog, enhanced with hypertext and visual materials. This sort of blog foregrounds the concept of audience in that students realize that the blogs they have created for a particular course may be broadcast worldwide.

In their article, "Blogging as Social Action: A Genre Analysis of the Weblog," Miller and Shepherd examine a large number of blogs and bloggers' reflections, concluding that the blog is a hybrid genre that derives from other antecedent genres, such as the diary, commonplace books and ship logs (2004, p. 11, cited in Bawarshi and Reiff, 2010, p. 164). They conclude that the blog is an emergent genre that combines the personal and public in its rhetorical form and allows bloggers to cultivate the self in a public way (p. 164).

The Influence of Antecedent Genres

The extent to which new media are likely to impact the genres in the writing class emerged in a classroom-based study of web-based writing assignments conducted by Mike Edwards and Heidi McKee (2005) in "The Teaching and Learning of Web Genres in First-Year Composition." Edwards and McKee asked students to develop a persuasive essay as a multipage website that incorporated links and graphics, and when students produced their essays, some tended to be more like argument essays associated with print while others were more multilinear, challenging the thought progression and reasoning patterns associated with argument. Both teachers discovered, however, that the choices students made and the effectiveness of those choices depended on their prior genre knowledge of the web genres—the antecedent genres—they were using. They also found that the web genres and websites that students were most familiar with were often not the same as those with which teachers were familiar—unsurprising but important to remember when considering the use of new media in a writing class.

For Further Discussion

Beach, R., Anson, C., Breuch, L. K., & Swiss, T. (2009). *Teaching writing using blogs, wikis, and other digital tools.* Norwood, MA: Christopher-Gordon.
Wysocki, A. F. et. al. (2004). *Writing new media: Theory and applications for expanding the teaching of composition.* Logan, UT: Utah State University Press.

ALTERNATIVE GENRES

Creative Nonfiction

In some academic writing scenes, teachers and scholars have focused on "creative nonfiction," a genre that combines the scholarly rigor and public concerns of academic writing with the energy and personal involvement of personal narrative. Because this genre often utilizes first-person perspectives as a means of developing a topic, creative nonfiction enables students to include relevant personal experience and opinion within an academic context. An advocate of introducing creative nonfiction to the composition class, Wendy Bishop (1997) noted that many of the journal articles in rhetoric and composition now include personal opinion and examples based on lived experience, allowing the writer to move back and forth between an informal, casual tone to the more formal, depersonalized tone associated with academic discourse. As rigid standards for academic writing are being examined, the text strategies associated with creative nonfiction are appearing with increasing frequency in the writing class.

Literary Genres

In a thought-provoking article, Amy Devitt (2000) called for rhetorical and literary genre theorists to recognize commonalities. Whereas literary genres tended to be regarded as a static categorization of textual features, recent concern with the "interactive nature of textual meaning" suggests that both rhetorical and literary genres "can be defined as a dynamic concept created through the interaction of writers, readers, past texts, and contexts" (p. 699). Devitt suggested that genre provides an important approach for examining all kinds of texts, because, as Derrida (1980) maintained, "every text participates in one or several genres, there is no genreless text; there is always a genre and genres, yet such participation never amounts to belonging" (p. 65). Similarly, Marjory Perloff (1989), addressing the question of whether genre is a necessary term in a postmodern world, observed that "even as we pronounce on the 'irrelevance' of genre in a time of postmodern openness, inclusiveness, and flexibility, we are all the while applying generic markers to the subjects of our discussion" (pp. 5–6).

OTHER TERMS ASSOCIATED WITH GENRE

Bawarshi and Reiff's book *Genre: An Introduction to History, Theory, Research and Pedagogy* (2010) concludes with a detailed glossary of terms associated with the concept of genre. For the purposes of this book, however, I will refer only to terms that are particularly relevant for teaching college composition.

Antecedent Genres. These are genres of the past that often influence a rhetorical response. The term is associated with Kathleen Jamieson's article, "Antecedent Genre as Rhetorical Constraint" (1975), which discusses several instances in which antecedent genres imposed inappropriate responses. Antecedent genres can help students learn new genres, but sometimes they may lead students in an inappropriate direction. Students' tendency to cling to the five-paragraph essay in all academic contexts is an example of how an antecedent genre can impose an incorrect response.

Discourse Community. The term "discourse" refers to all kinds of communication, and a discourse community refers to the people who utilize a particular type of discourse to achieve common goals. Swales (1990) found that a discourse community utilizes genres to achieve those goals and that membership in a discourse community is strongly connected to a member's familiarity and expertise with these genres.

Exigence. A term associated with Lloyd Bitzer's article, "The Rhetorical Situation" (1968), which refers to a problem, situation, or need that can be impacted or changed in some way through writing. Bitzer used the word "exigence" to refer to a defect, an obstacle, or "something that is other than it should be." In discovering a topic for writing, students should be encouraged to locate an exigence.

Genre Awareness. A pedagogical approach that aims to foster a critical understanding of genres, in terms of both their rhetorical purposes and ideological effects. Genre awareness focuses on developing insight into how a genre functions. It is not the same as explicitly teaching a particular genre.

Pedagogical Memory. The term "pedagogical memory" derives from a research study conducted at UC Irvine by Susan Jarratt and her colleagues. I first heard the term used at Jarratt's presentation at the Santa Barbara research conference and an article reporting on the research was published in the WPA journal. The study involved interviews with students several semesters after they had completed a first-year writing course to determine the extent to which they were able to transfer what they had learned to other writing tasks. What Jarratt discovered through the interviews is that although many students across the disciplines had "internalized the idea of writing as a process and a mode of learning ... even the most successful ... lacked fluency in basic writing terminology" (Jarratt, Mack, Sartor, & Watson, 2009, p. 48). On the basis of this study, the authors recommend helping students translate discourse about writing from one site to another.

Rhetoric. The term "rhetoric" refers to the effective use of language to persuade, inform or educate. Although people sometimes use the term to mean words that mean nothing, as in "that is just rhetoric," ancient Greek philosophers considered it a serious form of

communication that is oriented toward influencing an audience. Helping students understand the importance of rhetoric is essential to enabling them to write effectively, both academically and professionally.

The Rhetorical Situation. Lloyd Bitzer defined a rhetorical situation as "a complex of persons, events, objects, and relations presenting an actual or potential exigence which can be
completely or partially removed if discourse, introduced into the situation, can so constrain
human decision or action as to bring about the significant modification of the exigence"
(p. 18). The recognition of a rhetorical situation can enable students to develop ideas for
writing, helping them understand how the writer, audience, context, and purpose can be
utilized in addressing it effectively.

Uptake. The term "uptake" was originally associated with speech act theory, referring
to how an act or a statement can result in a subsequent action. For example, the statement
"it is hot in here" may be said in order to get someone to get someone to open a window.
Extending the concept, Anne Freedman (1994) maintained that genres can be defined by
the uptake they generate, that uptakes are learned, and that appropriate uptakes are necessary for membership in a discourse community. In the context of teaching writing, a writing assignment prompt generates a particular uptake in the form of an academic essay, and
the ability to respond appropriately is associated with academic success.

ADDRESSING GENRE IN THE WRITING CLASS

Pedagogical applications of genre have generated considerable controversy, and the extent to
which genre awareness can lead to enhanced genre performance has yet to be determined.
Nevertheless, the writing class can utilize a genre perspective in a number of ways, such as
those suggested below:

1. The writing class can help students understand that genres have political and social
   implications that provide access to power. Thus, genres can be presented in terms of discourse community, as a form of rhetorical etiquette that, like language, enables group
   membership. Students can then be encouraged to discover genres with which they are
   familiar as well as those that push linguistic, intellectual, and social boundaries.
2. The writing class can help students understand that both speaking and writing are
   strongly influenced by generic conventions, even when the goal is to break them.
3. The writing class can present generic form as the product of particular social relations between writer and audience. Students need to understand that "what counts as
   an example of a genre is historically determined and affected by social expectations"
   (Bazerman, 1991, p. 21).
4. The writing class can foster awareness of various genres.
5. The writing class can encourage creative variation by providing opportunities for students to push generic boundaries and examine the extent to which features from one
   genre can be transposed to another. Thus, a genre such as the argument essay can be
   presented in terms of more familiar ones, such as the advertisement.
6. The writing class can present the academic essay in terms of the writer's stance and
   definable features, "notably the use of an appropriate style in writing, the presentation
   and discussion of data, the use of hedging devices in the making of claims, and the use
   of sources" (Dudley-Evans, 2002).

7. Writing assignments can require students to define the rhetorical situation motivating the writing. The resulting essay can then be evaluated according to how well it achieved its purpose (Coe, 2002).

Whether the context is rhetorical or literary, genre is an important concept to introduce into the composition class because our students are already working in text genres that a short time ago did not exist—e-mail, blogs, Facebook pages, web pages, hypertext literature, and collaborative texts. Genre knowledge will enable students to examine texts in terms of their cultural function and to use their awareness of genre both to fulfill academic and professional expectations and, perhaps, to develop new genres as the need arises.

For Further Exploration

Essay Collections

Berkenkotter, C., & Huckin. T. N. (1995). *Genre knowledge in disciplinary communication.* Hillsdale, NJ: Lawrence Erlbaum.

Bishop, W., & Ostrom, H. (Eds). (1997). *Genre and writing: Issues, arguments, alternatives.* Portsmouth, NH: Boynton/Cook.

Freedman, A., & Medway, P. (Eds.). (1994). *Learning and teaching genre.* Portsmouth, NH: Boynton/Cook.

Freedman, A., & Medway, P. (Eds.). (1994). *Genre and the new rhetoric.* London: Taylor & Francis.

Johns, Ann M. (Ed). (2002). *Genre in the classroom: Multiple perspectives.* Mahwah, NJ: Lawrence Erlbaum.

The Explicit Teaching of Genre

Fahnestock, J. (1993). Genre and rhetorical craft. *Research in the teaching of English, 27* (3), 265–271.

Fahnestock responds to Aviva Freedman's article on explicit instruction of genre, which appears in the same issue of the journal. She questions Freedman's conclusions by asking how explicit instruction and genre should be defined and considers how craft, as opposed to a body of knowledge, can be learned.

Freedman, A. (1993). Show and tell? The role of explicit teaching in learning new genres. *Research in the Teaching of English, 27* (3), 222–251.

Freedman maintains that genre knowledge cannot be taught explicitly because it is only through immersion in a discourse community that students can develop a "felt sense" of a genre.

Mustafa, Z. (1995). Effect of genre awareness on linguistic transfer. *English for Specific Purposes, 14* (3), 247–256.

This article examines the effect of raising university students' awareness of term paper conventions through formal instruction in the second language in producing this genre in the same language or another language. The results indicate that although formal instruction is important, variation in professors' evaluation of these aspects is the main factor affecting whether this awareness is put into practice.

Williams, J., & Colomb, G. (1993). The case for explicit teaching: Why what you don't know won't help you. *Research in the Teaching of English, 27* (3), 252–264.

Academic Versus Personal Writing

Bawarshi, A. S. (1997). Beyond dichotomy: Toward a theory of divergence in composition studies. *JAC: Journal of Advanced Composition Theory, 17* (1), 69–82.

Bawarshi examines the dichotomy posited by Bartholomae and Elbow between institutional and personal writing, or, more generally, between social constructivism and expressivism. He attempts to propose a means of mediation between the two positions that goes beyond previous attempts.

Glasgow, J. (1995). Surface tension between two paradigms of writing instruction. *Teaching English in the Two-Year College, 22* (2), 102–109.

Glasgow reviews the tensions between discourse-centered writing instruction and expressivist approaches, considering the conflict that occurs when the writing instructor's approach differs from the writing tutor's approach. The article explores the possibilities of a reflective-response style of writing instruction and advocates that such an approach is a useful means of fostering writing development.

MacDonald, S. P. (1987). Problem definition in academic writing. *College English, 49* (3), 315–331.

MacDonald maintains that problem solving generates all academic writing and that, in this regard, writing about literature shares the same assumptions as other academic writing tasks. On the continuum of problem definition, the scientist is at one end and literary interpretation is at the other with its relatively undefined problems. Yet it is important for composition teachers to construct assignments that adequately define a problem.

Creativity in the Composition Class

Bawarshi, A. S. (1997). Beyond dichotomy: Toward a theory of divergence in composition studies. *JAC: Journal of Advanced Composition Theory, 17* (1), 69–82.

Bawarshi critiques the notion of creativity as unprecedented or passing, arguing instead that there can be no transcendence without derivation.

Bloom, L. Z. (1998). *Composition studies as a creative art*. Logan, UT: Utah State University Press.

Bloom discusses the role of creativity in the composition class through narratives of her own history as a compositionist. Advocates that compositionists write in the genres they teach.

Christie, F. (1987). Genres as choice. In I. Reid (Ed.), *The place of genre in learning: Current debates* (pp. 22–34). Australia: Deakin University Press.

Christie maintains that creativity and genre are not incompatible, and that genre awareness is a prerequisite for creative variation.

Dacey, J. S., & Lennon, K. H. (1998). *Understanding creativity*. San Francisco: Jossey-Bass.

Discusses various components of "creativity" as it has been defined, focusing on the interplay between biological, psychological, and social factors.

Weiner, R. P. (2000). *Creativity and beyond*. Albany, New York: State University of New York Press.

Discusses the importance given to creativity in Western culture and traces the concept from medieval times until the present in several societies.

Examining Particular Genres

Bazerman, C. (1991). *Shaping written knowledge: The genre and activity of the experimental article in science*. Madison, WI: University of Wisconsin Press.

Berkenkotter, C., & Huckin, T. N. (1995). Gatekeeping at an academic convention. In C. Berkenkotter, & T. N. Huckin, (Eds.), *Genre knowledge in disciplinary communication.* Hillsdale, NJ: Lawrence Erlbaum.

Paley, K. S. (1996). The college application essay: A rhetorical paradox. *Assessing Writing, 3,* 85–105.

Soven, M., & Sullivan, W. M. (1990). Demystifying the academy: Can exploratory writing help? *Freshman English News, 19* (1), 13–16.

Swales, J. M. (1990). *Genre analysis.* Cambridge: Cambridge University Press.

Swales, J. M., & Feak, C. B. (1994). *Academic writing for graduate students: Essential tasks and skills.* Ann Arbor: University of Michigan Press.

Genre and New Media

Beach, R., Anson, C., Breuch, L. K., & Swiss, T. (2009). *Teaching writing using blogs, wikis, and other digital tools.* Norwood, MA: Christopher-Gordon.

Gane, N., & Beer, D. (2008). *New media.* Oxford: Berg.

Wysocki, A. F., Johnson-Eilola, J., Selfe, C. L., & Sirc, G. (2004). *Writing new media: Theory and applications for expanding the teaching of composition.* Logan, UT: Utah State University Press.

REFERENCES

Bakhtin, M. (1986). The problem of speech genres. In C. Emerson, M. Holquist (Eds.), & V. W. McGee, (Trans.), *Speech genres and other late essays* (pp. 60–102). Austin, TX: University of Austin Press.

Bartholomae, D. (1995). Writing with teachers: A conversation with Peter Elbow. *College Composition and Communication, 46* (1), 62–71.

Barton, E. (1993). Evidentials, argumentation, and epistemological stance. *College English, 55* (7), 745–769.

Bawarshi, A. (2000). The genre function. *College English, 62* (3), 335–360.

Bawarshi, A. S., & Reiff, M. J. (2010). *Genre: An introduction to history, theory, research, and pedagogy.* West Lafayette, IN: Parlor Press and WAC Clearinghouse. http://wac.colostate.edu.

Bazerman, C. (1991). *Shaping written knowledge: The genre and activity of the experimental article in science.* Madison, WI: University of Wisconsin Press.

Bazerman, C. (2002). Genre and identity: Citizenship in the age of the internet and the age of global capitalism. In R. Coe, L. Lingard, & T. Teslenko (Eds.), *The rhetoric and ideology of genre* (pp. 13–38). Cresskill, NJ: Hampton Press.

Beaufort, A. (2007). *College writing and beyond: A new framework for university writing instruction.* Logan, UT: Utah State University Press.

Belmont, J. M., Butterfield, E. C., & Ferretti, R. P. (1982). To secure transfer of training instruct self-management skills. In D. Detterman, & R. Sternberg (Eds.), *How and how much can intelligence be increased?* (pp. 147–54). Norwood, NJ: Ablex.

Bishop, W. (1997). Preaching what we practice as professionals. In W. Bishop, & H. Ostrom (Eds.), *Genre and writing: Issues, arguments, alternatives* (pp. 3–16). Portsmouth, NH: Boynton/Cook.

Bitzer, L. (1968). The rhetorical situation. *Philosophy and Rhetoric, 1,* 1–14.

Britton, J., Burgess, T., Martin, N., McLead, A., & Rosen, H. (1975). *The development of writing abilities.* London: McMillan Education Ltd.

Burke, K. (1968). *Counterstatement.* Berkeley and Los Angeles: University of California Press.

Burke, K. (1969). *A rhetoric of motives.* Berkeley: University of California Press.

Christie, F. (1987). Genres as choice. In I. Reid (Ed.), *The place of genre in learning: Current debates* (pp. 22–34). Geelong, Australia: Deakin University Press.

Clark, I. L. (2010). Academic argument, genre awareness, and transferability. Paper given at *Conference on College Composition and Communication.* March 2010. Louisville, Kentucky.

Clark, I. L., Hale, C., & Neff-Lippmann, J. (2010, May). Perspectives on creativity from students and WAC. Faculty. Paper presented at European Writing Centers Association Conference, Paris, France.

Coe, R. M. (2002). The new rhetoric of genre: Writing political briefs. In A. M. Johns (Ed.), *Genre in the classroom: Multiple perspectives* (pp. 197–207). Mahwah, NJ: Lawrence Erlbaum.

Connors, R. J. (1987). Personal writing assignments. *College Composition and Communication, 38* (1), 166–183.

Cope, B., & Kalantzis, M. (Eds.). (1993). *The powers of literacy: A genre approach to teaching writing*. Pittsburgh, PA: University of Pittsburgh Press.

Derrida, J. (1980). The law of genre. *Critical Inquiry, 7*, 55–82.

Devitt, A. J. (1993). Generalizing about genre: New conceptions of an old concept. *College Composition and Communication, 44*, 573–586.

Devitt, A. J. (1997). Genre as language standard. In W. Bishop, & H. Ostrom (Eds.), *Genre and writing: Issues, arguments, alternatives* (pp. 45–55). Portsmouth, NH: Boynton/Cook.

Devitt, A. J. (2000). Integrating rhetorical and literary theories of genre. *College English, 62* (6), 697–718.

Downs, D., & Wardle, E. (2007). Teaching about writing, righting misconceptions: (Re)envisioning "first year composition" as "introduction to English Studies," *College Composition and Communication, 58* (4), 552–584.

Dudley-Evans, T. (2002). The teaching of the academic essay: Is a genre approach possible? In Ann M. Johns (Ed.), *Genre in the classroom: Multiple perspectives*. Mahwah, NJ: Lawrence Erlbaum.

Edwards, M., & McKee, H. (2005). The teaching and learning of Web genres in first-year composition. In A. Herrington, and C. Moran (Eds.), *Genre across the curriculum* (pp. 196–218). Logan, UT: Utah State University Press.

Elbow, P. (1991). Reflections on academic discourse: How it relates to freshmen and colleagues. *College English, 53* (2), 135–155.

Elbow, P. (1995). Being a writer vs. being an academic: A conflict in goals. *College Composition and Communication, 46* (1), 72–83.

Foertsch, J. (1995). Where cognitive psychology applies: How theories about memory and transfer can influence composition pedagogy. *Written Communication, 12* (3), 360–383.

Freedman, A. (1987). Learning to write again: Discipline specific writing at university. *Carleton Papers in Applied Language Students, 4*, 95–116.

Freedman, A. (1994). Anyone for tennis? In A. Freedman, & P. Medway (Eds.), *Genre and the new rhetoric* (pp. 43–66). London: Taylor & Francis.

Freedman, A. (1995). The what, where, when, why, and how of classroom genres. In J. Petraglia (Ed.), *Reconceiving writing, rethinking writing instruction*. Mahwah, NJ: Lawrence Erlbaum.

Freedman, A., & Medway, P. (Eds.). (1994). *Learning and teaching genre*. Portsmouth, NH: Boynton/Cook.

Freire, P. (1968). *The pedagogy of the oppressed*. New York: Seabury.

Gick, M., & Holyoak, K. J. (1983). Schema induction and analogical transfer. *Cognitive Psychology, 15*, 1–38.

Graff, G. (2003). *Clueless in academe: How schooling obscures the life of the mind*. New Haven: Yale University Press.

Heath, S. B. (1993). Rethinking the sense of the past: The essay as legacy of the epigram. In L. Odell (Ed.), *Theory and practice in the teaching of writing: Rethinking the discipline* (pp. 105–131). Carbondale, IL: Southern Illinois University Press.

Hernandez, A. (2010). *Genre awareness and transferability*. Unpublished thesis. California State University, Northridge.

Ivanic, R. (1998). *Writing and identity: The discoursal construction of identity in academic writing*. Amsterdam/Philadelphia: John Benjamins.

Jamieson, K. M. (Dec. 1975). Antecedent genre as rehtorical constraint. *Quarterly Journal of Speech, 61*, 406–415.

Jarratt, S. C., Mack, K., Sartor, A., & Watson, S. E. (2009). Pedagogical memory: Writing, mapping, translating. *Writing Program Administration, 33* (1–2), 46–74.

Knobel, M., & Lankshear, C. (2007). Sampling "the new" in new literacies. In M. Knobel and C. Landshear (Eds.), *A new literacies sampler* (pp. 1–24). New York: Peter Lang.

Kress, G. (1982). *Learning to write*. London: Routledge and Kegan Paul.

LeCourt, D. (2006). Performing working-class identity in composition: Toward a pedagogy of textual practice. *College English, 69* (1), 30–51.

MacDonald, S. P. (1987). Problem definition in academic writing. *College English, 49* (3), 315–331.

Macken-Horarik, M. (2002). Something to shoot for: A systemic functional approach to teaching genre in secondary school science. In A. Johns (Ed.), *Genre in the classroom: Multiple perspectives* (pp. 17–42). New Jersey: Lawrence Erlbaum.

Martin, J. R., & Rose, D. (2008). *Genre relations: Mapping culture*. London: Equinox.

Miller, C. (1984). Genre as social action. *Quarterly Journal of Speech, 70*, 151–167.

Miller, C., & Shepherd, D. (2004, June). Blogging as social action: A genre analysis of the weblog. In L. J. Gurak, S. Antonijevic, L. Johnson, C. Ratliff, & J. Reyman (Eds.), *Into the blogosphere: Rhetoric, community and culture of weblogs*. Retrieved from http://blog.lib.umn.edu/blogosphere/blogging_as_social_action_a_genre_analysis_of_the_weblog.html (accessed 10 April 2007).

Perkins, D. N., & Salomon, G. (1988). Teaching for transfer. *Educational Leadership 46* (1), 22–32.

Perloff, M. (Ed.) (1989). *Postmodern genres*. Norman, OK, and London: University of Oklahoma Press.

Rose, M. (1983). Remedial writing courses: A critique and a proposal. *College English, 45* (2), 109–122.

Russell, D. (1995). Activity theory and its implications for writing instruction. In J. Petraglia (Ed.), *Reconceiving writing, rethinking writing instruction* (pp. 51–78). Mahwah, NJ: Lawrence Erlbaum.

Sawyer, W., & Watson, K. (1987). Questions of genre. In I. Reid (Ed.), *The place of genre in learning: Current debates* (pp. 46–57). Geelong, Vic., Australia: Deakin University, Centre for Studies in Literary Education.

Swales, J. (1990). *Genre analysis.* Cambridge: Cambridge University Press.

Thaiss, C., & Zawacki, T. M. (2006). *Engaged writers, dynamic disciplines.* Portsmouth, NH: Boynton/Cook.

Wardle, E. (2009). "Mutt genres" and the goal of FYC: Can we help students write the genres of the university? *College Composition and Communication, 60* (4), 765–789.

Williams, J., & Colomb, G. G. (1993). The case for explicit teaching: Why what you don't know won't help you. *Research in the Teaching of English, 27* (3), 252–264.

Villanueva, V. (Ed.) (1997). *Cross-talk in comp theory: A reader.* Urbana, IL: NCTE.

Clifton Justice, who is now a lecturer at California State University, Channel Islands, wrote this essay when he was an undergraduate student at California State University , Northridge. Clifton had had previous experience in fundraising, and his essay shows how his knowledge of the fundraising genre enable him to raise funds successfully.

Essay

Clifton Justice

How Do You Raise That Money?

Without ever intending to become one, I have become an expert on soliciting and receiving foundation support for charitable programs. Over a four-year period of time I raised from both public and private sources more than $100,000.00 each year for a small nonprofit performing arts group. Arts organizations often get short shrift by foundations because they are not able to substantiate their community impact, but with issues of literacy dominating the field in the 1990s, I was able to find a way of blending foundation concerns and arts programming. To be successful in this arena, it was necessary that I learn to write the two-page request for support letter. This letter is the instrument whereby a nonprofit organization solicits money from a charitable foundation. This mechanism brings together features from academic writing and business writing in order to make a compelling case for funding an organization's project. The genre reveals a system that favors structured management, clear outcomes for complex problems, and measured advances in changing people's lives. It is conservative, like the people who established the foundations.

In the early part of the 20th century the U.S. developed tax codes that placed federal taxes on each citizen or resident of the country. The federal tax was a progressive act that allowed the federal government to raise additional revenue. Since there were no government services for those who faced personal or economic catastrophe, the government used the increased funds from taxes to lead the way in providing a social safety net for its citizens who had fallen on hard times. But conservatives in the government did not want citizens to look just to the government for assistance. Private individuals were encouraged to participate in the enterprise and if they did, their taxes would be exempted or reduced. The most popular method used by the wealthy to assist those less fortunate than themselves was to establish foundations designed to fund worthy enterprises by nonprofit organizations. Nonprofit organizations provide services to the community through their programs, and since their programs are offered free or at a reduced cost to the community, outside funds must be solicited in order to continue operations. Because of the federal government's tax codes, wealthy individuals and their foundations have financial as well as humanitarian reasons to give money to nonprofit organizations.

Now the two entities, foundation and nonprofit, have a reason to talk with one another, but how will they communicate? The last thing a wealthy individual wants is every director of a charity banging on his door with a personal appeal. In the beginning of a foundation, the man (sometimes a woman) with the money has pet projects, such as Carnegie and his libraries, and as long as the philanthropist is alive, giving his money away is a relatively simple task. The foundation donates to whatever organizations the gentleman (sometimes gentlewoman) prefers. But after that individual's passing, a professional staff and board of directors must decide each year how to give away a percentage of the founder's lifetime accumulation of wealth as mandated by the tax code. The staff and the board of foundations are usually well-educated, often holding advanced degrees, so asking nonprofits to put their requests in writing made sense and it was an easy solution to a pressing problem. From the 1960's forward, nonprofit growth skyrocketed and pleas to foundations increased each year. Foundations wanted an orderly way of communicating with nonprofits to be imposed. Personal visits and telephone calls could take up too much of the staff's day. Comfortable with academic writing, the grantsmakers borrowed the concept of "thesis" and "support" and merged it into "problem to be addressed" and "community impact," then imposed that all requests must be in writing. To assist fundraisers in conforming to the requirements, pamphlets, such as the PP & PG (Program Planning and Proposal Guide), were printed and widely distributed.

Another prominent reason for demanding that requests be in writing is to avoid personal involvement in projects. With the internal structure based in academic writing, the two-page request for support letter serves the foundation's need of creating a space between themselves and the nonprofit. Since a substantial percentage of the proposals, well over 50%, will be rejected, foundations want to maintain distance from the organizations. Distance allows them a more careful and objective examination. It also forces both sides to take a "cool" approach to the problem, viewing it with a dispassionate nature.

Of course, this style of discourse has its vagaries that favor college-educated, economically advantaged grant writers. These individuals, particularly those who come from a composition background, are able to communicate in a manner society has determined superior. Thus, their programs are deemed superior and receive funding. Rarely do you see awards given to organizations run by individuals without a strong writing background. At the time, I was one of those few exceptions.

The components of the two-page request for support letter are: 1) mission of the organization or the purpose of the group, 2) history of the organization focusing on recent accomplishments by the organization, 3) the community problem to be addressed—and you never say the problem is lack of money (even though it often is), 4) the actions your organization will take to address the problem, 5) the long term impact of your program and their money on the community to be addressed, and 6) how much money you want from the foundation along with who else is supporting the project. Funders rarely go it alone.

While the genre's internal structure is derived from academia, its appearance is similar to that of a business letter. It is most often single-spaced, printed on organization letterhead, and has a clean, no-fuss appearance. This appearance somehow conveys to the foundation strong management, fiscal responsibility, and community involvement. It does this through paragraphs borrowed from the business world that are ten to twelve lines long, often with a space between them and no indentation. On the page, the paragraphs form powerful-looking blocks meant to inspire trust in the organization. Letterhead, in and of itself, indicates the serious intent of the organization. It is printed, not photocopied, on heavy stock, and may include wood pulp mixed with cotton or linen. Generally, letterhead includes a listing of the board of directors, which indicates a system of hierarchy similar to the foundation's own structure. Familiarity, in this instance, breeds confidence rather than contempt.

Certainly the limit of two pages is derived from the genre's attachment to the business letter. In that form the writer needs to get to the point quickly and move on. Two pages are a limited amount of space to describe the project; great care must be taken with each word and phrase. Confusion is disastrous. If the foundation looks favorably on the request letter then the next step is usually to require a more formal proposal that can run many pages. The essence of that well-thought out proposal must be synthesized within the two-page appeal. This is challenging since the project is almost always over two years away from starting. Foundation's move at such a slow pace that even an affirmative response to a funding request can take over a year and a half. Negative responses to the request for support letter come quicker, usually within a few weeks or months, so no news can be good news to the grantwriter.

The organization I wrote grants for presented programs that were based on classic stories or poems—The Walrus and the Carpenter, Jabberwocky—and folk tales from Mexico, Africa, and Asia. I partnered with larger organizations, such as the Los Angeles City Library, to bring further attention to the company's work by local foundations. With support from the Parsons Foundation, the Weingart Foundation and the Norris Foundation, the company twice visited all 89-library sites in Los Angeles providing them with family programs designed to encourage reading. I believe much of my success came from knowing how to tailor my program to the foundation's goals of literacy, particularly for children. The more the nonprofit advances the goals of the foundation in their request, the more likely the organization will receive funding. This can have a detrimental aspect; organizations can lose their own sense of mission when they are chasing funds from a foundation. I believe, for the most part, I was able to avoid this error.

The skill I learned in writing two-page requests for support letters has served me well in college. First, it provided me a way to earn a living. By working part time out of my home, I have been able to pursue a career in teaching. My reputation as a grantwriter is such that I have numerous organizations desiring my services and I can choose for whom I want to write. Second, I find that determining what a professor wants and then giving it to them is remarkably similar to structuring a program that a foundation will fund. The ability to mold your idea to the vision of another without losing your way is central to success, not only in college, but also in life.

Reading

SITES OF INVENTION: GENRE AND THE ENACTMENT OF FIRST-YEAR WRITING

Annis Bawarshi

Genres themselves form part of the discursive context to which rhetors respond in their writing and, as such, shape and enable the writing; it is in this way that form is generative.
                                        Aviva Freedman, "Situating Genre"

We need to be aware not only that genres are socially constructed but also that they are socially constitutive—in other words, that we both create and are created by the genres in which we work.
                                        Thomas Helscher, "The Subject of Genre"

[A genre's discursive features] are united within the relatively stable discursive "type" to offer us a form within which we can locate ourselves as writers—that is, a form which serves as a guide to invention, arrangement, and stylistic choices in the act of writing.
       James F. Slevin "Genre Theory Academic Discourse, and Writing in the Disciplines"

Reflecting on the concept of invention in the classical rhetorical tradition, Jim Corder writes that "*inventio*, by its nature, calls for openness to the accumulated resources of the world a speaker lives in, to its landscapes, its information, its ways of thinking and feeling. ... *Inventio* is the world the speaker lives in" (109). Similarly, Sharon Crowley writes that "invention reminds rhetors of their location within a cultural milieu that determines what can and cannot be said or heard" (*Methodical* 168). Invention takes *place*, which is why classical rhetoricians recommended the topoi or commonplaces as the sites in which rhetors could locate the available means of persuasion for any given situation. As heuristics for invention, the topoi were thus rhetorical habitats—"language-constituted regions" (Farrell 116) and "resources, seats, places, or haunts" (Lauer, "Topics" 724)—which framed communal knowledge and provided rhetors with shared methods of inquiry for navigating and participating in rhetorical situations. Invention, as such, was not so much an act of turning inward as it was an act of locating oneself socially, a way of participating in the shared desires, values, and meanings already existing in the world. As Scott Consigny explains, the topoi were both "the *instrument* with which the rhetor thinks and the *realm* in and about which he thinks" (65; my emphasis). The topoi helped rhetors locate themselves and participate within common situations.

In much the same way, genres are also instruments and realms—habits and habitats. Genres are the conceptual realms within which individuals recognize and experience situations at the same time as they are the rhetorical instruments by and through which individuals participate within and enact situations. The Patient Medical History Form, for example, not only conceptually frames the way the individual recognizes the situation of the doctor's office; it also helps position the individual into the figure of "patient" by providing him or her with the rhetorical habits for acting in this situation. Likewise, George Washington "invents" the first state of the union address by rhetorically situating himself within the conceptual realm of an antecedent genre, the "king's speech," which provides him not only with a way of recognizing the situation he is in, but also a way of rhetorically acting within it. And similarly, D. H. Lawrence is motivated to invent his autobiography differently as he perceives and enacts it within different genres. As such, why individuals are motivated to act and how they do so depends on the genres they are using. These genres serve as the typified and situated topoi within which individuals acquire, negotiate, and articulate desires, commitments, and methods of inquiry to help them act in a given situation, thereby inventing not only certain lines of argument (logos), but also certain subjectivities (ethos—think of the subject position Washington assumes when he writes the "king's speech) and certain ways of relating to others (pathos—think of the relation Washington sets up between himself and Congress, and, as a result, how Congress reacts to Washington).[1] Conceived thus, invention does not involve an introspective turn so much as it involves the process by which individuals locate themselves within and devise ways of rhetorically acting in various situations. In this way, invention is a process that is inseparable from genre since genre coordinates both how individuals recognize a situation as requiring certain actions and how they rhetorically act within it.

Genres, thus, are localized, textured sites of invention, the situated topoi in which communicants locate themselves conceptually *before* and rhetorically *as* they communicate. To begin to write is to locate oneself within these genres, to become habituated by their typified rhetorical conventions to recognize and enact situated desires, relations, practices, and subjectivities in certain ways. I will now consider one such genre-constituted environment within which teacher and students "invent" various situated practices, relations, and subjectivities as they (re)locate themselves from one genre-situated topoi to the next: the first-year writing course.

In *Modern Dogma and the Rhetoric of Assent*, Wayne Booth speculates on a theory of interaction and self-formation similar to the one I have been proposing in my discussion of genre and agency. "What happens," he wonders, "if we choose to begin with our knowledge that we are essentially creatures made in symbolic interchange, *created in the process of sharing intentions*, values, meanings? … What happens if we think of ourselves as essentially participants in a field or process or mode of being persons together?" (134, my emphasis). In this chapter, I will examine the first-year writing course from the perspective of Booth's question, describing and analyzing the first-year writing course as an activity system coordinated by a constellation of genres, each of which constitutes its own topoi within which teachers and students assume and enact a complex set of desires, relations, subjectivities, and practices. By investigating how teachers and students make their way through these genres, we can observe the complex relations and repositioning that teachers and students negotiate as they participate within and between genred discursive spaces. Invention takes place within and between these genred spaces, as one genre creates the timing and opportunity for another. When they write their essays, for example, students are expected to perform a discursive transaction in which they recontextualize the desires embedded in the writing prompt as their own self-sponsored desires in their essays. Invention takes place at this intersection between the acquisition and articulation of desire. By analyzing the syllabus, writing prompt, and student essay as genred sites of invention, I hope to shed light on how students and teachers reposition themselves as participants within these topoi at the same time as they enact the activity system we call the first-year writing course.

The First-Year Writing Course and Its Genres

Elsewhere I have discussed how a site of activity (for example, a physician's office) is coordinated by a variety of genres, referred to as "genre sets" (Devitt, "Intertextuality") or "genre systems" (Bazerman "Systems"), each genre within the set or system constituting its own site of action within which communicants instantiate and reproduce situated desires, practices, relations, and subjectivities. Within a site of activity, thus, we will encounter a constellation of related, even conflicting situations, organized and generated by various genres. David Russell, adapting Vygotsky's concept of activity theory to genre theory, has described this constellation of situations that make up an environment as an "activity system," which he defines as "any ongoing, object-directed, historically conditioned, dialectically structured, tool-mediated human interaction" ("Rethinking" 510). Examples of activity systems range from a family, to a religious organization, to a supermarket, to an advocacy group. As Russell defines it, an activity system resembles what Guddens calls "struc-ture." Like structure, an activity system is constituted by a dialectic of agents or subjects, motives or social needs, and mediational means or tools (what Giddens refers to as "structura-tional prop-erties"). Each element of the dialectic is constantly engaged in supporting the other, so that, for instance, agents enact motives using tools which in turn reproduce the motives that require agents to use these tools and so on. As Russell explains, "activity systems are not static, Parsonian social forces. Rather, they are dynamic systems constantly re-created through micro-level interac-tions" (512). In their situated, micro-level activities and interactions, discursively and ideologically embodied as genres, participants in an activity system are at work "operationalizing" and, in turn, reproducing the ideological and material conditions that make up the activity system within which they interact. Each genre enables individuals to enact a different situated activity within an activ-ity system. Together, the various genres coordinate and synchronize the ways individuals define, interact within, and enact an activity system.

Russell's description of an activity system helps us conceptualize both how genres interact within a system of activity and how they help make that system possible by enabling individuals to participate within and in turn reproduce its related actions. The genres that constellate an activity system do not only organize and generate participants' activities within the system, however. They also, as Russell describes, link one activity system to another through the shared use of genres ("Rethinking"; "Kindness"). Participants in one activity system, for instance, use some genres to communicate with participants in other activity systems, thereby forming intra- and intergenre system relations. By applying the concept of activity system to school settings, especially to the interactions among micro-level disciplinary and administrative activity systems that together form the macro-level activity system of the university, Russell provides us with a model for analyzing the first-year writing course as one activity system within a larger activity system (the English depart-ment), within an even larger activity system (the College of Liberal Arts and Sciences), within an even larger activity system (the university), and so on. The constellation of genres within each of these related systems operationalizes the situated actions of participants within that system in order "to create stabilized-for-now structures of social action and identity" (Russell, "Rethinking" 514). The genres that coordinate each of the micro-level activity systems within a macro-level activity system function interactively as a series of uptakes, with one genre creating an opportunity for another, as in the example of the Department of Defense, in which requests for proposals generate funding proposals, which generate contracts, which generate reports and experimental articles, and so on (520). At the same time, not everyone involved in an activity system is or needs to be engaged in all its genres. As Russell explains, "in a typical school, for example, the teacher writes the assignments; the students write the responses in classroom genres. The administrators write the grade form; the teachers fill it out. The parents and/or the government officials write the checks; the administrators write the receipts and the transcripts and report to regents" (520). In this scenario, the various participants (teachers, students, parents, administrators) are all involved in micro-level activity systems which interact in close proximity to one another and which together comprise the macro-level activity system called a school. In what follows, I will focus on one par-ticular micro-level activity system within a college or university: the first-year writing course.

Like other college or university courses, the first-year writing (FYW) course takes place, for the most part, in a physical setting, a material, institutionalized site most often situated within a building on campus.[2] It is a place a teacher and students can physically enter and leave. But as in the case of the physician's office, the classroom is not only a material site; it is also a discursive site, one medi-ated and reproduced by the various genres its participants use to perform the desires, positions, relations, and activities that enact it. For example, one of the first ways that a classroom becomes a FYW course (or any other course for that matter) is through the genre of the syllabus, which, as I will describe shortly, organizes and generates the classroom as a textured site of action which locates teacher and students within a set of desires, commitments, relations, and subject positions.

At the same time, the syllabus also manages the set of genres that will enable its users to enact these desires, relations, and subjectivities. In this way, the syllabus and its related FYW course genres orient teachers and students in a discursive and ideological scene of writing which locates them in various, sometimes simultaneous and conflicting positions of articulation. The choices teachers and students make in this scene emerge from, against, and in relation to these positions. As such, "the classroom is always invented, always constructed, always a matter of genre" (Bazerman, "Where" 26). When we only identify students as writers in the writing classroom, then, we are ignoring the extent to which teachers (as well as those who administer writing programs) are also writers of and in the writing classroom—writers of the genres that organize and generate them and their students within a dynamic, multitextured site of action. The FYW course, thus, is a site where writing is already at work to make writing possible. Seen in this light, the FYW course is not as artificial as some critics make it out to be. It may be artificial when, chameleon-like, it tries to mimic public, professional, or disciplinary settings, or when it tries to imagine a "real" external audience for student writing. But the classroom in its own right is a dynamic, textured site of action mediated by a range of complex written and spoken genres that constitute student-teacher positions, relations, and practices.[3] As they reposition themselves within and between these genres, teachers and students acquire, negotiate, and articulate different desires, which inform the choices they make as participants in the FYW course.

The set of written genres that coordinates the FYW course includes, but is not limited to, the course description, the syllabus, the course home page, student home pages, the grade book, the classroom discussion list, assignment prompts, student essays, the teacher's margin and end comments in response to student essays, peer workshop instructions, student journals or logs, peer review sheets, and student evaluations of the class. These "classroom genres" (Christie, "Curriculum"; Russell, "Rethinking") constitute the various typified and situated topoi within which students and teacher recognize and enact their situated practices, relations, and subjectivities. I will now examine three of these classroom genres, the syllabus, the assignment prompt, and the student essay, in order to analyze how writers reposition and articulate themselves within these sites of invention. By doing so, I hope to demonstrate the extent to which, when they invent, writers locate themselves in a complex, multilayered set of discursive relations, so that by the time students begin to write their essays they do so in relation to the syllabus, the writing assignment, and the various other genres that have already located them and their teachers in an ideological and discursive system of activity.

The Syllabus

In many ways, the syllabus is the master classroom genre, in relation to which all other classroom genres, including the assignment prompt and the student essay, are "occluded" (Swales, "Occluded"). According to Swales, occluded genres are genres that operate behind the scenes and often out of more public sight, yet play a critical role in operationalizing the commitments and goals of the dominant genre, in this case, the syllabus. As such, the syllabus plays a major role in establishing the ideological and discursive environment of the course, generating *and* enforcing the subsequent relations, subject positions, and practices teacher and students will perform during the course. In some ways, the syllabus, like the architecture students' sketchbooks described in the previous chapter, functions as what Giltrow calls a "meta-genre," an "atmosphere surrounding genres" (195) that sanctions and regulates their use within an activity system. It is not surprising, thus, that the syllabus is traditionally the first document students encounter upon entering the classroom. Immediately, the syllabus begins to transform the physical setting of the classroom into the discursive and ideological site of action in which students, teacher, and their work will assume certain significance and value. That is, within the syllabus, to paraphrase Giddens, the desires that inform the structure of the course become textually available to the students and teacher who then take up these desires as intentions to act. No doubt, the syllabus is a coercive genre, in the same way that all genres are coercive to some degree or another. It establishes the situated rules of conduct students and teacher will be expected to meet, including penalties for disobeying them. But even more than that, the syllabus also establishes a set of social relations and subjectivities that students and teacher have available to them in the course.

It is curious that, as significant a genre as it is, the syllabus has received so little critical attention (Baecker 61). In fact, to the extent that it is discussed at all, the syllabus is mostly described in "how to" guidebooks for novice teachers. For instance, both Erika Lindemann's *A Rhetoric for Writing Teachers* and Robert Connors and Cheryl Glenn's *The St. Martin's Guide to Teaching Writing* describe the syllabus in terms of its formal conventions, listing them in the order they most often appear: descriptive information such as course name and number, office hours, classroom location, significant phone numbers; textbook information; course description and objectives; course policy, including attendance policy, participation expectations, policy regarding late work, etc.; course requirements, including kinds and sequence of exams and writing assignments; grading procedures; any other university or departmental statements; and then a course calendar or schedule of assignments. In addition to presenting these conventions, Lindemann and Connors and Glenn also describe the purpose of the syllabus, acknowledging its contractual as well as pedagogical nature. Lindemann, for example, cites Joseph Ryan's explanation of the informational and pedagogical purposes of the syllabus:

> Students in the course use the syllabus to determine what it is they are to learn (course content), in what sense they are to learn it (behavioral objectives), when the material will be taught (schedule), how it will be taught (instructional procedures), when they will be required to demonstrate their learning (exam dates), and exactly how their learning will be assessed (evaluation) and their grade determined. (256–57)

In this sense, Lindemann claims that "syllabuses are intended primarily as information for students" (256).

Connors and Glenn, however, recognize the more political function of the syllabus. For them, "the syllabus, for all intents and purposes, is a contract between teacher and students. It states the responsibilities of the teacher and the students as well as the standards for the course" (10). The syllabus, then, informs the students and the teacher, protecting both from potential misunderstanding. It also informs the "structure of the class" by developing "a set of expectations and intentions for composition courses" (10–11). In other words, the syllabus establishes the course goals and assumptions as well as the means of enacting these goals and assumptions—both the structure of the course and the rhetorical means of instantiating that structure as situated practices. As Connors and Glenn remind teachers, the syllabus is "the first written expression of your personality that you will present to your students" (10).

Neither Lindemann nor Connors and Glenn, however, go on to analyze exactly how the syllabus locates teachers and students within this position of articulation or how it frames the discursive and ideological site of action in which teacher and students engage in coordinated commitments, relations, subjectivities, and practices. What effect, for instance, does the contractual nature of the syllabus have on the teacher-student relationship? What positions does the syllabus assign to students and teacher, and how do these positions get enacted and reproduced in the various situations and activities that constitute the FYW course? An analysis of the typified rhetorical features of the syllabus, especially its use of pronouns, future tense verbs, and abstract nominalizations, helps us begin to answer some of these questions.[4]

One of the more obvious characteristics of the syllabus is the way it positions students and teachers within situated subjectivities and relations. The student is frequently addressed as "you" ("This course will focus on introducing *you* to ..."), as "students" ("*Students* will learn ..." or "The goal of this course is to introduce *students* to ..."), and as "we" ("We will focus on learning ...") quite often interchangeably throughout the syllabus but at times even within the same section. For example, one teacher addresses her students in the "Course Objectives" section as follows: "Over the course of the semester, *you* will develop specific writing strategies which will help *you* adapt *your* writing skills to different contexts and audiences. Also, *we* will discuss how to approach and analyze the arguments of other writers, and how to either adapt or refute their views in *your* writing." This interchange between "you" and "we" on the pronoun level reflects a larger tension many teachers face when writing a syllabus: between establishing solidarity with students and demarcating lines of authority (Baecker 61). This tension is especially heightened in FYW courses which tend to be taught mostly by inexperienced teachers, most often graduate students who are themselves struggling with the tension between being teachers and students. Diann Baecker, drawing on Mühlhäusler and Harré's work on pronouns and social identity, applies this tension within pronouns to the social relations they make possible in the syllabus. Pronouns such as "you" and, in particular, "we" not only create social distinctions among communicants; they also "blur the distinction between power and solidarity and, in fact, allow power to be expressed as solidarity" (Baecker 58).

It is perhaps this desire to mask power as solidarity that most characterizes the syllabus, a desire that teachers, as the writers of the syllabus, acquire, negotiate, and articulate. Positioned within this desire, the teacher tries to maintain the contractual nature of the syllabus while also invoking a sense of community. On the one hand, the teacher has to make explicit what the students will have to do to fulfill the course requirements, including the consequences for not doing so. On the other hand, the teacher also has to create a sense of community with the students so they can feel responsible for the work of learning. This balance is difficult, and, as we saw in the above example, many teachers will awkwardly fluctuate between "you" and "we" in order to maintain it. The following excerpt from another syllabus also reveals this fluctuation:

> The goals of the course are two-fold. During the initial part of the semester, *we* will focus on learning to read critically—that is, how to analyze the writing of others. The skills that *you* will acquire while learning how to read an argument closely ... will be the foundation for the writing *you* will do for the rest of the course. *Our* second objective ...

This "we"/"you" tension reflects the balance the teacher is attempting to create between community and complicity. As Baecker explains, citing Mühlhäusler and Harré, "*we* is a rhetorical device that allows the speaker(s) to distance themselves from whatever is being said, thus making it more palatable because it appears to come from the group as a whole rather than from a particular individual" (59). The "we" construction tries to minimize the teacher's power implicit in the "you" construction by making it appear as though the students are more than merely passive recipients of the teacher's dictates; instead, they have ostensibly acquiesced consensually to the policies and activities described in the syllabus. The teacher, then, uses "you" and "we" in order to position students as subjects, so that without knowing it, they seem to have agreed to the conditions that they will be held accountable for. In this way, the syllabus is an effective contract, incorporating the student as other ("you") into the classroom community ("we") at the same time as it distinguishes the individual student from the collective. "What the "you"/"we" construction seems to suggest is that "*we* as a class will encounter, be exposed to, and learn the following things, but *you* as a student are responsible for whether or not you succeed. *You* will do the work and be responsible for it, but *we* all agree what the work will be."

In her research, Baecker finds that "you" is by far the most common pronoun employed in syllabi (60), a finding supported by my own analysis. This "you," coupled with the occasional "we," the second most common pronoun, works as a hailing gesture, interpellating the individual who walks into the classroom as a student subject, one who then becomes part of the collective "we" that will operationalize this activity system we call the FYW course. As Mühlhäusler and Harré explain, it is "largely through pronouns and functionally equivalent indexing devices that responsibility for actions is taken by actors and assigned to them by others" (89). When a teacher identifies the student as "you," he or she is marking the student as the "other," the one on whom the work of the class will be performed: "You will encounter," "You will develop," "You will learn." But who exactly prescribes the action? Passive constructions such as the following are typical of the syllabus: "During the semester, *you* will be required to participate in class discussions," "*You* will be allowed a week to make your corrections." But who will be doing the requiring and the allowing? The teacher?

Not really. As much as the syllabus locates students within positions of articulation, it also positions the teacher within a position of articulation. The teacher's agency is seldom explicitly asserted through the first person singular; Baecker finds that "I" comprises an average of 24 percent of total pronoun usage per syllabus (60). More often, teachers mask their agency by using "we." Yet this "we" implicates the teacher into the collective identity of the goals, resources, materials, and policies of the course so that the teacher as agent of the syllabus becomes also an agent on behalf of the syllabus. The syllabus, in short, constructs its writer, the teacher, as an abstract nominalization in which the doer becomes the thing done. This is in part the genred subjectivity the teacher assumes when he or she writes the syllabus. For example, writers of syllabi rely on abstract nominalizations and nominal clauses to depict themselves as though they were the events and actions that they describe. Take, for instance, these typical examples: "Missing classes will negatively affect your participation grade," "Good class attendance will help you earn a good grade," "Acceptable excuses for missing a class include …," "Each late appearance will be counted as an absence," "Guidance from texts constitutes another important component," "Writing is a process," "Conferences give us a chance to discuss the course and the assignments," "Plagiarism will not be tolerated." In these examples, we find objects, events, and actions that are incapable of acting by themselves treated as if they in fact are performing the actions. When a verb that conveys action in a sentence is transformed into a noun, we have the effect that somehow the action is performing itself—is its own subject, as in "missing classes" or "attendance." Rather than being the identifiable agents of the syllabus they write, teachers become part of the action they expect students to perform. This way, students come to see teachers less as prescribers of actions and more as guiding, observing, and evaluating student actions. As such, activities become substitutes for the agents who perform them, activities that teachers recognize and value and students subsequently enact.

The syllabus, therefore, is not merely informative; if is also, as all genres are, a site of action that produces subjects who desire to act in certain ideological and discursive ways. It establishes the habitat within which students and teachers rhetorically enact their situated relations, subjectivities, and activities. Both the teacher and the students become habituated by the genre of the syllabus into the abstract nouns that they will eventually perform. It is here, perhaps, that the syllabus's contractual nature is most evident, as it transforms the individuals involved into the sum of their actions, so that they can be described, quantified, and evaluated. No wonder, then, that the most dominant verb form used in the syllabus is the future tense, which indicates both permission and obligation, a sense that the activities and behaviors (the two become one in the syllabus) outlined in the syllabus are possible and binding. To be sure, the overwhelming number of future tense verbs present in the syllabus ("you will learn," "we will encounter") indicate that it is a genre that anticipates or predicts future action. Yet the discursive and ideological conditions it initially constitutes are already at work from day 1 to insure that these future actions will be realized.

The syllabus, in short, maintains and elicits the desires it helps its users fulfill. When a teacher writes the syllabus, he or she is not only communicating his or her desires for the course, but is also acquiring, negotiating, and articulating the desires already embedded in the syllabus. These desires constitute the exigencies to which the teacher rhetorically responds in the syllabus. For example, the contractual nature of the syllabus, especially the way it objectifies agency by constituting actors as actions which can then be more easily quantified and measured, is socio-rhetorically realized by such typified conventions as the "we"/"you" pronoun constructions, the abstract nominalizations, and the auxiliary "will" formations. By using these rhetorical conventions, the teacher internalizes the syllabus's institutional desires and enacts them as his or her intentions, intentions that he or she will expect students to respect and abide by. The teacher's intentions, therefore, are generated and organized rhetorically by the generic conventions of the syllabus. Teachers invent their classes, themselves, as well as their students by locating themselves within the situated topoi of the syllabus, which functions both as the rhetorical instrument and the conceptual realm in which the FYW course is recognized and enacted. Indeed, the syllabus, as Connors and Glenn warn teachers, *is* "the first expression of your personality," but the syllabus does not so much convey this a priori personality as it informs it.

The syllabus, then, helps establish the FYW course as a system of activity and also helps coordinate how its participants manage their way through and perform the various genres that operationalize this system, each of which constitutes its own site of invention within which teachers and students assume and enact a complex set of textured actions, relations, and subjectivities. Within this scene of writing, one such genre, the assignment (or writing) prompt, plays a critical role in constituting the teacher and student positions that shape and enable student writing.

The Writing Prompt

While it does receive scholarly attention, mainly in handbooks for writing teachers such as Lindemann's and Connors and Glenn's (see also Murray and James Williams), the writing prompt remains treated as essentially a transparent text, one that facilitates "communication between teacher and student" (Reiff and Middleton 263). As a genre, it is mainly treated as one more prewriting heuristic, helping or "prompting" student writers to discover something to write about. As Connors and Glenn describe it, "a good assignment … must be many things. Ideally, it should help students practice specific stylistic and organizational skills. It should also furnish enough data to give students an idea of where to start, and it should evoke a response that is the product of discovering more about those data. It should encourage students to do their best writing and should give the teacher her best chance to help" (58). Indeed, the most obvious purpose of the writing prompt is to do just that, prompt student writing by creating the occasion and the means for writing.

To treat the writing prompt merely as a conduit for communicating a subject matter from the teacher to the student, a way of "giving" students something to write about, however, is to overlook the extent to which the prompt situates student writers within a genred site of action in which students acquire and negotiate desires, subjectivities, commitments, and relations before they begin to write. The writing prompt not only *moves* the student writer to action; it also *cues* the student writer to enact a certain kind of action. This is why David Bartholomae insists that it is *within* the writing prompt that student writing begins, not *after* the prompt. The prompt, like any other genre, organizes and generates the conditions within which individuals perform their activities. As such, we cannot simply locate the beginning of student writing in student writers and their texts. We must also locate these beginnings in the teachers' prompts, which constitute the situated topoi that the student writers enter into and participate within. As Bartholomae notes, a well-crafted assignment "presents not just a subject, but a way of imagining a subject as a subject, a discourse one can enter, and not as a thing that carries with it experiences or ideas that can be communicated" ("Writing Assignments" 306). This means that the prompt does not precede student writing by only presenting the student with a subject for further inquiry, a subject a student simply "takes up" in his or her writing, although that certainly is part of its purpose. More significantly, the prompt is a precondition for the existence of student writing, a means of habituating the students into the subject as well as the subjectivity they are being asked to explore so that they can then "invent" themselves and their subject matter within it.

As situated topoi, writing prompts are both rhetorical instruments and conceptual realms—habits and habitats. They conceptually locate students within a situation and provide them with the rhetorical means for acting within it. We notice examples of this in assignments that ask students to write "literacy narratives," narratives about their experiences with and attitudes relating to the acquisition of literacy. Teachers who assign them usually presume that these narratives give students the opportunity to access and reflect on their literacy experiences in ways that are transformative and empowering, ways that describe the challenges and rewards of acquiring literacy. What these assignments overlook, however, is that literacy narratives, like all genres, are not merely communicative tools; they actually reflect and reinscribe desires and assumptions about the inherent value and power of literacy. Students who are asked to write literacy narratives come up against a set of cultural expectations—embedded as part of the genre—about the transformative power of literacy as a necessary tool for success and achievement. Kirk Branch, for instance, describes how students in his reading and writing class at Rainier Community Learning Center struggled to invent themselves within the assumptions of these narratives. Aware of the social motives rhetorically embedded within these narratives, Branch explains, students wrote them as much to describe their experiences with literacy as to convince themselves and others of the transforming power of literacy. For example, commenting on one such student narrative, titled "Rosie's Story," Branch concludes,

> "Rosie's Story" *writes itself* into a positive crescendo, a wave of enthusiasm which tries to drown out the self-doubt she reveals earlier. "Rosie's Story" does not suggest an unbridled confidence in the power of literacy to solve her problems, but by the end of the piece she drops the provisional "maybes" and "shoulds" and encourages herself to maintain her momentum: "Just keep it up." Her story, then, reads as an attempt to quash her self-doubt and to reassert the potential of literacy in her own life. (220; my emphasis)

In the end, it seems, the power of genre and the ideology it compels writers to sustain and articulate wins out. Rosie does not seem to be expressing some inherent intention as she writes this narrative. Rather, she seems to be locating herself within the desires embedded within the literacy narrative, desires that inform how she recognizes and performs herself in the situation of the reading and writing class. To claim, then, that her narrative begins *with* and *in* her is to overlook the extent to which she herself is being written by the genre she is writing.

We notice a remarkable example of how genres shape our perceptions and actions when Lee, a student in Branch's class, writes in his literacy narrative: "Furthermore Mr. Kirk gives us our assignments and he has always wanted us to do our best. He said, 'If you hadn't improved your English, you wouldn't have got a good job.' Therefore I worry about my English all the time" (Branch 221). "Does it matter," Branch wonders afterwards, "that I never said this to Lee?" (221) Apparently, Branch does not have to say it; Lee's assumption about literacy as a necessary tool for success is already rhetorically embedded in the genre of the literacy narrative as understood by the student, an assumption that Lee internalizes as his intention and enacts as his narrative when he writes this genre. It is within the situated topoi of the genre that Lee "invents" his narrative.

Often, teachers of writing overlook the socializing function of their writing prompts and consequently locate the beginnings of student writing too simply in the students rather than in the prompts themselves. What these teachers overlook—and writing teacher guides are no exception—is that students first have to situate and "invent" themselves in our prompts before they can assume the position of student writer. In fact, as we will discuss momentarily, it is the prompt that tacitly invokes the position that student writers are asked to assume when they write, so that students read their way into the position of writer via our prompts. Given this, it is perhaps more than a little ironic that most guides to writing effective assignment prompts emphasize the importance of specifying an audience *in* the prompt while more or less ignoring the students as audience *of* the prompt. As one of her five heuristics for designing writing assignments, for instance, Lindemann includes the following: *"For whom are students writing?* Who is the audience? Do students have enough information to assume a role with respect to the audience? Is the role meaningful?" (215). Here, the student is perceived only as potential writer to the audience we construct in the prompt. But what about the student as audience to the teacher's prompt, the position that the student first assumes before he or she begins to write? The assumption seems to be that the student exists a priori as a writer who has only to follow the instructions of the teacher's prompt rather than as a reader who is first invoked or interpellated into the position of writer by the teacher's prompt. This process of interpellation involves a moment of tacit recognition, in which the student first becomes aware of the position assigned to him or her and is consequently moved to act out that position as a writer.

The prompt is a genre whose explicit function is to make another genre, the student essay, possible. Within the FYW course activity system, it helps to create a timeliness and an opportunity for student writing in what Yates and Orlikowski, following Bazerman, refer to as "kairotic coordination" (110). In coordinating this interaction, the writing prompt functions to transform its writer (the teacher) and its readers (the students) into a reader (the teacher) and writers (the students). It positions the students and teacher into two simultaneous roles: the students as readers and writers, the teacher as writer and reader. First of all, the prompt rhetorically positions the teacher as both a writer and a reader. As he or she writes the prompt, the teacher positions him or herself as reader for the student text that the prompt will eventually make possible. The challenge that the prompt creates for the teacher is how to create the conditions that will allow students to recognize him or her not as the writer of the prompt, but as the eventual reader of their writing. That is, the teacher has to find a way to negotiate a double subject position, a subject subject, one who is doing the action (the subject as writer) and one on whom the action is done (the subject as reader). One way the teacher manages this double position is through a series of typified rhetorical moves and statements. For example, the following phrases are typical of prompts: "You should be sure to consider," "You probably realize by now that," "As you have probably guessed," "As you all know."[5] These are loaded phrases, because they not only offer suggestions the teacher-writer is giving to the student-readers; they also offer hints about what the teacher-writer will be expecting as a teacher-reader. When the teacher writes, "You probably realize by now that one effective way to support YOUR evaluation of those reviews is to offer examples from them in the way of quotes," he is telling the students something about him as an audience. He is basically saying, "Look, I care about using quotes to support evaluation, so if you want to write an effective evaluation for me, use quotes." Writing "one effective way" allows the teacher-writer to covertly express what he cares about as a reader. The next example is even more covert—and clever. After describing the assignment to the students, the teacher writes:

> To do this, *you should be able* to explain why the scene is central to the story's plot, what issues are being dealt with, and how or why the characters change. *The trick here* is to employ as many specific details from the story as possible. *You have the responsibility* to explain to your audience why you made the decision you did. (my emphasis)

The teacher who begins this prompt as a writer describing the assignment to the students as readers here begins to emerge as a reader to the students as writers. "You should be able to" is a subtle, or perhaps not so subtle, way of letting students know what he as a teacher-reader expects from their writing. "The trick here" is even more effective, because it allows the teacher to enact the role of reader while seeming to be an objective observer giving helpful advice. In fact, however, there is no "trick" involved here, just a calculated rhetorical way for the teacher to let students know that he as a reader cares a great deal about the use of specific details. The only "trick" at work here is how the teacher creates the illusion that the writer addressing them is not the same person as the reader who will be reading their writing. It is this rhetorical sleight of hand that the prompt makes possible.

The prompt, therefore, allows the teacher to occupy two subject positions at once: writer/ coach and reader/evaluator. As a result, and at the same time, the prompt also constitutes the students as readers and writers. The students are prompted into position or invoked as writers by the prompt, within which they read and invent themselves. Indeed, every prompt has inscribed within it a subject position for students to assume in order to carry out the assignment. In FYW prompts, these roles can be quite elaborate, asking students to pretend that "you have just been hired as a student research assistant by a congressperson in your home state" or "you have been asked by *Rolling Stone* to write a critique of one of the following films." The prompts do not stop here, however. They go on to specify to students how they should enact these roles, as in the following example, in which the teacher asks students to pretend that they are congressional aides:

> You must not explain what you "think" about this subject; the congressperson is more inter-
> ested in the objective consideration of the issues themselves. And *of course*, you shouldn't
> recommend whether or not your employer should support the bill; *you are, after all, only an*
> *aide.* (my emphasis)

Words such as "of course," "obviously," "after all," "remember," and "certainly" all typically appear in prompts. Their function is to establish shared assumptions; however, we have to question just how shared these assumptions really are. How shared, for example, is the "of course" in the above example? Does the student-writer share this knowledge about congresspersons or is this a subtle way in which the prompt writer coerces complicity? The fact that the teacher-writer goes to the trouble of mentioning it suggests that perhaps the knowledge is not so obvious, that, in fact, "of course," "certainly," and "as we all know" are rhetorical means of presenting new information in the guise of old information (Pelkowski 7). If this is the case, then what we are witnessing is the prompt at work constituting the students as writers who assent to the ideology presented in the prompt, just as we saw in the case of the literacy narratives.

To a great extent, students have to accept the position(s) made available to them in the prompt if they are to carry out the assignment successfully. As all genres do, the prompt invites an uptake commensurate with its ideology, just as we saw in the example of the first state of the union address in which George Washington's choice of the "king's speech" prompted an appropriate congressional reply mirroring the echoing speeches of Parliament. While there is room for resistance, for students to refuse to accept the shared assumptions the prompt makes available to them, Pelkowski reminds us that "the power structure of the university denies students the ability to offer alternative interpretations of prompts. ... Rather, an alternative interpretation of the assignment is not seen as such, but as a 'failure to respond to the assignment' (the F paper is often characterized in this way in statements of grading criteria)" (16). The writing prompt, in short, functions as a site of invention in which teacher and student create the conditions in which they will eventually interact as reader and writer.

The Student Essay

The very coercion masked as complicity that we observe in the syllabus and writing prompt is also at work when students begin to write their essays. This time, though, rather than being objects of this discursive move, students are expected to become its agents. In this way, students learn to enact the desires they acquire as participants within the FYW course and its system of genres. For example, one of the tricks teachers often expect students to perform in their writing involves recontextualizing the desires embedded in the writing prompt as their own self-generated desires. That is, students are expected to situate their writing within the writing prompt without acknowledging its presence explicitly in their writing so that it appears as though their writing created its own exigency, that somehow their writing is self-prompted. This rhetorical sleight of hand appears most visibly in the introductions of student essays, because it is there that students are asked to create the opportunity and timing for their essays in relation to the opportunity and timing as defined by the writing prompt. Experienced student writers know that they must negotiate this transaction between genres and do so with relative ease. Less experienced student writers, however, sometimes fail to recognize that the prompt and essay are related but separate genres, and their essays can frustrate teachers by citing the prompt explicitly in a way that shatters the illusion of self-sufficiency we desire students to create in their writing. In what follows, I will look at several examples of student essays to examine to what extent and how students negotiate this difficult transaction between genres as they function as agents on behalf of the prompt and agents of their own writing.

Yates and Orlikowski's work on the function of chronos and kairos in communicative interaction can help us interrogate the relation between the writing prompt and the student essay. They describe how genre systems choreograph interactions among participants and activities chronologically (by way of measurable, quantifiable, "objective" time) and kairotically (by way of constructing a sense of timeliness and opportunity in specific situations) within communities (108–10). In terms of chronos, the writing prompt assigns a specific time sequence for the production of the student essay, often delimiting what is due at what time and when. In this way, the writing prompt defines a chronological relationship between itself and the student essay. At the same time, however, the writing prompt also establishes the kairos for the student essay by providing it with a timeliness and an opportunity. In this way, the writing prompt defines a recognizable moment that authorizes the student essay's raison d'Être. Participating within this kairotic relationship between two genres, the student must, on the one hand, recognize the opportunity defined for him or her in the prompt and, on the other hand, reappropriate that opportunity as his or her own in the essay. Carolyn Miller describes this interaction as "the dynamic interplay between ... opportunity as discerned and opportunity as defined" (312). Engaged in this interplay, the student writer must discern the opportunity granted by the prompt while writing an essay that seemingly defines its own opportunity. As such, the student writer needs to achieve and demonstrate a certain amount of generic dexterity, functioning within a genre system while masking its interplay. I will now look at some examples of how student writers negotiate this discursive transaction.

The following examples, from a FYW course, are all written in response to the same writing prompt. The students had read and discussed Clifford Geertz's "Deep Play: Notes on the Balinese Cockfight," had been assigned to take on the "role of 'cultural anthropologist' or 'ethnographer,'" had conducted some field observations, and were then prompted to write, "in the vein of Geertz in 'Deep Play,'" a

> claim-driven essay about the "focused gathering" [a term that Geertz uses] you observed. Your essay should be focused on and centered around what you find to be most significant and worth writing about in terms of the "focused gathering" you observed. ... Some issues you might want to attend to include: How does the event define the community taking part in it? What does the event express about the beliefs of the community? What does the event say about the larger society?

Not only does the prompt assign students a subjectivity (the role of cultural anthropologist), but it also grants them an opportunity to transform their observations into an argument. In taking up this opportunity, the students perform a range of transactions between their essays and the writing prompt. Below, I will describe a sample of these transactions, starting with essays in which the writing prompt figures prominently (so that the coercion is visible) and concluding with essays in which the writing prompt is recontextualized as the student's own self-generated opportunity.

In those examples where students fail to enact the desired relationship between the prompt and the essay, the writing prompt figures explicitly in their essays, fracturing the illusion of autonomy that the essay, although prompted, tries to maintain. In the most obvious cases, such as the following, the student narrates explicitly the process of the essay's production:

> In my last literary endeavor [ostensibly referring to an earlier draft of the essay] I focused on one facet of the baseball game that I had gone to see. This time I am going to try to bring a few more topics to the table and focus on one thing in particular that I feel is significant.[6]

In this excerpt, the student appears to be narrating the prompt's instructions (stated as "be focused on and centered around what you find to be most significant") as he fulfills them. That is, he is telling us what he has been asked to do from one stage of the assignment sequence to the next as he does it, thereby making the coercion visible, as in the words, "This time I am going to try to …" Purposefully or not, the student in this case fails to perform the desired uptake between the prompt and his essay so that the prompt essentially speaks through him.

In a similar but less explicit way, the next essay also fails to reappropriate the prompt's defined opportunity as its own, so that the essay remains overly reliant on the prompt. The essay begins:

> Cultural events are focused gatherings that give observers insights to that certain culture. Geertz observes the Balinese culture and gains insights on how significant cockfighting is to the Balinese: including issues of disquieting and the symbolic meaning behind the cockfights. My observations at a bubble tea shop in the International District also have similarities with Geertz's observations of the Balinese cockfight on the cultural aspect.

The phrases "cultural events" and "focused gatherings" locate the language of the prompt in the essay, but the first sentence simply rewords the language of the prompt rather than recontextualizing it as part of the essay's own constructed exigency. The question that would likely come to most teachers' minds, even though they already know the answer, would be, "So what? Why do we need to know this?" Similarly, in the second sentence, the only way to understand the relevance of the transition into Geertz is to know the prompt, which makes that connection. By the time the student describes her own observations in the third sentence, too much of the prompt's background knowledge is assumed, so that, for the logic of these opening sentences to work, a reader needs the prompt as context, yet this is the very relationship that the prompt and essay wish to downplay.

Compare the opening sentences of the above essay to the opening sentences of the following essay:

> When you want to know more about a certain society or culture what is the first thing that you need to do? You need to make and analyze detailed observations of that particular society or culture in its natural environment. From there you should be able to come up with a rough idea of "why" that particular culture or society operates the way it does. That's exactly what Clifford Geertz did. He went to Bali to study the Balinese culture as an observer.

As in the earlier example, this excerpt borrows the language of the prompt, but rather than rewording that language, it reappropriates it. This time, the reader meets Geertz on the essay's terms, after the student has provided a context for why Geertz would have done what he did. The same exigency that motivated Geetz becomes the student's exigency for writing his essay. Crude as it might be, the question that begins the essay performs the sleight of hand I described earlier, in which the student recontextualizes the question the prompt asks of him and asks it of his readers as if this is the question *he* desires to ask. In this way, the student becomes an agent of the agency at work on him. The student, however, seems unable or unwilling to sustain this uptake, for in the very next paragraph, he fractures the illusion he has begun to create. He writes:

> A couple of weeks ago I decided to go visit some friends in Long Beach Washington. Since it was something different from the norm of people in my class analyzing concerts and baseball games I decided to do my paper on Long Beach. I didn't have to look far for a cultural event to observe because the little ocean-side town was having a parade. … I pretty much took the Geertz approach and just tried to figure out what was going on.

Here, the student not only slips out of his assigned role as a "cultural anthropologist" by acknowledging his position as a student, along with other students writing a paper for class, but he also makes visible the coercion that prompted his essay when he writes that it did not take him long to find a cultural event to observe. Suddenly, he identifies himself as someone who has been prompted to find an event. At the same time, although he does refer to Geertz in the previous paragraph, the student's statement, "I pretty much took the Geertz approach," appears to be addressed to a reader who knows more than what the student has already explained about Geertz. That is, the statement imagines a reader who is familiar with the prompt that directed the student to take the Geertz approach in the first place. After all, the prompt asks students to write an essay "in the vein of Geertz."

In the previous example, we witness a student who begins to negotiate but does not quite sustain the complex interplay between the genred discursive spaces of the writing prompt and the student essay. In the next couple of examples, we observe students who manage this discursive transaction by recontextualizing the desires embedded in the prompt as their own seemingly self-prompted desires to write.

The following student begins her essay by describing the activities and interactions that typically occur at her church, thereby performing her role as a cultural anthropologist. Her third paragraph, which follows two paragraphs of observations, marks a transition. She writes:

> What purpose does all this serve? Geertz states in Deep Play: Notes on the Balinese Cockfight, "the cockfight is a means of expression." (Geertz 420) In much the same way the Inn [the name of the church] is the same thing. It is a gathering for college aged people to express their faith in God.

By asking, "What purpose does all this serve?" this student asks the question that the prompt asks of her. In so doing, she makes it appear as though the inquiry that follows stems from her own curiosity. In the context of this appropriation, Geertz is not so much a figure she inherits from the prompt as he is a figure she invokes to create an opportunity for her essay to analyze the significance of the Inn. The student recontextualizes the opportunity as well as the authority from the discursive space of the prompt to the discursive space of the essay.

The next student performs a similar uptake, and does so with greater elegance. The student begins her essay by describing underground hip-hop music and the function it serves for its listeners, and then poses the question: "Is music created from culture, or is culture created from music?" The second paragraph begins to compare hip-hop to symphonies. The student writes:

> On a different note, a symphonic band concert creates a congregation of different status people uniting to listen to a type of music they all enjoy. "Erving Goffman has called this a type of 'focused gathering'—a set of persons engrossed in a common flow of activity and relating to one another in terms of that flow" (Geertz 405). This type of "focused gathering" is an example of music created from culture. "Focused gatherings" provide different emotions according to preference. The flocking of similar interests in the form of "focused gatherings"

makes up a culture. Similar values are shared to create one group of equals producing music for the same reason." (my emphasis)

By posing the question, "Is music created from culture, or is culture created from music?" the student creates an opportunity for her essay rather than inheriting that opportunity from the prompt. This is the question the *student* is asking. In the above excerpt, the student does not rely on the prompt's authority to justify the claim that "a symphonic band concert creates a congregation of different status people uniting to listen to a type of music they all enjoy." Instead, she appropriates the authority the prompt grants her to assert this claim. Only in the context of her authority does Geertz then figure into the essay. Notice how cleverly the student uses the quotation from Geertz to make it appear as though his description of a "focused gathering" was meant to define her focused gathering, the symphonic band concert. The determiner "this" no longer modifies the cockfight as Geertz meant it to; instead, it refers back to the concert, which is the student's subject of inquiry. In a way, this move creates the impression that the student found Geertz rather than having been assigned to use Geertz. There is very little evidence of prompting here.

In the remainder of the above excerpt, the student appears to perform what Fuller and Lee have described as an interiorized uptake, in which the student becomes positioned, through her interaction with the writing prompt, as a desiring subject who speaks from that subjectivity (222). In this case, the student internalizes the authority embedded in the prompt as her own authority in statements such as, "The flocking of similar interests in the form of 'focused gatherings' makes up a culture. Similar values are shared to create one group of equals producing music for the same reason." The student has appropriated the subjectivity assigned to her and now speaks from that position as a "cultural anthropologist." Fuller and Lee refer to this process of negotiation as "textual collusion," a term they use to describe how writers and readers move "around inside relations of power" (215). More so than her peers, this student seems able to negotiate the textured relations between the prompt and the essay, repositioning herself in the interplay between genred spaces so that she becomes an agent of the agency at work on her.

Invention takes place at the intersection between the acquisition and articulation of desire. When teachers assign students a writing prompt, they position students at this intersection so that part of what students do when they invent their essays involves recontextualizing the desires they have acquired as their own self-prompted desires to write. As such, teachers expect students to manage the interplay between coercion and complicity that we saw teachers perform in the syllabus (manifested in the "you" and "we" formations). Not all students, as we see in the above examples, are able to perform this sleight of hand with the same dexterity. And the reason for this, I would argue, has partly to do with the fact that some students do not know that this transaction requires them to move around between two genred sites of action, each with its own situated desires, relations, subjectivities, and practices—in short, its own positions of articulation. When they conflate these two worlds, students not only fracture the illusion of self-sufficiency the essay desires them to maintain, but students also fail to reposition their subjectivity and their subject matter within the discursive and ideological space of the essay. One way teachers can help students reposition themselves within such spheres of agency is to make genres analytically visible to students so that students can participate within and negotiate them more meaningfully and critically. ...

Summary

Writing involves a process of learning to adapt, ideologically and discursively, to various situations via the genres that coordinate them. Writing is not only a skill, but a way of being and acting in the world in a particular time and place in relation to others. The FYW course bears this out. As an activity system, it is sustained and coordinated by its various genres. Teachers and students assume ways of being and acting in the classroom not only because of its material setting—although that certainly does play a major part (see Reynolds)—but also because of its multitextured sites of action as they are embodied within and between genres. As such, the writing that students do in the FYW course does not just begin with them by virtue of their being (enrolled) in this setting; it begins, rather, in the textured topoi that are already in place, shaping and enabling the writing that students as well as teachers do. As such, the environment of the classroom—or any other environment for that matter, including the doctor's office—is not only an ontological fact, but also a generic fact. It exists largely because we reproduce it in our genres, each of which constitutes a different but related topoi within which students and teacher function, interact, and enact sub-jectivities and practices. Since we reproduce the FYW course in the ways we articulate it, there is really little that is artificial or arbitrary about it, at least not in the way that Paul Heilker describes the FYW course as being artificial: "Writing teachers need to relocate the *where* of composition instruction outside the academic classroom because the classroom does not and cannot offer stu-dents real rhetorical situations in which to understand writing as social action" (71).

Part of my argument in this essay is that the FYW course *is* a "real rhetorical situation," one made up of various scenarios within which students (and their teachers) recognize one another, reposition themselves, interact, and enact their situated practices in complex social and rhetori-cal frameworks. Once we recognize this, once we acknowledge that the FYW course, like any activity system, is "not a container for actions or texts" but "an ongoing accomplishment" (Russell "Rethinking" 513), we are on our way to treating the FYW course as a complex and dynamic scene of writing, one in which students can not only learn how to write, but ... can also learn what it means to write: what writing does and how it positions writers within systems of activity. Partici-pating in the textual dynamics of the FYW course is as "real" a form of social action and interaction as any other textual practice.

As we have observed ..., genres position their users to perform certain situated activities by generating and organizing certain desires and subjectivities. These desires and subjectivities are embedded within and prompted by genres, which elicit the various, sometimes conflicting, inten-tions we perform within and between situations. To assume that the writer is the primary locus of invention, then, is to overlook the constitutive power of genre in shaping and enabling how writers recognize and participate in sites of action.

Rather than being defined as the agency of the writer, invention is more a way that writers locate themselves, via genres, within various positions and activities. Invention is thus a process in which writers act as they are acted upon. The Patient Medical History Form is a case in point. So are the examples of George Washington and the first state of the union address, the example of the social workers' assessment report, and the example of the student essay in relation to the assignment prompt. All these examples point to the fact that there is more at work in prompting discourse than simply the writer's private intentions or even, for that matter, the demands of the writer's immediate exigencies. After all, George Washington responded to the exigencies of an unprecedented rhetorical situation not by inventing something new, but by turning to an anteced-ent genre, the "king's speech," which carried with it a rhetorical form of social action very much at odds with his more immediate exigencies. The available genre, rhetorically embodying social motives so powerful as to override the inspired democratic moment at hand, not only shaped the way Washington recognized and acted within his rhetorical situation, but the way Congress did too.

We notice a similar phenomenon at work in the example of the writing prompt. The writing prompt does not merely provide students with a set of instructions. Rather, it organizes and gener-ates the discursive and ideological conditions which students take up and recontextualize as they write their essays. As such, it habituates students into the subjectivities they are asked to assume as well as enact—the subjectivities required to explore their subjects. By expanding the sphere of agency in which the writer participates, we in composition studies can offer both a richer view of the writer as well as a more comprehensive account of how and why writers makes the choices they do. ... .

Notes

1   It is worth noting here that the word *ethos* in Greek means "a habitual gathering place." Just like rhetorical strategy, then, the persona a rhetor assumes takes place within a place, a habitation or topoi, so that when rhetors invent, they are not only formulating the available means of persuasion, but also the rhetorical persona they need to carry out that rhetorical strategy. As LeFevre explains, "ethos ... appears in that socially created space, in the 'between,' the point of intersection between speaker or writer and listener or reader" (46). Considered as situated topoi, genres not only shape and enable how communicants recognize and enact social situations; genres also shape and enable how communicants recognize and enact their ethos or subjectivities within these situations.

2   With the increased use of computer technology in education, especially networked classes and distance learning, this claim becomes less generalizable. If anything, though, the emergence of the "virtual classroom" only strengthens my claims about genre and the classroom that follow.

3   It is worth noting that the FYW classroom is no more artificial than Epcot is "artificial" when compared to the "real" Florida. As I discussed in chapter 4, Epcot is as complex a rhetorical ecosystem as any wilderness-designated area. Both are rhetorical constructions, ways we define, conceptualize, and behave in our environments.

4   For this analysis, I randomly collected fifteen syllabi from colleagues at a research university and from published teaching guides. All the syllabi are from FYW courses, and reflect a balance between experienced and new teachers,

5   The examples I analyze in this section are culled from my examination of fifteen randomly collected writing prompts from experienced and new teachers of FYW at a research university.

6   I reprint this and the following student excerpts as they appear in the students' essays, errors and all.

Works Cited

Baecker, Diann L. "Uncovering the Rhetoric of the Syllabus: The Case of the Missing I." *College Teaching* 46.2 (1998): 58–62.

Bartholomae, David. "Writing Assignments: Where Writing Begins." *Forum: Essays on Theory and Practice in the Teaching of Writing.* Ed. Patricia L. Stock. Portsmouth: Boynton/Cook, 1983. 300–312.

Bazerman, Charles. "Systems of Genres and the Enactment of Social Intentions." Freedman and Medway: 79–101.

Bazerman, Charles. "Where is the Classroom?" Freedman and Medway: 25–30.

Bishop, Wendy, and Hans Ostrom, Eds. *Genre and Writing: Issues, Arguments, Alternatives.* Portsmouth: Boynton/Cook, 1997.

Booth, Wayne. *Modern Dogma and the Rhetoric of Assent.* Chicago: U of Chicago P, 1974.

Branch, Kirk, "From the Margins at the Center: Literacy, Authority, and the Great Divide." *College Composition and Communication* 50.2 (1998): 206–231.

Christie, Frances. "Curriculum Genres: Planning for Effective Teaching." *The Powers of Literacy: A Genre Approach to Teaching Writing.* Ed. Bill Cope and Mary Kalantzis. Pittsburgh: U of Pittsburgh P, 1993. 154–78,

Coe, Richard, Lorelei Lingard, and Tatiana Teslenko, eds. *The Rhetoric and Ideology of Genre.* Cresskill, NJ: Hampton, 2002.

Connors, Robert J., and Cheryl Glenn. *The St. Martin's Guide to Teaching Writing.* 3rd ed. New York: St. Martin's, 1995.

Consigny, Scott. "Rhetoric and Its Situations." Young and Liu: 59–67.

Corder, Jim. "Varieties of Ethical Argument," Young and Liu: 99–133.

Crowley, Sharon. *The Methodical Memory: Invention in Current Traditional Rhetoric.* Carbondale: Southern Illinois UP, 1990.

Devitt, Amy J. "Intertextuality in Tax Accounting: Generic, Referential, and Functional." *Textual Dynamics of the Professions: Historical and Contemporary Studies of Writing in Professional Communities.* Ed. Charles Bazerman and James Paradis Madison: U of Wisconsin P, 1991. 335–357.

Enos, Theresa, ed. *Encyclopedia of Rhetoric and Composition: Communication from Ancient Times to the Present.* New York: Garland, 1996,

Farrell, Thomas B. "Commonplaces." Enos: 116–117.

Freedman, Aviva, "Situating Genre: A Rejoinder." *Research in the Teaching of English* 27 (1993): 272–281.

Freedman, Aviva, and Peter Medway, eds. *Genre and the New Rhetoric.* Bristol: Taylor and Francis, 1994.

Fuller, Gillian, and Alison Lee. "Assembling a Generic Subject." Coe, Lingard, and Teslenko: 207–224.

Geertz, Clifford. *Local Knowledge.* New York: Basic, 1983.

Giltrow, Janet. "Meta-Genre." Coe, Lingard, and Teslenko: 187–205.

Heilker, Paul, "Rhetoric Made Real: Civil Discourse and Writing Beyond the Curriculum." *Writing the Community.* Ed, Linda Addler-Kassner, Robert Crooks, and Ann Watters, Washington D.C.: American Association for Higher Education, 1997. 71–76.

Helscher, Thomas P. "The Subject of Genre." Bishop and Ostrom: 27–36.

Lauer, Janice M. "Topics." Enos: 724–725.

LeFeve, Karen Burke, *Invention as a Social Act.* Carbondale: Southern Illinois UP, 1987.

Lindemann, Erika. *A Rhetoric for Writing Teachers.* 3rd. ed. New York: Oxford UP, 1995.

Miller, Carolyn R. "Kairos in the Rhetoric of Science." *A Rhetoric of Doing.* Ed. S. P. Witte, N. Nakadato, and R. D. Cherry. Carbondale: Southern Illinois U P, 1992. 310–27.

Mühlhäusler, P., and R. Harré. *Pronouns and People: The Linguistic Construction of Social and Personal Identity.* Oxford: Basil and Blackwell, 1990.

Murray, Donald *Expecting the Unexpected: Teaching Myself and Others to Read and Write.* Portsmouth: Boynton/Cook, 1989.

Pelkowski, Stephanie. "The Teacher's Audience is Always a Fiction." Unpublished Manuscript.

Reiff, John D., and James E. Middleton "A Model for Designing and Revising Assignments." *Fforum: Essays on Theory and Practice in the Teaching of Writing.* Ed. Patricia L. Stock. Portsmouth: Boynton/Cook, 1983. 263–68.

Reynolds, Nedra. "Composition's Imagined Geographies: The Politics of Space in the Frontier, City, and Cyberspace." *College Composition and Communication* 50.1 (1998): 12–35.

Russell, David R. "Rethinking Genre in School and Society: An Activity Theory Analysis." *Written Communication* 14.4 (1997): 504–554.

Russell, David R. "The Kind-ness of Genre: An Activity Theory Analysis of High School Teachers' Perceptions of Genre in Portfolio Assessment across the Curriculum." Coe, Lingard, and Teslenko: 225–242.

Slevin, James F. "Genre Theory, Academic Discourse, and Writing in the Disciplines," *Audits of Meaning: A Festschrift in Honor of Anne E. Berthoff.* Ed. Louise Z. Smith. Portsmouth: Boynton/Cook, 1988. 3–16,

Swales, John M. "Occluded Genres in the Academy: The Case of the Submission Letter." *Academic Writing: Intercultural and Textual Issues.* Amsterdam: Benjamins, 1996. 44–58.

Williams, James D. *Preparing to Teach Writing.* Belmont: Wadsworth, 1989.

Yates, JoAnne, and Wanda Orlikowski "Genres of Organizational Communication: A Structural Approach." *Academy of Management Review* 17 (1992): 299–326.

Young, Richard, and Yameng Liu, eds. *Landmark Essays on Rhetorical Invention.* Davis, CA: Hermagoaras, 1994.

7

Voice and Style

Darsie Bowden

- What is meant by "voice" in the context of composition theory and pedagogy?
- Is there such a thing as an authentic personal "voice"?
- How is "voice" related to "style"?

This chapter discusses the perplexing concept of "voice," examining what we mean when we talk about voice in writing and the relationship between voice and style.

One is hard pressed to avoid the mention of the term *voice* in talk about teaching and learning to write. Teachers of writing, professional writers, and students use it, generally to describe a feature or set of features of style in writing. Sometimes *stance* or *persona* can be substituted for voice; other times, it is *style* or *tone*. A longtime critic of voice, I rail against its use in my courses. Despite this, the term invariably emerges, often sheepishly from one of my students and, more frequently than I'd like to admit, from me as I stumble over my own inability to describe what I mean. What *do* we mean when we talk about voice in writing? What is understood by finding your own voice when you write? What relationship does voice have with *style*? Perhaps most important, why might voice be valuable and why might it be problematic?

Voice is a metaphor—a very powerful one. Metaphors, by their very nature, enable us to talk about abstract concepts (such as *love*, *war*, *time*, or *argument*) that are difficult if not impossible to talk about in any other way. As George Lakoff and Mark Johnson (1980) have pointed out, when we talk about argument, for example, battle metaphors often seem to creep in: "She challenged John and trounced him in the debate," or "I attacked him in open court and was victorious," or "The two sides could never agree and remain in an uneasy truce." *Writing* is no different. Despite the concreteness of production—you take a pen or computer and produce tangible text—composing text often seems as abstract and mysterious as love, war, or argument.

But as valuable and necessary as metaphors are in enabling us to understand phenomena, they also lead us down certain conceptual pathways that severely limit our perceptions. For example, framing argument in battle- or war-like terms suggests that when we argue we are in a contest, the goal of which is to win; the objective is conquest. But we could also consider argument as a method to engage in an exchange of differing points of view or the bringing together and sorting through of opinions that can help both parties come to new understandings. Here, argument is not a battleground, but, rather, a meeting place where the players are partners—not opponents.

So what avenues of perception does the use of voice open up when we refer to "voice in writing" and what does it foreclose? It helps to know where the concept of "voice" comes from.

A LITTLE HISTORY

Despite the frequency and effortlessness with which voice is used today, it hasn't always been part of our lexicon about writing. T. S. Eliot used it in his 1943 in his essay, "The Three Voices of Poetry" where he asserts that:

> [I]n writing [nondramatic] verse, I think that one is writing, so to speak, in terms of one's own voice: the way it sounds when you read it to yourself is the test. For it is yourself speaking. The question of communication, of what the reader will get from it, is not paramount. (p. 100)

But its first chronicled use in composition studies occurred, according to Walker Gibson, at the Dartmouth Conference in 1966 (see Chapter 1) and became broadly used in articles and essays about composition and composition classrooms in the 1970s, in which teachers were exhorted to help students find their own voices in their writing.

As Irene Clark points out in Chapter 1, the voice movement paralleled the process movement; some of the strongest supporters of process were also leading advocates of voice (Peter Elbow, Donald Stewart, Walker Gibson, and Ken Macrorie). And as with the process movement, voice was often associated with the so-called "expressionist school," which wasn't really a school at all, but rather a groundswell of sentiment reacting against traditional ways of teaching writing and toward self-expression. Traditional ways of teaching that most dismayed voice promoters included a primary focus on grammar and mechanics, the compartmentalizing of style into discrete categories (word, sentence, and paragraph), and the emphasis on style at the expense of self-expression and other aspects of discourse. (See Berlin's 1987 definition of *current-traditional rhetoric* in *Rhetoric and Reality: Writing Instruction in American Colleges, 1900–1985.*) Voicists argued that this kind of focus on form created a teaching and learning environment that stifled students' interest and left them with no option but to write boring, tedious, and listless prose. As a result, students emerged from their writing classes able to produce writing that was flawless mechanically, but which also seemed to indicate that they clearly had nothing to say.

Trends in composition tend to follow trends in politics. The 1960s and early 1970s were particularly volatile years in American history. There was trouble on college campuses in response to the unpopular and ultimately unsuccessful Vietnam War. The inner cities became much more explosive and dangerous than in previous decades as minorities and lower socioeconomic groups felt increasingly disenfranchised and excluded from the American ideal of prosperity and justice for all. Racism and poverty exacerbated conditions in a number of schools, which were already wretched and ineffective places to learn. The institutionalized government, business, and the university bureaucracies not only invited little confidence but also were presumed to be destructive to social values of individualism, personal expression, equality, and freedom. Hence, outlets for self-expression in writing were suddenly highly valued. It is small wonder that both the process movement (which paid attention to how writing was produced) and voice (which privileged the expression of emotions, passions, ideals, and a writer's inner character) not only took hold but also became quickly entrenched.

Certainly, individualism and self-expression were not new phenomena; they have been part of American identity since pre-Revolutionary War days. But trends both in education and in politics tended to force those values to a back burner. In 1957, the Soviets launched the Sputnik rocket, making the Soviet Union the first country to enter outer space. As a consequence, the United States decided it needed to dramatically improve its educational system—particularly the sciences—to catch up. There ensued an infusion of funding to support the sciences from which the other liberal arts, including English, were initially excluded. To compete with the sciences, English quickly redefined itself in more scientific terms. What emerged were programs that led students through a clearly and strictly specified sequence of literary works, designed primarily to promote a thorough understanding of the power and importance of American heritage. The progressive movement in education—which gained popularity in the 1920s and focused on individual interests, skills, and adjustment—was reviled and abandoned in favor of this new curriculum, which Arthur Applebee (1974) called the "academic" approach, an approach that was not unlike the "back to basics" lobbying that seems to be a familiar part of educational rhetoric today.

Thus, as historical trends most often are, the move to expressivism was essentially a reaction against what had existed previously, both politically and in the writing classroom. The strong connections between political trends and what is going on in composition are crucial to understanding the shifts and permutations in public and theoretical perceptions of writing and literacy, and the move to expressivism is no exception.

SELF-EXPRESSION IN THE WRITING CLASSROOM

What were the early explanations of voice in writing? In 1969, Robert Zoellner laid out his "Talk-Write" pedagogy in a well-known essay in *College English* where he attempted to explain the writer's voice:

> A striking characteristic of many students' verbal behavior is that they "sound" one way when talking, and quite another way when writing. If they have a consistent "voice" at all, it is in the speech area. In contrast, their writing is simply congeries of words, entirely lacking in any distinguishing "voice." One of the objectives of the talk-write pedagogy is to overcome this modal distinction: on the one hand, the rapid alternation between vocal and scribal activity should lead to a reshaping and vitalizing of the scribal modes, so that the students' written "voice" begins to take on some of the characteristics of the speaking "voice." (p. 301)

Peter Elbow, one of most vocal and persuasive proponents of voice in the 1970s and 1980s, portrayed his concept of voice as "what most people have in their speech but lack in their writing—namely, a sound or texture—the sound of 'them'" (1981, p. 288). Readers know that they have encountered the writer's real voice, Elbow continued, when they feel a "resonance" not necessarily with the writer, but with "the words and themselves" (p. 300). With Zoellner and Elbow, we have some of key components of early voice pedagogy, that of lending to writing the kind of identifiable imprint that the spoken voice has. In so doing, the writer's voice can be "heard" in the reading of her work; that voice is unique and consequently more compelling.

This perspective maintained that writers could find their own *writing voice* if they trusted themselves and did the appropriate exercises. Among the activities that Elbow suggested to facilitate the discerning of one's voice was "freewriting," which was usually a timed writing done *without* the reader in mind, in other words, before presentation. Because writing for an audience can potentially change a writer's voice and undermine a writer's power, Elbow advised writers to begin without imagining a reader. In other words, freewriting is intended to be truly free. There are no rules because there is no reader; it doesn't even necessarily need to make sense. It is a way for the writer to get at what he truly feels, to generate ideas that are his alone, to explore—or to find—his own words (his voice) on paper without risk.

Ken Macrorie's complaint about "Engfish" raised another aspect of the voice movement. "Engfish," Macrorie explained in *Telling Writing* (1985), lacks life, spontaneity, dynamism, and authenticity. The typical example of Engfish is standard academic writing in which students attempt to replicate the style and form of academia, or, in other words, prose written by professors. By contrast, writing with voice has *life* because it's ostensibly connected to a real speaker—the student writer herself. Here's what Macrorie said about a particular student paper that has voice:

> In that paper, a truthtelling voice speaks, and its rhythms rush and build like the human mind travelling at high speed. Rhythm, rhythm, the best writing depends so much upon it. But as in dancing, you can't get rhythm by giving yourself directions. You must feel the music and let your body take its instructions. Classrooms aren't usually rhythmic places. (p. 160)

The "truthtelling voice" is the authentic one. Good writers are authentic because they tap into their inner selves. Donald Stewart described that authenticity in *The Authentic Voice: A Pre-Writing Approach to Student Writing* (1972):

> Your authentic voice is that authorial voice which sets you apart from every living human being despite the number of common or shared experiences you have with many others: it is not a copy of someone else's way of speaking or of perceiving the world. It is your way. Because you were born at a certain time, in a certain place, to certain parents, with a particular position in the family structure, you have a unique perception of your experience. All the factors of your environment plus your native intelligence and particular response to that environment differentiate you from every other person in the world. Now the closer you come to rendering your particular perception of your world in your words, the closer you will come to finding your authentic voice. (pp. 2–3)

The valuing of the individual, both her experience and what she feels and thinks is still intoxicating, but in the volatile period of the 1960s and 1970s, it struck just the right chord with students learning to write. No longer would they be forced to replicate the stilted prose of the status quo, writing on topics that might have been "good for them" but about which they had no interest and could see no relevance. Instead, their own lives and words were validated. The classrooms were to become their own.

VOICE AS ROLE PLAYING

Another permutation of authentic voice emerged during this period as well, one that emphasized the representation of emotion and feeling in the classroom through drama and role playing. The concept can be traced to a new pedagogical model of the classroom imported from Great Britain in the late 1960s; it is an important one because it helps understand how voice evolved in the latter part of the last century (1980s and 1990s). This concept, defined below, conferred less value on the authentic individual voice than on assuming a voice for particular occasions (Gibson, 1969):

> [I]t is as if the author, as he "puts on his act" for a reader, wore a kind of disguise, taking on, for a particular purpose, a character who speaks to the reader. This persona may or may not bear considerable resemblance to the real author, sitting there at his typewriter; in any case, the created speaker is certainly less complex than his human inventor. He is inferred entirely out of the language; everything we know about him comes from the words before us on the page. In this respect he is a made man, he is artificial. (pp. 3–4)

Thus, in the service of conveying a message to an audience, voice—or persona—is created for specific rhetorical occasions, a concept stemming from the notion of *ethos* in classical rhetoric. Gibson's voice is constructed by "design" to change a reader's mind. Contrast this with Elbow's conception in *Writing Without Teachers* (1973):

> In your natural way of producing words there is a sound, a texture, a rhythm—a voice—which is the main source of power in your writing. I don't know how it works, but this voice is the force that will make a reader listen to you, the energy that drives the meanings through his thick skull. Maybe you don't *like* your voice; maybe people have made fun of it. But it's the only voice you've got. It's your only source of power. … If you keep writing in it, it may change into something you like better. But if you abandon it, you'll likely never have a voice and never be heard. (pp. 6–7)

Just as the spoken voice has the rhythm, tone, and intonations of the individual speaker, so can writing—and this, for Elbow, represents rhetorical power. Creating or designing a speaking voice does not seem to have a place here; it seems antithetical to the concept of one's "natural" voice.

More recently, the uses of voice have tended to echo Walker Gibson rather than Peter Elbow. Here is a fairly typical presentation of voice in a writing textbook, *Work in Progress: A Guide to Writing and Revising* by Lisa Ede (1995):

> We often associate style with the personal, referring, for instance, to a person's style of dress or style of interacting with others. And a writer's style does reflect his or her individual taste and sensibility. But just as people dress differently for different occasions, so too do writers vary their style, depending on the rhetorical situation … [S]ometimes writers present strong and distinctive voices [referring to an essay by Ken Kesey] … In other situations, writers don't wish to present a distinctive personal voice [referring to essay in *Rolling Stone*] … When you consider the degree to which you wish to draw on appeals to reason (*logos*), emotion (*pathos*), and your own credibility as a writer (*ethos*), you are led to consider your own *persona* or voice and your relationship with readers. (Italics in original, pp. 200–202)

Note the absence of any reference to authentic voice. For Ede, voice is created for specific rhetorical occasions and is not necessarily a phenomenon emanating from the author's character or inner being. Even so, authentic voice proponents are certainly not extinct, and there are, I would argue, important reasons why this is true, which I will cover in the next section.

CRITIQUE OF VOICE

Major developments emerged with the voice movement that have dramatically changed the composition classroom for the better. These include the emphasis on the writing process (see Chapter 1) and on collaborative work where students learn to rely on readers other than the teacher, creating for themselves environments that are less oppressive and threatening. As a consequence, the teacher's authority in controlling every aspect of the writing classroom was somewhat reduced, resulting—at least in principle—in the relegation of more responsibility to the student.

Up through 1960, personal writing was primarily considered the means to an end; that end was expository writing—critical, analytical, and argumentative writing that was both formal and academic (see Robert Connors, 1987). Personal writing served as invention or prewriting for the more valued type of texts, and was intended to help students segue more easily into formal exposition. By contrast, the voice period helped us to conceive of personal writing as a legitimate end product, and its value was reinforced by other studies, including Janet Emig's *The Composing Process of Twelfth Graders* (1971) where she argued for the value of reflexive (or personal) writing in the classroom, not only to get writers to write but also as a necessary component of the writer's development. Ultimately, the voice pedagogy introduced into the composition classroom the kinds of changes that were going on in politics and society: mistrust of the status quo; attention to the individual writer, especially those traditionally in marginalized social groups; and, in some sense, a politicization of the composition classroom.

Since the 1970s, voice has been appropriated to refer to a variety of textual phenomena including register, style, persona, and tone. It has been used by activists from a range of marginalized groups, including women, African Americans, Native Americans, and other minorities, to talk about power—both political and discursive.

But voice has also come under attack, particularly the notion of authentic voice, for a variety of reasons. In his 1987 article in *College Composition and Communication,* Hashimoto argued that the "evangelical" approach taken by some voice enthusiasts, notably Peter Elbow, promoted a kind of anti-intellectualism, particularly in the way voice proponents urged students to tap into their emotional selves for their writing, often consciously ignoring—even if temporarily—the intellectual and discursive values of the community within which they were writing. Others have questioned whether it is even possible to have one "true" voice and if this, indeed, leads to power in writing, as voice proponents have claimed.

As a metaphor, voice locates the source of its explanatory power in the human voice, which is audible, measurable, and identifiable. In the history of Western tradition beginning with Plato, the spoken voice was often understood as being closer to thought and an authentic self. However, although a writer himself, Plato dismissed writing as inferior to speech (see the *Phaedrus* dialogue, 1961) because, he argued, without the give and take of conversation, we cannot get at "truth"; we cannot fully understand the world. Writing, according to Plato, only gives us the semblance of permanence or objective truth and, consequently, is misleading and ultimately dangerous.

Furthermore, our spoken voice is one of the key features that identifies us and distinguishes us from others. Voice has often been considered to have presence, the presence of the speaker. It is in that presence that listeners can sense (or not sense) authenticity, genuineness, and passion. For many people, it follows that for writing to have presence, it must also have voice. Writing with presence is powerful writing; it resonates with the reader.

The idea that spoken language more accurately reflects thought than writing has been, since the late 1970s, a source of controversy. French philosopher Jacques Derrida (1976) argued that Western thought (including Platonic thought) presumes an ultimate point of reference, a transcendent truth that language—the spoken word or *phoné*—can express:

> Within ... logos [voice, speech, reason], the original and essential link to the *phoné* has never been broken. ... As has been more or less implicitly determined, the essence of the *phoné* would be immediately proximate to that which within "thought" as logos relates to "meaning," produces it, receives it, speaks it, "composes" it. If, for Aristotle, for example, "spoken words are the symbols of mental experience and written words are the symbols of spoken words," (*De interpretatione, 1,* 16a3) it is because the voice, producer of the first symbols, has a relationship of essential and immediate proximity with the mind. (1976, p. 11)

For many Western thinkers, voice has interiority—that is, "proximity" to the self; voice is the closest thing to being. Derrida maintains, however, that the spoken language is merely a set of symbols or signs that only vaguely (and inadequately) represents reality. Writing, as symbols representing spoken language, is even further removed, and the relationship between language and thought or meaning is not stable, as Western philosophers would have us believe. Both speech and writing give us the illusion of presence, but it is illusion only.

Derrida goes even further to argue that language (spoken or written) cannot express consciousness. In fact, it works the other way around: language makes consciousness possible. This reversal in thinking "deconstructs" Western assumptions about the function and primacy of consciousness and language. This movement, called *deconstruction,* is a fundamental component of postmodernism, which has been a major influence on the teaching of writing and the consideration of texts since the 1980s. It serves, among other things, to shift the emphasis from the author as the purveyor of meaning (and owner of the voice) and from text (as meaningful) to the rhetorical situation in which text, author, context, audience, and purpose all influence meaning. The idea that voice is definable and recognizable is incompatible with deconstruction, which tends to move us in the other direction, toward plurality, instability, and disintegration, which comes from understanding writing from perspectives other than the author's. The implications for teaching writing are significant. In the postmodern classroom—influenced by the project of deconstruction—writing does not originate and end with the author, but is subject to multiple forces that motivate the act of writing. Hence, writers must consider the context, purpose, and reader for their writing, and must also assume that texts cannot be simply conduits for the writer's intentions ... or voice. (For an excellent discussion of deconstruction, see Sharon Crowley, 1989.)

Nonetheless, the notion of voice remains very popular. In much of the recent work on voice, concerted efforts—particularly in Kathleen Blake Yancey's volume on voice, *Voices on Voice: Perspectives, Definitions, Inquiry* (1994)—have been made to reconfigure voice to make it fit in a postmodern, technological, and multicultural era. Drawing in part on M. M. Bakhtin's use of multiple voices (1981)—and his notion of heteroglossia in discourse—theorists, teachers, and textbooks now generally acknowledge that writers may not have one true voice, but, rather, many voices, each used for particular occasions and with particular audiences. Still, a writer's voice should be consistent, unified, and stable, if only for that rhetorical instance. And in a remarkable essay in the Yancey volume, Randall Freisinger argues for working toward a synthesis of expressionist and postmodern attitudes toward voice.

Even so, the continued use of voice in writing pedagogy seems to be an attempt to fit a square peg into a round hole. Efforts to reconfigure the voice metaphor in an environment that has significantly changed since the 1960s glosses over important conflicts that are not so easily dismissed. Among these conflicts are key distinctions between speaking and writing, differing individual and social perspectives on rhetoric, and even differences between literary and expository writing. (For more on this, see Bowden, 1999.) To explore the problem of voice in the theoretical and pedagogical climate of the new century, two examples are given here, one from women's studies and the other from electronic technology, to suggest just how perplexing voice has become in the face of some potentially much more powerful metaphors.

OTHER METAPHORS: WOMEN'S STUDIES

It is not uncommon in women's studies and feminist studies to assert that women have long been deprived of having a voice in politics and society. Well-known books such as Belenky, Clinchy, Goldberger, and Tarule's *Women's Ways of Knowing* (1986) and Carol Gilligan's *In a Different Voice: Psychological Theory and Women's Development* (1993) make much of women's voices. Gilligan, in particular, uses voice to mean a kind of communicative energy that emanates from deep inside a person, from the heart of a person's being. Voice, she explained, is "something like what people mean when they speak of the core of the self ... [it is] a powerful psychological instrument and channel, connecting inner and outer worlds" (Gilligan, 1993, p. 178).

In *Women's Ways of Knowing*, many of the women interviewed by the authors talk about their desire to find their voices, voices that will be heard, presumably in a world that is populated with other, often male voices that tend to drown out theirs. These uses of voice have considerable resonance with the way voice was used in the 1970s. Perhaps it is true that finding one's voice and using that voice leads to power in a male-dominated society where having a voice is seen to be the source of that power. However, in using voice, two different discourse behaviors are conflated, each having a different underlying assumption. The discourse of power seems to be one in which a person uses his voice to promote himself and his ideas and win over or dominate other voices. For one voice to speak, another must be silenced or somehow incorporated. For good or ill, this discourse style most often leads to acquisition of social goods in our society, that is, money, status, and power. By contrast, women's discourse—and this is a theory that Gilligan's book promotes so persuasively— tends to view the repair and maintenance of social networks as a priority. Here, voice may not come into play at all; in fact, silence has a value, because silence presumes listening, hearing, thinking, caring, and embracing. These are two different definitions of power; unfortunately, the discourse of self-assertion tends to be valued more than the other.

It might be argued, then, that those who use voice to refer to the source of their rhetorical power are subscribing to the very patriarchal discourse from which they are trying to break free. In other words, using voice plays into the hands of dominant voices because it configures power in terms that insist on silence and then devalue it. And, of course, women have commonly been accorded the devalued, silent voice.

Another metaphor suggested in *Women's Ways of Knowing*—one that seems far more in keeping with what many women's discourses seem to value—is the *web* or *network* because both focus more attention on interdependency, celebrating rather than debasing it. The idea of a network assumes that there is not necessarily one individual holding sway over another or others, but a web of interconnected strands—wherein much of the power lies in the connectedness and solidarity, and wherein the integrity of the individual is, although not irrelevant, certainly secondary.

Network has a strong affinity with text as texture, the weaving together of signs. One way of looking at this is to consider that in writing we must attend to the weave of interrelationships between authorial stance, impact or effect on listeners and readers, the text itself, and the context within which the act takes place. Networks and textures lead to the second illustration, this time from digital technology.

FROM ANOTHER ANGLE: DIGITAL WRITING

In *Writing Space: The Computer, Hypertext, and the History of Writing,* Jay Bolter (1991) wrote that "it is somehow uncanny how well the post-modern theorists seem to be anticipating electronic writing" (p. 156). Regardless of whether this is true, voice—however you define it (as persona, tone, style, etc.)—is unquestionably problematic in electronic or digital writing for a number of reasons.

First, electronic technology diffuses, in fact, often ravages the integrity of the authorial voice. Digital texts have multiple users; some log-on as readers, some as writers; users are often both, constantly and sometimes exuberantly blurring the boundary between writer and reader as they add to texts, collaborate on texts, and follow links from one text to another as their interest dictates, making the act of reading most ostensibly an example of textual construction. The digital text rarely remains static; it can potentially be rewritten each time some new user encounters it. Even though writers might plan for the reading of texts in certain ways, by programming links and connections, the reading/writing movement is often spontaneous and often haphazard.

One of the hallmarks of voice is that it helps identify, if not an author, at least a tone. In electronic texts, the lack of stability and integrity militates against the creation of a consistent persona or a consistent tone. In fact, although it frequently remains possible to find a voice, persona, or tone, it is just as frequently impossible. In fact, the technology often seems to defy that impulse to find unity and integrity by its nature: a user can disrupt entire textual configurations—and stable meaning—with a single keystroke or click of a mouse.

Furthermore, the strong visual component of digital writing, through the use of font styles, font sizes, colors, images, video, screen movement, hypertexts, screen configurations, and layering—all of which convey meaning—aren't as easily conceived of in oral terms, which is what gives the voice metaphor its explanatory power. In addition, texts can exist literally, virtually, or as a combination of the two.

If there is a voice, it is disrupted and disrupting. Responsibility is diffused; authority is scattered into cyberspace. It is hard to have power over someone who refuses to play. Thus voice, although it still might be possible to use as a metaphor, is in key ways antithetical to the medium.

WHAT ABOUT STYLE?

A student, John, is assigned to write an editorial about an issue on campus. For a topic, he selects the food in the cafeteria because he feels strongly (often a good place to start) that it lacks variety and is both unappetizing and unhealthy. In his first draft, he taps into what could easily be construed as his own voice. He's angry that he is put into a position where he has to eat the food or go hungry, and he wants to express that anger. The resulting essay is a sarcastic diatribe explaining why he hates the university's cafeteria food. The essay is informal, personal, and passionate. One could argue that it is possible to hear his voice as one reads the essay. And if it is believed, as it is believed by the voice proponents, that hearing that voice is powerful, then the essay should be powerful.

However John's essay is not necessarily powerful writing. His stylistic choices are based on whether the wording, sentencing, and structure conveyed his feelings accurately, on whether he clearly *expressed himself.* But the essay may not be effective rhetorically, unless the reader is purely interested in John and in understanding John's feelings. Even then, an accurate understanding of the complexity of John's feelings (if he even cares that much about this assignment) is difficult.

Powerful discourse is discourse that makes a difference. Sometimes that difference *is* personal; writing can *express* one's emotions in ways that are therapeutic. Writing can also help a writer make sense of something, as in writing to learn what one thinks or writing to organize one's thoughts. More often, powerful writing also has a transactional purpose: to inform, persuade, or move readers from their present state of mind to a new one. To do that, one needs to enter the game, to participate in the discursive network. Another approach John might have taken, then, is to determine what he wanted to *do* with his essay, given the context and purpose of the assignment. If he wants to change cafeteria policies, then he needs to determine who might be able to effect those changes. Assuming the school's food services is his target audience, he'd need to make *stylistic choices* that would be most effective in persuading that audience that changes need to be made. In this case, a more formal, even dispassionate tone might make him sound more objective and enhance his credibilty (rhetorical *ethos*). The use of rhetorical strategies or appeals that are crafted to be effective with his particular audience can serve to get readers on his side rather than to antagonize them; and the introduction of concrete evidence might be effective at getting the audience to believe his claims. This shift involves a *network* of choices in which he wants to demonstrate his authority, appeal to his readers, and adjust what he says to do both. It involves decisions about style.

STYLISTIC CHOICES—WHERE TO BEGIN

What is style? Is it voice? Is it something else? Grammar? Diction? Sentencing?

Walker Gibson's analysis of three writing styles in his well-known "Styles and Statistics: A Model T Style Machine" from his 1966 book *Tough, Sweet, and Stuffy* is a good example of the confluence of voice and linguistics. For this chapter, Gibson gathered around 3,000 words of nonfiction prose and sorted them into three categories—"tough," "sweet," and "stuffy"—based "impressionistically" (p. 115) on his sense of the "personality" that seems to govern each category. A sample from the "tough" category by Harold Taylor from the *Saturday Review,* 1961, begins:

> The temptation of the educator is to explain and describe, to organize a body of knowledge for the student, leaving the student with nothing to do. I have never been able to understand why educators do this so often, especially where books are concerned. (p. 134)

A passage by Irwin Edwin from the *Saturday Review*, 1950, falls into the "sweet" category. For example:

> The title of this essay may strike you as a typographical error. You may be saying to yourself that the writer really means required reading, and the phrase conjures up for you, I suspect, lists distributed on the first days of college courses. (p. 134)

And stuffy, by David H. Stevens in his book *The Changing Humanities*, 1953:

> Rapid and coherent development of programs in modern literature has led to the production of excellent materials for study from the earlier years of secondary education through the last of undergraduate study. The sole danger—if it be one, in the opinion of others—lies in easy acceptance of what is well done. (p. 134)

For each category he determines and tabulates the "grammatical-rhetorical qualities" (p. 113) that may account for the differences. The linguistic features, which include word size, verbs, modifiers, subordination, determiners, and punctuation, enable him to conclude that each passage has a distinctive style based on the co-occurrence of linguistic patterns. The connection between the labels ("stuffy," etc.) and the linguistic feature analysis suggests that voice has very specific constructs.

Voice as style (or style as voice) remains current. In the 2010 edition of *Rhetorical Grammar*, Martha Kolln and co-author Loretta Gray advise novice writers to:

> [t]hink of your writer's voice as the identity you create through choosing words and arranging them on the page. Just as different facets of your identity appear during the day, depending on whom you're talking to, your writing voice or identity will vary according to your imagined readers. Sometimes your voice will be angry, sometimes friendly, other times meditative … The key in writing is to be able to control your voice so that you convey the message you want to. You can gain this control by understanding certain features of language: **tone**, the writer's stance, or attitude toward the topic; **diction**, the choice of words; **point of view**, the perspective from which the writers voice the topic; and **metadiscourse**, the signals that help guide the reader through the text as well as communicate the writer's credibility and authority. (p. 122, emphasis in original)

Thus voice can be shaped by word choice and metadiscourse (cuing and transitions, for example), but also more vaguely through point of view and tone.

While this explanation reflects the concept that writers can have multiple voices, a few paragraphs later, the authors remind writers: "In all of your writing, however, your writer's voice should be your voice, your **personal voice**" (p. 122). What is personal voice? Is it the authentic voice that is featured so prominently in expressivism (Elbow et al.)? It is not entirely clear.

In the essay at the end of this chapter, Tom Pace points out that since 1980, teachers of writing have generally spent less time in their courses on style than they did previously. Most of the lay public is familiar with Strunk and White's *Elements of Style*, a style manual first published in 1918 that tends to offer prescriptive admonitions about style, much of which falls into the category of usage. The concept of "good style," independent of context or rhetorical situation, which is epitomized by current-traditional rhetoric, still holds sway in writing instruction with its heavy emphasis on grammar rules and small units of discourse (words and sentences), on rigid organizing principles (such as the five-paragraph essay), and on a focus on words, sentences and paragraphs. The emergence of authentic voice pedagogy with the process movement didn't contribute much either in terms of time spent on "craft" because of the abstract emphasis on helping writers find their unique, authentic "voices."

Despite Pace's contention, however, significant work has been done on the teaching of style. While the following cannot be comprehensive, I offer some representative examples of teaching practices post 1980.

Previously published in 1965, Chapter 4 in *Classical Rhetoric for the Modern Student* (1990) and *Style and Statement* (1999) by Edward P. J. Corbett and Robert J. Connors took students through considerations of diction, sentences, paragraphing, figures of speech and imitation. Corbett and Connors emphasized attention to flexibility: "The classical rhetoricians taught that a person acquired versatility of style in three ways: (1) through a study of precepts or principles (*ars*), (2) through practice in writing (*exercitatio*), (3) through imitation of the practice of others (*imitatio*)" (p. 3). Further, they drew a line between grammar and rhetoric. *Grammar*, they argued,

> is preoccupied with how a particular language works—how words are formed and how words can be put together in phrases and clauses. What we mean when we say that rhetoric is concerned with "effectiveness" is that rhetoric deals with the choice of the "best" from a number of possible expressions in a language. (p. 4)

One of the hallmark assignments of this book is a linguistic analysis of students' own prose. First students are asked to measure and tabulate sentence complexity and paragraphing in a passage they have previously written. Then they examine sentence openers, and finally they focus attention on diction. Then students are asked to do the same set of analyses with a passage of comparable length written by a professional writer. Finally they are asked to compare the two and comment on the difference between their own prose and that of the professionals. Based on observable features of style and close analysis, this methodology served to demystify style and help students perceive stylistic variables.

Also published in the 1980s were a number of books on metaphor and style, the best known is Lakoff and Johnson's *Metaphors We Live By* (1980; see also Paul Ricoeur's *The Rule of Metaphor,* 1987). What becomes clear is that the effectiveness of metaphors is dependent upon the rhetorical situation. If a metaphor is too familiar and has, hence, lost its explanatory power, it is considered a "dead" metaphor. Powerful metaphors have the potential to shape understanding and meaning.

Another well-known book is Joseph Williams' *Style: Lessons in Clarity and Grace*. First published in 1981 and now in its tenth edition (revised by Gregory Colomb, 2010), *Style* is based on a curriculum created through the Little Red Schoolhouse writing program at the University of Chicago. Early chapters focus on definitions of style and the vagaries and inconsistencies of grammar rules, but the bulk of this book works (according to Colomb in the preface to the tenth edition) to address the following questions:

- What is it in a sentence that makes readers judge it as they do?
- How do we diagnose our own prose to anticipate their judgments?
- How do we revise a sentence so that readers will think better of it? (p. xi)

Each chapter explains stylistic issues (clarity, coherence, concision, elegance) with particular emphasis on the sentence, then supplies exercises and examples. The only mention of voice has to do with active and passive verbs.

The relatively recent work on genre and genre studies (Cope & Kalantzis, 1993; Devitt, Bawarshi, & Reiff, 2004; Jolliffe, 1999) introduces an approach to style that is based on genre. Cope and Kalantizis argue for helping students understand the varying forms that a text can take and how the form relates to social purpose, adding a layer of complexity to the study of style that Williams deftly avoids. In their textbook *Scenes of Writing*, Devitt, Bawarshi, and Reiff provide ways that students can use genre analyses to help make choices for their own writing. Those choices critically involve stylistic choices. For example, in a section labeled "Guidelines for Analyzing Genres" they ask students to collect samples of the genre that they are writing and go through three important steps: first, identify the setting, subject, participants (readers and writers), purposes; second, identify and describe patterns of that genre, including rhetorical appeals, format, sentences and diction; and finally to think about what these patterns reveal about the situation and the scene.

THE FORMAL STUDY OF STYLISTICS

The formal study of style, called "Stylistics," has been out of favor since the 1980s, and this fact may have contributed to the perception that few writing classrooms deal with style. The traditional focus of stylistics was on the linguistic study of literary language, even though, as Leech and Short point out in their 1981 book, *Style in Fiction*, "style can be applied to both spoken and writing, both literary and non-literary varieties of language." (p. 11). For many language theorists working in stylistics, the study of style had a largely aesthetic function, and its reliance on linguistics to explain the impact of words, sentences, and paragraphs on a reader has been controversial. (For two good edited volumes on stylistics that explore the range of stylistics, see *Linguistics and Literary Style* (1970) and *Essays in Modern Stylistics* (1981), both edited by Donald C. Freeman. In 1986, Donald McQuade published an edited collection, *The Territory of Language: Linguistics, Stylistics, and the Teaching of Composition*, which features essays by David Bartholomae, Robert Connors, Edward P. J. Corbett, Lester Faigley, and Ross Winterowd. This volume is out of print.)

While is it not yet clear if stylistics is making a comeback, there have been a number of new books seeking to rehabilitate attention to style and stylistics—*Refiguring Prose Style* (2005), edited by T. R. Johnson and T. L. Pace, and *Out of Style* by Paul Butler, for example. (See Pace's chapter, "Style and the Renaissance of Composition Studies," at the end of this chapter.) Whether or not these contribute to a renewed interest, the fact remains that the study of style—much like the study of voice—is complex, controversial, and political. And important.

For Writing and Discussion

Becoming Familiar With Voice

Writing Before Reading: if you have a voice in writing, how would you characterize it? Do you feel you have your own, identifiable voice? If not, is having a voice in writing something you aspire to have?

Readings

Elbow, P. (1994). What do we mean when we talk about voice in texts? In K. B. Yancey (Ed.), *Voices on voice: Perspectives, definitions, inquiry* (pp. 1–35). Urbana, IL: NCTE.

Fulwiler, T. (1990). Looking and listening for my voice. *College Composition and Communication. 41* (2), 214–220.

Hashimoto, I. (1987). Voice as juice: Some reservations about evangelic composition. *College Composition and Communication, 38*, 70–80.

Follow-Up Questions and Activities

1. Do you adjust your voice for different speaking or writing occasions? Some definitions of voice assume that your voice can be adjusted for different rhetorical situations. Imagine that despite the warnings and misgivings of your parents who are currently living in Mexico City, you were skiing in some backcountry in Colorado—as you do every weekend—and were caught in an avalanche. This has happened before, only this time you couldn't just ski out of it. The impact of the avalanche broke your leg and buried you under eight feet of snow. Through pure dint of willpower, you were able to shovel a tunnel with your ski pole and drag yourself out, making it to safety. Rescuers found you shortly thereafter. Now that you are recovering, you find you need to do some writing about the event. This first is an e-mail to your best friend (also a skiier) who lives in Washington State; the second is a letter to your parents, explaining what happened, and the third is an opinion piece to a local newspaper who is interested in your story. Each should be about a page long.

2. If you can, determine and describe your voice for each passage in the previous exercise. Then write a stylistic assessment of how each piece of writing differs from the next. Here are some features to consider as you construct your response.

   - Diction (philosophical, polysyllabic, Latinate, formal, abstract, informal, monosyllabic, concrete nouns, slang, idiomatic expressions, etc.). What kinds of word choice are most effective? Why?
   - Sentencing (short, simple sentences, long sentences, complex sentences, fragments, imperatives, questions, etc.). What kinds of sentence would work best? Why?
   - Tone (ironic, sarcastic, humorous, serious, casual, objective, personal, etc.).
   - Paragraphing (short, long, meandering, direct, etc.).
   - Structure/organization (chronological, comparison/contrast, problem/solution, deductive/inductive, etc.).
   - Figures of speech (metaphors, similes, analogies, personification, etc.).

3. Is it easier to teach voice or style? What are the differences?

Reading for Voice and Style

The following are two first-year students' responses to a "reflective essay" assignment, which asked student writers to introduce their final writing portfolios and comment on (a) what the writer now understands to be good writing, (b) how their portfolios reflect this understanding, and (c) what they might still want to work on. Designated audience: first-year writing instructors. Note that these papers are used with little or no editing.

Which one has "voice"? Identify as many features as you can that contribute to this voice.

Student A (Eli Britt)

I have never done this before. I have never had to make something as utterly boring as the five-paragraph format seem interesting and appealing. My teacher gave me the final edits on the paper. Now suppose it all lies on my shoulders.

I kind of feel like a super hero, my grades are my Metropolis and I am Superman. O.K. Playtime is over please focus now Eli. Put on the headphones, bump the euro-trash techno and pump out a masterpiece you can be proud of.

Jen (My English 101 teacher) is right about this first sentence. "Five-paragraph essays suck serious a**." It needs to go. I have this sick compulsion to swear now that I don't have high school teachers salivating at the chance to slap a red mark on it. I'll go with a more intellectual form of shock value. Evil is such a good word, so vague, but you just know it's bad.

Audience. Oh man, how am I going write to two difference audiences. I just wanted write for people that didn't really know too much about five-paragraph essays. That way I so much easier, they are putty in my hands (cue menacing laugh) … delusional hands, you cocky little punk. I have to stop getting caught in this whole power of writing thing. Focus. So I have to focus on two audiences, those that know and those that don't. That means more evidence, stronger claims and an over-all wholesome feeling. I am going to have to give a lot of credit to Jen on this paper. Most of her ideas are really good. Moving the paragraph about our conversation is a good cure for a rather boring intro, I never would have thought about it that way. I need to elaborate on the conversation with Jen. People aren't going to know what made me think differently. It's difficult to articulate the process of my thought to others and yet I have had to do it so much in this class. I like it though, it is definitely something I want to get better at, maybe make it not so difficult.

Now I have to "go into more detail on my high school paper" says Jen. All right, I'll buy that and see where it goes. I can't really see the point but I'll trust her. Oh … evidence.

Always with the evidence it's like I have to prove everything. I know it's good. It's just difficult.

That clock had better not say 2:00 am, it is Saturday night I should be at a party. Yeah, the TA's grading this will be crying in their fourth lukewarm cup of Maxwell House for me. Focus… .

Student B (Lisa Cooper)

To begin with, defining the characteristics of audience impacted my style as a writer. I have come to understand that an audience consists of those who agree with you, those who disagree with you, and those who are undecided. For the most part, it's the undecided crowd that your writing needs to be directed to. The group that agrees with you will support what you say no matter how you say it to some degree. Those who disagree will tear your writing apart. The undecided will tear it apart but with an open mind. Understanding the audience plays a big part in informing or persuading diverse members. Read All About It (But Don't Believe It) by Caryl Rivers is a perfect example of the latter. She proclaims, "The American press greatly exaggerates the problems of women—especially working women." Although her arguments are strong and her support is sturdy, she is one-sided, judgmental, and close-minded. Even though I agree with her line of reasoning, the manner in which she presented the facts is clouded with a harsh and condescending tone of voice. She did not take the audience into account nor did she seem to care. Rivers gave me, as the reader, the sense that she was just an angry person venting to anyone willing to listen long enough. The piece by Kurt Vonnegut Jr., entitled "How to Write with Style" was similarly belittling to the reader. His use of imaginative language and word play captivated me, a word choice fanatic; however, it detracted from the actual point of the writing. Furthermore, he did not follow his own tips on "how to write with style." In my persuasive essay about night classes, I attempted to tailor the tone of my paper toward the undecided by focusing on my point while acknowledging arguments of the opposing side as well. I made it clear how I felt, that night classes are bothersome without becoming overly emotional. I had sound arguments supported by common sense and fact rather than judgment justified by opinion. Realizing that the audience will not always agree with what you are writing is a considerable step on the path to effective writing... .

Here is an excerpt from a different paper by the same student, Lisa Cooper. This time, the assignment was to "enter the conversation" about a controversial issue, do her own study of the data, and come up with a claim supported by evidence that in some way makes a contribution to the issue.

It has been stated that a picture is worth a thousand words, and in the case of describing events it is often true. Neil Postman and Steve Powers, authors of "The Bias of Language, the Bias of Pictures" state, "The words people use to describe [an] event are not the event itself and are only abstracts through re-presentations of the event." Each individual interprets an event using personal attitudes and points of view, which, when relaying that information to another, are injected into the event. This is where television comes into play. With the addition of pictures, the art of recounting worldwide happenings has attained a new level. But how much do the pictures really say? By examining one television newscast and comparing it to the newspaper version of the same story, it is possible to identify the differences. In contrast to conventional wisdom, the addition of moving pictures detracts from the accuracy and content of the story, thus causing the newspaper article to be more informative than the newscast.

Which of the three passages is "effective"? Note that you'll need to define "effective." Examine the success of each passage in terms of what you think might be intended by "voice."

For Writing and Discussion

In the early 1980s, a group in the Pacific Northwest (now known as Education Northwest), developed the "6-trait writing model." Eventually developed (and trademarked) as the 6+1 Trait® Writing Model of Instruction and Assessment, it is now used for state and district writing assessments in (as the Education Northwest website indicates) "virtually every state in the country, not to mention American Samoa, Amsterdam, France, Great Britain, Saudi Arabia, China, Venezuela, Australia, Turkey, and Bahrain."

Voice is one of the six traits in addition to *ideas* and *content, organization, word choice, sentence fluency,* and *conventions* (with the +1 being *Presentation*). Consider how four of these traits are defined below.

Voice

Voice is the writer coming through the words, the sense that a real person is speaking to us and cares about the message. It is the heart and soul of the writing, the magic, the wit, the feeling, the life and breath. When the writer is engaged personally with the topic, he/she imparts a personal tone and flavor to the piece that is unmistakably his/hers alone. And it is that individual something—different from the mark of all other writers—that we call Voice.

Word Choice

Word Choice is the use of rich, colorful, precise language that communicates not just in a functional way, but in a way that moves and enlightens the reader. In descriptive writing, strong word choice resulting in imagery, especially sensory, show-me writing, clarifies and expands ideas. In persuasive writing, purposeful word choice moves the reader to a new vision of ideas. In all modes of writing figurative language such as metaphors, similes and analogies articulate, enhance, and enrich the content.

Sentence Fluency

Sentence Fluency is the rhythm and flow of the language, the sound of word patterns, the way in which the writing plays to the ear, not just to the eye. How does it sound when read aloud? That's the test. Fluent writing has cadence, power, rhythm, and movement. It is free of awkward word patterns that slow the reader's progress. Sentences vary in length, beginnings, structure, and style, and are so well crafted that the writer moves through the piece with ease.

Conventions

The Conventions Trait is the mechanical correctness of the piece and includes five elements: spelling, punctuation, capitalization, grammar/usage, and paragraphing. Writing that is strong in Conventions has been proofread and edited with care. Since this trait has so many pieces to it, it's almost an analytical trait within an analytic system. As you assess a piece for convention, ask yourself: "How much work would a copy editor need to do to prepare the piece for publication?" (http://educationnorthwest.org/resource/503)

Write an essay in which you explore what you think voice means in this context, and what you might be looking for in students' writing. To what degree is voice different from word choice, sentence fluency, and conventions? What are the advantages in considering student writing in these terms? What are the liabilities? Develop an argument where you defend or disagree with the use of voice in this rubric.

If you believe that focusing on voice is an effective way to teach writing, develop a definition of voice and sketch out some activities that would help students develop their own voices. If, on the other hand, you believe in an alternative approach to understanding style, sketch this out with appropriate activities.

For Writing and Discussion

Read the excerpt at the end of this chapter, "How to Get Power Through Voice" by Peter Elbow (1981), from Chapter 26 of *Writing with Power: Techniques for Mastering the Writing Process* (pp. 304–313). New York: Oxford UP. Then respond to the following questions:

1. Draw up a list of features that you believe would exist in a text that has "real voice," as Elbow defines it. Are these features that you believe constitute good writing? Or powerful writing? If you can think of other features that might contribute to powerful writing, what are these? In other words, in what ways do you and Elbow see eye-to-eye and to what extent do you disagree? How do you account for this?
2. Find a piece of writing that you believe has "real voice" as described by this article. Justify your selection.
3. How would you teach students to use the kind of voice that Elbow talks about in this chapter?
4. What kinds of writing do you see yourself or your students doing in the next ten years? How might Elbow's techniques help? Where would they be of no help? Where would they be a problem?
5. Note that this excerpt is from a book designed to help writers "master the writing process." In other words, it's from a textbook of sorts. Describe how Elbow's style in this excerpt differs from that of other textbooks on writing that you are familiar with. How does this seem to support his argument about finding voice in writing? What do you think of his style? Does it seem to have "voice"? Why or why not?

For Writing and Discussion

Theories about writing always emerge from specific historical and political contexts. What was going on in 1981—in the field of teaching writing as well as in the political climate—that might have influenced the way Elbow conceptualized voice and treated voice in writing? Discuss the specific influences that you see.

Note that Peter Elbow's book from which this excerpt is taken was published in 1981. Since then he has somewhat revised his stance on voice. Locate some of Elbow's more recent articles or books in which he discusses voice and see if you can trace shifts in his thinking. Do you believe these changes are more or less productive in helping students learn to write?

For Further Exploration

Bowden, D. (1999). *The mythology of voice*. Portsmouth, NH: Heinemann-Boynton/Cook. A critique of the voice metaphor.

Elbow, P. (Ed.). (1994). *Landmark essays on voice and writing*. Davis, CA: Hermagorus Press.

Includes many of the essential readings on voice, including essays that lay out some of the important theoretical underpinnings.

Johnson, T. R., & Pace, T. (2005). *Refiguring prose style*. Logan, UT: Utah State Press.

Yancey, K. B. (Ed.). (1994). *Voices on voice: Perspectives, definitions, inquiry*. Urbana, IL: NCTE.

Contains newer essays on voice and on the use of voice in different genres of writing. Also includes a good annotated bibliography of work done on voice.

REFERENCES

Applebee, A. N. (1974). *Tradition and reform in the teaching of English: A history*. Urbana, IL: NCTE.

Bakhtin, M. (1981). *The dialogic imagination*. Ed. M. Holquist, & trans. C. Emerson. Austin: University of Texas Press.

Belenky, M. F., Clinchy, B., Goldberger, N., & Tarule, J. (1986). *Women's ways of knowing: The development of self, voice, and mind*. New York: Basic Books.

Berlin, J. (1987). *Rhetoric and reality: Writing instruction in American colleges, 1900–1985*. Carbondale: Southern Illinois University Press.

Bolter, J. D. (1991). *Writing space: The computer, hypertext, and the history of writing*. Hillsdale, NJ: Lawrence Erlbaum.

Bowden, D. (1999). *The mythology of voice*. Portsmouth, NH: Boynton/Cook Heinemann.

Connors, R. (1987). Personal writing assignments. *College Composition and Communication, 38* (2), 166–183.

Cope, B., & Kalantzis, M. (Eds.). (1993). *The powers of literacy: A genre approach to teaching writing*. Pittsburgh, PA: University of Pittsburgh Press.

Corbett, E. P. J. (1999). *Classical rhetoric for the modern student* (3rd ed.). Oxford: Oxford University Press.

Corbett, E. P. J., & Connors, R. (1999). *Style and statement*. Oxford: Oxford University Press.

Crowley, S. (1989). *A teacher's introduction to deconstruction*. Urbana, IL: NCTE.

Derrida, J. (1976). *Of grammatology*. Trans. G. C. Spivak. Baltimore and London: The Johns Hopkins University Press.

Devitt, A., Bawarshi, A., & Reiff, M. J. (2004). *Scenes of writing: Strategies for composing with genres*. New York: Pearson/Longman, 93–94.

Ede, L. (1995). *Work in progress: A guide to writing and revising* (3rd ed.). New York: St. Martin's Press.

Elbow, P. (1973). *Writing without teachers*. Oxford: Oxford University Press.

Elbow, P. (1981). *Writing with power: Techniques for mastering the writing process*. New York: Oxford University Press.

Eliot, T. S. (1943). The three voices of poetry. In *On poetry and poets* (pp. 96–112). New York: Farrar.

Emig, J. (1971). *The composing process of twelfth graders*. Urbana, IL: NCTE.

Freeman, D. C. (1970). *Linguistics and literary style*. New York: Holt, Rinehart and Winston, Inc.

Freeman, D. C. (Ed.). (1981). *Essays in modern stylistics*. New York: Methuen & Co.

Gibson, W. (1966). Styles and statistics: A model T style machine. In *Tough, sweet, and stuffy*. Bloomington, IN: Indiana University Press.

Gibson, W. (1969). *Persona: A style study for readers and writers*. New York: Random.

Gilligan, C. (1993). *In a different voice: Psychological theory and women's development*. Cambridge, MA: Harvard University Press.

Hashimoto, I. (1987). Voice as juice: Some reservations about evangelic composition. *College Composition and Communication, 38,* 70–80.

Johnson, T. R., & Pace, T. L. (Eds.). (2005). *Refiguring prose style: Possibilities for writing pedagogy*. Logan, UT: Utah State Press.

Jolliffe, D. A. (1999). *Inquiry and genre: Writing to learn in college*. Boston: Allyn and Bacon.

Kolln, M., & Gray, L. (2010). *Rhetorical grammar: Grammatical choices, rhetorical effects* (6th ed.). Boston: Longman.

Lakoff, G., & Johnson, M. (1980). *Metaphors we live by*. Chicago and London: University of Chicago Press.

Leech, G., & Short, M. (1981). *Style in fiction: A linguistic introduction to English fictional prose*. London: Longman.

Macrorie, K. (1985). *Telling writing* (4th ed.). Upper Montclair, NJ: Boynton/Cook.

McQuade, D. (1986). *The territory of language: Linguistics, stylistics, and the teaching of composition*. Carbondale: Southern Illinois University Press.

Plato. (1961). *The collected dialogues of Plato*. Ed. E. Hamilton, & H. Cairns. Princeton: NJ: Bollingen Series LXXI, Princeton University Press.

Ricoeur, P. (1987). *The rule of metaphor: Multi-disciplinary studies of the creation of meaning in language*. Toronto: University of Toronto Press.

Stewart, D. (1972). *The authentic voice: A pre-writing approach to student writing*. Dubuque, IA: Wm. C. Brown.

Williams, J. M., & Colomb, G. (2010). *Style: Lessons in clarity and grace* (10th ed.). Boston: Longman.
Yancey, K. B. (Ed.). (1994). *Voices on voice: Perspectives, definitions, inquiry.* Urbana, IL: NCTE.
Zoellner, R. (1969). Talk-write: A behavioral pedagogy for composition. *College English, 30* (4), 267–320.

Readings

HOW TO GET POWER THROUGH VOICE

Peter Elbow

What if this hypothesis about voice is correct? One thing follows from it that's more important than anything else: everyone, however inexperienced or unskilled, has real voice available; everyone can write with power. Even though it may take some people a long time before they can write well about certain complicated topics or write in certain formal styles, and even though it will take some people a long time before they can write without mistakes in spelling and usage, nevertheless, nothing stops anyone from writing words that will make readers listen and be affected. Nothing stops you from writing right now, today, words that people will want to read and even want to publish. Nothing stops you, that is, but your fear or unwillingness or lack of familiarity with what I am calling your real voice.

But this clarion call—for that's what I intend it to be despite my careful qualifiers—immediately raises a simple question: Why doesn't everyone use power if it is sitting there available and why does most writing lack power? There are lots of good reasons. In this section I will give advice about how to get real voice into your writing, but I will present it in terms of an analysis of why people so seldom use that power.

...

People often lack any voice at all in their writing, even fake voice, because they stop so often in the act of writing a sentence and worry and change their minds about which words to use. They have none of the natural breath in their writing that they have in the conditions for speaking. The list of conditions is awesome: we have so little practice in writing, but so much more time to stop and fiddle as we write each sentence; we have additional rules of spelling and usage to follow in writing that we don't have in speaking; we feel more culpable for our written foolishness than for what we say; we have been so fully graded, corrected, and given feedback on our mistakes in writing; and we are usually trying to get our words to conform to some (ill-understood) model of "good writing" as we write.

Frequent and regular freewriting exercises are the best way to overcome these conditions of writing and get voice into your words. These exercises should perhaps be called compulsory writing exercises since they are really a way to *compel* yourself to keep putting words down on paper no matter how lost or frustrated you feel. To get voice into your words you need to learn to get each word chosen, as it were, not by you but by the preceding word. Freewriting exercises help you learn to stand out of the way.

In addition to actual exercises in nonstop writing—since it's hard to keep writing *no matter what* for more than fifteen minutes—force yourself simply to write enormous quantities. Try to make up for all the writing you haven't done. Use writing for as many different tasks as you can. Keep a notebook or journal, explore thoughts for yourself, write to yourself when you feel frustrated or want to figure something out.

Practice revising for voice. A powerful exercise is to write short pieces of prose or poetry that work without any punctuation at all. Get the words so well ordered that punctuation is never missed. The reader must never stumble or have to reread a phrase, not even on first reading—and all without benefit of punctuation. This is really an exercise in adjusting the breath in the words till it guides the reader's voice naturally to each pause and full stop.

Read out loud. This is a good way to exercise the muscle involved in voice and even in real voice. Good reading out loud is not necessarily dramatic. I'm struck with how some good poets or readers get real voice into a monotone or chant. They are trying to let the words' inner resonance come through, not trying to "perform" the words. (Dylan Thomas reads so splendidly that we may make the mistake of calling his technique "dramatic." Really it is a kind of chant or incantation he uses.) But there is no right way. It's a question of steering a path between being too timid and being falsely dramatic. The presence of listeners can sharpen your ear and help you hear when you chicken out or overdramatize.

…

Real voice. People often avoid it and drift into fake voices because of the need to face an audience. I have to go to work, I have to make a presentation, I have to teach, I have to go to a party, I have to have dinner with friends. Perhaps I feel lost, uncertain, baffled—or else angry—or else uncaring— or else hysterical. I can't sound that way with all these people. They won't understand, they won't know how to deal with me, and I won't accomplish what I need to accomplish. Besides, perhaps I don't even know *how* to sound the way I feel. (When we were little we had no difficulty sounding the way we felt; thus most little children speak and write with real voice.) Therefore I will use some of the voices I have at my disposal that will serve the audience and the situation—voices I've learned by imitation or made up out of desperation or out of my sense of humor. I might as well. By now, those people think those voices are me. If I used my real voice, they might think I was crazy.

For real voice, write a lot without an audience. Do freewritings and throw them away. Remove yourself from the expectations of an audience, the demands of a particular task, the needs of a particular interaction. As you do this, try out many different ways of speaking.

But a certain *kind* of audience can help you toward real voice even though it was probably the pressures of audience that led you to unreal voices in the first place. Find an audience of people also committed to getting power in their writing. Find times when you can write in each other's presence, each working on your own work. Your shared presence and commitment to helping each other will make you more powerful in what you write. Then read your rough writing to each other. No feedback: just welcoming each other to try out anything.

Because you often don't even know what your power or your inner self sounds like, you have to try many different tones and voices. Fool around, jump from one mood or voice to another, mimic, play-act, dramatize and exaggerate. Let your writing be outrageous. Practice relinquishing control. It can help to write in settings where you never write (on the bus? in the bathtub?) or in modes you never use. And if, as sometimes happens, you know you are angry but somehow cannot really feel or inhabit that feeling, play-act and exaggerate it. Write artificially. Sometimes "going through the motions" is the quickest way to "the real thing."

Realize that in the short run there is probably a conflict between developing real voice and producing successful pragmatic writing—polished pieces that work for specific audiences and situations. Keeping an appropriate stance or tone for an audience may prevent you from getting real voice into that piece of writing. Deep personal outrage, for example, may be the only authentic tone of voice you can use in writing to a particular person, yet that voice is neither appropriate nor useful for the actual document you have to write—perhaps an official agency memo or a report to that person about his child. Feedback on whether something works as a finished piece of writing for an audience is often not good feedback on real voice. It is probably important to work on both goals. Work on polishing things and making sure they have the right tone or stance for that audience. Or at least not the wrong one: you may well have to play it safe. But make sure you also work on writing that *doesn't* have to work and doesn't have to be revised and polished for an audience.

And yet you needn't give up on power just because a particular writing situation is very tricky for you. Perhaps you must write an essay for a teacher who never seems to understand you; or a report for a supervisor who never seems able to see things the way you do; or a research report on a topic that has always scared and confused you. If you try to write in the most useful voice for this situation—perhaps cheerful politeness or down-to-business impersonality—the anger will probably show through anyway. It might not show clearly, readers might be unaware of it, yet they will turn out to have the kind of responses they have to angry writing. That is, they will become annoyed with many of the ideas you present, or continually think of arguments against you (which they wouldn't have done to a different voice), or they will turn off, or they will react condescendingly.

To the degree that you keep your anger hidden, you are likely to write words especially lacking in voice—especially dead, fishy, fake-feeling. Or the process of trying to write in a non-angry, down-to-business, impersonal way is so deadening to you that you simply get bored and sleepy and devoid of energy. Your mind shuts off. You cannot think of anything to say.

In a situation like this it helps to take a roundabout approach. First do lots of freewriting where you are angry and tell your reader all your feelings in whatever voices come. Then get back to the real topic. Do lots of freewriting and raw writing and exploration of the topic—writing still in whatever style comes out. Put all your effort into finding the best ideas and arguments you can, and don't worry about your tone. After you express the feelings and voices swirling around in you, and after you get all the insights you can while not having to worry about the audience and the tone, then you will find it relatively easy to revise and rewrite something powerful and effective for that reader. That is, you can get past the anger and confusion, but keep the good ideas and the energy. As you rewrite for the real audience, you can generally use large chunks of what you have already written with only minor cosmetic changes. (You don't necessarily have to write out *all* the anger you have. It may be that you have three hundred pages of angry words you need to say to someone, but if you can get *one* page that really opens the door all the way, that can be enough. But if this is something new to you, you may find you cannot do it in one page—you need to rant and rave for five or ten pages. It may seem like a waste of time, but it isn't. Gradually you will get more economical.)

By taking this roundabout path, you will find more energy and better thinking. And through the process of starting with the voices that just happen and seeing where they lead, often you will come to a *new* voice which is appropriate to this reader but also rings deeply. You won't have to choose between something self-defeatingly angry that will simply turn off the reader or something pussyfooting, polite, and full of fog—and boring for you to write.

A long and messy path is common and beneficial, but you can get some of the benefits quicker if you are in a hurry. Just set yourself strict time limits for the early writing and force yourself to write without stopping throughout the early stages. When I have to write an evaluation of a student I am annoyed at, I force myself to write a quick freewriting letter to the student telling him everything on my mind. I make this uncensored, extreme, exaggerated, sometimes even deliberately unfair—but very short. And it's for the wastepaper basket. Having done this, I can turn to my official evaluation and find it much easier to write something fair in a suitable tone of voice (for a document that becomes part of the student's transcript). I finish these two pieces of writing much more quickly than if I just tried to write the official document and pick my way gingerly through my feelings.

...

Another reason people don't use real voice is that it makes them feel exposed and vulnerable. I don't so much mind if someone dislikes my writing when I am merely using an acceptable voice, but if I use my real voice and they don't like it—which of course is very possible—that hurts. The more criticism people get on their writing, the more they tend to use fake voices. To use real voice feels like bringing yourself into contact with the reader. It's the same kind of phenomenon that happens when there is real eye contact and each person experiences the presence of the other; or when two or more people stop talking and wait in silence while something in the air gets itself clear. Writing of almost any kind is exhibitionistic; writing with real voice is more so. Many professional writers feel a special need for privacy. It will help you, then, to get together with one or more others who are interested in recovering their power. Feeling vulnerable or exposed with them is not so difficult.

Another reason people don't use their real voice is that it means having feelings and memories they would rather not have. When you write in your real voice, it often brings tears or shaking—though laughter too. Using real voice may even mean finding you *believe* things you don't wish to believe. For all these reasons, you need to write for no audience and to write for an audience that's safe. And you need faith in yourself that you will gradually sort things out and that it doesn't matter if it takes time.

Most children have real voice but then lose it. It is often just plain loud: like screeching or banging a drum. It can be annoying or wearing for others. "Shhh" is the response we often get to the power of our real voice. But, in addition, much of what we say with real voice is difficult for those around us to deal with: anger, grief, self-pity, even love for the wrong people. When we are hushed up from those expressions, we lose real voice.

In addition, we lose real voice when we are persuaded to give up some of our natural responses to inauthenticity and injustice. Almost any child can feel inauthenticity in the voices of many TV figures or politicians. Many grown-ups can't hear it so well—or drown out their distrust. It is difficult to get along in the world if you hear all the inauthenticity: it makes you feel alone, depressed, hopeless. We need to belong, and society offers us membership if we stop hearing inauthenticity.

Children can usually feel when things are unfair, but they are often persuaded to go along because they need to belong and to be loved. To get back to those feelings in later life leads to rage, grief, aloneness and—since one has gone along—guilt. Real voice is often buried in all of that. If you want to recover it, you do well to build in special support from people you can trust so you don't feel so alone or threatened by all these feelings.

Another reason people don't use real voice is that they run away from their power. There's something scary about being as strong as you are, about wielding the force you actually have. It means taking a lot more responsibility and credit than you are used to. If you write with real voice, people will say "You did this to me" and try to make you feel responsible for some of their actions. Besides, the effect of your power is liable to be different from what you intended. Especially at first. You cause explosions when you thought you were just asking for the salt or saying hello. In effect I'm saying, "Why don't you shoot that gun you have? Oh yes, by the way, I can't tell you how to aim it." The standard approach in writing is to say you mustn't pull the trigger until you can aim it well. But how can you learn to aim well till you start pulling the trigger? If you start letting your writing lead you to real voice, you'll discover some thoughts and feelings you didn't know you had.

Therefore, practice shooting the gun off in safe places. First with no one around. Then with people you know and trust deeply. Find people who are willing to be in the same room with you while you pull the trigger. Try using the power in ways where the results don't matter. Write letters to people that don't matter to you. You'll discover that the gun doesn't kill but that you have more power than you are comfortable with.

Of course you may accept your power but still want to disguise it. That is, you may find it convenient, if you are in a large organization, to be able to write about an event in a fuzzy, passive "It has come to our attention that ..." kind of language, so you disguise not only the fact that it was an action performed by a human being with a free will but indeed that *you did it*. But it would be incorrect to conclude, as some people do, that all bureaucratic, organizational, and governmental writing needs to lack the resonance of real voice. Most often it could do its work perfectly well even if it were strong and clear. It is the *personal, individualistic,* or *personality-filled* voice that is inappropriate in much organizational writing, but you can write with power in the impersonal, public, and corporate voice. You can avoid "I" and its flavor, and talk entirely in terms of "we" and "they" and even "it," and still achieve the resonance of real voice. Real voice is not the sound of an *individual personality* redolent with vibes, it is the sound of a *meaning* resonating because the individual consciousness of the writer is somehow fully behind or in tune with or in participation with that meaning.

I have stressed the importance of sharing writing without any feedback at all. What about asking people to give you feedback specifically on real voice? I think that such feedback can be useful, but I am leery of it. It's so hard to know whether someone's perception of real voice is accurate. If you want this feedback, don't get it early in your writing development, make sure you get it from very different kinds of people, and make sure not to put too much trust in it. The safest method is to get them to read a piece and then ask them a week later what they remember. Passages they *dislike* often have the most real voice.

But here is a specific exercise for getting feedback on real voice. It grows out of one of the first experiences that made me think consciously about this matter. As an applicant for conscientious objector status, and then later as a draft counselor, I discovered that the writing task set by Selective Service was very interesting and perplexing. An applicant had to write why he was opposed to fighting in wars, but there was no right or wrong answer. The draft board would accept any reasons (within certain broad limits); they would accept any style, any level of skill. Their only criterion was whether *they* believed that the *writer* believed his own words. (I am describing how it worked when board members were in good faith.)

Applicants, especially college students, often started with writing that didn't work. I could infer from all the arguments and commotion and from conversations with them that they were sincere but as they wrote they got so preoccupied with theories, argument, and reasoning that in the end there was no conviction on paper. When I gave someone this feedback and he was willing to try and try again till at last the words began to ring true, all of a sudden the writing got powerful and even skillful in other ways.

The exercise I suggest to anybody, then, is simply to write about some belief you have—or even some experience or perception—but to get readers to give you this limited, peculiar, draft-board-like feedback: where do they really believe that you believe it, and where do they have doubts? The useful thing about this exercise is discovering how often words that ring true are not especially full of feeling, not heavy with conviction. Too much "sincerity" and quivering often sounds fake and makes readers doubt that you really believe what you are saying. I stress this because I fear I have made real voice sound as though it is always full of loud emotion. It is often quiet.

...

In the end, what may be as important as these specific exercises is adopting the right frame of mind.

Look for real voice and realize it is there in everyone waiting to be used. Yet remember, too, that you are looking for something mysterious and hidden. There are no outward linguistic characteristics to point to in writing with real voice. Resonance or impact on readers is all there is. But you can't count on readers to notice it or to agree about whether it is there because of all the other criteria they use in evaluating writing (e.g., polished style, correct reasoning, good insights, truth-to-life, deep feelings), and because of the negative qualities that sometimes accompany real voice as it is emerging. And you, as writer, may be wrong about the presence or absence of real voice in your writing—at least until you finally develop a trustworthy sense of it. You have to be willing to work in the dark, not be in a hurry, and have faith. The best clue I know is that as you begin to develop real voice, your writing will probably cause more comment from readers than before (though not necessarily more favorable comment).

If you seek real voice you should realize that you probably face a dilemma. You probably have only one real voice—at first anyway—and it is likely to feel childish or distasteful or ugly to you. But you are stuck. You can either use voices you like or you can be heard. For a while, you can't have it both ways.

But if you do have the courage to use and inhabit that real voice, you will get the knack of resonance, you will learn to expand its range and eventually make more voices real. This of course is the skill of great literary artists: the ability to give resonance to many voices.

It's important to stress, at the end, this fact of many voices. Partly to reassure you that you are not ultimately stuck with just one voice forever. But also because it highlights the mystery. Real voice is not necessarily personal or sincere. Writing about your own personal concerns is only one way and not necessarily the best. Such writing can lead to gushy or analytical words about how angry you are today: useful to write, an expression of strong feelings, a possible *source* of future powerful writing, but not resonant of powerful for readers as it stands. Real voice is whatever yields resonance, whatever makes the words bore through. Some writers get real voice through pure fantasy, lies, imitation of utterly different writers, or trance-writing. It may be possible to get real voice by merging in your mind with another personality, pretending to be someone else. *Shedding* the self's concerns and point of view can be a good way to get real voice—thus writing fiction and playing roles are powerful tools. Many good literary artists sound least convincing when they speak for themselves. The important thing is simply to know that power is available and to figure out through experimentation the best way for you to attain it.

Reprinted from Peter Elbow. "How to Get Power Through Voice." *Writing With Power*. 2nd edition. Oxford: Oxford University Press, 1981, 304–313. Reprinted by permission of Oxford University Press, Inc.

STYLE AND THE RENAISSANCE
OF COMPOSITION STUDIES

Tom Pace

I must say, though, that An Alternative Style *is the only work I've published that has generated hate mail, and the only work I've ever done that was attacked at a national meeting by a colleague who knew I was in the audience.*

—Winston Weathers

Why is it that the one feature most popularly associated with writing is the one most ignored by writing instructors? Many of us who became English majors in college and later pursued careers as professionals in graduate programs did so because of a love for the written word, that feeling of magic and mystery that overcame us when we read a well-crafted sentence or a perfectly placed word in our favorite book, poem, play, or essay. We wanted our writing to achieve at least some semblance of that magic. We wanted our writing to be beautiful, our language to inspire, our words to mean something to someone. For those of us who became English teachers, perhaps we wanted to help others appreciate a well-wrought sentence or paragraph, to arouse others to be moved by beautiful language. Perhaps we wanted our students to appreciate the beauty of the way John Keats describes a centuries-old urn, the way Virginia Woolf describes the winds and waves during a journey to a distant lighthouse, or the way Toni Morrison relates the pain of a young girl upon being thrust into a terrifying world of racism and hate. Or perhaps we wanted our students to recognize the political power of language, its capacity to lead people to social justice—the way Martin Luther King, in a speech on a hot August day, inspired an entire generation to change the world. Whatever our reasons, all of us at one time or another came across words that stirred us enough to want to make that love of language our life's work.

But many writing teachers since the mid-1980s or so have gravitated away from teaching the actual craft of writing interesting sentences, well-chosen words, or finely tuned paragraphs. Many professionals in the field of composition studies have shunned, it seems, the one feature most readers and writers associate with good writing—style. While the public, as well as professors outside of English departments, complain loudly about student writers' lack of stylistic grace and control, many writing teachers devote very little of their courses to direct instruction in style or to analysis of stylistic choices. Part of the reason why many instructors neglect to introduce their students to style stems from their misunderstanding of the term and its place within rhetorical education.

In a 2002 opinion piece in *College English*, Peter Elbow makes a call for the field of composition and the field of literary studies to learn from, rather than oppose, one another. Elbow hopes that "both cultures could fully accept that a discipline can be even richer and healthier if it lacks a single-vision center. A discipline based on this multiplex model can better avoid either-or thinking and better foster a spirit of productive catholic pluralism" (544). In the course of this argument, he makes a confession: "I miss elegance." He also misses the fun of playing with language that the field of composition, he insists, has lost. Elbow continues: "I'm sad that the composition tradition seems to assume discursive language as the norm and imaginative, metaphorical language as somehow special or marked or additional. I'd argue that we can't harness students' strongest linguistic and even cognitive powers unless we see imaginative and metaphorical language as the norm—basic or primal" (536).

Elbow, in other words, misses style. He says as much late in the essay when he suggests a list of traits that the field of composition could learn from literary studies: "And what do I wish people in composition could learn from the culture of literature? More honoring of style, playfulness, fun, pleasure, humor. Better writing—and a more pervasive assumption that even in academic writing, even in prose, we can have playfulness, style, pleasure—even adornment and artifice—without being elitist snobs" (543).

Amen.

Elbow is insisting here that studying and teaching style—and playing with language in both scholarship and the classroom—are by no means an exercise in some type of dainty humanism for a few privileged souls, or dull regurgitation of rules. No. Rather, Elbow is suggesting that the study and teaching of style should reside at the very heart of what we should do as composition teachers—instruction in the craft, the skill, and the infinite richness of language. And, I would add, the teaching of style, the playing around with words, the messing around with metaphorical language is conducive, not adverse, to academic writing and to socially responsible writing instruction. But how did the field of composition find itself in this state? What is it about the condition of composition studies at the beginning of the twenty-first century that could lead Elbow to make such a confession? One answer to this question is that compositionists over the last twenty years or so have regarded style as a throwaway element of writing pedagogy, an element that has less to do with knowledge building and more to do with mere surface correctness. Many of these scholars operate within a linear narrative that assumes more complex writing theories supersede less complicated ideas about composing. A review of a key moment in composition and rhetoric's more recent past, the early process movement, will show that their multifaceted approaches to stylistics is not as simplistic as has been previously imagined.

Style and the Early Process Movement

This desire for disciplinary status in composition studies has led to a tension between the desire to tackle what John C. Gerber, in the very first issue of *College Composition and Communication* (CCC) in 1950, called the "practical needs of the professions" and the desire to elevate its "professional standards" (12). In her essay "Reading—and Rereading—the Braddock Essays," Lisa Ede reflects on the early days of the CCCC conference and of its journal, CCC. Ede recognizes that this tension informed much of the work during the early process years:

> Service to colleagues, students, and society—or progress as a scholarly discipline? Since the inception of the CCCC, many have believed that it is possible and necessary to achieve both goals. Indeed, many have hoped not only to achieve these goals but also to contribute broadly to progressive values and practices—to function, in other words, as agents of social, political, and economic changes. … Beliefs such as these have marked the field as transgressive within the academy, even as many in the field have worked to acquire accoutrements of traditional disciplinarity "such" accoutrements as graduate programs and specialized journals, conferences, and associations (all of which have had the effect of extending the scholarly and professional enterprise of composition beyond the domains of the CCCC and CCC) (1999, 11).

Ever since, the field of composition has been working through the tensions among its service mission, its agenda for social reform, and its desire for professional status. The early process movement of the 1960s and 1970s, in many ways, was an attempt "to achieve both goals," as Ede put it. The sense was that in studying how students learned to write, writing teachers could accomplish the two goals at once—one, discover practical, usable pedagogical methods to teach writing more effectively and two, build a body of research and methods of inquiry that could serve as the foundation for composition studies. These two results combined led the way for social reform.

Out of this work, style became an important aspect of writing pedagogy during the days of the early process movement. Style was often seen as a tool of writing instruction in which students could learn various writing strategies and learn to conceive of writing as choice. Certain compositionists drew from several areas of inquiry to develop pedagogies that used style as a key element of teaching writing: Ken Macrorie wrote a text-book, *Telling Writing* (1970), in which he encouraged students to break out of the routine of writing dull, monotonous prose—which he termed "Engfish" – and stretch their writing legs by using journals and analyzing word choice in an effort to make connections between language use and personal experience; and Peter Elbow published such works as *Writing without Teachers* (1973) and *Writing with Power* (1981), in which he provided numerous writing exercises and prompts in an effort to encourage people to think of themselves as writers, to break through the conventional roadblocks of traditional grammar instruction and drill exercises, and to write with vividness and magic. In many ways, these teachers were offering alternatives to the tradition-bound constraints of grammar instruction and the focus on surface error that process pedagogy also countered. For these teachers and scholars, the teaching of style formed the centerpiece of writing pedagogy, a type of pedagogy that connected language acquisition to its contexts.

Francis Christensen, for instance, drew from a background in linguistics to develop a method of teaching writing that focused on sentence- and paragraph-level writing instruction. Edward P. J. Corbett looked to the recovery of classical rhetorical texts as sources for the teaching of style. And Winston Weathers examined alternative writing styles as a way of teaching students to resist dominant, oppressive forms of language. Although these scholars drew from different sources and backgrounds, they all used studies in style as a gateway for students to become more sophisticated and proficient users of language.

Unfortunately, their work has not always been remembered in that way. In 1991, *The Politics of Writing Instruction: Postsecondary*, edited by Richard Bullock and John Trimbur, appeared. This collection features essays on the political implications of teaching writing in college and offers many examples of classrooms influenced by critical pedagogy. Yet, none of these essays says anything about the teaching of style, or even about the teaching of writing in general. That same year, Patricia Harkin and John Schilb published their collection titled *Contending with Words,* a series of essays that explores the role of composition studies in a postmodern world. As the introduction attests, this collection is "for college and university teachers of English who believe that the study of composition and rhetoric is not merely the service component of the English department, but also an inquiry into cultural values" (1991, 3). Again, nothing on style or on teaching the craft of writing appears in its pages. On the contrary, one of the essays, John Clifford's "The Subject in Discourse," regards the teaching of craft as antithetical to teaching critical pedagogy. Clifford argues that institutions of education, including writing classrooms, are subservient to dominant ideologies. He criticizes such composition textbooks as *St. Martin's Handbook* that make assumptions about apolitical subjectivity based on "romantic" notions of the individual writer. Clifford concludes; "We should do the intellectual work we know best: helping students to read and write and think in ways that both resist domination and exploitation and encourage self consciousness about who they are and can be in the social world" (1991, 51).

What strikes me about Clifford's argument is the dichotomy he establishes between teaching writing as a service and teaching writing as critical literacy. Clifford appears to suggest that teaching skills such as diction, sentence structure, and paragraph organization contradict the goals of teaching students that writing is a site "where hegemony and democracy are contested, where subject positions are constructed, where power and resistance are enacted, where hope for a just society depends on our committed intervention" (1991, 51). If we see style merely as a prescriptive set of colonizing rules—as Clifford argues such books as *St. Martin's Handbook* do—then, yes, it can be very destructive. But style is more than just a set of colonizing rules. Style can find a space within critical pedagogy.

Ten years later, Gary Tate, Amy Ruppier, and Kurt Schick edited a series of essays entitled *A Guide to Composition Pedagogies*, in which the only mention of style comes in William Covino's essay on "Rhetorical Pedagogy." Here, Covino refers to style only in his review of how Ramus placed it under "Rhetoric" as part of his method. These three collections of essays on writing pedagogy ignore completely the teaching of style as a viable element of writing pedagogy in the post-process era.

This dismissal suggests that the teaching of style has been ignored over the last twenty years, with many believing the work of the early process-movement compositionists to be "uncritical" or worse, elitist. But as a rereading of Christensen, Corbett, and Weathers will show, their work in style encourages students to become sophisticated language users and, in some instances, to resist dominant forms of discourse. In some ways, these collections had an unforeseen effect: while they were successful at articulating the political nature of writing instruction, they did so at the expense of lumping some early composition scholars into a collective heap that labeled their work as devoid of contextual concerns. In other words, those of us who came of age in composition and rhetoric graduate programs during the mid- to late 1990s, in the wake of "the social turn," often assumed that the work of scholars such as Christensen, Corbett, and Weathers was oversimplistic, too surface-oriented, and apolitical.

Francis Christensen's Generative Rhetoric

Francis Christensen was a composition and language scholar who was interested in discovering ways for students to write sentences and paragraphs in the manner of professional writers. His hope was that teachers could introduce the composing of sentences and paragraphs to their students in a fashion that would lead students to generate ideas at the same time that they learn new and varied writing strategies. Christensen called this idea "generative rhetoric," and he developed it in a pair of articles for CCC—"The Generative Rhetoric of the Sentence" (1963) and "The Generative Rhetoric of the Paragraph" (1965)—and later in a longer work, *Notes toward a New Rhetoric* (1967; I cite from the second edition of 1978). Christensen's method of using generative rhetoric to help students develop their style while inventing ideas in their writing at the same time enjoyed a brief period of popularity during the 1960s and 1970s.

"We need," he wrote, "a rhetoric of the sentence that will do more than combine the ideas of primer sentences. We need one that will generate ideas" (1978, 26). Rather than teach students how to develop sentences based on traditional classifications, such as loose, balanced, or periodic sentences, or on traditional grammatical structures—simple, compound, complex—Christensen's method asks students to examine the ideas expressed in the sentences and then rephrase the idea in a more effective way. In "The Generative Rhetoric of the Sentence," Christensen develops the idea of the "cumulative sentence," in which ideas are generated by student writers who add modifying words and phrases to their sentences, either before, after, or within the main clause of the sentence. The words or phrases that modify the base clause can have either a subordinate or coordinate relationship to the base clause. In other words, Christensen sees the sentence not as a simple list of words that convey ideas. The sentence, he says, "is dynamic rather than static, representing the mind thinking." He adds that "the mere form of the sentence generates ideas" (p. 28). For Christensen, therefore, instruction in sentence development is not a static exercise but is the very way writers construct meaning in their texts.

Christensen suggested that students practice studying multiple sentence types to recognize how meaning is developed by the addition of various clauses and clusters. Again, his assumption here is not for students to develop stylistic flourish and confidence in a decontextualized environment. Rather, he stressed that these exercises give students more options for their own compositions, as well as help them develop into stronger readers. In "The Generative Rhetoric of the Sentence," Christensen argues that his exercises go beyond decontextualized drill and provide students with the tools they need to develop confidence in their reading of texts and in their writing:

> What I am proposing carries over of itself into the study of literature. It makes the student a better reader of literature. It helps him thread the syntactical mazes of much mature writ-

ing, and it gives turn insight into that elusive thing we call style. Last year, a student told me of rereading a book by her favorite author, Willa Cather, and of realizing for the first time why she liked reading her: she could understand and appreciate the style. For some students, moreover, such writing makes life more interesting as well as giving them a way to share their interest with others. When they learn to put concrete details into a sentence, they begin to look at life with more alertness (1978, 37–38).

Here, Christensen makes the connection between instruction in style and instruction in larger, contextual factors that go into language learning. He insists that classroom focus on the stylistics of language allows students to make connections between their writing and their reading and, in the process, leads them to be able to make larger connections that go beyond the classroom.

Christensen's idea of coordinate and subordinate combine to create what he terms "cumulative sentences." In other words, students create new sentences and phrases at the same time they develop new ideas for composition. So, in a very concrete way, Christensen's rhetoric of the sentence is not merely a tool to develop style but is an invention technique as well. His rhetoric encourages student writers to examine their thoughts and the meanings that their words convey. Christensen's ideas provide students with a way to make their writing more textured, more rich, and less threadbare, They will create and make meaning as they write more complex sentences. Christensen points out the difference between teaching the cumulative sentence and teaching the periodic sentence, a type of sentence that combines a number of thoughts and statements in a number of balanced clauses. Christensen notes that the cumulative sentence is a more effective sentence for composition instruction because of its capacity to be used as a tool of invention:

> The cumulative sentence is the opposite of the periodic sentence. It does not represent the idea as conceived, pondered over, reshaped, packaged, and delivered cold. It is dynamic rather than static, representing the mind thinking. ... The additions stay with the same idea, probing its bearings and implications, exemplifying it or seeking an analogy or metaphor for it. ... Thus the mere form of the sentence generates ideas. It serves the needs of both writer and reader, the writer by compelling him to examine his thought, the reader by letting him into the writer's thought (28).

As students work and grapple with the base clause by adding modifiers and other clauses to it, they generate ideas. These ideas expand on the basic idea conveyed in the main clause and, in the process, lead students to develop and engage additional ideas. Christensen's rhetoric of the sentence, in many ways, hearkens back to Quintilian's call for *facilitas* with language, because the generative nature of cumulative sentences allow student writers to work with and play around with language in a manner that provides students with numerous options and choices. This generative quality is ethical and political, not merely formal and apolitical.

Here's a student example where additional description, via subordinate clauses, adds to the generative quality of the writing in a way that provides additional options for composing:

the hospital was set for night running,
smooth and silent, (A + A)
its normal clatter and hum muffled, (Abs)
the only sounds heard in the white walled room distant and unreal: (Abs)
a low hum of voices from the nurses' desk, (NC)
quickly stifled, (VC)
the soft squish of rubber-soled shoes on the tiled corridor, (NC)
starched white cloth rustling against itself, (NC)

and, outside, the lonesome whine of wind in the country night (NC) and the Kansas dust beating
against the windows. (NC). (34)

Here, the student sets the scene for the reader: a hospital at night. One by one, the writer adds
additional clauses that not only add description of the setting, but also add possibilities for new
ideas and circumstances: the "low hum of voices" introducing characters, the "lonesome whine"
suggesting a certain mood and atmosphere, "the Kansas dust" bringing in geographical possibilities.
In other words, the student has a long sentence in which a series of events and circumstances can
be further invented and developed in a manner that leads the student to more mature compositions and to a more mature style.

Christensen's generative method has not been completely forgotten. It is featured prominently
in two popular handbooks for first-time teachers of composition: *The St. Martin's Guide to Teaching Writing*, edited by Robert Connors and Cheryl Glenn (1995), and Erika Lindemann's *A Rhetoric
for Writing Teachers* (1995). Both texts feature chapters that introduce composition instructors to
teaching style, sentences, and paragraphs. But, while Christensen's rhetoric has found a space in
these popular handbooks, it seems to me that his placement in these texts merely reinforces the
popular critiques of his work—that his theories about rhetoric succeed for the more mundane,
uncritical work of actually teaching writing and have nothing to do with the social context surrounding students' writing experiences. For example, *The St. Martin's Guide* relegates Christensen
to the back of its text in a chapter titled "Teaching the Sentence and the Paragraph." This chapter
comes after lengthy chapters on invention and arrangement. Their placement of Christensen's
rhetoric suggests that his rhetoric of the sentence and paragraph should be reserved for matters
of composition outside of invention and arrangement, or other elements where ideas may be
discovered. Rather, assumptions at play in *The St. Martin's Guide* hold that Christensen's method is
a prescriptive one that teaches students rigid form without exploring the tension between form
and content. In *The St. Martin's Guide,* the editors write that Christensen's generative rhetoric reinforces a mechanistic, surface-driven pedagogy:

> Should you become uncomfortable with the prescriptive nature of any of the approaches
> in this chapter, you are not alone. We all may worry that in condensing writing to discrete,
> mechanical formulas, we are taking away from more than we are giving. But be assured that
> with continued reading and practice in writing, your students should eventually transcend
> rigid, formal rules. In the final analysis, a grasp of the rules seldom holds anyone down and,
> when understood correctly, can help keep one up (Connors and Glenn 1995, 262).

On the one hand, Connors and Glenn recognize that sentence rhetorics like Christensen's are
useful in teaching a student to write. On the other hand, they assume that Christensen's methods
reinforce "rigid, formal rules," and are "discrete, mechanical formulas" that are to be learned and
then quickly advanced upon. Christensen's call for a generative rhetoric of the sentence and the
paragraph gets at the very heart of the tension between form and content and, in the process,
provides students with tools to develop syntactic maturity while, at the same time, they develop
ideas to write about.

Edward P. J. Corbett and Classical Style

Corbett was among a coterie of scholars who rediscovered and made available to writing teachers classical rhetorical texts during the 1960s and 1970s. His first article for CCC was titled "The
Usefulness of Classical Rhetoric" (1963). In his preface to *Classical Rhetoric for the Modern Student,*
Corbett connects his interest in classical rhetoric to the preparation of students for civic participation. It is acknowledged that a knowledge of rhetoric helps citizens defend against demagogues and

other "exploiters of specious arguments, half-truths, and rank emotional appeals to gain personal advantage rather than to promote the public welfare" (1990, 30).

Style, of course, played a significant role in Corbett's recovery of classical rhetoric. For Corbett, style was not simply a matter of writing pretty language for the sake of artifice but was interwoven with discovering ideas and creating textual choices. In his textbook on rhetoric, Corbett connects style to Aristotle's definition of rhetoric:[1] "Style does provide a vehicle for thought, and style can be ornamental; but style is something more than that. It is another one of the 'available means of persuasion,' another of the means of arousing appropriate emotional responses in the audience, and of the means of establishing the proper ethical image" (1990, 381).

He dismissed the notion that style is merely "dressed up thought," and tried to remind the field that classical rhetoricians also rejected the idea that style is mere ornament, noting that "none of the prominent classical rhetoricians—Isocrates, Aristotle, Demetrius, Longinus, Cicero, Quintilian—ever preached such a doctrine" (1990, 381). But again, many in the field did not perceive these classical rhetoricians in this way—due in large part to the types of histories that were being written, as well as composition's desire to define itself differently from its classical predecessors.[2] Corbett understood that how something is written directly affects what is being conveyed in the writing. "A writer must be in command of a variety of styles," Corbett asserted, "in order to draw on the style that is most appropriate to the situation" (1990, 381). He stressed that the modern student could become a better writer by focusing primarily on invention.

In "The Usefulness of Classical Rhetoric" Corbett reminds readers that imitation is not merely slavish copying of someone else's style but rather the study and adaptation of multiple styles that assist students in gathering the "available means."

> Many of our students need exercise in constructing their own sentence patterns. They can be assisted in acquiring this skill by such exercises as merely copying passages of sophisticated prose, constructing their own sentences according to models, varying sentence patterns. The term imitation suggests to some people the attempt to encourage students to acquire someone else's style. Such a view betrays a total misunderstanding of what the rhetoricians meant by imitation and what they hoped to accomplish by it. (1963, 163).

In *Classical Rhetoric for the Modern Student,* Corbett put together a series of imitation exercises to help students develop an eloquent style. The point here is for students to draw from a whole host of prose styles and not focus solely on one style. Here, Corbett echoes the suggestion of Erasmus nearly five hundred years earlier, who implored students at St. Paul's not to imitate Cicero only but to draw from other writers as well. Corbett provides examples from a wide range of authors and prose styles, including the Bible, John Dryden, Edward Gibbon, Mary Wollstonecraft, Abraham Lincoln, James Baldwin, Susan Sontag, Alice Walker, and Toni Morrison, to name only a few. Corbett stresses that students who imitate writers do so with a pen or pencil, copying and imitating the authors slowly, paying attention to the sentence structure and placement of words. He encourages students to focus on a single passage each day, rather than try to cram many different passages into a single day's work. "You must have time to absorb what you have been observing in this exercise," Corbett advises, "and you will not have time to absorb the many lessons to be learned from this exercise if you cram it into a short period" (1990, 476).

After students copy passages, Corbett suggests they move toward imitation proper. He recommends that students begin with simple sentences and work up to more complex sentences and eventually to imitation of entire passages. Corbett wants students to use these imitation exercises to introduce novice writers to the complexity and variety of professional prose styles. "The aim of this exercise," Corbett cautions, "is not to achieve a word-for-word correspondence with the model but rather to achieve an awareness of the variety of sentence structures of which the English language is capable ... writing such patterns according to models will increase [students'] syntactical resources" (Corbett 1990, 495). Again, Corbett supplies a variety of sample sentences for students to imitate. Corbett also draws from Erasmus's method of expressing an idea in multiple ways. "Devising an alternate expression," Corbett notes, "often involves the choice of different words and different syntactical structures" (498). Here, he models several sentences, showing variations of the sentence patterns as well as an alternate way to express the idea in a different style. Again, the purpose here, much like in copying other authors' prose, is to be introduced to a variety of styles and to practice imitating and studying the sentence structure of various writers.

Corbett's work on style is viewed as part of composition's past that should we should acknowledge but move on from. Many compositionists today regard Corbett's work as part of the pre-professionalization era of composition studies, work that is not as exciting, as innovative, or as complex as the post-process era. I find it interesting, as Connors notes in his introduction to *Style and Statement* (Corbett and Connors 1999), that the individuals who find Corbett's work on style the most relevant are high school and college composition instructors, individuals who struggle every day with teaching students the actual craft of writing. I find this confession interesting because it suggests that the professionalization of rhetoric and composition has led scholars in the field away from the business of teaching writing. Indeed, many of us who came to the field in the mid- to late 1990s assumed Corbett's work on style was part of a distant past that did not speak to the more "complex" issues of composition: post-modern identity, the negotiation of difference, and discourse communities, to name only a few. For example, during my first graduate seminar on the teaching of writing, our instructor introduced us to Corbett's method of analyzing prose style. This method asks students to count the number of sentences in an essay and identify their type—simple, complex, and so on—and count the number of words in each sentence. The rationale behind such an exercise is to determine the readability of a piece of writing and to determine areas for possible revision and editing. As we sat in the seminar listening to the instructor and applying this method to our own writing sample, I noticed most of us—budding composition and rhetoric scholars—resisting this exercise by rolling our eyes, grumbling under our breaths—in general, not taking it very seriously. Later, during our break, one of my class colleagues complained bitterly in the hallway that the exercise was a total waste of time, that it was too hard. At the time, I tended to agree. How does counting sentences help students write? What we failed to understand then, and what many of us still fail to recognize, is that Corbett's pedagogy of style is not some series of surface-oriented exercises, but rather lies at the very heart of what rhetorical education attempts to provide: the ability in individuals to write eloquently and responsibly within numerous contexts, whether they be personal, academic, or public.

Corbett's work on style, and his insistence that style should be taught within the realm of the whole rhetorical canon, came out of his reading and recovery of classical rhetorical texts—namely, Aristotle, Cicero, and Quintilian. His ideas about style have a decidedly Western canonical bent to them and, as a result, Corbett's stylistic exercises do not cross the line into what we might think of as radical or alternative styles. But there is another scholar whose work attempts to break through traditional stylistic boundaries who has gone largely unrecognized for the past ten to fifteen years—Winston Weathers.

Winston Weathers: An Alternative

Weathers, a writing teacher and scholar from the 1960s and 1970s, overtly sought alternative styles and radical approaches to teaching writing. He published such titles as *A New Strategy of Style* (1978, with Otis Winchester) and *Alternative Style: Options in Composition* (1980). Weathers was interested in exploring a pedagogy of style that would lead students to resist dominant modes of discourse and write alternative prose styles. For Weathers, the teaching of style was itself a revolutionary act, which could lead to critical thinking against dominant forms of communication. One way that Weathers urged writing teachers and students to resist these dominant discourses was through the development of different styles, noting that "we can point out that with the acquisition of a plurality of styles (and we are after pluralities, aren't we? not just the plain style?) the student is equipping himself for a more adaptive way of life within a society increasingly complex and multi-faceted" (2000, 295).

He encouraged writing teachers to use style as a tool to break through rigid systems and to teach writing that was more socially responsible, writing that took into consideration multiple styles and not just the socially sanctioned conventional style prevalent in most American writing classrooms. Alternative styles, for Weathers, was a place where most writers— professional and nonprofessional alike—wrote. In a 1996 interview with Wendy Bishop, Weathers reflects on the inspiration for his 1980 book, *An Alternative Style: Options in Composition.*

> I'd long noticed that much of the great literature I was teaching was not written in the tradi-tional straight/linear mode. I'd noticed too, that out in the "real world," a great many of the messages presented in advertising, publicity, promotion, in personal letters, journals, diaries, and even in more daring book reviews, testimonials, meditations, etc. were using writing techniques that no one in the nation's English departments seemed to be teaching. The Acad-emy occasionally acknowledged the existence of "experimental writing" but never suggested that ordinary writers might also practice something like it. My goal in writing *An Alternative Style* was simply to say to students (and their teachers) that there's more to writing than the style usually found in the Freshman theme, the second semester research report, or the graduate literary essay. (Bishop and Weathers 1996, 76)

Style, for Weathers, is by no means some rigid, cold, mechanistic tool used to teach inflexible conventions of writing. For Weathers, style becomes a place where all people use language in fresh, inventive ways, ways that can be recast and used in socially responsible and democratic contexts. The rigid systems that Weathers recognized in most English departments needed to be challenged. One of those systems, of course, was the tradition of style as a surface-oriented tool of writing instruction that had been reinforced in the history of writing instruction since the Renaissance.

In an article originally published in CCC in 1970, "Teaching Style: A Possible Anatomy," Weath-ers argued that for the teaching of style to be a viable element of writing pedagogy, instructors must accomplish three tasks:

(1) make the teaching of style significant and relevant to our students,
(2) reveal style as a measurable and viable subject matter, and
(3) make style believable and real as a result of our own stylistic practices (2000, 294).

Weathers's call for a richer pedagogy of style is significant because he assumes an integration of style in all forms of writing instruction and not just a technique for editing or polishing students' prose. For example, he writes that students need a strategy of style so that they can accomplish two objectives in literacy acquisition, by "(1) identifying the categories of style, and (2) describing the constituency of those categories in terms of stylistic material" (2000, 297). In other words, Weathers wants teachers to incorporate the study of style into the larger purpose of writing instruction in a way that allows the student to develop a variety of prose styles to use in mul-tiple rhetorical situations. Weathers follows much of the same ideas about imitation that Corbett learned from the classical rhetoricians and that Erasmus encouraged students in the sixteenth century to practice. "We ask the student to write a sentence or a topic of his own choosing, but following the model he has just studied," Weathers writes. "In this process, the student is asked to recognize, copy, understand, and imitate creatively" (2000, 296–97). For Weathers, style becomes the very way students use language to make meaning in their worlds. The more styles students experiment with, Weathers argues, the more able they are to resist dominant structures of lan-guage and use language more democratically.

One of the more telling moments in this article occurs when Weathers associates alternative styles with democracy. Here, Weathers articulates the role that the teaching of style can play in a liberating pedagogy that teaches students to become responsible users of language:

> Style is a gesture of personal freedom against inflexible states of mind; that in a very real way—because it is the art of choice and option—style has something to do with freedom; that as systems—rhetorical or political—become rigid and dictatorial, style is reduced, unable to exist in totalitarian environments. We can reveal to students the connection between democracy and style, saying that the study of style is a part of our democratic and free experience. And finally we can point out that with the acquisition of a plurality of styles (and we are after pluralities, aren't we? not just the plain style?) the student is equipping himself for a more adaptive way of life within a society increasingly complex and multifaceted (2000, 295).

Even though Weathers is counseling writing teachers to resist rigid systems of writing instruction and encourage their students to write in a variety of styles, his caution against the totalitarianism of systems applies to the way histories are embraced and eventually become unyielding systems in their own right. Questioning the received history of style allows current composition scholars t break through a system of instruction that consigns style to a rigid, surface-only concern. Weathers wants the teaching of style to be much more. He argues that teachers of writing can show the connections between style and democracy to their students, encouraging them to practice and study multiple verbalizations. Weathers pushes students to play with multiple styles in a manner that could suggest stretching the boundaries of traditional stylistic grounds. In other words, it may lead them on a path toward recognizing how multiple styles are representative of multiple points of view—indeed, the very essence of democracy.

Weathers wants students to recognize and be able to incorporate a plurality of styles. Such plurality, Weathers insists, is necessary for educating students to become vital participants in a democracy. "We can reveal to students the connection between democracy and style," he writes, "saying that the study of style is part of our democratic and free experience" (2000, 295). Weathers wrote this call for an integrated pedagogy of style during a time when American society was being reminded of its own plurality in the form of the protest against the war in Vietnam, the civil rights movement, and the second-wave feminist movement. Such movements, of course, were particularly popular on college campuses. There, students were searching for ways to connect what they were learning in the classroom with their concerns for social justice. Weathers's call to make style, and writing itself, more relevant in students' lives shows how his work on style was not some exercise in getting students to prettify their language but rather to discover the richness of language and its uses in a democracy. "Many students write poorly and with deplorable styles simply because they do not care," Weathers insists (2000, 295). Weathers simply wanted to make writing more relevant to student experience.

In 1980, Weathers published *An Alternative Style: Options in Composition*. The purpose of this textbook, as Weathers notes in the preface, is to provide student writers with ways to develop a varied prose style. "And so this book," he writes, "Ready to be shared—as we become aware of more mentalities than one (left brain/right brain if nothing else), aware of more compositional goals than one, more life-styles than one, more human chemistries than one, more 'voices' than one" (2000, preface). Weathers wants student writers to be able to move in and out of different writing situations and adjust their writing styles accordingly, without being beholden to any one, dominant mode of writing. "I write for many reasons," he notes, "to communicate many things. And yet, much of what I wish to communicate does not seem to be expressible within the ordinary conventions of composition as I have learned them and mastered them in the long years of my education" (1). In an e-mail conversation with Wendy Bishop, almost twenty years after he published

An Alternative Style, Weathers echoes his desire for teaching student writers multiple styles. "A good writer—like a good architect—should know how to design and build all kinds of structures: traditional, art deco, baroque, functional, etc.," he declares. "Who knows what 'content' requirements will be presented to us day after day? A concern with style is a concern with being prepared to build the best composition we can whatever the content happens to be" (Bishop and Weathers 1996, p.75). And encouraging students to build the best compositions they can forms the focus of Weathers's interest in style.

In *Alternative Style,* Weathers offers a short explanation of his theory of alternative style and a variety of rhetorical devices and strategies that professional writers use to develop new and interesting styles. For Weathers, an alternate style means any type of style that seeks to go beyond tradition-bound notions of "good writing" in the effort to construct the best piece of writing possible. He distinguishes between what he calls Grammar A and Grammar B. Grammar A, according to Weathers, is the "traditional" grammar or instruction in style in most writing classrooms, which "has the characteristics of continuity, order, reasonable progression and sequence, consistency, unity, etc. We are all familiar with these characteristics, for they are promoted in nearly every English textbook and taught by nearly every English teacher" (1980, 6). Grammar B, on the other hand, seeks to expand Grammar A's rigidity and open students to alternative ways to express themselves. "It is a mature and alternate (not experimental) style used by competent writers and offering students of writing a well-tested set of options that, added to the traditional grammar of style, will give them a much more flexible voice, a much greater communication capacity, a much greater opportunity to put into effective language all the things they have to say" (Weathers 1980, 8). Later, Weathers describes a number of characteristics of Grammar B and does so in a manner that allows users of the book to apply them to their own writing—some tricks of the trade, as it were.[3]

What's important to keep in mind about Weathers's theory of Grammar A and Grammar B is that they are not mutually exclusive. Grammar B, for Weathers, is an expansion of Grammar A. He does not want to keep his students away from learning and understanding the dimensions of Grammar A. Not at all. He wants them to be able to break away from the conventions of Grammar A and become more imaginative and creative with their style, based on what the rhetorical constraints are. "Grammar B in no way threatens Grammar A," he insists, "It uses the same stylistic deck of fifty-two cards and embraces the same English language we are familiar with. Acknowledging its existence and discovering how it works and including it in our writing expertise, we simply become better teachers of writing, making a better contribution to the intellectual and emotional lives of our students" (1980, 8). Here, Weathers echoes Aristotle's definition of rhetoric as being the ability to discover the available means of persuasion. Grammar B becomes another of the available means. Playing around with and using crots, for example, allow student writers to find connections among ideas where they may not have looked before. His double-voice technique encourages students to examine ideas from various perspectives, while working on the stylistic features of their writing. Weathers's desire for student writers to develop multiple, even subversive, writing strategies also echoes Erasmus's call for teaching students to express ideas in a variety of ways. Students who incorporate Weathers's suggestions for labyrinthine sentences and sentence fragments, alongside the more traditional sentences of Grammar A, give themselves more options for phrasing ideas in new and interesting ways.

Weathers has largely been forgotten among many rhetoric and composition specialists. Although his essay "Teaching Style: A Possible Anatomy" appears in the latest edition of the perennially popular *The Writing Teacher's Sourcebook* (Corbett, Tate, and Myers 2000), most compositionists have ignored his work. Wendy Bishop notes that his "work didn't seem to be half as influential as I thought it should be" (Weathers and Bishop 1996, 72). His work is rarely, if ever, cited in the pages of CCC or *College English* anymore, and his textbooks are out of print. Graduate programs in composition and rhetoric rarely include Weathers's work as part of the curriculum or reading lists. It almost appears as if Weathers's work has disappeared completely.

Weathers himself tells stories of how the field resisted vehemently his theories and ideas about the teaching of style (see the epigraph to this chapter). Weathers also tells the story of how he was received by his colleagues during his keynote address at the 1982 CCCC convention in San Francisco, a city Bishop, in a delicious moment of irony, calls "the city of alternative styles" (Weathers and Bishop 1996, 79):

> It was, in effect, boycotted. I was invited to give the address by Donald Stewart. ... He had read some of my work, had written about it in an article, which led to some correspondence, which led to the invitation. He was the CCCC program chairman at the time, as I remember. Alas, though the conference attendance was large, I gave the address to about fifty people— in a vast, cavernous Hyatt Regency ballroom that would have held a thousand. It was obvious that the title of the address, or my reputation perhaps, had led vast numbers of people to stay away. (79)

That was twenty years ago, and it seems safe to say that Weathers's reputation has not changed much. My sense is that Weathers has been lumped into a group of compositionists—including Christensen and Corbett—whose work on style and rhetoric runs counter to the goals of critical and creative thinking espoused by the proponents of critical pedagogy.

As the 1970s turned into the 1980s, and social construction theories of composition slowly took precedence in composition programs and on the pages of composition journals, the stylistic and sentence-level pedagogies of Christensen, Corbett, and Weathers came under fire. Robert Connors argues that many of their critics pointed out that sentence-level rhetorics like Christensen's "were quintessentially exercises, context-stripped from what students really wanted to say themselves" (Connors 2000, 115). James Britton, for example, called such writing exercises "dummy runs," and condemned such writing instruction for its lack of contextual awareness, arguing that a student writer should be "called upon to perform a writing task in order (a) to exercise his capacity to perform that kind of task, and/or (b) to demonstrate to the teacher his proficiency in performing [the writing assignment]" (Britton et al., 1975, 104–5). Sabina Thorne Johnson, a contemporary of Christensen, voiced her critique by questioning Christensen's claim that students can generate ideas by merely adding modifiers to their sentences. In her article "Some Tentative Strictures on Generative Rhetoric," Johnson at first praises Christensen's method for offering a "revolution in our assessment of style and in our approach to the teaching of composition" (1969, 159). But later she wonders why Christensen seems to believe that form can generate content. "I don't believe it can, especially if the content is of an analytic or critical nature" (159), Later A. B. Tibbets chimed in on the complaint against Christensen, noting that the generative rhetoric method led students to produce clever sentences but not much else. Tibbets argues: "What we are generally after in expository writing is accuracy rather than cleverness" (1976, 144). Tibbets assumes here that interesting sentences can't produce interesting ideas. And he says as much later in his article when he notes that effective writing instruction leads students to separate content from form, as well as divide issues from one another (144). Tibbets's assumptions about the split between form and content resonate with the other critiques of Christensen's rhetoric. What most of these critiques assume, however, is that learning to write eloquent and interesting sentences and paragraphs is somehow antithetical to learning to express ideas effectively.

Conclusion

During the early process years of the late 1960s and 1970s, the teaching of style, via Christensen's generative rhetoric, Corbett's recovery of classical rhetoric, and the alternative style of Weathers, shared, along with the process movement, prominence across the composition landscape, As c mpositionists started to investigate more deeply the various social and political contexts that affect how students learn to write, the focus on stylistics became associated with oversimplistic, decontextualized writing pedagogy. The work of such figures as Christensen, Corbett, and Weathers subsequently became associated with this type of "uncritical" pedagogy. But reassessment of these scholars reveals that their work on style and the sentence was done under the assumption that the more stylistic options were available to students, the more likely that students would be able to demonstrate successful rhetorical activity.

Notes

1 Aristotle defines rhetoric as "an ability, in each particular case, to see the available means of persuasion" (1991, 36).
2 Two received histories of early modern rhetoric, Kennedy (1980) and Howell (1956), both dismiss style as a surface-oriented element of rhetoric that has little to do with the invention of ideas. Both texts are often cited as standard histories of the field. In their anthology *The Rhetorical Tradition,* Bizzell and Herzberg (1990) call Kennedy's history "the standard general historical source" and *The Bedford Bibliography for Teachers of Writing* call Howell's history "the standard history of this important period in the history of rhetoric" (2004, 40).
3 Some of these strategies include experimenting wildly with various types of sentences: short, one-word sentences he called crots and longer, complex sentences he called labyrinthine. Weathers also recommended writing in what he termed "double voice," a technique that allows writers to explore two sides of an argument and present the material on opposing sides of a composition. This practice reminds me of Ann Berthoff's "Double Entry Notebook" in her book *Forming, Thinking, Writing* (1982).

References

Aristotle. 1991. *On Rhetoric: A Theory of Civil Discourse.* Translated by George A. Kennedy. New York: Oxford University Press.

Berthoff, Ann E. 1982. *Forming, Thinking, Writing.* Portsmouth, NH: Boynton/Cook.

Bizzell, Patricia, and Bruce Herzberg, eds. 1990. *The Rhetorical Tradition: Readings from Classical Times to the Present.* Boston: Bedford/St. Martin's Press.

Britton, James, Tony Burgess, Nancy Martin, Alex McLeod, and Harold Rosen. 1975. *The Development of Writing Abilities (11–18).* London: MacMillan Educational for the Schools Council.

Bullock, Richard, and John Trimbur. 1991. *The Politics of Writing Instruction: Postsecondary.* Portsmouth, NH: Heinemann/Boynton Cook.

Christensen, Francis. 1963. A Generative Rhetoric of the Sentence. *CCC* 14:155–61.

———. 1965. The Generative Rhetoric of the Paragraph. *CCC* 16:144–56.

———. 1978. The Generative Rhetoric of the Sentence. In *Notes toward a New Rhetoric.* 2nd ed. New York: Harper and Row.

Clifford, John. 1991. The Subject in Discourse. In Harkin and Schilb 1991.

Connors, Robert. 2000. The Erasure of the Sentence. *CCC* 52:96–128.

Connors, Robert, and Cheryl Glenn, eds. 1995. *The St. Martin's Guide to Teaching Writing.* New York: St. Martin's Press.

Corbett, Edward P.J. 1963. The Usefulness of Classical Rhetoric. *CCC* 14.3:162–64.

———. 1990. *Classical Rhetoric for the Modern Student.* 3rd ed. New York: Oxford University Press.

Corbett, Edward P.J., and Robert J. Connors. 1999. *Style and Statement.* New York: Oxford University Press.

Corbett, Edward P.J., Gary Tate, and Nancy Myers, eds. 2000. *The Writing Teacher's Sourcebook.* New York: Oxford University Press.

Covino, William. 2001. Rhetorical Pedagogy. In Tate, Ruppier, and Schick 2001.

Ede, Lisa S. 1999. Reading—and Rereading—the Braddock Essays. In *On Writing Research: The Braddock Essays 1975–1998,* ed. Lisa Ede. Boston: Bedford/St. Martin's Press.

Elbow, Peter. 1973. *Writing without Teachers.* New York: Oxford University Press.

——. 1981. *Writing with Power*. New York: Oxford University Press.

——. 2002. The Cultures of Literature and Composition: What Could Each Learn from the Other? *College English* 64:533–46.

Gerber, John C. 1950. The Conference on College Composition and Communication. *CCC* 1:12.

Harkin, Patricia, and John Schilb, eds. 1991. *Contending with Words: Composition and Rhetoric in a Postmodern Age*. New York: MLA.

Howell, Wilbur S. 1956. *Logic and Rhetoric in England: 1500–1700*. Princeton: Princeton University Press.

Johnson, Sabina Thorne. 1969. Some Tentative Strictures on Generative Rhetoric. *College English* 31:155–65.

Kennedy, George A. 1980. *Classical Rhetoric and Its Christian and Secular Tradition: From Ancient to Modern Times*. Chapel Hill: University of North Carolina Press.

Lindemann, Erika. 1995. *A Rhetoric for Writing Teachers*. 3rd ed. New York: Oxford University Press.

Macrorie, Ken. 1970. *Telling Writing*. Rochelle Park, NJ: Hayden.

Reynolds, Nora, Bruce Herzberg, and Patricia Bizzell. 2004. *The Bedford Bibliography for Teachers of Writing*. Boston: Bedford/St. Martin's Press.

Tate, Gary, Amy Ruppier, and Kurt Schick, eds. 2001. *A Guide to Composition Pedagogies*. New York: Oxford University Press.

Tibbets, A.B. 1976. On the Practical Uses of a Grammatical System: A Note on Christensen and Johnson. In *Rhetoric and Composition: A Sourcebook for Teachers*, edited by E. Richard Graves. Rochelle Park, NJ: Hayden.

Weathers, Winston. 1980. *An Alternative Style: Options in Composition*. Rochelle Park, NJ: Hayden.

——. 2000. Teaching Style: A Possible Anatomy. In Corbett, Tate, and Myers 2000.

Weathers, Winston, and Wendy Bishop. 1996. Talking to Winston Weathers on E-Mail—An Interview. *Composition Studies* 24.1–2:72–87.

Weathers, Winston, and Otis Winchester. 1978. *The New Strategy of Style*. 2nd ed. New York: McGraw-Hill.

8

Teaching Grammar in the Context of Writing

James D. Williams

- Why has grammar been such a significant part of writing instruction?
- Does instruction in grammar improve student writing?
- How can grammar best be incorporated into a writing class?

This chapter examines some of the issues surrounding grammar and writing and summarizes what has been learned from the available research. It also suggests several best-practice strategies for effectively incorporating grammar into a writing class.

Writing is difficult. There are many reasons why it is difficult, but one of the more important is that it requires us to do something that doesn't come naturally—attend to linguistic form as we strive to convey meaningful content. The challenge this task presents is perhaps more understandable if we consider spontaneous speech. When we are having a conversation with a friend or colleague, our goal is to communicate a message. Few of us think about the structure of the language we produce or the turn taking it requires—we just talk. For their part, our friends and colleagues don't pay much attention to the structure of our speech because they are likewise focused on the message.

The process appears to work well. We typically finish a conversation feeling, more often than not, that the communication was successful. What's interesting, however, is that a transcript of any conversation suggests that the participants' sense of success may not be based solely—or even significantly—on the language itself but rather on mutually constructed notions (which may be inaccurate) of the conveyed message and on fairly complex and usually unconscious negotiations concerning the psychosocial relationships of the participants. The reason is that the underlying dynamic of our language is social, not the communication of information per se (see Dunbar, 1997).

Transcripts are illustrative in other respects. For example, to those who don't know the context of the conversation, they are often incomprehensible. The participants exchange little explicit information, usually only one or two points that are repeated several times, if the conversation is long enough. In addition, the participants frequently interrupt each other, and the topic may jump without transition to a reference point established in the past that has no explicit connection with the present. Fillers—such as *um, ah, I mean, you know,* and *ok*—regularly interrupt the flow of words. Among younger speakers, the word *like* is ubiquitous, generally conveying no meaning and often used with a form of *go* to replace the word *said*.[1]

Although most of the utterances in a conversation are well formed from a linguistic perspective, we nevertheless find consistent patterns of error, but only a few of the errors are grammatical, in part because spontaneous speech contains few constructions that can be accurately classified as sentences (see Biber, 1988; Du Bois, Schuetze-Coburn, Paolino, & Cummings, 1993). As Du Bois (2003) noted, spontaneous speech consists primarily of "intonation units" such as phrases, but what we generally think of as complete sentences do not occur regularly. Chafe (1998) found that subjects are commonly introduced as an intonation referent and that the predicate appears as a separate unit, often with a pronominal serving to link the verb to the referent. Thompson and Hopper (2001) reported that the transivity found in writing is rare in spontaneous speech.

The challenge of attending to form is easily demonstrated: during a conversation, or even during a class lecture, try to recall verbatim the last sentence someone uttered. Unless a person is concentrating on recalling the structure, this task is quite difficult. When a person is thus concentrating, he or she usually cannot recall the message. Stated simply, we are not very good at multitasking with regard to language. We can attend to message fairly easily; we can attend to form with some difficulty; but attending to both simultaneously is a challenge.

The point here is that while engaged in a conversation we tend to ignore matters of form and structure. Why is it, then, that these matters become so apparent as soon as we read a transcript? The explanation is that texts are static and visual, whereas speech is transitory and aural. The static nature of a transcript allows us to slow down our processing speed and to reread passages; in addition, its visual nature demands that we attend to orthography.

For Writing and Discussion

One of the problems we see in student writing is the tendency to import conversational features into the text. Here are two effective ways to help students begin reducing the gap between their spoken and written English. First, ask them to compose individually a text orally onto a recording device. When they are finished, have them transcribe the oral composition. Hold a workshop in which they then work in teams to identify and revise conversational features. Second, have students read two or three paragraphs of academic writing. Setting the paragraphs aside, they should write a paraphrase of what they read. Hold a workshop in which, with your help, they compare vocabulary and sentence structure of their summaries and the original.

This analysis helps us understand why writing is hard—and not just for student writers but for all writers. Among students, efforts to attend to form are hampered by lack of familiarity with the genre-driven structural patterns that characterize academic texts. Hence writing tends to be error-prone along a limited number of parameters. A writer may read his or her text with a determination to focus on correcting errors of form—and not succeed completely.

Even so, many teachers approach papers like copyeditors. They operate, often unconsciously, on the principle that most students in our public schools and undergraduate programs lack sufficient knowledge to provide much in the way of content, even when the assignment calls for a personal-experience narrative. They also understand that evaluating content for anything other than an essay exam is highly problematic, especially if students are writing about different topics, which leads to assessment with dubious validity (see J. Williams, 2003). As a result, they tend to focus by default on the form of student writing, concentrating on such elements as sentence structure, paragraph development, and punctuation. Because when talking to their students teachers seldom attend to errors in speech, many reach the unfortunate and incorrect conclusion that the errors in students' papers must be the result of laziness, for the students' spoken language seems just fine, annoying fillers and slang notwithstanding.

WHAT IS GRAMMAR?

Even though grammar is a central concern in writing classes, few teachers receive much training in the subject. Moreover, our understanding of what constitutes grammar is clouded by the fact that there are various definitions of grammar and various types of grammar. Some people define grammar as the words we use for labeling language, such a *noun*, *verb*, and *preposition*—the "eight parts of speech." Others define it as how we use words in sentences, such as *subject* and *object*. However, linguists—those who make a scientific study of language—define grammar as *syntax,* or *the order of words* in the natural sentences we construct. A basic word order in English, for example, is noun subject (N) plus verb (V) plus noun object (SVO), as in:

1. Rita kissed Fred.   *active*

I will use the linguistic definition of grammar throughout the chapter.

Few students encounter this definition, but not because grammar instruction is ignored in our schools. Indeed, whenever politicians take notice of writing skills in our schools, they blame poor writing on the failure to teach children grammar, and they nearly always propose a "back to basics" program that will force schools to teach even more grammar. When parents see the low test scores in language arts at their children's schools, they demand that more emphasis be placed on grammar. Ask students what they need to do to improve their writing, and more often than not the answer is "Work on my grammar."

But students *do* study grammar, and they study it for a long time. Instruction begins in 3rd grade and commonly doesn't end until completion of 10th or 11th grade. Most English textbooks for elementary, middle, and high school students focus on grammar. For example, *Houghton-Mifflin English* (2004), a popular text for middle school students, has little in it that isn't related to grammar in one way or another. Glencoe/Macgraw-Hill's *Glencoe Grammar and Composition Handbook* (2001) series spans elementary and secondary grades. The reality is that whenever students work on writing, grammar instruction tends to predominate. Nevertheless, as any university teacher of first-year composition will attest, students finish high school not only unable to do much more than recite the definitions of noun and verb but also unable to write an essay. The question is "Why?"

The answer to this question is not simple. We first need to understand that there are several different linguistic models of grammar. The major ones are summarized below. We also must examine what various studies have shown about the connection between grammar instruction and writing, as well as what linguists and psychologists have learned about language development.

TRADITIONAL GRAMMAR

When parents, students, and even most teachers think about grammar, they generally think about the eight parts of speech, the names that we assign to the different elements that make up language. This grammar—the grammar that most teachers know, the grammar of most handbooks, the grammar that gets taught in our schools—is known as "traditional" or "school" grammar. It is important to understand that when people talk about grammar and writing, they seldom, if ever, use the word "grammar" in the sense of its linguistic meaning. Instead, they are using the term to refer to punctuation, word choice, and similar issues that are actually unrelated to grammatical structure.

Traditional grammar and its place in education have ancient roots. Those roots extend all the way back to ancient Greece, where teachers known as *grammatici* taught grammar-school children how to read and write using literary models with the explicit aim of maintaining the purity of the language and instilling moral lessons. This pedagogy was adopted by the Romans and is at the core of how grammar is understood and taught in most of our schools.

Like the ancient Greeks, Romans differentiated literary Latin—used by the well-educated and influential members of society—from the Latin used by the common people. The aim of grammar instruction was to preserve the prestige dialect by giving students a set of tools—the parts of speech—that were believed to enable them to identify and then mimic the language of the elite. This goal was seldom realized, however, as illustrated by the accounts of wealthy Romans forced to adopt "the salty language of the poor" during political campaigns so as to appeal to common people (plebeians) and win their votes (J. Williams, 2009, p. 282).

After the Roman Empire collapsed in 476 A.D., Latin quickly became a dead language no longer spoken by any native speakers as it evolved into so-called "vulgar" tongues: French, Spanish, Portuguese, Romanian, and Italian. Among scholars, the need for a common language was great, and Latin, owing in part to the prestige of the Empire, served this need. From the Middle Ages through the early 19th century, it was the language of scholars, and the educated elite were expected to have reading proficiency.[2] But without any native speakers to model the language, mastering grammar and pronunciation was a problem. Scholars and educators therefore relied on two Latin grammar books: *Ars grammatica*, written by Donatus in the 4th century, and *Institutiones grammaticae*, written by Priscian in the 6th century. There were no grammar books for the vulgar tongues, but because these languages were derivatives of Latin, the Donatus and Priscian texts worked reasonably well to provide rules of correctness based on literary models. The same cannot be said, however, with regard to English, which is a Germanic language.

The notion of linguistic purity was embedded in the English grammatical treatises on how to write that began to appear in the late Middle Ages. Owing to the widely held perception that Latin was a perfect language, its grammar was embraced as the quintessential tool for analyzing English and for correcting the speech and writing of those who spoke a "vulgar" form, or nonprestige dialect, of the language. Constructions natural in English but ungrammatical in Latin were labeled violations of the grammar. The real differences between the dialects of the different social classes led to the conclusion among educators that the purity of English is preserved by the well educated, who speak and write a prestige dialect. People without a good education, on the other hand, corrupt the language by deviating from the norm prescribed by the grammar.

Although from a linguistic perspective changes in language are natural and ineluctable, the question of whether there is value in striving to maintain and disseminate a prestige dialect is open to debate and indeed has been a point of contention for decades. Nevertheless, our schools today, like those in the distant past, generally embrace the idea that grammar plays a major role in distinguishing between what people *do* with language and what they *ought to do* with it. Linguistic superiority, and thus social superiority, is associated with notions of correctness that are linked primarily to literary texts rather than to everyday speech.

Problems with Traditional Grammar

One of the more obvious problems associated with traditional grammar is the concept of "parts of speech." Although we may reference nouns, verbs, and so on in a general way, we cannot establish a fully consistent classification system because word classes resist a rigid scheme. *Run,* for example, can be a noun or a verb, depending on the structure of a sentence. Furthermore, an unavoidable result of using Latin-based traditional grammar to describe a non-Latin language like English is that much of what has been, and continues to be, taught to generations of students is just plain wrong. Consider the split infinitive:

2. I'm going to slowly open the door.

In this sentence, the infinitive verb form, *to open,* is "split" by the adverb *slowly.* Most English teachers in our nation's schools, as well as many handbooks, treat the split infinitive as a grammar error. From the perspective of Latin or one of the Latin-based languages, such as Spanish, this makes sense because the infinitive form in these languages is one word rather than two. In Spanish, for example, the infinitive form of *to open* is *abrir*—one word. It is impossible to split *abrir* in any way. We simply cannot have **Voy a ab-despacio-rir la puerta*[3] ("I'm going to slowly open the door"); we can only have something like *Voy a abrir la puerta despacio.*

A large majority—if not all—American students are taught that they cannot end a sentence with a preposition, and they sometimes are provided examples like the following that illustrate the ungrammaticality that results from such a construction:

3. *Juanita looked the number of the local pizza parlor that served her favorite beer up.

The problem here is twofold: first, the injunction itself has no basis in English grammar, and second, the word *up* in this and other such examples is not a preposition but a *particle.* English grammar allows particles, which are verbal elements, to move from their verbs to the noun object that immediately follows, but it does not allow movement elsewhere. Consequently, the sample sentence above is indeed ungrammatical, but not because it ends with a preposition.

English grammar actually allows prepositions at the end of certain sentence types:

4. Fritz bought the house in which the rock star had lived.
5. Fritz bought the house which the rock star had lived in.

Both sentences are grammatically correct. We can see why if we analyze them closely and recognize that they consist of two clauses, one of which has been relativized. They began, in other words, as two independent clauses:

6. Fritz bought the house. The rock star lived in the house.

The clauses were joined by replacing the second occurrence of "the house" with the relative pronoun "which." Because dependent clauses must be joined to their independent clause with a connector, the relative pronoun must be raised to the front of the dependent clause. The grammar allows the option of shifting the entire prepositional phrase "in which" to the front of the clause or just the relative pronoun. In most instances, the only difference between these options appears to be *stylistic,* not grammatical, which explains why we see the form of the first example in formal writing/speaking and the form of the second example in informal writing/speaking.

Some sentences, however, do not seem to allow the same degree of flexibility that we see in 4 and 5. Shifting the entire prepositional phrase results in a construction that may challenge our ability to judge its grammaticality, as in 7 below. In such constructions, ending the sentence with the preposition, as in 8, certainly sounds more natural.

7. ?An interesting puzzle is for what language is used. [4]

8. An interesting puzzle is what language is used for.

Also worth considering is the issue of tense. *Tense* is a technical term that describes how the form of verbs change to signify when an action occurred. There are three possibilities: past, present, and future. The change in form among Spanish verbs is easy to identify. The untensed form of *to speak,* for example, is *hablar.* The present-tense form is *habla,* the third-person past-tense form is *habló,* and the future-tense form is *hablaré.*

In English, we have *speak* and *spoke* for present and past, but there is no equivalent change that we can make to the verb to signify the future. Instead, we have two options. We may place the modal *will* in front of the present-tense form to signify the future, giving us *will speak,* or we may use an adverbial of time in conjunction with the present tense, as in *She speaks to the group tomorrow.* The form of the verb does not change in either instance. In other words, English does not have a future tense. Thus, English, unlike Latin and Latin-based languages, has only two tenses, not three. Even so, virtually all major handbooks claim that English has at least three tenses. *The Everyday Writer* by Lunsford (2009), for example, states that in English the "three simple tenses are the present tense, the past tense, and the future tense" (p. 285). *A Writer's Reference,* by Hacker (2007), as well as *The Norton Field Guide to Writing,* by Bullock and Weinberg (2009), take a further step, confusing progressive and perfect verb forms with tenses.[5] English uses progressive and perfect verb forms to signify when an action is ongoing and when it has been completed in the past, respectively. But these verb forms are not tenses because they do not involve any change in the verb itself—tense is indicated in the modal, not the verb.

For Writing and Discussion

To a great extent, learning involves imitating modeled behaviors. On this account, professional writers provide excellent models for student writers, which serves as a strong rationale for using published writing in the composition class. Too often, however, published writing is used as the basis for discussion of the content rather than for discussion and analysis of the form. To help students overcome some of the unfounded injunctions they received regarding writing—such as never begin a sentence with a conjunction—provide them with some professional models that violate these injunctions. Use these models as the foundation for analyzing the difference between grammaticality and style.

MODERN GRAMMARS

In the limited space available in this chapter, it is impossible to do more than offer a brief summary of modern grammars, all of which are significantly more complex than traditional grammar. Even the term "modern grammars" itself is somewhat misleading owing to the fact that modern grammars date to the early 20th century, when Franz Boas (1911) published his *Handbook of American Indian Tribal Languages*. Lamenting the inability of traditional grammar to describe tribal languages accurately, Boas argued that the prescriptive approach of this grammar was inadequate. Boas and his student Leonard Bloomfield therefore proposed a grammar that was entirely descriptive (see Bloomfield, 1933).

Phrase Structure Grammar

Today their effort is known as phrase structure grammar. Whereas traditional grammar is predicated on the idea that Latin serves as a tool for unveiling the universal features of languages, phrase structure grammar advocated the perception that every language is unique, with its own structure. The task of identifying and describing structure required extensive data collection, analysis, interpretation, and rule formation. As I've noted elsewhere, it required "an empirical approach to language" that traditional grammar never really considered (J. Williams, 2005, p. 99). This approach led Bloomfield (1933) to shift the focus of grammatical analysis away from matters of "correctness" to what he termed "acceptability," which is based on the context in which a given linguistic event occurs and on the specific word order of the construction. In this model, a statement might be deemed grammatical but unacceptable; likewise a statement might be ungrammatical but nevertheless acceptable. The following examples illustrate this point:

9. The determination of the cause of the crash that destroyed the car that Fritz had rented from the dealership where his own car was getting the brake job that he had foolishly delayed until he was faced with the unhappy and costly reality of metal against metal took weeks.

10. I am dining at 7 o'clock postmeridian and am solicitous of your companionship.

11. *Fritz feels badly about ruining the party.

12. Why am I leaving? *The reason is because I don't like your company.

Sentence 9 is perfectly grammatical but nevertheless is unlikely to be accepted in any context in which clarity and precision are valued. Anyone hoping to have a dinner date would probably fail if his or her invitation took the form of sentence 10, yet it, too, is perfectly grammatical. Sentence 11 is ungrammatical because adverbs (*badly*) cannot grammatically follow linking verbs (in this case, *feels*). Even so, this construction is almost universally accepted, especially among reasonably well-educated people (those with less education tend, ironically, to use the correct form of *bad* rather than *badly*). The statement in sentence 12 likewise is ungrammatical but widely accepted.

Transformational-Generative Grammar

Although phrase structure grammar was supplanted in 1957 by Noam Chomsky's transformational grammar (see Chomsky, 1957), its focus on description rather than prescription has been maintained by all modern grammars. Chomsky, however, did not believe that phrase structure grammar was sufficiently descriptive, nor did he believe that it was explanatory. He developed transformational-generative grammar in an effort to overcome these perceived limitations. Phrase structure grammar does not provide any insight into the relations between similar sentences, such as active and passive forms like the following:

13. Fritz kissed Rita. (active form)
14. Rita was kissed by Fritz. (passive form)

Phrase structure would, in fact, assign different grammatical descriptions to such sentences. Transformational-grammar, on the other hand, proposes that sentence 14 is derived from sentence 13 through the "passive transformation." We understand the relation between the two sentences by examining the transformational history of the passive form.

A large number of similar transformations, which supposedly occur in the language processing areas of the brain, govern a wide variety of constructions, such as adverbial movement, subordinate and relative clause formation, and particle movement. Because the grammar is not prescriptive, it is not concerned with the common injunction that writing teachers issue against using passive constructions; it is concerned only with the rule-governed mechanisms involved in generating these constructions. Use of passive voice, therefore, is a stylistic issue, not a grammatical one.

At the core of transformational-generative grammar was Chomsky's (1965) argument that a properly formulated grammar gives insight into mental operations, which had a strong appeal to many scholars devoted to understanding cognition. As part of this argument, he proposed that language is rule-governed, that language development in children consists of inducing the rules on the basis of limited and highly distorted input, and that sentences have a history that can be investigated to understand mental operations.

The Minimalist Program

Many of the claims related to transformational-generative grammar failed to hold up under scrutiny, and by the early 1970s, most people working in psychology had abandoned it as a viable tool. In response to many years of criticism, Chomsky (1995) revised the grammar and produced the minimalist program (MP). Like transformational-generative grammar, the MP maintains that language production begins in the brain and that each utterance undergoes various generative processes before expression. The rule-governed view of language was maintained, but there was more emphasis on linguistic universals.

Understanding what Chomsky means by linguistic universals can be facilitated by considering that, although we define ourselves as unique individuals, biologically we are very much the same (see Pinker, 2002). Our brains are anatomically similar and have an essentially identical architecture. As a result, we process information and thought itself in limited ways (see Tremlin, 2006). This limitation is manifested clearly in syntax, or word order. Sentences in all languages are made up of three core components: subject (S), verb (V), and object (O).[6] Thus, there are six possible combinations of these three components. Nevertheless, 95% of the world's languages fall into only two categories—either SVO (like English) or SOV (like Japanese). The other possible combinations are spoken by small groups of people. (OVS word order, the rarest of the possible combinations, governs Tamil, a language spoken in India, and Guarijio, an Uto-Aztecan language spoken in northwestern Mexico.) The overwhelming dominance of SVO and SOV word order suggests the existence of some universal factor related to cognitive processing and neural architecture.

The minimalist program proposes that language is innate and that the brain contains a language faculty responsible for language acquisition. This faculty contains a universal grammar that gives the newborn the potential to become a speaker of any human language. The child's exposure to adult language in the home sets specific principles and parameters associated with grammatical structure that in time limits this potential. As Chomsky (1995) stated, "language acquisition is interpreted as the process of fixing the parameters of the initial state [of the universal grammar] in one of the permissible ways" (p. 6).

Cognitive Grammar

The minimalist program is a powerful tool for analyzing and describing language, but it has many critics. Like transformational-generative grammar, the MP proposes that utterances begin with language. That is, in a sentence such as *Fritz kissed Rita,* the utterance or written expression begins with the individual words that make up the sentence; these words are extracted from the mental lexicon and then undergo specific cognitive operations that result in the sentence. As in the case of transformational-generative grammar, the MP proposes that grammar provides insight into how the brain operates.

Cognitive grammar takes a different approach (see Langacker, 2008; Taylor, 2002). First, it does not claim that utterances begin with language but rather that they are linked to life experiences that trigger concepts, relations, and images stored in the neural network. In *Fritz kissed Rita,* the sentence might begin with the observation (and the resulting image) of a male named Fritz engaged in the act of kissing a female named Rita. Underlying concepts and mental images are then connected with the words and syntactic patterns necessary to express them in language. The difference between cognitive approaches to language and transformational ones is therefore apparent: grammar does not determine the structure of the language we produce—situations determine the grammar we use.

Drawing on work in connectionism (see Rumelhart & McClelland, 1986), cognitive grammar dismisses the idea that language acquisition involves inducing grammar rules, proposing instead that children use their cognitive skill in pattern recognition to identify the grammatical patterns that govern their home language. Cognitive grammar also reverses Chomsky's perspective on the relation between language and mind: language does not provide insight into how the brain operates—understanding how the brain operates provides insight into language.

MODERN GRAMMARS AND WRITING

During the 1960s and 1970s, in what perhaps can be best described as an experiment of sorts, teachers at some public schools replaced traditional grammar with transformational-generative grammar in the hope that it would improve students' writing proficiency. These efforts were short-lived for several reasons, but among the more important was that modern grammars are challenging and require substantial formal education in them to understand fully. Few teacher-credential programs, then or now, provide such training. Furthermore, the move away from prescription to description that transformational-generative grammar entailed was derided by journalists who had no training in linguistics and yet who railed that schools were adopting an "anything goes" policy with regard to grammar and writing.

Today's handbooks contain no features or acknowledgment of modern grammars. A few include a comment related to dialects and how all dialects are legitimate, even grammatical, but such comments seem more aligned with multicultural politics than with the descriptive stance of modern grammars. Consequently, comparing a writing handbook published today with one published in the late 19th century shows that their discussions of grammar are nearly identical.

For Writing and Discussion

Survey students' history of grammar instruction to determine when it began and ended. Ask them to write a couple of paragraphs and then to report how much conscious attention they gave to grammar during writing. Then hold a workshop to analyze the grammatical structure of their paragraphs.

GRAMMAR AND WRITING: THE RESEARCH

The question of whether grammar instruction improves students' writing is an empirical one. That is, we should be able to measure the effect, if any, such instruction has on writing performance. The number of studies examining this question is considerable, although only a small number are unencumbered by design and method problems. Before summarizing these studies, we can use National Assessment of Educational Progress (NAEP) data to obtain a broad perspective on writing performance in our public schools.

National Assessment of Educational Progress

The National Assessment of Educational Progress (NAEP) provides regular reports on students' writing performance in grades 4, 8, and 12. Although changes in how results are

TABLE 8.1
Percentage of 17-, 13-, and 9-Year-Olds, by Amount of Time Spent Each Day on Homework, 1984 and 1999.

Year	Age	Had homework assigned	Did no homework	Less than 1 hour	1 to 2 hours	More than 2 hours
1984	17	77.5	11.4	26.2	26.8	13.2
1999	17	73.6	13.1	26.4	22.6	11.5
1984	13	77.4	3.7	35.9	29.2	8.6
1999	13	75.9	4.5	37.2	26.3	7.9
1984	9	64.4	4.2	41.5	12.7	6.1
1999	9	74.2	3.8	53.1	12.4	4.9

reported make long-term comparisons difficult, some trends do emerge over the shorter term. *The 1984 and 1999 Long-Term Trend Assessment* (US Department of Education, 2002) reported a drop between 1984 and 1999 in the amount of homework students were assigned as well as in the amount of time students spent on homework each day (see Table 8.1).[7] There is no evidence, however, that during this period grammar instruction diminished. Just the opposite. As Hudson (2001) reported, an upswing in grammar instruction was fueled by "more enthusiasm in some educational circles for the idea that … grammar … could have the … benefit of improving writing" (p. 1).

The decrease in the amount of homework assigned and the amount completed may be related to the findings of *The 1996 Trends in Writing* report (US Department of Education, 1996) that between 1984 and 1996 the percentage of run-on sentences in students' writing increased, as did the percentage of sentence fragments and other sentence-level errors. NAEP's 1998 report (US Department of Education, 1999) on writing indicated that only about 25% of 12th graders were capable of producing a coherent, well-developed essay. The writing of the 75% who were not capable of producing such an essay was characterized by the sort of errors that grammar instruction is supposed to eliminate.

The latest NAEP report (US Department of Education, 2010a) showed that students at the lowest level (basic) of performance in grades 8 and 12 realized modest increases in scores between 1998 and 2007. Students at the proficient level also increased their scores between 1998 and 2007, but not between 2002 and 2007. At the advanced level, however, scores declined among 12th graders but were unchanged among 8th graders. More problematic is that between 1998 and 2007 the number of students who scored at the basic level increased significantly. In 1998, 84% of 8th graders wrote at the basic level; in 2007, the figure was 88%. Among 12th graders, the number of students at the basic level of performance rose from 78% to 82%.[8]

Summarizing the Research Connection

A large body of research, going back many years, exists on the grammar/writing connection, and the results are uniform and consistent. In 1963, Braddock, Lloyd-Jones, and Schoer summarized the existing research at that time and reported the following:

In view of the widespread agreement of research studies based upon many types of students and teachers, the conclusion can be stated in strong and unqualified terms that the teaching of formal [traditional] grammar has a negligible or, because it usually displaces some instruction and practice in actual composition, even a harmful effect on the improvement of writing. (pp. 37–38)

In spite of this assessment, the assumed connection between grammar and writing was so ancient and so strong that other researchers continued to investigate the question. White (1965), for example, studied three 7th-grade classes: one class studied traditional grammar, one transformational grammar, and the third used the time to read popular novels. White found no significant differences in the students' writing skills at the end of the study. Whitehead (1966) compared two groups of high school students: one received grammar instruction; the other did not. At the end of the study, there were no measurable differences in writing performance. Gale (1968) studied 5th graders divided into four groups. Three of these groups received instruction in grammar, with each group studying a different type (traditional, phrase structure, and transformational-generative). The fourth group did not receive any grammar instruction. Although Gale reported that students who studied transformational-generative and phrase-structure grammars could write more complex sentences than the students in the other groups, there were no overall differences in writing quality across groups.

One of the more frequently cited studies on the question of grammar and writing was conducted by Bateman and Zidonis (1966). Starting with 9th-grade students, Bateman and Zidonis provided grammar instruction over a two-year period to half of the students; the other half received no grammar instruction. Like some previous researchers, Bateman and Zidonis found that, at the end of the study, students who studied grammar could write slightly more complex sentences than those who could not, but, again, there were no measurable differences in writing proficiency across the groups.

The strength of these findings, however, did not convince skeptics who believed that the lack of positive findings had to be the result of methodological flaws in the research. Some claimed, for example, that the studies failed to account for different teaching styles; the failure to find that grammar instruction improved writing was related to poor teaching. Elley, Barham, Lamb, and Wyllie (1976) responded to this issue by designing a three-year study that controlled, to the extent possible, for the effect of different teaching styles. They divided students into three groups. The first group, consisting of three classes of students, studied the following: 1) literature; 2) organizational modes, such as narration, analysis, comparison/contrast, and argument; and 3) transformational-generative grammar. The second group, also made up of three classes, studied the same topics as the first group, with one exception—they did not study grammar. The final group, made up of two classes, studied traditional grammar and read a large amount of popular fiction.

At the end of each year of the study, students were evaluated on a range of factors to assess their growth in vocabulary, reading comprehension, sentence complexity, usage, spelling, and punctuation. The results were compared across groups each year. In addition, students wrote four essays at the end of the first year and three at the end of the second and third years. The essays were scored on the basis of content, style, organization, and mechanics. Finally, students completed questionnaires periodically to assess their attitudes toward the content of their English classes.

The results were again consistent. The writing of students who studied grammar, whether traditional or transformational, was not judged to be any better along any dimension than the writing of students who did not study grammar. In addition, the attitude questionnaires showed that, at the end of the second year, students who had studied transformational grammar not only disliked writing more than their counterparts did but also felt that English was quite difficult—understandable, perhaps, given the complexity of transformational grammar.

At the end of the third year, the researchers evaluated specific features of the students' writing—such as spelling, punctuation, sentence structure and usage—using a variety of measures. A standardized test showed that the students who had studied grammar performed better on usage questions than did those students who had not studied grammar. However, no significant differences in any other area were found. The two groups who studied grammar also reported on their attitude surveys that they found English "repetitive" and that their English classes were boring and useless. The group that did not study grammar had a much more positive attitude toward English. More significant, perhaps, is that after three years of instruction, the writing of the students showed no differences in overall quality across groups.

Such unequivocal findings dampened the voices claiming some positive effect of grammar instruction on writing performance, but it did not silence them entirely. Kolln (1981), Holt (1982), and Davis (1984) argued that the studies showing no effect were flawed and that grammar did, in fact, lead to improved writing, but they were not able to provide any meaningful data to support their claim. An important factor in all these counter-arguments does, however, merit consideration: none of the studies that found no effect of grammar instruction on writing proficiency lasted more than three years. Longer exposure to grammar instruction, from this perspective, might show measurable effects. Unfortunately, this idea is offset by the fact that, as noted previously, the majority of children are taught grammar from elementary school into high school, with no measurable benefit.

In an effort to address the concerns of those who questioned the results of the empirical research, Hillocks (1986) performed a meta-analysis on thousands of studies on composition, including all those related to grammar and writing that met certain design criteria. Studies with flawed or inadequate designs were eliminated, which made his conclusions more substantial and difficult to dismiss. On the question of grammar and writing, Hillocks' conclusion was blunt and warrants full inclusion here:

> The study of traditional school grammar (i.e., the definition of parts of speech, the parsing of sentences, etc.) has no effect on raising the quality of student writing. Every other focus of instruction examined in this review is stronger. Taught in certain ways, grammar and mechanics instruction has a deleterious effect on student writing. In some studies a heavy emphasis on mechanics and usage (e.g., marking every error) resulted in significant losses in overall quality. School boards, administrators, and teachers who impose the systematic study of traditional school grammar on their students over lengthy periods of time in the name of teaching writing do them a gross disservice which should not be tolerated by anyone concerned with the effective teaching of good writing. We need to learn how to teach standard usage and mechanics after careful task analysis and with minimal grammar. (pp. 248–249)

Hillocks' work was compelling, at least among scholars in composition. A review of the following major journals in composition studies—*College Composition and Communication*,

Research in the Teaching of English, Written Communication, and *College English*—from 1986 to the present did not produce a single article addressing the question of grammar's effect on writing performance. The works that did emerge in this review were not empirical but theoretical. Parker and Campbell (1993), for example, argued that the theoretical framework of linguistics would find a significant theoretical vacuum in composition. Crowley (1989) and Noguchi (1991) reiterated on linguistic grounds the conclusion that direct grammar instruction does not improve writing performance. Examining the influence on composition studies of Chomskian grammar as a rule-governed model of language, I explored (J. Williams, 1993) the implications of cognitive linguistics and connectionism, concluding that:

> [If] structure is … determined by initial [cognitive] states, it seems reasonable to suggest that rhetorical knowledge is implicit in the performative act as well as in the intentional state that initiates a given discourse. The model [of writing that emerges] therefore predicts that at the text level non-performative tasks [such as grammar exercises] will do little to increase the … [cognitive connections] among mental representations of discourse, regardless of how frequently one engages in them. (p. 556)

In response to the British government's efforts to improve students' writing performance through the Grammar for Writing Initiative, Wyse (2001) reviewed the major studies of grammar's effect on writing that were conducted in the United Kingdom. Wyse's conclusions were similar to those of other investigators, finding that grammar instruction had no significant effect on writing performance. He noted that "the teaching of grammatical 'technical vocabulary' such as adjective; noun: collective, common, proper; pronoun: personal, possessive; verb, and verb tense to six and seven year-old children … is highly questionable" (p. 422).

Hudson (2004) reviewed several studies related to punctuation (Laurinen, 1955), spelling (Bryant, Devine, Ledward, & Nunes, 2002; Bryant, Nunes, & Bindman, 2004), number of sentences (G. Williams, 1995), and reading (Chipere, 2003). On the basis of this review, he argued that teaching grammar improved children's syntactic maturity. What remains uncertain, however, is whether the children's increase in syntactic maturity was related to instruction or to cognitive/linguistic growth as a result of natural development (see Hunt, 1964, 1965).

Andrews et al. (2004a) conducted a similar review. Using relevance criteria comparable to those of Hillocks (1986), the authors examined the reported effects of grammar instruction on the writing performance of 5–16-year-old students. Their results were consistent with all previous studies: "there is no high-quality evidence … that the teaching of … syntax has … [any] influence on the writing quality or accuracy of 5 to 16 year-olds" (p. 4).

WHY ISN'T GRAMMAR INSTRUCTION TRANSPORTABLE TO WRITING?[9]

Many people resist the conclusion that grammar instruction fails to improve writing because it seems to fly in the face of common sense. After all, before we teach children how to read, we first teach them the alphabet. Letters form words, words form sentences, and so on. Common sense, therefore, tells us that writing instruction should follow a similar bottom-up approach, with grammar being the building block for sentences and paragraphs, just as the alphabet is the building block for words and reading.

Common sense fails us here. Foreign students, especially those from Asia, illustrate the problem. English language instruction in some parts of Asia follows what is known as the *grammar-translation method*. This method was originally designed to teach people how to read a language, like Latin or Greek, that they would never have to speak or write. It is grammar intensive. Japanese students who attend universities in the United States after having studied English through grammar-translation commonly arrive with a good knowledge of grammar. Some have better technical knowledge of English grammar than their American teachers. Nevertheless, they tend to be poor writers. In some respects, such students are in the same situation as their American counterparts, for both have studied grammar but cannot write well.

The building-block approach fails with writing because it is inconsistent with the nature of grammar and how the mind processes language. The cognitive perspective proposes that language acquisition involves internalizing mental models of the basic sentence patterns and their acceptable permutations. Although these structural patterns cannot be neurologically separate from the lexicon, the connections in the neural network seem to be relatively remote. Sentence production in this account is not based on a bottom-up process in which individual words and grammatical units are merged, building-block style, to form sentences. Instead, production is largely top down.

The process of language acquisition is extremely powerful. As I've noted elsewhere (J. Williams, 1999), "on a neurophysiological level … [mental models of language consist] of modifications to the cerebral structure" (p. 232). In other words, the brain literally changes in response to linguistic input, developing new cells and a network of neural pathways to connect these cells within the communicative system. As language develops, the neural network expands, grows more dense, and becomes richer.

The linguistic input children receive comes primarily from adults, who provide models of the language. Although children go through a period of development in which their language is characterized as "baby talk," this period is short-lived; they fairly quickly begin reproducing the grammatical patterns of the language around them. What is fascinating is that during the acquisition process parents commonly correct their children's pronunciation of individual words, and children respond to the parents' modeling. The result is a matching procedure that leads to a "best fit" that approximates the home dialect. Yet when parents correct grammar, children rarely respond, and parental efforts have little or no effect. In other words, the sort of matching procedure that works so well with pronunciation of individual words does not work with grammar. We don't know why, but we do know, obviously, that children manage to produce sentences that follow standard syntax.

The connection between the home/community environment and a child's emerging language is important and accounts for the fact that children reared in the South grow up speaking a Southern dialect, that children reared in Boston grow up speaking a New England dialect, and so on. Children acquire not only the accents but also the grammar of these dialects, simply by being immersed in the language community. Although the language that children acquire may or may not be congruent with Standard English, depending on the home dialect, it is almost never congruent with formal Standard English because so few people use the formal standard dialect when speaking. Formal standard English is principally the dialect of writing.

Nevertheless, regardless of which dialect children develop, their language is largely grammatical. There are several reasons for this. Perhaps the most important is that the architecture of our brains limits how we process information (Cosimides & Tooby, 1994; Fingelkurts, Fingelkurts, & Neves, 2009; Karmiloff-Smith, 1992; Leslie, 1994; Pinker, 1994). Although cognition appears to involve parallel distributed processes, mental representations have a hierarchical and/or sequential structure owing to the linear flow of input sensory data (Perlovsky, 2009; Rumelhart & McClelland, 1986). A sense of agency, which is among the first emergent cognitive functions in infant development, operates in conjunction with hierarchical/sequential processing to emphasize agents in mental representations (Barrett & Johnson, 2003; Bering, 2002; Scholl & Tremoulet, 2000). This emphasis seems to be reflected in word order: the majority of the world's 5,000 or so languages front the subject in clauses. The subject is then followed either by the verb or by the object. What this means in practical terms is that sentences cannot be significantly ungrammatical because we cannot process or produce ungrammatical utterances naturally. They do not follow the neural pathways of the brain's architecture, and thus they are not meaningful.

It is therefore important to recognize that, by the time students enter school, grammar is already embedded in their brains. Grammar instruction is not transportable to writing, ultimately, because students already have the grammar. Their writing *is* grammatical when viewed from the linguistic perspective because it conforms to the basic word order of English and is meaningful.

BAD GRAMMAR OR BAD USAGE?

Even though student writing is essentially grammatical, no one would be so bold as to call it error-free. The challenge is to understand that most of the errors we find in student writing are problems of usage, not grammar.

Usage can best be understood as conventions associated with language that govern how we use it in different contexts. On this account, we can recognize that a formal context will expect usage that is different from what is expected in an informal context. Linguists often refer to these different forms of usage as *register* or style. With the concept of acceptability, register explains why the language we use when talking with friends and family is in nearly every instance unlike the language we use in, say, a job interview.

The most widely accepted dialect is Standard English, whereas the least accepted is nonstandard English. With good reason, then, national news anchors use Standard English rather than Black English, Southern English, Indian English, or some other dialect. Academic writing is at a higher level of formality and is governed by even stricter conventions; thus, academic writing represents formal Standard English. When we ask students to write an academic paper, we essentially are asking them to use a dialect of English that they have rarely encountered and therefore have not mastered.

Note that issues of usage generally do not have any connection with issues of grammar. Some of the more egregious problems we find in student writing are errors in *word-choice* (using the wrong word, such as *impact* for *affect* or *immolate* for *emulate*), *punctuation* (resulting in sentence fragments, run-on sentences, improper placement of the comma vis-à-vis quotation marks, separating verbs in a compound verb phrase), *agreement* (using a singular antecedent and a plural pronoun or a singular subject and plural verb), and *tense* (shifting from past to present—or vice versa—in a given sentence). Word choice has little to do with grammar—spelling nothing at all. The punctuation problems that cause sentence fragments and run-ons are typically the result of students' inability to differentiate conversational patterns, in which fragments and run-ons are common, from formal writing conventions. Asking students to study the parts of speech cannot have any effect on their ability to spell, punctuate, or use words correctly. These skills are developed through reading and writing. By reading widely, students internalize English spelling and a variety of genre conventions, and they enlarge their vocabularies so that they are more inclined not only to use the right word but also to use words more precisely.

The other problems in student writing are equally unaffected by grammar instruction because they are unrelated to grammar. This point will become clearer if we consider a type of sentence that teachers often hold up as an example of bad grammar: *I ain't got no money.* This sentence supposedly has two problems. First, many argue that *ain't* is not a word, although it is listed in most dictionaries as a word and looks, sounds, and feels like a word. Those who accede that it is a word argue that, as a forced contraction of *am not,* as well as *are not, is not, has not,* and *have not,* it is ungrammatical in this instance. The second problem is the double negative—created by *ain't* and *no*—for as every self-respecting English teacher knows from basic math (and their handbooks), two negatives make a positive.

Let's address the second problem first. Although it is the case in math that two negatives make a positive, language is different, and the idea that what holds in math holds in English is fundamentally flawed. There isn't a single native speaker of English anywhere who would read or hear *I ain't got no money* and understand it to mean that the subject in fact has money. Moreover, the double negative has existed in English for centuries; we find it in Chaucer and Shakespeare, obviously well-established writers. The double negative also exists in other languages, such as French and Spanish. Therefore, rejecting our example sentence on the grounds that it fails to communicate the speaker/writer's intention—that its meaning is positive rather than negative—is not only silly but also contrary to fact.

But is *I ain't got no money* grammatical? Answering this question requires that we return to what grammatical actually means. A sentence is grammatical when it follows, at least generally, the word order of native speakers and when those speakers accept a given utterance or written statement as meaningful. In English, a truly ungrammatical sentence would be one that does not follow the SVO word order, such as the sentences below:

15. *Cat my rat a chased.
16. *The into wind over blew hills the valley and.

Although, as an exercise, we can rearrange the words, putting them in their proper order, and understand what the utterances mean, they have no meaning as they stand, and they violate the SVO word order of English. They therefore are ungrammatical. It is important to emphasize that a native speaker of English will never and can never spontaneously produce sentences such as 15 and 16. In fact, native speakers have a difficult time producing truly ungrammatical sentences even when they try.[10]

There are certain exceptions that emerge in spoken English as a result of widespread distribution of nonstandard forms. One of the more common examples, as noted on page 273, involves the response to Why-questions. Consider the following:

Speaker A: Why did you fail the exam?
Speaker B: *The reason is because I didn't study.

For native Standard English speakers of a certain age, B's response is unacceptable and ungrammatical. The explanation is based on the fact that the predicate in B's response is governed by the linking verb *is*. Linking verbs in English are followed by predicate adjectives, predicate nominatives, or prepositional phrases. Yet *because I didn't study* is a subordinate clause. This example illustrates two important points about grammaticality: first, most speakers today do not recognize the grammatical problem associated with following a linking verb with a subordinate clause, and second, language is always in a state of flux that can result in changes in what is deemed grammatical. Note, however, that such changes occur more readily in speech than in writing, especially with regard to grammatical structure. Writing is not subject to the same social influences that affect speech. Consequently, structures like *The reason is because I didn't study* may be deemed grammatical and acceptable in speech but not in formal writing. Formal texts tend to fossilize linguistic features. The more formal the text, the more rigid the fossilization.

With this information in mind, let's return to *I ain't got no money* and consider its structure:

Subject: I

Verb phrase: ain't got

Object: no money

This analysis shows that the sentence structure follows the standard SVO pattern, with *ain't* functioning as an auxiliary to the verb *got,* much in the way that *don't* functions in sentence 17:

17. I don't have any money.

Every native speaker of English understands the intended meaning of the sentence (the speaker/writer really is broke), and the sentence follows the standard SVO pattern of English. It therefore meets all the requirements of a grammatical sentence and, indeed, is grammatical. Nevertheless, we would not want students to produce such a sentence in a typical writing assignment. Such sentences are unacceptable because they violate the usage conventions that govern academic writing, not because they are ungrammatical. They are the equivalent of wearing cutoff jeans, a tank top, and sandals to an elegant wedding service—simply unacceptable.

We can analyze in a similar fashion nearly all of the difficulties in student writing that usually are described as grammatical errors. For example, faulty punctuation, which can sometimes produce run-on sentences, fused sentences, and sentence fragments, may appear on the surface to be the result of students' failure to understand the grammatical structure of a sentence, but closer examination reveals something very different. Let's consider the following example:

18. Plato had a great influence on Western civilization and his student Aristotle may have had an even greater influence.

Anyone who *heard* this sentence would find nothing unusual about it. The sentence has meaning, and it follows English word order, so it is grammatical. However, a person reading the sentence who happens to know something about punctuation would immediately recognize that it violates the convention that calls for a comma plus a conjunction in compound sentences. Punctuation is largely a visual aid for readers and has little to do with grammar. Until the end of the 16th century, punctuation as we know it did not exist. Not until the end of the 17th century, when there was a widespread shift from oral to silent reading, did scholars and printers begin using something approaching modern punctuation conventions. But then, as now, punctuation was understood to be somewhat arbitrary, depending on the writer's style (see Freeborn, 2006).

A simple modern example illustrates this point. Currently, there are two different conventions governing the use of the comma in lists. One convention, advocated by the Modern Language Association in its *MLA Handbook* (2009) as well as by the American Psychological Association in its *APA Publication Manual* (2009), specifies that a comma should separate each item in a list, including the last item, as illustrated below:

19. Hobbes wrote that the life of man in his natural state is dirty, nasty, brutish, and short.

The second convention, advocated by journalists in the *Associated Press Guide* (Christian, 2010), specifies that a comma should not be used for the last item in a list, which gives us:

20. Hobbes wrote that the life of man in his natural state is dirty, nasty, brutish and short.

In the anaerobic environs of the English class, the sentence fragment is deemed to be an even more egregious error than the run-on, but here again close examination reveals that what underlies the fragment is not an ignorance of grammar. The passage below comes from a paper written by a 5th grader who was asked to report on a field trip to a museum. The sentence fragments are in italics:

We arrived at the Field Museum almost an hour late. *Because there was an accident on the highway.* We went first to the dinosaur exhibit on the second floor. The exhibit was about the life of the dinosaurs. They lived a long time ago. *Long before humans.* The exhibit showed us what the earth was like during the time of the dinosaurs. *Hot and humid.* I liked the exhibit very much and want to go back again soon.

What we notice is that in each instance the problem is one of punctuation, not grammar. If we hear the passage read aloud, the lack of commas is not an issue. The same is true if we put in the proper punctuation. But there is nothing structurally wrong with the paragraph. Providing this student opportunities to see how other writers handled similar constructions, as well as some help understanding punctuation conventions through examining his own writing, would go a long way toward giving him better control over his sentences. Professional writers have such control, and we are not surprised or dismayed when we encounter fragments in their work. Yet we shine a harsh spotlight on students because we know that, in most cases, they do not yet have this control.

In addition, it is worth noting that speech allows for fragmented constructions. For example, if my wife asked me why I was late arriving home, I might correctly respond with, *An accident on the highway.* No one would label this response as ungrammatical because

English allows for reduction of responses through ellipsis. I do not need to respond with, *I am late arriving home because of an accident on the highway.* In fact, if I were to offer that response rather than the elliptical one, my utterance would be judged stilted at best, unnatural at worst.

The writing of the 5th grader above—and the writing of students who produce sentence fragments—manifests conventions of speech that have been transferred to writing. There are several reasons why students use conventions of speech when they write, perhaps the most obvious being their lack of experience with the written word. To a significant degree, writing is an artificial representation of language, governed by conventions that are much more rigorous than anything we find in speech, and it takes people many years to master these conventions fully.

For Writing and Discussion

A key to modeling professional writing lies in knowing with some specificity what professionals do with regard to sentence structure—what often is labeled as style but what is actually inseparable from structure and usage choices. Ask students to select two essays by different writers dealing with the same topic. They should then select four paragraphs from each essay. Using those paragraphs, they should calculate: 1) the average sentence length, 2) the different types of sentence opener (subject, introductory modifier, coordinating conjunction, verb phrase, etc.), 3) the average number of adverbs and adjectives per sentence, and 4) the average number of subordinate clauses. Have students use these data to write a short essay comparing and contrasting the styles of the two writers.

Follow-up activity: While working on their next out-of-class paper, hold a work-shop in which students perform the same stylistic analysis on it. Have them compare these data with the data they obtained from their analysis of one of the professional essays. Where their data don't match the professionals, they should revise their papers accordingly.

READING AND WRITING

Acquisition of writing conventions occurs primarily though reading, yet, with the exception of text messages, our students do very little reading. The National Endowment for the Arts (2007) reported, for example, that 21% of high school seniors and 39% of college freshman read "little or nothing" for pleasure. Given the correlation between skill growth and practice, especially during adolescence (Krashen, 1981, 1985), we should not be surprised that reading proficiency has been declining for decades (Alwin, 1991; Glenn, 1994; Stedman & Kaestle, 1987; Wilson & Gove, 1999). The 2005 NAEP report (US Department of Education, 2005) indicated that reading scores for 12th graders had declined steadily since 1992, and the 2010 report (US Department of Education, 2010b) on reading found that nearly 30% of 12th-grade students were reading below grade level (also see Ravitch, 2004; Simmons & Kameenui, 1998; Stotsky, 1999; Sykes, 1995).

In a cross-sectional analysis of 800 elementary, middle, and high school books published between 1919 and 1991, Hayes, Wolfer, and Wolfe (1996) found that reading materials designed for 8th-grade readers were simpler than 5th-grade readers were before World War II. Their analysis also showed no significant differences in the current reading levels of required English texts used in 9th through 12th grades. As they noted, "The average literature text required in 12th grade English classes is ... simpler than the average 7th or 8th grade reader published before World War II" (p. 499). In addition, the data showed no significant differences in text difficulty across academic tracks, including AP English. Hayes, Wolfer, and Wolf concluded that simplification of textbooks since the end of World War II, involving decreasing sentence length and complexity along with replacing domain-specific vocabulary with nondomain-specific words, accounted for a decrease in reading levels across all age groups and also effected a "cumulative knowledge deficit" in the population (p. 501).

NEW MEDIA: TEXTING, BLOGGING, AND INSTANT MESSAGING

Texting, messaging, blogging, and social networking—often subsumed under the concept of *new media* (also *digital media*)—have experienced a remarkable increase in popularity over a very short time. Two factors are central to new media: digitalization and interactivity. Texting and messaging have attracted a great deal of journalistic attention owing to the frequency with which young people, especially teenagers, engage in these activities and the common use of abbreviations and emoticons.

New media also has become a major subject of academic interest in various fields, especially psychology and sociology. The American Psychological Association, for example, established a task force in 1996 on new media psychology with the goal of investigating "the new media technologies and their impact and promise for psychologists and applying psychology in their occupations" (Luskin & Friedland, 1998, p. 1). In sociology, the recently established *Journal of New Media & Society* aims to examine global and local dimensions of the relationship between media and social change as well as the individual, social, cultural and political dimensions of new media.

The popularity of texting and its associated technology has led some composition scholars to advocate integrating new media into composition classes. Among the first to do so were Schroeder, Bizzell, and Fox (2002), whose *Alt Dis: Alternative Discourses and the Academy* predicted that the unique forms that characterize new media would find their way into formal writing and also advocated their acceptance. Other texts have followed, such as *Writing New Media: Theory and Applications for Expanding the Teaching of Composition* (Wysocki, Johnson-Eilola, Selfe, & Sirc, 2004); *The Two Virtuals: New Media and Composition* (Reid, 2007); and *Rhetorics and Technologies: New Directions in Writing and Composition* (Selber, 2010). Meanwhile, composition faculty at various schools have shifted the focus of instruction away from the academic essay to new media. According to the school's campus newspaper, the University of Kentucky, for example, announced in 2010 that by 2011 its composition courses will focus on digital media "to help students acquire the social media skills necessary to function in today's workplace" (Bailiff, 2010, p. 2). The writing program director, Roxanne Mountford, was quoted as stating that "there's Facebook and YouTube videos now, it's [communication] becoming easier and faster. There's a broad integration of skills and I think it's high time to teach this way. This is a 2020 future" (p. 3).

An underlying assumption in the new media movement among those in composition studies is that the abbreviations and emoticons that are part of digitally generated text messages will—and should—affect grammar and writing proficiency. A growing number of anecdotal reports claim that this is indeed the case (e.g., Brown-Owens, Eason, & Lader, 2003; Lee, 2002; O'Connor, 2005). None of these reports, however, is based on empirical data; in addition, the reports are often conflicting, with some claiming that the new media have a positive effect and with others claiming a negative effect.

Until well-designed empirical studies shed light on this question, it seems wise to reserve judgment. Yet it bears noting that the enthusiasm of those in composition studies for embracing alternative discourse structures does not appear to be shared by those in other disciplines. The submission guidelines for *New Media & Society,* for example, specify that all manuscripts must conform to the Harvard style, without deviation. The entries on Wikipedia, arguably the most successful model of new media collaborative interaction, all conform to Standard or formal Standard English grammar.

There are several obvious problems associated with the idea that the textual features characteristic of texting and instant messaging might affect students' grammar. Historically, when changes in grammar have occurred, they evolved over periods longer than one or two decades, making it unlikely that the features we find in texting have had sufficient time to affect existing grammatical patterns. But two other factors are perhaps more important. First, as noted previously, formal texts tend to fossilize linguistic features, making them very resistant to change. Second, examination of new media texts show that, abbreviations and emoticons notwithstanding, they are grammatical. On this account, the unique features of these texts resemble slang, especially when we consider that the majority of the people texting and instant messaging are, at least at this point, teenagers and young adults.

NONSTANDARD DIALECTS

Although some teachers are willing to grant that the problems of their Anglo students are due to usage rather than grammar, the majority refuse to do so when it comes to black and Chicano students. Many resist the suggestion that structures like the following are grammatical:

21. I is hungry.
22. I'm is thirsty.
23. He like da woman has blonde hair.

Nevertheless, both Black English Vernacular (BEV) and Chicano English are grammatical—but their grammatical structures are different from Standard English.

Few children grow up immersed in a language environment that consists of formal Standard English. In fact, if we think of language acquisition as existing on a continuum, with formal standard on one end and nonstandard on the other, most children's home language is probably located somewhere south of the midpoint. For children of color, the home language can be very far south, indeed. The result is a gap between the language of the home and the language of the school, a gap that students are expected to bridge fairly quickly. They face major difficulties because their home language/dialect is already established firmly in the neural network. It is not readily malleable, and it is quite resistant to direct instruction. Fogel and Ehri (2000) reported, however, that indirect instruction involving intensive reading in Standard English and guided practice in translation between BEV and Standard English showed promise in helping children in their study apply the school dialect.

Unfortunately, many black and Hispanic students have little motivation to master Standard English, for a wide variety of social reasons rooted in lack of socioeconomic opportunity, discrimination, and injustice. In theory, school provides all students the opportunity to master Standard, if not formal Standard, English. Working-class children, upper-class children, black, white, brown, and yellow all come together under the great umbrella of compulsory education where they are taught Standard English grammar. The aim of instruction, as in the case of Fogel and Ehir (2000), is additive in most instances rather than subtractive and is intended to allow students to code switch from the home dialect to the school dialect in keeping with their individual situations.

But in practice, this theory does not work in the face of current realities. Traditional grammar continues to be anchored solidly in our language arts and English classes. It is not only arcane but also incomprehensible to a large number of students. Moreover, the concept of the school as a great melting pot is obsolete, proven false by the failure of bussing and forced integration, the subsequent self-segregation of students, and the dramatic influx of illegal immigrants that has resulted in many schools that are 80 or 90% limited English proficient. Unwilling or unable to read books that help them develop genre and syntactic awareness, the only models students have for Standard or formal Standard English are their teachers, but here, too, reality intervenes. In a landmark study, Labov (1970) tabulated grammatical and ungrammatical sentences in a variety of social settings for several social classes. Although most sentences were technically grammatical, Labov found that working-class subjects had a higher percentage of grammatical utterances than middle-class subjects. More interesting still, *academics had the highest percentage of ungrammatical sentences.* The situation has become more problematic over the last two decades, as the language skills of teachers have continued to decline. On college and university campuses, it has become commonplace to hear students—and increasingly, faculty—using a whole range of nonstandard speech.

For Writing and Discussion

Do you speak Standard English? Is Standard English your home dialect? Do you have friends whose first language is English who do not speak Standard English? If not, does their dialect bother you in any way? Do you feel compelled to correct them?

Write a brief essay discussing your views on whether our schools should help students produce Standard as well as formal Standard English.

TEACHING GRAMMAR AND USAGE

If grammar instruction doesn't help students become better writers, if it doesn't even help them with simple issues such as case, does it have any value? Yes. Grammar can be one of the more interesting subjects a person can study—when it is taught the right way. The right way does not link it with writing but instead treats grammar as a way of studying the intricacies of language. Also, there is value in knowing how to talk about language. Teachers and students benefit when they have a common vocabulary for analysis and when they share concepts of English structure. (Consider in this regard, how difficult it is to analyze poetry without knowing poetic terminology.)

The first step toward solving the problem is to recognize that direct instruction is certainly not effective in the early grades and not particularly effective in the later grades when it relies on textbooks and exercises. More effective are approaches that immerse students in language itself, approaches that give students opportunities to analyze not only their own language but also the language of everyone around them. Asking students to act as amateur linguists and to observe closely and record the language that people use serve as great learning opportunities. Students are fascinated when with minimal training in grammar and usage they discover that highly paid and well-educated people frequently produce language that is carelessly constructed.

Such approaches also need to be linked to other activities, reading in particular. Discussions of reading inevitably involve questions of meaning as students and teacher explore what a given author means in a text. And questions of "what" lead naturally to questions of "how," which is where issues of structure and usage come in. This strategy can be enhanced, at any grade level, when teachers read aloud to their students and make comments that focus student attention on a particular word or phrase. This indirect approach to grammar and usage reinforces concepts in ways that direct instruction cannot. Remarking, for example, that a certain word is an "interesting adjective" draws students to the word, and it also models the important idea that some words are more interesting than others while simultaneously reinforcing the concept of "adjective."

A vital part of such teaching involves understanding that grammar is related to the structure of language, not its production per se. Usage, on the other hand, does involve production. It requires an understanding of the conventions that govern register, word choice, and genre. The pervasive nature of usage problems can be addressed by helping students read more and motivating them to be more reflective when writing. Activities that separate composing from editing and that encourage students to examine the precise meaning of words will yield substantial results. No doubt the greatest challenge for the public school teacher is finding ways to individualize writing instruction, making it one-on-one. We know that this kind of instruction works best for writing; we know that pointing out and then showing students how to correct their usage blunders again and again, day after day, results in a substantial improvement. What we don't know is how to fit this kind of instruction into a teacher's schedule. Until we do, it is likely that grammar instruction will be viewed, incorrectly, as a shortcut panacea for the usage problems we find in our students' writing.

For Writing and Discussion

Give students a lesson on the semantic features of commonly confused subordinating conjunctions: while/because, while/whereas, since/because. Have them form small groups to examine newspaper and/or magazine articles to determine whether the writers used subordinating conjunctions consistently in keeping with their semantic content. They should share their findings with the whole class. Next, have them pair up and exchange drafts of a paper in progress. Then ask them to examine each subordinate clause to determine whether its subordinating conjunction semantically matches the nature of the information the clause provides.

SENTENCE COMBINING

Lessons in usage, unlike grammar exercises, are hands-on, embedded in the act of writing. They necessarily engage students in the complexities of language as a communicative tool. Students nevertheless need a way to manipulate sentence structures to best convey messages. Sentence combining pedagogy emerged in the 1960s and early 1970s to address this need. It consists of showing students how to combine short clauses into single sentences so as to produce more complex and more varied constructions. Consider the following examples:

I danced with excitement.

I wound myself around my mother's legs.

I tugged at her dress.

I stepped on her toes.

    24. I danced with excitement, winding myself around my mother's legs, tugging at her dress, stepping on her toes.

The participants ranged in age from 18 to 24.

They consisted of 15 males and 21 females.

They received a copy of the PF-16.

    25. The participants, ranging in age from 18 to 24 and consisting of 15 males and 21 females, received a copy of the PF-16.

Several early studies (e.g., Combs, 1977; Daiker, Kerek, & Morenberg, 1978; Howie, 1979) found that students who were taught this technique gained better control over sentence structure and produced more mature writing. Other studies noted, however, that these gains in performance were short-lived (e.g., Callaghan, 1978; Sullivan, 1978). By the late 1980s, when composition studies began focusing on political issues rather than on students' difficulties with writing, sentence combining had all but disappeared from composition pedagogy. Connors (2000), however, argued that the field had made a mistake and that sentence combining provides valuable teaching and composing tools. More recently, Andrews et al. (2004b) conducted a meta-analysis of more than 4,500 studies to examine the effects of sentence combining. They found that gains in syntactic maturity were immediate. Moreover, in the single study that undertook a delayed posttest, "syntactic maturity gains are maintained, albeit less dramatically than immediately after the event" (p. 2).

    These results are particularly important in light of the fact that teaching sentence combining does not involve teaching grammar. Forty years ago, O'Hare (1972) reported that students were able to understand and apply combining techniques quickly after merely being introduced to the available combinatory patterns. In addition, teaching sentence combining has been demonstrated to improve students' writing performance. Teaching grammar has not.

For Writing and Discussion

How would you describe your experience with grammar as a student in public school? For example, did you study traditional grammar? How many years did you study grammar? Was the instruction based on the idea that knowledge of grammar would improve your writing? Did it? If so, explain how. Did your teacher ever comment that some feature of your writing was "ungrammatical"? Did your teacher ever issue injunctions, such as never begin a sentence with a coordinating conjunction or never end a sentence with a preposition? Did you ever feel conflicted when you saw published writing that violated those injunctions? How would you describe your perception of the relation between grammar and writing prior to reading this chapter? Has this chapter changed your view? Why or why not? Consider some ways that you might use grammar and usage instruction to improve student writing. What approach would you advocate?

Write a lesson plan or essay describing how you might teach grammar using the principles described in this chapter.

Classroom Activity

In *The Teacher's Grammar Book,* I provided the following "make-believe" grammar (J. Williams, 1999), which is designed to illustrate how learning grammar rules and applying them to writing tasks require significantly different abilities. Complete the activity and then write about what you learned from it.

A Make-Believe Grammar

Directions: Study the following grammar rules.

Rule 1: All adjectives must follow the nouns they modify.

Example: The car *old* stopped at the light *red.*

Exception: Any adjective that modifies a noun signifying or related to a person will come before the noun, but the noun will take the suffix -o.

Example: The old *man-o* gave the flower to the young *woman-o* because he liked her pretty *face-o.*

Rule 2: The indefinite article is *zot.* (Indefinite articles are *a* and *an.*)

Example: At the circus, the clown tooted *zot* horn.

Exception: Indefinite articles that come before an adjective are *zots.*

Example: We saw *zots* old policeman riding *zots* brown horse.

Rule 3: The progressive verb form consists of *be + verb + ing,* but tense is marked as follows—*x* for past, and *y* for present.

Example: The man *be-y* washing his car.

Exception: All actions involving nonhumans form the progressive with *be + verb + ing,* but tense in all instances is marked with *k.*

Example: My dog *be-k* running in the yard.

Part 1

Directions: Use these rules to correct the following "ungrammatical" sentences:

1. The wind blew in over the dark mountains and chilled the young boys.
2. There was a strange look on the woman's face, as though she was thinking deep thoughts.
3. The waves were crashing against the beach, but the hardy surfers were waiting until the foamy crests were higher.
4. Several people strolled down the boardwalk and tossed a handful of bread crumbs at the screeching gulls that were flying overhead.
5. Macarena was getting cold because she had forgotten to bring even a light jacket.
6. Fritz was bundled up snug and warm in a down parka, but he was not going to offer his warm coat to Macarena.
7. Macarena began walking to her old Ford as the noisy gulls were swooping down at her.
8. Fritz was following slowly behind when one of the gulls stole a piece of a derelict's soggy Big Mac.
9. A few more birds distracted the derelict until he dropped the burger, and then a huge gull grabbed it in his yellow beak.
10. Meanwhile, a sullen Macarena slid into the driver's seat and drove off, leaving Fritz standing in the lot with a silly look on his silly face.

Part 2

Directions: In about ten minutes, write a description of the things you did before going to campus today. Be sure to use our make-believe grammar in your writing.

For Further Exploration

Amastae, J. (1984). The writing needs of Hispanic students. In B. Crannell (Ed.), *The writing needs of linguistically different students.* Washington, DC: SWRL Educational Research and Development.

Although the focus of this work is on broad social and pedagogical issues, the author notes that too often writing instruction for Hispanic students has been rooted in bottom-up, grammar-based approaches that do little to teach the skills students need to succeed.

Andrews, R., Torgerson, C., Beverton, S., Freeman, A., Locke, T., Low, G., Robinson, A., & Zhu, D. (2004). *The effect of grammar teaching (sentence combining) in English on 5 to 16 year old's accuracy and quality in written composition.* London: EPPI Centre.

The authors of this report performed a meta-analysis on 4,691 papers using inclusion/exclusion criteria to determine the strength of research design and methodology. From this initial pool, only 20 papers were deemed to be relevant to the question of whether sentence combining instruction had an effect on student writing performance. The authors concluded that such instruction is, indeed, effective.

Christensen, F. (1967). *Notes toward a new rhetoric: Six essays far teachers.* New York: Harper & Row.

This slim volume broke new ground in the area of sentence combining. The author explains how to teach sentence combining without requiring students to know much at all about grammar.

Connors, R. (2000). The erasure of the sentence. *College Composition and Communication, 52,* 95–128.

An important review of the efficacy of sentence combining, a technique that builds syntactic maturity without reliance on grammar instruction.

Coulson, A. (1996). Schooling and literacy over time: The rising cost of stagnation and decline. *Research in the Teaching of English, 30,* 311–327.

This article examines the decline in SAT scores since 1967, focusing on the precipitous decline in verbal scores. A leading cause of this decline is deemed to be the failure of schools to teach reading and writing effectively.

Crowhurst, M., & Piche, G. (1979). Audience and mode of discourse effects on syntactic complexity in writing at two grade levels. *Research in the Teaching of English, 13,* 101–109.

Although many people assume that grammar instruction results in syntactic complexity, there is no evidence to support this assumption. In fact, the authors show that this important factor in good writing is significantly influenced by audience and genre.

Gundlach, R. (1983). *How children learn to write: Perspectives on children's writing for educators and parents.* Washington, DC: National Institute of Education.

Grammar instruction is predicated on a bottom-up model of language learning. The author examines how top-down processes, related to the desire to communicate and use of symbols to convey information, underlie how children learn to write.

Parker, R. (1979). From Sputnik to Dartmouth: Trends in the teaching of composition. *English Journal 68,* 32–37.

This article analyzes some of the major trends in teaching composition from the 1950s through the 1960s. It addresses the role grammar played in composition instruction.

NOTES

1 Consider the following excerpt from a conversation recorded in a university cafeteria:
   A: "And so, like, what happened?"
   B: "Well, like, she like walks up to him, and she goes like, 'Where were you last night?' And he goes like, 'I was, you know, like hanging with Tom.' And she goes like, 'I talked to Tom like this morning,' and he goes like 'I've not seen him in like days.'"

2 Worth noting is the fact that colleges and universities in the US required a solid knowledge of Latin as well as Greek for admission until the 1930s.

3 Ungrammatical sentences are marked with an asterisk.

4 Constructions with questionable grammaticality are indicated by a question mark.

5 In these examples the present progressive and perfect verb forms, respectively, are shown in italics: Progressive—Maria *is going* to the dance with Raul. Perfect: Sarah *has left* the building.

6 In highly inflected languages, such as Japanese and Spanish, the subject is often identified by the form of the verb. In Spanish for example, a speaker has two ways of saying *I am hungry: Yo tengo hambre* or *Tengo hambre.* The second option, however, with the dropped subject *yo,* is far more common than the first.

7 Since the mid-1990s, many schools and school districts nationwide have actually banned homework, which may be a factor in the reported decline.

8 Also worth noting is that SAT writing scores dropped a total of five points between 2006, when the writing section was added, and 2010.

9 Note that the discussion in this section does not apply to students for whom English is their second language.

10 I sometimes ask my linguistics students to produce an ungrammatical sentence. At least 90% of the time, they offer the equivalent of *I ain't got no money.* After I explain why this sentence is grammatical, they try again and succeed, but it can take them ten seconds or more of visibly intense thought. They then struggle to articulate the construction because it is so unnatural.

REFERENCES

Alwin, D. (1991). Family of origin and cohort differences in verbal ability. *American Sociological Review, 56,* 625–638.

American Psychological Association. (2009). *Publication manual of the American Psychological Association* (6th ed.). Washington, DC: American Psychological Association.

Andrews, R., Torgerson, C., Beverton, S., Locke, T., Low, G., Robinson, A., & Zhu, D. (2004a). *The effect of grammar teaching (syntax) in English on 5 to 16 year olds' accuracy and quality in written composition.* London: EPPI Centre.

Andrews, R., Torgerson, C., Beverton, S., Locke, T., Low, G., Robinson, A., & Zhu, D. (2004b). *The effect of grammar teaching (sentence combining) in English on 5 to 16 year olds' accuracy and quality in written composition.* London: EPPI Centre.

Bailiff, M. (2010). New class combines composition, social media as part of general education reform. *Kentucky Kernel.* Lexington, KY: University of Kentucky. Retrieved December 23, 2010, from www.kykernel.com.

Barrett, J. L., & Johnson, A.H. (2003). The role of control in attributing intentional agency to inanimate objects. *Journal of Cognition and Culture, 3,* 208–217.

Bateman, D., & Zidonis, F. (1966). *The effect of a study of transformational grammar on the writing of ninth and tenth graders.* Champaign, IL: National Council of Teachers of English.

Bering, J. M. (2002). The existential theory of mind. *Review of General Psychology, 6,* 3–24.

Biber, D. (1988). *Variation across speech and writing.* Cambridge: Cambridge University Press.

Bloomfield, L. (1933). *Language.* New York: Holt, Reinhart, & Winston.

Boas, F. (1911). *Handbook of American Indian tribal languages.* Washington, DC: Smithsonian Institution.

Braddock, R., Lloyd-Jones, R., & Schoer. L. (1963). *Research in written composition.* Champaign, IL: National Council of Teachers of English.

Brown-Owens, A., Eason, M., & Lader, A. (2003). What effect does computer-mediated communication, specifically instant messaging, have on 8th grade writing competencies? Retrieved September 20, 2010, from www.usca.edu/medtech/courses/et780.

Bryant, P., Devine, M., Ledward, A., & Nunes, T. (2002). Spelling with apostrophes and understanding possession. *British Journal of Educational Psychology, 67,* 91–110.

Bryant, P., Nunes, T., & Bindman, M. (2004). The relations between children's linguistic awareness and spelling: The case of the apostrophe. *Reading and Writing, 12,* 253–276.

Bullock, R., & Weinberg, F. (2009). *The Norton field guide to writing* (2nd ed.). New York: W. W. Norton & Company.

Callaghan, T. (1978). The effects of sentence-combining exercises on the syntactic maturity, quality of writing, reading ability, and attitudes of ninth grade students. *Dissertation Abstracts International, 39,* 637-A.

Chafe, W. (1998). Language and the flow of thought. In M. Tomasello (Ed.), *The new psychology of language: Cognitive and functional approaches to language structure* (vol. 1) (pp. 111–150). Mahwah, NJ: Lawrence Erlbaum Associates.

Chipere, N. (2003). *Understanding complex sentences: Native speaker variation in syntactic competence.* London: Palgrave Macmillan.

Chomsky, N. (1957). *Syntactic structures.* The Hague, The Netherlands: Mouton.

Chomsky, N. (1965). *Aspects of the theory of syntax.* Cambridge, MA: MIT Press.

Chomsky, N. (1995). *The minimalist program.* Cambridge, MA: MIT Press.

Christian, D. (Ed.). (2010). *The Associated Press stylebook* (45th ed). New York: Basic Books.

Combs, W. (1977). Sentence-combining practice: Do gains in judgments of writing "quality" persist? *Journal of Educational Research, 70,* 318–321.

Connors, R. (2000). The erasure of the sentence. *College Composition and Communication, 52,* 96–128.

Cosimides, L., & Tooby, J. (1994). Origins of domain specificity: The evolution of functional organization. In L. A. Hirschfeld, & S. A. Gelman (Eds.), *Mapping the mind: Domain specificity in cognition and culture* (pp. 85–116). Cambridge: Cambridge University Press.

Crowley, S. (1989). Linguistics and composition instruction: 1950–1980. *Written Communication, 6,* 480–505.

Daiker, D., Kerek, A., & Morenberg, M. (1978). Sentence-combining and syntactic maturity in freshman English. *College Composition and Communication, 29,* 17–33.

Davis, F. (1984). In defense of grammar. *English Education, 16,* 151–164.

Du Bois, J. W. (2003). Discourse and grammar. In M. Tomasello (Ed.), *The new psychology of language: Cognitive and functional approaches to language structure* (vol. 2). New York: Psychology Press. (Original work published 2003, Lawrence Erlbaum Associates)

Du Bois, J. W., Schuetze-Coburn, S., Paolino, D., & Cumming, S. (1993). Outline of discourse transcription. In J. A. Edwards, & M. D. Lampert (Eds.), *Talking data: Transcription and coding in discourse research* (pp. 45–89). Hillsdale, NJ: Lawrence Erlbaum Associates.

Dunbar, R. (1997). *Grooming, gossip, and the evolution of language.* Cambridge, MA: Harvard University Press.

Elley, W., Barham, L., Lamb, H., & Wyllie, M. (1976). The role of grammar in a secondary school English curriculum. *New Zealand Journal of Educational Studies, 10,* 26–42. Reprinted in *Research in the Teaching of English, 10,* 5–21.

Fingelkurts, A. A., Fingelkurts, A. A., & Neves, C. (2009). Phenomenological architecture of a mind and operational architectonics of the brain: The unified metastable continuum. *New Mathematics and Natural Computation, 5,* 221–244.

Fogel, H., & Ehri, L. (2000). Teaching elementary students who speak black English vernacular to write in standard English: Effects of dialect transformation practice. *Contemporary Educational Psychology, 25,* 212–235.

Freeborn, D. (2006). *From Old English to Standard English: A course book in language variation across time* (3rd ed.). Ottawa: University of Ottawa Press.

Gale, I. (1968). An experimental study of two fifth-grade language-arts programs: An analysis of the writing of children taught linguistic grammar compared to those taught traditional grammar. *Dissertation Abstracts, 28,* 4156A.

Glencoe/McGraw-Hill, (2001). *Glencoe grammar and composition handbook, grade 10.* Boston: Glencoe/McGraw-Hill.

Glenn, N. D. (1994). Television watching, newspaper reading, and cohort differences in verbal ability. *Sociology of Education, 67,* 216–230.

Hacker, D. (2007). *A writer's reference* (6th ed.). New York: Bedford/St. Martin's.

Hayes, L. T., Wolfer, M. F., & Wolfe, D. P. (1996). Schoolbook simplification and its relation to the decline in SAT-verbal scores. *American Educational Research Journal, 33,* 489–508.

Hillocks, G. (1986). *Research on written composition: New directions for teaching.* Urbana, IL: National Conference on Research in English.

Holt, R. (1982). In defense of formal grammar. *Curriculum Review, 21,* 173–78.

Houghton-Mifflin. (2004). *Houghton-Mifflin English.* Boston: Houghton-Mifflin.

Howie, S. (1979). A study: The effects of sentence combining practice on the writing ability and reading level of ninth grade students. *Dissertation Abstracts International, 40,* 1980-A.

Hudson, R. (2001). Grammar teaching and writing skills: The research evidence. *Syntax in the Schools, 17,* 1–6.

Hudson, R. (2004, May). *Grammar for writing.* Paper presented at New Perspectives Conference, Exeter University.

Hunt, K. (1964). *Differences in grammatical structures written at three grade levels* (Cooperative Research Project No. 1998). Tallahassee: Florida State University.

Hunt, K. (1965). *Grammatical structures written at three grade levels* (NCTE Research Report No. 3). Champaign, IL: National Council of Teachers of English.

Karmiloff-Smith, A. (1992). *Beyond modularity: A developmental perspective on cognitive science.* Cambridge, MA: MIT Press.

Kolln. M. (1981). Closing the books on alchemy. *College Composition and Communication, 32,* 139–151.

Krashen, S. (1981). *The role of input (reading) and instruction in developing writing ability.* Working paper. Los Angeles: University of Southern California.

Krashen, S. (1985). *Writing research, theory, and applications.* New York: Pergamon.

Labov, W. (1970). *The study of nonstandard English.* Urbana, IL: National Council of Teachers of English.

Langacker, R. W. (2008). *Cognitive grammar: A basic introduction.* Oxford: Oxford University Press.

Laurinen, I. (1955). *The development of sentence sense in the light of the results attained in the teaching of writing in Finnish primary schools.* Unpublished doctoral dissertation, Helsinki University.

Lee, J. (2002). I think, therefore IM. *New York Times,* p. G1.

Leslie, A. M. (1994). ToMM, ToBy, and agency: Core architecture and domain specificity. In L. A. Hirschfeld, & S. A. Gelman (Eds.), *Mapping the mind: Domain specificity in cognition and culture* (pp. 119–148). Cambridge: Cambridge University Press.

Lunsford, A. (2009). *The everyday writer* (4th ed). New York: Bedford/St. Martin's.

Luskin, B. J., & Friedland, L. (1998). Task force report: Media psychology and new technologies. Retrieved September 20, 2010, from www.apa.org/divisions/div46/articles/luskin.pdf.

Modern Language Association. (2009). *MLA handbook for writers of research papers* (7th ed.). New York: The Modern Language Association.

National Endowment for the Arts. (2007). *To read or not to read: A question of national consequence* (Report No. 47). Washington, DC: National Endowment for the Arts.

Noguchi, R. (1991). *Grammar and the teaching of writing: Limits and possibilities.* Urbana, IL: NCTE.

O'Connor, A. (2005). Instant messaging: Friend or foe of student writing? Retrieved September 16, 2010, from www.newhorizons.org/strategies/literacy/oconnor.htm.

O'Hare. F. (1972). *Sentence combining: Improving student writing without formal grammar instruction.* NCTE Committee on Research Report Series, Number 15. Urbana, IL: National Council of Teachers of English.

Parker, F., & Campbell, K. (1993). Linguistics and writing: A reassessment. *College Composition and Communication, 44,* 295–314.

Perlovsky, L. I. (2009). Language and cognition. *Neural Networks, 22,* 247–257.

Pinker, S. (1994). *The language instinct: How the mind creates language.* New York: William Morrow.

Pinker, S. (2002). *The blank slate.* New York: Penguin Books.

Ravitch, D. (2004). *The language police: How pressure groups restrict what children learn.* New York: Random House.

Reid, A. (2007). *The two virtuals: New media and composition.* Anderson, SC: Parlor Press.

Rumelhart, D., & McClelland, J. (1986). *Parallel distributed processing: Explorations in the microstructure of cognition* (vol. 1). Cambridge, MA: MIT Press.

Scholl, B. J., & Tremoulet, P. D. (2000). Perceptual causality and animacy. *Trends in Cognitive Sciences, 4,* 299–309.

Schroeder, C., Bizzell, P., & Fox, H. (2002). *Alt dis: Alternative discourses and the academy.* Upper Montclair, NJ: Boynton-Cook.

Selber, S. (2010). *Rhetorics and technologies: New directions in writing and composition.* Columbia, SC: University of South Carolina Press.

Simmons, D. C., & Kameenui, E. J. (Eds.). (1998). *What reading research tells us about children with diverse learning needs.* Mahwah, NJ: Lawrence Erlbaum Associates.

Stedman, L. C., & Kaestle, C. E. (1987). Literacy and reading performance in the United States from 1880 to the present. *Reading Research Quarterly, 22,* 8–46.

Stotsky, S. (1999). *Losing our language: How multicultural classroom instruction is undermining our children's ability to read, write, and reason.* New York: Free Press.

Sullivan, M. (1978). The effects of sentence-combining exercises on syntactic maturity, quality of writing, reading ability, and attitudes of students in grade eleven. *Dissertation Abstracts International, 39,* 1197-A.

Sykes, C. J. (1995). *Dumbing down our kids: Why American children feel good about themselves but can't read, write, or add.* New York: Macmillan.

Taylor, J. R. (2002). *Cognitive grammar.* Oxford: Oxford University Press.

Thompson, S. A., & Hopper, P. J. (2001). Transitivity, clause structure, and argument structure: Evidence from conversation. In J. L. Bybee, & P. J. Hopper (Eds.), *Frequency and the emergence of linguistic structure* (pp. 27–60). Amsterdam: John Benjamins.

Tremlin, T. (2006). *Minds and gods: The cognitive foundations of religion.* Oxford: Oxford University Press.

US Department of Education, National Center for Education Statistics. (1996). *NAEP 1996 trends in writing: Fluency and writing conventions.* Washington, DC: US Government Printing Office.

US Department of Education, National Center for Education Statistics. (1999). *1998 writing: Report card for the nation and the states.* Washington, DC: US Government Printing Office.

US Department of Education, National Center for Education Statistics. (2001). *The 1984 and 1999 long-term trend assessment.* Washington, DC: US Government Printing Office.

US Department of Education, National Center for Education Statistics. (2002). *National Assessment of Educational Progress 1984 and 1999 long-term trend assessment in the condition of education 2001.* Retrieved September 12, 2010, from http://nces.ed.gov.

US Department of Education, National Center for Education Statistics. (2005). *The nation's report card: Reading 2005.* Washington, DC: US Government Printing Office.

US Department of Education, National Center for Education Statistics. (2010a). *The nation's report card: Writing 2007: National assessment of academic progress at grades 8 and 12.* Washington, DC: US Government Printing Office.

US Department of Education, National Center for Education Statistics. (2010b). *The nation's report card: Reading 2009.* Washington, DC: US Government Printing Office.

White, R. (1965). The effect of structural linguistics on improving English composition compared to that of prescriptive grammar or the absence of grammar instruction. *Dissertation Abstracts, 25,* 5032.

Whitehead, C. (1966). The effect of grammar diagramming on student writing skills. *Dissertation Abstracts, 26,* 3710.

Williams, G. (1995). *Learning systemic functional grammar in primary schools.* Sydney: Macquarie University Style Council.

Williams, J. D. (1993). Rule-governed approaches to language and composition. *Written Communication, 10,* 542–568.

Williams, J. D. (1999). *The teacher's grammar book.* Mahwah, NJ: Lawrence Erlbaum.

Williams, J. D. (2003). *Preparing to teach writing: Research, theory, and practice* (3rd ed.). Mahwah, NJ: Lawrence Erlbaum Associates.

Williams, J. D. (2005). *The teacher's grammar book* (2nd ed.). New York: Routledge.

Williams, J. D. (2009). *An introduction to classical rhetoric: Essential readings.* London: Wiley-Blackwell.

Wilson, J. A., & Gove, W. R. (1999). The intercohort decline in verbal ability: Does it exist? *American Sociological Review, 64,* 253–266.

Wyse, D. (2001). Grammar for writing? A critical review of empirical evidence. *British Journal of Educational Studies, 49,* 411–427.

Wysocki, A. F., Johnson-Eilola, J., Selfe, C., & Sirc, G. (2004). *Writing new media: Theory and applications for expanding the teaching of composition.* Logan, UT: Utah State University Press.

Reading

GRAMMAR, GRAMMARS, AND THE TEACHING OF GRAMMAR

Patrick Hartwell

For me the grammar issue was settled at least twenty years ago with the conclusion offered by Richard Braddock, Richard Lloyd-Jones and Lowell Schoer in 1963.

> In view of the widespread agreement of research studies based upon many types of students and teachers, the conclusion can be stated in strong and unqualified terms: the teaching of formal grammar has a negligible or, because it usually displaces some instruction and practice in composition, even a harmful effect on improvement in writing.[1]

Indeed, I would agree with Janet Emig that the grammar issue is a prime example of "magical thinking": the assumption that students will learn only what we teach and only because we teach.[2]

But the grammar issue, as we will see, is a complicated one. And, perhaps surprisingly, it remains controversial, with the regular appearance of papers defending the teaching of formal grammar or attacking it.[3] Thus Janice Neuleib, writing on "The Relation of Formal Grammar to composition" in *College Composition and Communication* (23 [1977], 247–50), is tempted "to sputter on paper" at reading the quotation above (p. 248), and Martha Kolln, writing in the same journal three years later ("Closing the Books on Alchemy," *CCC* 32 [1981], 139–51), labels people like me "alchemists" for our perverse beliefs. Neuleib reviews five experimental studies, most of them concluding that formal grammar instruction has no effect on the quality of students' writing nor on their ability to avoid error. Yet she renders in effect a Scots verdict of "Not proven" and calls for more research on the issue. Similarly, Kolln reviews six experimental studies that arrive at similar conclusions, only one of them overlapping with the studies cited by Neuleib. She calls for more careful definition of the word grammar—her definition being "the internalized system that native speakers of a language share" (p. 140)—and she concludes with a stirring call to place grammar instruction at the center of the composition curriculum: "our goal should be to help students understand the system they know unconsciously as native speakers, to teach them the necessary categories and labels that will enable them to think about and talk about their language" (p. 150). Certainly our textbooks and our pedagogies—though they vary widely in what they see as "necessary categories and labels"—continue to emphasize mastery of formal grammar, and popular discussions of a presumed literacy crisis are almost unanimous in their call for a renewed emphasis on the teaching of formal grammar, seen as basic for success in writing.[4]

An Instructive Example

It is worth noting at the outset that both sides in this dispute—the grammarians and the antigrammarians—articulate the issue in the same positivistic terms: what does experimental research tell us about the value of teaching formal grammar? But seventy-five years of experimental research has for all practical purposes told us nothing. The two sides are unable to agree on how to interpret such research. Studies are interpreted in terms of one's prior assumptions about the value of teaching grammar: their results seem not to change those assumptions. Thus the basis of the discussion, a basis shared by Kolln and Neuleib and by Braddock and his colleagues—"what does educational research tell us?"—seems designed to perpetuate, not to resolve, the issue. A single example will be instructive. In 1976 and then at greater length in 1979, W. B. Elley, I. H. Barham, H. Lamb, and M. Wyllie reported on a three-year experiment in New Zealand, comparing the relative effectiveness at the high school level of instruction in transformational grammar, instruction in traditional grammar, and no grammar instruction.[5] They concluded that the formal study of grammar, whether transformational or traditional, improved neither writing quality nor control over surface correctness.

> After two years, no differences were detected in writing performance or language competence; after three years small differences appeared in some minor conventions favoring the TG [transformational grammar] group, but these were more than offset by the less positive attitudes they showed towards their English studies. (p. 18)

Anthony Petrosky, in a review of research ("Grammar Instruction: What We Know," *English Journal*, 66, No. 9 [1977], 86–88), agreed with this conclusion, finding the study to be carefully designed, "representative of the best kind of educational research" (p. 86), its validity "unquestionable" (p. 88). Yet Janice Neuleib in her essay found the same conclusions to be "startling" and questioned whether the findings could be generalized beyond the target population, New Zealand high school students. Martha Kolln, when her attention is drawn to the study ("Reply to Ron Shook," *CCC*, 32 [1981], 139–151), thinks the whole experiment "suspicious." And John Mellon has been willing to use the study to defend the teaching of grammar; the study of Elley and his colleagues, he has argued, shows that teaching grammar does no harm.[6]

It would seem unlikely, therefore, that further experimental research, in and of itself, will resolve the grammar issue. Any experimental design can be nit-picked, any experimental population can be criticized, and any experimental conclusion can be questioned or, more often, ignored. In fact, it may well be that the grammar question is not open to resolution by experimental research, that, as Noam Chomsky has argued in *Reflections on Language* (New York: Pantheon, 1975), criticizing the trivialization of human learning by behavioral psychologists, the issue is simply misdefined.

> There will be "good experiments" only in domains that lie outside the organism's cognitive capacity. For example, there will be no "good experiments" in the study of human learning.
>
> This discipline ... will, of necessity, avoid those domains in which an organism is specially designed to acquire rich cognitive structures that enter into its life in an intimate fashion. The discipline will be of virtually no intellectual interest, it seems to me, since it is restricting itself in principle to those questions that are guaranteed to tell us little about the nature of organisms. (p. 36)

Asking The Right Questions

As a result, though I will look briefly at the tradition of experimental research, my primary goal in this essay is to articulate the grammar issue in different and, I would hope, more productive terms. Specifically, I want to ask four questions:

1. Why is the grammar issue so important? Why has it been the dominant focus of composition research for the last seventy-five years?
2. What definitions of the word *grammar* are needed to articulate the grammar issue intelligibly?
3. What do findings in cognate disciplines suggest about the value of formal grammar instruction?

4. What is our theory of language, and what does it predict about the value of formal grammar instruction? (This question—"what does our theory of language predict?"—seems a much more powerful question than "what does educational research tell us?")

In exploring these questions I will attempt to be fully explicit about issues, terms, and assumptions. I hope that both proponents and opponents of formal grammar instruction would agree that these are useful as shared points of reference: care in definition, full examination of the evidence, reference to relevant work in cognate disciplines, and explicit analysis of the theoretical bases of the issue.

But even with that gesture of harmony it will be difficult to articulate the issue in a balanced way, one that will be acceptable to both sides. After all, we are dealing with a professional dispute in which one side accuses the other of "magical thinking," and in turn that side responds by charging the other as "alchemists." Thus we might suspect that the grammar issue is itself embedded in larger models of the transmission of literacy, part of quite different assumptions about the teaching of composition.

Those of us who dismiss the teaching of formal grammar have a model of composition instruction that makes the grammar issue "uninteresting" in a scientific sense. Our model predicts a rich and complex interaction of learner and environment in mastering literacy, an interaction that has little to do with sequences of skills instruction as such. Those who defend the teaching of grammar tend to have a model of composition instruction that is rigidly skills-centered and rigidly sequential: the formal teaching of grammar, as the first step in that sequence, is the cornerstone or linchpin. Grammar teaching is thus supremely interesting, naturally a dominant focus for educational research. The controversy over the value of grammar instruction, then, is inseparable from two other issues: the issues of sequence in the teaching of composition and of the role of the composition teacher. Consider, for example, the force of these two issues in Janice Neuleib's conclusion: after calling for yet more experimental research on the value of teaching grammar, she ends with an absolute (and unsupported) claim about sequences and teacher roles in composition.

> We do know, however, that some things must be taught at different levels. Insistence on adherence to usage norms by composition teachers does improve usage. Students can learn to organize their papers if teachers do not accept papers that are disorganized. Perhaps composition teachers can teach those two abilities before they begin the more difficult tasks of developing syntactic sophistication and a winning style. ("The Relation of Formal Grammar to Composition," p. 250)

(One might want to ask, in passing, whether "usage norms" exist in the monolithic fashion the phrase suggests and whether refusing to accept disorganized papers is our best available pedagogy for teaching arrangement.)[7]

But I want to focus on the notion of sequence that makes the grammar issue so important: first grammar, then usage, then some absolute model of organization, all controlled by the teacher at the center of the learning process with other matters, those of rhetorical weight—"syntactic sophistication and a winning style"—pushed off to the future. It is not surprising that we call each other names: those of us who question the value of teaching grammar are in fact shaking the whole elaborate edifice of traditional composition instruction.

The Five Meanings of "Grammar"

Given its centrality to a well-established way of teaching composition, I need to go about the business of defining grammar rather carefully, particularly in view of Kolln's criticism of the lack of care in earlier discussions. Therefore I will build upon a seminal discussion of the word *grammar* offered a generation ago, in 1954, by W. Nelson Francis, often excerpted as "The Three Meanings of Grammar."[8] It is worth reprinting at length, if only to re-establish it as a reference point for future discussions.

> The first thing we mean by "grammar" is "the set of formal patterns in which the words of a language are arranged in order to convey larger meanings." It is not necessary that we be able to discuss these patterns self-consciously in order to be able to use them. In fact, all speakers of a language above the age of five or six know how to use its complex forms of organization with considerable skill; in this sense of the word—call it "Grammar 1"—they are thoroughly familiar with its grammar.
>
> The second meaning of "grammar"—call it "Grammar 2"—is "the branch of linguistic science which is concerned with the description, analysis, and formulization of formal language patterns." Just as gravity was in full operation before Newton's apple fell, so grammar in the first sense was in full operation before anyone formulated the first rule that began the history of grammar as a study.
>
> The third sense in which people use the word "grammar" is "linguistic etiquette." This we may call "Grammar 3." The word in this sense is often coupled with a derogatory adjective: we say that the expression "he ain't here" is "bad grammar." ...
>
> As has already been suggested, much confusion arises from mixing these meanings. One hears a good deal of criticism of teachers of English couched in such terms as "they don't teach grammar any more." Criticism of this sort is based on the wholly unproven assumption that teaching Grammar 2 will improve the student's proficiency in Grammar 1 or improve his manners in Grammar 3. Actually, the form of Grammar 2 which is usually taught is a very inaccurate and misleading analysis of the facts of Grammar 1; and it therefore is of highly questionable value in improving a person's ability to handle the structural patterns of his language. (pp. 300–301)

Francis' Grammar 3 is, of course, not grammar at all, but usage. One would like to assume that Joseph Williams' recent discussion of usage ("The Phenomenology of Error," *CCC*, 32 [1981], 152–168), along with his references, has placed those shibboleths in a proper perspective. But I doubt it, and I suspect that popular discussions of the grammar issue will be as flawed by the intrusion of usage issues as past discussions have been. At any rate I will make only passing reference to Grammar 3—usage—naively assuming that this issue has been discussed elsewhere and that my readers are familiar with those discussions.

We need also to make further discriminations about Francis' Grammar 2, given that the purpose of his 1954 article was to substitute for one form of Grammar 2, that "inaccurate and misleading" form "which is usually taught," another form, that of American structuralist grammar. Here we can make use of a still earlier discussion, one going back to the days when *PMLA* was willing to publish articles on rhetoric and linguistics, to a 1927 article by Charles Carpenter Fries, "The Rules of the Common School Grammars" (42 [1927], 221–237). Fries there distinguished between the scientific tradition of language study (to which we will now delimit Francis Grammar 2, scientific grammar) and the separate tradition of "the common school grammars," developed unscientifically, largely based on two inadequate principles—appeals to "logical principles," like "two negatives make a positive," and analogy to Latin grammar; thus, Charlton Laird's characterization, "the grammar of Latin, ingeniously warped to suggest English" (*Language in America* [New York: World, 1970], p. 294). There is, of course, a direct link between the "common school grammars" that Fries criticized in 1927 and the grammar-based texts of today, and thus it seems wise, as Karl Dykema suggests ("Where Our Grammar Came From," *CE*, 22 (1961), 455–465), to separate Grammar 2, "scientific grammar," from Grammar 4, "school grammar," the latter meaning, quite literally, "the grammars used in the schools."

Further, since Martha Kolln points to the adaptation of Christensen's sentence rhetoric in a recent sentence-combining text as an example of the proper emphasis on "grammar" ("Closing the Books on Alchemy," p. 140), it is worth separating out, as still another meaning of *grammar,* Grammar 5, "stylistic grammar," defined as "grammatical terms used in the interest of teaching prose style." And, since stylistic grammars abound, with widely variant terms and emphases, we might appropriately speak parenthetically of specific forms of Grammar 5—Grammar 5 (Lanham); Grammar 5 (Strunk and White); Grammar 5 (Williams, Style); even Grammar 5 (Christensen, as adapted by Daiker, Kerek, and Morenberg).[9]

The Grammar in Our Heads

With these definitions in mind, let us return to Francis' Grammar 1, admirably defined by Kolln as "the internalized system of rules that speakers of a language share" ("Closing the Books on Alchemy," p. 140), or, to put it more simply, the grammar in our heads. Three features of Grammar 1 need to be stressed; first, its special status as an "internalized system of rules," as tacit and unconscious knowledge; second, the abstract, even counterintuitive, nature of these rules, insofar as we are able to approximate them indirectly as Grammar 2 statements; and third, the way in which the form of one's Grammar 1 seems profoundly affected by the acquisition of literacy. This sort of review is designed to firm up our theory of language, so that we can ask what it predicts about the value of teaching formal grammar.

A simple thought experiment will isolate the special status of Grammar 1 knowledge. I have asked members of a number of different groups—from sixth graders to college freshmen to high-school teachers—to give me the rule for ordering adjectives of nationality, age, and number in English. The response is always the same: "We don't know the rule." Yet when I ask these groups to perform an active language task, they show productive control over the rule they have denied knowing. I ask them to arrange the following words in a natural order:

French   the   young   girls   four

I have never seen a native speaker of English who did not immediately produce the natural order, "the four young French girls." The rule is that in English the order of adjectives is first, number, second, age, and third, nationality. Native speakers can create analogous phrases using the rule—"the seventy-three aged Scandinavian lechers"; and the drive for meaning is so great that they will create contexts to make sense out of violations of the rule, as in foregrounding for emphasis: "I want to talk to the French four young girls." (I immediately envision a large room, perhaps a banquet hall, filled with tables at which are seated groups of four young girls, each group of a different nationality.) So Grammar 1 is eminently usable knowledge—the way we make our life through language—but it is not accessible knowledge; in a profound sense, we do not know that we have it. Thus neurolinguist Z. N. Pylyshvn speaks of Grammar 1 as "autonomous," separate from common-sense reasoning, and as ""cognitively impenetrable," not available for direct examination.[10] In philosophy and linguistics, the distinction is made between formal, conscious, "knowing about" knowledge (like Grammar 2 knowledge) and tacit, unconscious, "knowing how" knowledge (like Grammar 1 knowledge). The importance of this distinction for the teaching of composition—it provides a powerful theoretical justification for mistrusting the ability of Grammar 2 (or Grammar 4) knowledge to affect Grammar 1 performance—was pointed out in this journal by Martin Steinmann, Jr., in 1966 ("Rhetorical Research," *CE,* 27 [1966], 278–285).

Further, the more we learn about Grammar 1—and most linguists would agree that we know surprisingly little about it—the more abstract and implicit it seems. This abstractness can be illustrated with an experiment devised by Lise Menn and reported by Morris Halle,[11] about our rule for forming plurals in speech. It is obvious that we do indeed have a "rule" for forming plurals, for we do not memorize the plural of each noun separately. You will demonstrate productive control over that rule by forming the spoken plurals of the nonsense words below:

thole   flitch   plast

Halle offers two ways of formalizing a Grammar 2 equivalent of this Grammar 1 ability. One form *of the rule* is the following, stated in terms *of* speech sounds:

a.   If the noun ends in /s z š ž č Ĵ/, add /ɪz/;

b.   otherwise, if the noun ends in /p t k f Ø/, add /s/;

c.   otherwise, add /z/.[11]

This rule comes close to what we literate adults consider to be an adequate rule for plurals in writing, like the rules, for example, taken from a recent "common school grammar," Eric Gould's *Reading into Writing: A Rhetoric, Reader, and Handbook* (Boston: Houghton Mifflin, 1983):

> *Plurals* can be tricky. If you are unsure of a plural, then check it in the dictionary. The general rules are
> Add *s* to the singular: *girls, tables*
> Add *es* to nouns ending in *ch, sh, x* or *s: churches, boxes, wishes*
> Add *es* to nouns ending in *y* and preceded by a vowel once you have changed *y* to *i: monies, companies.* (p. 666)

(But note the persistent inadequacy of such Grammar 4 rules: here, as I read it, the rule is inadequate to explain the plurals of *ray* and *tray,* even to explain the collective noun *monies,* not a plural at all, formed from the mass noun *money* and offered as an example.) A second form of the rule would make use of much more abstract entities, sound features:

a.   If the noun ends with a sound that is [coronal, strident], add /+z/;
b.   otherwise, if the noun ends with a sound that is [non-voiced], add /s/;
c.   otherwise, add /z/.

(The notion of "sound features" is itself rather abstract, perhaps new to readers not trained in linguistics. But such readers should be able to recognize that the spoken plurals of *lip* and *duck,* the sound [s], differ from the spoken plurals of *sea* and *gnu,* the sound [z], only in that the sounds of the latter are "voiced"—one's vocal cords vibrate—while the sounds of the former are "non-voiced.")

To test the psychologically operative rule, the Grammar 1 rule, native speakers of English were asked to form the plural of the last name of the composer Johann Sebastian *Bach,* a sound [x], unique in American (though not in Scottish) English. If speakers follow the first rule above, using word endings, they would reject a) and b), then apply c), producing the plural as /baxz/, with word-final /z/. (If writers were to follow the rule of the common school grammar, they would produce the written plural *Baches,* apparently, given the form of the rule, on analogy with *churches.*) If speakers follow the second rule, they would have to analyze the sound [x] as [non-labial, noncoronal, dorsal, non-voiced, and non-strident], producing the plural as /baxs/, with word-final /s/. Native speakers of American English overwhelmingly produce the plural as /baxs/. They use knowledge that Halle characterizes as "unlearned and untaught" (p. 140).

Now such a conclusion is counterintuitive—certainly it departs maximally from Grammar 4 rules for forming plurals. It seems that native speakers of English behave as if they have productive control, as Grammar 1 knowledge, of abstract sound features (± coronal, ± strident, and so on) which are available as conscious, Grammar 2 knowledge only to trained linguists—and, indeed, formally available only within the last hundred years or so. ("Behave as if," in that last sentence, is a necessary hedge, to underscore the difficulty of "knowing about" Grammar 1.)

Moreover, as the example of plural rules suggests, the form of the Grammar 1 in the heads of literate adults seems profoundly affected by the acquisition of literacy. Obviously, literate adults have access to different morphological codes: the abstract print -s underlying the predictable /s/ and /z/ plurals, the abstract print -ed underlying the spoken past tense markers /t/, as in "walked," /əd/, as in "surrounded," /d/, as in "scored," and the symbol /q/ for no surface realization, as in the relaxed standard pronunciation of "I walked to the store." Literate adults also have access to distinctions preserved only in the code of print (for example, the distinction between "a good sailer" and "a good sailor" that Mark Aranoff points out in "An English Spelling Convention," *Linguistic Inquiry*, 9 [1978], 299–303). More significantly, Irene Moscowitz speculates that the ability of third graders to form abstract nouns on analogy with pairs like *divine::divinity* and *serene::serenity*, where the spoken vowel changes but the spelling preserves meaning, is a factor of knowing how to read. Carol Chomsky finds a three-stage developmental sequence in the grammatical performance of seven-year-olds, related to measures of kind and variety of reading; and Rita S. Brause finds a nine-stage developmental sequence in the ability to understand semantic ambiguity, extending from fourth graders to graduate students.[12] John Mills and Gordon Hemsley find that level of education, and presumably level of literacy, influence judgments of grammaticality, concluding that literacy changes the deep structure of one's internal grammar; Jean Whyte finds that oral language functions develop differently in readers and non-readers; José Morais, Jésus Alegria, and Paul Bertelson find that illiterate adults are unable to add or delete sounds at the beginning of nonsense words, suggesting that awareness of speech as a series of phones is provided by learning to read an alphabetic code. Two experiments—one conducted by Charles A. Ferguson, the other by Lary E. Hamilton and David Barton—find that adults' ability to recognize segmentation in speech is related to degree of literacy, not to amount of schooling or general ability.[13]

It is worth noting that none of these investigators would suggest that the developmental sequences they have uncovered be isolated and taught as discrete skills. They are natural concomitants of literacy, and they seem best characterized not as isolated rules but as developing schemata, broad strategies for approaching written language.

Grammar 2

We can, of course, attempt to approximate the rules or schemata of Grammar 1 by writing fully explicit descriptions that model the competence of a native speaker. Such rules, like the rules for pluralizing nouns or ordering adjectives discussed above, are the goal of the science of linguistics, that is, Grammar 2. There are a number of scientific grammars—an older structuralist model and several versions within a generative-transformational paradigm, not to mention isolated schools like tagmemic grammar, Montague grammar, and the like. In fact, we cannot think of Grammar 2 as a stable entity, for its form changes with each new issue of each linguistics journal, as new "rules of grammar" are proposed and debated. Thus Grammar 2, though of great theoretical interest to the composition teacher, is of little practical use in the classroom, as Constance Weaver has pointed out (*Grammar for Teachers* [Urbana, Ill.: NCTE, 1979], pp. 3–6). Indeed Grammar 2 is a scientific model of Grammar 1, not a description of it, so that questions of psychological reality, while important, are less important than other, more theoretical factors, such as the elegance of formulation or the global power of rules. We might, for example, wish to replace the rule for ordering adjectives of age, number, and nationality cited above with a more general rule—what linguists call a "fuzzy" rule—that adjectives in English are ordered by their abstract quality of "nouniness": adjectives that are very much like nouns, like *French* or *Scandinavian*, come physically closer to nouns than do adjectives that are less "nouny," like *four* or *aged*. But our motivation for accepting the broader rule would be its global power, not its psychological reality.[14]

I try to consider a hostile reader, one committed to the teaching of grammar, and I try to think of ways to hammer in the central point of this distinction, that the rules of Grammar 2 are simply unconnected to productive control over Grammar 1. I can argue from authority: Noam Chomsky has touched on this point whenever he has concerned himself with the implications of linguistics for language teaching, and years ago transformationalist Mark Lester stated unequivocally, "there simply appears to be no correlation between a writer's study of language and his ability to write."[15] I can cite analogies offered by others: Francis Christensen's analogy in an essay originally published in 1962 that formal grammar study would be "to invite a centipede to attend to the sequence of his legs in motion,"[16] or James Britton's analogy, offered informally after a conference presentation, that grammar study would be like forcing starving people to master the use of a knife and fork before allowing them to eat. I can offer analogies of my own, contemplating the wisdom of asking a pool player to master the physics of momentum before taking up a cue or of making a prospective driver get a degree in automotive engineering before engaging the clutch. I consider a hypothetical argument, that if Grammar 2 knowledge affected Grammar 1 performance, then linguists would be our best writers. (I can certify that they are, on the whole, not.) Such a position, after all, is only in accord with other domains of science: the formula for catching a fly ball in baseball ("Playing It by Ear," *Scientific American,* 248, No. 4 [1983], 76) is of such complexity that it is beyond my understanding and, I would suspect, that of many workaday centerfielders. But perhaps I can best hammer in this claim—that Grammar 2 knowledge has no effect on Grammar 1 performance—by offering a demonstration.

The diagram below is an attempt by Thomas N. Huckin and Leslie A. Olsen (*English for Science and Technology* [New York: McGraw-Hill, 1983]) to offer, for students of English as a second language, a fully explicit formution of what is, for native speakers, a trivial rule of the language—the choice of definite article, indefinite article, or no definite article.

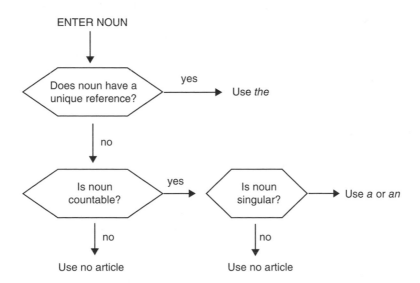

There are obvious limits to such a formulation, for article choice in English is less a matter of rule than of idiom ("I went to college" versus "I went to a university" versus British "I went to university"), real-world knowledge (using indefinite "I went into a house" instantiates definite "I looked at the ceiling," and indefinite "I visited a university" instantiates definite "I talked with the professors) and stylistic choice (the last sentence above might alternatively end with "the choice of the definite article, the indefinite article, or no article") Huckin and Olsen invite non-native speakers to use the rule consciously to justify article choice in technical prose, such as the passage below from P. F. Brandwein (*Matter: An Earth Science* [New York: Harcourt Brace Jovanovich, 1975]). I invite you to spend a couple of minutes doing the same thing, with the understanding that this exercise is a test case: you are using a very explicit rule to justify a fairly straightforward issue of grammatical choice.

> Imagine a cannon on top of ___ highest mountain on earth. It is firing ___ cannonballs horizontally. ___ first cannonball fired follows its path. As ___ cannonball moves, gravity pulls it down, and it soon hits ___ ground. Now ___ velocity with which each succeeding cannonball is fired is increased. Thus, ___ cannonball goes farther each time. Cannonball 2 goes farther than ___ cannonball 1 although each is being pulled by ___ gravity toward the earth all ___ time. ___ last cannonball is fired with such tremendous velocity that it goes completely around ___ earth. It returns to ___ mountaintop and continues around the earth again and again. ___ cannonball's inertia causes it to continue in motion indefinitely in ___ orbit around earth. In such a situation, we could consider ___ cannonball to be artificial satellite, just like ___ weather satellites launched by ___ U.S. Weather Service. (p. 209)

Most native speakers of English who have attempted this exercise report a great deal of frustration, a curious sense of working against, rather than with, the rule. The rule, however valuable it may be for non-native speakers, is, for the most part, simply unusable for native speakers of the language.

Cognate Areas of Research

We can corroborate this demonstration by turning to research in two cognate areas, studies of the induction of rules of artificial languages and studies of the role of formal rules in second language acquisition. Psychologists have studied the ability of subjects to learn artificial languages, usually constructed of nonsense syllables or letter strings. Such languages can be described by phrase structure rules:

$$S \Rightarrow VX$$
$$X \Rightarrow MX$$

More clearly, they can be presented as flow diagrams, as below:

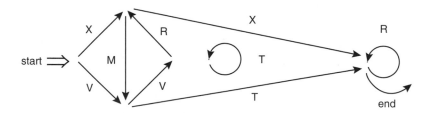

This diagram produces "sentences" like the following:

VVTRXRR.	XMVTTRX.	XXRR.
XMVRMT.	VVTTRMT.	XMTRRR.

The following "sentences" would be "ungrammatical" in this language:

*VMXTT.	*RTXVVT.	TRVXXVVM.

Arthur S. Reber, in a classic 1967 experiment, demonstrated that mere exposure to grammatical sentences produced tacit learning: subjects who copied several grammatical sentences performed far above chance in judging the grammaticality of other letter strings. Further experiments have shown that providing subjects with formal rules remarkably degrades performance: subjects given the "rules of the language" do much less well in acquiring the rules than do subjects not given the rules. Indeed, even telling subjects that they are to induce the rules of an artificial language degrades performance. Such laboratory experiments are admittedly contrived, but they confirm predictions that our theory of language would make about the value of formal rules in language learning.[17]

The thrust of recent research in second language learning similarly works to constrain the value of formal grammar rules. The most explicit statement of the value of formal rules is that of Stephen D. Krashen's monitor model.[18] Krashen divides second language mastery into *acquisition*—tacit, informal mastery, akin to first language acquisition—and formal learning—conscious application of Grammar 2 rules, which he calls "monitoring" output. In another essay Krashen uses his model to predict a highly individual use of the monitor and a highly constrained role for formal rules:

> Some adults (and very few children) are able to use conscious rules to increase the grammatical accuracy of their output, and even for these people, very strict conditions need to be met before the conscious grammar can be applied.[19]

In *Principles and Practice in Second Language Acquisition* (New York: Pergamon, 1982) Krashen outlines these conditions by means of a series of concentric circles, beginning with a large circle denoting the rules of English and a smaller circle denoting the subset of those rules described by formal linguists (adding that most linguists would protest that the size of this circle is much too large):

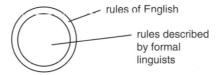

(p. 92)

Krashen then adds smaller circles, as shown below—a subset of the rules described by formal linguists that would be known to applied linguists, a subset of those rules that would be available to the best teachers, and then a subset of those rules that teachers might choose to present to second language learners:

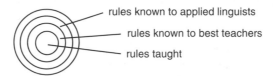

(P. 93)

Of course, as Krashen notes, not all the rules taught will be learned, and not all those learned will be available, as what he calls "mental baggage" (p. 94), for conscious use.

An experiment by Ellen Bialystock, asking English speakers learning French to judge the grammaticality of taped sentences, complicates this issue, for reaction time data suggest that learners first make an intuitive judgment of grammaticality, using implicit or Grammar 1 knowledge, and only then search for formal explanations, using explicit or Grammar 2 knowledge.[20] This distinction would suggest that Grammar 2 knowledge is of use to second language learners only after the principle has already been mastered as tacit Grammar 1 knowledge. In the terms of Krashen's model, learning never becomes acquisition (*Principles*, p. 86).

An ingenious experiment by Herbert W. Seliger complicates the issue yet further ("On the Nature and Function of Language Rules in Language Learning," *TESOL Quarterly*, 13 [1979], 359–369). Seliger asked native and non-native speakers of English to orally identify pictures of objects (e.g., "an apple," "a pear," "a book," "an umbrella"), noting whether they used the correct form of the indefinite articles *a* and *an*. He then asked each speaker to state the rule for choosing between *a* and *an*. He found no correlation between the ability to state the rule and the ability to apply it correctly, either with native or non-native speakers. Indeed, three of four adult non-native speakers in his sample produced a correct form of the rule, but they did not apply it in speaking. A strong conclusion from this experiment would be that formal rules of grammar seem to have no value whatsoever. Seliger, however, suggests a more paradoxical interpretation. Rules are of no use, he agrees, but some people think they are, and for these people, assuming that they have internalized the rules, even inadequate rules are of heuristic value, for they allow them to access the internal rules they actually use.

The Incantations of The "Common School Grammars"

Such a paradox may explain the fascination we have as teachers with "rules of grammar" of the Grammar 4 variety, the "rules" of the "common school grammars." Again and again such rules are inadequate to the facts of written language; you will recall that we have known this since Francis' 1927 study. R. Scott Baldwin and James M. Coady, studying how readers respond to punctuation signals ("Psycholinguistic Approaches to a Theory of Punctuation," *Journal of Reading Behavior, 10* [1978], 363–83), conclude that conventional rules of punctuation are "a complete sham" (p. 375). My own favorite is the Grammar 4 rule for showing possession, always expressed in terms of adding -'s or -s' to nouns, while our internal grammar, if you think about it, adds possession to noun phrases, albeit under severe stylistic constraints: "the horses of the Queen of England" are "the Queen of England's horses" and "the feathers of the duck over there" are "the duck over there's feathers." Suzette Haden Elgin refers to the "rules" of Grammar 4 as "incantations" (*Never Mind the Trees*, p. 9: see footnote 3).

It may simply be that as hyperliterate adults we are conscious of "using rules" when we are in fact doing something else, something far more complex, accessing tacit heuristics honed by print literacy itself. We can clarify this notion by reaching for an acronym coined by technical writers to explain the readability of complex prose—COIK: "clear only if known." The rules of Grammar 4—no, we can at this point be more honest—the incantations of Grammar 4 are COIK. If you know how to signal possession in the code of print, then the advice to add -'s to nouns makes perfect sense, just as the collective noun *monies* is a fine example of changing-*y* to -*i* and adding *es* to form the plural. But if you have not grasped, tacitly, the abstract representation of possession in print, such incantations can only be opaque.

Worse yet, the advice given in "the common school grammars" is unconnected with anything remotely resembling literate adult behavior. Consider, as an example, the rule for not writing a sentence fragment as the rule is described in the best-selling college grammar text, John C. Hodges and Mary S. Whitten's *Harbrace College Handbook*, 9th ed. (New York: Harcourt Brace Jovanovich, 1982). In order to get to the advice, "as a rule, do not write a sentence fragment" (p. 25), the student must master the following learning tasks:

Recognizing verbs.
Recognizing subjects and verbs.
Recognizing all parts of speech. (*Harbrace* lists eight.)
Recognizing phrases and subordinate clauses. (*Harbrace* lists six types of phrases, and it offers
    incomplete lists of eight relative pronouns and eighteen subordinating conjunctions.)
Recognizing main clauses and types of sentences.

These learning tasks completed, the student is given the rule above, offered a page of exceptions, and then given the following advice (or is it an incantation?):

> Before handing in a composition, ... proofread each word group written as a sentence. Test each one for completeness. First, be sure that it has at least one subject and one predicate. Next, be sure that the word group is not a dependent clause beginning with a subordinating conjunction or a relative clause. (p. 27)

The school grammar approach defines a sentence fragment as a conceptual error—as not having conscious knowledge of the school grammar definition of *sentence*. It demands heavy emphasis on rote memory, and it asks students to behave in ways patently removed from the behaviors of mature writers. (I have never in my life tested a sentence for completeness, and I am a better writer—and probably a better person—as a consequence.) It may be, of course, that some developing writers, at some points in their development, may benefit from such advice—or, more to the point, may think that they benefit—but, as Thomas Friedman points out in "Teaching Error, Nurturing Confusion" (*CE*, 45 [1983], 390–399), our theory of language tells us that such advice is, at the best, COIK. As the Maine joke has it, about a tourist asking directions from a farmer, "you can't get there from here."

Redefining Error

In the specific case of sentence fragments, Mina P. Shaughnessy (*Errors and Expectations* [New York: Oxford University Press, 1977]) argues that such errors are not conceptual failures at all, but performance errors—mistakes in punctuation. Muriel Harris' error counts support this view ("Mending the Fragmented Free Modifier," *CCC*, 32 [1981], 175–182). Case studies show example after example of errors that occur *because of* instruction—one thinks, for example, of David Bartholmae's student explaining that he added an *-s* to *children* "because it's a plural" ("The Study of Error," *CCC*, 31 [1980], 262). Surveys, such as that by Muriel Harris ("Contradictory Perceptions of the Rules of Writing," *CCC*, 30 [1979], 218–220), and our own observations suggest that students consistently misunderstand such Grammar 4 explanations (COIK, you will recall). For example, from Patrick Hartwell and Robert H. Bentley and from Mike Rose, we have two separate anecdotal accounts of students, cited for punctuating a *because*-clause as a sentence, who have decided to avoid using *because*. More generally, Collette A. Daiute's analysis of errors made by college students shows that errors tend to appear at clause boundaries, suggesting short-term memory load and not conceptual deficiency as a cause of error.[21]

Thus, if we think seriously about error and its relationship to the worship of formal grammar study, we need to attempt some massive dislocation of our traditional thinking, to shuck off our hyperliterate perception of the value of formal rules, and to regain the confidence in the tacit power of unconscious knowledge that our theory of language gives us. Most students, reading their writing aloud, will correct in essence all errors of spelling, grammar, and, by intonation, punctuation, but usually without noticing that what they read departs from what they wrote.[22] And Richard H. Haswell ("Minimal Marking," *CE*, 45 1983], 600–604) notes that his students correct 61.1% of their errors when they are identified with a simple mark in the margin rather than by error type. Such findings suggest that we need to redefine error, to see it not as a cognitive or linguistic problem, a problem of not knowing a "rule of grammar" (whatever that may mean), but rather, following the insight of Robert J. Bracewell ("Writing as a Cognitive Activity," *Visible Language*, 14 [1980], 400–422), as a problem of metacognition and metalinguistic awareness, a matter of accessing knowledges that, to be of any use, learners must have already internalized by means of exposure to the code. (Usage issues—Grammar 3—probably represent a different order of problem. Both

Joseph Emonds and Jeffrey Jochnowitz establish that the usage issues we worry most about are linguistically unnatural, departures from the grammar in our heads.)[23]

The notion of metalinguistic awareness seems crucial. The sentence below, created by Douglas R. Hofstadter ("Metamagical Themes," *Scientific American*, 235, No. 1 [1981], 22–32), is offered to clarify that notion; you are invited to examine it for a moment or two before continuing.

Their is four errors in this sentance. Can you find them?

Three errors announce themselves plainly enough, the misspellings of *there* and *sentence* and the use of *is* instead of *are*. (And, just to illustrate the perils of hyperliteracy, let it be noted that, through three years of drafts, I referred to the choice of *is* and *are* as a matter of "subject-verb agreement.") The fourth error resists detection, until one assesses the truth value of the sentence itself—the fourth error is that there are not four errors, only three. Such a sentence (Hofstadter calls it a "self-referencing sentence") asks you to look at it in two ways, simultaneously as statement and as linguistic artifact—in other words, to exercise metalinguistic awareness.

A broad range of cross-cultural studies suggest that metalinguistic awareness is a defining feature of print literacy. Thus Sylvia Scribner and Michael Cole, working with the triliterate Vai of Liberia (variously literate in English, through schooling; in Arabic, for religious purposes; and in an indigenous Vai script, used for personal affairs), find that metalinguistic awareness, broadly conceived, is the only cognitive skill underlying each of the three literacies. The one statistically significant skill shared by literate Vai was the recognition of word boundaries. Moreover, literate Vai tended to answer "yes" when asked (in Vai), "Can you call the sun the moon and the moon the sun?" while illiterate Vai tended to have grave doubts about such metalinguistic play. And in the United States Henry and Lila R. Gleitman report quite different responses by clerical workers and PhD candidates asked to interpret nonsense compounds like "house-bird glass": clerical workers focused on meaning and plausibility (for example, "a house-bird made of glass"), while PhD candidates focused on syntax (for example, "a very small drinking cup for canaries" or "a glass that protects house-birds").[24] More general research findings suggest a clear relationship between measures of metalinguistic awareness and measures of literacy level.[25] William Labov, speculating on literacy acquisition in inner-city ghettoes, contrasts "stimulus-bound" and "language-bound" individuals, suggesting that the latter seem to master literacy more easily.[26] The analysis here suggests that the causal relationship works the other way, that it is the mastery of written language that increases one's awareness of language as language.

This analysis has two implications. First, it makes the question of socially nonstandard dialects, always implicit in discussions of teaching formal grammar, into a non-issue.[27] Native speakers of English, regardless of dialect, show tacit mastery of the conventions of Standard English, and that mastery seems to transfer into abstract orthographic knowledge through interaction with print.[28] Developing writers show the same patterning of errors, regardless of dialect.[29] Studies of reading and of writing suggest that surface features of spoken dialect are simply irrelevant to mastering print literacy.[30] Print is a complex cultural code—or better yet, a system of codes—and my bet is that, regardless of instruction, one masters those codes from the top down, from pragmatic questions of voice, tone, audience, register, and rhetorical strategy, not from the bottom up, from grammar to usage to fixed forms of organization.

Second, this analysis forces us to posit multiple literacies, used for multiple purposes, rather than a single static literacy, engraved in "rules of grammar." These multiple literacies are evident in cross-cultural studies.[31] They are equally evident when we inquire into the uses of literacy in American communities.[32] Further, given that students, at all levels, show widely variant interactions with print literacy, there would seem to be little to do with grammar—with Grammar 2 or with Grammar 4—that we could isolate as a basis for formal instruction.[33]

Grammar 5: Stylistic Grammar

Similarly, when we turn to Grammar 5, "grammatical terms used in the interest of teaching prose style," so central to Martha Kolln's argument for teaching formal grammar, we find that the grammar issue is simply beside the point. There are two fully-articulated positions about "stylistic grammar," which I will label "romantic" and "classic," following Richard Lloyd-Jones and Richard E. Young.[34] The romantic position is that stylistic grammars, though perhaps useful for teachers, have little place in the teaching of composition, for students must struggle with and through language toward meaning. This position rests on a theory of language ultimately philosophical rather than linguistic (witness, for example, the contempt for linguists in Ann Berthoff's *The Making of Meaning: Metaphors, Models, and Maxims for Writing Teachers* [Montclair, N.J.: Boynton/Cook, 1981]); it is articulated as a theory of style by Donald A. Murray and, on somewhat different grounds (that stylistic grammars encourage overuse of the monitor), by Ian Pringle. The classic position, on the other hand, is that we can find ways to offer developing writers helpful suggestions about prose style, suggestions such as Francis Christensen's emphasis on the cumulative sentence, developed by observing the practice of skilled writers, and Joseph Williams' advice about predication, developed by psycholinguistic studies of comprehension.[35] James A. Berlin's recent survey of composition theory (*CE*, 45 [1982], 765–777) probably understates the gulf between these two positions and the radically different conceptions of language that underlie them, but it does establish that they share an overriding assumption in common: that one learns to control the language of print by manipulating language in meaningful contexts, not by learning about language in isolation, as by the study of formal grammar. Thus even classic theorists, who choose to present a vocabulary of style to students, do so only as a vehicle for encouraging productive control of communicative structures.

We might put the matter in the following terms. Writers need to develop skills at two levels. One, broadly rhetorical, involves communication in meaningful contexts (the strategies, registers, and procedures of discourse across a range of modes, audiences, contexts, and purposes). The other, broadly metalinguistic rather than linguistic, involves active manipulation of language with conscious attention to surface form. This second level may be developed tacitly, as a natural adjunct to developing rhetorical competencies—I take this to be the position of romantic theorists. It may be developed formally, by manipulating language for stylistic effect, and such manipulation may involve, for pedagogical continuity, a vocabulary of style. But it is primarily developed by any kind of language activity that enhances the awareness of language as language.[36] David T. Hakes, summarizing the research on metalinguistic awareness, notes how far we are from understanding this process: [the optimal conditions for becoming metalinguistically competent involve growing up in a literate environment with adult models who are themselves metalinguistically competent and who foster the growth of that competence in a variety of ways as yet little understood. ("The Development of Metalinguistic Abilities," p. 205: see footnote 25)]

Such a model places language, at all levels, at the center of the curriculum, but not as "necessary categories and labels" (Kolln, "Closing the Books on Alchemy," p. 150), but as literal stuff, verbal clay, to be molded and probed, shaped and reshaped, and, above all, enjoyed.

The Tradition of Experimental Research

Thus, when we turn back to experimental research on the value of formal grammar instruction, we do so with firm predictions given us by our theory of language. Our theory would predict that formal grammar instruction, whether instruction in scientific grammar or instruction in "the common school grammar," would have little to do with control over surface correctness nor with quality of writing. It would predict that any form of active involvement with language would be preferable to instruction in rules or definitions (or incantations). In essence, this is what the research tells us. In 1893, the Committee of Ten (*Report of the Committee of Ten on Secondary School*

Studies [Washington, D.C.: U.S. Government Printing Office, 1893]) put grammar at the center of the English curriculum, and its report established the rigidly sequential mode of instruction common for the last century. But the committee explicitly noted that grammar instruction did not aid correctness, arguing instead that it improved the ability to think logically (an argument developed from the role of the "grammarian" in the classical rhetorical tradition, essentially a teacher of literature—see, for example, the etymology of *grammar* in the *Oxford English Dictionary*).

But Franklin S. Hoyt, in a 1906 experiment, found no relationship between the study of grammar and the ability to think logically; his research led him to conclude what I am constrained to argue more than seventy-five years later, that there is no "relationship between a knowledge of technical grammar and the ability to use English and to interpret language" ("The Place of Grammar in the Elementary Curriculum," *Teachers College Record*, 7 [1906], 483–484). Later studies, through the 1920s, focused on the relationship of knowledge of grammar and ability to recognize error; experiments reported by James Boraas in 1917 and by William Asker in 1923 are typical of those that reported no correlation. In the 1930s, with the development of the functional grammar movement, it was common to compare the study of formal grammar with one form or another of active manipulation of language; experiments by I. O. Ash in 1935 and Ellen Frogner in 1939 are typical of studies showing the superiority of active involvement with language.[37] In a 1959 article, "Grammar in Language Teaching" (*Elementary English*, 36 [1959], 412–421), John J. DeBoer noted the consistency of these findings.

> The impressive fact is ... that in all these studies, carried out in places and at times far removed from each other, often by highly experienced and disinterested investigators, the results have been consistently negative so far as the value of grammar in the improvement of language expression is concerned. (p. 417)

In 1960 Ingrid M. Strom, reviewing more than fifty experimental studies, came to a similarly strong and unqualified conclusion:

> direct methods of instruction, focusing on writing activities and the structuring of ideas, are more efficient in teaching sentence structure, usage, punctuation, and other related factors than are such methods as nomenclature drill, diagramming, and rote memorization of grammatical rules.[38]

In 1963 two research reviews appeared, one by Braddock, Lloyd-Jones, and Schorer, cited at the beginning of this paper, and one by Henry C. Meckel, whose conclusions, though more guarded, are in essential agreement.[39] In 1969 J. Stephen Sherwin devoted one-fourth of his *Four Problems in Teaching English: A Critique of Research* (Scranton, Penn.: International Textbook, 1969) to the grammar issue, concluding that "instruction in formal grammar is an ineffective way to help students achieve proficiency in writing" (p. 135). Some early experiments in sentence combining, such as those by Donald R. Bateman and Frank J. Zidonnis and by John C. Mellon, showed improvement in measures of syntactic complexity with instruction in transformational grammar keyed to sentence combining practice. But a later study by Frank O'Hare achieved the same gains with no grammar instruction, suggesting to Sandra L. Stotsky and to Richard Van de Veghe that active manipulation of language, not the grammar unit, explained the earlier results.[40] More recent summaries of research—by Elizabeth I. Haynes, Hillary Taylor Holbrook, and Marcia Farr Whiteman—support similar conclusions. Indirect evidence for this position is provided by surveys reported by Betty Bamberg in 1978 and 1981, showing that time spent in grammar instruction in high school is the least important factor, of eight factors examined, in separating regular from remedial writers at the college level.[41] More generally, Patrick Scott and Bruce Castner, in "Reference Sources for Composition Research: A Practical Survey" (*CE*, 45 [1983], 756–768), note that much current research is not informed by an awareness of the past. Put simply, we are constrained to reinvent the wheel. My concern here has been with a far more serious problem: that too often the wheel we reinvent is square.

It is, after all, a question of power. Janet Emig, developing a consensus from composition research, and Aaron S. Carton and Lawrence V. Castiglione, developing the implications of language theory for education, come to the same conclusion: that the thrust of current research and theory is to take power from the teacher and to give that power to the learner.[42] At no point in the English curriculum is the question of power more blatantly posed than in the issue of formal grammar instruction. It is time that we, as teachers, formulate theories of language and literacy and let those theories guide our teaching, and it is time that we, as researchers, move on to more interesting areas of inquiry.

Notes

1 *Research in Written Composition* (Urbana, Ill.: National Council of Teachers of English, 1963), pp. 37–38.

2 "Non-magical Thinking: Presenting Writing Developmentally in Schools," in *Writing Process, Development and Communication,* Vol. II of *Writing: The Nature, Development and Teaching of Written Communication,* ed. Charles H. Frederiksen and Joseph F. Dominic (Hillsdale, N.J.: Lawrence Erlbaum, 1980), pp. 21–30.

3 For arguments in favor of formal grammar teaching, see Patrick F. Basset, "Grammar—Can We Afford Not to Teach It?" *NASSP Bulletin,* 64, No. 10 (1980), 55–63; Mary Epes, et al., "The COMP-LAB Project: Assessing the Effectiveness of a Laboratory-Centered Basic Writing Course on the College Level" (Jamaica, N.Y.: York College, CUNY, 1979) ERIC 194 908; June B. Evans, "The Analogous Ounce: The Analgesic for Relief," *English Journal,* 70, No. 2 (1981), 38–39; Sydney Greenbaum, "What Is Grammar and Why Teach It?" (a paper presented at the meeting of the National Council of Teachers of English, Boston, Nov. 1982) ERIC 222 917; Marjorie Smelstor, *A Guide to the Role of Grammar in Teaching Writing* (Madison: University of Wisconsin School of Education, 1978) ERIC 176 323; and A.M. Tibbetts, *Working Papers: A Teacher's Observations on Composition* (Glenview, Ill.: Scott, Foresman, 1982).

    For attacks on formal grammar teaching, see Harvey A. Daniels, *Famous Last Words: The American Language Crisis Reconsidered* (Carbondale: Southern Illinois University Press, 1983); Suzette Haden Elgin, *Never Mind the Trees: What the English Teacher Really Needs to Know about Linguistics* (Berkeley: University of California College of Education, Bay Area Writing Project Occasional Paper No. 2, 1980) ERIC 198 536; Mike Rose, "Remedial Writing Courses: A Critique and a Proposal." *College English,* 45 (1983), 109–128; and Ron Shook, "Response to Martha Kolln," *College Composition and Communication,* 34 (1983), 491–495.

4 See, for example, Clifton Fadiman and James Howard, *Empty Pages: A Search for Writing Competence in School and Society* (Belmont, Cal.: Fearon Pitman, 1979); Edwin Newman, *A Civil Tongue* (Indianapolis, Ind.: Bobbs-Merrill, 1976); and *Strictly Speaking* (New York: Warner Books, 1974); John Simons, *Paradigms Lost* (New York: Clarkson N. Potter, 1980); A. M. Tibbetts and Charlene Tibbetts, *What's Happening to American English?* (New York: Scribner's, 1978); and "Why Johnny Can't Write," *Newsweek,* 8 Dec. 1975, pp. 58–63.

5 "The Role of Grammar in a Secondary School English Curriculum." *Research in the Teaching of English,* 10 (1976), 5–21; *The Role of Grammar in a Secondary School Curriculum* (Wellington: New Zealand Council of Teachers of English, 1979).

6 "A Taxonomy of Compositional Competencies," in *Perspectives on Literacy,* ed. Richard Beach and P. David Pearson (Minneapolis: University of Minnesota College of Education, 1979), pp. 247–272.

7 On usage norms, see Edward Finegan, *Attitudes toward English Usage: The History of a War of Words* (New York: Teachers College Press, 1980), and Jim Quinn, *American Tongue in Cheek: A Populist Guide to Language* (New York: Pantheon, 1980); on arrangement, see Patrick Hartwell, "Teaching Arrangement: A Pedagogy," *CE,* 40 (1979), 548–554.

8 "Revolution in Grammar," *Quarterly Journal of Speech,* 40 (1954), 299–312.

9 Richard A. Lanham, *Revising Prose* (New York: Scribner's, 1979); William Strunk and E. B. White, *The Elements of Style,* 3rd ed. (New York: Macmillan, 1979); Joseph Williams, *Style: Ten Lessons in Clarity and Grace* (Glenview, Ill.: Scott, Foresman, 1981); Christensen, "A Generative Rhetoric of the Sentence,"

CCC, 14 (1963), 155–161; Donald A. Daiker, Andrew Kerek, and Max Morenberg, *The Writer's Options: Combining to Composing,* 2nd ed. (New York: Harper & Row, 1982).

10   "A Psychological Approach," in *Psychobiology of Language,* ed. M. Studdert-Kennedy (Cambridge, Mass.: MIT Press, 1983), pp. 16–19. See also Noam Chomsky, "Language and Unconscious Knowledge," in *Psychoanalysis and Language: Psychiatry and the Humanities,* Vol. III, ed. Joseph H. Smith (New Haven, Conn.: Yale University Press, 1978), pp. 3–44.

11   Morris Halle, "Knowledge Unlearned and Untaught: What Speakers Know about the Sounds of Their Language," in *Linguistic Theory and Psychological Reality,* ed. Halle, Joan Bresnan, and George A. Miller (Cambridge, Mass.: MIT Press, 1978), pp. 135–140.

12   Moscowitz, "On the Status of Vowel Shift in English," in *Cognitive Development and the Acquisition of Language,* ed. T. E. Moore (New York: Academic Press, 1973), pp. 223–60; Chomsky, "Stages in Language Development and Reading Exposure," *Harvard Educational Review,* 42 (1972), 1–33; and Brause, "Developmental Aspects of the Ability to Understand Semantic Ambiguity, with Implications for Teachers," *RTE,* 11 (1977), 39–48.

13   Mills and Hemsley, "The Effect of Levels of Education on Judgments of Grammatical Acceptability," *Language and Speech,* 19 (1976), 324–342; Whyte, "Levels of Language Competence and Reading Ability: An Exploratory Investigation," *Journal of Research in Reading,* 5 (1982, 123–132; Morais, et al., "Does Awareness of Speech as a Series of Phones Arise Spontaneously," *Cognition,* 7 (1979), 323–331; Ferguson, *Cognitive Effects of Literacy: Linguistic Awareness in Adult Non-readers* (Washington, D.C.: National Institute of Education Final Report, 1981) ERIC 222 85; Hamilton and Barton, "A Word Is a Word: Metalinguistic Skills in Adults of Varying Literacy Levels" (Stanford, Cal.: Stanford University Department of Linguistics, 1980) ERIC 222 859.

14   On the question of the psychological reality of Grammar 2 descriptions, see Maria Black and Shulamith Chiat, "Psycholinguistics without 'Psychological Reality'," *Linguistics,* 19 (1981), 37–61; Joan Bresnan, ed., *The Mental Representation of Grammatical Relations* (Cambridge, Mass.: MIT Press, 1982); and Michael H. Long, "Inside the 'Black Box': Methodological Issues in Classroom Research on Language Learning," *Language Learning,* 30 (1980), 1–42.

15   Chomsky, "The Current Scene in Linguistics," *College English,* 27 (1966), 587–595; and "Linguistic Theory," in *Language Teaching: Broader Contexts,* ed. Robert C. Meade, Jr. (New York: Modern Language Association, 1966), pp. 43–49; Mark Lester, "The Value of Transformational Grammar in Teaching Composition," *CCC,* 16 (1967), 228.

16   Christensen, "Between Two Worlds," in *Notes toward a New Rhetoric: Nine Essays for Teachers,* rev. ed., ed. Bonniejean Christensen (New York: Harper & Row, 1978), pp. 1–22.

17   Reber, "Implicit Learning of Artificial Grammars," *Journal of Verbal Learning and Verbal Behavior,* 6 (1967), 855–863; "Implicit Learning of Synthetic Languages: The Role of Instructional Set," *Journal of Experimental Psychology: Human Learning and Memory,* 2 (1976), 889–894; and Reber, Saul M. Kassin, Selma Lewis, and Gary Cantor, "On the Relationship Between Implicit and Explicit Modes in the Learning of a Complex Rule Structure," *Journal of Experimental Psychology: Human Learning and Memory,* 6 (1980), 492–502.

18   "Individual Variation in the Use of the Monitor," in *Principles of Second Language Learning,* ed. W. Richie (New York: Academic Press, 1978), pp. 175–185.

19   "Applications of Psycholinguistic Research to the Classroom," in *Practical Applications of Research in Foreign Language Teaching,* ed. D. J. James (Lincolnwood, Ill.: National Textbook, 1983), p. 61.

20   "Some Evidence for the Integrity and Interaction of Two Knowledge Sources," in *New Dimensions in Second Language Acquisition Research,* ed. Roger W. Anderson (Rowley, Mass.: Newbury House, 1981), pp. 62–74.

21   Hartwell and Bentley, *Some Suggestions for Using Open to Language* (New York: Oxford University Press, 1982), p. 73; Rose, *Writer's Block: The Cognitive Dimension* (Carbondale: Southern Illinois University Press, 1983), p. 99; Daiute, "Psycholinguistic Foundations of the Writing Process," *RTE,* 15 (1981), 5–22.

22   See Bartholomae, "The Study of Error"; Patrick Hartwell, "The Writing Center and the Paradoxes of Written-Down Speech," in *Writing Centers: Theory and Administration,* ed. Gary Olson (Urbana, Ill.: NCTE, 1984), pp. 48–61; and Sondra Perl, "A Look at Basic Writers in the Process of Composing," in *Basic Writing: A Collection of Essays for Teachers, Researchers, and Administrators* (Urbana, Ill.: NCTE, 1980), pp. 13–32.

23   Emonds, *Adjacency in Grammar: The Theory of Language-Particular Rules* (New York: Academic, 1983); and Jochnowitz, "Everybody Likes Pizza, Doesn't He or She?" *American Speech,* 57 (1982), 198–203.

24   Scribner and Cole, *Psychology of Literacy* (Cambridge, Mass.: Harvard University Press, 1981); Gleitman and Gleitman, "Language Use and Language Judgment," in *Individual Differences in Language Ability and Language Behavior,* ed. Charles J. Fillmore, Daniel Kempler, and William S.-Y. Wang (New York: Academic Press, 1979), pp. 103–126.

25   There are several recent reviews of this developing body of research in psychology and child development: Irene Athey, "Language Development Factors Related to Reading Development," *Journal of Educational Research,* 76 (1983), 197–203; James Flood and Paula Menyuk, "Metalinguistic Development and Reading/Writing Achievement," *Claremont Reading Conference Yearbook,* 46 (1982), 122–132; and the following four essays: David T. Hakes, "The Development of Metalinguistic Abilities: What Develops?," pp. 162–210; Stan A. Kuczaj, II, and Brooke Harbaugh, "What Children Think about the Speaking Capabilities of Other Persons and Things," pp. 211–227; Karen Saywitz and Louise Cherry Wilkinson, "Age-Related Differences in Metalinguistic Awareness," pp. 229–250; and Harriet Salatas Waters and Virginia S. Tinsley, "The Development of Verbal Self-Regulation: Relationships between Language, Cognition, and Behavior," pp. 251–277; all in *Language, Thought, and Culture,* Vol. II of *Language Development,* ed. Stan Kuczaj, Jr. (Hillsdale, N.J.: Lawrence Erlbaum, 1982). See also Joanne R. Nurss, "Research in Review: Linguistic Awareness and Learning to Read," *Young Children,* 35, No. 3 [1980], 57–66.

26   "Competing Value Systems in Inner City Schools," in *Children In and Out of School: Ethnography and Education,* ed. Perry Gilmore and Allan A. Glatthorn (Washington, D.C.: Center for Applied Linguistics, 1982), pp. 148–171; and "Locating the Frontier between Social and Psychological Factors in Linguistic Structure," in *Individual Differences in Language Ability and Language Behavior,* ed. Fillmore, Kempler, and Wang, pp. 327–340.

27   See, for example, Thomas Farrell, "IQ and Standard English," *CCC,* 34 (1983), 470–84; and the responses by Karen L. Greenberg and Patrick Hartwell, *CCC,* in press.

28   Jane W. Torrey, "Teaching Standard English to Speakers of Other Dialects," in *Applications of Linguistics: Selected Papers of the Second International Conference of Applied Linguistics,* ed. G. E. Perren and J. L. M. Trim (Cambridge, Mass.: Cambridge University Press, 1971), pp. 423–428; James W. Beers and Edmund H. Henderson, "A Study of the Developing Orthographic Concepts among First Graders," *RTE,* 11 (1977), 133–148.

29   See the error counts of Samuel A. Kirschner and G. Howard Poteet, "Non-Standard English Usage in the Writing of Black, White, and Hispanic Remedial English Students in an Urban Community College," *RTE,* 7 (1973), 351–355; and Marilyn Sternglass, "Close Similarities in Dialect Features of Black and White College Students in Remedial Composition Classes," *TESOL Quarterly,* 8 (1974), 271–283.

30   For reading, see the massive study by Kenneth S. Goodman and Yetta M. Goodman, *Reading of American Children whose Language Is a Stable Rural Dialect of English or a Language other than English* (Washington, D.C.: National Institute of Education Final Report, 1978) ERIC 175 754; and the overview by Rudine Sims, "Dialect and Reading: Toward Redefining the Issues," in *Reader Meets Author/Bridging the Gap: A Psycholinguistic and Sociolinguistic Approach,* ed. Judith A. Langer and M. Tricia Smith-Burke (Newark, Del.: International Reading Association, 1982), pp. 222–232. For writing, see Patrick Hartwell, "Dialect Interference in Writing: A Critical View," *RTE,* 14 (1980), 101–118; and the anthology edited by Barry M. Kroll and Roberta J. Vann, *Exploring Speaking-Writing Relationships: Connections and Contrasts* (Urbana, Ill.: NCTE, 1981).

31   See, for example, Eric A. Havelock, *The Literary Revolution in Greece and its Cultural Consequences* (Princeton, N.J.: Princeton University Press, 1982); Lesley Milroy on literacy in Dublin, *Language and Social Networks* (Oxford: Basil Blackwell, 1980); Ron Scollon and Suzanne B. K. Scollon on literacy in central Alaska, *Interethnic Communication: An Athabascan Case* (Austin, Tex.: Southwest Educational Development Laboratory Working Papers in Sociolinguistics, No. 59, 1979) ERIC 175 276; and Scribner and Cole on literacy in Liberia, *Psychology of Literacy* (see footnote 24).

32   See, for example, the anthology edited by Deborah Tannen, *Spoken and Written Language: Exploring Orality and Literacy* (Norwood, N.J.: Ablex, 1982); and Shirley Brice Heath's continuing work: "Protean Shapes in Literacy Events: Ever-Shifting Oral and Literate Traditions," in *Spoken and Written Language,* pp. 91–117; *Ways with Words: Language, Life and Work in Communities and Classrooms* (New York: Cambridge University Press, 1983); and "What No Bedtime Story Means," *Language in Society,* 11 (1982), 49–76.

33   For studies at the elementary level, see Dell H. Hymes, et al., eds., *Ethnographic Monitoring of Children's Acquisition of Reading/Language Arts Skills In and Out of the Classroom* (Washington, D.C.: National

Institute of Education Final Report, 1981) ERIC 208 096. For studies at the secondary level, see James L. Collins and Michael M. Williamson, "Spoken Language and Semantic Abbreviation in Writing," *RTE,* 15 (1981), 23–36. And for studies at the college level, see Patrick Hartwell and Gene LoPresti, "Sentence Combining as Kid-Watching," in *Sentence Combining: Toward a Rhetorical Perspective,* ed. Donald A. Daiker, Andrew Kerek, and Max Morenberg (Carbondale: Southern Illinois University Press, in press).

34 Lloyd-Jones, "Romantic Revels—I Am Not You," *CCC,* 23 (1972), 251–271; and Young, "Concepts of Art and the Teaching of Writing," in *The Rhetorical Tradition and Modern Writing,* ed. James J. Murphy (New York: Modern Language Association, 1982), pp. 130–141.

35 For the romantic position, see Ann E. Berthoff, "Tolstoy, Vygotsky, and the Making of Meaning," *CCC,* 29 (1978), 249–255; Kenneth Dowst, "The Epistemic Approach," in *Eight Approaches to Teaching Composition,* ed. Timothy Donovan and Ben G. McClellan (Urbana, Ill.: NCTE, 1980), pp. 65–85; Peter Elbow, "The Challenge for Sentence Combining"; and Donald Murray, "Following Language toward Meaning," both in *Sentence Combining: Toward a Rhetorical Perspective* (in press; see footnote 33); and Ian Pringle, "Why Teach Style? A Review-Essay," *CCC,* 34 (1983), 91–98.

   For the classic position, see Christensen's "A Generative Rhetoric of the Sentence"; and Joseph Williams' "Defining Complexity," *CE,* 41 (1979), 595–609; and his *Style: Ten Lessons in Clarity and Grace* (see footnote 9).

36 Courtney B. Cazden and David K. Dickinson, "Language and Education: Standardization versus Cultural Pluralism," in *Language in the USA,* ed. Charles A. Ferguson and Shirley Brice Health (New York: Cambridge University Press, 1981), pp. 446–468; and Carol Chomsky, "Developing Facility with Language Structure," in *Discovering Language with Children,* ed. Gay Su Pinnell (Urbana, Ill.: NCTE, 1980), pp. 56–59.

37 Boraas, "Formal English Grammar and the Practical Mastery of English." Diss. University of Illinois, 1917; Asker, "Does Knowledge of Grammar Function?" *School and Society,* 17 (27 January 1923), 109–111; Ash, "An Experimental Evaluation of the Stylistic Approach in Teaching Composition in the Junior High School," *Journal of Experimental Education,* 4 (1935), 54–62; and Frogner, "A Study of the Relative Efficacy of a Grammatical and a Thought Approach to the Improvement of Sentence Structure in Grades Nine and Eleven," *School Review,* 47 (1939), 663–675.

38 "Research on Grammar and Usage and Its Implications for Teaching Writing," *Bulletin of the School of Education,* Indiana University, 36 (1960), pp. 13–14.

39 Meckel, "Research on Teaching Composition and Literature," in *Handbook of Research on Teaching,* ed. N. L. Gage (Chicago: Rand McNally, 1963), pp. 966–1006.

40 Bateman and Zidonis, *The Effect of a Study of Transformational Grammar on the Writing of Ninth and Tenth Graders* (Urbana, Ill.: NCTE, 1966); Mellon, *Transformational Sentence Combining: A Method for Enhancing the Development of Fluency in English Composition* (Urbana, Ill.: NCTE, 1969); O'Hare, *Sentence-Combining: Improving Student Writing without Formal Grammar Instruction* (Urbana, Ill.: NCTE, 1971); Stotsky, "Sentence-Combining as a Curricular Activity: Its Effect on Written Language Development," *RTE,* 9 (1975), 30–72; and Van de Veghe, "Research in Written Composition: Fifteen Years of Investigation," ERIC 157 095.

41 Haynes, "Using Research in Preparing to Teach Writing," *English Journal,* 69, No. 1 (1978), 82–88; Holbrook, "ERIC/RCS Report: Whither (Wither) Grammar," *Language Arts,* 60 (1983), 259–263; Whiteman, "What We Can Learn from Writing Research," *Theory into Practice,* 19 (1980), 150–156; Bamberg, "Composition in the Secondary English Curriculum: Some Current Trends and Directions for the Eighties," *RTE,* 15 (1981), 257–266; and "Composition Instruction Does Make a Difference: A Comparison of the High School Preparation of College Freshmen in Regular and Remedial English Classes," *RTE,* 12 (1978), 47–59.

42 Emig, "Inquiry Paradigms and Writing," *CCC,* 33 (1982), 64–75; Carton and Castiglione, "Educational Linguistics: Defining the Domain," in *Psycholinguistic Research: Implications and Applications,* ed. Doris Aaronson and Robert W. Rieber (Hillsdale, N.J.: Lawrence Erlbaum, 1979), pp. 497–520.

Non-Native Speakers of English

John R. Edlund and Olga Griswold

- How can theories of language acquisition enable writing teachers to work effectively with students whose first language is not English?
- What is contrastive rhetoric and how can it be used in the teaching of writing?
- What role should grammar and error correction play in helping ESL students learn to write?

This chapter addresses several ideas associated with the field of second language acquisition that can help composition teachers work effectively with ESL students. These include theories of language acquisition, insights from contrastive rhetoric, and the role of grammar and error correction.

A recent post on the Writing Program Administrator's e-mail list (WPA-L) asked if most composition programs "segregate ESL students into separate sections or mainstream them into existing sections of composition?" The responses indicated that both models are common across the country, but many other issues also arose that are appropriate for composition teachers to consider. Who is an ESL student? What are the advantages and disadvantages of segregating and mainstreaming? At what level is a student ready for mainstream composition, and how is this determined? Should students choose which program suits them best? How is an ESL composition course different from a mainstream one?

In "Broadening the Perspective of Mainstream Composition Studies: Some Thoughts from the Disciplinary Margins" (1997), Tony Silva, Ilona Leki, and Joan Carson note that "English as a Second Language (ESL) writing, or, more generally, second language writing, is uniquely situated at the intersection of second language studies and composition studies," but they lament the fact that "the transfer of knowledge between the fields has primarily been a one way affair, from composition studies to second language studies" (p. 399). In their essay, they argue that there is much that mainstream composition could learn from second language writing research, and that without such influence, mainstream composition is too narrow, reduced to making "universalist claims about the phenomenon of writing almost exclusively on the basis of Western (Greco-Roman and Anglo-American) rhetorical traditions and/or on the findings of empirical research conducted primarily on undergraduate college students in North American colleges and universities" (p. 399).

Thus, there are two strong reasons why mainstream composition teachers should be interested in second language writing research: first, ESL students are already in mainstream classes; and second, without theory, research, and experience from the field of second language acquisition, mainstream composition is too provincial, basing grand claims on monolingual, monocultural evidence. This chapter addresses several ideas associated with the field of second language acquisition that can help composition teachers work effectively with ESL students. These include:

- theories of language acquisition
- the role of culture and rhetoric
- insights from contrastive rhetoric
- characteristics of Generation 1.5
- the role of grammar and error correction.

SECOND LANGUAGE ACQUISITION (SLA)

In making the case that second language writing research has something to offer the mainstream composition tradition, Silva, Leki, and Carson provide a good overview of second language writing as a field. The overall thesis of their article "Broadening the Perspective of Mainstream Composition Studies: Some Thoughts from the Disciplinary Margins" (1997) is that composition needs a "broader and more inclusive view of writing," and that it "could profit from the perspectives and insights of second language studies" (p. 402). However, there is always danger in importing theories from outside disciplines, even closely related ones, if they are not clearly understood. Silva, Leki, and Carson open their discussion of SLA research with a critique of Horning's *Teaching Writing as a Second Language,* apparently one of the few books in mainstream composition that refers to SLA research, but they do so to problematize her idea that the acquisition of written language, or academic language, is similar to second language acquisition (1987). They say specifically that Horning relies too much on Stephen Krashen's distinction between conscious learning and unconscious acquisition as unrelated processing mechanisms. They claim that this distinction has been "frequently and convincingly challenged in second language acquisition research" (Silva, Leki, & Carson, 1997, p. 403).

Composition has struggled with the role of grammar teaching for decades. Although the research indicates that teaching grammar has either no effect, or a negative effect, on writing skills, there is still considerable pressure from administrators, parents, and even the students themselves, to teach it. The often-cited article by Patrick Hartwell, "Grammar, Grammars, and the Teaching of Grammar" (included in this book at the end of Chapter 7), actually cites Krashen in making the argument against grammar teaching (1985).

Krashen's Language Acquisition theory consists of five hypotheses, of which the acquisition/learning distinction is the most important. For Krashen, second language *acquisition* is a natural unconscious process very similar to first language acquisition. Babies, after all, do not study grammar books or dictionaries, but acquire language naturally from the surrounding linguistic environment. Language *learning,* on the other hand, involves the conscious study of grammatical rules, vocabulary lists, practice exercises, memorized dialogues, and other such strategies. Some researchers have assumed that while children acquire language, adults must learn it through an entirely different process. Krashen (1982) argues that these processes are, indeed, separate, but that adults are not merely *capable* of acquiring language naturally, it is, in fact, the most powerful method.

The other hypotheses in the theory concern the natural order of the acquisition of specific grammatical structures, which appears to be invariable regardless of instructional sequence, and the conditions under which natural acquisition occurs. The key factor is the presence of "comprehensible input." Krashen maintained, "We acquire by understanding language that contains structure a bit beyond our current level of competence" (1982, p. 21). From this perspective, the job of the language teacher is not to provide a carefully sequenced and well-explained series of grammatical rules and exercises. Instead, the ideal classroom is a comfortable, nonthreatening place with rich opportunities for communicative interaction, lots of comprehensible input, and no grammar drills. Because direct teaching of rules and forms is not useful, the main task of a language teacher is to facilitate language acquisition by creating the proper linguistic environment. Krashen himself noted:

> The input hypothesis runs counter to our usual pedagogical approach in second and foreign language teaching. ... our assumption has been that we first learn structures, then practice using them in communication, and this is how fluency develops. The input hypothesis says the opposite. It says we acquire by "going for meaning" first, and as a result, we acquire structure! (1982, p. 21)

For many language teachers, this is a profoundly counterintuitive approach, and a number of researchers have challenged Krashen's theory, mostly focusing on the "non-interface" position, the claim that conscious learning cannot turn into acquisition. Rod Ellis provided a useful summary of the issues in his book *Understanding Second Language Acquisition* (1985, p. 264). First, the theory has been challenged because it is defined in terms of "subconscious" and "conscious" processes that are not open to empirical investigation. In other words, it is a "black box" theory that discusses inputs and outputs but does not describe or investigate the mental processes involved. Second, the lack of connection between conscious learning and unconscious acquisition, the "non-interface position," has been challenged by many researchers.

Ellis (1985) noted that a number of researchers have articulated softer versions of the "non-interface" position arguing that learned knowledge can become "automatized" through practice and so become "acquired" and available for spontaneous conversation. However, without a clear distinction between the cognitive processes that lead to conscious learning, and those that lead to acquisition, or how these types of knowledge are different, it is impossible to distinguish between conscious knowledge of grammatical forms that has been "automatized" and subsequent acquisition of the same forms.

William Rutherford, a colleague of Krashen's at the University of Southern California, argued that when an adult language learner begins the process of acquiring a second language, that person is not a *tabula rasa*. The new learner already knows a lot about how language works and how people communicate, based on experiences with the first language. To begin to learn a new language is to embark on a journey across the *interlanguage continuum*, which we can imagine as a line that stretches from the L1 grammar (first language) to the L2 grammar (second language). Progress is made across the continuum by making and testing hypotheses about how the L2 grammar works. At first, the interlanguage system is based almost entirely on the L1 grammar, but as the learner acquires more of the L2 and makes further hypotheses about how it works, the interlanguage system becomes more and more like the "standard" grammar of the L2 (Rutherford, 1987).

Rutherford argued that this hypothesis-testing process can be facilitated by what he calls "grammatical consciousness-raising" (C-R). Consciousness-raising is a process in which "data that are crucial for the learner's testing of hypotheses, and for his forming generalizations, are made available to him in somewhat controlled and principled fashion" (p. 18). Rutherford noted that traditional grammar teaching can be a form of C-R, but that C-R is typically "a *means* to attainment of grammatical competence in another language (i.e., necessary but not sufficient, and the learner contributes), whereas 'grammar teaching' typically represents an attempt to *instill* that competence directly (i.e., necessary *and* sufficient, and the learner is a *tabula rasa*)" (p. 24).

In Rutherford's consciousness-raising theory, language acquisition is still more powerful than conscious learning, but there is the potential that pointing out a nonstandard form or teaching a grammatical rule might facilitate acquisition of that particular grammatical concept. In other words, there *is* an interface between conscious learning and unconscious acquisition. The nice thing about this theory is that it justifies what is common practice in both mainstream and second language composition classes: selectively marking errors.

Silva, Leki, and Carson (1997) discussed language acquisition largely in terms of a dichotomy between external or social factors, and internal factors related to cognition and psychology. The line between external and internal is a difficult one to maintain when talking about linguistic issues. The authors quickly blurred the distinction when they began to discuss the role of "sociopsychological" attitudes in language acquisition. Clearly, such concepts as "integrative" and "instrumental" motivation have both external and internal poles. However, Silva, Leki, and Carson (1997) maintained that this dichotomy serves to emphasize the overwhelming importance of social factors:

> Social factors play a major but indirect role in second language acquisition, insofar as acquisition is mediated by learner attitudes as well as by the nature and extent of input. ... Learner attitudes are both cognitive and affective, and they tend to be learned and persistent, but modifiable. Learner attitudes toward the acquisition of the target language are related to learner attitudes toward target language speakers, the target language culture, the social value of learning the target language, the particular uses that the target language might serve, and the learners' perceptions of their own culture. (p. 408)

The characterization of learner attitudes as "learned and persistent, but modifiable" is important for both the classroom and research. One of the goals of classroom instruction might be to facilitate language acquisition through changing learner attitudes toward the target language and target language speakers. Learner attitudes may also be an uncontrolled variable in many SLA studies, in part explaining the lack of convincing results for one pedagogical method over another. Age, gender, social class, cultural background, personal history, goals, motivation, and temperament all have the potential to influence language acquisition.

Implications for the Classroom

All of the various forms of Second Language Acquisition theory imply that non-native speakers learning to write in English will benefit from lots of comprehensible input, both oral and written. Large quantities of reading material, classroom discussions, videos and films, and one-on-one interactions with tutors or native-speaking peers will all help students acquire vocabulary, context-building background knowledge, and grammatical forms. Selective error marking can focus attention on particular linguistic features and facilitate acquisition of those features through consciousness-raising.

For Writing and Discussion

1. Think about your own experiences learning a foreign language, including grammar study, opportunities for comprehensible input, attitudes toward the new language and its speakers, and communicative success. How well does Second Language Acquisition theory account for your own experiences?

2. Take a popular writing handbook that includes information for ESL writers and look up the rules for using perfect tenses, the rules for articles, and the rules for using commas. Write a paragraph about your experience as a writing teacher or tutor, paying close attention to the rules in the handbook, so that nothing you write will deviate in any way from these rules. In class, discuss how the focus on rules affected your writing process.

CULTURE AND RHETORIC

Because affective and motivational issues are such important factors in language learning, and because the student's *native* language and culture may have a strong influence on his or her writing, it is useful to know basic information about the backgrounds of your ESL students. As Silva, Leki, and Carson (1997) noted, cultural background influences everything from conceptions of audience to organizational patterns. Your strategies for working with a particular student, even what you say to that student, may be influenced by what you know about the student's background. The questions below could be put into a survey administered on the first day of class, but in many cases a few questions of this sort asked as part of an early writing conference are enough to clarify the situation:

- What is the student's native language?
- What other languages does the student speak?
- Is the student able to read and write in his or her native language?
- How much does the student read in English?
- How much does the student read in his or her native language?
- Is English the student's most comfortable language of literacy?
- What language(s) does the student speak at home?
- Is the student an "international" student? (Is the student studying in the United States on an F-1 student visa and returning home on completion of study?)
- If the student is an immigrant, how long has he or she been in this country?
- Why did the student come to this country?
- How does the student feel about being here?
- Where was the student educated, and what was the language of instruction?
- What is the student's major? What are the student's career goals?

These questions can be rather personal, and should be asked tactfully. Unless you are doing this in survey form, it would be best to ask these questions informally, and to ask only the ones that seem relevant to the student's situation at the time.

ESL Students/International Students

If the student was educated primarily outside of the United States in a language other than English, second language acquisition is probably in process, and the student's writing is likely to be strongly influenced by the attitudes and rhetorical patterns of his or her home culture. For example, Silva, Leki, and Carson (1997) noted that cultural attitudes toward knowledge range from valuing the conservation of knowledge to valuing the extension of knowledge. Asian cultures tend to value the former, and, thus, emphasize the reproduction of information and strategies such as memorizing and imitating. Thus, although Scardamalia and Bereiter (1987) characterized knowledge telling in writing as "immature" writing, and knowledge transforming as characteristic of "mature" writing, this distinction does not pertain in the context of working with students from Asian cultures. "What would appear to be a developmental continuum, then, from immature to mature writing in a knowledge extending culture, is recast as an issue of social context when viewed from the larger cross-cultural perspective" (p. 416).

CONTRASTIVE RHETORIC

The field of study known as "contrastive rhetoric" was essentially invented by Robert Kaplan in a 1966 article titled "Cultural Thought Patterns in Intercultural Education." He later expanded the concept in a 1972 book titled *The Anatomy of Rhetoric: Prolegomena to a Functional Theory of Rhetoric: Essays for Teachers*. In both works, Kaplan analyzed numerous examples of foreign student writing in English, and represented his findings as a series of five simple diagrams. These diagrams are not reproduced here, because although these "squiggles" have provoked both interest and controversy, once people see them they tend to remember the squiggles and forget the caveats. It is enough to say that "Semitic" writing is represented by a series of parallel lines with dotted connections, "Oriental" by a spiral, "Romance" by a crooked single line, and "Slavic" by a similar crooked, but dotted, line. The English pattern is represented as a single, direct, and vertical line. The squiggles have been criticized as simplistic, both in the patterns they represent and in breadth of their categories. Even Kaplan, responding to this criticism, acknowledged, "It is probably true that, in the first blush of discovery, I overstated both the difference and my case" (Conner & Kaplan, 1987, p. 9).

Contrastive rhetoric deals with organizational patterns, stylistic preferences (especially in terms of subordination and coordination), and other conventional aspects of specific genres, viewed across cultures. In general, this research contrasts American English rhetorical patterns with those of a second culture. This research is complex and difficult to do, because to be credible, the researcher must be fluent in both languages and cultures, or have access to bilingual, bicultural informants, and any insights gained by research into the patterns of one culture are unlikely to be applicable to another. In most cases, it would be unreasonable to expect composition teachers to be familiar with the rhetorical patterns of every culture they might deal with. Why then, is contrastive rhetoric important to composition teachers?

Contrastive rhetoric can help explain the following situation, described by a Chinese-speaking student in her Writing Proficiency Exam:

> *My friend and I read an article. Although my English-speaking friend thought it was very good convincing article, I, on the other hand, did not agree with him. What I thought was that it was very pushing one way argument. … Most of native-speaker agreed with him. Some foreigner agreed with him, some agreed with me … all Asian who have strong Asian background agreed with me.*

This writer has conducted her own survey research on an important issue in contrastive rhetoric, and found American patterns to be one-sided and narrow from an Asian point of view. Many non-native speakers would agree with her.

Kaplan said in his original article, "One should not judge the construction of a composition merely by the standards of a rhetoric which one takes for granted" (1966, p. 34). In other words, an essay that appears to be illogical or incoherent by American standards may be well crafted by the standards of another culture. This is not to say that the foreign pattern should simply be accepted as a cultural difference, but it is also clear that calling the paper "illogical" or "incoherent" probably won't help the student improve. A student is not a blank slate or an empty vessel, and a writing teacher must be prepared to help integrate new learning with what has been learned before. In the case of a foreign student, what has been learned previously may be very different from what American teachers expect.

Kaplan (2001) noted that "genres are nothing more nor less than conventional solutions to recurring communication problems" (p. xi). The problem for students and teachers arises when two cultures have conflicting solutions. In discussing the pedagogical issues raised by contrastive rhetoric, this chapter will focus first on Japanese patterns. Again, the most important concept for the composition teacher is the idea that there *are* different patterns, and that they may be influencing the writing of your students.

An Example from Japanese Composition

Shinshu Kokugo Soran (*New Japanese Conspectus*), a textbook or reference book commonly used in Japanese secondary education, contains an article titled "How to Construct a Sentence/Composition." Ema (Ema, Taniyama, & Ino, 1981) writes, "There are two main formats in the design of Japanese compositions: (1) a three-step construction called *jo ha kyu* (literally opening—breaking—rushing) and (2) a four-step construction *ki-shô-ten-ketsu* (introduction—development—turn—conclusion)" (pp. 294–295). The author continues:

> The term *jo ha kyu* was originally used to name the three movements of music accompanying traditional Japanese Court dances, *bugaku*. Later, this idea was adapted for the method of dramatizing *nô* drama (creating dynamic movement, expression, or emphasis). Applied to the design of a written composition, it is considered as follows:
>
> <jo> Beginning. An introductory part or opening section.
> <ha> The portion which makes the center of a composition. A development part on a main subject.

<kyu> Ending of a composition. The conclusion. (1981, pp. 294–295 [translated by Miri Park from the Japanese original])

On the surface, this sounds similar to the introduction—body—conclusion pattern that Americans are taught. However, the character that is here represented by *jo* can also be translated as "overture," and this section is seen as establishing a mood or a context for the rest of the communication. It would be unlikely for this section to contain a thesis statement. For example, in Japan, it is conventional to begin a business letter with a reference to the weather, using specific words appropriate to the season. This is felt to establish a personal connection before the business at hand is broached. A Japanese professor was once drafting a letter to a distinguished British colleague who was receiving an award, but who was gravely ill. To an American sensibility, the information about the weather seemed to be trivial and unimportant, especially in this serious context, but to the Japanese writer, it seemed essential.

Examining *jo ha kyu* also reveals differences in reader/writer roles that affect the extent to which topics are expected to be developed or explained. The character *ha* literally means "breaking" as in "daybreak" or even in the sense of breaking something open, such as a nut. It signifies new development and the introduction of new themes. However, in Japanese texts, topics may be "opened" without real development, in a mode that reminds the English reader of an encyclopedia, or even a laundry list, requiring more involvement from the reader than is expected from texts written in English and highlighting differences in the Japanese sense of the roles of writer and reader. Linguist John Hinds proposed a typology of language based on relative reader/writer responsibility. Hinds classified Japanese as a reader-responsible language, English as writer-responsible, and Mandarin as a language in transition from reader-responsibility to writer-responsibility (Kaplan, 1988). This means that in Japanese the reader is expected to read between the lines, to supply missing connections and information, and in general to tolerate far more ambiguity than an American reader would be comfortable with. Thus, Kaplan argued, "the fact that a student understands audience in one language does not mean the student understands audience in any other language system" (1988, p. 296).

Kyu carries the sense of "rushing" as water rushes into a drain. It means "processing with force." In this section, the writer gets to the point, and brings all the themes and topics together.

Shinshu Kokugo Soran noted that the alternative four-part construction *ki-shô-ten-ketsu* is adapted from the poetic form of a Chinese quatrain, *zekku:*

<ki> Beginning. A problem is shown.
<shô> In response to *ki*, it describes further detail.
<ten> A example which contrasts or is opposed to the idea presented in the former two
    steps is given to enhance the development of the subject.
<ketsu> Integrating the contents discussed in *ten* section, the whole comes to a conclusion
    with one theme. (Ema, Taniyama, & Ino, 1981, p. 295 [trans. Miri Park])

K. Takemata defined the *ten* section in a slightly different way: "At the point where this development is finished, turn the idea to a subtheme where there is a connection, but not a directly connected association [to the major theme]." Takemata also pointed out that a

Japanese *ketsu* "need not be decisive [*danteiteki*]. All it needs to do is to indicate a doubt or ask a question" (cited in Hinds, 1983, p. 80).

The *ki-shô-ten-ketsu* pattern can be seen as roughly analogous to the five-paragraph essay formula in English, and is often used for short essays and academic paper writing. However, the *ten* and *ketsu* sections are especially problematic for English readers. Linguist John Hinds points out that:

> In *ten,* an abrupt shift takes place in which information only indirectly relevant to the major point is brought up with minimal syntactic marking. This obviously causes problems for English readers who do not expect "digressions" and "unrelated information" to come up suddenly. ... In *ketsu,* the major difficulty involves the Japanese definition of this term and the difference between that and the English definition of "conclusion." (1983, p. 80)

Intermediate Japanese ESL students who are new to writing in English tend to produce four-paragraph essays in which the third paragraph seems to be entirely off topic. Japanese readers who know this pattern expect the third section to make some kind of away from the topic; American readers are confused; and American instructors are likely to ask, "How does this relate to your topic?" or "What's your point?"

For example, a Japanese graduate student came to the Writing Center because he was having trouble passing the university's writing proficiency test. He said that the writing center tutors told him that his problem was not grammatical errors, but, rather, that he kept going off the topic. The tutor talked about this *ki-shô-ten-ketsu* pattern, and explained that American readers have trouble following the *ten* section. The tutor asked if the writer could simply leave that section out. The writer understood what the tutor was saying, but he did not seem to think he could leave one section out. However, encouraging students to reflect on this problem in this way may lead to adoption of more American patterns.

Japanese rhetorical patterns are influenced by earlier Chinese patterns. Kaplan found that some Korean and Chinese writing is marked by what may be called an "approach by indirection." In this kind of writing, the development of the paragraph may be said to be turning in circles around the subject, showing it from a variety of tangential views, but never looking at the subject directly. Things are developed in terms of what they are not, rather than in terms of what they are (Kaplan, 1966).

Kaplan also found that Chinese students writing in English were influenced by the Chinese eight-legged essay, the required form for the civil service exam from the middle of the 15th century to the early 20th. Cai (1993) said that the eight-legged essay is still a powerful organizing principle for many Chinese students and that a newer, four-part model, *qi-cheng-jun-he,* is commonly used to organize paragraphs. *Qi* prepares the reader for the topic, *cheng* introduces and develops the topic, *jun* turns to a seemingly unrelated subject, and *he* sums up the paragraph. In Cai's example, the *qi* section states that we learn about ourselves from songs and stories, the *cheng* section notes that we "realize" or understand ourselves and mutually understand people through books, and the *jun* section names places where we learn and use literacy, and also interact with others, but does not directly mention literacy or books. The [*he*] section, what an English reader might call the "topic sentence," appears at the end of the paragraph: "Hence, literacy is not an ornament, but a necessity" (Cai, 1993, as cited in Connor, 1996, p. 39).

Hinds (1990) demonstrated that writing in Japanese, Chinese, Thai, and Korean follows an organizational pattern he calls "quasi-inductive." Generally, writing in English is deductive, with the thesis at the beginning. If the thesis is not at the beginning, readers expect an inductive pattern, with the thesis at the end. Instead, in this pattern, the thesis is implied or buried in the passage, involving what Hinds called "a delayed introduction of purpose." Hinds (1990) noted:

> Seen in this light, we must recognize that the traditional distinction that English-speaking readers make between deductive and inductive writing styles is inappropriate to the writing of some nonnative authors. We may more appropriately characterize this writing as quasi-inductive, recognizing that this technique has as its purpose the task of getting readers to think for themselves, to consider the observations made, and to draw their own conclusions. The task of the writer, then, is not necessarily to convince, although it is clear that such authors have their own opinions. Rather, the task is to stimulate the reader into contemplating an issue or issues that might not have been previously considered. (p. 42)

Additional Cultural Influences

Literature, culture, and education have rhetorical influences beyond organizational patterns. The Asian writer's tendency toward an approach through indirection may also result in a preference for the passive voice, which allows actors and agents to remain unspecified. Kaplan found that native speakers of Arabic tend to favor coordination over subordination, because of the stylistic influence of the Koran. "While the literary traditions of the Judeo-Greco literary influence do not penetrate in English much beyond the 17th century, the literary influences of the Koran in Arabic extend into the present day" (Kaplan, 1966, p. 35). Since the 17th century, the fashion in English prose has been to favor subordination over coordination. However, in Arabic, the stylistic preference is for elaborate coordination. Kaplan shows that when Arabic-speaking students revise compositions in English, they create *more* coordinated structures. (To get an idea of what such elaborate coordination sounds like, look at the beginning of Genesis in the King James version.)

An Example from Mexican-Spanish Composition

In "Discourse Features of Written Mexican Spanish: Current Research in Contrastive Rhetoric and Its Implications," Maria Montaño-Harmon described a study of four groups of student writers: Mexican students in Mexico, who are native-speakers of Spanish, writing in Spanish; ESL students, who are native speakers of Mexican Spanish, writing in English; Mexican-American/Chicano students, who are English-dominant, writing in English; and Anglo-American students writing in English. She found that the compositions written in Mexican Spanish were longer overall than those written in English, but contained fewer sentences. Sentences in the Spanish compositions were longer and tended to be what English readers would characterize as run-ons, connected by conjunctions, commas, or no separation at all. On occasion, one sentence would occupy an entire paragraph. Anglo-American writers used simple subject–verb complement constructions or short complex sentences subordinated with "because" (Montaño-Harmon, 1991).

Montaño-Harmon also found that students in Mexico:

> relied heavily on synonyms to unify their compositions, a skill that is emphasized and taught explicitly in the schools in Mexico. Their basic strategy was to state an idea, place a comma,

and then repeat the same idea using a synonym, the same word, or a semantically related word (collocation) to create a build-up effect. This building on an idea was emphasized many times via the use of hyperbole. Thus, the result was a repetition of the same idea several times within a run-on sentence, each repetition becoming more fancy or formal. (p. 421)

Note that this pattern was explicitly taught by the Mexican teachers.

The compositions also differed in the representation of logical relationships. Anglo-American students most often used enumeration of ideas, represented by such connectors as *first*, *second*, *then*, and *finally*. On the other hand, the Spanish compositions were organized via additive or explicative relationships, in which the writer states an idea and adds restatements and explanations for why he or she believes it.

Perhaps the most important feature of the Spanish compositions was that they had many more deviations in their logical development, in some cases complete breaks in the connection between one idea and the next. As Montaño-Harmon explained:

> These deviations were *conscious deviations*, which are part of the discourse pattern of Mexican Spanish, for the writer was aware that he/she had gone off the topic and would often use transitional words or phrases to return to the previous idea before the deviation. (p. 422)

The Anglo-American students, if they deviated from the topic, did so unconsciously, without transitional phrases.

On the other hand, the writing of Mexican-American, or Chicano, students was unlike that of any of the other groups. These students "exhibited composition problems due to a clash between a nonstandard dialect of English, Chicano English—used for oral, informal interaction with peers—and the standard/academic English" (p. 419). They did not exhibit Spanish language interference problems.

Implications for the Classroom

Students whose primary literacy is in a language other than English may write in English using rhetorical patterns that are appropriate to their native language and culture, but are confusing or seem disorganized to American readers. It is very difficult to cast aside ingrained habits of thought and organization. Rather than labeling such texts disorganized, or identifying particular sections as tangential or unnecessary, the instructor can approach the problem as a matter of writing to the appropriate audience, and explain that American readers have different expectations than Japanese, Chinese, Mexican, or Arabic readers.

GENERATION 1.5

In the past, most writing programs divided developmental writing students into two categories: native speakers of English (or basic writers) and non-native speakers (or ESL students). In many programs, the non-native speakers were generally assumed to be international students, quite unfamiliar with American language and culture, or first-generation immigrants who had been in the United States for a short time. Time in the United States was seen as a major factor in determining who belonged in the ESL course. Second-generation students, born in the United States, were assumed to be assimilated and fluent. These categories have now become inadequate to describe current student populations, if indeed they ever were adequate. Now researchers are talking about "Generation 1.5," and many programs have begun developing basic writing courses designed specifically for this student population (see Holten, 2002; Holten & Mikesell, 2007; Goen, Porter, Swanson, & van Dommelen, 2002, for specific examples of such curricula and teaching practices). *Generation 1.5 Meets College Composition: Issues in the Teaching of Writing to U.S.-Educated Learners of ESL* (1999), edited by Linda Harklau, Kay M. Losey, and Meryl Siegal, is an excellent introductory resource for issues related to this population.

Some researchers have defined Generation 1.5 students as immigrants who arrive in the United States as children or adolescents, and obtain a large part of their K-12 education in U.S. schools, thus sharing characteristics of both the first and second generations. However, there are also students who were born in the United States who speak a foreign language at home and in the community. For this latter group, English is an academic language, and the language of literacy, but the home environment does not support the development of English-language skills. Another possibility is a home environment in which English is spoken by parents or siblings who are in the midst of language acquisition themselves. In this case, some children may acquire someone else's interlanguage as a native language. Finally, being what Roberge (2002) defined as "aural/oral" learners, i.e., learners who acquire language through natural interaction, Generation 1.5 English users often incorporate into their speech the features of community dialects, such as African-American English Vernacular or Chicano English, that are generally considered nonstandard and, therefore, undesirable in the academic environment.

Roberge (2002, 2003) also pointed out that Generation 1.5 learners' educational histories play a significant role in the process of their acquiring English as an additional language. Their schooling experiences are often riddled with interruptions, inconsistencies in pedagogical practices, premature mainstreaming or, on the contrary, persistent ESL tracking based on ethnicity or the length of residency in the United States rather than on language skills, and relative inattention to academic literacy. This tends to result in the learners' gaining significantly higher oral communicative proficiency than grammatical competency or academic reading and writing skills.

Lastly, recent studies, for example Chiang and Schmida (1999), Destandau and Wald (2002), Holten (2002), and Roberge (2002, 2003), have found that Generation 1.5 students develop complex cultural and linguistic identities. While some may still waver in their cultural affiliations, most such learners, especially those who are born in the United States or who arrive in the United States at a very young age, tend to identify with the American culture and frequently consider themselves native speakers of English (e.g. Holten, 2002). Nevertheless, their writing often displays features typical of second language users, such as errors in verb forms, verb tense use, predication, subject–verb agreement, and complementation (Holten, 2002; Holten & Mikesell, 2007; Mikesell, 2007). However, since the paths of language acquisition differ between international students and Generation 1.5 English users, pedagogies employed in traditional ESL classes may not be appropriate for the latter.

It is important for composition teachers to keep in mind, then, that international students and recent immigrants tend to have strong influences from the rhetorical patterns and epistemological attitudes of their home cultures, with which they strongly identify. In this group, language acquisition is ongoing, and the instructor's job is to negotiate an understanding between the rhetorical patterns and stylistic preferences of the student's home culture and those of the English-speaking world, as well as facilitating progress along the interlanguage continuum toward grammatical proficiency in standard written English. As language acquisition progresses, the goal is for nonstandard grammatical forms to be discarded in favor of standard ones. Generation 1.5 students, on the other hand, are likely to be familiar with American rhetorical patterns, especially the more formulaic ones, but may speak a nonstandard dialect of English. This dialect may be an essential part of home life, or communication with peers, and, thus, it is questionable whether the nonstandard forms—which are a feature of this dialect—can or should be discarded. In this case, standard written English must be considered as a new dialect to be acquired.

Implications for the Classroom

The growing presence of Generation 1.5 writers in both ESL and composition classes presents a challenge for both types of instructors. Composition instructors, who until recently, needed to focus only on rhetorical and stylistic issues, now have to contend with grammatical errors, which can affect both the comprehensibility of student texts and the credibility of their authors. College-level ESL instructors, on the other hand, have been generally trained to teach students with high levels of declarative knowledge of English grammar but limited procedural skills in applying it. They now have to educate students who compose their texts and construct their sentences based on intuitions about language, on the feeling of what "sounds right." Unfortunately for Generation 1.5 writers, for the reasons discussed above, these intuitions are often flawed when it comes to academic language use. Lacking the tools that typical ESL students usually receive in the course of learning English, such as grammatical terminology and overtly stated rules regarding grammatical structures, Generation 1.5 writers often find themselves unable to correct their syntactic and morphological errors because they do not see what it is they are supposed to correct or how they are supposed to correct it.

What, then, are instructors to do? How can they help their students become more proficient writers? Recent research and practice suggest that a balance between rhetoric and grammar instruction is necessary in classrooms with significant numbers of Generation 1.5 writers irrespective of the official designation of the classroom as either composition or ESL (Goen, Porter, Swanson, & van Dommelen, 2002; Holten, 2002; Holten & Mikesell, 2007; Singhal, 2004; Thonus, 2003). Generation 1.5 writers certainly do need to master common rhetorical patterns used in academic texts, but because such patterns are already culturally familiar to the students educated in American secondary schools, even if only on the subconscious level, instruction in rhetoric and style can be informed by the same theories and pedagogies as used for teaching composition to native speakers. Instructors can focus on helping students write for specific purposes and for specific audiences who share the writers' cultural references and expectations.

With respect to grammar, many researchers and practitioners agree that Generation 1.5 English users need explicit tools they can rely on in editing their own writing for linguistic accuracy and fluency. As Thonus (2003) has pointed out, appealing to these students' native-speaker intuitions is counterproductive precisely because these intuitions may not be quite "native."[1] In other words, what may sound odd to a monolingual native speaker of the standard dialect may not sound odd at all to a Generation 1.5 bilingual. Generation 1.5 writers, therefore, are not always able to correct their grammatical and lexical mistakes based on "what sounds right." On the other hand, Foin and Lange (2005) have found that

Generation 1.5 students who were taught grammatical terminology and rules and whose linguistic errors in essays were then marked with a familiar grammatical code were able to correct up to 89% of the marked errors on their own when they revised the essays.

Holten (2002; Holten & Mikesell, 2007) and Goen, Porter, Swanson, & van Dommelen (2002) advocate a discourse-based approach to teaching grammar to Generation 1.5 writers. Instructors of both advanced ESL users and native speakers may find this approach equally effective, especially when it comes to helping students polish their writing by eliminating language problems common to all groups of writers: misplaced modifiers, run-on sentences, fragments, or abrupt and unmarked shifts between different rhetorical moves. In this approach, grammar is taught not as a subject in and of itself, but as a tool that allows writers to manipulate language in such a way as to make their texts accessible, persuasive, and credible to their audiences. Holten (Holten, 2002; Holten & Mikesell, 2007), in particular, suggests using readings not only as models of good writing, as is already done in composition classes, but also as models of the rhetorical effects that different grammatical choices produce. Students can analyze academic texts in order to understand how passive and active voice allow them to refocus the reader's attention, how cohesion in a text can be created through the appropriate use of verb tenses or logical connectors, how smooth flow is achieved through parallel structure and the use of participial phrases, and so on. The form and function of each structure can be taught simultaneously during mini-lessons or grammar workshops designed in response to specific linguistic problems arising in student writing. The focused analysis of the functions of grammatical forms in well-written texts is consistent with the consciousness raising practice discussed above.

Goen, Porter, Swanson, and van Dommelen (2002) propose using the students' own original texts, complete with their authentic errors, as the foundation for teaching self-editing strategies. Learning such strategies may require also learning a limited amount of grammatical terminology, but only as a means of providing students with a "handle" on the problematic lexicogrammatical patterns. Holten (2002) found that students were more engaged and personally invested if they learned grammatical rules, terms, and patterns as a tool to make their sentences clearer, their paragraphs more cohesive and coherent, and their essays better flowing. Another technique that composition instructors may find useful is teaching students to use the dictionary as a source of grammatical information, such as the countability of nouns, transitivity of verbs, and the existence of irregular forms. Armed with this information, students are less likely to make errors in article use, predication, or complementation (Holten & Mikesell, 2007).

To sum up, the balance of explicit discourse-based grammar instruction and rhetoric creates a learning environment where Generation 1.5 writers can gain both metalinguistic and metarhetorical awareness and, thus, become independent authors, proofreaders, and editors of their work.

For Writing and Discussion

1. Develop a survey based on the types of question at the beginning of this section. Administer the survey to a writing class, and write a paper discussing the results.
2. Choose a topic related to language pedagogy or language policy, perhaps "grammar teaching" or "English-only" policies. Write an essay using an unfamiliar form

of organization such as inductive or quasi-inductive. When finished, write a post-script about your experience of writing this essay.

RESPONDING TO STUDENT WRITING

ESL writing generally contains more errors, and different kinds of error, than the writing of native speakers. The natural instinct of most teachers who encounter papers written by non-native speakers is to begin correcting the errors one by one as they encounter them in the first reading of the paper. Students often encourage this type of response by saying that they want every error corrected. However, students also tend to believe that an error-free paper is an "A" paper, which might be the case in an ESL classroom, but is not the case in an academic course, or in business or industry. The paper must also be appropriate for its audience and achieve its rhetorical purpose. As we have seen in the discussion above, non-native speakers are often unaware of the rhetorical expectations of American readers and apply different organizational strategies and argumentation styles. It is important to address the problem of error, but it is equally important to address rhetorical issues in responding to student writing.

Addressing Rhetorical Concerns

Response to Student Writing: Implications for Second Language Students, provides a very useful summary of research regarding the effects of different kinds of response to student writing, in both the L1 and L2 literature. Ferris finds a convergence between the two fields in the 21st century, with both developing somewhat parallel analytical frameworks for evaluating comments and finding that while students value feedback and appreciate both praise and constructive criticism on their writing, both L1 and L2 students struggle with vague, cryptic comments, abbreviations, and correction codes.

Ferris recommends designing a rubric or grading criteria sheet to use in responding to assignments. Her example includes categories for quality of the response to the assignment, the content, the use of readings, the organization, and language and mechanics. The sheet saves time because the instructor does not end up writing the same comments on every paper. It also keeps the instructor and the students appropriately aware of rhetorical issues. The technology that is often available to students and teachers in 21st-century university settings can be used to make response sheets even more powerful. If students submit papers electronically, it is easy for the instructor to copy good and bad examples from the current papers and paste them into a copy of the response sheet, to be projected in class for discussion of different possibilities for improvement. This practice reinforces awareness of the issues the rubric is designed to reflect and provides an opportunity both to demonstrate success and to negotiate improvement.

Addressing Grammatical Concerns

Silva, Leki, and Carson (1997) characterize errors as "windows on the acquisition process," but note that it is hard to know if a particular error is a feature of the writer's interlanguage or simply a mistake. As we have seen above, Krashen's Second Language Acquisition theory implies that teaching grammar directly will not be effective except perhaps in special cases. Consciousness-raising implies that selective attention to particular grammatical features could facilitate acquisition of those features. Whatever theory is true, it remains common practice in both ESL classes and mainstream composition classes to correct errors in written texts. Is this an effective practice?

In "The Case against Grammar Correction in L2 Writing Classes," John Truscott set off a storm of controversy by describing a comprehensive survey of research he conducted on this question, both in mainstream and ESL composition. His conclusion is as follows:

> Grammar correction has no place in writing courses and should be abandoned. The reasons are (a) research evidence shows that grammar correction is ineffective; (b) this lack of effectiveness is exactly what should be expected, given the nature of language learning; (c) grammar correction has significant harmful effects; and (d) the various arguments offered for continuing it all lack merit. (1996, p. 328)

Truscott reached these conclusions after carefully evaluating many different kinds of study covering many different kinds of grammar correction, including explicit correction, correction codes, and highlighting errors without explanation. Of selective correction, he says:

> One might think that at least some of these problems could be greatly reduced if teachers selected a few important errors and consistently corrected them over a long period, ignoring other, less important errors. ... Not surprisingly then, selective correction seems to be the generally accepted approach these days. ... However, the evidence is not encouraging on this matter. (1996, p. 352)

Truscott noted that various studies of L1 writing found that it makes no difference whether corrections are comprehensive or selective: "For L2, Hendrikson (1981) failed to find any difference between comprehensive correction and correction restricted to communicative errors. Thus, the evidence suggests that limiting the number of corrections is not a solution" (1996, pp. 352–353). Silva, Leki, and Carson (1997) noted that according to the "Teachability Hypothesis" (Pienemann, 1984) learners will learn what they are taught only if they are developmentally ready, but agreed with Truscott that "although many second language learners believe in the importance of correction, there is little evidence that correction has much effect on developing proficiency" (Silva, Leki, & Carson, 1997, p. 414). Truscott left open the possibility that selective correction carefully timed in accordance with a developmental sequence might be effective, but he is not sanguine about the possibility.

Ferris (1999) is a response to Truscott's arguments, but at that point the evidence that error correction is effective in improving student writing was slim to none. Subsequently, in Ferris (2003), she again reviews the literature, including new studies of her own, taking great care to note study design and which variables are controlled and which are not, and concludes, "despite design inconsistencies and the lack of a true control group in most instances, the majority of studies suggest that error feedback is beneficial to student writers" (p. 140). This review makes it clear that studies of the effectiveness of teacher response are very difficult to design and implement because of the complexity of the task and the number of variables that are almost impossible to control.

What should teachers do? In our summary and response to Ferris's review of the research we focus on five general questions:

- Should instructors correct errors, or simply indicate where they are (direct versus indirect feedback)?
- If direct feedback is given, should the instructor use a correction code?
- Should feedback on rhetorical and content problems come in early drafts with feedback on grammatical problems later, or can different kinds of feedback be combined?
- Should instructors include mini-lessons on grammatical problems?
- Will making students responsible for the linguistic accuracy of their texts help them improve?

The following suggestions address each of these points in turn.

The Directness of Feedback

For errors in structures that are teachable or rule-governed, indirect feedback is most effective. This means making an underline in the text or a checkmark in the margin to indicate that there is a problem that the student must fix. However, non-native English-speaking students do not necessarily have the same language intuitions as native speakers even when they are highly proficient. Merely indicating to these learners that something is wrong in a sentence or a phrase may not assist them in correcting it if the problem is part of their interlanguage. It is, therefore, important not to forget the "teachable" aspect of the "teachable structure."

For structures that are not rule-governed or are idiomatic, such as preposition use or lexical choices, or where the rules are too elaborate and complicated to be taught, let alone acquired, in a single workshop, such as article usage or complementation, it may be best to give direct feedback, i.e., correct the error. Indirect feedback is also generally ineffective for complex sentence structure errors. In such sentences, multiple problems usually compound each other, creating an overall effect of incomprehensibility or awkwardness, but it is often impossible to tease out a single factor that, if fixed, would resolve the problem. Instructors may find it useful to address such errors in individual conferences with the students, guiding them in the process of reformulating problematic stretches of language so as to make the meaning clearer to the reader. Another approach is to project a particularly tangled sentence on a screen or write it on the board for a class editing session, being careful to focus on the meanings created by different alternatives. If the errors in complex structures are pervasive, it may be good to add the clarity of language as a component of regular peer-editing practice and let students collaborate in reformulating anonymous problematic stretches from their peers' essays.

The Use of Correction Codes

Ferris notes that codes or abbreviations such as "Awk." for "awkward sentence" or "WC" for "word choice" can be confusing to students and do not appear to cause effective revisions, and she recommends that if correction codes are used, they should be simple, consistent, and clearly explained. On error codes and direct feedback in general Ferris says, "it is important to note that the scant research evidence that exists on this point suggests that it makes little difference whether such errors are treated by direct or indirect feedback" (2003, p. 147).

However, here, we must again draw attention to the fact that non-native speaking students (and often speakers of nonstandard dialects coming from disadvantaged educational backgrounds) do not have the same intuitions about awkwardness and register- and genre-appropriate word use as native speakers of the standard dialect with a strong academic background. Vague codes appealing to native intuitions enhanced by extensive schooling that privileges the standard dialect can frustrate those learners who have no access to the said resources. Research on grammatical feedback to Generation 1.5 learners (e.g., Foin & Lange, 2005; Goen, Porter, Swanson, & van Dommelen, 2002; Holten, 2002) suggests that providing *specific* codes and demonstrating to the students what they mean and how the errors can be fixed has beneficial effects. It is best to use excerpts from student writing as authentic examples on the correction symbol guide and to provide this guide to the students at the beginning of the course.

The Use of Combined Feedback

Composition instructors need not worry about stumping students with two different types of feedback. Giving feedback on content and rhetorical issues at the same time as feedback on errors does not appear to confuse students, and can lead to successful revisions. In fact, as per Ferris's suggestion discussed in the preceding section, teachers may want to include a section on grammar and mechanics in the same rubric that they use to respond to the students' rhetorical issues. Analytical rubrics with language and mechanics as components have been successfully used in developmental writing classes in many programs, including, for example, UCLA's ESL Service Courses and Writing Programs and Cal Poly Pomona's Composition for Multilingual Speakers program.

Grammar Mini-lessons

The effectiveness of the direct teaching of grammar has little support in either L1 or L2 research. However, it is hard to hold students responsible for errors they cannot recognize or understand. Composition instructors who find themselves marking the same types of error over and over in multiple students' essays might find it useful to devote part of their instructional time to targeted grammar workshops aimed at teaching the students what makes a particular structure problematic and how it may be fixed. Using the students' own sentences as good or bad examples of the structure's use is likely to keep them more invested in learning. This approach is often called teaching "grammar in context." If the errors are not patterned or particular to only one or two students, it may be more efficient for the teacher to refer the students to outside resources, such as grammar books or reference texts, from which the students can learn the appropriate use of the structure in question.

Student Responsibility for Linguistic Accuracy

It is important for composition teachers to assign a large portion of responsibility for linguistic accuracy to the students themselves. Studies on the writing of Generation 1.5 learners conducted both in classrooms (Foin & Lange, 2005) and University Writing Centers (Goen, Porter, Swanson, & van Dommelen, 2002; Destandau & Wald, 2002; Holten, 2002; Thonus, 2003) show that when students find their own corrections to the grammatical errors they have made, they are more likely to retain the command of the target structure in the future. Furthermore, encouraging students to fix problematic sentences in their own way allows them to retain the ownership of the text and their voice as authors. These properties of authorship may be jeopardized if the instructor imposes his or her choice of wording or grammatical structure on the writer. With respect to timing, self-editing immediately after receiving the feedback may help long-term improvement.

Another way of making students accountable for linguistic accuracy is keeping error logs. Error logs help students track their success in reducing errors and may help with consciousness raising. These can be tailored to individual students. Logs with broader, more inclusive categories seem to be more effective than those with a larger number of more precisely defined categories.

CONCLUSIONS

The theories outlined in this chapter have strong implications for what an ESL writing course should look like. The course should provide ample opportunities for comprehensible input, via both reading and listening. The atmosphere in the classroom should be positive and comfortable, so that anxiety is diminished, and there should be numerous opportunities for real communication. As Silva, Leki, and Carson (1997) noted, "It is thought that interactive input focused on communicating comprehensible messages of importance to both partners in a communicative event (rather than corrective feedback) is what helps learners most to progress in their second language" (p. 412).

The rhetorical expectations of English speakers, and the organizational patterns of academic genres such as the college essay, research essay, report, memo, and letter, may have to be explicitly taught, especially to international students. John Swales, in *Genre Analysis: English in Academic and Research Settings* (1990), noted that case studies indicate that "there may be value in sensitizing students to rhetorical effects, and to the rhetorical structures that tend to recur in genre-specific texts," and that "formal schemata ... need to be activated and developed, not so much as rigid templates against which all texts are forced to fit, but more as *caricatures* which self-evidently simplify and distort certain features in an attempt to capture general identity" (p. 213). However, instructors should use care when presenting formulaic approaches such as the five-paragraph essay, because students may over-generalize the formula to inappropriate genres, and may become so reliant on the formula that they are unable to grow as writers.

Feedback on the writing should include selective attention to nonstandard forms, so that acquisition of standard forms can be facilitated. As Rod Ellis said, "formal instruction is best seen as facilitating natural language development rather than offering an alternative mode of learning." He noted that formal instruction seems to work best when combined with opportunities to experience the structures taught in real communication, and recommended approaches that focus both on forms and the meanings they create (Ellis, 1994, p. 659).

Tony Silva, Ilona Leki, and Joan Carson (1997) are correct in arguing that research in ESL composition has much to teach mainstream composition, especially regarding language acquisition theory, which connects easily with reading theory, vocabulary acquisition, and other matters of concern to all writing teachers. Contrastive rhetoric and the study of cross-cultural communication also offer important insights into the rhetorical patterns of English. In the matter of error correction, there is still research to be done and many questions to answer, but these questions are also relevant to mainstream composition.

For Futher Exploration

Ellis, R. (1994). *The study of second language acquisition.* Oxford: Oxford University Press.
This work is an authoritative compendium of research and theory concerning the problems of language acquisition.

Ferris, D. (2003). *Response to student writing: Implications for second language students.* Mahwah, NJ: Lawrence Erlbaum.
Dana Ferris provides a thorough summary of the research on responding to student writing in both L1 and L2 classrooms, draws conclusions about implications for teaching practice, and provides a wealth of suggestions for new and experienced teachers.

Ferris, D., & Hedgcock, J. S. (1998). *Teaching ESL composition: Purpose, process, and practice.* Mahwah, NJ: Lawrence Erlbaum.
This work by Dana Ferris and John S. Hedgecock is a very thorough presentation of almost every aspect of teaching ESL writing, including theoretical issues, reading–writing connections, syllabus design, lesson planning, text selection, oral and written feedback, and improving grammatical accuracy.

Silva, T., & Matsuda, P. K. (Eds.) (2001). *Landmark essays on ESL writing.* Mahwah, NJ: Hermagoras Press.
Landmark essays on ESL writing, edited by Tony Silva and Paul Kei Matsuda, reprints 16 articles that have been influential in the field, including Kaplan's original 1966 contrastive rhetoric article "Cultural Thought Patterns in Inter-cultural Education."

Silva, T., & Matsuda, P. K. (Eds.) (2001). *On second language writing.* Mahwah, NJ: Lawrence Erlbaum Associates.
On second language writing (2001), also edited by Silva and Matsuda, presents 15 new articles.

Swales, S. M. (1990). *Genre analysis: English in academic and research settings.* Cambridge: Cambridge University Press.
This work is an insightful and interesting analysis of the problems of genres and discourse communities, very applicable to the problems of ESL composition and contrastive rhetoric.

For Writing and Discussion

1. Look up the aforementioned articles by John Truscott and Dana Ferris. Write a paper analyzing their arguments and presenting your own case for or against grammar correction.

2. Do a web search on "learn hiragana," "learn Chinese characters," "learn Greek alphabet," or "learn Arabic alphabet," or try a search on another writing system. Using the materials you find, try to learn to write five or six letters or characters from an unfamiliar writing system. Write a description of your experiences, noting your successes and problems. Discuss your experiences with the class.

NOTE

1 The concept of nativeness is a complex and controversial one within second language studies. Here, the term "native intuitions" is used to refer to the idealized intuitions of monolingual speakers of the standard dialect, which they acquired from birth, which they use (primarily or exclusively) in their everyday communication, schooling, and professional life, and which underlie written academic English.

REFERENCES

Cai, G. (1993, March). Beyond bad writing: Teaching English composition to Chinese ESL students. Paper presented at the Conference of College Composition and Communication. San Diego, CA.

Chiang, Y. D., & Schmida, M. (1999). Language identity and language ownership: Linguistic conflicts of first-year university writing students. In L. Harklau, K. M. Losey, & M. Siegal (Eds.), *Generation 1.5 meets college composition: Issues in the teaching of writing to U.S.-educated learners of ESL*. Mahwah, NJ: Lawrence Erlbaum.

Connor, U. (1996). *Contrastive rhetoric: Cross-cultural aspects of second-language writing.* Cambridge: Cambridge University Press.

Connor, U., & Kaplan, R. (Eds.). (1987). *Writing across languages: Analysis of L2 text.* Reading, MA: Addison Wesley.

Destandau, N., & Wald, M. (2002). Promoting Generation 1.5 learners' academic literacy and autonomy: Contributions from the Learning Center. *The CATESOL Journal, 14* (1), 207–234.

Ellis, R. (1985). *Understanding second language acquisition.* New York: Oxford University Press.

Ellis, R. (1994). *The study of second language acquisition.* Oxford: Oxford University Press.

Ema, T., Taniyama, S., & Ino, K. (Eds.). (1981). Bunshô no kakikata [How to construct a sentence/composition]. In *Shinshu kokugo soran [New Japanese conspectus]* (rev. ed., pp. 294–295). Kyoto: Kyoto Shobô.

Ferris, D. (1999). The case for grammar correction in L2 writing classes: A response to Truscott (1996). *Journal of Second Language Writing, 8* (1), 1–11.

Ferris, D. (2003). *Response to student writing: Implications for second language students.* Mahwah, NJ: Lawrence Erlbaum.

Foin, A. T., & Lange, E. J. (2005). Error coding effects on revision in Generation 1.5 writing. Proceedings of the CATESOL State Conference. Retrieved on October 7, 2010, from http://www.catesol.org/Foin_Lange.pdf.

Goen, S., Porter, P., Swanson, D., & van Dommelen, D. (2002). Working with Generation 1.5 students and their teachers: ESL meets composition. *The CATESOL Journal, 14* (1), 131–171.

Harklau, L., Losey, K. M., & Siegal, M. (Eds.) (1999). *Generation 1.5 meets college composition: Issues in the teaching of writing to U.S.-educated learners of ESL.* Mahwah, NJ: Lawrence Erlbaum.

Hartwell, P. (1985). Grammar, grammars, and the teaching of grammar. *College English, 47,* 105–127.

Hendrikson, J. M. (1981). *Error analysis and error correction in language teaching.* Singapore: SEAMEO Regional Language Centre.

Hinds, J. (1976). *Aspects of Japanese discourse structure.* Tokyo: Kaitakusha.

Hinds, J. (1983). Linguistics and written discourse in English and Japanese: A contrastive study. In R. B. Kaplan (Ed.), *Annual review of applied linguistics 1982* (pp. 78–84). Rowley, MA: Newbury House.

Hinds, J. (1990). Inductive, deductive: Expository writing in Japanese, Korean, Chinese and Thai. In U. Connor & A. M. Johns (Eds.), *Coherence in writing: Research & pedagogical perspectives* (pp. 87–110). Alexandria, VA: TESOL.

Holten, C. (2002). Charting new territory: Creating an interdepartmental course for Generation 1.5 writers. *The CATESOL Journal, 19* (1), 173–189.

Holten, C., & Mikesell, L. (2007). Using discourse-based strategies to address lexicogrammatical development of Generation 1.5 ESL writers. *The CATESOL Journal, 19* (1), 35–52.

Horning, A. S. (1987). *Teaching writing as a second language.* Carbondale: Southern Illinois University Press.

Kaplan, R. B. (1966). Cultural thought patterns in intercultural education. *Language Learning, 16,* 1–20.

Kaplan, R. B. (1972). *The anatomy of rhetoric: Prolegomena to a functional theory of rhetoric: Essays for teachers. Language and the teacher: A series in applied linguistics* (Vol. 8). Philadelphia, PA: The Center for Curriculum Development.

Kaplan, R. B. (1988). Contrastive rhetoric and second language learning: Notes toward a theory of contrastive rhetoric. In A. C. Purves (Ed.), *Writing across languages and cultures: Issues in contrastive rhetoric* (pp. 275–304). *Written Communication Annual* (Vol. 2). Newbury Park: Sage.

Kaplan, R. B. (2001). Forward: What in the world is contrastive rhetoric? In C. G. Panetta (Ed.), *Contrastive rhetoric revisited and redefined* (pp. vii–xx). Mahwah, NJ: Lawrence Erlbaum.

Krashen, S. (1982). *Principles and practice in second language acquisition.* Oxford: Pergamon Press.

Mikesell, L. (2007). Differences between Generation 1.5 and English as a Second Language writers: A corpus-based comparison of past participle use in academic essays. *The CATESOL Journal, 19* (1), 7–29.

Montaño-Harmon, M. (1991). Discourse features of written Mexican Spanish: Current research in contrastive rhetoric and its implications. *Hispania, 74,* 417–425.

Pienemann, M. (1984). Psychological constraints on the teachability of languages. *Studies in Second Language Acquisition, 6,* 186–214.

Roberge, M. M. (2002). California's Generation 1.5 immigrants: What experiences, characteristics, and needs do they bring to our English classes? *The CATESOL Journal, 14* (1), 107–129.

Roberge, M. M. (March, 2003). Academic literacy scaffolds for Generation 1.5 students: What special experiences, characteristics and educational needs do they bring to our English classes? Paper presented at the 37th Annual TESOL Convention, Baltimore, MD.

Rutherford, W. E. (1987). *Second language grammar: Learning and teaching.* New York: Longman.

Scardamalia, M., & Bereiter, C. (1987). Knowledge telling and knowledge transforming in written composition. In S. Rosenberg (Ed). *Advances in applied psycholinguistics. Volume 2: Reading, writing and language learning* (pp. 142–175). Cambridge: Cambridge University Press.

Silva, T., Leki, I., & Carson, J. (1997, July). Broadening the perspective of mainstream composition studies: Some thoughts from the disciplinary margins. *Written Communication, 14* (3), 398–428.

Singhal, M. (2004). Academic writing and Generation 1.5: Pedagogical goals and instructional issues in the college composition classroom. *The Reading Matrix, 4* (3), 1–13.

Swales, J. M. (1990). *Genre analysis: English in academic and research settings.* Cambridge: Cambridge University Press.

Thonus, T. (2003). Serving Generation 1.5 learners in the University Writing Center. *TESOL Journal, 12* (1), 17–24.

Truscott, J. (1996). The case against grammar correction in L2 writing classes. *Language Learning, 46* (2), 327–369.

Reading

BROADENING THE PERSPECTIVE OF MAINSTREAM COMPOSITION STUDIES: SOME THOUGHTS FROM THE DISCIPLINARY MARGINS

Tony Silva
Purdue University

Ilona Leki
University of Tennessee

Joan Carson
Georgia State University

In this article we (a) argue that mainstream composition studies is at present too narrow in its scope and limited in its perspective and (b) offer some thoughts, from our unique interdisciplinary position, that we feel could help mainstream composition professionals improve this situation. In our article, we first provide evidence that we feel suggests an unfortunate pattern of neglect in mainstream composition studies of writing in English as a second language (ESL) and writing in languages other than English. We then introduce a number of concepts from second language studies (primarily from second language acquisition and second language writing instruction) that we believe could help mainstream composition studies address its limitations; develop a more global and inclusive understanding of writing; and thus avoid being seen as a monolinguistic, monocultural, and ethnocentric enterprise.

Native language teachers have much to learn from ESL research and pedagogy.

—Smith, 1992

We agree.

English as a Second Language (ESL) writing, or more generally, second language writing is uniquely situated at the intersection of second language studies and composition studies. This position requires us as second language writing researchers and teachers to keep up on scholarship in two fairly distinct disciplines and invites us to compare developments in each and to observe how each influences the other. In our view, both disciplines have a lot to offer each other. A number of ideas and insights from composition studies have proved quite valuable for second language studies and have both broadened its perspectives and added depth to its discussions. Unfortunately, the transfer of knowledge between the fields has primarily been a one way affair, from composition studies to second language studies.[1]

There is no disputing that in recent years mainstream composition studies has been at great pains to articulate and promote a multicultural perspective that honors diversity. Composition studies has gained a great deal from attention to feminist, critical, postcolonial, and postmodernist perspectives imported from literary and cultural studies.[2] Yet from our vantage point, mainstream composition studies remains troublingly narrow in its scope. Mainstream composition scholars make what seem to us to be universalist claims about the phenomenon of writing almost exclusively on the basis of Western (Greco-Roman and Anglo-American) rhetorical traditions and/or on the findings of empirical research conducted primarily on undergraduate college students in North American colleges and universities. Muchiri, Mulamba, Myers, and Ndoloi (1995) propose a similar argument supported by compelling examples from the perspective of African writing researchers. They urge composition researchers to

> see how much of [their] work is tied to the particular context of the U.S. When composition researchers make larger claims about academic knowledge and language, it [sic] needs to acknowledge these ties. The very diversity rightly celebrated in the composition literature may lead a teacher to forget that it is diversity joined in a peculiarly American way, within American institutions, in an American space. The teacher in New York or Los Angeles may look out over a classroom and think, "the whole world is here." It isn't. (p. 195)

Canagarajah (1996) likewise provides a glimpse into the material conditions of scholars in third world countries, conditions so unlike those taken for granted, for example, in North America. But in mainstream composition studies little consideration has been given to writing in languages other than English—for example, there seems to be negligible concern for Asian, African, or Middle Eastern writing or rhetorics—or to writing done by individuals in a language that is not their mother tongue. This limited perspective is troubling to us in that we feel it could lead to inadequate theories of composition and consequently to instructional practices that are ineffective or even counter productive. We believe that the attention to issues raised by the examination of writers learning and composing in a second language can result in a broadening of perspectives that may enrich mainstream composition studies in the same way as feminist, critical, postcolonial, and postmodernist considerations have done.

Our discussion is in two parts. First, we offer evidence to support our claim about the limitations of mainstream composition studies. Second, we introduce and discuss some concepts from second language studies that we believe could help mainstream composition studies address these limitations.[3]

A Pattern of Neglect

The neglect of second and other language writing in mainstream composition studies becomes evident when some of the field's basic documents are examined. For example, a perusal of the program books for the Conference on College Composition and Communication (CCCC) conferences will reveal a very small number of sessions devoted to second and other language concerns, and a substantial percentage of the sessions labeled as such actually relate only marginally to second or other language matters. The *CCCC Bibliography of Composition and Rhetoric*, though it includes a subsection on ESL (placed under the heading of curriculum and thus implicitly put on a par with areas like research and study skills), devotes only a tiny percentage of its entries to second and other language matters. Furthermore, many of the relevant entries do not deal with writing issues, thus providing a partial and distorted picture of scholarship in second and other language writing.

A look at almost any of the monographs of the most widely known mainstream composition scholars (for example, those of Berlin, Berthoff, Elbow, Emig, Kinneavy, Flower) will turn up little if anything regarding second or other language writing. This also holds true for important collections and reviews of research in the field. For example, in Bizzell and Herzberg's (1990), *The Rhetorical Tradition: Readings from Classical Times to the Present* (our bold), all of the selections are from the Western (Greco-Roman and Anglo-American) rhetorical tradition; we found no focus on Asian, African, Middle Eastern, or other rhetorical traditions and no mention of this exclusion in the book's preface or elsewhere. Given the contents of this collection, its title is problematic; it is at best misleading and at worst exclusionary in its ethnocentricity.

With regard to reviews of empirical research, Braddock, Lloyd-Jones, and Schoer (1963) note as "unexplored territory" (p. 53) the effectiveness of "... procedures of teaching and learning composition ... for pupils learning to write English as a second language" (p. 54). Although none of the studies considered for this report focused on second or other language writing, the authors' recognition of the need to look at ESL writing is promising. Thus, it is disappointing and ironic to find in the introduction to Hillocks' (1986) follow up volume, *Research on Written Composition: New Directions for Teaching*, that "... research dealing with spelling, vocabulary, initial teaching alphabet, or English as a second language was excluded" (p. xvii). Hillocks goes on to say that "Research written in languages other than English was not examined" (p. xviii)—with the exception of one review of research in Dutch—an exclusion that would certainly seem to work against globalization of the research base on writing.

An examination of scholarly journals in mainstream composition over the last 10 years would reveal a similar pattern. Although a few of these journals (*Journal of Basic Writing, Writing Center Journal*, and *Written Communication*) give what we would consider a meaningful amount of space to second and other language writing issues, in the majority of mainstream composition journals the treatment of second and other language writing concerns seems to us to be largely absent or negligible.

An examination of mainstream composition textbooks, handbooks, and readers reveals a more encouraging but not wholly satisfactory situation. Though many of the newest composition text-books and handbooks include notes or sections to address ESL writers, these treatments are often limited to morphosyntactic considerations (for example, verb use, articles, adjective/adverb position, present and past participles). Although this is a step in the direction of inclusion, it implies a simplistic view of ESL writers, that is, that their differences from native English speaking writers are merely a matter of a few morphosyntactic oddities and that no consideration of discoursal, rhetorical, or cultural differences is necessary. The case with mainstream composition readers is similar. Although many focus on cross-cultural or multicultural issues, these issues are typically addressed in the North American context, thus making them somewhat culture bound and difficult to use with those ESL writers who are new to this context. That is, many of these readers assume knowledge or experience that many ESL writers do not possess.

On the basis of the foregoing, it is fair to suggest that, overall, mainstream composition studies' perspective on second and other language writing is indeed limited. We believe that such a limited perspective is problematic on both theoretical and practical levels. A theory of writing based only on one rhetorical tradition and one language can at best be extremely tentative and at worst totally invalid. Such a theory could easily become hegemonic and exclusionary; that is, English/Western writing behaviors could be privileged as somehow being "standard," thus stigmatizing other writing behaviors as "substandard" or "deviant." Such a theory could be seen as monolingual, monocultural, and ethnocentric. Pedagogical insights so based would seem inadequate even for those whose concerns are limited to North America because the population here is increasingly diverse and multicultural. For those with more global concerns, such narrowness of scope is untenable and unacceptable.

Clearly composition studies needs a broader and more inclusive view of writing, one that we feel could profit from the perspectives and insights of second language studies. Therefore, we will introduce and discuss insights from two wide domains of second language studies: second language acquisition (SLA) and ESL writing pedagogy. We believe these insights could help mainstream composition studies develop a more global and inclusive view of writing. Here it is not our intention to show explicitly how each issue we raise would play out in mainstream composition classrooms or research. We leave that to mainstream composition instructors and researchers. Rather we seek primarily to point to directions of potentially fruitful inquiry and reflection. Though we recognize that some mainstream composition professionals may find some of these concepts familiar, we expect that the second language spin provided here will be less familiar. We also believe that the examination of the large area of studies of writing in languages other than English, though regretfully beyond the scope of this article, would repay consideration by adding a needed depth to theories of rhetoric and writing.

Insights from Second Language Studies

Second Language Acquisition Research

The idea that inexperienced first language writers are like learners of a second language, most often the language of the academy, has been suggested by Horning (1987) whose central hypothesis is that "basic writers develop writing skills and achieve proficiency in the same way that other adults develop second language skills, principally because, for basic writers, academic, formal, written English is a new and distinct linguistic system" (p. 2). Although this hypothesis makes intuitive sense, Horning's account of SLA falls short in several crucial respects. We mention Horning's work here because reviewers' comments on previous drafts of this article indicate that it is one of the few sources of information about second language writing known by mainstream compositionists, and yet Horning's account is at best incomplete. Horning relies heavily on Krashen's learning-acquisition distinction in which conscious (learned) and unconscious (acquired) acquisition are said to result in distinct and unrelated processing mechanisms (see, for example, Krashen, 1981, 1982), a distinction that has been frequently and convincingly challenged in second language acquisition research. Furthermore, Horning's work presents, at best, an uneven explanation of concepts in second language acquisition and, at worst, explanations of complex phenomena (errors, for example) that do not accord with the findings of relevant research. Finally, she does not address some of the crucial aspects of second language acquisition theory that would be most relevant to an understanding of first language writing development (explanations of variability, for example). Thus, whereas Horning's initial analogy may be appealing, we hope to supplement and modify this account through a closer look at what second language acquisition theory has to offer first language composition studies.

Those who are developing expertise in writing already command a first—oral—language and through exposure to and practice with writing are expected to move progressively closer to the language norms of those in the community of writers they seek to join. However, this perspective describes developing writers primarily in terms of proficiency, or lack thereof. For example, in his review of 1,557 composition studies from 1984–1989, Durst (1990) notes that the most influential composition research has been with English speaking high school students (Emig, 1971); high school, college, and more experienced writers (Bridwell, 1980; Faigley & Witte, 1981; Sommers, 1980); expert and novice writers (Flower & Hayes, 1981); basic college writers (Perl, 1979); and early elementary students (Graves, 1978). This literature on composing processes provides a picture of writers arrayed on a developmental continuum from less to more proficient. Proficiency has been portrayed in mainstream composition research as an issue of development and as the primary factor distinguishing among first language writers. Research in second language studies, on the other hand, has been more concerned with *explaining* differential proficiency. In general, second language acquisition research seeks to answer four fundamental questions:

1. What does learner language look like? (This description needs to account for both synchronic and diachronic aspects of learner language.)
2. How do learners acquire a second language? (This explanation needs to include both internal and external factors.)
3. What accounts for the differences in learners' achievements? (This explanation attends to the fact that second language learners as a rule experience differential success.)

4. What are the effects of formal instruction? (This question investigates the extent to which instruction plays a role in the acquisition process.)

In the following section, we will review some of the major findings in each of these areas.

Question #1. What does learner language look like? In general, learner language can be characterized as having three dimensions: (a) it has errors; (b) it exhibits developmental pat terns; and (c) it is variable.

Perspectives on error in second language acquisition are similar to those of Shaughnessy (1977) in that they are seen as windows on the acquisition process. Errors, however, are difficult to define and identify for several reasons. First, it is not always clear whether a learner is producing an error (generated by the learner's linguistic competence) or a mistake (generated by the learner's linguistic performance). Second, the variety of language that the learner has chosen to acquire is an intervening factor: what might be an error in one variety is not necessarily so in another. Finally, because learners' intended utterances are not always clear to native speakers, what constitutes the specific error in an utterance is not always immediately obvious. These issues of error definition and identification are undoubtedly applicable, as well, to the development of written language proficiency by providing different ways of interpreting possible errors in students' work.

Because error analysis does not provide a complete picture of learner language (a focus on errors fails to provide information about what learners are doing correctly, for example), errors are only a preliminary source of information about learner language. The recognition of developmental patterns allows a clearer picture of the general regularities that characterize second language acquisition. Typically, in the early stages of acquisition, learners use formulaic speech that consists of memorized language formulas or routines. This strategy allows learners to produce whole "chunks" of language, reducing the learning burden while maximizing communicative ability. These chunks are available later for analysis as learners figure out the items and rules used in creative speech. Do we see similar processes among inexperienced writers who try on the written language forms of the academy, for example, in chunks of overly academic phrasings? Borrowing unanalyzed chunks of such written language can be seen not negatively as indicating a lack of proficiency but rather positively as moving the learner forward toward target and flexible use of written forms.

The development of second language proficiency is understood as occurring on what Selinker (1972) calls the interlanguage continuum, in which the learner moves successively toward closer and closer approximations of the target language. This continuum is characterized by the acquisition of general patterns of language in a relatively predictable order, and this order does not vary regardless of the learner's first language background. In other words, all learners will develop linguistically along the same general route of acquisition. But a learner's interlanguage rules are not necessarily the rules of the target language; rather, they represent the learner's hypotheses at a single point in time about the target language.

Although the interlanguage continuum provides a perspective on the regularities in second language learners' acquisition patterns, there is an apparent contradiction between this systematicity and the variation that is evident in, and characteristic of, learner language. Variation is exhibited when learners apply a rule in one context but not in another. For example, a learner who writes "You depend on other people and they depend of you" has produced the target language rule in the first clause but not in the second.

What accounts for this variability? Variability of this type is described as occurring in three contexts: linguistic, situational, and psycholinguistic. Linguistic context refers to the language elements that precede and/or follow the variable in question. For example, a second language learner might easily produce subject-verb agreement in simple sentences (My sister lives in Washington), but might not in complex sentences (My sister, who live in Washington, is older than me.)

Situational context refers to many factors including speech styles (style shifting in socially appropriate ways), social factors (such as age, gender, class, ethnicity), and stylistic factors (situation and topic, for example). Each of these factors can result in the differential application of interlanguage rules. For example, producing an essay on a topic related to the learner's experiences in their native country might result in more first language interference (see discussion of Friedlander, 1990, below) than would an essay based on experiences in the learner's second language. This might be the case, too, with writers who speak a non-standard dialect, where certain topics might elicit more non-standard forms. Social Accommodation Theory (Beebe, 1988) can help explain some of the variability as well, to the extent that writers seek to converge with, diverge from, or maintain a social connection to the reader. (See issues of motivation and social distance below.)

Psycholinguistic context refers to the cognitive processing constraints imposed by the task in question. Learners must balance the demands of language production with the cognitive demands inherent in producing the text (oral or written). Speaking on a complex or abstract topic or under time constraints means that the language learner must focus not only on the difficulty of what s/he is trying to say, but also on the language that is needed to express her/his ideas. When attention is divided in this way, the speaker often attends primarily to the content of the utterance rather than to its form, resulting in language that is less native-like than would be the case if the speaker were talking about familiar, more concrete topics. With less complex tasks, in terms of topic or lack of time constraints or as the result of a process approach in which the writer focuses on language issues only in later drafts, a writer is likely to have time to employ a careful style, which is the most attended form. However, the attended style does not necessarily result in the most correct form. Monitoring in the careful style allows the learner/writer the time to consider competing hypotheses about language forms. Because writing eventually requires the selection of a single form—even when more than one possibility exists for the writer—the text may not only exhibit variability (when the writer in one place chooses one form and in another place the competing form) but may also give the reader an inaccurate perspective on the writer's developing competence.

Most adult second language learners never reach target language proficiency (this is commonly seen in the persistence of non-native pronunciation—foreign accents), and this failure to move toward native speaker norms is called "fossilization" (Selinker, 1972). Cognitive and social forces appear to intersect in the phenomenon of fossilization, in which a second language learner stops progressing toward proficiency in the second language despite continuing access to target or "correct" forms. Second language learners reach a level of competence in the target language that allows them to accomplish their communication tasks to their own satisfaction, and though they may assert that they want to continue to move toward target forms, they do not move farther. In fact, they may no longer even perceive the difference between their own production and target forms.

The construct of fossilization might apply to novices writing in their first language and help explain lack of progress toward target goals of institutionally accepted writing. It is possible that, despite conscious belief that they want to produce a change in their writing, novice writers considered unsuccessful are in fact satisfied with the communicativeness of what they produce and have no profound motivation to unfossilize. In the complex interaction between social and cognitive factors, an exploration of the implications of fossilization for mainstream composition studies might yield new insights.

Given this complex picture of learner language, it become clear that writers' errors are a window on the acquisition process. Errors exhibit the variability inherent in the acquisition process, and as such can be interpreted as evidence of the writer's potential (not unlike Vygotsky's (1978) zone of proximal development), rather than as a lack of proficiency.

Question #2. How do learners acquire a second language? Explaining second language acquisition requires a consideration of both external and internal factors. (Although linguistic universals are an important part of second language acquisition theory, they are probably not of relevance to composition studies and will not be discussed here.) Significant external factors are primarily social in nature; internal factors involve issues of language transfer and cognition.

External factors. Social factors play a major but indirect role in second language acquisition, insofar as acquisition is mediated by learner attitudes as well as by the nature and extent of input (as determined by learning opportunities related to such things as ethnic background and socio-economic class). Learner attitudes are both cognitive and affective, and they tend to be learned and persistent, but modifiable. Learner attitudes toward the acquisition of the target language are related to learner attitudes toward target language speakers, the target language culture, the social value of learning the target language, the particular uses that the target language might serve, and the learners' perceptions of themselves as members of their own culture.

Social factors related to second language acquisition include sociolinguistic aspects of age (younger learners between the ages of 10 and 19 are more influenced by their peer group whereas middle aged learners from 30 to 60 are more influenced by mainstream social values, including standard language norms), sex (women tend to have more positive attitudes and to use more standard forms than men), and social class. In particular, social class is related to the role of socio-psychological attitudes, to the extent that second language acquisition implies the loss of the first language (referred to as subtractive bilingualism) or the maintenance of the first language as the second language is acquired (referred to as additive bilingualism). Subtractive bilingualism is typical of what happens in this country to immigrants and refugees who are expected to become "Americanized" linguistically by giving up their first language and adopting English. In this perspective, the first language is perceived as a problem that language learners must overcome. Additive bilingualism, on the other hand, is typical of middle- and upper-class bilinguals for whom knowing more than one language is seen as an advantage. In this view, bilingualism is seen as a resource that can be used for social, political, and economic gain.

The social context of subtractive bilingualism influences learners' attitudes and language acquisition in subtle but profound ways, having to do with the learner's identification with the first language social group. A parallel can be drawn here for middle- and upper-class writers who typically control a more or less standard variety of English (given regional variation). These writers are given the opportunity in school to develop the type of writing proficiency used in academic contexts, with no expectation that they will need to abandon/"correct" their oral language or their written language in nonacademic contexts. In other words, their writing development is more nearly like additive bilingualism. However, students who speak a nonstandard variety of English, typically associated with working-class writers, are most often taught that their oral and written language is "incorrect" and they are put in the position of subtractive bilinguals who feel that they must give up their first language to acquire the standard forms.

Related to this notion of ethnolinguistic vitality, Schumann's (1977) Acculturation Model of second language acquisition sees language as one aspect of becoming acculturated to the second language cultural context. According to Schumann, successful language acquisition depends on the learner's perceived social and psychological distance from the target language group. When the learner maintains this distance, pidginization is likely to occur in which the learner fossilizes on a relatively nonproficient point on the interlanguage continuum, resulting in the ability to produce limited language functions. (See Peirce, 1995 for a cogent critique of Schumann and others who appear to make language acquisition contingent on giving up first language social identities.)

This perspective on fossilization evokes issues of learner motivation, central to studies of second language acquisition. A widely used distinction in second language acquisition work that might be useful to mainstream writing research is the distinction between integrative motivation and instrumental motivation, originally proposed by Gardner and Lambert (1972). A learner who shows integrative motivation wants to become like the people who speak the target language. (See Alice Kaplan's [1993] autobiography of a French major for a striking example of this concept.) The target culture is admired and its representatives are sought out and imitated. A learner who shows instrumental motivation, on the other hand, is less interested in the target language, culture, and people for their inherent qualities, but more interested in developing skilled use of the target language for particular purposes. This might be the type of motivation of, for example, Chinese graduate students in physics studying in the United States for an advanced degree making some English speaking friends, but primarily interested in English to participate in, perhaps, the international dialogue in professional journals in physics.

Neither type of motivation is necessarily superior to the other; both have been shown to correlate with success in language learning. But the discussion in mainstream writing literature has implicitly focused almost exclusively on integrative motivation, urging an integrative desire on writing students. If we think of, for instance, the teachers of writing as the "native speakers" of the target culture, first language students with integrative motivation would want to become like those native speakers, to imitate their behavior and attitudes. Bartholomae (1985) speaks of students having to invent the university; more dramatically, students are required to re-invent themselves, ideally to see themselves as indistinguishable from the people already there, already a part of the university culture. Although there has been recognition in the mainstream writing literature of the fact that students may not want to bring their image of themselves in line with the image projected by the "natives" of the university culture, second language writing research explicitly acknowledges the legitimacy and efficacy of instrumental, not just integrative, motivation in the pursuit of the second language, including writing.

The issue of social context for learning a second language that predominates in Schumann's work focuses on the importance of the social distance between the native and the target culture. A few of the conditions favorable to the acquisition of the second language that might be considered in thinking about mainstream writing instruction include the following: The learner's culture and the target culture admire each other and see each other as equals; both the learner's culture and the target culture expect the learner to succeed; the learner and the target culture share social environments; the learner plans to spend a great deal of time in the target culture. If we look at the first language learners' task in developing into proficient writers, we must question whether the optimal conditions laid out here for second language acquisition are met for first language writing students. When viewed from this perspective, we might feel humbled by the enormity of the social barriers faced especially by writing students from minority cultures not admired by the target culture, not seen as equal, not expected to succeed, and not socialized with. These barriers may be insurmountable for first language students from poor, rural, or minority cultures or backgrounds whose relationship to the majority culture is not optimal for acquisition of majority norms, even when such acquisition is desired.

Internal factors. The question of how the learner's first language knowledge influences the acquisition of the second language has long been an issue for second language theory. Second language acquisition researchers see a complex role for the first language in the acquisition of the second: sometimes negative, when reliance on first language intuitions causes errors in the second language; sometimes positive, when taking a chance using a first language form succeeds and results in appropriate use of the second language. This work has implications for mainstream writing research if extended to include attempts to understand, for example, the relationship between a student's oral language and that student's acquisition of written language. What features of the target language are difficult for writing students to acquire and which come easily? Which features of a student's oral language help in the acquisition of the written language and which do not? With a better sense of the answers to these questions, teachers might be more sensitive to the efforts students are required to make in order to function in written language and might have more realistic expectations of individual students and of writing curriculums.

The role of consciousness is also of interest to second language theorists. Bialystok (1978) claims that conscious and unconscious knowledge interact in second language acquisition.

Explicit knowledge arises when there is a focus on the language code, and the acquisition of explicit knowledge is facilitated by formal practice. Implicit knowledge is developed through exposure to communicative language use that is facilitated by functional practice. Bialystock's perspective is one that Is relevant to composition theory to the extent that it can account for the fact that techniques such as explicit grammar teaching have been shown to be ineffective in improving writing proficiency. Functional practice, resulting in implicit knowledge, highlights the importance of audience and purpose in writing and suggests why a focus on these aspects of the writing process is more likely to lead to the development of writing ability.

Such internal factors interact with the external linguistic environment, a feature of the acquisition context stressed in second language research but perhaps underplayed in first language contexts. Target language input is presumed to be data that the learner must use to develop and adjust an internal picture (the interlanguage system) of how the target language is constructed. It is thought that interactive input focused on communicating comprehensible messages of importance to both partners in a communicative event (rather than corrective feedback) is what helps learners most to progress in their second language.

In terms of mainstream writing instruction, the question then would be: What kind of input are the learners getting? Are they aware of what the target language looks like? Do they get repeated samples of what they are expected to produce? Research in Canada shows high school writers able to adapt their writing for sixth graders but not for adult newspaper readers (Lusignan & Fortier, 1992). Is this perhaps because these young writers know from personal experience what sixth grade texts look like, but have no real internalized sense of what the other target language, here, the written language of newspaper readers, looks like? If this is the case, how can they be expected to produce similar language or rhetorical forms? Do first language writing students read material that they can realistically be expected to produce, or is it far too complicated, too far beyond their reach for them to be able to produce similar types of writing within the short amount of time designated as appropriate for learning to write, for example, during a first-year composition class? Clearly the role of input is as significant in composition studies as it is in second language acquisition research.

Question #3. What accounts for the differences in learners' achievements? It is a fact that few adult second language learners (perhaps only 5%) will acquire native-like proficiency in the target language, although many if not most learners will attain the ability to communicate relative to their needs. This fact of differential success requires explanation in second language acquisition theory and has resulted in many studies of learner differences.

In the context of writing, the recognition of learner differences and of differential success can lead to a deeper institutional acceptance of the idea that different students have differing goals and agendas in their study of writing. Second language research explicitly recognizes that because of differing motivations or differing amounts of contact with speakers of the target language some learners will become more proficient than others. Teachers and researchers in second language writing also acknowledge that those who are learning to write in a second language in an institutional setting may be doing so only to satisfy the requirements of the institutional setting and may never again need to write, or perhaps even to read, a single word in their second language in the rest of their lifetimes, particularly if these learners return to their native countries. These acknowledgments help to discourage an inappropriately inflated view of the importance of learning to write and a concomitant inappropriate negative evaluation of those who do not become particularly proficient. Although little attention is given in mainstream composition studies to gaining a sense of native English speaking students' goals and agendas in learning to write, such a focus might be revealing and might lead to a reconsideration of why students should necessarily learn to write for higher educational settings at all. (See discussion below on functions of writing.) Or, perhaps such a focus might lead to a refinement of notions of "proficiency" to include the recognition of student goals and agendas—that is, that students may be proficient when they have achieved what they want to achieve and not when they achieve what the academy wants them to. Proficiency might be seen as an individual concept rather than an institutional one.

Characterizations of good language learners parallel those of proficient writers: These learners are typically said to show a concern for form, concern for meaning/communication, an active task approach, an awareness of the learning process, and the capacity to use strategies flexibly vis-à-vis task requirements. Second language acquisition researchers distinguish between learning styles, understood as a consistent way of functioning, and learning strategies, assumed to be modifiable. (In mainstream composition studies, much of the work leading to the process paradigm in composition focuses on writer's strategies, e.g., Emig, 1971.) However, although open to modification and conscious manipulation, according to research by Bialystock (1985), learning strategies must be internally governed. That is, teaching the strategies of good learners to poor learners and urging the struggling learners to adopt them will not result in improvement. Such a claim has clear implications for composition instruction that is based on the notion that struggling writers are best served by being taught the composing strategies of successful writers. SLA research suggests that requisite internal government may not develop through instruction on composing processes.

Recognition in mainstream composition studies of differences in learner styles and strategies has not seemed to move far beyond noting that certain minority students are more orally or visually oriented than traditional, majority-culture students. Mainstream composition research may need to examine these preference among individuals (in either the majority or minority cultures) and propose alternative teaching methods to accommodate them. (See Carson & Nelson, 1996 for a second language perspective on culture-related problems of peer review in an ESL composition class, for example.) Such a focus seems particularly desirable in light of recent challenges to progressive and expressivist forms of writing instruction that assert that expressivist forms of instruction are effective primarily for White middle-class students and not for less advantaged writers (Cope & Kalantzis, 1993; Graff, 1996; Gore, 1993; Stotsky, 1995).

Question #4. What are the effects of formal instruction? One of the surprising findings of second language acquisition research is that there has been no convincing evidence for method superiority. Several explanations have been offered for this finding. First, lessons of any type often result in relatively little progress in language acquisition. Second, individual learners benefit from different types of instruction. Finally, language classes tend to offer similar opportunities for learning irrespective of method. The most important question about formal classroom instruction, though, is whether learners learn what they are taught. The answer to this question may lie with what is referred to as the Teachability Hypothesis (Pienemann, 1984). According to this hypothesis, learners will learn what they are taught only if they are developmentally ready.

This perspective calls into question the role of error correction. Although many second language learners believe in the importance of correction, there is little evidence that correction has much effect on developing proficiency, although it may lead to undesirable types of communication. Chaudron's (1988) review of research on teachers' error correction behaviors concludes that many errors are not treated and that the more often an error is made, the less likely a teacher is to correct it. This may be due to teachers' tacit understanding that error treatment should be conducted in a manner compatible with general interlanguage development; that is, teachers may correct only errors that learners are ready to eliminate. In mainstream composition pedagogy, errors appear to be regarded somewhat monolithically (either we should pay attention to them or not), with seemingly little attention given to the relationship between error production/correction and learner development.

One hypothesis about the effects of formal instruction is that negotiation may be the most crucial aspect of classroom interaction. In this respect, closed task tend to produce more negotiation and more useful negotiation work than open tasks (where there is no predetermined solution). This would be analogous to the difference between (a) writing an essay exam in a history class (a closed tasks in which content is either correct or not and, thus, discussable/explainable/negotiable) and (b) writing an expressive essay in a composition class (an open task in which there is no one predetermined correct response). Furthermore, teachers play a central role in formal acquisition because language learners need grammatical input that is unavailable in sufficient quantity from peers. This may explain recent findings (e.g., Zhang, 1995) in second language composition research that nonnative English speaking writers much prefer teacher feedback to peer response group input.

Second Language Writing Instruction

Second language writing research takes place against a background of insights developed from second language acquisition research. Taking into consideration what is known about second language acquisition and about composition theory and pedagogy, second language writing instruction has developed perspectives that are in some respects different from first language writing instruction but that may provide insights for mainstream composition studies.

Epistemological Issues   In second language writing instruction, cultural context is understood as a significant determinant of writers' purposes. Ballard and Clanchy (1991) argue that cultural attitudes toward knowledge range on a continuum from valuing the conservation of knowledge to valuing the extension of knowledge. "These different epistemologies are the bedrock of different cultures, yet they are so taken for granted, each so assumed to be 'universal,' that neither the teachers nor the students can recognize that they are standing on different ground" (p. 21). Ballard and Clanchy suggest that many Asian cultures favor conserving knowledge, with an emphasis on reproduction of information, and strategies such as memorizing and imitating. This is quite a different approach from the mainstream composition perspective of Scardamalia and Bereiter (1987), which highlights Western values of extending knowledge. Scardamalia and Bereiter characterize knowledge telling in writing as "immature" writing, and knowledge transforming as characteristic of "mature" writers. "What we see in the performance of expert writers is the execution of powerful procedures that enable them to draw on, elaborate, and refine available knowledge. For novices, however, writing serves more to reproduce than to refine knowledge" (p. 171). Asian writers who value the conservation of knowledge might be classified as "immature" knowledge tellers in the dichotomy Scardamalia and Bereiter present, although within their own cultural framework they would be "mature" writers. What would appear to be a developmental continuum, then, from immature to mature writing in a knowledge extending culture, is recast as an issue of social context when viewed from the larger crosscultural perspective.

Function of Writing   Mainstream composition research, beginning with Emig's (1971) groundbreaking study, turned away from a conventional focus on the message or text toward an investigation of the writer or encoder, highlighting writers' composing processes. This perspective emphasizes the importance of writing as a way of knowing, as well as the place of writing in the writer's mental development. For example, Freedman, Pringle, and Yalden (1979) note that Britton and the British educationists talk about the value of writing in acquiring knowledge and in allowing writers to come to terms with their lives. In this view, "writing is seen ultimately as the great humanizing force; it is not the practical, mundane, communicative advantages of writing that are celebrated but rather its power to give form and significance to our lives" (p. 9).

The mainstream composition literature very much gives the sense that writing experiences have the potential for producing thoughtful, critical-thinking citizens, and the development of such citizens has appeared an important goal in mainstream writing instruction. Also, the idea of using writing to learn has been a strong theme, particularly in the Writing Across the Curriculum Movement. But these views seem to assume that all writers will have the same priorities—an assumption that is not validated by the experience of second language writers. For many second language writers, for example, writing in a nonnative language will never have a function beyond the "practical, mundane, and communicative," as may well be the case for some first language writers. Clearly an adequate theory must acknowledge more pointedly that in a multicultural society, as in the world, the role of writing in writers' lives has varying functions and even for first language writers may legitimately remain limited, never becoming an instrument for life changing experiences.

Writing Topics   Teachers of second language writing try to be sensitive to a given writing topic's potential for being culture bound and not addressable by or appropriate for all cultural groups. Although some groups have no problem with writing on personal topics that require a great deal of personal disclosure, other groups find topics like these invasive and are not comfortable writing on them. Some groups may be reluctant to take issue with what they read; others may take an automatically contestatory stance in relation to what they read.

The point is that none of these preferences is beyond the range of possibilities for individual writers in any culture, including native English speaking writers. Although a given topic may be inappropriate for some native English speaking writers, they may nevertheless feel compelled to address some topics without protest when assigned because they find no cultural support for rejecting them. In thinking about what is appropriate for a native English speaking population, mainstream writing professionals might consider taking into account the kinds of differences in preference and comfort levels that are displayed in an international population.

Knowledge Storage   The issue of appropriateness arises from another angle in research (Friedlander, 1990) that suggests that experiences committed to memory in one language and written about in another are more difficult to write about than experiences committed to memory and written about in the same language. It is then also possible that native English speaking students may have particular difficulty using written (or academic) language to relate an experience stored in oral language. They not only need to access the memory but also, in effect, translate the experience from one language (oral) to another (written). Yet assignments that ask for this very translation are not unusual and in fact are considered especially easy because they only call upon writers to recount what they have experienced, with perhaps a "what I learned from this experience" tacked on. Friedlander's research suggests that such assignments may be more difficult than teachers realize.

Writing from Reading   Although writing from reading is common in mainstream composition studies, what is less typical is recognition of the difficulty first language student writers have reading. For second language readers it is assumed that texts may be opaque and that, therefore, learners may need help with reading, but it is not clear that such consideration is granted to native English speaking readers who appear to be expected to understand college level reading without help. The mainstream composition literature has carefully and repeatedly considered the reciprocity of reading and writing, and many mainstream writing classes use readings to stimulate writing, yet there is little evidence that actual instruction in reading has played much of a role in writing instruction in mainstream classrooms. Discussions of how to teach first language reading at the college level appear to be limited to teaching students how to read literary texts. Might native English speaking students perhaps also benefit from help in constructing meaning not only from literary texts, but also from texts from other genres?

Audience Awareness   Another dimension of composition studies that seems somewhat limited is that of the writer's awareness of the reader or audience and the role that such awareness plays in composing. Flower's (1979) distinction between reader- and writer-based prose, for example, has been extremely influential in mainstream composition studies. In this view, writer-based prose is the result of the writer's lack of cognitive awareness of the reader; the resultant text is insufficient for readers who lack the writer's ability to "fill in the gaps" with necessary information that the writer has in her or his mind but that does not appear in the text. Mature writers are able to move beyond writer-based prose and can develop a text that is reader-sensitive.

This "cognitive problem," as Flower described it, receives a different interpretation when we consider Japanese writers, who, according to Hinds (1987), are socialized in their literacy development (a) to read between the lines to interpret a writer's intention, and (b) to assume that readers will be able to "fill in the gaps" of the texts writers produce. It is asserted that Japanese writers believe that readers have a significant responsibility for understanding text, and comprehensible texts are more the result of "reader responsible" prose than they are of typical Western "writer responsible" texts wherein the writer's obligation is to clarify for the reader's understanding. Thus, what the prevailing paradigm sees as an issue of cognitive development is understood from a larger multicultural perspective as an issue of social context. It is not always clear in developmental studies which aspects of development should be attributed to cognition and which to social forces, but unqualified valuing of reader-based over writer-based prose points to a culture-specific view of this distinction. A broader perspective would look for common features in cognitive processes, recognizing that cognitive performance is inevitably shaped by social forces.

Textual Issues One area of study completely indigenous to second language research has emerged in the large body of work examining cross-cultural discourse patterns, or contrastive rhetoric. Although initial findings (Kaplan, 1966) have been criticized (see Connor, 1996, for a thorough discussion of contrastive rhetoric), there is general recognition that rhetorical form is a product of a culture's world view and social conventions, and that the degree to which texts are logical, well-formed, and successful depends on their sociocultural context.

The findings of contrastive rhetoric research are unique within second language research because they are the only elements of second language research that have piqued the interest of mainstream writing studies to any noticeable degree. Unfortunately, that interest has been limited primarily to a focus on the varying patterns of organization that have been said to prevail in different cultures (e.g., English is direct; Romance languages, digressive; Asian languages, indirect). Other contrastive rhetoric areas of potential interest to mainstream composition studies might include the exploration of varieties of text-types written within and across cultures; in genre studies, for example, culture-based expectations for such genres as grant writing; types of appeals that are persuasive across cultures; citation patterns that point to different ways of belonging to a scholarly tradition; appropriate tone to adopt in writing that will signal one's right to speak; cross-cultural perspectives on various rhetorical devices (for example, the importance and value placed on ornateness, beauty of language, or moral exhortations); the role of literacy and the methods of literacy training across cultures. Even as brief a listing as this indicates something of the enormous variety and richness available in studies of writing that go beyond concerns with writing in English by North American college students.

Within second language composition studies contrastive rhetoric research has helped us to view variations from the text structure expected in the culture of the U.S. university not as examples of failure to think logically or failure to learn to write. Instead they are viewed from the broader perspective contrastive rhetoric provides as examples of alternative rhetorics. The idea is not to eliminate their traces and replace them with the correct rhetoric, but rather to add English rhetoric to the second language student's repertoire of possible rhetorical solutions. Difference, then, is regarded as explanation, not as deficit.

Mainstream composition studies might consider pursuing answers to the question contrastive rhetoric poses: What assumptions do native English speaking learners already have about writing that might not match those of their academic audience? In terms of pedagogy, mainstream writing classes might do as second language writing classes do and make part of the instructional strategy to discuss with students in class and individually their assumptions about writing and the assumptions of the academy. Addressing differences in assumptions explicitly validates the students' background and acknowledges that college students do not come to first-year writing classes as blank slates but with a culturally developed image of what good writing is and of how to go about producing it. The study of contrastive rhetoric suggests that these images have a place in writing classrooms. It is clear, in any case, that text cannot be defined from a monocultural perspective and that the influence of culturally-preferred text structures must be considered as one of the factors that affect writers' composing processes.

Plagiarism   Mainstream views of plagiarism provide a further example of the limitations of conceptions that grow out of monocultural models of writing. The issue of plagiarism becomes more complex than the standard view allows for with a look at other cultures that view intellectual heritage differently. In cultures beyond the borders of North America the use of another's words or ideas can have the function of demonstrating the writer's familiarity with those words and ideas and of honoring historically important writers by finding them pertinent again. It is a mark of intellectual accomplishment to be able to select and use these words and ideas, an attitude that we have vestigially as well when we quote Shakespeare or Plato. If we cite a line from, say, Emma Goldman, and give its source, we interpret that as intellectual honesty. Another culture interprets the lack of need to cite Lao Tzu as the source of a quotation as a sign of respect for the reader of the line, an acknowledgment of the reader's scholarly achievement, the ability to recognize the line without the need for a gloss. (See Pennycook, 1996, for an extensive discussion of plagiarism and cross-cultural contexts.)

Memorization, Imitation, Quotation   Another angle to consider in thinking about plagiarism is from the point of view of the learner of any new language, including the language of the academy. In effect, all the language that the second language student uses is a borrowing without credit. Imitation, necessary in all language learning, is a way of trying on the target language and gradually transforming the internal representation of that language until the target language and the learner's internal representation of it, or the learner's interlanguage, coincide. This imitation may take the form of memorization of poems, facts, or chunks of language, a form of learning valued in many cultures. Western culture's argument for dismissing both memorization and extensive direct quotation rest on the opinion that when a learner does this, the learner is not learning, only repeating mindlessly what someone else has said. Yet other cultures view these as valid forms of learning. How can they reasonably be simply dismissed as mindless in this culture? In what sense can Western culture make the claim that those trained by its methods are better educated than those trained using other methods? (See also Sampson, 1984, who questions the importance of "superior" North American teaching methods in China.) Thus, other cultural practices call into question our confidence that learning is *not* accomplished by having the exact phrasings rolling around in the learner's head in all their complexity instead of in simplified versions translated into teenage language and understanding. The experiences of other cultures complexify our own understandings and must be accounted for in any legitimate theory of writing or learning. These examples clearly demonstrate the importance of broadening the dimensions of context-specific categories.

Students' Right to Their Own Language   The notion of students having a right to their own languages has been an issue of concern to first language writing researchers. The issue has usually been examined essentially as a question of additive or subtractive bidialectalism, similar to additive or subtractive bilingualism, with discussion nearly always centered around the status of the students' home, usually oral, dialect and the role this home dialect can take in academic writing instruction. The Conference of College Composition and Communication long ago moved to officially support the idea of students' right to their own language, although critics like Delpit (1988) have wondered whether this "right" in fact denies access to powerful academic languages to the students whose home dialects are most dissimilar from academic language.

For years, the picture in second language writing instruction was different. Students' right to their own language was, in one sense, a non-issue. It seemed obvious that Chinese international students had a right to Chinese and, perhaps more pertinently, French students a right to French.[4] These languages and cultures are admired. Speakers of these languages are proud of their languages and cultures, and their pride is supported by our admiration of their ability to speak, read, and write in another language. But the picture has become more complicated as second language writing researchers have begun questioning the role of English, particularly internationally, as the gatekeeper to power and wealth. Those with access to English could expect to accrue to themselves that power and wealth; those without, often could not. And those who could not afford English lessons that would allow them to obtain a high enough score on the TOEFL to be admitted to, for example, a North American university would perhaps never study abroad.

Further complicating the picture is the question: Whose English? That is, ESL professionals have come to recognize the importance of the many varieties of world English, such as those spoken in India, Singapore, Nigeria—Englishes whose structures and vocabulary vary from those of speakers from the monolingual English speaking countries like the United States, Great Britain, and Australia. Indeed, scholars from multilingual Third World countries have helped those from monolingual English speaking countries to see the anomaly of our monolingualism in a world where *most* humans negotiate in more than one language.

With the many challenges to the status of English coming from second language researchers, particularly from the "outer circle" (Kachru, 1985), those teaching ESL are thus being required to develop a more humble conception of the place of "our" English in the world. Can this more humble view also challenge the hegemony of academic English as taught, for example, in first-year composition classes? And for those who disdain the supposed stodginess of academic English and look instead for authenticity and voice, can this more humble sense of ourselves, combined with a more sophisticated knowledge of conditions in which English is used world wide, shake our faith in the notion that finding one's voice is a preeminent concern in learning to write? Ramanathan and Kaplan (1996) raise these very questions for ESL writing instruction. Should they also be considered in mainstream composition?

Conclusion

As ESL researchers, in reading and listening to the discourse of mainstream composition research, we often find ourselves in the same kind of awkward position as women sometimes experience when someone refers to "mankind" or uses "he" to refer to mixed genders. We want to add the equivalent of "or she"; we want to say "look at our research." Our voices here come from the margins of U.S. academic life but we nevertheless have something to contribute. First language writing researchers and practitioners lose by remaining unaware of findings and thinking in second language research.

Limited perspectives are likely to cause problems not only for writing teachers with ESL students in their classes but also for teachers of other ethnic minorities, including African, Asian, Hispanic, and Native Americans who might have native English proficiency but different sociocultural and sociocognitive contexts for writing. The attitudes and practices of second language writing classrooms challenge assumptions underlying first language writing pedagogy by taking for granted such notions as: Writers are heterogeneous; they have differing agendas in learning the second language and learning to write in that language; they are all developmental in that their tackling of academic writing will be a new experience; they will achieve differing ultimate success in their second language; they bring to the classroom specific culturally determined educational, social, and linguistic characteristics to which they claim an undisputed right and to which academic English is merely one addition. When second language writing classrooms refuse to regard ESL writers as simply writers who are deficient in English language, this perspective specifically acknowledges the importance of their contexts for writing, including writers' goals (conserving or extending knowledge), their perceptions of audience (text as reader-responsible or writer-responsible), and the influence of culturally-specified rhetorical forms on their writing processes and products. These views of the second language writer are supported by instructional practices that regard difference as an explanation rather than as a deficit; that acknowledge and openly address different learning (and teaching) styles and strategies; that assume and often openly address students' previous writing experiences and the way they contrast with rhetorical expectations in English; and that recognize that instruction is only one of many variables in writing development. These are all areas that might be considered in an attempt to broaden perspectives on teaching writing to native English speakers as well. Beyond classroom practices, a theory of composition that looks only at English writers, readers, texts, and contexts is an extremely narrow one. What can we know from a perspective limited to monolingual, monocultural writers and writing? Is the question really how a monolingual community learns culture-specific forms? Or is it the wider question of how different writers learn to deal with variable demands in various situations? Second language writers present the clearest picture of linguistic and cultural differences, yet they tend to be ignored by mainstream composition studies. Multilingualism and multiculturalism cannot be explored only from within the political borders of North America. Mainstream composition studies has given a great deal to second language writing research and teaching; it is time to take something in return. We feel that this something should be a larger, more inclusive, more global perspective on writers and writing, a perspective that can only enhance the validity and viability of mainstream composition theory.

Notes

1   In this article, we would like to begin to make this transfer a bit more balanced, and in doing so we will say some things about mainstream composition studies that may strike the reader as negative or uncomplimentary. However, we would like to make it clear up front that our purpose is not to chastise or impugn the motives of mainstream composition scholars or denigrate their work in any way. We respect these individuals and greatly value their efforts, which, we feel, are typically of the highest quality. Rather, our aim is to draw attention to what we see as a pattern of neglect of second and other language writing issues in the discipline today and to explore the potential consequences of that neglect.

2   We are also forced to recognize that second language composition studies has only just begun similar self-examinations, having for many years operated under an applied linguistics paradigm that viewed research into language learning, and by extension second language writing, as a question of science somehow free of ideological, social, and political constraints (see Santos, 1992). Given the highly charged nature of English teaching both in North America and around the world, such a parochial perspective seems quite astonishing. For discussions of the political, social, and ideological dimensions of teaching English, particularly worldwide, see work by, among others, Pennycook (1994, 1995, 1996), Phillipson (1988, 1991, 1992), and Tollefson (1989, 1995).

3   Second language studies in general and second language acquisition theory in particular have been accused of having a monolingual, ethnocentric bias (Kachru, 1994; Sridhar, 1994). The validity of this position is being discussed by second language researchers and theorists in professional forums and our goal in this article is to initiate the same type of discussion among mainstream composition researchers and theorists.

4   The picture has obviously never been as rosy for immigrants to this country who have always experienced strong pressure to assimilate and to suppress their connections to their native languages.

References

Ballard, B., & Clanchy, J. (1991). Assessment by misconception: Cultural influences and intellectual traditions. In L. Hamp-Lyons (Ed.), *Assessing second language writing in academic contexts* (pp. 19–36). Norwood, NJ: Ablex.

Bartholomae, D. (1985). Inventing the university. In M. Rose (Ed.), *When a writer can't write* (pp. 134–165). New York: Guilford.

Beebe, L. (1988). Five sociolinguistic approaches to second language acquisition. In L. Beebe (Ed.), *Issues in second language acquisition: Multiple perspectives* (pp. 43–77). New York: Newbury House.

Bialystock, E. (1978). A theoretical model of language learning. *Language Learning, 28,* 69–84.

Bialystock, E. (1985). The compatibility of teaching and learning strategies. *Applied Linguistics, 6,* 255–262.

Bizzell, P., & Herzberg, B. (1990). *The rhetorical tradition: Readings from classical times to the present.* Boston: Bedford.

Braddock, R., Lloyd-Jones, R., & Schoer, L. (1963). *Research in written composition.* Urbana, IL: National Council of Teachers of English.

Bridwell, L. (1980). Revising strategies in twelfth grade students' transactional writing. *Research in the Teaching of English, 14,* 197–222.

Canagarajah, A. S. (1996). "Nondiscursive" requirements in academic publishing, material resources of periphery scholars, and the politics of knowledge production. *Written Communication, 13,* 435–472.

Carson, J. G., & Nelson, G. L. (1996). Chinese students' perceptions of ESL peer response group interaction. *Journal of Second Language Writing, 5,* 1–19.

Chaudron, C. (1988). *Second language classrooms: Research on teaching and learning.* Cambridge, UK: Cambridge University Press.

Connor, U. (1996). *Contrastive rhetoric: Cross-cultural aspects of second language writing.* New York: Cambridge University Press.

Cope, B., & Kalantzis, M. (Eds.). (1993). *The powers of literacy: A genre approach to teaching writing.* London: Falmer.

Delpit, L. (1988). The silent dialogue: Power and ideology in education of other people's children. *Harvard Educational Review, 58,* 280–298.

Durst, R. K. (1990). The mongoose and the rat in composition research: Insights from the RTE annotated bibliography. *College Composition and Communication, 41,* 393–408.

Emig, J. (1971). *The composing process of twelfth graders.* Urbana, IL: National Council of Teachers of English.

Faigley, L., & Witte, S. (1981). Analyzing revision. *College Composition and Communication, 32,* 411–414.

Flower, L. (1979). Writer-based prose: A cognitive basis for problems in writing. *College English, 41,* 19–37.

Flower, L., & Hayes, J. R. (1981) A cognitive process theory of writing. *College Composition and Communication, 32,* 365–387.

Friedlander, A. (1990). Composing in English: Effects of first language on writing in English as a second language. In B. Kroll (Ed.), *Second language writing: Research Insights for the classroom* (pp. 109–125). New York: Cambridge University Press.

Friedman, A., Pringle, I., & Yalden, J. (1979). *Learning to write: First language/second language.* London: Longman.

Gardner, R. C., & Lambert, W. (1972). *Attitudes and motivation in second language learning.* Rowley, MA: Newbury House.

Gore, J. (1993). *The struggle for pedagogies: Critical and feminist discourses as regimes of truth.* London: Routledge.

Graff, G. (1996, May 27). Is progressive education growing up? *In These Times, 20,* 30–31.

Graves, D. (1978). *Balance the basics: Let them write.* New York: Ford Foundation.

Hillocks, G. (1986). *Research on written composition.* Urbana, IL: National Council of Teachers of English.

Hinds, J. (1987). Reader versus writer responsibility: A new typology. In U. Connor & R. B. Kaplan (Eds.), *Writing across languages: Analysis of L2 text* (pp. 141–152). Reading, MA: Addison Wesley.

Horning, A. (1987). *Teaching writing as a second language.* Carbondale: Southern Illinois University Press.

Kachru, B. (1985). Standards, codification and sociolinguistic realism: The English language in the outer circle. In R. Quirk & H. G. Widdowson (Eds.), *English in the world* (pp. 11–30). New York: Cambridge University Press.

Kachru, Y. (1994). Monolingual bias in SLA research. *TESOL Quarterly, 28*(4), 795–800.

Kaplan, A. (1993). *French lessons.* Chicago: University of Chicago Press.

Kaplan, R. B. (1966). Cultural thought patterns in inter-cultural education. *Language Learning, 16,* 1–20.

Krashen, S. (1981). *Second language acquisition and second language learning.* Oxford, UK: Pergamon.

Krashen, S. (1982). *Principles and practice in second language acquisition.* Oxford, UK: Pergamon.

Lusignan, G., & Fortier, G. (1992). Revision de textes et changement d'audience. *Canadian Journal of Education, 17,* 405–421.

Muchiri, M., Mulamba, N., Myers, G., & Ndoloi, D. (1995). Importing composition: Teaching and researching academic writing beyond North America. *College Composition and Communication, 46,* 175–198.

Peirce, B. (1995). Social identity, investment, and language learning. *TESOL Quarterly, 29,* 9–31.

Pennycook, A. (1994). *The cultural politics of English as an international language.* New York: Longman.

Pennycook, A. (1995). English in the world/the world in English. In J. Tollefson (Ed.), *Power and inequality in language education* (pp. 34–58). New York: Cambridge University Press.

Pennycook, A. (1996). Borrowing others' words: Text, ownership, memory, and plagiarism. *TESOL Quarterly, 30,* 201–230.

Perl, S. (1979). The composing process of unskilled college writers. *Research in the Teaching of English, 13,* 317–336.

Phillipson, R. (1988). Linguicism: Structures and ideologies in linguistic imperialism. In J. Cummins & T. Skutnabb-Kangas (Eds.), *Minority education: From shame to struggle* (pp. 339–378). Clevedon: Multilingual Matters.

Phillipson, R. (1991). Some items on the hidden agenda of second/foreign language acquisition. In R. Phillipson, E. Kellerman, L. Selinker, M. Sharwood-Smith, and M. Swain (Eds.). *Foreign/second language pedagogy research* (pp. 38–51). Bristol, PA: Multilingual Matters.

Phillipson, R. (1992). *Linguistic imperialism.* New York: Oxford University Press.

Pienemann, M. (1984). Psychological constraints on the teachability of languages. *Studies in Second Language Acquisition, 6,* 186–214.

Ramanathan, V., & Kaplan, R. B. (1996). Audience and voice in current L1 composition texts: Some implications for ESL student writers. *Journal of Second Language Writing, 5*(1), 21–24.

Sampson, G. P. (1984). Exporting language teaching methods from Canada to China. *TESL Canada, 1,* 19–31.

Santos, T. (1992). Ideology in composition: L1 and ESL. *Journal of Second Language Writing, 1,* 1–15.

Scardamalia, M., & Bereiter, C. (1987). Knowledge telling and knowledge transforming in written composition. In S. Rosenberg (Ed.), *Advances in applied psycholinguistics, Volume 2: Reading, writing, and language learning* (pp. 142–175). Cambridge, UK: Cambridge University Press.

Schumann, J. (1977). Second language acquisition: The pidginization hypothesis. *Language Learning, 26,* 391–408.

Selinker, L. (1972). Interlanguage. *International Review of Applied Linguistics, 10,* 209–231.

Shaugnessy, M. P. (1977). *Errors and expectations: A guide for the teacher of basic writing.* New York: Oxford University Press.

Smith, L. Z. (1992). Profession and vocation: Trends in publication. *Focuses, 6,* 75–86.

Sommers, N. (1980). Revision strategies of student writers and experienced adult writers. *College Composition and Communication, 31,* 378–388.

Sridhar, S. N. (1994). A reality check for SLA theories. *TESOL Quarterly, 28*(4), 800–805.

Stotsky, S. (1995). The uses and limitations of personal or personalized writing in writing theory, research, and instruction. *Reading Research Quarterly, 30,* 758–776.

Tollefson, J. (1989). *Alien winds: The re-education of America's IndoChinese refugees.* New York: Praeger.

Tollefson, J. (Ed.). (1995). *Power and inequality in language education.* New York: Cambridge University Press.

Vygotsky, L. (1978). *Mind in society.* Cambridge, MA: Harvard University Press.

Zhang, S. (1995). Reexamining the affective advantage of peer feedback in the ESL writing class. *Journal of Second Language Writing, 4,* 209–222.

10

Language and Diversity

Sharon Klein

- How are language and writing related?
- What is meant by the term "linguistic diversity?"
- What is the difference between a "language" and a "dialect?"
- How can teachers work effectively with linguistically diverse writers?

INTRODUCTION

Composition faculty regularly encounter sentences, paragraphs, and essays, which, to varying degrees, are not consistent with the expectations of college writing. Such discoveries require responses—both to the contents of such pieces, and to the lexical and syntactic choices made by the student writer. Of course, these responses are inevitably informed by what faculty believe about language, its nature and capacity to represent what its users think (if perhaps not how they think), as well as their ideas about how language should be used. These beliefs may be explicit, implicit, or even inchoate, and, thus, difficult to specify, much less make explicit. But these ideas have a significant influence on how teachers work with students on their writing, and, therefore, an important goal of this chapter is to engender an awareness of how language, thought, and writing interact and to help prospective teachers understand linguistic diversity so that they can work with their students more effectively. Some of this material addresses the sources of the friction that can occur when diversity and institutional expectations meet. But awareness of these sources (and of the friction) and knowledge about linguistic diversity and its relationship to writing can contribute to writing teachers' success in responding to their students, enabling students to develop control over the form and substance of their writings.

Toward these goals, readers will find the following in this chapter:

- Ways of thinking and talking about language and linguistic variation.
- Discussion of a sampling of the actual forms found in some of the varieties.
- Attitudes toward the varieties.
- The connections between all of these strands and issues pertaining to composition.

SOME PRELIMINARIES AND TERMS

Any discussion about the connections between language and composition must at least acknowledge the complex relationship between *writing* and *speaking*. Writing and speaking are generally agreed to be the primary communicative outlets for language (also signing, as we should recognize the existence of roughly 130 (Lewis, 2009) languages whose perceptual and delivery systems exclusively involve hand, arm, and facial movements and positions, and eye contact). But speaking and writing are distinct, and the distinction itself raises many issues, not the least of which is the question of what comes "first." The very phrase *written language* hints at one position; the unmodified—unmarked—system, *language* is "first." Nonetheless, many do not agree about the relative primacy of these two outlets, arguing on both sides that one, more than the other, provides a better lens through which one can examine the nature of language (or communication, as we should keep the referents of these two words distinct). It is enough for us to recognize that the relationship is complex, having tantalized thinkers from Plato, Rousseau, Condillac, Saussure, and Husserl to Derrida, who himself challenges any attempt to establish either as exclusively fundamental to the other.

On one hand, it is the case that although all written representations—or otherwise inscribed forms—of language may be traced to a spoken (or signed) system, the reverse is not true. A little under two-thirds of the world's six thousand or so languages do not have writing systems. And although every human develops at least one language without explicit instruction, very few are able to acquire the ability to write (or read) without fairly involved instruction. Conversely, the sort of inscribing that writing provides for changes our mental maps of language—almost irretrievably—once we become writers (and readers). The general focus of this book is on the nature of these reading and writing abilities and how to teach them at relatively advanced levels. Nonetheless, it is reasonable to keep these observations about "language" and "writing" in mind.

For Writing and Discussion

Four terms here, *language* and *communication* and *language* and *writing* have been distinguished. What are your thoughts about *language* and *communication*? How do they overlap? In what ways are they distinct? How might both this overlap and distinction be reflected in the context of composition? What, in turn, are some of the differences between *language* and *writing* that require attention when thinking about how to talk with student writers?

When we teach writing, of course, we are working with students to develop a facility in using a system of structural conventions to represent and communicate a range of thoughts, some of which they may already be representing in spoken or signed languages. So, despite our careful separation of the written and nonwritten forms of expression, the two are related, albeit complexly. For that reason, we need to look at nonwritten linguistic systems, their workings, and the ways in which they are viewed, because this is where students' thoughts are initially represented.

But there is also a wrinkle. When we speak of written forms, we can be fairly confident that we are referring to a relatively established set of conventional structures, discourse patterns, and expected genres; many of them are represented and duplicated in handbooks, for example. This set, however, is assuredly different from virtually any of the nonwritten forms of expression that students bring to writing classes. No student's language corresponds completely to "the language" of writing. But all students ultimately will be asked to align the language(s) they know and to use the set of written conventions established, as that is, in somewhat oversimplified terms, what "learning to write" entails. The wrinkle is that we will not be engaged in a mapping of one system on to another. Rather, perhaps, we are talking of a many-to-one mapping. In other words, we are engaged in mapping any number of languages onto the relatively small set of forms of written discourse that are recognized and valued in American college classrooms.

In their chapter on non-native English speakers included in this volume, John Edlund and Olga Griswold acknowledge this situation, providing good reasons for developing stronger connections between the fields of second language acquisition studies and composition studies. They also talk about a group of student writers who are currently often referred to as "Generation 1.5." These are young people who immigrated to the United States as children, and who grew up primarily in the American educational system, but whose home and community languages may be Spanish, Tagalog, Bikol, Hmong, Korean, Mandarin, Armenian, or any other language distinct from some targeted form of American English.

The discussion in this chapter moves one step beyond, looking at linguistic systems that are part of the worlds of students who are sometimes also included in the Generation 1.5 category, but whose experiences also diverge from immigrant students. These are students who were born in the United States, but who, for any number of reasons, speak another language or dialect. As these linguistic systems rub up against the linguistic systems used in American writing courses (and the expectations of courses and faculty who ask students to write), students and their instructors may find themselves at odds with one another. Success in these classes requires students to develop and maintain a facility in this written system. But developing this facility has long challenged both students and their instructors. To understand a bit about why and how the process is challenging, and how the coexisting systems affect each other, it is crucial to understand something about the nature of language diversity and the relative positions of the varieties. The next section considers these questions.

LANGUAGE AND VARIATION: SOME FUNDAMENTAL NOTIONS

Acknowledging that students arrive with fully developed linguistic systems, and that these languages are likely to be quite different from the language associated with writing, we turn briefly to a distinction that may be helpful in identifying some of the difficulties that arise in moving between the two.

I-Language and E-Language

A pair of language terms, introduced by Noam Chomsky (Chomsky, 1986), can be useful in understanding linguistic phenomena. The pair is *I-language* and *E-language*. *I-language* (roughly, "internalized language") refers to the *internal* system of tacit knowledge that grows in every human being as he or she develops a language from infancy.[1] The language developed is just that: I-language. It is a system that assigns structure to sequences of seeable (in sign languages) or hearable (in spoken languages) elements and allows for them to be connected to meanings systematically associated with them. There are a number of assumptions about the first language embedded here: that it develops—virtually "grows" in every human child—and is not taught; that it develops as a result of an intricate interaction between the child's environment and her biology; and that, in this way, language shares a number of important developmental features with lots of other human systems, including digestive or visual systems, for example.

E-language refers to everything else. The irony is that even though its reference—everything else—makes it virtually impossible to define (much less study), it is what all of us typically use the word *language* for. We talk about the *English language*, or *writing in English* (or French, Armenian, or Korean, for that matter), or we say *"Julia speaks Hungarian and Hebrew."* But exactly what are our references in these expressions? Whenever we talk about speakers of Bikol, or of Swedish Sign Language, or when we're talking about "global English," AAVE, or Spanglish, we are using E-language terms. The terms don't really refer to anything tangible; they refer to our *ideas* of what the languages are, tacitly including social and political components. And typically it is these *ideas* of language—rather than the realities of the linguistic systems in the heads of the individuals—that guide teachers in their work with student writers.

For Writing and Discussion

Do two small experiments. First, do a survey. Find out what the language backgrounds of your classmates or students are (perhaps anonymously; language, as this chapter will continue to note, is a club (either one to which we may belong or one some might brandish as a weapon), and as students begin to talk about their language and their own language profiles, it may be more comfortable to do so anonymously, at least at first). Ask them about differences they notice in the languages they use outside of the classroom—on campus or off—and what they find in textbooks, lectures, and what they do in discussions. Ask them to jot down what they mean when they specify the language they speak. What, in other words, do they mean when they say "'I' or 'we' speak Spanish," for example? Consider the answers you get, and how people talk about such issues. Next, do some observations of your own language use and of language around you. Listen to talk radio, interviews with public figures, or your friends and family and note (preserving anonymity) how people use various forms of language. How many "complete sentences" do you hear? Record pronunciations, or words and expressions that you find interesting, and save them to use later in the chapter.

Language and Dialect

The distinction between *I-language* and *E-language*, although only roughly drawn here, also helps us in understanding the terms *language* and *dialect*, critical terms in this chapter. The distinction between these terms has been part of our language consciousness for a long time and has been perpetuated in many of the texts that teachers of writing consult; nonetheless, the distinction is not linguistically motivated. The following epigrammatic statement about the distinction summarizes the point best. "A language," it says, "is a dialect with an army and a navy."[2] That definition suggests that when we use the terms *dialect* and *language*, we are making, at best, an E-language distinction, but in fact, more precisely, the distinction between the terms is a political one.

Examples of how the term *language* and its companion *dialect* range over the world's linguistic systems and our perceptions of them abound. There are at least nine identifiable linguistic systems—many that are mutually unintelligible—in Chinese. But they are referred to as dialects, a reference that corresponds to the writing system and national identity. And what was known for much of the 20th century as the Serbo-Croatian language was, in fact an attempt to interweave two related, but distinct languages into a unified and, presumably, a unifying language. But the two have always used different writing systems, and have distinct vocabularies. Languages more similar than these two have remained separate for converse political reasons: Flemish and Dutch, Hindi and Urdu, or Norwegian and Danish, for example. And now, for the very same reasons, Serbian and Croatian are recognized as distinct languages (McAdams, 1989).

Sometimes, in fact, we speak of something as a language that is not considered a language at all—Spanglish, for example. The term *Spanglish* grows out of our need to categorize and label a set of very real, recognizable, but complexly changing language patterns; perhaps the label will suffice for understanding and describing the patterns.[3]

For Writing and Discussion

The Klingon Dictionary, Marc Okrand, 1985.

As part of the Star Trek enterprise, a non-Terran language identified with the Klingon beings was developed for Paramount Pictures by Marc Okrand, a linguist. The introduction to the dictionary providing a detailed description of the language is quite instructive for us—in a number of ways—working as a mirror of sorts for the ways we think about linguistic variation and privileged (or Standard, or Standardized) forms. Consider some of the assertions in this excerpt. What comments does the piece make about the roles of dialect and language in society? What parallels can you draw in universes with which you are more familiar? What is *Standard Klingon*, for example? How is it defined?

Although Klingons are proud of their language and frequently engage in long discussions about its expressiveness and beauty, they have found it impractical for communication outside the Klingon Empire. For intra- and intergalactic communication, the Klingon government, along with most other governments, has accepted English as the lingua franca. In general, only those Klingons of the upper classes (which include higher-level governmental and military officials) learn English. As a result, English has taken on two additional functions in Klingon society. First, it is used as a symbol of rank or status. Those Klingons who know English will use it among themselves to show off their erudition and make their place in society known to all who happen to be listening. Second, English is used when it is thought best to keep servants, soldiers, or even the general

populace uninformed. Thus, on a Klingon vessel, the commanding officer will often speak
Klingon when giving orders to his crew, but choose English when having discussions with
his officers. On the other hand, a Klingon officer may use Klingon in the presence of non-
Klingons to prevent them from knowing what is going on. This use of Klingon seems to be
quite effective.

There are a number of dialects of Klingon. Only one of the dialects, that of the current
Klingon emperor, is represented in this dictionary. When a Klingon emperor is replaced,
for whatever reason, it has historically been the case that the next emperor speaks a dif-
ferent dialect. As a result, the new emperor's dialect becomes the official dialect. Those
Klingons who do not speak the official dialect are considered either stupid or subversive,
and are usually forced to undertake tasks that speakers of the official dialect find distaste-
ful. Most Klingons try to be fluent in several dialects.

Some dialects differ only slightly from the dialect of this dictionary. Differences tend to
be in vocabulary (the word for forehead, for example is different in almost every dialect)
and in the pronunciation of a few sounds. On the other hand, some dialects differ signifi-
cantly from the current official dialect, so much so that speakers have a great deal of diffi-
culty communicating with current Klingon officialdom. The student of Klingon is warned
to check into the political situation of the Klingon Empire before trying to talk. (pp. 10–11)

So, specifying what one means in the assertion "Students should write in Standard English" requires that we understand what *English* refers to even before we try to lay out the territory of *Standard English*. No mean feat. This is another distinction related to our general
idea of language, again, influenced by all the forces that we've seen can contribute to it.

One more preliminary term requires attention before the discussion turns directly to
language varieties and what understanding them can contribute to the ultimate goal: writing teachers' success with their students. That term is *grammar,* and it will be discussed
briefly, as it is treated in some detail in the chapter by James D. Williams.

GRAMMAR

When most people think of the word *grammar,* they tend to associate it with what they
were taught in high school—parts of speech, rules of punctuation, and the marking of
error. Linguists, however, conceive of the term as more complex, using the word to refer
at once to the linguistic description of internalized mental systems and some sort of representation that could correspond to the I-language we have described. Teachers inhabit
a sort of odd conceptual territory along the boundaries of these two definitions, a territory that has been recognized and, consequently, has been labeled the area of *pedagogical*
grammar. The goal of a pedagogical grammar is to provide a description of a particular
linguistic system (the term used here to avoid the danger of using either the terms *dialect*
or *language* arbitrarily) that would allow someone to understand the system well enough to
learn to use it. Of course the phrase *learn to use the system* raises the questions of what happens when learners go through this process consciously (usually learning a new system in
addition to the one they have developed as children) and what they come out with. Another
way to ask this question is to examine the connection between I-language, E-language,

and pedagogical grammar. And this is why we say that pedagogical grammars inhabit the borderlands between them.

As this discussion turns to language varieties, readers should keep in mind two points about the notions under the umbrella of the term *grammar*. First, presentations of descriptions in specific varieties are not representations of any single individual's I-language, but, rather, a rough characterization of some of the features, and they border on E-language type descriptions. Second, in examining the nature of language diversity and the general structure of linguistic systems themselves, the term *grammar* more closely parallels its use in linguistic work.

LINGUISTIC VARIATION AND DIVERSITY

However the terms *language* and *dialect* are defined, it is important to recognize that there are multiple linguistic forms across groups of people (as well as within individuals for use across situations). The organization of these varieties and their sources have kept linguists working for some time now and offer multiple challenges for attempts to develop descriptions that would lead to an understanding of how the systems work. Fundamental to the work is the understanding that at their most elemental level, all linguistic systems must correspond to the universal principles and conditions that define human language, and that make up the grammatical system linguists refer to as "Universal Grammar." *Human language* has been proposed as describing the epiphenomenon that an extraterrestrial scientist might observe when she first arrived to study Earthlings. They all would seem to be speaking variants of some common language. As she moved on to understanding the nature of this common language—what linguistically unites the Earthlings, the scientist would move into constructing hypotheses about the nature of Universal Grammar—its defining principles and conditions.

These principles range over *phonology* (the features of sounds that structure themselves into recognizable sound patterns in spoken languages, and the features of hand shape and movement that structure themselves into parallel systems in sign languages), *morphology* (the patterns structured from minimal-meaning-bearing units in a linguistic system), syntax (the patterns of phrases, clauses, and sentences), and *semantics* (the ways in which words, phrases, and sentences constitute meanings). There is no linguistic system that does not correspond precisely to the possibilities these principles provide for. Additionally, human beings make use of their knowledge of the world, their respective cultural identities, and of how these interact with communicative expectations in particular situations. The range of generalizations here are referred to collectively as *pragmatics,* and are a significant component of human communicative competence in any linguistic system.

These constants encompass a range of variation, which develops across a number of boundaries: actual geographical boundaries (including the political boundaries that define *language*), gender boundaries, boundaries of income (translating into boundaries of "class"), and ethnic boundaries. In turn, these boundaries interact, as one might imagine, complicating the picture somewhat, but also providing a way to understand the interplay that contributes to attitudes toward divergent linguistic forms. The boundaries and contacts between and among speakers with different linguistic systems interact in complex ways, providing for the crucibles of language.

For Writing and Discussion

If what we have described can underlie a strong and consistent hypothesis about human linguistic systems, and if we consider some of the social networking systems to be communities in which individuals gather and use language, we might ask if these systems (Twitter, Facebook, and texting, or whatever has developed between the writing of this and your reading of it) affect the existing language, or, whether or not users develop linguistic systems that are particular to these modes. What would you never do on Twitter, for example, or what forms do you or do you not favor for texting? Why? Have you ever been conscious of doing this? And see Eisenstein, O'Connor, Smith, & Xing (2011) for some interesting effects of Twitter—also, Crystal (2008) and Baron (2008).

The Blending of Language: Pidgin, Creole, and Interlanguage

The meetings of languages and the linguistic products of prolonged contact of various kinds have become an important focus of study. Over the years, they have been labeled in various ways, and these names are likely to come up in any discussion about language that readers might have with their students. An overview of the labels and an introduction to some of the results of current, closer scrutiny appear here.

One set of contact products, *pidgins,* may be loosely defined as varieties of language that develop out of contact between some nonstandard (i.e., already stigmatized) and accepted forms of colonial European languages, including English. Often there would be one European language and multiple non-European ones. The European languages are referred to as the *lexifiers,* because it is from them that most of the vocabulary in pidgins comes, and the non-European languages are known as the *substrate* languages.[4] These contact languages developed primarily in the context of trade and the initial stages of colonization, and would have identifiable features, varying with respect to how close the created language was to the forms of the lexifier language—or even more educated forms of it—or how much like itself (and different from either the lexifier or any one of the substrate languages) the pidgin became. The forms closest to the lexifier are what linguists call the *acrolects,* and the forms most different from the lexifier are referred to as *basilects.*

The companion term, *creole,* has an interesting history, as it was first used to describe a people: that is, nonindigenous, but clearly not European people, born in the colonies of the Americas in the 1500s (Mufwene, 2001). Gradually, the term came to refer to other such transplants and mixes involving plants and animals, until it came to refer to the languages that grew out of the experiences.

Linguists have used the term *creole,* along with *pidgin,* to define not only a language type but also a process of language formation, with *pidgins* first, then *creoles* developing as children learn a pidgin as their first language. Linguists embraced this continuum enthusiastically, because the connections between the creation of languages out of the crucible of contact (however difficult the surrounding social conditions may be) and the recreation of language by children provided a compelling set of questions, and the opportunity to delve further into a developing understanding of the universal nature of language and the development of I-language. But many argue that the picture is not so clear, and that there may be creoles without pidgins; pidgins without creoles; and contact-language situations with features of both.

Of particular relevance to writing teachers in this vein is that the set of language-creation processes share a number of features with the contact-language situation we call second (or subsequent) language acquisition. Second language acquisition occurs when one speaker of some language is encountering a new (presumably *target*) language. The intermediate result, often called *interlanguage* (a term with a history as well, related to all of these contact-language situations[5]), bears some resemblance both to pidgin and creole situations. Thus, the ESL[6] students that Edlund and Griswold discuss are themselves involved in the process of language creation. And speakers of a number of varieties of English that garner attention mostly in the context of the classroom are also involved in various processes of language creation.

One such process that may be familiar to readers, and that the chapter has already mentioned briefly, is *Spanglish*. Ilan Stavans (2000) traces the historical underpinnings of the language back to the beginnings of Spanish colonialization of the Americas in the 1500s (which brought an already heterogeneous language into contact with multiple indigenous ones—the crucible) and the subsequent Anglo colonization, introducing English into the mix, the two interacting most dramatically with the treaty of Guadalupe Hidalgo in 1848, signing over almost one-third of what had been Mexican territory to the United States. But most importantly, he notes that the history of this contact between two languages— neither homogeneous—has resulted in a multiple of linguistic forms. One might say many "Spanglishes." Cuban Americans have different vocabulary and sound patterns from the "Nuyorican" ones, and both differ from the various forms that are found in the Los Angeles area—from East Los Angeles (with roots in Pachuco and Caló) to the San Fernando Valley. And other parts of the Southwest have varying forms as well, traceable to the interaction of indigenous languages, English, and Spanish.

Linguists are involved in trying to understand the extent to which Spanglish could be considered a linguistic system in and of itself—a type of interlanguage of the sort previously defined—or whether the name Spanglish is a label for the complex *code switching* that speakers who are relatively competent in more than one language do. Speakers take words and phrases from one language and reanalyze them using forms from the other: *parkear*, "to park" uses an English word with Spanish verb suffixes; *el maus*, the label for a computer "mouse," which already involves a lexical appropriation, uses spelling that obeys Spanish conventions, and *llamar pa'tras*, "to call back" borrows syntax, keeping the Spanish words. And such examples illustrate code switching, which entails moving back and forth between (at least) two languages, in conversation, sentences, phrases, and words. The smaller the switching moves (the selection of systematically chosen forms even smaller below than the level of "word," for example), and the more frequently the moves occur (a frequency whose nature and design are also the objects of linguistic study: cf. Poplack 1980/2000), the more the process begins to resemble what we think of as a "new" language—out of the crucible.

Paralleling this intricate code switching, necessarily the purview of bilingual speakers, is a system that is observable in Mexican-American communities (and plausibly Central American-American ones, as well, although this issue is not consistently treated) where young people do not necessarily grow up bilingual, but do use a lect (we use "lect" neutrally, to avoid labeling something a dialect) with identifiable and systematic features. This lect has been called Chicano English (CE) in a range of sources (Fought, 2003; Santa Ana,

1991; Wald, 1984—among others). These features include characteristics in the phonology, in the syntax, and in the area of word choice and word meaning. Detailed and documented descriptions of CE are found in the resources cited above, and most accessibly in either Fought (2003) or on the website specifically designed for educators that serves as a companion to the 2005 PBS documentary, "Do you Speak American?" (Fought, 2005).

Because speakers of all these varieties are living in the midst of another, dominant language culture, they are all also involved in moving back and forth—in situations that call for such moving—between these systems and other forms of English, which are collectively referred to as **m**ainstream **U.S.** English[7]—MUSE (Lippi-Green, 1997)—the term we will use here. In a writing classroom, speakers, who are also students, are directing their attention to learning yet another set of codes related to the conventions of written exposition. It is important, then, that writing teachers attempt to understand the linguistic systems from which their students work, the processes underlying their travels across the linguistic borders they must navigate, and the various distances involved in such journeys.

The issues around the classification and nature of pidgins, creoles, and interlanguages, and questions of code switching are relevant for trying to understand a range of issues. Some linguists are currently enthusiastic about what seems a fruitful perspective. Mufwene (2001) uses the notion of an ecology of language evolution. Sifting multiple factors together, Mufwene notes that differing situations will inescapably result in slightly different outcomes for developing (and endangered) languages. Some of the determinants are linguistic, and others are a mix of social, cultural, and political factors. Careful observation of what has happened in a number of language contact situations has allowed Mufwene to suggest this framework; and it seems helpful to keep in mind when we examine any of the lects that both diverge from MUSE and exist in its sphere of influence.

AFRICAN-AMERICAN ENGLISH (AAE)

We turn next to African-American English, AAE,[8] a linguistic system available to most African Americans, as well as to any speakers who are part of and identify with the African-American community. However, African-American English is not necessarily spoken by everyone who is African American, and certainly is not spoken by all Black people (for example, in Haiti communities, Haitian Creole, a French-based language, is spoken predominately, and other communities speak Jamaican Creole, which differs from AAE, or the Garifuna language, spoken by many Belizian Americans).

There has long been agreement about the connections between AAE and the African languages brought (predominately from the languages of the Niger-Congo family spoken in West Africa) by the imported slaves who were likely to have been among the agents of language creation. There is little controversy over that connection. What remains a question is whether contemporary AAE still derives from a creole that formed out of the extended contact between the slaves and their captors, traders, and owners. Gullah, a language of the South Sea Islands off the coast of South Carolina, and Jamaican Creole, along with a number of other related linguistic systems, are thought to reflect such a process. But the AAE generally spoken in various areas in the United States not only has a strong core of specific characteristics, which the discussion here will present, but also has a number of features that are not unlike other vernacular Englishes, notably those spoken in lower-income areas of some southern states and of northern cities, as well as in some identifiable vernacular areas in Britain. Such findings about common features have led some linguists to lean in the direction of claiming that AAE has stronger roots in English, or is certainly developing them. It may ultimately not be possible to categorize the origins of AAE as creole or argue that it has other, noncreole origins; this chapter certainly will not (for a helpful and accessibile overview, see Green (2002, pp. 8–11)). What is important is that AAE has features that it shares with other non-MUSE forms of English and others that make it noticeably and systematically distinct and that its speakers are generally required to replace with MUSE in "appropriate situations" (most notably, in academic written work). And, while it is important to understand that the written language of university writing is no one's first language, Mainstream U.S. English (MUSE) speakers have the advantage of not being required to learn AAE, Spanglish, Chicana/o English or any other other non-MUSE systems (cf. O'Neil, 1972).

For Writing and Discussion

Issues of income, ethnicity, and hierarchy are inevitably part of any conversation about the linguistic systems that are not part of MUSE. Knowing how our perceptions about these issues affect our attitudes toward forms of language and their speakers is crucial for teachers. Hence, this small exercise. Look up the words *churlish*, *villain*, and *vulgar*. What sort of etymologies do you find? What might the semantic changes observable in these words tell us about the perspectives used to categorize people into desirable and less desirable groups, and thus, how we come to think about the characteristics—such as their language forms, for example—that identify them?

Moving back to language, one might also say that *language is a club* (see our discussion in the text, as well). What are the relevant meanings of such an assertion in the context of discussing these linguistic varieties? Consult a good dictionary with etymological information (*The American Heritage Dictionary of the English Language*, 4th edition, has such information) and consider both the current definitions and the respective histories of the words *shibboleth* and *barbarian*. How do these meanings contribute to your developing view of how people come to make judgments about others, and what such judgments reflect? Of what relevance are such findings to working with students' writing?

For Writing and Discussion

Note that MUSE is the language of this chapter, which includes discussion of other forms, predominately AAE. Imagine the reverse—that this chapter was written in AAE, or forms from Chicano English. What is the likelihood of that happening? What challenges (or refreshing opportunities) might it present to you? You have additional opportunities to imagine this reverse in chapter 8, in the "Bad Grammar or Bad Usage?" section. Which speakers do you suppose would be wearing the "cutoff jeans, tank top, and sandals?" Why?

THE OAKLAND DECISION AND AAE

This divergence between AAE and MUSE—and the requirement that students develop reading and writing skills in MUSE—brought AAE to the attention of the courts in the context of education famously for the first time in 1978. Based on the testimony of a number of linguists, Judge Joiner in Ann Arbor, Michigan found for the plaintiffs, a group of 15 school children, in a decision about language barriers and discrimination. He ruled, essentially, that the school district in question take appropriate action to overcome a clear language barrier impeding the children's access to equal educational opportunity. And the language barrier, he had been convinced, was largely a function of teachers' lack of knowledge about AAE in sufficient detail to permit them to understand what the children were saying. Teachers had not been given the opportunity to learn about this language system.

Nevertheless, despite subsequent attempts to introduce teachers at all levels to forms of the language, topics related to language variation, and interwoven pedagogical issues, a fair level of institutionalized misunderstanding continues to prevail. In December of 1996, the Oakland School District in California tried to respond (again) to a similar situation. The discussion here focuses on the educational goals of the District's decision. But their position also had the effect of popularizing the label *Ebonics,* which had not been previously used widely. The label was coined, from *ebony* and *phonics,* by Robert Williams, an African-American psychologist, in the 1970s, but in those 20 years, the term had not gained the usage accorded it almost overnight after the Oakland proposal became public.

Observations by Oakland educators and others had revealed that the longer African-American children stayed in school, the more poorly they performed on tests, as reported by the National Assessment of Educational Progress. The School Board was primarily interested in building students' English language proficiency, and sought to use their primary language as a vehicle for instruction. Note the clause in the proposal:

> Be it further resolved that the Superintendent in conjunction with her staff shall immediately devise and implement the best possible academic program for *imparting instruction to African-American students in their primary language* for the combined purposes of *maintaining the legitimacy and richness of such language* [**facilitating the acquisition and mastery of English language skills, while respecting and embracing the legitimacy and richness of the language patterns**] whether it is [**they are**] known as "Ebonics," "African Language Systems," "Pan African Communication Behaviors," or other description, *and to facilitate their acquisition and mastery of English language skills.* (Rickford & Rickford, 2000, p. 168)

Italicized language was in the original, December, 1996 document, but was deleted from the January, 1997 document; boldfaced print in brackets includes language substituted in January.

The board was interested in "transitioning students from the language patterns they bring to school to English." Again, it was a matter of educating students in MUSE. But the middle step, which involved recognizing AAE long enough for teachers to understand it and to use such knowledge to acknowledge students' linguistic identity and to add MUSE to their linguistic portfolios, set off wildfires among whose smoldering coals we continue to walk, even more than a decade later. Because language does play such a central role in constructing and maintaining one's identity, as well as in representing one's world, it seems reasonable to understand and use students' languages to support their acquisition and use of MUSE. The following discussion of AAE aims to further these goals.

GRAMMATICAL PROPERTIES OF AAE

In the context of working with students who speak AAE, the term *grammar* has two potential applications for writing teachers. Some of what are generally called "surface errors" in exposition are structures that parallel but diverge from those in MUSE. In composition classes, there are occasions to see through such surface errors and focus on other features of the writing—treatments of topics, persuasiveness of an argument, or the quality of a narrative, for example. Outside of writing classes, however, such differences in sentence structure are what readers and evaluators may emphasize. Students should be able to choose whether to translate; writing teachers are in the best positions to help them be able to have the choice. The second and corollary application has to do with standardized testing of writing proficiency. These tests often use just such differences in questions about sentence structures. In other words, such tests are asking questions about fluency in MUSE. Again, writing teachers are in positions to provide students with insight about the two language systems and, with sufficient fluency in MUSE, to be able to call on it in these situations.

The description below begins with an overview, summarizing a number of the syntactic structures that characterize sentences in the system, and explaining some of the terminology. Examples and descriptions come from Green (1998, 2002), Pullum (1999), Wolfram, Temple-Adger, and Christian (2007), Smitherman (1977, 1994), and Rickford and Rickford (2000), where readers can find much more information. It is also important to acknowledge, as have others (and as we alluded to earlier), that the extensive contact AAE has had with other forms of English—some nonstandard and some closer to MUSE—will result in some of the non-MUSE features we discuss being not precisely unique to AAE, but also part of other non-MUSE systems.

Copula Sentences

It is generally possible to isolate about five sentence patterns in languages, based on what sorts of meanings a verb has and what structures that meaning provides for. One of those patterns involves a subject coupled to a predicate whose basic function is to provide more information about the subject. In the following examples, the subject and additional information are in bold, and the connecting verb form (the copula) is underlined.

> *Her comment <u>was</u> mysterious.*
>
> *Writing instruction <u>is</u> a complicated process.*
>
> *My friends <u>will be</u> at the beach.*

Many languages do not use a verb form in positions with the underlined forms from MUSE. Or they'll put the verb form in only to mark a past or future as in the first and third examples, respectively. Russian is such a language, using the copula only in nonpresent tense forms. When systems have patterns of omission, the patterns are referred to as *zero copula* patterns.[9] AAE has such patterns, and these patterns, along with the tense/aspect structures explained in the next section, may have attracted the most attention from scholars and non-AAE speakers alike.

Tense/Aspect

Although readers may not be aware of making the distinction, human language has two ways of talking about events. They can be aligned in a chronological relation to one another from the perspective of the speaker, or they can be described as ongoing, habitual, or continuous, on the one hand, or punctual, momentary, or complete, on the other. The formal systems typically expressing chronological alignment are generally referred to as *tense,* whereas those that provide for these other features of events are called *aspect systems.* The two can—and regularly do—co-occur and intermingle, and they are not always indicated by what we consider to be markers. The MUSE sentence *He does windows,* for example, has a present-tense marking, but is making a general statement about a habitual activity. AAE has borrowed forms from MUSE (remember, MUSE is the *lexifier* language) and put them to work in a different system. This borrowing/reanalysis process is very common in the language contact situations out of which AAE has evolved; reanalysis itself is part of what any human language does over time and space. When the two systems (AAE and MUSE, in this case) are in constant contact, however, the combination of common vocabulary and the different uses can cause difficulties. Unraveling the respective systems is important for writing teachers, as well as for anyone seeking to understand the two systems.

Another strand to keep track of in the unraveling is the actual form *be.* In both AAE and MUSE, *be* has two functions. And the two interact. It is, as previously noted, the copula. In other words, it functions as what is called a *main* verb. Alternatively, the *be* is what texts refer to as an *auxiliary* verb. It can signal either the progressive, with a (*main*) verb ending in the *-ing* suffix (*Students are writing in a range of forms*), or the passive, with a (main) verb carrying the perfective marking, which may take a range of forms (e.g., *eaten, rung,* or *refuted* [*Most of his comments were refuted quite easily*]). Sometimes the copula connects the subject with an adjective phrase that is constructed by making use of what started out its life as an *-ing* verb (e.g., *writing, going, leaving,* or *sweeping*) or a perfective one (*written, gone, left,* or *swept*). Speakers of all forms of MUSE or AAE must rely on context to distinguish between these progressives and passives and the respective but distinct adjectival meanings. The patterns for marking them in the two systems differ. Consider, for example, what happens when the string in parentheses is removed from either of these two sentences: *The toddlers were charming (the pants off their grandparents)./The ship was painted blue (by a crew of teenagers).* Knowing which meaning writers intend is critical for writing teachers, as is the ability to make certain that the writers are in control of what they intend for their readers.

Be is a complicated form, marking a number of meanings in AAE, with both its presence and absence, and its different forms (*am, is, were, was*) alternating with its infinitive form (*be*) indicating these meanings. For example, *be* used in its infinitive form marks the habitual aspect. This *be* is always translated as "typically" or "generally" in contrast to "now," which is the interpretation of sentences with no form of 'be' at all:

> *He be singing* translates as "*He sings.*"
>
> *He singing* translates as "*He is singing.*"
>
> *She be testy* translates as "*She is typically testy.*"
>
> *She testy* translates as "*She is testy now.*"

In its participle form, *been,* this verb has a specific aspectual meaning in AAE, and it is pronounced with special stress, which we indicate here with uppercase letters. First, note these two MUSE sentences and their meanings (uppercase letters here indicate increased loudness, what linguists call greater "stress"):

She's BEEN married means *She was married for a while, but certainly is not now.*

She's been married (for a while, since yesterday, for five minutes) means *She got married and still is.*

In AAE, the *BEEN* (stressed *been*) means specifically that the event or condition not only still exists but also began in the distant past, never five minutes ago, or yesterday, for example. So, in AAE, the sentence *She BEEN married* must be interpreted as meaning that the person in question got married in the distant past and remains married now. That meaning is different from either of the two MUSE meanings with *been.*

Another example will lead us to a third aspectual form. Consider this sentence and its meaning:

I BEEN finish(ed) my homework translates as *I have COMPLETELY finished my homework (a while back).*

This example provides a form of 'perfective,' the aspect associated with completeness and related senses.

The third aspectual form (distinct from invariant *be,* and stressed *BEEN*) is the use of *done,* which also provides a sense of completedness. Used without stress, *done* with a past-tense-marked verb indicates the perfective—as in the following examples:

The mirror done broke translates as *The mirror has (just) broken.*

The chef done cooked the food translates as *The chef has (just/already) cooked the food.*

The students done went/gone to class translates as *The students have (just/already) gone to class.* (Green, 1998, pp. 51–52)

The *done* combines with other verb forms, including the *be,* and *BEEN* (here BIN) to form a range of constructions with related meanings (Green, 1998):

I/you/s/he shoulda done ate/run.	I/you/s/he should have already eaten/run.
I/you/s/he BIN done ate/run.	I/you/s/he (had) already ate (eaten)/ran (run).
I/you/s/he ain't BIN done ate/run.	I/you/s/he hadn't (yet) eaten/run.
I/you/s/he be done ate/run.	I/you/s/he usually have already eaten/run.
I/you/s/he don't be done ate/run.	I/you/s/he usually won't have already eaten/run.
I/you/s/he'uh be done ate/run.	I/you/s/he will have already eaten/run.

A fairly striking application of knowledge about the uses of unstressed *done* and the fact that it must be used with a marked form of the verb (e.g., *ate* or *run*) comes from the sort of worksheet one might find in the context of SAT II preparation materials. As it turns out, the portions of the test that ask students to look for sentence errors, and to identify and correct them, are quite explicitly in pursuit of identifying dialect knowledge (Wolfram, Temple-Adger, & Christian, 2007, pp. 138–144). A speaker of AAE would be stopped if he or she were confronted with a test question such as the following: "Select the best word form to complete the sentence: *He ___ what he had to. [done/did]*" A well-formed, meaningful AAE sentence would require both *done* and *did,* in that order, in the remote perfective, and some speakers might use the form *done,* with stress, for a simple past. Without context, the student would be at a clear disadvantage without carefully designed preparation including strategic work for maneuvering around such questions.

Negation

This term is fairly self-explanatory, and refers to how linguistic systems negate expressions. Primary forms of AAE negation include *don't* and *ain't*. *Ain't* is the most frequent, but *don't* must occur in negative forms of habitual *be* sentences (sentences with the unchanged—the invariant—*be*):

> *I been here three days, the boy ain't move a muscle.* (from a Richard Pryor monologue, 1975, from Rickford & Rickford, 2000, p. 59)
>
> *Ain't nobody gonna spend no time going to no doctor.* (translation: Nobody is gonna spend any time going to a/any doctor; Martin & Wolfram, 1998, p. 18)
>
> *An she don't be listenin'.* (translation: And, she doesn't listen.; Rickford & Rickford, 2000, p. 114)
>
> *An she ain't listening.* (translation: And, she is not listening.)

So, *don't* and *ain't* are not interchangeable; each has a specific sense.

MUSE has an interesting pattern referred to as *negative polarity,* which requires speakers to use forms such as *any* or *ever* in the structural vicinity of a negative (e.g., *no, not,* or *none*). AAE uses *negative concord,* putting a second negative element in places where a negative *polarity* one would appear in MUSE: *Ain't* **nobody** *gonna spend* **no** *time going to* **no** *doctor.* *Ain't* is the primary negative marker here, and the boldfaced elements are concord markers. A MUSE translation might be something like (with optional elements in parentheses, indicating that either, both, or neither might be in the sentence. The second 'any' would alternate with 'a' '*Nobody is going to spend (any) time going to (any) doctor.*'

Often, AAE negation will be at the beginning of the sentence:

> *Ain't nobody done nothing.*
>
> *Couldn't nobody in the place do more than they did.*
>
> *Wouldn't nobody help the poor man?*
>
> *Ain't no car in that lot got a speck of rust on it.*
>
> *Can't no man round here get enough money to buy their own farm.*

For Writing and Discussion

How would these sentences be expressed in MUSE? Compare these and your translations to MUSE forms such as the following: *Never would I consider reading that book. Seldom did he utter even a greeting.* What differences and similarities do you find? What sort of "diction" is involved in the MUSE examples here? And what is "diction"?

Existential Sentences

This term refers to a construction that speakers of many forms of English are familiar with. Sentences with indefinite subjects and linking (copula) verbs such as *be*, *seem*, or *appear* may take one of two forms:

No shelf is **without books.**	There is **no shelf without books.**
Two women are **in the administration.**	There are **two women in the administration.**
We want **clean dishes** to be **in the cupboard.**	We want there to be **clean dishes in the cupboard.**

The sentences in the right-hand column are referred to as *existential sentences*.

For Writing and Discussion

What do you think the pattern of existential sentences might be? Try to provide a general statement of the pattern, and construct additional examples to test your hypothesis. If a speaker or writer may be said to put the information s/he wants readers or speakers to attend to most at the ends of sentences, rather at the beginnings, what sorts of communicative functions might you see for these so-called "existential sentences" sentences with *there* as the stand-in subject?[10]

Another type of sentence also uses a stand-in subject. Here are some examples:

It seemed that **the students were a bit overwhelmed.**

The students seemed (to be) **a bit overwhelmed.**

It bothers me **that not everyone can study language.**

That not everyone can study language bothers me.

We will not discuss this second set of sentences in any detail, but they, too, are quite common in a number of forms of English, and have interesting communicative functions. What is important here is that although non-AAE forms of English alternate between *there* and *it* as stand-in subjects, using the *it* in these sentences and the *there* in the existential ones, the *it* typically appears in both these sorts of sentences and the existential ones in AAE.

> *It a big closet filled with junk.* (translation: There's a big closet filled with junk).[11]

Some Other Structures

Pronouns

Rickford and Rickford (2000) note two places where AAE uses pronouns in ways that non-AAE forms of English do not. Both are interesting and may appear in the writing of AAE speakers. But because both can also be found in some non-AAE forms of English, they may not appear only as part of AAE systems. The first has to do with using a pronoun as a subject even after the sort of logical subject has already been introduced. Some grammarians refer to this construction as a "topic" structure, noting that the *that man* and the *my mother* respectively act as topics, setting the stage for what the sentence tells, and the pronouns *he* and *she* do the work of subjects:

> *That man **he** walks to the store.* [That man typically walks to the store.]

> *My mother **she** told me, "There's a song I want you to learn."* [My mother told me … .]

The second involves the introduction of pronouns in the indirect object position when they are also identical to the subject. MUSE typically omits the indirect object in this context.

> *Ahma git **me** a gig.* (translation: I'm going to get (me/myself) a job/gig.)

Relative Clauses

As readers may know, relative clauses are clauses that modify a noun in a noun phrase; they have a missing piece which corresponds to that noun. The following examples include relative clauses (in boldfaced type) with a parenthesized line indicating the missing piece. The noun they modify is also underlined, corresponding to the missing piece.

> *The <u>children</u> **who(m) we saw** (__) **in the library** are working on a project.*
> *We saw the <u>people</u> **who** (__) **were trying to get on the airplane** wandering around the airport.*
> *We noticed the <u>book</u> **that you wanted** (__).*
> *No one knows the <u>person</u> **from whom this letter came** (__).*

Sometimes in MUSE, it is possible to replace the *who(m)* with *that,* or to omit the marker completely. Here, parentheses indicate that the *that* is optional, giving us a zero marker:

> The children (that) we saw in the library are working on a project.
> We noticed the book (that) you wanted.

Yet when the missing element is the subject in MUSE, the *who* or *that* must appear. In AAE (e.g., as in a number of languages, including Japanese), it is also possible to have a zero marker setting off relative clauses with missing subjects. You can see this structure at work in the next example:

He the man got all the old records. (translation: He is the man who/that got all the old records; Martin & Wolfram, 1998, p. 32)

Embedded Questions

In AAE, when questions are embedded in sentences themselves, the order of the subject (boldfaced) and the auxiliary (italicized) may be inverted unless the embedded question begins with *if* as the asterisk—indicating that any speaker of AAE would simply reject the third example as ill-formed—indicates:

> They asked *could* **she** go to the show.
>
> I asked Alvin whether *did* **he** know how to play basketball.
>
> *I asked Alvin if *did* **he** know how to play basketball.

These are the syntactic features of AAE you are most likely to encounter, either in exchanges with students or in readings. These features also constitute the subset that plays a central role for researchers who are asking questions about the beginnings of AAE and its relationship to other linguistic systems—whose origins have to do with the interaction their speakers have had with multiple languages. Sustained study and analysis continue to uncover explanatory patterns and raise new questions.

We turn now to the sound patterns that contribute to the system of AAE.

SOUNDS AND SOUND PATTERNS IN AAE[12]

The furor surrounding the Oakland decision highlights the necessity for teachers at all levels to understand how the linguistic system of human language is structured, including the relevance of sounds and sound patterns to spoken languages. Why are these important? We talk about "accents" all the time. They define people as being "from somewhere else," and they define "us" as well—as we remember that the reference of "us" changes with the sets of readers turning these pages, as the forms of language used may also change. Opera singers who know nothing of the languages in which they may be singing an aria may study the sounds and sound patterns of the language with a coach so that their pronunciations make them sound like native speakers. Actors may similarly study the speech patterns of people who are from the same communities as characters they are portraying to learn such "accents." The nature and distribution of these accents may also contribute to the way speakers spell words. Finally, researchers have found that even recorded babbling in babies as young as eight months old from French, Arab, and Cantonese language communities is recognizable by adults as being in or out of their own language communities. And experimentation with the babies of similar ages have yielded long acknowledged evidence that by ten months of age, children have organized their mental systems related to phonology. They recognize the sounds that are part of the language and distinguish between sound differences that affect meaning and those whose distributions are patterned and do not affect meaning consistently (de Boysson-Bardies, 1999). The sound patterns of language are learned early and stay with us in ways that linguists are still trying to understand.[13]

Therefore, sound—both the patterning of consonants and vowels into syllables, and the relative volume and pitch of these syllables as they group into larger structures (what linguists refer to as prosodic units)—is a critical part of the linguistic system of every spoken language. When humans who have developed a spoken language go on to learn to use the alphabet, and to read, and write, a number of events occur that make dialect study, the role of sounds and sound patterns, and the role of syntax and word structure important. For example, the interaction of the way *-'ve* (as in *I'd've* or *she'd've*) is pronounced and the insight that many pieces of inflection in a language (including English) use the same sounds (think about the range of meanings that the sound represented by the letter *'s'* makes: plural, so-called possessive, and the third-person-singular present tense marking on regular verbs) results in many writing students spelling *-ve* as 'of' without "confusing" it with the meaning of the preposition.

Thus, if writing teachers study at least one system, and have some developing ideas about how linguists believe that system works, they should be in a stronger position to analyze what their students are doing, whatever system it is that students may be using.[14]

To facilitate discussion, Table 10.1 is provided and adapted, with annotations and some changes from Bailey and Thomas (1998, pp. 88–89; who attribute the observations there to Wolfram (1994) and Stockman (1996)). In this table, readers will find selected forms and descriptions of the observed sounds and sound patterns. It is difficult to represent pronunciations using alphabet letters, an observation that should, by itself, initiate some thought and discussion about the nature of alphabets in general. There are, as well, some other points to make, and terms to explain. The terms *voicing* and *stops* (or "obstruents") need some definition. The smallest pieces of phonology are the articulatory and acoustic features of sounds. Readers can hear themselves using the features, but you have probably rarely, if ever, talked about the internal structure of sounds, and how they combine. Voicing is such a feature, and although every speaker of English uses it to know how to pronounce the past tense of a verb such as *walk* or of a verb such as *cry* or *sob,* most are quite unaware of what knowledge they're appealing to in order to do this. It is possible to perceive voicing at work, nonetheless. Consider the two sentences *"It's a Sue!"* and *"It's a zoo!"* By placing the palm of your hand gently over the front of your neck, where your larynx is (this is our "voicebox"—where our vocal cords are), and saying these two phrases slowly, but without stopping between the article *"a"* and the following words, you should be able to feel a continuous vibrating in the *"a zoo"* phrase, yet feel a short cessation of vibration in the *"a Sue"* phrase (you can protract the effect by saying these slowly). That cessation reflects the "voicelessness" of the /s/ in the pronunciation of the name *Sue.*

Obstruent is a term that refers to whether or not the air coming up from our lungs and passing between the vocal cords (they're really folds of tissue, but calling them cords allows us to think of stringed instruments, and may help understand how their vibration works) moves unobstructed through the mouth or nose. The unobstructed sounds include roughly four sets: first, the vowels; second, what some books call "liquids"—the sounds we think of as 'l' or 'r' (although there are at least two pronunciations of 'l', if you think about the words *let* and *tell,* and there are many sorts of 'r', which you'll notice if you stop to think about it); third, the glides—what some people call 'y' (the first sound in *yes,* the sound after 'p' in *computer,* and also the sound that makes *ah* into what rhymes with *eye* in words such as *sigh,* or even *I*), and 'w' (the first sound in *wither* and the sound after the 'k' sound in *quick,* as well as the sound that makes *ah* into what rhymes with *Ow!* in *sound,* or *crowd*); and fourth, nasals, the sounds whose noise comes through our noses. (Try to say *mom, nose,* or *thing* while you hold your nose tightly closed and see what happens.) All four of these unobstructed categories, although each is different, as we can see, are also categorized as sonorants; they resonate. Not only can some start syllables but some can also be almost entire syllables (taking on some of the work of the vowel), which we can hear in the unstressed (less loud, roughly) second syllables of words such as *paper, table, bottom,* or *common,* for example.

The obstructed sounds—which interfere with what comes out of the mouth (we leave the air coming through our noses alone) can be categorized into three groups: stops—the sounds typically represented by the letters *p, t, k* and *b, d, g* (until we say them, our vocal area is pretty much shut, and air is stopped, literally); fricatives (relatively noisy sounds)— including the sounds typically represented by *f* and *v,* the two pronunciations of *th* (in **thigh** and **thy,** for example, where voicing is at work, distinguishing meaning), the sounds in *s*eal and li*c*e or in *z*eal and lie*s* (often represented by the letters *s* and *z*) *s* and *z,* the sounds in *sh*ield or *cr*u*sh,* and the sounds in the beginning of the second syllables of *pleasure,* or *treasure*; and finally, a set called affricates, which begin with a stop and finish with a fricative. We hear both affricates in the word *change,* and hear one each in *lunch* and *lunge.* A way to distinguish the sounds, and to see, again, how the feature voicing works in the language to make meaning distinctions, is to contrast the word *lunge* with the word *lunch.* It is this feature that is at work in final position of those two words, creating the meaning distinction, signaled by the distinct affricates.

Now you have made a working acquaintance with terms, sounds, and some sound features that are at work in all varieties of language; they are part of the human language faculty. These sound features work to define sounds and sound patterns, resulting in identifiable linguistic systems; they interact in systematic (if complex) ways with the writing systems that provide ways to represent, preserve, and sometimes even change the original systems.

Table 10.1 indicates whether each feature is specifically an AAE feature or is also found in the other vernacular Englishes that AAE has had the most contact with. Many of the forms may be familiar, but readers should take care to pronounce and consider them.

TABLE 10.1

Feature	Example	Linguistic systems where observed
final consonant cluster reduction	'cold' *col* 'hand' *han* 'desk' *des*	most Engl. varieties, more frequent in AAE
unstressed syllable deletion (at the beginnings and middles of words)	'about' *'bout* 'government' *go(v)'mint*	most Engl. varieties, more frequent in AAE
haplogogy (deletion of reduplicated syllable)	'mississippi' *misipi* general' *genrl* (with the 'l' representing its own syllable)	most AAE and non-AAE forms
making the syllable-final l more like a vowel	'bell' *beuw* 'pool' *poow* 'will' -> 'll-> *uw*	most AAE and non-AAE forms
loss of 'r' after 'th' and in initial clusters of unstressed syllables	'throw' *thow* 'professor' *puhfessor*	general vernacular feature
word-final 'th' sounds become 'f' and 'v' sounds depending on voicing	'bath' *baff* 'baths' *bavz*	AAE and southern vernaculars (also found in some British dialects)
word-initial 'th' sounds become stops	'those' *doze* 'these' *deeze* 'thing' *ting*	vernacular forms
word-final voiceless 'th' becomes a stop, especially after a nasal	'tenth' *tint* 'with' *wit*	vernacular forms

(continued)

TABLE 10.1 Continued

Feature	Example	Linguistic systems where observed
metathasis (inversion) of 's' and a voiceless stop consonant at the ends of words	'ask' *aks*	older general Southern speech and AAE
vocalization or deletion of end of syllable 'are'	'bird' *buhd* 'father' *fathuh* 'four' *fahw*	older white Southern speech and AAE
deletion of 'are' before an unstressed syllable	'carol' *ca(r)uhl* 'hurry' *huh(r)y*	older white Southern speech and AAE
change of the diphthong sound 'eye' to 'ah' before b, d, g, v, and z, and at word ends	'tied' *tahd* 'wise' *wahz* 'pie' *pah*	older general Southern speech and AAE
change of the diphthong 'oy' to 'awh' before l	'boil' *bawhl* 'soil' *sawhl*	older general Southern speech and AAE
merger of short 'e' and short 'i' sounds before n and m at the ends of syllables	'pin' *pin* 'pen' *pin* 'Wednesday' *winsday*	older general Southern speech and AAE
changing of z, v and th to d, b, and d, respectively, before nasals	'wasn't' *wahdn't* 'seven' *seb'm* 'heathen' *heed'n*	southern midland and AAE
stressing of first syllables in two syllable words	'police' *POlice* 'supper' *SUHpuh* 'Detroit' *DEtroit* 'hotel' *HOtel*	AAE (Rickford & Rickford, 2000)
changing of the sound of /d/ at the ends of words to /t/ (this sometimes happens also to /b/ and /g/, which change to /p/ and /k/, respectively)	'bad' *bat*	AAE
making word-final /t/ a glottal /t/ or a glottal stop (a glottal stop is the sound between the /uh/ and /oh/ in /uh-oh/ and for most speakers' of the sound—spelled by /tt/—in /kitten/, or /mitten/)	'bat' *bat?*	a number of non-AAE forms and AAE

Note: This table and material are adapted from Pullum (1999, p. 39), Mufwene et al. (1998), and Green (2002).

For Writing and Discussion

Some of these patterns may, indeed, sound familiar. Listen carefully to speakers that you interact with, and that you hear on the radio or on television. Do you notice some of the features described here? Do any of them contribute to making people sound a certain way? What sound patterns, for example, would you think of in saying that someone "sounds French," "Spanish," "Southern," "Texan," or "Latina"? Listen again to the speakers you recorded earlier, too.

A number of the characteristic regularities described in Table 10.1, as well as a number of the syntactic characteristics previously described, have developed the status of shibboleth, the meaning of which readers have discovered on page 367. This status seems to provide these particular linguistic features with two functions. They flag speakers as part of the African-American community and they are used as foci for discussions about the nature and origins of AAE. Probably the most "notorious" of features is the pronunciation *aks*. Consider the following:

> One of the most salient points of phonological variation which is strongly stigmatized from outside the [b]lack community might be called the great *ask-aks* controversy. ... The Oxford English Dictionary establishes this variation ... as very old, a result of the Old English metathesis *asc-acs-*. From this followed Middle English variation with many possible forms: *ox, ax, ex, ask, esk, ash, esh, ass, ess*. Finally, *ax* (aks) survived to almost 1600 as the regular literary form, when *ask* became the literary preference. Most people know nothing of the history of this form, and believe the *aks* variant to be an innovation of the AAVE community. In fact, it is found in Appalachian speech, in some urban dialects in the New York metropolitan area, and outside the US in some regional varieties of British English. Non-AAVE speakers are eager and willing to point out this usage, which is characterized as the most horrendous of errors. (Lippi-Green, 1997, pp. 179–180)

The "most horrendous of errors," speakers are told. In fact, the difference merely reflects an arbitrary victory of one form over another. There is no logical superiority of one pronunciation over another. But "aks" is a shibboleth. And this particular form eclipses other similar processes, resulting in pronunciation differences that may affect written forms. Listening to popular pronunciations of the words *jewelry, realtor,* or *nuclear* (a pronunciation that became a notorious marker for the 43rd president of the USA) for example, should reveal some interesting changes, none as marked (and thus not as well-noticed or well-studied) as the ask/aks example.

Some other examples of more or less shibbolethed regularities in AAE are found in the changes of the *th* interdental voiceless and voiced sounds to *f* or *v* respectively at the ends of words, and to *t* or *d* at the beginnings of words, the stressing of the first syllables, and the influences of the *r* and *l* sounds in syllable ending or word-ending positions. Equally noteworthy is the observation that non-AAE forms—quite standard ones—make use of a number of the same or parallel processes. The absence of the *d* in *hand*, for example, is much like the absence of *g* in *long* and the absence of *b* in *bomb*. All three reappear in other contexts, viz., *handy, longest,* and *bombast*, for example.[15]

Some of the changes interact with other patterns. The absence of /t/ after /p/ or /k/ and the absence of /d/ after /n/ can affect the marking of past tense in verbs such as *wipe, walk,* or *loan*, for example. So, a MUSE speaker might imagine that an AAE speaker has "failed" to acknowledge that a verb is in the past tense in a sentence, such as the following (where the ' indicates the absence of a pronounced /d/) *Yesterday I loan' her a table*. In reality, the sound pattern has hidden the marker (but of course, the *yesterday* arguably obviates a marker for past, as it would be redundant). These changes may also have consequences in writing, and the response to a spelling that seems to indicate a misuse of tense should take into consideration the possibility that it reflects a sound pattern. Thus, intervention would recognize a student's understanding of tense, and might begin with a conversation about sound and spelling, rather than one about tense marking. An analogous example in MUSE is the increasingly frequent menu entry "ice tea." Once, it read "iced tea," but the juxtaposition of the two identical sounds, at the end of "iced" and at the beginning of "tea," led to the loss of one, and this new spelling—and expression—evolved. This occurs also when the sounds are almost identical, as it did, as well, in "ice cream."

The inflectional forms, syntactic markers, and these sound patterns make up the structure of clauses and sentences in AAE. But as important as these characteristics are for writing, features beyond—discourse and narrative styles—are also important. These patterns beyond the sentence have been described in the context of oral traditions as well as written ones. We turn now to them, looking briefly at each, as they are mutually dependent.

DISCOURSE, NARRATIVE STRUCTURE, AND BEYOND

We have seen that there are differences in the forms of the language that student writers are expected to access as they construct college essays. But there are also differences in the presentation, flow, and organization of ideas. A natural question arises: What can teachers do to ensure that all students have an opportunity to learn multiple languages and multiple discourses? An obvious beginning to an answer is to have teachers develop the linguistic, composition, and cultural savvy requisite to describing the languages and discourses. The chapters in this text, including this one, along with the readings, have as their collective goal to lead readers in that direction.

That step itself is important, and involves at least two preliminary steps. For a discourse to be described, it must be visible. Very often the dominant discourse seems invisible because it is dominant; certainly its speakers are often as unaware of it as Earth dwellers are unaware of the multiple effects of gravity or the presence of the atmosphere. Learning explicitly about the dominant language and discourse, as well as the myths (e.g., the describable existence of MUSE), is critical. The next step is to learn about the structure and nature of the nondominant languages and discourses.

When there is no question about the national status of a language or a discourse, scholars and students are enthusiastic and willing to consider it as one among many. When, however, there is some question—whatever the sources or the validity of the questions may be—about the status of the language, its rhetorical patterns, its speakers and their discourses, the situation is more complex. People question the need to look at different styles or discourses, and deny the very existence of any framework or different system, as in the case of the Oakland School Board crisis. However, as the discussion here has indicated, it is important for teachers to acknowledge and work with the language variations students bring to the classroom. The following suggestions for doing so are offered by Lisa Delpit (2001, p. 553):

> First, teachers must acknowledge and validate students' home language without using it to limit students' potential. Students' home discourses are vital to their perception of self and sense of community connectedness. ... Second, teachers must recognize the conflict ... between students' home discourses and the discourse of school. They must understand that students who appear to be unable to learn are in many instances choosing to "not-learn," as Kohl puts it [a response which, as Claude Steele (1999) has shown, is influenced by school culture itself], choosing to maintain their sense of identity in the face of what they perceive as a painful choice between allegiance to "them" [an often unaccepting or critical "other"] or "us" [themselves].

Bridging this chasm in the context of sometimes hostile environments is complex. Delpit notes effective use of Afrocentric curriculum, providing students with some rediscovery and ownership of areas whose content otherwise seems more central to what are taken as Eurocentric values. She reminds her readers of the *Stand and Deliver* story of Jaime Escalante's admonishing of his Latino students from poor neighborhoods, as he taught them calculus and the dialogue that his film persona is given: "You have to learn math. The Mayans discovered zero. Math is in your blood" (p. 554). Finally, she argues that teachers

> can acknowledge the unfair "discourse-stacking" that our society engages in. They can discuss openly the injustices of allowing certain people to succeed, based not on merit, but on which family they were born into, and on which discourse they had access to as children [given that some discourses are privileged and some are not]. The students, of course, already know this, but the open acknowledgement of it in the very institution that facilitates the sorting process is liberating in itself. (p. 554)

A next step is to provide descriptions of the discourses, both those that students know and the ones they are being asked to develop proficiency in, insofar as comprehensive and objective description is possible. For that reason, it is crucial to look carefully at descriptions of distinct modes of discourse, and to put them in context. References to what has come to be called "contrastive rhetoric," the study of varying styles of presentation, organization, and infusion of voice are particularly helpful in this context, as they provide descriptions of such styles (e.g., the work of Kaplan (1966) and Connor (1996)). Readers have already encountered this spectrum in the ESL chapter, where Edlund discusses the range of rhetorical styles and their resulting organizational features in some detail. The writing differences across languages are not unlike those that distinguish AAE and MUSE writing, as the selection by Paul Kei Matsuda observes.

Furthermore, it is often the case that different organizational modes match up differently with particular contexts to create genres. So, for example, a topic-centered approach, laying out the thesis and circling around it, may alternate with a topic-associated approach, which more or less concatenates a set of related topics, leading "up" to the one central to the thesis of the essay, depending on the goal or the discipline of the writing. The two may not just exist as mutually exclusive approaches in different linguistic/cultural systems. Thus, students writing in MUSE, whatever their first language, must also learn all of these patterns and their perceived matchings to genres or other contexts.

Understanding how writers may vary not only across discourse cultures, but also across genres and contexts, offers new possibilities for writing instruction. It may not be a particular narrative style that is "different" and that must be supplanted for student writing to meet expectations. Instead, the "difference" may be due to a matching of a particular framework to a context, which must be observed, demonstrated, and practiced. The goal becomes learning alignment skills: learning to align style and contexts. This goal entails access to, and developing proficiency in more than one style.

With this understanding, writing teachers can develop a greater range of expectations and understandings, as well as an increased awareness of their own modes of discourse, their own assumptions about their uses, and the assumptions about them that prevail in academic communities. This triangle—descriptions of multiple rhetorical frameworks, clear understanding of the structures of target frameworks and their preferred matchings (those privileged in university classrooms and academic disciplines, for example, that create genres), and a well-developed awareness of one's own writing patterns in relation to these frameworks—is a critical piece of geometry. It outlines the context for understanding what is said about variation in discourse strategies.

For example, consider the following description: "traditional African American discourse characteristics [incorporate] the quality of a performance in [texts]"; techniques that create a performance may vary across different communities, and "within the African American tradition those techniques include such musical phenomena as the rhythmic use of language, patterns of repetition and variation, expressive sounds, and phenomena encouraging participatory sense making, like using dialogue, tropes, hyperbole, and call and response patterns within the text" (Ball, 1996, p. 30, with indicated changes). On the surface, such performance seems different from (orderly) presentation, involving aspects of author presence, and even orality—another feature often attributed to the discourses of many students categorized as nonmainstream. Although these features do exist, and certainly play a role in affecting how readers of student essays respond to them, they are all features of writing that can appear in various genres across discourse cultures as well.[16] They should not, in other words, become stereotypes or be seen as obstacles to overcome in pursuit of a particular approach to exposition. The chapters that treat audience and genre in this text provide more detailed explanations that can, in turn, be woven in with the topics discussed here.

Recognizing the sorts of structures that their own exchanges involve—another leg of the triangle—requires instructors to learn something about discourse, including some study of what seems the most quotidian conversational or written experiences. Asking questions about how requests are made; how one is convinced of a position by a colleague, friend, or adversary; what it means to "be polite"; where to look for the point, or the new information in a sentence or a paragraph; or about how simple conversations are structured (how one knows when to take a turn speaking, for example, or how one might flout such principles) provide first (but not uncomplicated) steps.[17] As instructors learn about their own patterns, and how they may be described, they are also learning about some of the more "dominant" patterns, and how these come to be accepted as mainstream, thus structuring our expectations.

Writing teachers and their students are in complex positions, juggling multiple objects—including conceptual triangles of the sort we have been constructing. Collectively, students are seeking admission to and recognition from institutional systems—universities—that both present and challenge prevailing values. Admission and recognition require some level of control over the means of exchange—language. We have seen further that there is significant variation in language—some of which we notice more, and some less, for complex reasons—and that admission and recognition seem to require attention to the variation, demanding that students make some choices.

University (writing) instructors are asked both to staff the admission booth and to provide students with the means of achieving recognition—or at least to point them to the most promising paths in that direction. But we are not just guides and gatekeepers. As our students navigate the paths, juggling their own and institutional values (their baggage—but also ours), we must help them learn to develop their own sense of the territory—to become language savvy themselves. Engaging in explicit—and well-informed—discussion of language variation—in writing classes, across students' languages and ethnicities, and between students' usages in speaking or engaging with contemporary social media (texting,

Twitter, and Facebook, for example, current at the time of this writing) should help them develop such savvy, which, in turn, empowers them both to comment on and to choose among a variety of pathways in the territories of composition classrooms and beyond. Their choices—their navigational strategies—are then informed by clear legends and labels that such maps require.

Knowledge of this sort of metaphoric geography, of course, requires at least an understanding of how forms and the meanings we make of them interact, not only with each other but also with the cultural/communicative contexts in which we use them. Such knowledge seems critical, and if students are to develop it, it must be part of the faculty toolkit. It has been the goal of this chapter to introduce readers to some small foundational parts of that knowledge in ways that will provide not only for applications, but also for fruitful study.

For Writing and Discussion

1. How is dialect or language diversity treated in popular media? Consider seeing *The Sound of Music*, or one of the following animated features: *Lion King, Aristocats, Dumbo, Shrek, Toy Story*, or *Lady and the Tramp* (you may think of others, as well). What do you notice about forms of language used by the actors doing the voiceovers? (Cf. Lippi-Green "Teaching children how to discriminate," in *English with an Accent* ([1997).) How might you discuss such treatment in a writing class?

2. Consult the Conference on College Composition and Communication website. (Note that websites do change, so some hunting may be required.) One of the conference's early position statements about language variation is available (www.ncte.org/ccc/12/sub/) on the website. Compare the positions taken there to some of what is written currently about the relationship between individual languages and the expectations of college composition classrooms. Visit the website of the Linguistic Society of America (www.lsadc.org) and look there for the LSA statements about language rights and Ebonics. You can find these by selecting the virtual button labeled *Resolutions*.

3. Consult the website for educators, associated with the PBS documentary, "Do you speak American?": http://www.pbs.org/speak/education/, where there are several instructive resources regarding both the nature of linguistic variation and our perceptions of it. Take the Chicano English quiz, and see how you do. Consider both the "Perspectives on written and spoken English," and the "African American English" sections.

4. Read the O'Neil essay "Dealing With Bad Ideas: Twice is Less" from the *English Journal* at the end of this chapter. O'Neil investigates Orr's assumptions about the connection between language (more precisely, the way someone uses vocabulary and syntax) and thought. Consider the implications for interpreting student writing, and for understanding the student performance that O'Neil's insights about Orr's misunderstanding have.

5. Read the piece by Paul Kei Matsuda, "The Myth of Linguistic Homogeneity in U.S. College Composition" at the end of this chapter. What connections can you draw between what he observes and asserts and what we have discussed here? Together, what sorts of implications might these have for your own teaching? What sorts of

preparation might you engage in as you anticipate the students in your writing classes?

6. What connections do you see between the O'Neil critique and the Matsuda paper? What do the lects we have discussed and "foreign" languages have in common? How might we use those common features to (all) our students' benefits?

For Further Exploration

Language Variation, Pidgins, Creoles, and Related Issues

Bonvillain, N. (2000). *Language, culture and communication* (3rd ed.). Upper Saddle River, NJ: Prentice Hall.

Finegan, E. (2008). *Language: Its structure and use* (5th ed.). Boston, MA: Thompson Wadsworth.

Fromkin, V., Rodman, R, & Hyams, N. (2010). *An introduction to language* (9th ed.). Boston, MA: Wadsworth-Cengage Learning.

Pinker, S. (1994). *The language instinct.* New York: Harper Collins.

Linguistic Ideas

Anderson, S. R., & Lightfoot, D. W. (2002). *The language organ: Linguistics as cognitive physiology.* Cambridge: Cambridge University Press.

Baker, M. C. (2001). *The atoms of language.* New York: Basic Books.

Jackendoff, R. (1994). *Patterns in the mind.* New York: Basic Books.

Pinker, S. (1994). *The language instinct.* New York: Harper Collins.

Dialects, Attitudes, and Classrooms

Gilyard, K. (1996). *Let's flip the script.* Detroit, MI: Wayne State University Press.

Lippi-Green, R. (1997). *English with an accent.* London: Routledge.

Wolfram, W., Temple-Adger, C., & Christian, D. (2007). *Dialects in schools and communities* (2nd ed.). Mahwah, NJ: Lawrence Erlbaum.

AAE

African American English and the DEA. http://linguisticanthropology.org/blog/2010/08/25/dea-and-ebonics/

Black Sign Language. http://blackaslproject.gallaudet.edu/BlackASLProject/Welcome.html

Center for the Study of African American English: University of Massachusetts at Amherst. http://www.umass.edu/csaal/

Green, Lisa J. (2002). *African American English: A linguistic introduction.* Cambridge: Cambridge University Press.

Rickford, J., & Rickford, R. (2000). *Spoken soul.* New York: John Wiley and Sons.

Smitherman, G. (1977). *Talkin and testifyin.* Detroit: Houghton Mifflin. Republished by Wayne State University Press, 1986.

General

Adler-Kassner, Linda, & Harrington, Susanmarie. (2002). *Basic writing as a political act: Public conversations about writing and literacies.* Cresskill, NJ: Hampton Press, Inc.

Baldwin, J. (1979, July). If Black English isn't a language, then tell me, what is? *New York Times* editorial.

Ball, A., & Lardner, T. (1997, December). Dispositions toward language: Teacher constructs of knowledge and the Ann Arbor Black English case. *College Composition and Communication, 48,* 469–485.

Ball, A. F., & Larnder, T. (2005). *African American literacies unleashed: Vernacular English and the composition classroom*. Carbondale, IL: Southern Illinois University Press.

Baugh, J. (1983). *Black street speech: Its history, structure and survival*. Austin: University of Texas Press.

Baugh, J. (2000). *Beyond Ebonics: Linguistic pride and racial prejudice*. Oxford: Oxford University Press.

Bayley, Robert, & Santa Ana, Otto. (2004). Chicano English grammar. In B. Kortmann, E. W. Schneider, K. Burridge, R. Mesthrie, & C. Upton (Eds.), *A handbook of varieties of English: Morphology and syntax* (vol. 2, pp. 167–183). Berlin: Mouton de Gruyter.

Cameron, D. (1995). *Verbal hygiene*. New York and London: Routledge.

Chomsky, N. (2000). *New horizons in the study of language and mind*. Cambridge: Cambridge University Press.

Coleman, C. F. (1997, December). Our students write with accents—oral paradigms for ESD students. *College Composition and Communication, 48* (4), 486–500.

Culler, J. (1983). *On deconstruction*. Ithaca, NY: Cornell University Press.

Cushman, E., Kintgent, E. R., Kroll, B, & Rose, M. (Eds.). (2001). *Literacy: A critical source book*. Boston: Bedford/St. Martin's.

Daniell, B. (1996). Deena's Story: The discourse of the other. *JAC: A Journal of Composition Theory, 16* (2), 253–264.

Dillard, J. L. (1973). *Black English*. New York: Vintage Books.

Dillard, J. L. (1992). *A history of American English*. New York: Longman.

Durant, Alan, & Lambrou, Marina. (2009). *Language and media: A resource book for students*. New York, NY: Routledge.

Farr, Marcia, Lisya Seloni, & Juyoung Song. (Eds.) (2010). *Ethnolinguistic diversity and education: Language, literacy, and culture*. New York, NY: Routledge.

Field, F. (2002). *Linguistic borrowing in bilingual contexts*. Amsterdam: John Benjamins.

Field, F. (Forthcoming). *Chicano-Latino blingualism in the U.S*. Amsterdam, The Netherlands: John Benjamins.

Field, F. (Forthcoming). *Key concepts in bilingualism*. New York: Palgrave Macmillan.

Field, F. (2007). *The double-whammy: Linguistic minority writers, rhetorical strategies and salient grammatical features*. Presentation at the annual Society for Pidgins and Creoles meeting.

Finegan, Edward, & Rickford, John. (2004). *Language in the USA: Themes for the twenty-first century*. Cambridge: Cambridge University Press.

Fought, Carmen. (2006). *Language and ethnicity*. Key Topics in Sociolinguistics. New York: Cambridge University Press.

Gilyard, K. (1991). *Voice of the self*. Detroit: Wayne State University Press.

Gilyard, K. (Ed.). (1999). *Race, rhetoric and composition*. Portsmouth, NH: Boynton/Cook-Heineman.

Haake, K. (2000). *What our speech disrupts: Feminism and creative writing studies*. Urbana, IL: NCTE.

Hartwell, P. (1985). Grammar, grammars, and the teaching of grammar. *College English, 47*, 105–127.

Honda, M., & O'Neil, W. (1996). On making linguistics useful for teachers: What can you learn from plural nouns and R? In D. L. Lillian (Ed.), *Papers of the Annual Meeting of the Atlantic Provinces Lingustic Association/Actes du Colloque Annuel de l'Association de Linguistique de Provinces Atlantiques*, pp. 81–92. Ontario, Canada: York University Press.

hooks, b. (1994). Language. In *Teaching to transgress* (pp. 167–175). London and New York: Routledge.

Horner, Bruce, Min-Zhan Lu, & Matsuda, Paul Kei (Eds.) (2009). *Cross-language relations in composition*. Carbondale, IL: Southern Illinois University Press.

Howard, R. M. (1996, January). The great wall of African American Vernacular English in the American college classroom. *JAC, 16* (2), 265–283. *Special Issue: Who's Doing the Teaching?*

Hudson, G. (2000). *Essential introductory linguistics*. Malden, MA: Blackwell.

Hughes, Pam (2008). Working with speakers of non-standard dialects in an academic ESL writing class. MATESOL presentation. Retrieved from http://www.sfsu.edu/~matesol/conferences/spring2008/abstracts.htm#Pamela.

Jackendoff, R. (1994). *Patterns in the mind*. New York: Basic Books.

Jordan, J. (1972). White English/Black English: The politics of translation. In *Civil Wars* (1981) (pp. 59–73). Boston, MA: Beacon Press.

Kochman, T. (1981). *Black and white styles in conflict*. Chicago: University of Chicago Press.

Kohl, H. (1991). *I won't learn from you! The role of assent in education*. Minneapolis, MN: Milkweed Editions.

Kozol, J. (1975, December). The politics of syntax. *English Journal, 64,* (9), 22–27.

Krapp, G. P. (1925). *The English language in America*. New York: Modern Language Association.

Labov, W. (1972). *Language in the inner city: Studies in the Black English vernacular*. Philadelphia: University of Pennsylvania Press.

Labov, W. (1995). The case of the missing copula: The interpretation of zeroes in African-American English. In L. R. Gleitman, & M. Liberman (Eds.), *Language, an invitation to cognitive science* (2nd ed., Vol. 1). Cambridge, MA: MIT Press.

Lanehart, S. (1998). African American vernacular English and education: The dynamics of pedagogy, ideology, and identity. *Journal of English Linguistics: Special Issue: Ebonics, 26,* (2), 8.

LePage, R. (1986). Acts of identity. *English Today, 8,* 21–24.

Lovejoy, Kim Brian (Ed.). (2004). Language, dialects, and writing. *Journal of Teaching Writing, 21,* 1–2, 1–7.

Makoni, Sinfree, Smitherman, Geneva, Ball, Arnetha, F., & Spears, Arthur K. (Eds.). (2003). *Black linguistics: Language, society, and politics in Africa and the Americas*. New York: Routledge.

Marback, R. (2001). Ebonics: Theorizing in public our attitudes toward literacy. *The Journal of the Conference on College Composition and Communication, 53,* (1), 11–32.

Matsuda, Paul Kei. (2003). Basic writing and second language writers: Toward an inclusive definition. *Journal of Basic Writing, 22,* (2), 67–89.

Matsuda, Paul Kei. (2010). The myth of linguistic homogeneity in U.S. college composition. In Bruce Horner, Min-Zhan Lu, & Paul Kei Matsuda (Eds.), *Cross-language relations in composition*. Carbondale, IL: Southern Illinois University Press.

McIntosh, P. (1989, July/August). White privilege: Unpacking the invisible knapsack. Excerpt from Working Paper 189, *Peace and freedom*. Philadelphia: Women's International League for Peace and Freedom.

Morales, Ed. (2002). *Living in Spanglish: The search for a Latino identity in America*. New York: St. Martins Press.

Mufwene, S. (1998, October). *The ecology of language: New imperatives in linguistics curriculua* (pp. 30–31). Paper presented at the Symposium on *The Linguistic Sciences in a Changing Context*, University of Illinois, Urbana-Champagne. Retrieved from www.uchicago.edu/linguistics/faculty/mufw_ecol.html.

Mufwene, S. (1999). North American varieties of English. In R. Wheeler (Ed.), *The workings of language*. New York: Praeger Press.

Mufwene, S., Bailey, R. G., & Baugh, J. (Eds.). (1998). *African-American English*. London and New York: Routledge.

Myers-Scotton, Carol. (2002). *Contact linguistics: Bilingual encounters and grammatical outcomes*. Oxford: Oxford University Press.

Myers-Scotton, Carol (2006). *Multiple voices: An introduction to bilingualism*. Malden, MA: Blackwell Publishers.

Nero, Shondel J. (Ed.) (2006). *Dialects, Englishes, Creoles, and education*. Mahwah, NJ: Lawrence Erlbaum Associates, Inc.

Okrand, M. (1985). *The Klingon dictionary*. New York: Pocket Books.

Olson, D. R. (1994). *The world on paper*. Cambridge: Cambridge University Press.

O'Neil, W. (1990, April). Dealing with bad ideas: Twice is less. *English Journal, 79* (4), 80–88.

O'Neil, W. (1991). Ebonics in the media. *Radical Teacher, 54*, 13–17.

Palacas, A. L. (2001, January). Liberating American Ebonics from Euro-English. *College English, 63* (3), 326–352.

Perry, T., & Delpit, L. (Eds.) (1999). *The real ebonics debate: Power, language and the education of African American children*. Boston: Beacon Press.

Peñalosa, F. (1980). *Chicano sociolinguistics: A brief introduction*. Rowley, MA: Newbury House.

Read, C. (1975). *Children's categorization of speech sounds in English*. Urbana, IL: NCTE.

Reaser, Jeffrey and Carolyn Temple Adger (2008). Vernacular language varieties in educational settings: Research and development. In Bernard Spolsky, & Frances M. Hult (Eds.), *The handbook of educational linguistics*. Malden, MA: Blackwell Publishers.

Rickford, J. (1998). *African American vernacular English*. London: Blackwell.

Shopen, Timothy, & Williams, Joseph M. (Eds.). (1980). *Standards and dialects in English*. Under the auspices of the Center for Applied Linguistics. Cambridge, MA: Winthrop Publishers, Inc.

Sebba, M. (1997). *Contact languages*. New York: St. Martin's Press.

Sledd, J. (1969). Bi-dialectalism: The linguistics of white supremacy. *English Journal, 58*, 1307–1315.

Smith, N. (1999). *Chomsky: Ideas and ideals*. Cambridge: Cambridge University Press.

Stavans, I. (2003). *Spanglish*. New York, NY: Rayo: an imprint of HarperCollins.

Stavans, I. (Ed.) (2008). *Spanglish*. Westport, CN: Greewood Press.

Turner, L. (1949). *Africanisms in the Gullah dialect*. Chicago: University of Chicago Press.

Wallace, D. F. (2001, April). Tense present: Democracy, English, and the wars over usage. *Harper's*, 39–58.

Wardaugh, R. (1999). *Proper English*. Malden, MA: Blackwell.

Wei, Li. (Ed.) (2000). *The bilingualism reader*. New York: Routledge.

Wheeler, R. (1999). *The workings of language*. New York: Praeger Press.

Williams, J. (1998). *Preparing to teach writing: Research, theory, and practice* (2nd ed.) Mahwah, NJ: Lawrence Earlbaum.

Wolfram, W., & Schilling-Estes, N. (1998). *American English*. New York: Blackwell.

Wolfram, W., & Whiteman, M. (1971, Spring/Fall). The role of dialect interference in composition. *Florida FL Reporter, 9*, 34–48.

Wright, Laura (Ed.). (2000). *The development of standard English 1300–1800: Theories, descriptions, conflicts*. Cambridge: Cambridge University Press.

NOTES

1 If you look up the word *infancy* in a dictionary with etymological information (the text mentions the fourth edition of the *American Heritage Dictionary of the English Language*), you will find that it refers directly to language itself.

2 This epigram is traceable to a coterie of scholars—Max Weinreich, his son Uriel Weinreich, and Joshua Fishman, all grandparents of the field of sociolinguistics, whose complex object of study is the intersection of language structure with the forces of social structure.

3 Spanglish receives more attention in the general discussion of language varieties.

4 In the context of our discussion about linguistic variation and the sources of attitudes about the varieties, it seems appropriate to note the language of terms here. *Lexifier* has an *-er* agentive suffix: lexifier languages provide words; they have an active role. Compare the term *substrate,* which translates roughly to "bottom layer."

5 In *An Introduction to Second Language Acquisition Research* (1991), Diane Larsen-Freeman and Michael Long note that the term was first used by a pidgin/creole scholar, John Reinecke, in 1935, when he talked of the plantation contact language that developed in Hawaii, and gained use as a *lingua franca* (a common language, used by speakers of different languages to speak to one another, accorded some prestige by its very commonality and function).

6 We have used "ESL" here, because it represents the most widely used label for describing the concept and process of learning English as a new language. But we use it reluctantly, as it detracts from the fact that although it is new to them, many speakers learning English may be encountering it as a third or fourth language.

7 We say "perceived of" because it is in a chapter entitled "The Myth of Standard English" that Rosina Lippi-Green introduces the term *MUSE*. In recent work, Peter Elbow (2003, 2008) has used the term "Standardized English," which is attractive for the message its morphology provides. The "-ize" suggests that someone has constructed a system; it doesn't merely exist, and the passive allows us to understand that there are agents, even if we cannot identify them.

8 It is worth spending a few words on the label for this linguistic system. Since it was first recognized as a discrete lect worthy of study (Labov, 1969, 1970), AAE has been referred to as Nonstandard (Negro) English (NNSE), Black English, Black English Vernacular (BEV), Ebonics, and African American Vernacular English (AAVE). "Ebonics" is a label originally used publicly by the psychologist Robert Williams in 1975, and was adopted by the Oakland School Board in its initiative. The names of the linguistic system differ insofar as they often reflect different positions concerning its origin and its relationship to English. There is some discussion of this naming issue in Green (2002, p. 3). We will adopt AAE (rather than AAVE or Ebonics) because it is most currently widely accepted in linguistic circles.

9 In some texts, readers may find the expression *be deletion* instead of *zero copula*. The term *be deletion* suggests that the copula verb *be* was there and was then taken out. Because they do not wish to make that claim with the term, many linguists have taken to using *zero copula* as the label.

10 Your pattern description should have the subject "moved" from its sentence-initial position to the position directly adjacent to the predicate. The "vacated" sentence-initial subject position is filled with **there**. You might notice sentences such as *There's three guys out on the porch*. Why do you think the copula might change from the plural, matching *three guys* to the singular?

11 In AAVE, this sentence could also mean that the speaker is referring to some big closet, and describing it. The sentence here could translate into *It is a big closet, filled with junk,* depending on how it is uttered when spoken or on the context in which it appears in written form. But a teacher would want to ask before making any suggestions for changes or translations.

12 It is perilously difficult to talk about sounds with recourse only to the representations that letters of the alphabet provide for us. We are all readers (evident from the fact that you are here), and the very process of learning to read does change our awareness of sound and the patterning of sound in the language. I will try to describe the sounds without engaging in a phonetics and phonology course, but show how they are distinct from the letters that we typically use to represent them, and how this distinction, along with different systems in AAVE and non-AAVE phonologies may affect students' writing. A particular danger in using letters to represent the sounds is that there is a long tradition of what is called "eye-dialect," where such forms as *wuhz* for 'was', or *kumbine* for 'combine' are used in written forms of dialogue in narratives, and are frequently used to derogate the characters who utter them, although they represent not any particularly stigmatized pronunciations of the words at all, but the typical ones. Readers should take care to avoid making any such connections when they look through the letter representations in the chart provided here. No symbol (especially letter) can make a sound, of course. Symbols may only represent sounds, more or less precisely. And for readers new to linguistic notation, the symbols between /.../ or [...] are those of the International Phonetic Alphabet (IPA) and are used to represent sounds as directly as any written form can; they do not belong to any particular language and are used to represent the sounds at different levels of analysis of any language.

13 Importantly, the parallel features related to hand shapes, positions, and movements work in precisely the same ways for sign languages. Deaf babies born amidst speakers of a signed language show babbling behaviors using their hands that are linguistically identical to the oral babbling of hearing infants. There are "accents" in signed languages, and the same issues about variation and its effects are raised. There are also important questions that must be considered when hearing impaired and deaf students are required to write in MUSE. We cannot consider such questions in this chapter, but encourage readers to consult relevant materials that do treat them (Emmorey, 1998; Hickok, Bellugi, & Klima, 2002; Meier, 1991; Padden, 1998; Supalla, Wix, & McKee, 2001; and Weisel, 1998, among others).

14 In the writing of a sixth-grade English learner whose first language is Spanish, for example, a teacher discovered the spelled form "verer" in the phrase "a verer day." Working with context and the insights of understanding the sound–letter correspondences in Spanish, the teacher was able to discover that the student's intended word was "better," and that his spelling was very systematic, involving hypotheses based on how Spanish orthography could represent English words.

15 The nasals and the stops in each of the words match as to where they are pronounced (place of articulation, more precisely), and there is often either a predilection for such matching, or there are processes centered around it.

16 Having taken these descriptions from Ball (1996), I do not wish to suggest that she is herself categorizing or stereotyping. In fact, in her discussion, Ball invokes the work and views of Bakhtin, noting the dialogic and multivoiced nature of writing itself.

17 Introductory linguistics textbooks can be helpful here, as they provide entry-level information about such areas as ethnographies of communication and components for describing them, as well as how communicative structures are understood. Two such resource texts are Nancy Bonvillain, 2000, *Language, Culture, and Communication*, 3rd edition, Upper Saddle River, NJ: Prentice-Hall (particularly Chapters 4 and 5, which address how speakers address one another, forms of politeness, conversational expectations, etc.) and E. Finegan, 1999, *Language: Its Structure and Use*. Fort Worth, TX: Harcourt Brace (particularly Chapters 8, 9, and 10, which deal with the ways in which information is organized, the structures of conversations, and the interaction of situational conditions and linguistic forms). All of these topics are relevant to writing classrooms. Another resource is *An Introduction to Functional Grammar*, 2nd edition (1994) by M. A. K. Halliday (New York: Arnold), whose work connecting structure to communicative function is often cited. But this text is more involved than the first two, which also make mention of Halliday's contributions.

REFERENCES

Bailey, G., & Thomas, E. (1998). Some aspects of AAVE phonology. In S. Mufwene, J. R. Rickford, G. Bailey, & J. Baugh (Eds.), *African-American English*. London and New York: Routledge.

Ball, A. (1996, January). Expository writing patterns of African American students. *English Journal, 85* (1), 27–36.

Ball, A., & Lardner, T. (1997, December). Dispositions toward language: Teacher constructs of knowledge and the Ann Arbor Black English case. *College Composition and Communication, 48*, 469–485.

Baron, Naomi (2008). *Always on: Language in an online and mobile world*. Oxford: Oxford University Press.

Baugh, J. (1983). *Black street speech: Its history, structure and survival*. Austin: University of Texas Press.

Chomsky, N. (1986). *Knowledge of language: Its nature, origin, and use*. New York: Praeger.

Connor, U. (1996). *Contrastive rhetoric: Cross-cultural aspects of second-language writing*. Cambridge: Cambridge University Press.

Crystal, David. (2008). *Txting: The gr8 db8*. Oxford: Oxford University Press.

de Boysson-Bardies, B. (1999). *How language comes to children*. Trans. M. DeBevoise. Cambridge, MA: MIT Press.

Delpit, L. (2001). The politics of teaching literate discourse. In E. Cushman (Ed.), *Literacy: A critical sourcebook* (pp. 545–554). Boston, MA: Bedford/St. Martin's.

Eisenstein, Jacob, Brendan O'Connor, Noah A. Smith, & Eric P. Xing (January 2011). A latent variable model for geographic lexical variation. Paper presented at the Linguistic Society of America (LSA). Pittsburgh, PA.

Elbow, Peter. (2003). Should we invite students to write in home languages? Complicating the yes/no debate. *Composition Studies, 31* (1), 25–42.

Elbow, Peter. (2006). Forward. In Shondel J. Nero (Ed.), *Dialects, Englishes, creoles, and education*. Mahwah, NJ: Lawrence Erlbaum Associates, Inc.

Elbow, Peter. (2008). Coming to see myself as a vernacular intellectual. *College Composition and Communication, 59* (3), 519–524. Retrieved from http://works.bepress.com/peter_elbow/22.

Emmorey, K. (1998). Sign language. In V. Clark, P. Eschoholz, & E. Rosa (Eds.), *Language* (6th ed.) (pp. 78–95). New York: St. Martins.

Fought, C. (2003). *Chicano English in context*. New York: Palgrave Macmillan.

Fought, C. (2005). American varieties: Talking with Mi Gente. In *Do you speak American?* Retrieved April 30, 2008, from http://www.pbs.org/speak/seatosea/americanvarieties/chicano/.

Green, Lisa J. (1998). Aspect and predicate phrases in African American vernacular English. In S. Mufwene, J. R. Rickford, G. Bailey, & J. Baugh (Eds.), *African-American English*. London and New York: Routledge.

Green, Lisa J. (2002). *African American English: A linguistic introduction*. Cambridge: Cambridge University Press.

Hickok, G., Bellugi, U., & Klima, E. S. (2002, June). Sign language in the brain. *Scientific American*, Special edition, *The Hidden Mind*, *12* (1) (updated from *Scientific American*, June 2001).

Kaplan, R. B. (1966). Cultural thought patterns in intercultural education. *Language Learning*, *16*, 1–20.

Labov, William. (1969). *The study of non-standard English*. Washington, DC: National Council of Teachers of English.

Labov, William. (1970). *The study of non-standard English*. Champaigne, IL: National Council of Teachers of English.

Larsen-Freeman, D., & Long, M. (1991). *An introduction to second language acquisition research*. Reading, MA: Addison Wesley.

Lewis, M. Paul (Ed.) (2009). *Ethnologue: Languages of the world* (16th ed.). Dallas, TX: SIL International. Online version retrieved from http://www.ethnologue.com/.

Lippi-Green, R. (1997). *English with an accent*. London and New York: Routledge.

Maher, J., & Groves, J. (1996). *Introducing Chomsky*. New York: Totem Books.

Martin, S., & Wolfram, W. (1998). The sentence in AAVE. In S. Mufwene, J. R. Rickford, G. Bailey, & I. Baugh (Eds.), *African-American English* (pp. 11–36). London and New York: Routledge.

McAdams, C. M. (1989). Croatia: Myth and reality. Retrieved from www.hrvatska.org/mcadams/myth.

Meier, R. P. (1991). Language acquisition by deaf children. *American Scientist*, *79*, 60–70.

Moore, Matthew (2010) Facebook and Twitter "helping spread regional dialects." *The Telegraph*, September 2. Retrieved from http://www.telegraph.co.uk/technology/facebook/7977765/Facebook-and-Twitter-helping-spread-regional-dialects.html.

Mufwene, S. (2001). Pidgins and Creoles. Retrieved from www.uchicago.edu/linguistics/faculty/mufw_pdgcreo.html.

Mufwene, S., Bailey, R. G., & Baugh, J. (Eds.). (1998). *African-American English*. London and New York: Routledge.

O'Neil, W. (1972). The politics of bidialectalism. *College English*, *33*, 433–438.

Padden, Carol. (1998). Early bilingual lives of deaf children. In Ila Parasnis (Ed.), *Cultural and language diversity and the deaf experience* (Chapter 6). Cambridge: Cambridge University Press.

Poplack, Shana. (1980/2000). Sometimes I'll start a sentence in Spanish y termino en español: Toward a typology of code switching. In Li Wei (Ed.), *The bilingualism reader*. London: Routledge.

Pullum, G. (1999). African American English is not standard English with mistakes. In R. Wheeler (Ed.), *The workings of language*. New York: Praeger Press.

Rickford, J. R., & Rickford, R. J. (2000). *Spoken soul*. New York: John Wiley and Sons.

Santa Ana, Otto. (1991). Phonetic simplification processes in the English of the barrio: A cross-generational sociolinguistic study of the Chicanos of Los Angeles. University of Pennsylvania dissertation (cited in Fought 2003).

Smitherman, G. (1977). *Talkin and testifyin*. New York: Houghton Mifflin. Republished by Wayne State University Press, 1986.

Smitherman, G. (1994). *Black talk*. New York: Houghton Mifflin.

Stavans, I. (October 13 2000). The gravitas of Spanglish. *The Chronicle of Higher Education*, *47* (7), B7.

Steele, C. (1999). Thin ice. *The Atlantic Monthly*, *284* (2), 44–54.

Stockman, I. J. (1996). Phonological development and disorders in African American children. In A. G. Kamhi, K. E. Pollock, & J. L. Harris (Eds.), *Communication development and disorders in African American children* (pp. 117–153). Baltimore: H. Brookes.

Supalla, S. J., Wix, T. R., & McKee, C. (2001). Print as a primary source of English for deaf learners. In J. Nicol (Ed.), *One mind, two languages: Bilingual language processing*. Malden, MA: Blackwell.

Wald, Benji. (1984). The status of Chicano English as a dialect of American English. In Jacob Ornstein-Galicia & Allan Metcalf (Eds.), *Form and function in Chicano English* (pp. 14–31). Rowley, MA: Newbury House.

Weisel, A. (Ed.) (1998). *Issues unresolved: New perspectives on deaf education*. Washington, DC: Gallaudet University Press.

Wolfram, W. (1994). The phonology of a sociocultural variety: The case of African American vernacular English. In J. Bernthal, & N. Bankston (Eds.), *Child phonology: Characteristics, assessment, and intervention with special populations*. New York: Thieme.

Wolfram, W., Temple-Adger, C., & Christian, D. (2007). *Dialects in schools and communities* (2nd ed.). Mahwah, NJ: Lawrence Earlbaum.

Readings

DEALING WITH BAD IDEAS: TWICE IS LESS

Wayne O'Neil

It is an unfortunate fact about intellectual life in the United States, and certainly in other places as well, that bad and discredited ideas from the past keep reappearing. Particularly vulnerable to their reappearance are the "softer" areas of inquiry and work: the study of mind and of education and teaching. For there seems always to be the hope that human nature is less interesting and complex than it is; that there is somewhere to be found a quick educational fix for the overwhelming social problems of the day; that there is a science and technology that will solve all. From my particular vantage point, nowhere do these bad ideas roll so badly back, penny-like, than in discussions that link language with this or that aspect of education. These general remarks and the detailed ones that follow are largely motivated by the recent reappearance of many such bad ideas in the form of Eleanor Wilson Orr's *Twice as Less: Black English and the Performance of Black Students in Mathematics and Science* (1987).

Whatever her concerns, Orr's *Twice as Less* falls exactly into this category of research and band-aiding, with its attendant simplistic and wishful thinking. For her work sustains the fantasy of the intellectual that the basic injustices of society are subject to relatively simple technical correction. Thus—in education, for example—armed with the proper science and a derivative technology, the "experts" lead teachers to expect to find solutions to their problems close and easily at hand. In Orr's case, her goal is to explain the failure of urban, poor African American students to survive educationally in school, in particular in mathematics and science. Linguistics is then brought to bear on these problems. This brings Orr to an Ann Arbor-type solution (for more about this matter, see below, "Some Further Points"), according to which educators are enjoined to "seek out the knowledge of linguists" so that they can understand what their African American students are saying–thinking as well as what they are not saying–thinking (Orr 215: all page references are to Orr's book unless otherwise noted). (The wavering mark [–] between *saying* and *thinking* is to indicate that Orr does not distinguish between language and thought very carefully, if at all: see the following section for further discussion.) African American students then need only get "in the habit of ... using the conventions of standard [= international] English" (48) and "to gain control over the construction of complex sentences that depend on relative pronouns and conjunctions and contain many prepositional phrases" (212) in order to get on with an understanding of science and mathematics.

The nature of the educator's task is then clear enough—though the job is not an easy or pleasant one, as it never seems to be in these "hard" cases: some basic concepts supposedly have to be drummed or built into the minds of African American students. Allegedly great difficulty is experienced due to the underlap between two varieties of a language. For by proclamation it is supposed to be easier for a speaker of a foreign language to get international English down perfectly than it is for a speaker of a nonstandard form of the language (125–26, citing several such unsupported assertions). This is a familiar enough truth about language learning, and thus, like all such "truths" held to be true without examination, should be considered suspect.

Scientific Critique: Language and Thought

However, as with any scientific-technical solution to a problem, we need to evaluate its intellectual foundations. In this case, an evaluation requires that we look not only at linguistic theory but at the cognitive sciences more generally. To her credit, Orr has a sense that she is treading on some pretty unsteady ground: Harvard's Roger Brown has warned her about the Sapir-Whorf hypothesis (11), that rather vague notion that "one's cognitive structure is largely determined by the structure (including the vocabulary) of the language one speaks" (Fodor, Bever, and Garrett 1974, 384). Unfortunately, however, Brown has misinformed Orr about the status of this hypothesis (which, indeed, we dignify by so labeling it). For the Sapir-Whorf hypothesis has just the standing and just the persistency as, for example, the notion that the earth is flat: it conforms to our common-sense view of things in nature, but it is dead wrong and is not a serious candidate for the explanation of the things in nature.

Thus misinformed and misled, Orr is encouraged to march into the swamp, with predictable and disastrous results. For, like a lot of people, Whorf included, Orr has great difficulty distinguishing concepts from their labels in language (words, more or less). Thus, she (half-)believes that in giving her students the words, she is giving them the concepts involved. In her discussion of location and distance, for example, Orr concludes that the fundamental question is,

> Does Jane think in terms of two distinct entities—location and distance—even though she uses the same symbol for both? Or does she think in terms of only one entity, which she accordingly represents by a single symbol? And if she does think in terms of only one entity, is it some kind of hybrid of the conventional notions of location and distance? (25)

Moreover, Orr adds a curious wrinkle of her own to Sapir-Whorf by expressing the nonstandard belief that "in the case of the three modes of expressing comparisons [the noun mode, the *than* mode, and the *as* mode], the grammar of Standard English has been shaped by what is true mathematically" (158), a remarkable observation, if true. For her observation here is rather like assuming that in language as in logic, two negatives make a positive. But we know that, in fact, two negatives in *natural* language make an emphatic negative, as distinct from their canceling effect in the *artificial* language of logic.

Indeed, my co-worker Morris Halle (1988, personal communication) has carried out a small and contrary experiment on this point with fluent MIT graduate-student speakers of international English in connection with Orr's statement (192) that the synonymity of "John does not have as much money as Sam" with "John has less money than Sam" is paralleled by the synonymity of "John does not have as little money as Sam" and "John has more money than Sam." All of the students agreed that the members of the first pair were clearly synonymous but disagreed widely about the second pair. One person said that "only logical consistency" convinced him that the second set of sentences contained synonymous members. Thus, it seems obvious that it is the requirements of scientific discourse that ensure synonymity in the second pair, not the language of everyday use.

In thinking this way, Orr fails to notice that the mathematical and scientific education of us all involves our learning narrow and fixed definitions of the words of ordinary language. These new definitions correspond only partially, if at all, to those of ordinary language. Take the word *hypothesis*, for example, or nearly any word from among those that Orr finds her students having difficulty with. Each of them has a meaning, indeed several meanings in the language of everyday speech, different from its narrower technical or scientific one(s). The word *distance*, for example, has several abstract nominal meanings ("the fact or condition of being apart in space or time"; "the interval separating any two specified instants in time"; "a point removed in space or time"; "chilliness of manner, aloofness"; and the like.) In addition, the word *distance* has three meanings special to geometry—not to mention the fact that it functions as a verb as well with its particular, nontechnical definitions. Moreover, some terms of science (*quantum potential*, for example) and of even quite ordinary discourse have no sense outside of scientific or technical discourse. The label *live oak*, for example, refers to a tree of the sort that an expert tells me is a live oak; indeed I may always need an expert to tell me or point out to me which are the live oaks as distinct from the other trees in the world.

Moving beyond mere matters of vocabulary, we know that great numbers of students, both younger and older than Orr's, as well as at the same age, have difficulty with mathematical and arithmetical problems. The extent of this difficulty in the United States is urgently reported to us from time to time, recently, for example, in "The Mathematics Report Card: Are We Measuring Up," from the National Assessment of Educational Progress (NAEP, see Fiske 1988), in which it is revealed that only 6.4% of the tested seventeen-year-olds (down from 7.4% in 1978) could handle multistep problems and algebra, problems far simpler than those administered by Orr. Given the general scope of the difficulties reported, clearly something here runs far deeper than the specifics of the grammar of Black English. What is it?

Language and Thought: An Alternative View

However, more reasonable assumptions about human nature exist than the ones Orr unquestioningly adopts: namely, that on the basis of their species-specific genetic endowment, human beings are equipped as a matter of course with all the natural concepts there are. The maturation of a child in this respect is then simply the child's learning which labels (words, crudely speaking) go with the concepts that receive expression in its language and world. (For some discussion, see Noam Chomsky 1988 passim.) Among languages and among varieties of what we loosely call a language, differences as to how the concepts are labeled will occur. There will also be minor variation over which concepts are labeled and about whether the mapping between concepts and labels is many-to-one, one-to-many, one-to-one, and the like.

Most obvious and trivial is the fact that different languages will label the same concept in phonologically very different ways: thus, the notion "reflexive" is generally (but not only) labeled with some form of -self in English, with a form of -ziji (including the "plain" form, without a personal pronoun attached) in Chinese, and the like. More interestingly, for example, many languages label the number concepts beyond "two" with only two additional terms roughly equivalent to "few" and "many." Moreover, in some varieties of English (in the Creole English of Nicaragua, for example), the concepts that many of us separate with the labels learn and teach are covered with the single label learn—a concept-to-label mapping that is common in the languages of the world. This offers no difficulties of communication apart from those that arise from the sort of elitism recently exhibited by the English Prince Charles.

Closer to Orr's concerns are the many varieties of English marked by subtle differences in the way the prepositional labels are tied up with the relational concepts involved. In Appalachian speech, for example, at labels the directional concept to; in other varieties at labels the locational in, and the like. The varieties of American English exhibit fine differences in the exact forms that comparative constructions take, with the label as doing the work of the standard than in some varieties, for example. (See Cassidy 1985 for details.)

In this view, we do not expect to find that a person or a group of people will lack certain concepts. Nor are we surprised to find languages that lack labels for particular concepts. (See Hale 1975 for discussion.) Presumably, if nothing in the culture focuses attention on particular concepts, then there is no reason to label them. For example, in English (as distinct from many other languages of the world) a rudimentary set of labels for kinship relations exists. From this observation, we conclude nothing about the human mind, however much we may want to conclude about the culture to which the language gives partial expression. For under the normal notions of translatability, where there is a mind and time there is a way to go from one language to another, in principle. That is, all the mind's concepts are hypothesized to be available for labeling in language—any language. Thus, when it became crucial for the Walpiri (an aboriginal people of Australia) to have mathematics, words for the number concepts involved became easily available to their language, which had previously lacked labels for the distinct number concepts beyond "two" (having cover terms roughly equivalent to "few" and "many" for larger sets). Indeed, it is an interesting fact about human beings that they continue to learn new labels (i.e., words) throughout their lives, whether in their native language or in a second, third, or nth language, this being a major insight of work on second language acquisition about the difference between the acquisition of grammar and of the lexicon (or mental dictionary).

Orr's Problem

In this light, consider again Orr's concern with the notions "location" and "distance," which the African American students she works with seem to confuse so badly as to lead her to wonder whether they have the two distinct concepts at all. Yet these particular concepts are so fundamental to human nature as to be necessarily labeled in all languages. Indeed, in one widely respected view, they are at the foundation of the interplay between language and conceptual structure. (See Jackendoff 1983.)

If this view is accepted, then how are we to explain the behavior typical of Orr's students with respect to such problems as those in Figure 1? Instead of a standard diagram of the sort shown in square brackets, the students drew diagrams in which the various cities were expressed as lines and in which the lines were connected in various relational ways reflecting the notion "distance" in the statement of the problem.

12 The distance from Washington, DC, to New York City is equal to the distance from Washington to Cleveland. Ohio Johnstown, Ohio, is fifty miles further from Washington than Cleveland is Springsville. New York, is fifty miles further from Washington than New York City is.

a) In the space below draw a labeled diagram that depicts the distance from Washington to New York City and the distance from Washington to Cleveland

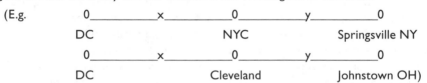

b) To the diagram you drew for 12a, add whatever is necessary in order to also show the locations of Springsville, New York, and Johnstown, Ohio. Label these locations.

FIG. R10.1.

How, then, do we explain their behavior? As I read Orr's distance and location problems, I was struck by how much their proper expression, which absolutely requires that cities be represented by points and the distances between them by connecting lines, depends on a familiarity with the conventions of maps. In fact, if you are too familiar with maps and with the geography of the United States, you will be astounded by some of the assertions made in the problems—the relative location of Cleveland and New York City with respect to Washington, DC, for example. Thus, without an acceptance of or familiarity with the abstraction from reality that mapping conventions demand—not to mention the suspension of beliefs that is required by the problems themselves—it is difficult to see why anyone should imagine Washington, DC, Cleveland, and New York City to be points: that is, to have no extension—especially if one travels each day from some *point* in DC to another and back again. Now since it is unbelievable that the students lack the concepts or the language required to solve these problems, it is quite likely that Orr's problems simply lack any semblance of reality of interest for the students. Indeed, from the NAEP report cited above, we learn that "most students see mathematics as having little use in their future work life" (Fiske A28), that is that they find it irrelevant. Thus, from this behavior, it is wrong to conclude that the students lack the relevant concepts, however much we might want to conclude about the limited imagination of those who would try to delve into their minds.

Science Education

In fact, the problems cited throughout Orr's book bear little relation to anything in the real world, and they often involve so many unknowns that they are unsolvable, emphasizing the form of a solution rather than the satisfaction of a solution itself. In this connection, it is worth examining Orr's notion that it was "more effective to have these students not take any science until they had successfully completed algebra and geometry" (211). The misconception here is to believe that science is principally formalism, when, in fact, modern science arose out of the realization that it was the simplest things in the physical world that defied our understanding, and that our common-sense misunderstanding of them (that the earth is flat, for example) could give way to widely appreciated explanations through the careful exercise of the human science-forming capacity (Noam Chomsky 156–59). As Randolph Bourne somewhere wrote, "Scientific method is simply a sublimely well-ordered copy of our own best and most fruitful habits of thought." And as we go about trying to understand "our own best and most fruitful habits of thought," formalism will play little role, as it plays only a small role in science itself except at its most advanced and technical levels.

Orr's book, however, is subtitled in such a way as to make the reader think that Orr is going to deal with science education in some serious way as well as with mathematics (severely limited in her case to algebra and geometry), but in fact, what little attention she does pay to science is disappointingly devoted to following one of her students through a logical maze of someone else's making (211–14), working out a rather sophisticated problem little different in structure from her usual type that involves "two people start[ing] from the same place at the same time and travel[ing] in opposite directions. One of these travels twenty mph faster ..." (67).

Our own work in science education, at the middle- and high-school levels, derives from a view of science as cooperative intellectual interplay between the human, science-forming capacity and things in nature. From this point of view, we have developed an introduction to the style and activity of modern scientific thinking based on very simple things: on the careful observation and explanation of simple linguistic phenomena, the behavior of floating and sinking objects, and the properties of dry yeast, for example. (See Carol Chomsky et al.; Carey et al. 1986, *A Progress Report*; Carey et al. 1988, *A Technical Report*; Bemis et al. 1988.)

Setting these important considerations about the general nature of scientific inquiry and science education aside, we conclude that Orr is naive about the relationships between language and thought. And it is this naiveté that simply cuts the scientific ground out from under her technical solution to the problems of education on which she fixes her attention.

Linguistic Critique: Black English

I turn now to other, increasingly more serious matters that Orr has gotten wrong: On the dust jacket of Orr's book, Roger Brown is quoted as saying that "this book is not naive about the Black English Vernacular and it is untainted by racism"—basic prerequisites, one would hope, given the topics that Orr addresses. However, neither of these judgments is true.

First about Black English. Although Orr writes as if there is little controversy over the origins and development of Black English and of the so-called creole languages generally, she has come to this conclusion by walking lightly past the incompatible views that she cites of Derek Bickerton and Joe Dillard (in Newmeyer 1988, 268–84), among others. The former claims that creoles are what they are because of the human bioprogram; the latter, that creolized European languages have become what they are through the intermixture of the lexicon of the European language and the syntax of African languages. (See Newmeyer 268–84; 285–301; 302–06; Holm 1988.)

A third view, one that I share, is that the so-called creole languages are largely varieties of the European languages from which they principally derive—on a par with the Englishes, the Spanishes, and the like found many places in the world (O'Neil, Joiner, and Taylor 1987; O'Neil and Honda 1987). It should be clear, then, that a great deal of controversy about these matters is now the basis of much lively and interesting linguistic research. Thus, what is known about creoles and about the creole basis for Black English cannot be assumed to be fixed. The answers to these interesting questions are, indeed, wide open, as is the formulation of the questions themselves. Thus, some of the conclusions that Orr reaches about, say, the differences between the ways prepositions work in Black English and in international English are easily challenged.

Moreover, Orr's discussion of several aspects of the grammar and the history of Black English is quite misleading. For example, she misunderstands the double-negative construction in Black English as somehow a hybrid of the international English "I don't know/anything about it" plus "I know/nothing about it" equaling "I don't know nothing about it" (148) and thoroughly neglects the thousand-year history of the double-negative construction in the English language. She also fails to see that an African American child's repetition of the sentence "he's not as smart as he thinks he is" as "he ain't as … he not so smart as what he thinks he be" (186) shows a perfect perception of the international English sentence through an exact translation of it into Black English. The translation even contains the relative pronoun *what*, clearly indicating the relative-clause structure of the comparative construction characteristic of all varieties of English at a sufficient level of abstraction.

As this last observation suggests, the linguistic goals for the study of Black English ought to be the same as for any language or language variety: linguists are concerned to understand the variety of human linguistic expression as well as its underlying and universal sameness. They pursue their studies in order to try to understand one aspect of human knowledge.

It is then intriguing to ask why so much emphasis has been put on the study of Black English in the recent history of dialect studies in the United States and not on its other varieties? In part, the answer to this question goes back to my opening (and what will be part of my closing) remarks: intellectuals want narrow, technical solutions to broad, nontechnical social problems. So funds get directed toward research on and dissection of the perceived sources of the problems, in this case the African American community. Whether such research is done in Vietnam, in Central America, or in the cities of the United States, the underlying goal of this sort of anthropological and socio-logical research, though not necessarily of the researchers themselves, is for the ruling class to seek to understand potential enemies in all ways so as to try to control and contain them. On the domestic side, such work serves to convince people that something important is being done for them, but in the end, the work is directed against them, toward preventing redistribution of the present imbalance of economic and cultural capital. It is for this reason that we know as much as we do about urban African American society and its varieties of English but so little about the Englishes and other languages of the many economically impoverished people of the United States: the urban rebellions of twenty or so years ago, which threaten always to recur, were rebellions of African American people, not rural rebellions of the farmers of Iowa, say, about whose language and social structure we know very little, consequently. It is in this way that the social sciences in general have served (since their birth in the United States) and continue to serve the interests of the state. In China, the government keeps its people down by shooting them: in the United States, the people are kept down by social science and propaganda, with shooting reserved for special occasions only.

Political Critique: Racism and Other Issues

Racism

As far as the question of racism is concerned, it is a matter of considerable insensitivity and extremely condescending—to say the least—for Orr to deny "these students" fundamental con-cepts of human mind: to suggest, for example, that they do not have the perceptions and the language to distinguish between where they are and where they would like to be and what it takes to get from here to there. In the literature of racism as well as that of sexism and classism, typically the racists (and other -ists) dehumanize the object of their attacks. (For discussion, see among many others, Gould 1981; Lewontin et al. 1984.) Orr's approach here may be gentler, superficially more understanding, and more nicely packaged than those discussed by Stephen J. Gould and R. C. Lewontin, Steven Rose, and Leon J. Kamin, but it is no less dehumanizing.

Some Further Points

Turning to other large political issues, which Orr neglects almost entirely, I began by saying that whatever her intentions, Orr's book falls into a category of research that comforts and sustains certain fantasies of the intelligentsia—two very favorable reviews in the *New York Times* (1 and 19 November 1987) exhibiting this perception of her work. Her study presents the calming view that there is a more or less simple answer to one of the many trying problems of our time—that in this case the answer lies in education, the last refuge of the intellectual being an unwarranted faith in education, a retreat from the political center and struggles of society into one of its marginal institutions.

Finally, by her silence, Orr appears to show no understanding of or concern for what I will refer to (in paraphrase of Jesse Jackson) as the social and economic violence of poverty and, in this case, its educational consequences.

Return for a moment to the Ann Arbor case: the central legal question there was whether Black English was a separate language or "just a dialect," a variety of English—an unanswerable question from a scientific point of view, although clearly answerable from, say, a political point of view. (See, for example, James Baldwin's "If Black English Isn't a Language, Then Tell Me, What Is?" 1985.) If the former, then its speakers were protected under the body of law supporting bilingual education. Not so if Black English was "merely" a variety of English. With the help of a battery of expert linguistic witnesses, the judge decided that Black English was not a separate language, but since the educators at the King school were not sufficiently sensitive to the language variety and culture of their African American students, he sentenced the teachers to inservice instruction about these matters.

However, few people remember, or even know, that the Ann Arbor case was originally more than a legal action about language, that it was a broad-based suit against the Ann Arbor school system, a suit demanding social and economic justice. It was the court that narrowed the case to a trial about the sociolinguistic status of Black English because, in the United States, the poor are not legally protected from the social and economic violence which they must endure, however marginally protected they may be by the various languages they speak. (See Perry 1980; Perry 1982.)

Conclusion

As far as I can see, technical answers of the type that Orr, the Ann Arbor judge, and others give us offer no way out of the present situation in which the gap between the educational achievements of the African American poor and other poor minority groups and those of the white majority correlates so strongly with other gaps: IQ and SAT scores, dropout rates, illiteracy rates, wage and salary ratios, unemployment rates, malnutrition rates, infant mortality rates, serious illness and longevity rates, violent-death rates, and so on. An understanding of the grammar of Black English will explain none of this. Perhaps the recent work that sees these differences to be the result of the caste-liké structure of our society will lead to an explanation of its present disgraceful state. But still better explanations will not eliminate the Third World conditions that characterize much of urban existence in the United States: for to change the world in a nonviolent way requires that those with social, political, and economic privilege and power give up much of what they have and work together with those without privilege and power in order to eliminate the economic and social violence of poverty and to participate in the building of a just society in which human differences are celebrated, human dignity restored, one in which material and cultural resources are shared equally and not hoarded through privilege.

Massachusetts Institute of Technology
Cambridge, Massachusetts 02139

Works Cited

Baldwin, James. 1979. "If Black English Isn't a Language, Then Tell Me, What Is?" *New York Times* 29 July: Op Ed Page. (Rpt. in James Baldwin. 1985. *The Price of the Ticket: Collected Nonfiction 1948–1985*. New York: St. Martin's. 649–52.)

Bemis, Diane, et al. 1988. *Nature of Science: Lesson Plans*. Cambridge, MA: Educational Technology Center.

Carey, Susan, et al. 1986. *What Junior High School Students Do, Can, and Should Know about the Nature of Science: A Progress Report*. Cambridge, MA: Educational Technology Center.

—— 1988. *What Junior High School Students Do, Can, and Should Know about the Nature of Science and Scientific Inquiry: A Technical Report*. Cambridge, MA: Educational Technology Center.

Cassidy, Frederic G., chief ed. 1985. *Dictionary of American Regional English. Vol. 1: Introduction and A-C*. Cambridge: Harvard UP.

Chomsky, Carol, et al. 1985. *Doing Science: Constructing Scientific Theories as an Introduction to Scientific Method: A Technical Report*. Cambridge, MA: Educational Technology Center.

Chomsky, Noam. 1988. *Language and Problems of Knowledge: The Managua Lectures*. Cambridge: MITP.

Fiske, Edward B. 1988. "Back-to-Basics in Education Produces Gains in Arithmetic." *New York Times* 8 June: A1, A28.

Fodor, Jerry A., Thomas G. Bever, and Merrill F. Garrett. 1974. *The Psychology of Language: An Introduction to Psycholinguistics and Generative Grammar*. New York: McGraw.

Gould, Stephen J. 1981. *The Mismeasure of Man*. New York: Norton.

Hale, Ken. 1975. "Gaps in Grammars and Cultures." *Linguistics and Anthropology: In Honor of C. F. Voegelin*. Ed. M. Dale Kinkade, Ken Hale, and O. Werner. Lisse: Peter de Ridder, 295–315.

Holm, John. 1988–89. *Pidgins and Creoles*. 2 vols. Cambridge: Cambridge UP.

Jackendoff, Rav. 1983. *Semantics and Cognition*. Cambridge: MIT P.

Lewontin, R. C., Steven Rose, and Leon J. Kamin. 1984. *Not in Our Genes: Biology, Ideology, and Human Nature*. New York: Pantheon.

Newmeyer, Frederick J., ed. 1988. *Linguistics: The Cambridge Survey: Volume II. Linguistic Theory: Extensions and Implications*. Cambridge: Cambridge UP.

O'Neil, Wayne, Dora Joiner, and Shirley Taylor. 1987. "Notes on NP Pluralization in Nicaraguan English." *Historical Studies in Honour of Taizo Hirose*. Tokyo: Kenkyusha. 81–91.

O'Neil, Wayne, and Maya Honda. 1987. "Nicaraguan English/El Inglés Nicaraguense." *Wani: Revista sobre la Costa Atlantica* 6: 49–60.

Orr, Eleanor Wilson. 1987. *Twice as Less: Black English and the Performance of Black Students in Mathematics and Science*. New York: Norton.

Perry, Theresa. 1980. "Towards an Interpretative Analysis of the Martin Luther King Jr., v. Ann Arbor School District Board Case." Harvard Graduate School of Education Qualifying Paper.

—— 1982. *An Interpretative Analysis of the Martin Luther King Jr. v. Ann Arbor School District Board Case*. Diss., Harvard.

Author's note: These comments constitute an extensively revised and expanded version of remarks presented at a 1988 Harvard Graduate School of Education panel discussion with Orr about her research. Thanks to Carol Chomsky, Morris Halle, Maya Honda, Ben Nelms, and to Don M. Lance for reading earlier drafts of these comments and for their own helpful comments.

THE MYTH OF LINGUISTIC HOMOGENEITY
IN U.S. COLLEGE COMPOSITION

Paul Kei Matsuda

In "English Only and U.S. College Composition," Bruce Horner and John Trimbur identify the tacit policy of unidirectional English monolingualism, which makes moving students toward the dominant variety of English the only conceivable way of dealing with language issues in composition instruction. This policy of unidirectional monolingualism is an important concept to critique because it accounts for the relative lack of attention to multilingualism in the composition scholarship. Yet it does not seem to explain why second language issues have not become a central concern in composition studies. After all, if U.S. composition had accepted the policy of unidirectional monolingualism, all composition teachers would have been expected to learn how to teach the dominant variety of English to students who come from different language backgrounds. This has not been the case. While Geneva Smitherman and Victor Villanueva argue that coursework on language issues should be part of every English teachers' professional preparation (4), relatively few graduate programs in composition studies offer courses on those issues, and even fewer require such courses. As a result, the vast majority of U.S. college composition programs remain unprepared for second language writers who enroll in the mainstream composition courses. To account for this situation, I want to take Horner and Trimbur's argument a step further and suggest that the dominant discourse of U.S. college composition not only has accepted "English Only" as an ideal but already assumes the state of English Only, in which students are native English speakers by default.

That second language writing has not yet become a central concern in composition studies seems paradoxical given the historical origin of U.S. college composition as a way of "containing" language differences from the rest of U.S. higher education. Robert J. Connors has suggested that U.S. composition arose in response to perceived language differences—texts written by ostensibly some of the brightest native English speakers that included numerous errors in "punctuation, capitalization, spelling, [and] syntax" (*Composition* 128). Susan Miller also points out that college composition "has provided a continuing way to separate the unpredestined from those who belong … by encouraging them to leave school, or more vaguely, by convincing large numbers of *native speakers* and otherwise accomplished *citizens* that they are 'not good at English'" (Miller 74; emphasis added). To a large extent, however, issues that prompted the rise of the composition requirement are weak forms of language differences that affect native speakers of English—matters of convention and style as well as performance errors that arise from factors such as unfamiliar tasks, topics, audiences, or genres. While U.S. composition has maintained its ambivalent relationship with those weak forms of language differences, it has been responding to the presence of stronger forms of language differences—differences that affect students who did not grow up speaking privileged varieties of English—not by adjusting its pedagogical practices systematically at the level of the entire field but by relegating the responsibility of working with those differences to second language specialists (Matsuda, "Composition"; Shuck).

I am not trying to imply that there has not been *any* effort to address second language issues in composition studies. I recognize that a growing number of writing teachers who face those issues in their classes on a daily basis have developed, often on their own initiative, additional expertise in issues related to language differences. What I want to call into question is why the issue of language difference has not become a central concern for *everyone* who is involved in composition instruction, research, assessment, and administration. I argue that the lack of "a professionwide response" (Valdés 128) to the presence of strong forms of language differences in U.S. composition stems from what I call the myth of linguistic homogeneity—the tacit and widespread acceptance of the dominant image, of composition students as native speakers of a privileged variety of English. To show how the myth of linguistic homogeneity came into being, I examine here the early history of various attempts at linguistic containment, which created a condition that makes it seem acceptable to dismiss language differences. My intention is not to argue against all forms of linguistic containment. Rather, I want to problematize its long-term implication—the perpetuation of the myth of linguistic homogeneity—that has in turn kept U.S. composition from fully recognizing the presence of second language writers who do not fit the dominant image of college students.

The Image of College Students and the Myth of Linguistic Homogeneity

Behind any pedagogy is an image of prototypical students—the teacher's imagined audience. This image embodies a set of assumptions about who the students are, where they come from, where they are going, what they already know, what they need to know, and how best to teach them. It is not necessarily the concrete image of any individual student but an abstraction that comes from continual encounters with the dominant student population in local institutional settings as well as from the dominant disciplinary discourses. Images of students are not monolithic; just as teachers incorporate pedagogical practices from various and even conflicting perspectives, student images are multiple and complex, reflecting local institutional arrangements as well as teaching philosophies and worldviews of individual teachers. Although there is no such thing as a generalized college composition student, overlaps in various teachers' images of students constitute a dominant image—a set of socially shared generalizations. Those generalizations in turn warrant the link between abstract disciplinary practices and concrete classroom practices.

Having a certain image of students is not problematic in itself; images of students are inevitable and even necessary. Without those images, discussing pedagogical issues across institutions would be impossible. An image of students becomes problematic when it inaccurately represents the actual student population in the classroom to the extent that it inhibits the teacher's ability to recognize and address the presence of differences. Just as the assumption of whiteness as the colorless norm has rendered some students of color invisible in the discourse of composition studies (Prendergast 51), theoretical practices that do not recognize and challenge inaccurate images reinforce the marginal status of those students by rendering them invisible in the professional discourse. By the same token, pedagogical practices based on an inaccurate image of students continue to alienate students who do not fit the image.

One of the persisting elements of the dominant image of students in English studies is the assumption that students are by default native speakers of a privileged variety of English from the United States. Although the image of students as native speakers of privileged varieties of English is seldom articulated or defended—an indication that English Only is already taken for granted—it does surface from time to time in the work of those who are otherwise knowledgeable about issues of language and difference. A prime example is Patrick Hartwell's "Grammar, Grammars, and the Teaching of Grammar," a widely known critique of grammar instruction in the composition classroom. In his analysis of a grammar exercise, he writes that "the rule, however valuable it may be for non-native speakers, is, for the most part, simply unusable for native speakers of the language" (116). While this is a reasonable claim, to argue against certain pedagogical strategies based on their relevance to native speakers seems to imply the assumption of the native-English-speaker norm. Hartwell also claims that "native speakers of English, regardless of dialect, show tacit mastery of the conventions of Standard English" (123), which seems to trivialize important structural differences between privileged varieties of U.S. English and many other domestic and international varieties of English.

Language issues are also inextricably tied to the goal of college composition, which is to help students become "better writers." Although definitions of what constitutes a better writer may vary, implicit in most teachers' definitions of "writing well" is the ability to produce English that is unmarked in the eyes of teachers who are custodians of privileged varieties of English or, in more socially situated pedagogies, of an audience of native English speakers who would judge the writer's credibility or even intelligence on the basis of grammaticality. (As a practicing writing teacher, I do not claim myself to be immune to this charge.) Since any form of writing assessment—holistic, multiple-trait, or portfolio assessment—explicitly or implicitly includes language as part of the criteria, writing teachers regularly and inevitably engage in what Bonny Norton and Sue Starfield have termed "the covert language assessment" (292). As they point out, this practice is not problematic in itself, especially if language issues are deliberately and explicitly included in the assessment criteria and if students are receiving adequate instruction on language issues. In many composition classrooms, however, language issues beyond simple "grammar" correction are not addressed extensively, even when the assessment of student texts is based at least partly on students' proficiency in the privileged variety of English. As Connors has pointed out, "the sentence ... as an element of composition pedagogy is hardly mentioned today outside of textbooks" and has become a "half-hidden and seldom-discussed classroom practice on the level of, say, vocabulary quizzes" ("Erasure" 97, 120). It is not unusual for teachers who are overwhelmed by the presence of language differences to tell students simply to "proofread more carefully" or to "go to the writing center"; in the same classrooms, non-native speakers of dominant varieties of English are being held accountable for what is not being taught.

The current practice might be appropriate if all students can reasonably be expected to come to the composition classroom having already internalized a privileged variety of English—its grammar and rhetorical practices associated with it. Such an expectation, however, does not accurately reflect the student population in today's college composition classrooms. In the 2003/2004 academic year, there were 572,509 international students in the United States (Institute of International Education, *Open Doors 2004*), most of whom came from countries where English is not the dominant language. Although the number has declined slightly in recent years, international students are not likely to disappear from U.S. higher education any time soon. In fact, many institutions continue to recruit international students—because they bring foreign capital (at an out-of-state rate), increase visible ethnic diversity (which, unlike linguistic diversity, is highly valued), and enhance the international reputation of the institutions—even as they reduce or eliminate instructional support programs designed to help those students succeed (Dadak; Kubota and Abels).

In addition, there is a growing number of resident second language writers who are permanent residents or citizens of the United States. Linda Harklau, Meryl Siegal, and Kay M. Losey estimate that there are at least 150,000–225,000 active learners of English graduating from U.S. high schools each year (2–3). These figures do not include an overwhelmingly large number of functional binguals—students who have a high level of proficiency in both English and another language spoken at home (Valdés)—or native speakers of traditionally underprivileged varieties of English, including what has come to be known as world Englishes. The myth of linguistic homogeneity—the assumption that college students are by default native speakers of a privileged variety of English—is seriously out of sync with the sociolinguistic reality of today's U.S. higher education as well as the U.S. society at large. This discrepancy is especially problematic considering the status of first-year composition as the only course that is required of virtually all college students in a country where, according to a 2000 U.S. census, "more than one in six people five years of age and older reported speaking a language other than English at home" (Bayley 269).

The Policy of Linguistic Containment in U.S. College Composition

The perpetuation of the myth of linguistic homogeneity in U.S. college composition has been facilitated by the concomitant policy of linguistic containment that has kept language differences invisible in the required composition course and in the discourse of composition studies. Since its beginning in the late nineteenth century at Harvard and elsewhere, the first-year composition course has been a site of linguistic containment, quarantining from the rest of higher education students who have not yet been socialized into the dominant linguistic practices (Miller 74). While using the composition course as a site of linguistic containment for native speakers of privileged varieties of English, institutions have found ways to exclude more substantive forms of language differences even from the composition course by enacting several strategies for linguistic containment. The first and most obvious strategy is to exclude language differences from entering higher education altogether by filtering them out in the admission process. Another common strategy, especially when the number of students from unprivileged language backgrounds is relatively small, is to ignore language issues, attributing any difficulties to individual students' inadequate academic preparation. Even when language differences are recognized by the teacher, those differences are often contained by sending students to the writing center, where students encounter peer tutors who are even less likely to be prepared to work with language differences than composition teachers (Trimbur 27–28).

The policy of containment is enacted most strongly through the placement procedure, which is unique to composition programs in the sense that students do not normally have the option of choosing a second language section—perhaps with the exception of speech communication courses. The all-too-common practice of using language proficiency tests for composition place-ment (Crusan 20) is a clear indication that the policy of linguistic containment is at work. Even when direct assessment of writing is used for placement, the use of holistic scoring may lead raters to give disproportionate weight to language differences because "a text is so internally complex (e.g., highly developed but fraught with grammatical errors) that it requires more than a single number to capture its strengths and weaknesses" (Hamp-Lyons 760). Based on the placement test results, many students are placed in non-credit "remedial" courses where they are expected to erase the traces of their language differences before they are allowed to enroll in the required composition course. In other cases, students are placed—sometimes after their initial placement in mainstream composition courses—in a separate track of composition courses for non-native English speakers that can satisfy the composition, requirement. These courses, though sometimes costly to students, provide useful language support for students and are necessary for many who will be entering the composition course as well as courses in other disciplines where the myth of linguistic homogene-ity prevails. At the same time, these placement practices also reify the myth by making it seem as if language differences can be effectively removed from mainstream composition courses.

In the remainder of this chapter, I examine the emergence of the myth of linguistic homogene-ity and the concomitant policy of linguistic containment in the late nineteenth and early twenti-eth centuries—the formative years of U.S. college composition. U.S. higher education during this period is marked by several influxes of international students, many of whom came from countries where English was not the dominant language. Each of these influxes was met not by attempts to reform composition pedagogy but by efforts to contain language differences—efforts that continue even today. I focus on developments before the 1960s because it was the period when a number of significant changes took place. Although English had long been part of U.S. higher education, the English language began to take center stage in the late nineteenth century through the use of English composition as part of the college entrance exam (Brereton 9) and through the creation of the English composition course that tacitly endorsed the policy of unidirectional monolingualism (Horner and Trimbur 596–97). It was also during this period that language differences in the com-position classroom became an issue because of the presence of a growing number of international students, and many of the placement options for second language writers were created (Matsuda and Silva; Silva). My focus is on international students because, until the latter half of the twen-tieth century, resident students from underprivileged language backgrounds were systematically excluded from higher education altogether (Matsuda, "Basic" 69–72).

Waves of International Students and the Policy of Containment

The image of U.S. college students as native speakers of more or less similar, privileged varieties of English had already been firmly established by the mid-nineteenth century. Although the larger U.S.

society had always been multilingual (Bayley 269), language differences were generally excluded from English-dominated higher education of the nineteenth century. The assumption of the native-English-speaker norm was, at least on the surface, more or less accurate in the mid-nineteenth century, when access to college education was restricted to students from certain ethnic, gender, religious, socioeconomic, and linguistic backgrounds. As David Russell notes, U.S. colleges before the end of the Civil War were "by modern standards extraordinarily homogeneous, guaranteeing a linguistic common ground" (35). While U.S. higher education began to shift from exclusive, elitist establishment to a more inclusive vehicle for mass education during the latter half of the nineteenth century, the traditional image of college students remained unchallenged for the most part. Although the creation of what have come to be known as Historically Black Universities and Colleges provided African American students access to higher education since the early nineteenth century, they did not affect the dominant image because they were physically segregated from the rest of the college student population. In fact, those colleges served as sites of containment—ethnic as well as linguistic. The Morrill Act, first passed in 1862 and then extended in 1890, gave rise to land-grant institutions across the nation that made college education open to women as well as students from a wider variety of socioeconomic groups. Yet, non-native speakers of privileged varieties of English did not enter higher education in large numbers because the ability to speak privileged varieties of English was often equated with the speaker's race and intelligence.

One of the major institutional initiatives that contributed to the exclusion of language differences was the creation of the entrance exam—first instituted at Harvard in 1874 and then quickly and widely adopted by other institutions. The entrance exam at Harvard was motivated in part by "a growing awareness of the importance of linguistic class distinctions in the United States" (Connors, *Composition* 128). Harvard course catalogs during this period indicate that the entrance exam included "reading English aloud" or writing with "correct spelling, punctuation, grammar, and expression" (quoted in Brereton 34). Miller also points out that "forms of this examination became the most powerful instrument for discriminating among students in higher education" (63), effectively excluding students who did not fit the dominant linguistic profile. Even in the nineteenth century, however, the assumption of linguistic homogeneity in higher education was not entirely accurate, and it moved farther and farther away from the sociolinguistic reality of U.S. higher education. One group of students who brought significant language differences was made up of international students who entered U.S. higher education through different admission processes; they therefore were not subject to linguistic filtering (Matsuda, "Basic" 71–72).

The history of international ESL students in U.S. higher education goes at least as far back as 1784, when Yale hosted a student from Latin America; in the mid-1800s, students from China and Japan also attended Yale and Amherst College (King 11). The first influx of international students came in the latter half of the nineteenth century, when U.S. higher education began to attract an increasing number of students from other countries as it developed research universities modeled after German institutions. Most of these international students were from Asian countries that were "undergoing modernization with the help of knowledge acquired from Western countries" (Bennett, Passin, and McKnight 26). During the late nineteenth century, European students also came to U.S. higher education "not so much seeking an education that was not available to them at home, as out of a desire to see America, the 'country of the future'" (Institute of International Education, *Handbook* [1955] 6).

In the late nineteenth century, when many of the international students were sponsored by their governments, language preparation was generally considered to be the responsibility of individual students or their sponsoring governments, and U.S. colleges and universities usually provided little or no institutional support for international students' cultural and linguistic adjustments. For instance, students from China and Japan, most of whom were sponsored by their respective governments, usually received language instruction before coming to the United States. In many cases, however, their language preparation was less than adequate by the standard of U.S. institutions, and they were sent to preparatory schools, where they were "placed in classes with the youngest children" (Schwantes 194). The Japanese government continued to send students to U.S. colleges; however, they were selected by a rigid examination, and their progress was monitored by a supervisor sent by the Japanese government (Institute of International Education, *Handbook* [1955] 4). By the 1880s, the practice of holding the sponsoring government responsible for providing language preparation became difficult to sustain as the number of government-sponsored students declined, giving way to an increasing number of privately funded students (Bennett, Passin, and McKnight 32).

The second influx came in the early part of the twentieth century, when internationally known research institutions began to attract a growing number of international students, most from countries where English was not the dominant language. Although there were only 3,645 international students in U.S. higher education in 1911, the number began to grow rapidly after the conclusion of World War I (1914–18). This change was due partly to European students' dissatisfaction "with their own traditions of education" as well as Asian students' need for "new foundations for modern systems of education" (Kandel 39). Another factor that contributed to the growth was the national interest of the United States. The U.S. government's growing concern with post-World War I international relations—especially with European nations—prompted the establishment in 1919 of the Institute of International Education (IIE) with support from the Carnegie Endowment for International Peace. The IIE was successful in "stimulat[ing] interest in student exchange, encouraging public and private groups to sponsor international students" (Institute of international Education, *Handbook* [1955] 7). By 1920, the number of international students had reached 6,163 and was continuing to increase (Institute of International Education, *Handbook* [1961] 230). In 1930, U.S. colleges and universities reported the presence of 9,961 international students (Darian 105).

The growing presence of international students from non-English-dominant countries became an issue among hosting institutions. Some educators recognized the problem of the traditional pedagogy based on the dominant image of students. Isaac Leon Kandel, for example, wrote that international students did not benefit as much from the instruction, not because of their lack of ability but because "courses were organized primarily with the American student, familiar with American ideals, aims, history, and social and political background, in mind" (50). The solution, however, was not to challenge the dominant image but to contain issues of linguistic and cultural differences by providing additional instruction—an approach that might have seemed reasonable when the number of international students was relatively small. To provide linguistic support for those who did not fit the traditional image of college students, institutions began to develop special English language courses. According to a 1923 survey of four hundred institutions, all but two stated that they had "provision for special language help by official courses or by voluntary conversation classes" (Parson 155). Although it continued to be "a common rule to refuse admission to students who are unable to speak and read English," about 50 percent of institutions offered "special courses for backward students" (155).

In 1911, Joseph Raleigh Nelson in the Engineering College at the University of Michigan created the first English courses specifically designed for international students (Klinger 1845–47), followed by Teachers College of Columbia University, which created special courses for matriculated international students in 1923 (Kandel 54). Harvard University created its first English courses for international students in 1927, and George Washington University and Cornell University followed suit in 1931 (Allen 307; Darian 77). While there were some exceptions—such as the program at Michigan, which continued for several decades—many of these early programs were ad hoc in nature. The initial innovation at Harvard ceased to exist after a while, and by the 1940s, second language writers at Harvard had come to be mainstreamed into "regular" sections of composition courses with additional help from individual tutoring services (Gibian 157). At George Washington, the separate section of composition used "the same materials as the sections for Americans and . . . was conducted by the same teacher"; however, "none of the English instructors really desired to teach that group," and this program was later found to be unsuccessful (Rogers 394). The courses at Columbia, which allowed students to enroll simultaneously in college-level courses, were also found to be ineffective in containing language differences (Kandel 54). Other institutions, especially where the number of international students was relatively small, dealt with language differences "by a process of scattering foreigners through different courses, so that they must mingle freely with others, rather than segregating them for group study in classes where they may persist in using their own language" (Parson 155).

Following the announcement of the Good Neighbor Policy in 1933, the State Department began to bring international students from Latin America to provide scientific and technical training. This development led to the creation, in 1941, of the English Language Institute (ELI) at the University of Michigan. As an intensive program, it separated students from the college-level courses for a period of several months while students focused on developing their English language proficiency. Although the program was initially intended for Spanish-speaking graduate students from Latin America, it later broadened its scope to include undergraduate students and students from other language backgrounds. The Michigan ELI provided a model for intensive English programs through-out the United States and in many other countries, paving the way for the next wave of ESL courses that were created in response to the post-World War II influx of international students (Matsuda, "Composition" 701–6).

Although the number of international students declined somewhat during the Depression and World War II, the conclusion of the war brought another influx of international students. The international student population surged from less than 8,000 in 1945 to 10,341 in 1946 (Darian 105), when the United States replaced Germany as the most popular destination for international students. The number doubled in the next two years, and by 1949, there were 26,759 international students (Institute of International Education, *Open Doors* 7, 14). To contain the language differ-ences these students brought with them, an increasing, number of institutions—including those that had relatively small but steady enrollments of international students—began to create sepa-rate English courses and programs on a permanent basis (Schueler 309). In 1949, Harvard once again created a special non-credit course for small groups of students from Europe, providing a preparation for the required composition course (Gibian 157). At about the same time, Queens College developed a multilevel intensive English language program with its own teaching and testing materials (Schueler 312–14). Tulane University also created a non-credit English course for sec-ond language writers. Sumner Ives reported that all non-native English speakers at Tulane, unless "individually excused," were required to enroll in a special English course for non-native speakers before taking the required English course. This program was unique in that the status of the course was determined after the beginning of the semester. Based on a reading test during the orienta-tion, the teacher would decide whether each student should move to a "regular section" or remain in the remedial course. When most of the remaining students had limited English proficiency, the course was taught as a remedial English language course, using the materials developed by the ELI at Michigan. The course became credit-bearing when a large number of students had reached advanced English proficiency and the textbooks for regular sections of composition courses were used (Ives 142–43).

The number of ESL writing courses continued to grow. In 1953, according to Harold B. Allen, about 150 institutions reported the existence of ESL programs for international students; by 1969, the number had nearly doubled. In addition, 114 institutions reported that they offered summer programs for international students (308). Initially, many of those courses were offered on a non-credit basis as preparation for a regular English requirement. These courses focused not only on writing but also on reading and oral communication skills. Non-credit English courses for non-native speakers offered at many institutions adopted the textbook series developed by the ELI at Michigan. Intensive language courses modeled after the Michigan ELI also became widespread, providing systematic instruction before second language writers were allowed to enroll in regular college-level courses.

Yet, a semester or two of extra language instruction was often not enough to help students fit the dominant image of students—after all, learning a second language is a time-consuming process, especially for adult learners—and they continued to bring language differences to college composition courses. For this reason, institutions began to develop a separate track of required composition courses for second language writers—courses that were designed to keep language differences out of the required composition course. In 1954, Michigan's Department of English Language and Literature in the College of Literature, Science and Art created one of the first credit-bearing ESL composition courses that paralleled the sections of English courses for native speakers of English (Klinger 1849). University of Washington followed suit with a three-credit composition course for second language writers, which emphasized purposeful cross-cultural communication with an audience rather than the language drills or linguistic analyses commonly used in intensive language programs at the time (Marquardt 31).

Embracing Language Differences as the New Norm

The assumption of linguistic homogeneity, which was more or less accurate in U.S. higher education institutions of the mid-nineteenth century, became increasingly inaccurate as linguistic diversity grew over the last two centuries. Yet, the growing presence of international students did not lead to a fundamental reconsideration of the dominant image of students in the composition classroom. It was not because the separate placement practices were able to eliminate language differences. For a number of reasons, none of these programs was able to contain language differences completely: because language learning is a time-consuming process, because students often come with a wide range of English language proficiency levels, and because developing placement procedures that can account for language differences is not an easy task. As Ives wrote, "Neither a frankly non-credit course for all, nor their [non-native English speaking students'] segregation into separate but parallel courses, nor their distribution throughout the regular courses is completely satisfactory" (142). Instead, the dominant image of students remained unchallenged because the policy of containment kept language differences in the composition classroom from reaching a critical mass, thus creating the false impression that all language differences could and should be addressed elsewhere. In other words, the policy of unidirectional monolingualism was enacted not so much through pedagogical practices in the mainstream composition course but through delegation of students to remedial or parallel courses that attempted to keep language differences from entering the composition course.

The policy of containment and the continuing dominance of the myth of linguistic homogeneity have serious implications not only for international second language writers but also for resident second language writers as well as for native speakers of unprivileged varieties of English. Many institutions place students into basic writing classes without distinguishing writing issues and language issues partly because underlying language differences are not easily discernible by observing student texts that seem, at least on the surface, strikingly similar to one another (Matsuda, "Basic" 74). As a result, basic writing courses often enroll many second language writers—both international and resident—although many basic writing courses, like the credit-bearing composition courses, are often designed for U.S. citizens who are native speakers of a variety of English (68).

By pointing out the problem of the policy of containment, however, I do not mean to suggest that these placement practices should be abandoned. On the contrary, many students do need and even prefer these placement options. As George Braine suggests, many—though certainly not all—second language writers prefer second-language sections of composition, where they feel more comfortable and where they are more likely to succeed. To deny these support programs would be to further marginalize non-native speakers of English in institutions of higher education where the myth of linguistic homogeneity will likely continue to inform the curriculum as well as many teachers' attitude toward language differences. Instead, composition teachers need to resist the popular conclusion that follows the policy of containment—that the college composition classroom can be a monolingual space. To work effectively with the student population in the twenty-first century, all composition teachers need to reimagine the composition classroom as the multilingual space that it is, where the presence of language differences is the default.

Works Cited

Allen, Harold B. "English as a Second Language." *Current Trends in Linguistics: Linguistics in North America*. Vol. 10. Ed. Thomas A. Sebeok. The Hague: Mouton, 1973. 295–320.

Bayley, Robert, "Linguistic Diversity and English Language Acquisition." *Language in the USA: Themes for the Twenty-First Century*. Ed. Edward Finegan and John R. Rickford. Cambridge, UK: Cambridge UP, 2004. 268–86.

Bennett, John W., Herbert Passin, and Robert K. McKnight. *In Search of Identity: The Japanese Overseas Scholar in America and Japan*. Minneapolis: U of Minnesota P, 1958.

Braine, George. "ESL Students in First-Year Writing Courses: ESL Versus Mainstream Classes." *Journal of Second Language Writing* 5.2 (1996): 91–107.

Brereton, John C. *The Origins of Composition Studies in the American College, 1875–1925: A Documentary History*. Pittsburgh: U of Pittsburgh P, 1995.

Connors, Robert J. *Composition-Rhetoric: Backgrounds, Theory, and Pedagogy*. Pittsburgh: U of Pittsburgh P, 1997.

———."The Erasure of the Sentence." *College Composition and Communication* 52 (2000): 96–128.

Crusan, Deborah. "An Assessment of ESL Writing Placement Assessment." *Assessing Writing* 8 (2002): 17–30.

Dadak, Angela. "No ESL Allowed: A Case of One College Writing Program's Practices." Matsuda, Ortmeier-Hooper, and You.

Darian, Stephen G. *English as a Foreign Language: History, Development and Methods of Teaching*. Norman: U of Oklahoma P, 1972.

Gibian, George. "College English for Foreign Students." *College English* 13 (1951): 157–60.

Hamp-Lyons, Liz. "Rating Nonnative Writing: The Trouble with Holistic Scoring." *TESOL Quarterly* 29 (1995): 759–62.

Harklau, Linda, Meryl Siegal, and Kay M. Losey. "Linguistically Diverse Students and College Writing: What is Equitable and Appropriate?" *Generation 1.5 Meets College Composition: Issues in the Teaching of Writing to U.S.-Educated Learners of ESL*. Ed. Linda Harklau, Kay M. Losey, and Meryl Siegal. Mahwah, NJ: Erlbaum, 1999. 1–14.

Hartwell, Patrick. "Grammar, Grammars, and the Teaching of Grammar." *College English* 47 (1985): 105–27.

Horner, Bruce, and John Trimbur. "English Only and U.S. College Composition." *College Composition and Communication* 53 (2002): 594–630.

Institute of International Education. *Handbook on International Study: A Guide for Foreign Students and for U.S. Students on Study Abroad*. New York: Institute of International Education, 1955.

———. *Handbook on International Study: For Foreign Nationals*. New York: Institute of International Education, 1961.

———. *Open Doors: 1948–49*. New York: Institute of International Education, 1949.

———. *Open Doors 2004*. New York: Institute of International Education, 2005.

Ives, Sumner. "Help for the Foreign Student." *College Composition and Communication* 4 (1953): 141–44.

Kandel, Isaac Leon. *United States Activities in International Cultural Relations*. Washington, DC: American Council on Education, 1945.

King, Henry H, "Outline History of Student Migrations." *The Foreign Students in America*. Ed. W. Reginald Wheeler, Henry H. King, and Alexander B. Davidson. New York: Association Press, 1925. 3–38.

Klinger, Robert B. "The International Center." *The University of Michigan: An Encyclopedic Survey in Four Volumes*. Vol. 4. Ed. Walter A. Donnelly, Ann Arbor: U of Michigan P, 1958, 1843–49.

Kubota, Ryuko, and Kimberly Abels, "Improving Institutional ESL/EAP Support for International Students: Seeking the Promised Land." Matsuda, Ortmeier-Hooper, You.

Marquardt, William F. "Composition in English as a Second Language: Cross Cultural Communication." *College Composition and Communication* 17 (1966): 29–33.

Matsuda, Paul Kei. "Basic Writing and Second Language Writers: Toward an Inclusive Definition." *Journal of Basic. Writing* 22.2 (2003): 67–89.

——. "Composition Studies and ESL Writing: A Disciplinary Division of Labor." *College Composition and Communication* 50 (1999): 699–721.

Matsuda, Paul Kel, Christina Ortmeier-Hooper, and Xiaoye You, eds. *Politics of Second Language Writing: In Search of the Promised Land.* West Lafayette, IN: Parlor Press, forthcoming.

Matsuda, Paul Kei, and Tony Silva. "Cross-Cultural Composition: Mediated Integration of U.S. and International Students." *Composition Studies* 27.1 (1999): 15–30.

Miller, Susan. *Textual Carnivals: The Politics of Composition.* Carbondale: Southern Illinois UP, 1991.

Norton, Bonnie, and Sue Starfield. "Covert Language Assessment in Academic Writing." *Language Testing* 14.3 (1997); 278–94.

Parson, A. B. "The Foreign Student and the American College." *The Foreign Students in America.* Ed. W. Reginald Wheeler, Henry H. King, and Alexander B. Davidson. New York: Association Press, 1925. 149–74.

Prendergast, Catherine. "Race: The Absent Presence in Composition Studies." *College Composition and Communication* 50 (1998): 36–53.

Rogers, Gretchen L. "Freshman English for Foreigners." *School and Society* 61 (1945): 394–96.

Russell, David. *Writing in the Academic Disciplines: A Curricular History.* 2nd ed. Carbondale: Southern Illinois UP, 2002.

Schueler, Herbert. "English for Foreign Students." *Journal of Higher Education* 20 (1949): 309–16.

Schwantes, Robert S. *Japanese and Americans: A Century of Cultural Relations.* New York: Harper and Brothers and the Council on Foreign Relations, 1955.

Shuck, Gail. "Combating Monolingualism: A Novice Administrator's Challenge." *WPA: Writing Program Administration* 30.1–2 (2006): 59–82.

Silva, Tony. "An Examination of Writing Program Administrators' Options for the Placement of ESL Students in First Year Writing Classes." *WPA: Writing Program Administration* 18.1–2 (1994): 37–43.

Smitherman, Geneva, and Victor Villanueva, eds. *Language Diversity in the Classroom: From Intention to Practice.* Carbondale: Southern Illinois UP, 2003.

Trimbur, John. "Peer Tutoring: A Contradiction in Terms?" *Writing Center Journal* 7.2 (1987): 21–28.

Valdés, Guadalupe. "Bilingual Minorities and Language Issues in Writing: Toward Professionwide Response to a New Challenge." *Written Communication* 9 (1992): 85–136.

11

Writing in Multiple Media

Lisa Gerrard

- How can computers support current practices in composition instruction?
- What is digital literacy?
- How might students combine writing print-based texts with composing audio, visual, and interactive media?
- Why and how might an instructor bring web design, social networking sites, and virtual reality environments into the writing classroom?

This chapter discusses the role of computers in the teaching of writing. It includes a historical overview of how computers have been integrated into composition pedagogy, a discussion of multimedia writing, and suggestions for using computers in the writing class. Where once "computer-based composition" designated courses that made word processing available to student writers, today these courses are designed in a range of ways: in distance writing classes, the computer is the exclusive medium of instruction, whereas in face-to-face courses, the instructor typically combines computer-based practices with noncomputerized ones, often in the same physical space. A third type of course, known as a "hybrid," meets part of the time online and part of the time in a physical classroom.

Regardless of how the course is delivered, computer-based writing has gone far beyond word processing and is often labeled "digital," "new media," or "multimedia" writing. This language reflects a much broader concept of "text" than the traditional, paper-based essay: students' texts are as likely to be web pages, visual images, wikis, blogs, video files, and audio files as they are to be words on paper. Often students' writing combines several media, so that a single document may interweave graphics, animation, sound, interactive elements, and hyperlinks—hence the terms "multimedia writing" and "new media" (to distinguish writing from earlier digital forms—static text and images). Furthermore, the expressions "digital" and "multimedia" writing reveal not just a change in writing products, but also an expanded view of writing practices. Students in a multimedia writing course usually plan, discuss, construct, and publish their work online, often in contexts such as virtual reality environments and blogs, with one or more co-authors, and for audiences that go far beyond the classroom.

THE BEGINNING

Computers were first used in composition in the 1960s—before process-based pedagogy took hold—in an effort to automate the teaching of grammar, spelling, and punctuation, and the evaluation of student compositions (Daigon, 1966; Engstrom & Whittaker, 1963; Page & Paulus, 1968). These computer systems were principally the experiments of a few English teachers, linguists, and educational psychologists, rather than commercial products designed for a wide audience. Nevertheless, they illustrated an emerging interest in combining computers with writing instruction. In the late 1970s, commercial systems such as PLATO (Control Data Corporation) were developed as multisubject teaching tools, which included electronic grammar drills, where students encountered grammar rules and corrected flawed sentences. These systems found a limited audience, largely because few English departments were interested in computers, even fewer could afford the equipment (the hardware and software had to be purchased as one expensive package), and, not incidentally, grammar-based writing instruction was beginning to lose favor around that time, the late 1970s to early 1980s.

WORD PROCESSING

The development of word processing software in the late 1970s marked the first and most pervasive influence of computers on composition. In the mid-1970s, I was writing my doctoral dissertation on a yellow pad, typing up my notes each night on an electric typewriter, and laying the typed pages across a table, where I revised them with scissors and tape—literally cutting my text apart and taping it back together. When I finished my dissertation in 1979, word processors had started to appear in offices, allowing typists, and later, writers, to edit with unprecedented ease.

Word processing coincided neatly with the development of process-based writing instruction. Several writing instructors surmised that if students were to write on a word processor, they would be far more likely to revise—and to make wholesale changes in concept and organization rather than limit themselves to local editing (Daiute, 1983; Gerrard, 1982).[1] As we shifted from product-based composition, where instructors commented only on the completed essay and never required a rewrite—to process pedagogy, which required multiple drafts of our students, taught them to view these drafts as malleable works in progress, and guided them toward a successful writing strategy—word processing, which invited repeated revision, became an invaluable tool. In addition to encouraging students to view writing as a process, word processing made writing less intimidating for novice writers (Bean, 1983), invited them to take risks (Feldman, 1984), gave them more control over their composing strategies (Gerrard, 1989), and led them to create more complex sentences and longer (if not necessarily better) papers (Collier, 1983).

Word processing has a variety of classroom uses. If you are fortunate enough to have a classroom outfitted with computers, you can use this room as your everyday classroom (as I do) or bring your students to the computer room occasionally. The advantage of having the computers available is that they make it easy to construct a class as a hands-on writers workshop, where students spend much of the class time writing. In preparation for discussing a reading, for example, students might write their reactions to it—then read each other's responses and comment on them.

like collab !

For Writing and Discussion

1. Go with your class to a computer lab. Using a word processor, open a new file, and type a response to one or more of the following assertions:
   - "The rapid proliferation of electronic media … is now the most significant contributing factor to society's growing physical estrangement. Whether in or out of the home, more people of *all* ages in the UK are physically and socially disengaged from the people around them because they are wearing earphones, talking or texting on a mobile telephone, or using a laptop or Blackberry" (Sigman, 2009).
   - "If the plasticity of the electronic text is a great liberation for the author, it can also license the forger, the plagiarist, the swindler, the impostor" (Hayes, 1993).
   - "It is easy to become unsettled by privacy-eroding aspects of [Facebook, Flickr, and Twitter]. But there is another—quite different—result of all this incessant updating: a culture of people who know much more about themselves. Many of the avid Twitterers, Flickrers and Facebook users I interviewed described an unexpected side-effect of constant self-disclosure. The act of stopping several times a day to observe what you're feeling or thinking can become, after weeks and weeks, a sort of philosophical act. It's like the Greek dictum to 'know thyself,' or the therapeutic concept of mindfulness" (Thompson, 2008).
2. When you finish writing, move to another computer, and read someone else's commentary. Write a response to it; for example, add a new idea, give an example to illustrate the idea, disagree with the commentary, explain your point of view.
3. Do the second step two more times.

Another advantage of having word processing software in the classroom is that students can bring their drafts to class on a flash drive or email them to themselves, and apply what they're studying in class that day directly—immediately—to their paper-in-progress. After introducing a rhetorical device (e.g., the thesis statement), discussing it with students, and looking at examples, you can set students to work, applying the principles just discussed to their drafts. While my students revise their thesis statements (or whatever the day's curriculum is), I walk around the room, offering help as requested. Colleagues who have never taught with computers often worry that I'll have nothing to do, that after 10 or 15 minutes of lecture/discussion, I'll sit back and stare at the ceiling while students revise their papers.

creates a new student-teacher relationship

This has never happened; instead, there is rarely enough of me to go around. Students are eager for the instructor's reactions to their writing, and by responding to their sentence or paragraph or outline immediately after they compose it, the instructor can provide guidance not only when students are most receptive but also when they can go back to their work—right then and there—and implement the suggestion.

Although critics of computer-based composition often imagine a cold, mechanistic environment—students staring at machinery and ignoring one another—the opposite is true. Computers socialize the classroom. At the outset of the term, computers break down the initial reticence students have finding themselves among strangers: students notice a classmate looking for the online assignment folder and offer to help, they peek at the website their neighbor is reading and comment on its contents, and so on. Regardless of whether students are novices or computer whizzes, they have one thing in common: they're working with the same technology; this fact helps build community. This socializing phenomenon was one of the most obvious results of the early experiments in computer-based composition (Gerrard, 1983; Sommers; 1985), one of the most powerful benefits of teaching in a classroom outfitted with computers, and an especially important one for courses that emphasize collective knowledge building and a pedagogy of collaboration.

eases up editing

Word processing also makes it easy for students to respond to one another's writing. The monitor displays text clearly enough for small groups of students (gathering around one computer) to see, so that groups of three students coauthoring a project (perhaps doing stylistic revision of a passage or preparing an oral presentation) can work together, with one "scribe" doing the typing. In a classroom outfitted with laptops, students can simply exchange computers; with desktop machines, students can move from chair to chair. Peer editing—of an entire paper, a paragraph, or a sentence—also works well on the computer. The display provides unlimited room to insert comments; these comments can be highlighted with colors, fonts, or other graphic features. Although simply typing comments into a text file works quite well, some instructors take advantage of the special features found on many word processors. Microsoft Word has a "track changes" feature (under the "Tools" menu) that allows an editor to insert comments, draw a line through deleted text, and color-code different kinds of changes. It also allows students to set up a "shared documents" folder, so that students can leave documents for their classmates to read. Many word processing programs (such as Microsoft Word) also have an "outline view," which allows writers to look at their (or their classmate's) paper in outline form, and isolate the headings or opening sentence of each paragraph—a view that shows how the draft is organized.

For Writing and Discussion

Consider your own use of computers—e.g., for social networking, web surfing, commenting on student papers, political blogging, sharing research with colleagues, and so on. Explain which computer applications best support your research, writing, teaching, or relationship with colleagues, and why.

INVENTION

By treating invention as a separate stage of writing, writers can explore what they want to say before striving to find the right style or form for their ideas. Composition researchers have found invention exercises, or heuristics, useful for helping writers discover what they know about a subject (Flower & Hayes, 1977), generate new information (Murray, 1978), and relieve writer's block (Rose, 1980). Many kinds of invention assignments are possible using word processing alone. For example, students can do a form of freewriting called "invisible writing" by simply turning down the brightness of the monitor so that they cannot see what they're writing. Freewriting, promoted by Peter Elbow (1973), is intended to break down blocks to getting started; the writer writes continuously for a period of time, writing anything that pops into her head. The object is to produce words and ideas without prematurely censoring them. "Invisible writing" on the computer serves this purpose because it is impossible to edit—the writer cannot see her writing until she turns the brightness back up. In their early experiments with invisible writing, Stephen Marcus and Sheridan Blau found that, unlike freewriting on paper, the computer-based version "encouraged a quality of attention to the topic at hand" (1983) that didn't take place with pen and paper.

In the 1980s, several writing instructors developed invention software to stimulate students' ideas.[2] Although such software was usually specific to a single operating system and is rarely used any more, composition courses make extensive use of readily available social networking software—e.g., chat rooms, wikis, and blogs—in which students generate information and ideas for their papers and discuss them with each other. Chat, which allows for real-time communication, can be used during or outside of class time for class discussion of readings or other materials students will use in their writing. Chat has numerous advantages for class discussion: it focuses the conversation away from the instructor, giving students more control over the discussion, and it engages far more students than traditional face-to-face discussions typically do. Students who are shy, self-conscious about speaking with an accent or a stutter, silenced by louder or more aggressive classmates, or those who like to think about an idea before they respond—and in the process, miss their chance to speak—are especially helped by this form of discussion. Research has shown that students in online forums also respond directly to one another, addressing comments to each other rather than to the instructor, and seem to respond to the instructor more often as well (Hartman et al., 1991). They also are more willing to take risks and speak more openly than they would in other contexts, to "do away with the niceties and express their opinions more readily" (Eldred, 1991).

Students also share ideas on blogs. A blog (short for "weblog") is a website where many different users contribute posts; an instructor or student can begin the discussion by posting a comment; then students log in and respond to the conversation. Blogs are asynchronous, so they are often used outside of class time, when students can post at their convenience. They are usually highly informal spaces where students can try out ideas, post quotations, links, or images, and thus stimulate each other's thinking about the paper topic. A blog feature is often included in course management software, and is also available for free in such services as Blogger, WordPress, and LiveJournal.

Many writing courses also use wikis for idea generation. A wiki is a type of website that can be edited by its users (Wikipedia is the most famous example), and thus is a form of collaborative knowledge building. As a brainstorming tool, it allows students to post and edit content related to their papers, such as quotations, facts, links, images, video, sound; any file that can sit on a web page can be added to the wiki. Students can take notes on the wiki, and add outlines, bibliographies, study guides, or other resources, so that the wiki becomes a collaborative invention project that students create and continually edit.

GRAMMAR AND STYLE

Some of the earliest writing-software designers hoped that computers would identify grammar errors and teach students to write correctly. IBM worked throughout the late 1970s and 1980s on a program (first called Epistle, later Critique) that would do this kind of identification. Although it made impressive use of artificial intelligence principles, this program never identified errors with more than 80% accuracy. In the 1980s, writing instructors experimented with online workbooks, drill and practice programs, such as Little, Brown, and Company's Grammarlab and Houghton Mifflin Co.'s Microwriter, which contained modules on noun and verb forms, sentence structure, punctuation, and similar mechanics.

These programs fell out of use, largely because they ran only on certain operating systems, and because many instructors found little carryover from the sentences students practiced in the tutorial to the ones they wrote in their essays. The web does, however, provide many grammar websites where students can look up grammar rules or parts of speech and do tutorials (such as http://www.englishpage.com/minitutorials/index.htm, of particular value to ESL writers; http://odl.vwv.at/english/odlres/res8/Grammar/grammar.htm; and http://www.englishgrammar101.com/). Popular word processors, such as MS Word, also include grammar checkers that identify flawed usage, but they are frequently inaccurate. Grammar checkers can be useful for alerting students to a *potential* error, and thus for getting them to reconsider a particular sentence structure, but students should never assume that the checker is correct. In fact, they should be cautioned that grammar checkers don't understand their writing and thus can flag correct usage as incorrect and fail to identify genuine errors.

Style checkers highlight common stylistic lapses, such as clichés, redundancy, and vagueness, and sometimes offer quantifiable information on the text, such as a bar graph showing sentence lengths or statistics on the number of "to be" verbs, prepositional phrases, or abstract nouns. Early ones, such as *Homer* (1981), *Writer's Workbench* (1982), and *HBJ Writer* (1984) provided extensive information about a text's surface features, and some of them offered alternatives to constructions the program flagged as undesirable, e.g., "'Its.' Wrong pronoun. Replace with 'It's.'" Word processors like MS Word also identify possible stylistic problems, but as with grammar checkers, it is up to the writer to decide whether a construction needs to be changed.

Having seen students ruin perfectly good sentences on advice from their computer's style checker, I make a point of warning them not to rely on this feature. However, used with an instructor's guidance, these programs can be excellent teaching tools. They can be used with poor writing as well as text by Hemingway or Woolf to show how much usage depends on context—how a sentence structure, such as a fragment or a very long sentence, that disrupts meaning in one instance, creates a strategic effect in another. By running the grammar or style checker on different texts, including student writing, and deciding how to interpret the computer's analysis, the class has an opportunity to discuss the relationship between sentence structure and meaning. This kind of software can also be used to initiate thought on how grammatical and stylistic norms come about. Who decides what practices are regarded as good writing? How might widely used programs such as Word or WordPerfect institutionalize certain language conventions? Why does Word label some usages matters of grammar and others matters of style? Why does WordPerfect allow writers to opt for a "Student Composition" style or other (business or professional) styles? What is the distinction between them? What other linguistic features might these checkers look for (Vernon, 2000)?

For Writing and Discussion

1. Choose two to five pages of either your own, a student's, or a piece of published writing available to you online. Copy it into a word processor that has a grammar/ style checker.
2. Run the checker on this piece of writing and analyze the results.
3. What was most and least informative in the output? What features of the text did the checker assess accurately? What was inaccurate?
4. Consider what the checker's responses reveal about the dependence of style on content. Does the checker seem to validate or criticize any particular kind of writing? Do you see social or political implications in these responses?

OWLS

For computerized help with grammar and style, students working alone or with assistance might do well consulting On-Line Writing Labs (OWLs), websites that offer help on sentence structure, grammar, organization, audience, and other rhetorical concerns. Most OWLs have been designed for a particular writing center at a university and offer tutorial help— comments from a live person—only to students enrolled at that school. But the generic advice is available to all users and is generally well written, up to date, and visually appealing and can supplement or replace a rhetoric text or grammar handbook. Most OWLs have a wide range of other resources and links to other sites, so that a student who consulted an OWL for help with apostrophes could easily discover something else he needed. OWLs typically offer information on specialized writing (e.g., for literature, science, journalism), the research process, and formatting conventions, along with links to such resources as dictionaries, thesauruses, and the MLA style manual. Purdue University's Online Writing Lab (http://owl.english.purdue.edu/owl/) is one of the most comprehensive and highly regarded, but there are many others; the writing center website at the University of Maine offers links to other colleges' OWLs (http://www.umaine.edu/wcenter/other-online-writing-centers/).

COURSE-MANAGEMENT SOFTWARE

Course-management software, such as Blackboard Learning System, WebCT, Sakai, Moodle, Drupal, and Mambo, are web-based products that provide a suite of generic teaching tools that instructors can customize for their courses. These systems were developed primarily for large lecture classes and are often used for distance education, but many of their features work well for small face-to-face writing workshops. This software typically includes administrative tools, such as a grading feature that calculates a student's grade according to the value the instructor gives each assignment; a roster that allows instructors to add and drop students and keep track of each student's contribution to the course; a "dropbox," where students can submit their work; an announcements page where students and instructors can post news; and a calendar for showing the class schedule, due dates, and other events. Instructors can add content: links to other websites, quizzes that students take and instructors grade online, and documents uploaded from other sources—multimedia files or text (e.g., readings, student papers, exams, etc.) for students to access. These materials can be concealed and then automatically released on dates the instructor specifies. These programs usually have a blog and bulletin board for asynchronous discussion, a chat room for real-time communication, and a wiki and workshop for collaborative projects. Instructors can divide these discussion places into individual forums where small groups of students can meet, make these spaces private, so that only group members participate in or see the discussion, and organize the output of a completed discussion by subject or the name of each participant.

Some instructors use the workshop feature for peer editing. Students comment on one another's work online, leaving a written record not just for the author to see, but also for viewing by other students and the instructor. The public nature of this workshop can prompt student editors to be more careful in analyzing each other's work than they might be in face-to-face peer groups.

Advocates of these packages praise their flexibility: because this software is modular, instructors can use as much or as little of the system as they choose and have considerable opportunities to customize both the content and physical appearance of the website. Others praise the convenience and completeness of these systems, their potential to meet all a course's electronic needs in a single package, so that students and instructors don't need to acquire and learn to use several separate pieces of software (i.e., a browser, chat program, bulletin board, or grading program). Critics of course-management software deride it as a "course in a box"; that is, they believe it is not a neutral conduit for an instructor's pedagogy, but that it molds a course toward a rigid teaching approach that discourages face-to-face contact between instructor and student, promotes lock-stop progress through a set of materials, and encourages excessive oversight of students.

SOCIAL NETWORKING

Chat

Chat and other forms of real-time networked communication allow students to share their work with their peers during scheduled class time—over a local area network, which connects computers located in the same building—as well as outside of class—over the Internet. As described in the Invention section of this chapter, synchronous communication, in which the participants are all reading and sending messages concurrently, has proved especially successful for class discussion. The earliest use of synchronous, or "realtime," communication for class discussion took place in 1984, at Gallaudet University, in an effort to help deaf students—who, because they cannot hear language, have difficulty with its written form—become proficient writers. The ENFI (Electronic Networks for Interaction) project,[3] as it was called, had students writing to each other to discuss readings and to do prewriting activities, peer editing, and other forms of collaboration. The effect of this experiment was to shift the students' attention from the teacher to each other, thus creating different audiences for the writing class and moving responsibility for learning back onto the students. It soon became apparent that electronic communication could have similar benefits for hearing students, and software—such as Interchange (Daedalus Corporation) and Realtime Writer (Realtime Learning Systems)—began to be developed for this purpose.

Today, most of our students are familiar with social networking software and take easily to chat or other forms of real-time conversation. Online discussions can be fun, and students tend to stay with them longer than they might with a face-to-face encounter. Talking online also frees students of inhibitions they may have talking in front of the class, and students are more likely to joke around, play with language, experiment with new ideas, and build a sense of community. At the same time, if students get carried away with this freedom and spend too much time off topic, the instructor, as moderator, needs to guide the conversation back to the day's agenda. Instructors also need to be alert to flaming and to students whose posts may be consistently ignored—both of which can inhibit conversation and undermine community. Many instructors advocate teaching students how to use this discourse to ensure that they "assume responsibility for dialectic exchange" (Hogsette, 1995). As David Hogsette points out, despite its potential for freeing student voices, online discussion can, used destructively, achieve the opposite effect:

> Students talk about what they want or what they are interested in, and if a student's ... posting ... presents a view that is radically different from other postings in that group, it will be quickly dismissed, simply ignored, or deleted from the list. When a student's post is ignored and not read, that student is silenced. (1995, p. 67)

Despite these drawbacks, the majority of online discussions have tremendous potential for creativity, awareness of audience, and community building. Instructors have reported that their students come to see their writing in its rhetorical context and can instantly gauge the reaction of the audience. Others praise chat for giving students a vehicle for writing in a conversational tone, developing a personal voice that can carry over into their more formal writing (Batson, 1992). From the beginning, proponents of social networking in composition have argued that it provides students with "rich and valuable writing experiences": "Students showed intelligent, creative thought and self-expression on the network that the constraints of more formal compositions ... may not have encouraged them to do" (Peyton, 1990).

Many instructors link their classes with classes at other schools; students from both schools meet online to discuss a shared reading or exchange and critique drafts of papers. Students often find these exchanges eye-opening, especially when they communicate with a class in a different part of the country or world, with a demographic and worldview unlike their own. Such exchanges also teach students to write for a real audience: in their online conversations, they have to make themselves clear to someone other than their teacher. If they are vague, insensitive, overly informal, or insulting, however inadvertently, they will get feedback that lets them know right away. In online exchanges, students practice expressing their ideas publicly, reading messages carefully, and responding to people they cannot see or hear; and because they depend entirely on words to communicate, they have an opportunity to learn to read and choose language thoughtfully. Most chat software allows a conversation to be archived, so that students can read it later and draw on it for their papers, or, in a separate assignment, analyze the rhetoric of the exchange.

Blogs

Unlike chat, blogs are asynchronous—that is, the conversation does not need to take place in real time. A blog is a web page where each participant can read and post messages at any time. The posts sit on the web page to be retrieved later. Used during class time, they can function as slightly delayed real-time communication, but many instructors prefer to assign them out of class for slightly more formal writing than chat: students can write responses to articles, create brief arguments, and post links and images to support these arguments. Blogs are a much less structured vehicle for expressing ideas than an essay, and the posts are short—usually a few lines—but they allow students to create entries that are more focused and permanent than comments in a typical chat would be. They provide an unthreatening space for students to publish their writing, try out different writing styles and personae, and get feedback from real audiences.

For Writing and Discussion

Go to http://www.blogger.com, start, and maintain a blog for your class that begins by discussing the following topic:

In 1997, the NCTE adopted the resolution "On Viewing and Visually Representing as Forms of Literacy," which argued that visual literacy was "a necessary feature of literacy in general" and that teachers should guide students both "to interpret [and] to produce visual arrangements."

Discuss how you might implement this resolution in your composition courses. What assignments might you give students? How might you guide students to look critically at visual images in art, advertising, film, websites, and other media? How might students integrate in their essays analysis of visual media with analysis of verbal texts?

Twitter

Like blogs, Twitter is an asynchronous communication medium, but it can work well during class discussion. Twitter is a "microblogging" tool that allows users to send and receive messages from a computer or cell phone and view them on a web page. Posts, called "tweets," are very short—limited to 140 characters—and go out to everyone subscribed to the broadcast. After establishing a Twitter account at www.twitter.com, and having the students register as "friends," the instructor can instruct students to send tweets during a face-to-face class discussion, so that the class is simultaneously talking face to face and intermittently sending brief written comments. This practice of multiple conversations may seem chaotic, but it pulls every single student into the discussion. The instructor can project the Twitter page on a screen for all to see, so that students are alternately talking out loud as in a traditional class discussion, reading the tweets others are producing, and writing their own tweets. This assignment shifts the conversation from the instructor and toward the ideas themselves, as created by students. It also encourages students to reflect on the issues under discussion as they are raised and makes it easy for them to contribute their thoughts, however shy they may be in a traditional setting. It also expands the conversation to multiple conversations:

the principal discussion taking place orally and several simultaneous Twitter discussions occurring in the background, known as a "backchannel." Like all social networking tools, Twitter turns a class into a community very quickly. It also leaves an archive students can return to and review ideas they may have missed during the discussion. You can find other ideas on using Twitter in the classroom here: http://academhack.outsidethetext.com/home/2008/twitter-for-academia/.

For Writing and Discussion

Go to http://www.groups.yahoo.com or http://www.blogspotsearch.com/ and search for a blog or public discussion forum of interest to you. Subscribe to the list or blog and participate in the discussion for at least three weeks. Then evaluate the experience. How would you define the culture of this list? What kinds of relationships do participants establish? What is the style of writing? How do participants present themselves rhetorically?

COLLABORATIVE WRITING

A natural extension of social networking in the writing classroom is collaborative writing, in which students work together with one or more classmates to plan their papers, generate content, write, and revise. Some instructors use collaboration software, such as Google Docs, a free web-based tool that includes a word processor and presentation feature. Rather than writing individual sections of their text separately, and then cutting and pasting the sections together, students access a central document online at anytime and write their essay together or paste in portions of text they have written on a word processor. Google Docs functions with a wide range of file formats, so compatibility with students' word processors is rarely a problem, and it can be accessed from any browser.

Another tool for collaborative writing are social bookmarking sites, such as del.icio.us, Diigo, and Digg. Social bookmarking sites allow users to keep a list of preferred websites in the same way they do by bookmarking favorite sites in browsers such as Firefox, Safari, and Explorer; but they offer the additional advantage of storing these URLs online, thus making them accessible from anywhere, not just from a single computer. Thus, co-authors can keep online a file of websites relevant to their paper, which they can access from anywhere and edit as they wish. Even if students are writing separate papers, they can collaborate on knowledge collection by sharing their online research this way; every student can see and contribute to the bookmarks produced by everyone else in the class. Social bookmarking sites have a number of features to facilitate searching; for example, users can sort the bookmarks by category by assigning "tags" to each one and even pull the information together to create a search engine (Santos, 2009).

Wikis, websites that students can create and edit without having to learn a web-composing program like Dreamweaver, are ideal tools for collaboration. Students can use a wiki not just for brainstorming, but also for the entire writing process—for collectively generating ideas, taking notes, building a bibliography, outlining, drafting, and revising. The wiki itself becomes a text that students discuss and negotiate as they design, write, edit, and publish it.

And because a wiki can be accessed from any browser, students can collaborate with others not just in the same class, but with students across campus or at schools anywhere in the world.

Wherever their co-authors, because all the students who have access to the wiki contribute to it, the co-authors have equal control over the wiki pages, and must discuss with each other how they will proceed, what information to include, how to arrange it, what style is appropriate, and what kind of editing they need to do; thus the process of collective writing is democratic and requires students to be conscious of, articulate, and negotiate their decisions. By distributing responsibility among all co-authors, wiki writing also gives students a large stake in the outcome: all writers have authority over the process from start to finish. That is, assigning students to write a wiki text puts the student, rather than the instructor, at the center of the writing project (Garza & Hern, 2005).

Furthermore, a wiki feature called "page histories" allows students to view the editing history of their text and see how it has developed over time. This characteristic makes manifest the concept of writing as both a social activity and a recursive process. Some instructors assign a self-evaluation paper at the end of the term, in which students review the full wiki history, which includes not just the process of creation and revision, but also the feedback they received from peers and the instructor, which is stored on the wiki along with the wiki text. Students can draw on this record to write a reflective essay on the collaborative process and their development as writers, and then post this essay on the wiki. Instructors have also found that the public nature of collaborative writing, evaluating, and reflecting motivates many students to revise more than they would in a single-authored paper delivered only to the instructor (Lamb, 2004; Lamb & Johnson, 2007).

MULTIMEDIA COMPOSITION

Collaboration is one of the hallmarks of Web 2.0,[4] so it is not surprising that as students write in computer-mediated spaces, their work too has become more collaborative. The other defining characteristic of Web 2.0 is multimedia, and multimedia essays have also become important to computers and writing courses. Increasingly, instructors are asking students to write documents that combine several different modes of communication in place of or alongside traditional print essays. The multimedia or "multimodal" essay makes meaning by interconnecting words with interactive features such as blogs and wikis; links to other websites; visual elements, such as graphs, photographs, clip art, and diagrams; moving media, such as animations, film, and video clips; audio files that play music, sound effects, and speech; or any combination of these media.

Although some instructors may be concerned that multimedia documents are inappropriate assignments for a writing course, research and writing are done very differently today than they were a generation ago: students need to understand multiple media and be able to create them. The purpose of a writing course in which students study and create these media is not to shift the focus from writing to computer science, art, film, or music, but to extend students' ability to express themselves in interactive, visual, and auditory media as well as written ones. A writing course in which students are taught to code a web page or create and edit a Podcast or video has not shifted its focus away from writing, but instead has extended the genres in which students write and the contexts in which their writing takes place. Creating a web page that incorporates several media is an excellent way for students to practice researching, selecting, organizing, and focusing information; choosing an appropriate style and content for a particular audience; establishing a consistent viewpoint on a subject; arguing through visual and auditory materials as well as words; and publishing their writing to real audiences. In creating these documents, students also learn how to express themselves not just in words, but in sound and image as well, a valuable practice in a world that increasingly depends on nonverbal forms of expression.

Many free applications are available online to help students collect text, images, audio, animations, and video. Audacity, for example, is an open-source program that gives students the ability to manipulate sound files—to record, edit, distort, and cut and paste files, capture and assemble sound files from other sources, and create new ones. Using this kind of software, students have created audio compositions, combining speech (recording interviews, making speeches), music, and sound effects. Other free or inexpensive applications, such as the video editing packages Microsoft Movie Maker and iMovie, are available for creating and editing video.

Some instructors have students create podcasts as a form of new media composition. A podcast is an audio file that is posted to a website and made available for listeners to download. A podcast may be a composition in itself or may be linked to other media, including print essays, to create a multimedia document. A podcast can also be a medium for discussing course readings: it can be linked to a discussion that has taken place earlier on a blog or wiki, or function as a standalone invention strategy. Typically, students write a script, record the podcast, and edit it to produce a live broadcast. They can publish their podcast either on the class website or more widely, on a publicly accessible site such as iTunes University.

In a typical multimedia assignment, students might create a web page that advances an argument on a current social or political controversy—integrating the written word with photographs and sound and video clips to present their viewpoint. Some classes produce webzines (also called "zines"), web-based magazines, a project in which they assemble knowledge in an interesting and fresh way, choose a style that will attract the audience they want to reach, and create a persona as a writer. Instructors have found that this kind of public writing increases students' personal commitment to their writing, motivates them to consider alternative views, and to see their writing as a "political endeavor" (Alexander, 2002). One way to combine a zine or other multimedia assignment with a print essay is to have students write about the experience of producing the zine or to have them analyze one another's zines as rhetorical documents. For example, after creating their zines as individuals or in small groups of three or four, students might analyze their classmates' zines, considering such criteria as these:

- rhetorical stance: audience, writer's persona, purpose, content, argument strategies
- visual appearance: color, font style and size, background images, placement of images
- technical features: interactive elements, navigational tools, ease of use, links
- ideological stance: values and assumptions, political and cultural beliefs.

Other instructors have had students create a web page of photo/text collage to interpret a quotation (Sorapure, 2006). Another multimedia assignment that investigates the complexity of postmodern identity asks students to alter a photograph of themselves to represent their multiple identities (Writing in Digital Environments (WIDE) Research Center Collective, 2005). And other assignments ask students to create a web page that investigates the role of technology in society (Jones, 2002).

For Writing and Discussion

Read Elizabeth Losh's (2002) online syllabus for her course, "The War from the Web: Reading for Rhetoric in September 11 Documents on the Internet": http://kairos.technorhetoric.net/7.2/binder.html?sectionone/losh.

Then create an online syllabus for one week of a course on the rhetoric of a social or political event of your choice. Include in your web page at least three graphic images and links to at least four online sources.

For the instructor in a computer-based writing course, a principal concern is how to give students the tools they need to create a digital product—for example, how to produce and edit a sound file or video clip—without turning over a majority of class time to teaching technical skill. Finding a balance between teaching technical and rhetorical skills can be tricky (Mauriello, Pagnucci, & Winner, 1999), but teaching students how to use a digital medium is part of literacy instruction. Instructors must either feel comfortable with the software or have a reliable technical consultant in the classroom, but either way, teaching students some rudimentary skills does not need to be time-consuming. I teach my students very basic HTML—the language that makes a document readable on the web—over a few days for a total of two to three hours. Students code simple pages by hand using free cross-platform text editors such as NoteTab and BBEdit. Students—especially those with no background in computer languages—take great pride in the pages they create from scratch and gain a deeper understanding of how a website "thinks." Regardless of the specific application you choose, some students will catch on more quickly than others, so putting students in groups to help each other speeds up learning.

Another concern is that most composition instructors, trained in literature, linguistics, or rhetoric, are far more comfortable in a verbal medium than a visual one and may not feel they have the skills to teach web design or podcasting. And when a multimedia assignment replaces a traditional print essay, it requires new instruments for evaluation, with attention paid to links, the visual layout, a nonlinear structure, and the relationship among the different media incorporated into the document. Although they may seem intimidating, these are not overwhelming problems, and instructors who have already confronted them have provided ample resources for those starting out (Rea & White, 1999; Jones, 2002; Nellen, 2000; Selfe, 2007).

For Writing and Discussion

In his article, "Tuning In: Infusing Media Networks into Professional Writing Curriculum," Alexander Reid (2008) describes how his students create individual and group podcasts as part of their work in new media composition. Read about this assignment at http://kairos.technorhetoric.net/12.2/binder.html?praxis/reid/index.html. Listen to the student podcasts provided there. Then discuss podcasting as an assignment for composition. What strikes you as valuable or problematic about using this technology? How committed do the students seem to be? How might you integrate podcasting into your writing course?

VIRTUAL ENVIRONMENTS

MOOs

The earliest virtual spaces used in composition were MOOs (MOO stands for "MUD, object oriented"),[5] computer programs that allow multiple users to enter the same virtual environment where they can interact with one another in real time. Although a few MOOs have some graphic features, most are made up entirely of words. They are entire worlds that exist as verbal description: rooms, objects, and people, many of them programmed to respond to "actions" the users type in. For example, a user might type "walk Violet's Garden," and see text that tells her she is being transported to a place named Violet's Garden. When she gets there she will see a verbal description of this place that might look like this:

Violet's Garden

A grassy field bordered by a grove of blooming, fragrant lilac bushes and sprinkled here and there with flower beds densely populated by daffodils, irises, and freesias. A long comfortable bench welcomes you. So does the grass; it's fresh and green and invites you to sit down. You notice a peach tree, leaning slightly toward you and covered with warm, rosy peaches. Sweetpea is peering through the daffodils, while Fritz dances around near the lilacs and Christopher Wren keeps watch from the peach tree.

This is part of the description of the room that I wrote when I created Violet's Garden. In any room, the visitor can look at "objects":

I type:

look Christopher Wren

and get a description of a bird I created named Christopher Wren:

a small brown grey bird with a short temper

A user can also interact with these objects. I type:

pet Christopher Wren

and see this on my screen:

You pet Christopher Wren. Christopher Wren flits nervously to another branch.

All this text is created by the person who created the specific room and the objects in it—in this case, me. Students can use MOO building to express their interpretation of a social issue or literary text. In one MOO project, an instructor had students create rooms to illustrate Emerson's ideas on education. In designing their virtual space, students had to use the skills of argument: to develop a thesis, design supporting evidence, and to determine a structure (possibly one room per idea) and a navigation scheme for the reader/user. However unconventional the presentation, the rhetorical features engaged here are the same as in a traditional essay (Walter, 2001).

As textual environments, MOOs are a powerful medium for writing classes: the only way to experience them is through writing. Thus, working in a MOO can help writers refine their style; users must develop verbal strategies for avoiding ambiguity, learn to convey emotion and gesture through text, ground their writing in a context, and use explanatory devices, emotes,[6] and other tools that compensate for the brevity of online discourse and the lack of face-to-face clues. Furthermore, when students create characters, rooms, and objects, they practice writing descriptively—using concrete, precise language and managing text in inventive, flexible ways.

Graphical Online Environments

Many composition courses take place all or in part in graphical online spaces such as Second Life. These are cartoon-like worlds which the user experiences primarily through visual images: one's avatar is not a bit of descriptive text, as it is in a MOO, but a cartoon-like figure the user sees walking around this world. Students can change the appearance of their avatar to make it resemble them or to look entirely nonhuman, a zebra or an orange blob, for example. These environments typically look like cartoon versions of our first lives, with libraries, amusement parks, beaches, universities, and other places rendered in convincing detail. The avatar can do most of the things people do in real life—laugh, drive a car, dance, spend money, even have (virtual) sex. Many instructors conduct all or some of their class meetings in a virtual classroom, where the instructor and students are represented by their avatars, and conversation occurs as it does in a chat. Thus, like chat and MOO, graphic environments make it easy for students to collaborate on projects, promote writing as a social activity, and prepare students to write for a public audience, not just for the instructor.

A virtual space, whether a graphical or verbal one, that has been specifically set up for teaching can function as a true online classroom. Educational virtual environments provide tools such as recorders that create a printed transcript of conversations, blackboards and notes that allow users to write and display information, and slides and slide projectors that allow a virtual slide show. Instructors can create virtual handouts, reserve readings in a virtual library, set up lectures with guest speakers in a virtual auditorium, and use virtual cameras, tapes, VCRs, and TV sets. Students can analyze recorded transcripts of their discussion, take quizzes on virtual "notes," and make virtual presentations. Although these features are immediately relevant to distance writing courses, where students never meet face to face, they are flexible, inventive, and playful tools for students in face-to-face courses, and I find that combining traditional classroom practice with meetings in Second Life makes students take charge of their learning, gravitate toward collaboration, and reflect both about online experiences and their role as students.

Although online graphical environments are not games, in that they do not have a built-in objective, some writing instructors have organized their courses around computer games. Their students study the ways in which computer games act as rhetorical events and engage multiple literacies. Students study the games, create them, and often work with students in other disciplines, sharing approaches to understanding gaming media. A collection devoted to gaming across the curriculum, which includes composition courses, is *Currents in Electronic Literacy, 2010: Gaming Across the Curriculum* (Holmevik & Haynes, 2010).

again, no experience w/this

STUDYING DIGITAL RHETORIC

What all these uses of computer media imply is that by creating and directly experiencing digital media, students will also explore them as rhetorical phenomena. Most, if not all, multimedia writing courses ask students not just to create but also to think critically about the media they use. Thus, in addition to composing in digital media, students analyze how adventure games use narrative techniques, how avatars may illustrate a fractured postmodern identity, whether blogs create or inhibit participatory democracy, whether social networking brings people together or isolates them, and similar rhetorical issues.

Whatever we call these writing courses—"computers and composition," "multimedia literacy," "digital rhetoric"—they all assume that for students to be literate in a digital culture, they need to think critically about the social networking sites, audio and video media, blogs, and other applications they are using. Thus, in addition to engaging in cultural and philosophical inquiry, students are also asked to analyze how the different elements that make up an online medium create a point of view or argument. Many composition courses focus on "media literacy," the ability to understand an online medium of communication by analyzing the strategies it uses to send its message as well as its context, its author(s), audience, message, and social issues it may raise, such concepts of privacy, intellectual ownership of online materials, and controls on antisocial behavior, such as bullying.

Many courses also focus on making students more savvy web consumers. Although the world wide web entered the composition classroom in the early 1990s and most of our students have grown up with the web as a primary source of information and entertainment, students still need instruction in evaluating what they find there. Most college libraries (e.g., at the University of California, Berkeley: http://www.lib.berkeley.edu/instruct/guides/evaluation.html) have web pages to help students determine whether an online source is credible. Typically, they pose questions for the students to consider (e.g., What is the authority behind the information? Who is the author? How up-to-date are the links?). Some classes ask students to explore a few websites together and analyze them according to rubrics such as these. One classroom activity is to send students on a scavenger hunt looking for four to six websites on a specified topic, and then show students how to use search engines and indexes to locate material on the topic. Afterwards, they can compare their sites and evaluate their completeness and apparent authority.

ELECTRONIC PORTFOLIOS

As Julie Neff-Lippman describes in Chapter 5 of this book, instructors sometimes require students to submit a portfolio of their work for evaluation at the end of the term. In a multimedia writing course, students may be asked to create a similar document, but in electronic form. The e-Portfolio is usually a webbed document that contains examples of the student's work, as well as the student's reflections on how this work evolved through the term, and a self-evaluation. Often these are online texts that may be linked to each other as well as to the multimedia documents the student has created. In addition, the ePortfolio may contain text pasted from discussions in such media as chat, Twitter, Second Life, or blogs, as well as images that show virtual reality spaces the student has created. Instructors may send feedback on this portfolio back to the student electronically.

ONLINE PLAGIARISM

Although there is no evidence that web-derived plagiarism is any more widespread than other kinds (e.g., the paper mills that operate in student residence halls), instructors are understandably concerned about the ease with which students can plagiarize, either intentionally or not. Online information doesn't always have a discernible author, and sometimes so many ideas emerge from collaborative spaces like blogs that it isn't clear to students which sources they need to cite (Gabriel, 2010). When students lift information or cut and paste text and images from websites, they don't always realize that they need to reference these sources or understand that they are plagiarizing. Other times they knowingly buy term papers from online paper vendors such as schoolsucks.com. To help them understand what plagiarism is and how to avoid it, an instructor can discuss with students sites such as "Plagiarism and the Web" (http://www.wiu.edu/users/mfbhl/wiu/plagiarism.htm). To track the source of potentially plagiarized work, one can type a brief passage into a search engine such as google.com, putting the suspect passage in quotation marks. Some schools have purchased plagiarism detection systems such as Turnitin.com, which require students to upload their papers to the system's database and compare the student's writing to that stored in its databases. Some instructors find that this software helps them to identify and deter fraud, and helps students learn what plagiarism is. Those who dislike such systems believe it invades students' privacy, violates intellectual property laws, and promotes a suspicious relationship between instructor and student.

CONCLUSION

Computers offer different ways to deliver some of our best practices in composition teaching: pedagogy that gives students ample opportunities to write, rewrite, and talk about their writing, fosters collaboration among students, guides students while their work is in progress, supports intellectual content along with verbal proficiency, and puts the student, rather than the instructor, at the center of the course. Computer-based writing instruction is almost always driven by research and theory in composition and rhetoric, and as new technologies have emerged, practitioners have experimented to see which of them would support their teaching. As writing, from drafting to publishing, takes place increasingly online, the composition classroom has become an ideal venue for teaching students digital literacy.

For Further Exploration

Anson, C., Beach, R., Breuch, L., & Swiss, T. (2009). *Teaching writing using blogs, wikis, and other digital tools*. Norwood, MA: Christopher-Gordon.

Cummings, R. E. (2009). Are we ready to use Wikipedia to teach writing? Inside higher education. Retrieved on March 12, from: http://www.insidehighered.com/views/2009/03/12/cummings.

Flew, T. (2003). *New media, an introduction*. New York: Oxford University Press.

Manovich, L. (2001). *The language of new media*. Cambridge, MA: MIT Press.

Thomas, D., & Brown, J. (2009). Why virtual worlds can matter. *International Journal of Learning and Digital Media, 1*, 37–49. Retrieved from http://www.mitpressjournals.org/doi/pdfplus/10.1162/ijlm.2009.0008.

Wysocki, A., Johnson-Eilola, J., Selfe, C., & Sirc, G. (2004). *Writing new media: Theory and applications for expanding the teaching of composition.* Logan, UT: Utah State University Press.

Classroom Activities

Analyzing a Website that Addresses a Social Issue

1. Choose a website that is concerned with a social issue (e.g., immigration law, same sex marriage, legalizing marijuana).
2. Divide the class into small groups to explore this site and discuss the message it communicates. Have the group respond to the following questions:
   - What is the mission of the site?
   - Who is the intended audience?
   - How would you describe the site's attitude toward its subject?
   - What are the writers worried about?
   - What social changes would they support?
   - What are some of the issues the site raises? What is the writer's stance on each issue?
   - If there are graphics, how do the visual images support or contradict the site's ideas?
   - What kinds of site does this site link to?
   - What information does the site give, and where does this information come from?
   - To what extent do you trust this information? Explain your reasons.
   - Using chat, MOO, a blog, or face-to-face communication, let the groups discuss their findings with the class as a whole.

Analyzing a Short Story

Directions

1. Assign a story to the class and break the class into groups, giving each group one feature of the story to analyze.
2. Have students in each group create a brief outline of their ideas, using a word processor and an 18-point font.
3. Give each group about 5 minutes to report its findings to the class and pose questions or problems they encountered. Project their outline on a large screen as they speak.
   - Group 1: Questions concerning plot.
   - Group 2: Questions concerning characterization.
   - Group 3: Questions concerning theme.
   - Group 4: Questions concerning setting.
   - Group 5: Questions concerning point of view.
   - Group 6: Questions concerning irony and symbolism.
4. Using a word processor or a wiki, have the students combine each group's outline to create a single document, a study guide for the class.

Conceptualizing a Digital Writing Project

1. Divide students into groups of four or five, and assign each group a different student-produced video from this site: http://unixgen.muohio.edu/~dwc/student_projects/projects.htm.

2. Have each group collaborate on an analysis of the video, possibly responding to these questions:
   - What is the relationship between the spoken narrative and the visual images?
   - What do you think is the video's objective?
   - How does the music or other sound support the purpose of the video?
   - What is the emotional impact of the video? What elements create this impression?

3. Ask each group to choose a topic for their own video and collectively to write a one-page "treatment," explaining the goal of the proposed video and detailing what images they would show and what text, music, or sounds they would pair with each image.

NOTES

1 Technically, the software I used for my earliest computer-based classes (1980–1982) was a text editor (ours was called Wylbur), not a word processor. Although word processors were originally written for secretaries and writers, text editors were meant for programmers—for typing computer code—and were far more cumbersome than word processors, which came later. For example, to format a paper, my students had to run a separate program (called Script) and learn a few programming commands. Desktop computers were not yet widely available, so we worked on remote terminals, connected to mainframe computers hidden away in the math/sciences building. Print-outs took hours to appear, and when they did, students had to walk across campus to retrieve them. Still, even this awkward experience was an improvement over the pad/typewriter method.

2 These included Topoi (Burns and Culp, 1979), Prewrite (Schwartz, 1981), WANDAH (Von Blum & Cohen, 1984) and Writer's Helper (Wresch, 1984).

3 The acronym originally stood for "English Natural Form Instruction," but was changed as classroom-based synchronous discussion became widespread.

4 The term "Web 2.0" refers to the innovations that developed after the large-scale failure of dotcom companies in 2001: one of these innovations was that software and files were increasingly stored on the web rather than on a user's personal computer, thus facilitating collaboration. Tim O'Reilly, who is credited with coining the term "Web 2.0," gives a more detailed definition: http://www.oreilly.de/artikel/web20.html.

5 A MOO is a type of MUD. A MUD, a "multiuser domain," or "multiuser dungeon," originated in adventure games such as Dungeons and Dragons, where several players interact with one another and with virtual objects in real time. In a MOO or MUD, users take an avatar, and through the avatar, move around, talk to other users, and interact with virtual objects. Everything a user sees on a MUD is presented in text; for example, when the user moves his or her avatar into a room on a MUD, he or she is presented with a text description of the room. On many MUDs, users are able to add their own rooms and objects to the MUD. MUDs are frequently used for serious purposes, and several have been designed specifically as sites for professional meetings or virtual classrooms.

6 An emote is a way of showing action or emotion through words.

> For example, if I type:
> *waves enthusiastically*
> those I'm conversing with will see:
> *LisaG waves enthusiastically.*

REFERENCES

Alexander, J. (2002). Digital spins: The pedagogy and politics of student-centered e-zines. *Computers and Composition*, *19* (4), 387–410.

Batson, T. (1992, May). Findings and directions in the network-based classroom. Paper presented at the Eighth Conference on Computers and Writing, Indianapolis, Indiana.

Bean, J. (1983). Computerized word processing as an aid to revision. *College Composition and Communication, 34*, 146–148.

Collier, R. (1983). The word processor and revision strategies. *College Composition and Communication, 34*, 149–155.

Daigon, A. (1966). Computer grading and English composition. *English Journal, 55*, 46–52.

Daiute, C. (1983). The computer as stylus and audience. *College Composition and Communication, 34*, 134–145.

Elbow, P. (1973). *Writing without teachers.* New York: Oxford University Press.

Eldred, J. (1991). Pedagogy in the computer-networked classroom. *Computers and Composition, 8*, 47–61.

Engstrom, J., & Whittaker, J. (1963). Improving students' spelling through automated teaching. *Psychological Reports, 12*, 125–126.

Feldman, P. (1984). Personal computers in a writing course. *Perspectives in Computing, 4*, 4–9.

Flower, L., & Hayes, J. (1977). Problem-solving strategies and the writing process. *College English, 39*, 449–461.

Gabriel, T. (2010). Plagiarism lines blur for students in digital age. *The New York Times*, August 1. Retrieved from http://www.nytimes.com/2010/08/02/education/02cheat.html.

Garza, S., & Hern, T. (2005). Using wikis as collaborative writing tools: Something wiki this way comes—or not! *Kairos, 10.1.* Retrieved from http://kairos.technorhetoric.net/10.1/binder2.html?http://falcon.tamucc.edu/wiki/WikiArticle/Home.

Gerrard, L. (1982). Using a computerized text-editor in freshman composition. (ERIC Document Reproduction Service No. Ed227512).

Gerrard, L. (1983). Writing with Wylbur: Teaching freshman composition with a mainframe computer. (ERIC Document Reproduction Service No. ED239299).

Gerrard, L. (1989). Computers and basic writers: A critical view. In G. Hawisher, & C. Selfe (Eds.), *Critical perspectives on computers and composition instruction* (pp. 94–108). New York: Teachers College Press.

Hartman, K., Neuwirth, C., Kiesler, S., Sproull, L., Cochran, C., Palmquist, M., & Zubrow, D. (1991). Patterns of social interaction and learning to write: Some effects of network technologies. *Written Communication, 8* (1), 79–113.

Hayes, B. (1993). The electronic palimpsest. *The Sciences, 33* (5), 10.

Hogsette, D. (1995). Unstable conditions: Dynamics of dissent in electronic discursive communities. *Works and Days, 25* (26), 63–80.

Holmevik, J., & Haynes, C. (2010*). Currents in Electronic Literacy. 2010: Gaming Across the Curriculum.* Retrieved from http://currents.dwrl.utexas.edu/2010.

Jones, B. J. (2002). Great ideas: A collaborative web assignment. *Kairos, 7.2.* Retrieved from http://kairos.technorhetoric.net/7.2/binder.html?sectiontwo/jones/TechPopJones.html.

Lamb, A., & Johnson, L. (2007). An information skills workout: Wikis and collaborative writing. *Teacher Librarian, 34* (5), 57–59.

Lamb, B. (2004). Wide open spaces: Wikis ready or not. *Educause Review,* September/October, 36–48.

Losh, E. (2002). The war from the Web: Reading for rhetoric in September 11 documents on the Internet. *Kairos, 7.2.* Retrieved from http://kairos.technorhetoric.net/7.2/binder.html?sectionone/losh.

Marcus, S., & Blau, S. (1983). Not seeing is relieving: Invisible writing with computers. *Educational Technology,* April, 12–15.

Mauriello, N., Pagnucci, G., & Winner, T. (1999). Reading between the code: The teaching of HTML and the displacement of writing instruction. *Computers and Composition, 16*, 409–419.

Murray, D. M. (1978, December). Write before writing. *CCC, 29*, 375–382.

Nellen, T. (2000). Using the Web for high school student writers. In S. Gruber (Ed.), *Weaving a virtual web: Practical approaches to new information technologies* (pp. 219–225). Urbana, IL: NCTE.

Page, E., & Paulus, D. (1968). The analysis of essays by computer. (ERIC Document Reproduction Service No. ED028633).

Peyton, J. K. (1990). Technological innovation meets institution: Birth of creativity or murder of a great idea. *Computers and Composition, 7*, 15–32.

Rea, A., & White, D. (1999). The changing nature of writing: Prose or code in the classroom. *Computers and Composition, 16*, 421–436.

Reid, A. (2008). Tuning in: Infusing media networks into professional writing curriculum. *Kairos, 12.2.* Retrieved from http://kairos.technorhetoric.net/12.2/binder.html?praxis/reid/index.html.

Rose, M. (1980). Rigid rules, inflexible plans, and the stifling of language: A cognitivist's analysis of writer's block. *College Composition and Communication, 31*, 389–400.

Santos, M. (2009). Del.icio.us: Social bookmarking as pedagogical tool. *Computers and Composition Online.* Retrieved from http://www.bgsu.edu/cconline/Web_2_0_Reviews/delicious_Santos/intro.html.

Selfe, C. (Ed.) (2007). *Multimodal composition: Resources for teachers.* Cresskill, NJ: Hampton Press.

Sigman, A. (2009). Well connected? The biological implications of "social networking." *Biologist, 56*, 14–20.

Sommers, E. (1985). Integrating composing and computing. In J. Collins, & E. Sommers (Eds.), *Writing on-line: Using computers in the teaching of writing* (pp. 3–10). Upper Montclair, NJ: Boynton/Cook.

Sorapure, M. (2006). Between modes: Assessing students' new media compositions. *Kairos*, 10.2. Retrieved from http://kairos.technorhetoric.net/10.2/binder2.html?coverweb/sorapure/index.html.

Thompson. C. (2008). Brave new world of digital intimacy. *The New York Times*. Retrieved July 17, 2010 from http://www.nytimes.com/2008/09/07/magazine/07awareness-t.html.

Vernon, A. (2000). Computerized grammar checkers 2000: Capabilities, limitations, and pedagogical possibilities. *Computers and Composition, 17*, 329–349.

Walter, J. (2001). American scholar MOO project assignment. Retrieved from http://www.geocities.com/Col-lege-Park/1305/emerson_assignment.html/.

Writing in Digital Environments (WIDE) Research Center Collective. (2005). Why teach digital writing? *Kairos,* 10.1. Retrieved from http://kairos.technorhetoric.net/10.1/binder2.html?coverweb/wide/index.html.

Reading

BETWEEN MODES: ASSESSING STUDENT NEW MEDIA COMPOSITIONS

Madeleine Sorapure

The Problem of Assessment

> If we agree that computers can challenge and thus change not only pedagogies but also writing and reading processes, then it follows that these changes necessitate a transition from assessment practices based in theories about print literacy to assessment practices based in computer-assisted composition theory.
>
> Pamela Takayoshi, "The shape of electronic writing" (1996)

> We attribute the gap between the quality of our online assignments and our ability to assess them largely to the mismatch between our assessment criteria and digital environments.
>
> Meredith Zoetewey & Julie Staggers, "Beyond 'current-traditional' design" (2003)

> ...we seem comfortable with intertextual composing [in which print and digital literacies overlap], even with the composed products. But we seem decidedly discomforted when it comes time to assess such processes and products.
>
> Kathleen Yancey, "Looking for sources of coherence in a fragmented world" (2004)

In three of the very few articles to focus on the assessment of writing in new media, the authors—Pamela Takayoshi, Meredith Zoetewey and Julie Staggers, and Kathleen Yancey—ask how the strategies and criteria that we use to assess students' print writing apply to our assessment of their digital writing. How do we evaluate the coherence of a hypertextual essay, for example, or the clarity of a visual argument? Or do familiar assessment criteria such as coherence and clarity need to be substantially revised or even rejected when we are evaluating work in new media?

In all three articles, we see something of a balancing act between old and new, as the authors detail suggestions for adapting current approaches and inventing new ones to help us assess writing in new media. For instance, Zoetewey and Staggers (2003) provided a sample rubric with familiar categories (e.g., narrative structure, point of view) containing new questions designed to assess the visual and hypertextual elements of a Web-based personal writing assignment. Yancey (2004) focused on how the specific criterion of coherence shifts as we move from print to digital compositions.

On the one hand, we need to attend to the differences between digital and print compositions in order to be able to see accurately and respond effectively to the kind of work our students create in new media. Yancey warned against using the "frameworks and processes of one medium to assign value and to interpret work in a different medium" (90) because by doing so we lose the chance to see new values emerging in the new medium. On the other hand, we need to work from what we know and to see computers as, in Takayoshi's (1996) words, "new lenses through which to look at the central issues of writing instruction" (247).

My own suggestion in this webtext involves another adaptation of familiar practices to the new situation of student new media production. Rather than assessing individual modes in a multimodal work, I suggest an assessment strategy that focuses on the effectiveness with which modes such as image, text, and sound are brought together or, literally, composed. Moreover, I propose that we draw on our familiarity with rhetorical tropes—and specifically with the tropes of metaphor and metonymy—to provide us with a language with which to talk to our students about the effectiveness of their work.

Although few publications have focused on the assessment of students' new media compositions, there may be something of a turn toward assessment evident in Yancey's (2004) recent article on this subject in *Computers and Composition* as well as in some of the discussions of assessment at the 2005 Computers and Writing conference. Prior to the conference, Victoria Szabo and Jeremy Sabol of Stanford University conducted a half-day workshop on "Design and Assessment of Digital Media Assignments" (http://cw2005.stanford.edu/workshopshtm.htm).

In presentations at the conference, Marcia Hansen discussed "good, better, and best" assignments and assessment strategies for weblogs; Krista Homicz Millar presented results from an empirical study of how teachers and students assessed the effectiveness of new media arguments; Anthony Ellerston described an eportfolio assessment system in use at Iowa State that allows students to display their work in new media. Even in this small sampling, we can see the lively diversity of approaches that discussions of assessment elicit.

I think that underlying this interest in assessment is the recognition of its importance in connecting new media assignments to broader curricular goals. As with print assignments, when we grade students' work we are assessing their success in achieving goals that we value and that, ideally, are made explicit to our students. How we evaluate and grade student work is—or should be—connected to everything else in the course, from the assignments themselves to the readings, the class activities, and the software we use.

Discussions of new media assessment should therefore help us articulate why new media matters and should help us in establishing, for ourselves and for our students, the key continuities and differences between composing in print and composing in new media.

Examining how student work in new media is currently assessed, it is clear that we are at a transitional stage in the process of incorporating new media into our composition courses. As Yancey (2004) noted, we give multimodal assignments but often draw on what we are far more familiar with—that is, print—to assess student work.

For instance, a common assessment strategy is to ask students to write an essay or a report to accompany a new media project—and to then derive the grade for the project wholly or mostly from the print part of the assignment. To be sure, pairing a paper with a new media composition is a useful strategy: it gives students a clear comparison between these modes and media, and it gives teachers insight into students' composing processes. However, this practice can also allow us to avoid assessing the new media work on its own, and in general it reflects an uneasiness with assessing something other than a written text.

Another common strategy is to draw on rules and models developed other areas (most notably, graphic design) to determine how to teach and assess specific features of new media production. But as Zoetewey and Staggers (2003) pointed out, "By relying on the rules as indices of successful execution of new media composition, we run the risk of decontextualizing graphic design guidelines from the theory that informs them. Even more problematic, we run the risk of depriviledging rhetoric" (145). While we should certainly consider incorporating guidelines from other disciplines into our assessment of new media, we should not expect these guidelines to function as our only evaluative measures. Indeed, by defining our approaches to assessment, compositionists can articulate our own disciplinary perspectives on new media production.

Complicating discussions of new media assessment is the fact that there are so many different types of projects being assigned: websites, images, image/text combinations, videos, audio projects, Flash projects, and others. With each type, somewhat different considerations come into play.

A broadly rhetorical approach can accommodate these differences—that is, an approach that focuses assessment on how effectively the project addresses a specific audience to achieve a specific purpose. The weakness of a broad rhetorical approach is that it doesn't in itself offer any specific guidance or criteria for handling the multimodal aspects of the composition.

Moreover, assessment is very much about context and needs to take into account the particular circumstances of the course, the students, and the teacher, as well as the possibilities afforded by the assignment, the modes, and the medium. Even if it were possible, then, it would be unwise to apply a set of assessment criteria to all types of assignments at all places.

The approach I suggest in this webtext is, I hope, flexible enough to be useful in a variety of contexts.

Looking between Modes

We have defined multimodality as the use of several semiotic modes in the design of a semiotic product or event, together with the particular way in which these modes are combined.

Kress & Van Leeuwen (2001), *Multimodal discourse*

In using the term "new media texts," I mean to refer to texts created primarily in digital environments, composed in multiple media (e.g., film, video, audio, among others), and designed for presentation and exchange in digital venues.

Cynthia Selfe (2004), "Students who teach us"

I offer a focused definition of *new media* as texts that juxtapose semiotic modes in new and aesthetically pleasing ways and, in doing so, break away from print traditions so that written text is not the primary rhetorical means.

Cheryl Ball (2004), "Show, not tell"

As the citations from Kress and van Leeuwen, Selfe, and Ball make clear, composing in new media usually involves bringing together multiple modes—text, image, sound, animation, and/or video—in order to convey a meaning or create an effect. The question for assessment is how this bringing together or composing of modes can be described and then evaluated.

Bringing together multiple modes in a single composition is often a difficult task. After all, in writing essays students have to worry only about working with text, and this is challenging enough. In new media compositions, students are being asked not only to use several different individual modes, but also to bring these modes together in space and time. In essence, they are orchestrating or directing these different resources.

This focus on the relations between modes in a multimodal composition fits into Yancey's (2004) broader discussion of coherence in digital texts. She noted that "Digital compositions *weave* words and context and images: They are exercises in *ordered complexity*—and complex in some different ways than print precisely because they include more kinds of *threads*" (95). Though Yancey offered a broad heuristic for assessing digital texts—one that includes the text's multiple arrangements, its reception, and the intent of its author—the narrow question of the relations between modes is, I believe, essential in understanding not only how a multimedia text coheres but also how it creates meaning.

Focusing assessment on the relations of modes might alleviate part of what Yancey described as the "discomfort" of assessment: that part that comes from our sense that we are not the most qualified people on campus to judge the effectiveness of the individual modes of image, audio, or video in a multimodal composition. But I think that we are indeed qualified to look at the relations between modes and to assess how effectively students have combined different resources in their compositions.

Assessing how students design relations between modes appeals to me on practical grounds because it addresses of the two most common problems I've seen in the new media compositions my students have done. First, some students seem inclined to match modes, so that, for instance, a Flash project will have a song playing in the background while on the screen the lyrics to the song appear along with images depicting exactly what the lyrics say. While some repetition across modes may be useful in focusing attention or highlighting key ideas, too much mode matching diminishes the potential of multimedia composing by, in essence, leveling the modes so that they each express something more or less equivalent. Productive tension between modes here is at a minimum.

The opposite sort of problem occurs when students include an element in a project simply because it looks good or because it is a cool effect, despite the fact that the element adds nothing to the meaning of the project and bears little, if any, relation to the other components of the project. For instance, text may be put in motion in a Flash animation for no reason other than that it is possible to do so; the animation in this instance is a distraction in reading the text rather than an element that enhances or expands its meaning. Here the potential of multimedia composing is diminished because the different modes are brought together more or less arbitrarily.

In talking with my students about their work, I warn against these extremes of pure repetition or pure arbitrariness, of course. But I also search for ways to describe more positively the kinds of relations that can apply between modes. Here the concepts of metaphor and metonymy can be useful.

Metaphor and metonymy, broadly understood, can designate two primary ways in which meaning emerges from the bringing together of modes in a multimodal work.

Metaphor designates a relation based on substitution; in a multimodal work, one mode can metaphorically represent or stand in for another, as when an animation of a word dynamically represents its meaning. It is a relation based on similarity between elements in different modes.

Metonymy designates a relation based on combination; modes can be metonymically related when they are linked by an association, as when lines from a poem are combined with a melody from a song. It is a relation based on contiguity between elements in different modes.

Using metaphor and metonymy in this way gives us a language for talking to students about the relations they are composing between modes and a way of explaining where a multimodal project is effective or weak.

While we typically think of metaphor and metonymy as verbal tropes, a broader understanding of these terms can be derived from Roman Jakobson's (1956) influential essay, "Two Aspects of Language and Two Types of Aphasic Disturbances." Jakobson posited that two basic types of aphasia correspond to impairments either in the faculty for selection and substitution or in the faculty for combination and contexture. Selection is equated with the metaphoric use of language and combination with the metonymic use of language. Further, Jakobson argued that the metaphoric and metonymic processes are not confined to language but occur in other art forms such as painting and film.

Metaphor and metonymy, in the broader sense proposed by Jakobson, name two different forces at work in the production of meaning. Metaphor exploits similarity and substitution, while metonymy exploits contiguity and association. Because metaphor and metonymy designate relations between two or more entities, they can be used to describe the relations between modes.

Between Verbal and Visual

> Whoever controls the media—the images—controls the culture.
>
> Allen Ginsberg

Students in my Winter 2004 "Writing in New Media" course were asked to use Photoshop to create a collage that interpreted the previous quotation by Allen Ginsberg. I present several student projects here in order to demonstrate how the concepts of metaphor and metonymy can be used to describe and assess the relations between verbal and visual modes.

I should note that the assignment lends itself to an assessment strategy focused on the relations between modes since it explicitly asks students to work back and forth across modes by creating an image that interprets a text.

Leading up to the collage assignment were several shorter exercises that invited students to explore relations between text and image. First, students added some text to a digital image of a coastal scene that they had all downloaded. This exercise allowed students to experiment with the color, font, and placement of the text but also with the creation of meaning(s) from juxtaposition of text and image. The second exercise asked students to create an image out of the text of a word; in other words, the word itself functioned as the image, and the visual qualities students gave to the word/image were intended to convey the meaning of the word.

Feedback on these exercises was intended to help students discover areas for exploration between modes. They saw, I hope, that the modes should not simply repeat each other. For example, adding the words "a coastal scene" to the image of a coastal scene is less interesting than, for instance, adding lines from a poem or statistics about ocean pollution. The choices students made in these exercises showed that meaning emerges in part from the interplay of word and image.

Comparing these collages, it is possible to say that one of them is better than the others, and that as a writing teacher I can make that determination. All of the collages are visually pleasing and are well executed in Photoshop, so an assessment of them as purely visual compositions would be quite positive.

But Gabe's is clearly the most effective multimodal composition, and this is because the relation between the written mode and the visual mode is richer and more productive than in the other collages. In particular, as I explain, Gabe's collage activates both metaphor and metonymy to create meaning whereas the other collages are weak in one or both areas.

Student Work

Gabe Mann

In interpreting the first part of the quotation—"Whoever controls the media"—Gabe's collage points the finger at Bush and the White House. The collage interprets the word "control" with the image of Bush as a puppeteer, and this image elaborates on and refines an understanding of "control" by suggesting that the control in question has certain qualities: for instance, that the entity in control is behind the scenes and is completely manipulative of characters who only seem to be independent and to act on their own.

This is a strong metaphor, in which Bush-as-puppeteer stands in or substitutes for the controlling force to which Ginsberg's words refer.

The reference to the "media" in Ginsberg's quotation elicits a series of metonymic connections. Gabe personifies the "media" in the images of Sean Hannity, Bill O'Reilly, and Rush Limbaugh—conservative TV and radio hosts who, the collage suggests, are merely puppets of the Bush administration. This is metonymic rather than metaphoric because the three commentators are part of the larger group of conservative media (and perhaps all media) that Bush manipulates.

The fact that Bush is holding crucifixes to join together the puppet strings evokes another metonymic association, bringing the particular manipulations of religion into this dynamic.

Finally, the background images are metonymically related to the "images" mentioned in Ginsberg's quotation; photographs taken from the war in Afghanistan and the collapse of the World Trade Center are among the many images that, the collage suggests, are controlled by Bush and the conservative media.

By activating both metaphorical and metonymic relations between the visual and verbal modes in this collage, Gabe creates a work rich in meaning and allusion. Through a strong central metaphor, Gabe's collage offers a straightforward interpretation of Ginsberg's quotation, and through the metonymic associations of media and images, the interpretation gains a certain breadth.

Stacy Johnson

In Stacy's collage, Ginsberg's quotation figures prominently, but there is much less of a connection between the images and the text here than there is in Gabe's collage. Most notably, Stacy's collage doesn't comment on or interpret what "control" means or who is in control. Although several elements in the collage interact, there is no sense that one character or element in the collage controls another. In addition, there is no indication of the repercussions of this control or of the ways in which control of the media effectively controls the culture.

Stacy's collage is highly metonymic; it activates a series of associations between pop culture icons (Madonna, Ben Affleck, Jennifer Lopez), a television, a small child, and a psychedelic 1960's background pattern. These associations are evocative but also quite difficult to interpret, in part because the collage lacks a controlling metaphor. In particular, it is difficult to identify how text and image are related since there seem to be no direct, metaphorical substitutions for any of the key terms in the quotation— "control," "media," "images"—but rather just a series of associations around these terms.

Kelley Kaufmann

Unlike Gabe and Stacy, Kelley focuses her collage almost exclusively on the second part of the quotation: "controls the culture." Kelley's collage shows a TV with an image of Britney Spears smoking, and then a magazine with a model smoking on the back, and finally the girl reading the magazine is smoking. There is a clear cause and effect being suggested here.

We can say that Kelley's collage is highly metaphorical. It offers a series of direct substitutions: Britney smokes, the model smokes, the reader smokes. These three elements are made equivalent, and taken together they provide a visual representation of the word "control." The collage lacks the kind of broader metonymic associations that would establish context or suggest the implications of these metaphoric substitutions.

Behzad Khorsand

Like Kelley's collage, this one by Behzad provides a fairly simplistic interpretation of the quotation. MTV has "caught" the world and holds the world on a fishhook. For the first part of the quotation—"Whoever controls the media"—the collage points to MTV, and perhaps by extension to the kind of media that MTV stands for.

But the characteristics of that control are not explained visually, nor are its consequences. Gabe's puppet show image—with the puppeteer and puppets clearly identified—offers a richer interpretation of the way the word "control" is used in the quotation than does Behzad's more vague world-on-a-fishhook image.

In addition to a vague central metaphor, Behzad's collage offers relatively weak metonymic associations. The background of the image is a black outer space and so it provides no clues as to the context in which MTV operates or the images it controls. Assessment of this collage in terms of metaphor and metonymy, then, would highlight the relatively weak and simplistic relations between the visual and verbal modes.

Modes and Models

> The alternative predominance of one or the other of these two processes [of metaphor and metonymy] is by no means confined to verbal art. The same oscillation occurs in sign systems other than language.
>
> Roman Jakobson (1956), "Two Aspects of Language and Two Types of Aphasic Disturbances"

In my "Writing in New Media" course, a multimodal project in Flash follows the static verbal/visual assignments discussed in the "between verbal and visual" section of this webtext. Ideally students will have had experience and success in combining text and image, and so will be better prepared to bring additional modes into a composition.

In this section, I discuss a student project—"Starry Night" by Casey Curtis—that adds sound and motion into the mix. I also briefly discuss two "professional" new media projects—both published at Poems That Go (http://www.poemsthatgo.com)—that can serve as models for students as they create their compositions and that establish clear and rich relations between modes.

Casey Curtis, "Starry Night"

(starrynite.swf)

Casey Curtis's project, "Starry Night," brings together word, image, and sound in a way that is mostly metonymic; however, elements from the project, particularly the animation, operate metaphorically and help give the project coherence.

"Starry Night" combines the lyrics from Bob Dylan's "Mr. Tambourine Man," paintings by Vincent Van Gogh, and the jazz piece "In a Sentimental Mood" by Duke Ellington and John Coltrane. These three diverse elements are composed in an evocative way and create associations through their juxtaposition.

It is at first a bit disconcerting to see the lyrics of one song on the screen as another song plays in the background; adding to the oddness is the visual experience of seeing very famous paintings fading in and out on the screen with words superimposed on them. The three basic elements of word, image, and sound all come from very well known sources. Casey's project takes these elements out of their context—for instance, presenting the lyrics of the song without its melody—and puts them in a new context with new associations.

In addition to the metonymic associations generated by the word, image, and sound combinations, other elements of the project use more of a metaphoric relation between modes.

For instance, the title "Starry Night" appears at first on the screen as small yellow dots; the dots converge to form the words of the title, and then they dissolve again into the small yellow dots before disappearing entirely. Against a dark blue background, this animation has the effect of making the title seem composed of twinkling stars; here the animation repeats or visually represents the words of the title.

Other text animations in the project also evoke the meaning of the text being animated. For instance, the words "but still not sleeping" throb, and the words "my weariness amazes me" gradually stretch out across the screen. These animations aren't exact replications of the meanings of the words, since we don't directly associate throbbing with sleepiness or stretching with weariness. In these cases, the animations expand on the meanings of the words they represent.

There are also metaphoric relations between text and image in some scenes, bringing Dylan's words and Van Gogh's images more closely together. For instance, the words "take me, yes, to dance beneath the diamond sky / silhouetted by the sea" appear against a backdrop of VanGogh's painting "Starry Night Over the Rhone," which shows lights reflecting on the water.

In her report that accompanied this project, Casey wrote that she wanted to "create an experience for the audience": "I wanted the combination [of text, image, and sound] to give the audience the impression of being lonely and in a daze." Placing well known text, images, and sounds together in a new context evokes new connections between these elements, creating something like an environment of associations that the audience can experience.

The associative logic of metonymy is appropriate here. However, without the metaphoric resonances and substitutions that offer connections between elements at various points in the project, the different modes might seem too disconnected and the associations too loose or random.

Mitchell Kimbrough, "Sky"

(http://www.poemsthatgo.com/gallery/summer2002/sky/launch.htm)

"Sky," by Mitchell Kimbrough, brings together the words of a poem he wrote (entitled "Sky") with Norah Jones's song "Don't Know Why." Two animated images make up the visual component of the project: first, a forest scene as evening turns to night, and second, a flower that grows and then dies. In addition, the words of the poem are animated, appearing and disappearing from the screen.

The modes in this project are related to each other mostly in a metaphorical way. That is, the song and the animated images metaphorically represent the poem, substituting for elements of the poem by conveying its meaning in terms and with techniques specific to each mode.

The poem seems to be about an opportunity that the speaker failed to take up. Although it is written in fragments of sentences, the verbs—"didn't," "might have," "could've," "didn't," "won't," "might have"—all express negation and point to the possibility of something that ultimately didn't occur. The repetition of the words "little," "almost," and "next time" suggest that this missed opportunity isn't tragic but is more like something upon which the speaker muses, perhaps with just a bit of longing or regret.

The images and sound point to some of the same meanings as the poem does. Visually, the two animated images of "Sky" convey a mild sense of loss. In the animated images of nightfall and in a flower's growth and death we see the passage of time and the end of something, but in a way that is natural, inevitable, perhaps sad but not tragic. The use of these two images evokes the cycles of nature, and this represents or stands in for phrases in the poem like "next time" and "always tomorrow though."

The audio component of "Sky" similarly represents some elements of the poem and the images. The lyrics and melody of Norah Jones's song suggest a mild, somewhat bewildered sense of melancholy and regret. There is a sense of longing for something that might have been, but also a certain acceptance conveyed both by the lyrics and by the smooth and calm style of the song.

In "Sky," then, all three modes work toward expressing more or less the same meaning; they substitute or stand-in for each other, though in a way that isn't simple repetition. The text, sound, and images each add their own part to the meaning, drawing of course on the resources of each mode.

Ingrid Ankerson, "Murmuring Insects"

(http://www.poemsthatgo.com/gallery/fall2001/murmuring/launch.htm)

"Murmuring Insects," by Ingrid Ankerson, was published at Poems That Go, shortly after 9/11. The text in the project comes from a poem entitled "Murmuring Insects," written by Otagaki Rengetsu, an 18th century Japanese poet. There are several still images (the twin towers of the World Trade Center after having been hit by airplanes, the exhaust trails of an airplane, a photograph of an eye) and several animated images (geese flying, words forming into a tear which then becomes a crescent moon). Finally, the audio element of the project includes sound clips of crickets chirping and a violin playing, along with sound clips taken from broadcasts on or shortly after 9/11.

As Ankerson (2001) commented in her brief description of the project at Rhizome.org, "This piece uses Rengetsu's language combined with simple imagery in the spirit of her words, but is starkly contrasted with the media sound bytes the American nation would hear for days in a row" following the events of 9/11.

In the terms I've been using here, the text and images metaphorically substitute for each other, whereas the sound (the sound clips related to 9/11, though not the crickets or violin sound clips) introduces a metonymic element.

For the most part, the images and text in "Murmuring Insects" express a similar meaning. For instance, in the "sky" scene, the animation of geese flying repeats a phrase in the poem ("flocks of departing geese"). In the water scene, the words "tears like dew / well up in my eyes" are animated so as to appear to well up and then drop from the eye of the photograph in the background.

But the sounds in "Murmuring Insects" bring a new dimension to the project and interact differently with the images and the text. In fact, audio is the mode that brings the events of 9/11 most clearly into the body of the project and places this reference next to the images and words. This is a metonymic relation because the sounds are not meant to translate or substitute for the words or images, but rather to extend their meaning by association—that is, to bring the words and images into association with 9/11, and with the particular expressions of 9/11 rendered in each audio clip.

While the images and text of the project provide mostly calming references to nature, the voiceovers that are part of the sound clips introduce the terror and fear and great sorrow of 9/11. This juxtaposition may, as Cheryl Ball (under review) noted in her insightful interpretation of "Murmuring Insects," allow readers to memorialize 9/11 in a "more productive and peaceful way than simply by reacting with fear."

As I have suggested, looking at the relations between modes helps us focus assessment on a unique and challenging element of multimodal composing. Metaphor and metonymy provide a language with which to talk to our students about how the different modes in their projects come together to make meaning.

This approach certainly doesn't offer a quantitative assessment measure, and it doesn't address the technical or aesthetic challenges of new media composition. Rather, the approach I have described here is one element—though I believe an essential element—in our assessment of student work in new media.

Citations

Text

Ankerson, Ingrid. (2001). Introduction to "Murmuring insects." Available: http://www.rhizome.com/object. rhiz?2865.

Ball, Cheryl E. (under review). Not just visual: Reading "Murmuring insects" as a new media text. *Computers and Composition* [Special issue: Multimedia composition].

Ball, Cheryl E. (2004). Show, not tell: The value of new media scholarship. *Computers and Composition*, 21 (4), 403–425.

Kress, Gunther & Van Leeuwen, Theo. (2001). *Multimodal discourse: The modes and media of contemporary communication.* London: Arnold.

Jakobson, Roman. (1956). Two aspects of language and two types of aphasic disturbances. In Jakobson, Roman & Halle, Morris, *Fundamentals of language* (115–133). The Hague: Mouton.

Selfe, Cindy. (2004). Students who teach us. In Wysocki, Anne et. al. (Eds.), *Writing new media* (pp. 43–66). Logan, UT: Utah State University Press.

Takayoshi, Pamela (1996). The shape of electronic writing: Evaluating and assessing computer-assisted writing processes and products. *Computers and Composition*, 13 (2), 245–257.

Yancey, Kathleen Blake. (2004). Looking for sources of coherence in a fragmented world: Notes toward a new assessment design. *Computers and Composition*, 21 (1), 89–102.

vey, Meredith W. & Staggers, Julie. (2003). Beyond "current-traditional" design: Assessing rhetoric in
w media. *Issues in Writing*, 13, 133–157.

Image

Photograph of Stanford's Memorial Court and the "Burghers of Calais" sculptures by Bipin Rajendran. Used with permission.

Audio

Sounds from The Freesound Project: http://freesound.iua.upf.edu/.

Design & Code

Design concept from The ABC: http://www.the-abc.org/. Code help from ActionScript.org: http://action-script.org.

Thanks

I benefitted greatly from the feedback offered by the Kairos editorial team. Many thanks to Cheryl Ball, Beth Hewett, Leah Cassorla, and the two anonymous Editorial Board reviewers. Their insightful comments helped me to improve substantially on the earlier version of this webtext.

And many thanks also to Bob Samuels, who gave me help and support at all stages of this project.

Appendix 1

Effective Writing Assignments

WRITING ASSIGNMENTS

Here is an important maxim for teaching a writing class: well-constructed, thoughtful writing assignments enhance the possibility for effective student writing, and poorly developed assignments, to which an instructor has not given adequate thought, are likely to minimize that possibility. This is probably one of the most important ideas for teachers to understand, whether they are teaching a stand-alone writing class or a subject matter class that includes writing. I cannot stress enough how important it is for composition instructors to devote sufficient time to developing thoughtful assignments—to give yourself enough time to plan, revise, confer with other instructors, even to try responding to the assignment yourself. This section provides some suggestions for constructing and presenting effective assignments, focusing on purpose, structure, audience, and sources of information.

DEVELOPING EFFECTIVE ASSIGNMENTS

Writing assignments work best when they are carefully planned, discussed thoroughly in class, and segmented into various components or "scaffolded." Assignments should include a number of pieces that build upon one another, each aimed at fostering students' understanding of the writing task, and each with a specific due date. Without the building blocks of a scaffolded assignment, students tend to procrastinate, delaying writing or even thinking about the assignment until the night before it is due. This habit is likely to cause writing anxiety or writer's block—and the writing produced under such circumstances is not likely to be very good, no matter how strongly students claim that they "work best under pressure." More likely—if a student works well under pressure, he or she will do even better work when the assignment is scaffolded!

The suggestions below can help you develop effective writing assignments, and I also include a model that might inform the assignments you develop for your own students:

1. Introduce the topic for a writing assignment in class, using exploratory writing, discussion questions, response to a reading, or another classroom activity that will help students understand the topic and engage with it.

Be sure to prepare students for the assignment. Explain it carefully. Do not simply hand out an assignment in class, or, worse, scribble the assignment on the board at the end of class.

2. Have students write responses to exploration questions.

Exploration questions enable students to become aware of what they already know or believe about the topic. They can respond to these questions either in class, at home, or online, using discussion lists of course management programs such as WebCT or Moodle. It is helpful for students to share their responses in groups or with the whole class.

Example exploration questions:
- When you were growing up, what experiences did you have with this topic?
- To what extent was the topic discussed in your home?
- To what extent was the topic discussed in your high school?
- Describe your feelings about this topic.
- Do you think this topic is important for people to understand or explore? Why or why not?
- Are there controversies concerning this topic? If so, has the topic always been controversial?

3. Assign an initial reading(s) concerned with the topic. Students can then summarize the content of these readings and/or write a response.

To use readings as springboards for writing, you can begin with one reading, go over it carefully in class (depending on the level of the students) and ask students to summarize the article and then write a letter or some form of response to the author, indicating points of agreement or disagreement. You can also assign two articles on the topic, each presenting a different perspective. In preparation for class discussion, students should summarize and respond to these essays. Indicate to students that this component of the assignment will count toward the final grade.

Example assignment using summary and response:
Read Professor X's essay on the topic. In one or two paragraphs, summarize Professor X's perspective and indicate why you think that perspective is important to understand. In a second paragraph, discuss the extent to which you agree with that perspective.
Read Professor Y's essay on the topic. In one or two paragraphs, summarize Professor X's perspective and indicate why you think that perspective is important to understand. In a second paragraph, discuss the extent to which you agree with that perspective.

4. Have students create a short annotated bibliography.

Locate __ additional articles on this topic from the (library, Internet, etc.). These articles might support the positions of Professors X and Y, take a more moderate position, or present a different position. Create an annotated bibliography in which you summarize the main positions of these articles.

5. Present the assignment in writing.

Here is an example you can use as a model. It includes the following sections: background, writing task, requirements, schedule of activities and due dates.

Background:

The topic of __ has increasingly attracted public attention, generating considerable debate among scholars. One perspective, presented in the essay by Professor X, maintains that __. Presenting another perspective, however, Professor Y maintains that __. Moreover, other scholars, presenting less extreme positions, have argued that __. (Elaboration depends on the complexity of the topic.)

Writing task:

Consider the perspectives of both Professor X and Professor Y on the topic of __ and those expressed in the additional articles you have obtained. Then, in a well-organized essay of __ pages, develop and support a position on the topic of __.

Requirements:

Keep in mind that this assignment requires you to develop and support a **position**—that is, a thesis or main point that you support throughout the essay. You should not simply summarize various perspectives on this topic although you should acknowledge the positions of Professors X and Y as well as those of the additional articles you have located.

Schedule of activities and due dates:

Exploration questions due __.

Reading, summary, and response due __.

Annotated bibliography due __.

One paragraph overview due __.

Bring a paragraph to class in which you summarize the position you plan to support in your essay. (Depending on time constraints, students can hand these in to the instructor, or read them aloud in small groups.)

First polished draft due __. (Depending on time constraints, the instructor can make comments, but not assign a grade.)

Peer review comments due __.

Final draft due. (This is assigned a grade.)

PROBLEMS STUDENTS HAVE WITH ASSIGNMENTS

The following is a list of problems students typically have in understanding the requirements of their writing assignments:

1. Students are often unaware of the necessity of having a thesis.

Students are often unaware that the assignment requires a thesis, position, or main idea that is developed and supported throughout the essay. As a result, they simply respond literally to the questions in the assignment prompt without focusing their essays around a central point. For example, when students are asked to "compare and contrast" two articles on a given subject, they simply discuss one article, then the other, without realizing that they are supposed to be deriving a main point or perspective that will structure the essay as a whole. Similarly, if the assignment uses the word "describe," students assume that description is an end in itself, whereas an instructor may conceive of description as a mode of presentation used to support a thesis. In my classes, I ask students to evaluate whether their writing is concerned with "an idea worth considering."

2. Students often do not understand the role of definition in academic writing.

In working with assignments, students may not understand that definition can be used to provide a context for discussing other facets of the topic. For example, in a prompt that asks students to consider the extent to which television could be considered "harmful" to society, it is necessary for students to establish what they mean by "harmful." Becoming aware of values is an important element in academic writing. But many students are unaware of how values impact what they want to say.

3. Students are often confused by an assignment that asks a lot of questions. Instead of synthesizing the prompts into a central question, they attempt to answer each one separately.

Here is an assignment that asks a lot of questions
> In the film Avatar, what is being suggested about society? Do the aliens represent a particular group in contemporary society? What image does the show provide of science and corporate development? Of racial tendencies? Of moral leadership? Does the film have an ethical message? Is the message consistent with the narrative?

Students may not understand that these questions are intended to generate thinking and that they don't have to answer every question in their essay.

4. Students will often write a bifurcated response to an assignment with a double focus.

A question such as "Is the political correctness movement helpful or harmful to a college campus and should the rules regarding political correctness be changed?" is likely to lead to a double answer.

5. Students often do not know how to narrow an unfocused or vague assignment prompt.

A prompt that asks students to "discuss political correctness" on campus is likely to generate description and perhaps many examples, but little analysis.

TO HELP STUDENTS UNDERSTAND A WRITING ASSIGNMENT

1. Scaffold the assignment—that is, divide it into parts. Assign a due date to each part.
2. Read all components of the assignment aloud in class as students follow along. Do not simply distribute the assignment and assume that students will figure it out on their own.
3. Point to key terms in the assignment that explain what students must do to write the paper. Encourage students to circle these terms.
4. Define the nature of the writing task that the assignment requires. If the paper requires a main point or thesis, provide a few examples. Caution students about selecting a thesis too soon, before they have had time to explore the topic adequately. Explain that ideas change through the process of reading, research, and writing.
5. Clarify terms, such as "discuss," "explicate," "trace," "examine," "analyze," or "develop" that students may not understand in the context of a writing assignment.
6. Discuss potential sources of information for the paper. Will the information be based primarily on personal experience or opinion? Are there particular sources that students

should access before writing the paper? Should students locate information from the library or the Internet?

7. Clarify any implicit requirements that may not be directly stated, but are necessary for the assignment to be completed satisfactorily. For example, many college writing assignments require students to define terms, consider questions of degree, or establish a relationship between ideas.

8. If possible, identify a possible audience or audiences for this paper aside from the teacher who gave the assignment. Explain that although the teacher is, of course, going to read the paper, many college essays are written for what is ambiguously termed a "general audience." To help the students understand this concept, have them imagine that the paper has been left on a desk in the college library and read by another student. Would this student be able to understand the paper without having access to the assignment? What sort of background information on the topic is this unknown college student likely to have? What sort of information needs to be included in the paper in order for a general audience to understand it?

A useful strategy for enabling students to think about audience is to have them respond to the following questions:

Before the people in my audience have read this paper, they are likely to think

_____

about this topic.

After the people in my audience have read this paper, I would like them to think

_____

about this topic.

Below is an example of a writing prompt that you can use as a model:

COMPONENTS OF A WRITING ASSIGNMENT

Assignment #2   **Changing the Law**

Purpose: **Goals of the assignment are**
- To formulate a thesis concerning a law that you think **made explicit.**
  should be changed;
- To support that thesis with convincing reasons
- To provide development and support for your ideas
- To demonstrate your understanding of essay structure

Readings: **Readings specified**
At least three short readings that you find online. These
may not be from Wikipedia. We will have a library session
to help you locate appropriate sources.

Background:

This assignment requires you to choose a law that exists today at the federal or local level that is currently enforced but which you believe needs to be changed. Examples can include seatbelt laws, helmet laws, drinking laws, voting laws, drug laws, cigarette laws, speed limit laws—the list is inexhaustible—but whatever you choose, it should be something that interests you, something with which you have some personal experience.

Questions to consider:

To help you develop ideas and prepare the background section of your paper, find out as much as you can by answering the following questions:

- Have you had personal experience with this law? If so, describe it.
- Why was this law passed in the first place?
- When was it passed?
- Who was in favor of its passage and who was against it?
- Who is most affected by it?
- Who benefits from it?
- What purpose did it originally serve?
- Is it outdated?/Why?
- What is wrong with it as it stands now?
- How would society benefit if it were changed?

Writing task:

Once you have learned as much as you can about this law, respond to the following question in a well-argued essay:

To what extent should this law be changed?

Further explanation:

This essay will be constructed as an academic argument and therefore should be well-reasoned, supported with logic-based evidence, and balanced through the inclusion of a counter-argument. Preparation for this paper must include brainstorming, a fact–idea list, and a points list. It should be oriented toward a general, academic audience and will be evaluated according to the grading rubric for this course.

Sidebar annotations:

A context is set for the assignment

Questions to generate thinking are included. But these are part of the *preparation*, not necessarily questions that must be answered within the essay itself.

The writing task is specified, isolated in a bolded prompt. It is desirable to have a short prompt.

Students are reminded of the type of essay this assignment requires. Audiences and grading rubrics are specified.

Appendix 2

Developing a Syllabus

A syllabus is a very important document, serving as a contract between you and your students. It describes as comprehensively as possible the focus and structure of the course, explains course policies, and indicates responsibilities students will have to fulfill. Although many elements of syllabus will be dictated by the requirements of a particular program or department, your syllabus will reflect your personality as a teacher and orientation toward the teaching of writing. It is, therefore, important to reflect on what sort of persona you want to project and the philosophy of writing and writing pedagogy you want to endorse. Whether the syllabus is in electronic or paper form, be sure to go over it carefully so that students can ask questions. Do not assume that students will read it carefully on their own.

Necessary components of a syllabus are listed here:

1. Course number and contact information.

These include course number; classroom location; class meeting time; and instructor's name, phone number, office location, e-mail address, and office hours.

2. Textbook information.

These include author, title, publisher, edition, and any supplementary information included in the assigned readings.

3. Overview of course and rationale.

This includes an overview of the course, and an explanation of its goals and the theoretical underpinnings on which they are based. Indicate how you are planning to structure the course, focusing on your primary concern of helping students develop an effective writing process and acquire a writing style appropriate to an intended audience. If you are incorporating online work into your course, such as blogs or courseware programs, you should schedule some time to teach students how to work with them.

4. Requirements and policies.

Requirements include the number of essays students will be writing, the necessity for submitting multiple drafts, and other required elements such as in-class exercises, homework activities, journals, listserves, and portfolios. Explain the format and style you require for written work; your grading policies; and your attitude toward class and group attendance, tardiness, and late papers. Be sure to address the issue of plagiarism.

5. Additional information.

This might include the location of a Writing Center or services available for the disabled or handicapped.

6. Course calendar.

Indicate in detail what is required for each class: readings, responses, activities, presentations, conferences, due dates for papers—including first, second, and third drafts, and portfolio submissions. Although it is useful to prepare your course in advance, feel free to alter it according to the needs of your students.

Below is an example of a syllabus for a first-year writing course at California State University, Northridge, which focuses on academic argument. Note how the various components of the syllabus are explained in this syllabus and feel free to copy parts of it. However, in constructing your own syllabus, you should also obtain copies of syllabi that pertain to the courses at your own college or university.

Welcome to English 155:
Introduction to Academic Writing, Applied Rhetoric and Critical Reasoning
for Spring 2008

A writer is someone for whom writing is more difficult than it is for other people
—Thomas Mann
How do I know what I think until I see what I say?—E.M. Forster
Fill the paper with the breathings of your heart—William Wordsworth

Professor:	*Office Location:*
Class Location:	*Office Hours:*
E-mail:	*Phone:*

Course Description

English 155 is a course in expository writing designed for freshman and transfer students. Its emphasis is on helping you gain experience with academic writing—that is, the text genres you will be using in your college courses. You will practice exploring ideas, conveying information, thinking critically about ideas in published works, and adopting a thoughtful position about complex and substantive topics. You will also develop skills in organizing an essay, using logical reasoning in support of a thesis, and expressing ideas clearly through appropriate language choices. Beyond these fundamental concerns, the course will encourage you to develop a degree of grace and style which will make your writing interesting and readable.

Essentially, this course is designed to improve your writing and prepare you for the variety of writing tasks that you will meet throughout your college careers and probably in your life beyond college. Thus, we will spend much time on learning strategies to approach a given writing task and to carry it through to its conclusion. In short, we will attempt to improve your individual writing process. While some writers have difficulty getting started, others have problems developing their ideas as they write, or experience varying degrees of writing anxiety. Still, others have problems revising their writing; however, no two writers have the exact same problems. Your writing process is as unique and complex as you are as a person. For this reason, we will attempt to individualize as much as possible through teacher–student conferences, peer reviews, and by exercising any other necessary measures to foster success.

Course Objectives

- To reinforce the theory and practice of composition as a recursive process—this entails exercises in invention, drafting, revision and editing.
- To encourage an understanding of the various contexts for writing, including timed and extemporaneous expository writing, and the utilization of effective strategies for writing in a variety of forms appropriate for a writer's multiple purposes. These include an awareness of purpose, audience, and genre (the rhetorical situation); the use of effective rhetorical appeals; and the use of the rhetorical methods of development.
- To develop fluency and style by practicing sentence variety, increasing vocabulary, and using the conventions of Edited American English.
- To increase proficiency in research and documentation techniques required by various disciplines, i.e., MLA, APA, annotated bibliographies, etc.
- To become acquainted with culturally diverse texts and encourage practice in the written analysis of rhetorical strategies, the potential effects of biased language on both writers and readers, and the interdependence between critical thinking and college-level reading and writing.
- To promote writing as a means of participation in democracy and social change.

Required Texts and Materials

- Textbooks and readings are listed.
- One standard two-pocket folder for the final portfolio project.
- One **small** bluebook for UDWPE practice exams (available at Matador Bookstore).
- A flash drive, memory stick, or floppy disk to save work completed in the computer laboratory.
- An active <u>CSUN</u> e-mail account (**use of CSUN email is mandatory and non-negotiable for this course**).

Assignments

Major Essays   **(40% of final grade)**

You are required to compose (4) substantive, thesis-driven essays four to six pages in length. These are department requirements; failure to meet any of these requirements will result in a lowered grade. You will develop your work through multiple drafts, revisions, course readings and other various assignments. During the semester, you will be introduced to a variety of helpful revision strategies that include tips on style, structure, focus, grammar/punctuation, and more to help you through this part of the process.

Draft and Revision Requirements—

Drafts and revisions are department requirements for **each** major essay; therefore, drafts submitted with your essays must demonstrate significant development from copy to copy. They may **not** be carbon copies of each other with only slight cosmetic changes. Please compose drafts that are distinguished from one another; those that demonstrate the beginning and evolution of each of your essays into a finished product. This requirement helps me to examine your personal process and transitions through them.

Submission Requirements and Essay Format—

Please see individual instructions listed on the essay prompts you are given for each assignment. These will inform you of the specific tasks being asked of you for your writing, i.e., genre, style, document layout, submission procedures, etc., and will include a specialized grading rubric so that you may gauge your work as you write.

Portfolio Requirement   **(30% of final grade)**

All English 155 students are required to submit a final portfolio that consists of their best writing from the semester. For this reason, **do not throw away any of your writing and save copies of each essay draft.** Your portfolio should contain the following items:

- A two-to-three page reflective essay discussing the contents of your portfolio and the knowledge you have absorbed as a student in English 155CMP.
- One in-class timed essay with the assignment sheet attached.
- Two individually stapled essay packets which will include: the assignment sheet; at least one polished draft; and one final draft of your essay that has been revised beyond its final submission stage.

Keep in mind that the appearance and quality of your work are a reflection of you and your commitment to excellence. When you submit the portfolio, your work will be examined by a panel of English Department faculty.

Examinations   **(20% of final grade)**

Quizzes—
A few small, unannounced quizzes will be given at random points during the semester. These are *gravy* so to speak. **Here is a helpful tip**—stay on top of your readings, remain attentive in class, and take good notes—if you do, you will succeed. I do not allow make-ups for quizzes unless severe and verifiable circumstances prevent you from taking them on the day administered. These quizzes help me to gauge your grasp of the material and other concepts while preliminarily indicating potential weaknesses you may have.

In-Class Essay Exams—
One timed essay, composed in your bluebook during class, will be assigned. An assignment sheet will be given with the essay prompt instructing you to develop and discuss a topic based upon certain issues/ideas. You will then address issues/ideas in-depth, thus creating

coherent essays. This helps to develop your ability to write on command and helps me to determine where you need improvement. The exam is a simulation of CSUN's required Upper Division Writing Proficiency Exam, and will provide good practice for tackling this and other essay examinations you will undoubtedly encounter in other courses.

Homework   **(10% of final grade)**

Small homework assignments will be given occasionally, and shall encompass a random variety of topics: questions regarding the readings; rhetorical techniques/writing strategies; research methods, etc. Homework is a great way to stay actively engaged in learning outside of the classroom.

If You Need Help

Let's face it—we all need a little help with our writing every now and again. As always, I am very approachable, and delighted to help you whenever possible. If you have questions or problems regarding any part of this course, please contact me **immediately**! I also encourage you to seek the professional assistance of our writing lab staff at the Learning Resource Center located in **408 Bayramian Hall**. They provide tutors, at no additional cost, who are trained to work exclusively with students in ENG. 155 and other composition courses. Appointments are encouraged, but walk-ins are available on a limited basis. Look for the writing lab hours on CSUN's website, or call 677-2033. In my professional opinion, only the writing center staff and your in-class peer critique groups are advisable forms of assistance in my absence.

General Policies and Course Business

Late Policy
Late assignments are not acceptable at any time unless severe and verifiable circumstances are the cause. All work is due *at the start of class, on the due date specified*. If you are knowingly going to miss class I must receive the assignment(s) before class begins. ***No e-mail attachments will be accepted per university policy.*** Failure to submit work in a timely manner will result in a full letter grade reduction for the assignment.

Attendance
You are permitted to miss up to **two** class meetings during the semester for whatever reason you choose; no excuses are necessary for these. I will excuse additional absences due to university business and *severe* personal emergencies, but only with *verifiable* documentation. ***If you have more than two unexcused absences, I will automatically deduct one letter grade from your final semester score for each class you miss beyond the second.*** In addition, you are solely responsible for finding out the assignments that will be due for the following class. Please contact a classmate to obtain this information. Finally, I take attendance at the beginning of each class, so if you arrive late, you will be recorded as absent.

Classroom Etiquette
Always arrive to class on time and treat the instructor and classmates with the same respect that you would want to receive in return. In addition, anything that beeps, buzzes, rings,

sings, chimes or vibrates—*anything at all along those lines*—*must be turned off before entering class. No exceptions!* Also, you *must refrain* from chit-chatting while class is in progress. If you have questions during class, i.e. what did he say? What page? Where are we? Rather than ask your neighbor, please ask me instead.

Participation

I do not grade, nor do I devote any component of the final grade, to participation or participation points. Participation is neither a reward, nor is it a representation of your skills; it is an expectation of you as a student in this course. Come fully prepared with assigned work, necessary course materials, collaborate constructively with your classmates, and be prepared to contribute to class discussion.

Minimum Academic Performance Limit

Any student earning a grade of (C) or less on any of the four major essay assignments *will be required to meet with a member of the writing center staff at the aforementioned Learning Resources Center.* In doing so, you must:

- Make an appointment at the center in a timely manner.
- Provide to me a legible and verifiable receipt detailing the date and time of your visit in addition to the name of the staff member with whom you consulted.
- Submit this information promptly before I will accept your next assignment and/or record a final grade.

This policy is non-negotiable, and enforced because I care deeply about the quality of your work. Failure to comply will result in a grade of (F) for the assignment.

Plagiarism

Don't do it! According to the CSUN catalog, plagiarism is *"intentionally or knowingly representing the words, ideas or work of another as one's own in any academic exercise."* Specific forms of plagiarism include the following:

- Turning in material that was written for *any* other class (high school included).
- Offering a restructured, reworded, version of someone else's text as your original work.
- Downloading essays from the internet, or paper mills, and offering them as your own work.
- Practicing any variation of not turning in original work for grades.

Academic dishonesty by cheating, plagiarism or collusion (collaborative work designated solely as your own) will result in your **immediate failure of the course—no questions asked!** Furthermore, you may subsequently be suspended or even expelled from the university, and I will urge CSUN's administration to do so. Rest assured we will discuss ways to avoid plagiarism and the proper citation of outside sources. If you are ever in doubt, please consult me, your text, your handbook, or a writing consultant at the Learning Resources Center (located in 408 Bayramian Hall).

Special Accommodations

Any student requiring special accommodations for specific learning needs should speak with me early in the semester. I am extremely sensitive to these requests and will put forth my greatest efforts to assure your needs are met in order to achieve success in the course.

Adjustments to Syllabus

As the course instructor, I reserve the right to modify any and/or all parts of this syllabus including policies, procedures, timelines, work schedules, etc., as necessary in order to best serve the collective needs of the class.

Tentative Work Schedule for Spring 2008

Please read selections below in the order that they are listed prior to the due date, and be prepared to discuss in class for the date scheduled

Week 1:

January 22   Introduction to course, review of syllabus, and discussion of chapter 1 on why writing is important and how it is learned.

January 24   Discussion of rhetorical genre theory, and the rhetorical situation. Begin rhetorical exercise.

Week 2:

January 29   Complete rhetorical exercise and begin discussing elements of applied rhetoric.
Discussion of chapter 3 (pp. 72–98) on the genre of writing profiles.

January 31   Continue discussion of chapter 3 (pp. 100–124) and chapter 20 on planning class exercise.

Week 3:

February 5   Continue discussion of chapter 3 (pp. 125–133) and chapter 25 (pp. 808–823) on document designs for writing.

February 7   **DRAFT DUE: Essay (1), peer critique training, peer critique workshop.**

Week 4:

February 12   *ESSAY (1) DUE*, discussion of chapter 13 on cueing a reader.

February 14   Discussion of chapter 16 on defining, class exercise.

Week 5:

February 19   Discussion of chapter 4 (pp. 134–163) on explaining a concept.

February 21   Continue discussion of chapter 4 (pp. 164–165), class exercise.

Week 6:

February 26   Continue discussion of chapter 4 (pp. 166–190), and read chapter 21 (pp. 702–737) on conducting library and Internet research.

February 28   **DRAFT DUE: Essay (2), peer critique workshop,** discussion of chapter 22 (pp. 738–779) on using and acknowledging sources.

Week 7:

March 4   *ESSAY (2) DUE,* discussion of chapter 19 (pp. 670–685) on arguing.

March 6   *Wings TBD*, class exercise.

Week 8:
March 11   Discussion of chapter 6 (pp. 272–293) on arguing a position.
March 13   Continue discussion of chapter 6 (pp. 294–295).

Holiday:
March 18   **SPRING BREAK: NO CLASSES**
March 20   **SPRING BREAK: NO CLASSES**

Week 9:
March 25   Continue discussion of chapter 6 (pp. 296 – 318).
March 27   **DRAFT DUE: Essay (3), peer critique workshop,** continue chapter 6
                (pp. 319–341).

Week 10:
April 1   *ESSAY (3) DUE,* discussion of chapter 7 (pp. 326–359) on proposing a
                solution.
April 3   **CLASS CANCELED FOR 4 C'S CONFERENCE**

Week 11:
April 8   Continue discussion of chapter 7 (pp. 360–392), class exercise.
April 10   Discussion of chapter 9 (pp. 457–481) on speculating about causes.

Week 12:
April 15   Continue discussion of chapter 9 (pp. 482–507), class exercise.
April 17   **DRAFT DUE: Essay (4), peer critique workshop,** continue
                chapter 9 (pp. 509–513).

Week 13:
April 22   *ESSAY (4) DUE,* discussion of chapter 23 on essay examination and
                timed writing.
April 24   Practice with essay examinations.

Week 14:
April 29   *Essay Exam* ***Please bring bluebook***
May 1   **DRAFT DUE: Reflective Essay, peer critique workshop,** review of
                chapter 23.

Week 15:
May 6   *ESSAY DUE: Reflective Essay,* portfolio assembly process.,
May 8   **Final Class—*Fully assembled portfolios due at the start of class.***

Grading Scale
Please consult this document before submitting writing assignments

100–94 = A	86–83 = B	76–73 = C	66–63 = D
93–90 = A–	82–80 = B–	72–70 = C–	62–60 = D–
89–87 = B+	79–77 = C+	69–67 = D+	59 or $<$ = F

Scoring Rubric

(A) Papers: Represent a superior, well-polished, level of writing that satisfies all assignment requirements

- Thesis is thoughtful, considerably clear, and skillfully supported.
- Sentences are free of grammatical errors, careless mistakes, and exhibit noticeable variety.
- Paragraphs are extremely well developed, organized effectively with a strong focus, and represent clear, connected units of thought.
- Essay is rich in detail with exemplary rhetorical control, stylistic fluency, and a wealth of critical thinking.

(B) Papers: Represent a commendable level of writing that satisfies all assignment requirements

- Thesis is thoughtful, clear, and well supported.
- Sentences are free of *major* grammatical errors, careless mistakes, and exhibit sufficient variety.
- Paragraphs are well developed, organized effectively, clearly focused, and represent complete, connected units of thought.
- Essay contains noticeable detail, sufficient rhetorical control, and substantial evidence of critical thinking.

(C) Papers: Represent an adequate level of writing that satisfies basic assignment requirements only

- Thesis is present, but possibly inadequate and/or ill-conceived.
- Sentences demonstrate lapses in proofreading/editing with enough careless mistakes to significantly catch a reader's attention in a negative manner, and exhibit little or no variety. Grammatical and structural errors may affect readability.
- Paragraphs are adequately organized, but contain only modest levels of focus and support necessary to effectively illustrate assertions, or represent clear, connected units of thought.
- Essay contains a minimally acceptable level of detail, rhetorical control, and critical thinking.

(D) Papers: Represent an inadequate level of writing that ineffectively and/or inappropriately satisfies basic assignment requirements

- Thesis is poorly conceived, ineffective, or absent.
- Sentences demonstrate significant lapses in proofreading/editing, insufficient variety, and several grammatical and/or structural errors that significantly diminish readability.
- Paragraphs are inadequately organized, and lack sufficient coherence, support, and focus necessary to appropriately illustrate assertions, or represent clear, connected units of thought.
- Essay contains insufficient levels of detail, rhetorical control, and little or no evidence of critical thinking.

(F) Papers: Represent an unacceptable level of writing that fails to satisfy core assignment requirements

- Thesis is absent, erroneous, or completely unacceptable.
- Sentences demonstrate severe lapses in proofreading/editing, lack variety or appropriateness, and contain an abundance of grammatical and/or structural errors that significantly diminish readability.
- Paragraphs are not organized, and lack any coherence, support, and focus necessary to appropriately illustrate assertions, and represent clear, connected units of thought.
- Essay contains little or no detail, and exhibits a complete absence of rhetorical control and critical thinking.

ONLINE SYLLABI

Increasingly, writing instructors are posting their syllabi online, sometimes through a course management system such as WebCT, Blackboard, or Moodle, or on a website. In some instances, the online syllabus is in exactly the same form as the paper version; students download the syllabus, print it out, and bring it to class. In other instances, the format of the syllabus may be quite different, reflecting the map-like configuration of visual texts. Whichever type of syllabus you decide to post, the same precepts pertain as those discussed above: be as specific as possible about all components of your course and go over the syllabus with your students in class through whatever means you use to communicate with your students.

An online syllabus can include a number of frames and attachments, but however you decide to structure it, it is important to construct a "welcome page" or some form of entrance to the syllabus so that students will be able to find it easily. An online syllabus, like a paper syllabus, constitutes a contract between students and instructors, defining requirements and expected responsibilities, including due dates. One element that can be particularly confusing for students if you are teaching in an online format is the definition of "participation." Does it mean sending messages to a discussion board, participating in real-time, or simply logging on and doing the assigned reading and writing? Clarify as much as you can, so students will know what is expected of them.

Given the increasing importance of new media and new models of coursework, it is likely that online syllabi will become more prevalent and that new structures will be developed. To get ideas about how an online syllabus might look, please access the template that is located at http://www.elearning.tcu.edu/resources/onlinesyllabustemplate.htm and there are others online you can use as a model. Like all syllabi, an online syllabus should reflect your philosophy of teaching writing and provide necessary information for your students about the requirements of your course. It should be easy to navigate and clearly structured. But it doesn't have to be a work of art. Some instructors like to include pictures, videos, and various elements that can make the syllabus visually attractive. Keep in mind, though, that a syllabus does not have to be beautiful. It just has to fulfill its function.

Author Index

Subject Index